比利时在天津的历史遗迹

Belgium's Historical Traces in Tianjin

张畅　刘悦

〔美〕杨溢（Yi Edward Yang）　著

社会科学文献出版社
SOCIAL SCIENCES ACADEMIC PRESS (CHINA)

天津社会科学发展研究中心课题成果

张畅，1973年生于天津，南开大学历史学博士，天津大学马克思主义学院副教授，天津社会学学会理事。长期从事天津城市史研究以及近代来华外国侨民口述史资料的搜集整理工作。学术专著《李鸿章的洋顾问：德璀琳与汉纳根》（合著）于2012年在台湾出版。译著《比利时—中国：昔日之路（1870—1930）》（合著）于2021年在北京出版。参与撰写的《近代中国看天津——百项中国第一》一书获2008年度天津市社会科学优秀成果二等奖，合作撰写的项目研究报告获2015年度天津市政府决策咨询优秀建议奖，发表论文十余篇。

Zhang Chang, born in 1973 in Tianjin, holds a PhD in history from Nankai University. She is an associate professor in the School of Marxism of Tianjin University, and a board member of Tianjin Sociological Society. She has been engaged in researching the urban history of Tianjin and collecting and organizing the oral history of foreigners who came to China in modern times. Her co-authored book *Li Hongzhang's Foreign Advisors: Gustav Detring and Constantin von Hanneken* was published in Taiwan in 2012. Her co-authored book *A Belgian Passage to China (1870-1930)* (translated from English to Chinese) was published in Beijing in 2021. Her co-authored book *Modern China through the Eyes of Tianjin - 100 Chinese Firsts* won the second prize of 2008 Tianjin Social Science Excellent Achievement. Her co-authored research report won the 2015 Tianjin Municipal Government Policy-making Advisory Excellence Award. She has published more than a dozen scholarly research papers.

刘悦，1971年生于天津，毕业于天津外国语学院、天津大学。1995年赴澳大利亚墨尔本MONASH大学金融系学习，回国后长期从事英文翻译工作。现任天津社会科学发展研究中心主任，原任近代天津博物馆馆长、副研究员。主要作品有《扛龙旗的美国大兵：美国第十五步兵团在中国（1912—1938）》（译著）、《李鸿章的洋顾问：德璀琳与汉纳根》（合著）、《李鸿章的军事顾问：汉纳根传》（合著）、《近代中国看天津——百项中国第一》（合著）、《天津的桥》（合著）、《清宫的门缝儿》（合著）、《比利时—中国：昔日之路（1870—1930）》（译著，与他人合作）、《翻译手记》等。

Liu Yue, born in Tianjin in 1971, graduated from Tianjin Foreign Language Institute and Tianjin University. In 1995, he went to Melbourne, Australia to study in the Department of Finance at Monash University. After returning to China, he worked as an English translator for many years. He is now the directorw of Tianjin Social Science Development Research Center. He previously served as the director and senior researcher of Tianjin Museum of Modern History. His main works include: *The United States 15th Infantry Regiment in China 1912-1938* (translated from English to Chinese), *Li Hongzhang's Foreign Advisors: Gustav Detring and Constantin von Hanneken* (co-authored), *Li Hongzhang's Military Advisors: A Biography of Constantin von Hanneken* (co-authored), *Modern China through the Eyes of Tianjin - 100 Chinese Firsts* (co-authored), *The Bridges of Tianjin* (co-authored), *The Doorway to the Qing Palace* (co-authored), *A Belgian Passage to China (1870-1930)* (translated from English to Chinese, co-authored), *Translation Notes*, etc.

杨溢（Yi Edward Yang），天津市人，现任美国詹姆斯麦迪逊大学政治学系教授，美国*Asian Survey* 编委。主要研究领域为国际关系、对外政策分析，政治心理学等。

我为本书所做的编译工作得到美国詹姆斯麦迪逊大学文理学院（College of Arts and Letters, James Madison University）小型研究资助项目的支持。特此表示感谢。谨以此书献给我的母亲魏学戴、父亲杨振民及所有远在故乡天津的亲朋好友。

Yi Edward Yang, a native of Tianjin, is currently a professor in the Department of Political Science at James Madison University and a member of the editorial board of *Asian Survey*. His main research areas include international relations, foreign policy analysis, and political psychology.

* Author's (Yi Edward Yang) note: Research for this book was supported by a small research grant from the College of Arts and Letters, James Madison University, USA. I would like to dedicate this book to my mother, Wei Xuedai, my father, Yang Zhenmin, and all my friends and family in my hometown of Tianjin.

目录

CONTENTS

序言一　8　Foreword Ⅰ
序言二　12　Foreword Ⅱ

Part I: Belgium and China
第一部分　比利时与中国

第一章　蒙着面纱的交往
Chapter 1: Veiled Interactions

欧洲的十字路口	3	Europe at the Crossroads
中世纪与东方的贸易	8	Trade with the East in the Middle Ages
蒙古帝国时期的中西交流	16	Exchanges between China and the West during the Mongol Empire
以书传教的金尼阁	23	Nicolas Trigault - Preaching through Books
康熙大帝的科学启蒙老师南怀仁	31	Emperor Kangxi's Scientific Enlightenment Teacher - Ferdinand Verbiest
把孔子学说介绍到欧洲的柏应理与助手沈福宗	43	Introducing the Teachings of Confucius to Europe - Philippe Couplet and His Assistant Shen Fuzong
比利时的"东印度公司"——奥斯坦德公司	52	Belgium's "East India Company" - Ostend

第二章　被火车头牵引的交往
Chapter 2: Interactions Led by the Locomotive

工业革命与国家独立	65	Industrial Revolution and National Independence
公司董事长——国王利奥波德父子	71	Chairman of the Company - King Leopold and His Son
开启近代中比外交的《中比通商条约》	75	The Treaty that Started Modern Sino-Belgian Diplomacy - Treaty of Commerce between China and Belgium
首次到访比利时的斌椿使团	82	First Visit to Belgium by the Bin Chun Mission
1896 年李鸿章访比	94	Li Hongzhang's Visit to Belgium in 1896
中比之间的第一次合作——京汉铁路	104	The First Cooperation between China and Belgium - Beijing-Hankou Railroad
林辅臣与黄河第一桥	118	Paul Splingaerd and the First Bridge over the Yellow River

第三章　日益密切的交往
Chapter 3: Increasingly Close Contacts

近代中国留比教育	131	Studying Overseas in Belgium and Modern Chinese Education
曾在比利时求学的中国名人	139	Famous Chinese Who Have Studied in Belgium
一战后中国劳工与比利时的重建	146	Chinese Laborers and the Reconstruction of Belgium after World War I
废除《中比通商条约》	160	Abolition of the Treaty of Commerce between China and Belgium
"盖世太保枪口下的中国女人"	175	"The Chinese Woman at the Gunpoint of the Gestapo"

Part II: Belgium and Tianjin

第二部分 比利时与天津

第四章 比利时在旧天津的遗迹

Chapter 4: The Traces of Belgium in Old Tianjin

为什么是天津？	185	Why Tianjin?
"殖民主义之王"利奥波德二世在中国谋夺租界的历次尝试	189	The Various Attempts by Leopold II - the "King of Colonialism" - to Seize the Concessions in China
股票上的租界	197	The Underdeveloped Concession
华比银行	208	Sino-Belgian Bank
天津比商电车电灯公司	221	Compagnie de Tramways et d'Eclairage de Tientsin (CTET)
天津比商义品放款公司	248	Crédit Foncier d'Extreme-Orient (CFEO)
义品公司设计建造的主要建筑	255	Major Buildings Designed and Constructed by CFEO
义品公司中的比利时建筑设计师沃卡特	267	A Belgian Architect at CFEO - Gustave Volckaert
"天津人"雷鸣远	273	"Tianjiner" Vincent Lebbe
一个比利时家族在天津	283	A Belgian Family in Tianjin

Part III: Belgium and China Today

第三部分 今日比利时与中国

第五章 新时代的交往

Chapter 5: Interactions in a New Era

1978 年谷牧访问比利时	299	Vice Premier Gu Mu's Visit to Belgium in 1978
从"欧亚大陆桥"到"一带一路"	304	From "Eurasian Continental Bridge" to "Belt and Road Initiative"
九次访华的菲利普国王	309	King Philippe Who Has Visited China Nine Times
比利时的文化名人与文化符号	311	Belgium's Cultural Figures and Cultural Symbols

后记	330	Afterword

我的案头放着《比利时—中国：昔日之路（1870—1930）》和《比利时在天津的历史文化遗存》两部书稿，两部书稿的主题完全一样，都是写历史上比利时与中国特别是与天津的关系，但书稿的作者一部是比利时人，一部是中国人。两部书稿从不同的视角描述它们共同的书写对象，两者互为参照，相得益彰，可谓双璧。

两书的作者为什么要选择这个看似冷门的题目呢？有两个原因：一是比利时和中国特别是和天津有着悠久而密切的关系，但为许多国人所不知；二是有一本比利时已故人士在华工作和生活的日记被发现，再现了欧洲人眼中清末民初中国社会的情境，弥足珍贵，引起了作者的兴趣。

比利时是欧洲一个小国，领土面积不过相当于两个北京大，人口 1000 万出头，还不如北京多，但这个小国却有许多独一无二的特点，使其在世界政治和经济生活中占有一席之地，其中有两大特点尤为突出：一是它是继英国工业革命之后在欧洲大陆率先实现工业革命的国家，它的钢铁和机械工业在当时的欧洲居于领先地位；二是它以小国之身立足于世界列强之林，却能在当时掠夺中国资源和侵犯中国主权的大国竞争中分享一杯羹。在近代史上，主要是这两个原因助成比利时同中国特别是同天津发生了密切的关系。然而，这一段历史鲜为人知，或知之不详。正是因为在诸多近代史册的叙说中存在这一段空白，上述两

I have two book manuscripts, *A Belgian Passage to China (1870-1930)* and *Belgium's Historical Traces in Tianjin,* on my desk, both on exactly the same subject - the historical relationship between Belgium and China in general and Tianjin in particular. But one manuscript's author is Belgian, the other's authors are Chinese. Although approaching their common subject from different perspectives, these two books cross reference and complement each other. They are a perfect pair.

Why did the authors of the two books choose this seemingly obscure topic? There are two reasons. First, Belgium has a long and close relationship with China, especially with Tianjin. But it is unknown to most people in China. Secondly, a diary of a deceased Belgian who worked and lived in China was discovered. Recreating the Chinese society in the late Qing dynasty and early Republican period through the lens of the Europeans, this diary is precious and piqued the authors' interest.

Belgium is a small country in Europe, with a territory twice the size of Beijing and a population of about 10 million, less than that of Beijing. But this small country has many unique features that give it a special place in the political and economic life of the world. Two features stand out. First, Belgium was the first country to achieve an industrial revolution on the European continent after Great British. Its iron and steel and machinery industries were at the forefront of Europe at the time. Second, although a small country, it was able to take part in the competition among the world powers to plunder China's resources and violate China's sovereignty. In modern history, it was mainly these two reasons that contributed to Belgium's close relations with China and especially with Tianjin. However, little is known or known about this part of history. It is because of this gap in the numerous narratives of modern histories that the authors of the

书的作者才花费力气挖掘被忘却的历史的积淀，钩沉众多尘封的史料，爬罗剔抉，编写成书，完成了这段历史的补缺。

两书把历史上的中比关系划分为两大阶段：比利时于1830年成为独立的主权国家之前的二三百年间同中国的关系；1830年之后百年间同中国的关系。

1830年之前中比关系的主要内容，是比利时众多的天主教传教士被派到中国进行传教活动。据统计，这一时期的来华传教士累计达700多人，其中不少人死在中国或来中国的途中。到达中国的传教士多在中国各地城镇乡村传教，籍籍无名，最有名的是南怀仁，但他未接触下层人民，而是和康熙皇帝建立了密切关系，并且做了钦天监监正。他向康熙皇帝传授了许多科学知识，得到康熙极大的信任，但未被允许向老百姓普及这些知识。他的最大贡献是建立了更科学的中国历法，在北京建立了观象台。中比关系在这个历史阶段的特点是比利时单向输出天主教教义，而不是基于外交关系的双向交流；而1830年之后约百年时间的历史阶段中，传教士的活动仍然活跃，中比关系的范围也扩大了，其重点逐渐转移到另一个群体——比利时实业家在中国的活动，主要体现在比利时政府发起和支持的重大建设工程，如天津和上海的有轨电车工程、京汉铁路的修建、天津部分电力供应系统的修建、兰州黄河铁桥的修建等。与上一历史阶段不同，中比关系在这一历史阶段不

above-mentioned two books have taken the trouble to dig up the historical archives and artifacts, comb through them, and compile them into these two books, henceforth filling the gap in history.

The two books divide historical Sino-Belgian relations into two major phases: first, Belgium's relations with China in the 200-300 years before it became an independent sovereign state in 1830; and second, Belgium's relations with China in the roughly 100 years after 1830.

The main element of Sino-Belgian relations before 1830 was the numerous Belgian Catholic missionaries sent to China for missionary activities. According to statistics, more than 700 people were sent China, many of whom died in China or on their way to China. Most of the missionaries who arrived in China preached in towns and villages all over the country and most were unknown to the world. The most famous missionary was Ferdinand Verbiest, although he did not reach out to the lower classes. Instead he formed a close relationship with the Kangxi Emperor and became the superintendent of the Imperial Observatory. He imparted a lot of scientific knowledge to the Kangxi Emperor and was greatly trusted by him. But Verbiest was not allowed to popularize this knowledge to the common people. His greatest contribution was the establishment of a more scientific Chinese calendar and the establishment of the Observatory in Beijing. Sino-Belgian relations during this phase of history were characterized by a one-way export of Catholic doctrine from Belgium, rather than a two-way exchange based on diplomatic relations. In the period of about a century after 1830, although missionary activities were still active, the scope of Sino-Belgian relations expanded and the focus gradually shifted to another group - Belgian industrialists in China. Their activities were mainly reflected in the major construction projects initiated and supported by the Belgian

仅出现了商务联系的双向交流，而且双方建立了正式的外交关系。这是在中国社会开始引进现代工业的洋务运动风起云涌的背景下中比关系更为重要的阶段。这里需要强调的是，上述这些工程固然有利于中国现代化进程，但它也伴随着比利时许多损害中国国家主权和尊严的殖民主义的无理要求，诸如胁迫中国签订不平等的《中比通商条约》，强行获取领事裁判权，强行在天津设立租界，等等。这些特权直到1949年新中国成立时才彻底终止。因此，这一阶段也是国家尊严蒙尘的屈辱时期。后来，在1927年，当时的中国政府顺应人民的强烈要求，经过反复的据理力争，促使比利时接受中方要求，废除了不平等的《中比通商条约》。1929年，比利时主动归还了天津的租界。二战结束后，又把天津电车电灯公司归还中国。这些举措为比利时后来和新中国顺利建立外交关系和此后不断发展友好合作关系扫清了障碍。

我是天津人，很小的时候就听长辈说过"天津电车电灯公司"，在我的青少年时期，经常乘坐天津的有轨电车，所以"比利时"是我除去英、美、法、俄、日之外最早听到的国名。更意外的是我于1997年初被任命为驻比利时大使，在比利时工作将近5年，很自然地对比利时这个国家有着浓厚兴趣，对这个国家的情况也有所了解，2012年我还专门写了一本介绍比利时的书并出版。但是，拜读

government, such as the tramway projects in Tianjin and Shanghai, the construction of the Beijing-Hankou railroad, the construction of part of the electricity supply system in Tianjin, and the construction of the Yellow River iron bridge in Lanzhou. Unlike the previous phase, Sino-Belgian relations during this phase not only saw a two-way exchange of commercial ties, but also the establishment of formal diplomatic relations. This was a more important phase in Sino-Belgian relations against the background of the upsurge of the Self-Strengthening Movement, which began to introduce modern industry into Chinese society. It should be emphasized here that while these aforementioned projects were certainly beneficial to China's modernization process, it was also accompanied by many unreasonable Belgian colonial demands that undermined China's national sovereignty and dignity, such as the coercion of China to sign the unequal Treaty of Commerce between China and Belgium, the forced acquisition of consular extraterritorial jurisdiction, the forced establishment of a concession in Tianjin, and so on. These privileges were not completely terminated until the founding of the People's Republic of China in 1949. This period was therefore also a time of humiliation and disgrace for the China's national dignity. Later, in 1927, in response to the strong demand of the people, the then Chinese government, after repeated arguments, urged Belgium to accept the Chinese demand and abrogate the unequal Treaty of Commerce between China and Belgium. In 1929, Belgium took the initiative to return the leased territory in Tianjin. After the end of World War II, it returned the Tianjin Tramway and Electric Lighting Company to China unconditionally. These initiatives cleared the way for the subsequent smooth establishment of diplomatic relations between Belgium and the new China and the continuous development of friendly and cooperative relations thereafter.

了这两本书稿以后，我发现我所了解的比利时和比利时与中国关系的历史在我的头脑中还有不少空白，这使我受益匪浅。我认为，这两本书对历史上中比关系客观的、细微的考察和描述，既包含了正面的，也历数了负面的史实，这对广大读者全面地了解比利时和中比关系的历史也是大有裨益的，是两本好书。因此，当两本书的作者刘悦、张畅约我写序言时，我欣然应命草就此文，诚挚地向广大读者做出推荐。是为序。

宋明江

2021 年 3 月 10 日

I am a native of Tianjin, and I heard my elders talk about "Belgian Tramway and Electric Light Company" when I was very young. The name "Belgium" was the first country name I heard besides England, America, France, Russia and Japan. Even more unexpectedly, I was appointed ambassador to Belgium in early 1997. Having worked there for almost five years, it was natural for me to take a keen interest in the country and get to know it a little better. In 2012, I also wrote and published a book about Belgium. However, after reading these two manuscripts, I found that there are still a lot of gaps in what I know about Belgium and the history of Belgian-Chinese relations in my mind. Reading them benefited me a lot. In my opinion, these two books are excellent. They provide an objective and nuanced examination and description of historical Sino-Belgian relations, containing both positive and negative historical facts, which will also be of great benefit to the general readers in gaining a comprehensive understanding of the history of Belgium and Sino-Belgian relations. Therefore, when Liu Yue and Zhang Chang, the authors of the two books, asked me to write the preface, I was happy to oblige. Such is the preface and I sincerely recommend both books to the readers.

Song Mingjiang
March 10, 2021

天津是我国历史名城，由于地处首都门户和濒临渤海的优越位置，她成为我国北方最早的开放城市之一，从一个运河边的小镇迅速发展成一个国际化大城市。近代，众多重大历史事件在这里上演，社会文化发生急速变迁，许多重要历史人物曾在这里活动，天津堪称中国近代风云变幻的缩影。

在近代天津城市发展的进程中，天津深受外来文化特别是西方文化影响，逐渐成为工业化产生的摇篮、新观念传播的温床、各种新事物发展的试验场。今天，这里仍然随处可见具有浓郁西洋风格的城市建筑、奋发图强的市民精神面貌以及兼容并蓄的生活方式。这些即是发生过东西方文化从冲突到交流、以融合促共存的丰富例证。

近代天津历史上，曾经先后有九个国家在这里留下了深深的历史痕迹。天津租界的设立及其每一次扩张都与近代中国的政治形势紧密相关，都是列强攻占天津的产物。那段悲剧是天津人也是中国人永远无法忘记的耻辱和负重前行的动力。

天津居民是最早接触外来者的中国人之一，早在荷兰使团和马戛尔尼使团进京观见皇帝之时，他们就表现出了强烈的好奇心。近代被迫开埠后，一次次毁城之灾、割裂之痛的现实发生后，天津人逐渐认识到"落后就要挨打"，必须奋发自强才能屹立于世界民族之林。他们逐渐接受了外国侨民带来的西方工业文明和城市文明，众采东西方文化之长，淬砺天津使其成为多元文化荟萃之地。快速的工业化、城市化进程，与农村的长期停滞形成了强烈对比，强烈地冲击并改变着以农耕文明为特征的传统中国社会。

Tianjin is a famous historical city in China. Its superior location at the gateway to the capital and closeness to the Bohai Sea made it one of the earliest northern Chinese cities opening up to the world. It developed rapidly from a small town by a canal into an internationalized city. In the modern era, many major historical events took place in Tianjin; its society and culture changed rapidly; many important historical figures were active here. Tianjin can indeed be described as a microcosm of China's modern changes.

In the process of modern Tianjin's urban development, Tianjin was deeply influenced by foreign culture, especially Western culture, and gradually became the cradle of industrialization, the hotbed for the spread of new ideas, and the testing ground for the development of various new things. Today, we can still see the rich Western style of the city's architecture, the spirit of the citizens and the eclectic lifestyle. These are rich examples of how the East and the West have moved from conflict to communication, and from integration to coexistence.

In the history of modern Tianjin, nine countries have left deep historical traces here. The establishment and expansion of the Tianjin Concessions were closely related to the political situation of modern China. They were the products of the brute force of the foreign powers that seized Tianjin. That tragedy is a shame that Tianjin people and Chinese people can never forget and the motivation to move forward.

The inhabitants of Tianjin were among the first Chinese to come into contact with outsiders, and they showed their strong curiosity as early as when the Dutch and Macartney missions went to Beijing to visit the Qing emperor. After the forced opening of the port, Tianjin people gradually realized that "being backward will be beaten" and that they had to strive for self-improvement in order to stand tall among the world's nations. They gradually accepted the Western industrial civilization and urban civilization brought by foreigners. The fusion of the eastern and western cultures turned Tianjin into a place of multi-culturalism. The rapid

农民不断涌入城市成为新的市民阶层，进而衍化出复杂的近代社会结构和城市体系，为后来的学生运动和工人革命提供了土壤，为新中国的建设打下了工业基础。

新中国成立之后，特别是改革开放以后，天津开始重新走上对外开放的道路，张开双臂欢迎来自世界各地的客人。1984年成立的天津经济技术开发区是中国首批国家级经济技术开发区之一，在全国54个国家级开发区、工业园区投资环境评价中，天津开发区曾连续14年位居第一。这是自1860至1984年的120多年的历史进程中，天津从被迫对外开放到日益主动开放的结果。

在九个曾在天津留下深刻历史痕迹的国家中，比利时是最小也是最独特的一个。比利时是一个欧洲小国——国土面积小，只有30688平方公里，在欧洲50个国家里排第33（与我国的海南岛差不多大）；立国时间也不长，1830年独立，不到200年历史。然而，它却是有着"欧洲心脏"和"欧洲首都"美誉的政治经济中心。欧洲联盟三个主要的机构当中，欧盟委员会和欧盟部长理事会位于布鲁塞尔，另一个重要机构欧洲议会在布鲁塞尔也有分处（全体议会在法国斯特拉斯堡），另外北大西洋公约组织的总部也设在布鲁塞尔。

虽然国土面积小，但比利时却是一个工业国家，是19世纪初欧洲大陆最早进行工业革命的国家之一。它的经济高度对外依赖，80%的原料靠进口，50%以上的工业产品出口，长期居世界进出口总额排名前十，近年居第12位，按人均出口量计算则排名世界第一。它最著名的产品有钻石、巧克力、平板玻璃和轻机枪。

process of industrialization and urbanization contrasted sharply with the long-term stagnation in the countryside, which strongly influenced and changed the traditional Chinese society characterized by agrarian civilization. As peasants continued to flock to the city to become a new class of citizens, there emerged a complex modern social structure and urban system that provided the soil for the subsequent student movement and workers' revolution, thus laid the industrial foundation for the construction of new China.

After the founding of New China, especially after the reform and opening up, Tianjin started to reopen its doors to the outside world and welcomed guests from all over the world with open arms. Established in 1984, Tianjin Economic and Technological Development Area (TEDA) is one of the first national economic and technological development zones in China. Among 54 national-level development zones and industrial parks in China, TEDA has ranked first in the evaluation of investment environment for 14 consecutive years. This is the result of Tianjin's transition from being forced to open to the outside world to an increasingly active opening in the course of more than 120 years (1860-1984) of history.

Among the nine countries that have left deep historical traces in Tianjin, Belgium is the smallest and most unique. Belgium is a small European country - a small area of 30,688 square kilometers, ranking 33rd among the 50 countries in Europe (about the same size as Hainan Island in China). Belgium has not been established for a long time. It became independent in 1830 and has a history of less than 200 years. However, it is a political and economic center with the reputation of "heart of Europe" and "capital of Europe". Among the three main institutions of the European Union, the European Commission and the Council of Ministers of the European Union are located in Brussels, and another important institution, the European Parliament, has a branch in Brussels (the full Parliament is in Strasbourg, France). In addition, the headquarters of the North Atlantic Treaty Organization is also located in Brussels.

Despite its small size, Belgium is an industrial country,

比利时人非常务实，重视在华的商业利益。历史上，比利时曾在天津留下深刻印记。天津比商电车电灯公司为天津兴建并成功运营了中国城市交通的第一条轨道交通线路。天津比商义品放款公司在天津修建了许多宏伟美丽的建筑，直到今天它们还装点着城市的很多街区。

如今伴随着中国的崛起，往昔的文化现象，为构建新世纪东西方关系提供了值得借鉴的历史经验。改革开放前后，比利时在西方国家中创造了数个第一：它是最早向中国提供政府贷款的西方国家，是最早向中国输出先进技术、同中国建立产业投资基金的西方国家之一。1979年比利时与中国签订了框架协议，两国的经济合作关系由此掀开了新篇章。中比建交50年来，中国已成为比利时在亚洲投资最多的国家。中比关系是中欧关系的一个典范。

本书以2017年天津与布鲁塞尔市合作举办的"中国与比利时共享历史文化交流展览"为基础，介绍中国与比利时的历史关系及近代天津的比利时历史文化遗存，旨在促进"一带一路"框架下的中欧经济文化交流、增进中国与比利时人民的友好往来。

本书为中英双语，诚挚地向对中比友好往来感兴趣的各国人士介绍这段历史。本书作者充分搜集了比利时外交部档案馆、伊泊尔市法兰德斯一战战地博物馆、巴黎银行档案馆、鲁汶大学档案馆、近代天津博物馆的馆藏史料，多年来采访了多位近代来华比利时侨民的后代，对其家族史进行了专业细致的资料搜集和整理，因此本书具有较高的史料价值。此外，本书还搜集了大量的历史图片、老照片，图文并茂，生动形象，亦可为旅游者和读者穿越古今中外

and was one of the first countries in mainland Europe to carry out the industrial revolution in the early 19th century. Its economy is highly externally dependent, importing 80% of its raw materials and exporting more than 50% of its industrial products. Belgium has long ranked among the top ten in the world in terms of total imports and exports, ranking 12th in recent years and first in the world in terms of exports per capita. Its most famous products are diamonds, chocolate, flat glass and light machine guns.

Belgians are very pragmatic and value their business interests in China. Historically, Belgium has left a deep imprint in Tianjin. The Belgian company, Compagnie de Tramways et d'Eclairage de Tientsin (CTET), successfully operated the first rail line in the history of urban transportation in China. The Belgian Tianjin Credit Foncier d'Extreme-Orient (CFEO) built many magnificent and beautiful buildings in Tianjin, which to this day still adorn many of the city's neighborhoods.

Today, with the rise of China, the cultural phenomena of the past provide a worthy historical experience for building East-West relations in the new century. Before and after the reform and opening up, Belgium created several firsts among Western countries: it was the first Western country to provide government loans to China; one of the first Western countries to export advanced technology to China and establish an industrial investment fund with China. In 1979, Belgium and China signed a framework agreement, which opened a new chapter in the economic cooperation between the two countries. In the 50 years since the establishment of diplomatic relations between Belgium and China, China has become the country where Belgium invests the most in Asia. The relationship between Belgium and China has become a model for China-Europe relations.

Based on the - "A Joint Exhibition of the China-Belgium Shared History" organized by Tianjin and Brussels in 2017, this book introduces the friendly relations between China and Belgium and the historical and cultural relics of Belgium in modern Tianjin. The aim is to promote the economic and

比利时外交部档案馆收藏的关于天津旧比利时租界的档案
Archives on the Belgian Concession in Tianjin in the
Archives of the Belgian Ministry of Foreign Affairs

的想象提供丰富依据。

　　本书付梓之际，我们还要特别感谢以下诸位师友的支持和帮助：中国驻比利时及欧共体原大使宋明江及夫人张幼云；天津社会科学院原秘书长李桐柏；比利时学者查尔斯·拉格朗日、约翰·麦特勒博士、冯浩烈；比利时国家档案馆卡罗琳·希克斯；比利时一战战地博物馆馆长邓多文；林辅臣后裔安芝拉·艾利奥特、安妮·梅戈文；沙多后裔让·沙多；山东滨州收藏家窦希仑。

张　畅

2021 年 6 月 6 日

cultural exchanges between China and Europe, and to enhance the friendly exchanges between the Chinese and Belgian people under the "Belt and Road Initiative" framework.

　　This book is bilingual in Chinese and English, and introduces this history to people from all over the world who are interested in friendly exchanges between China and Belgium. The authors have collected and studied historical materials from the archives of the Belgian Ministry of Foreign Affairs, the Flanders Fields Museum in Ypres, the archives of the Bank of Paris and the University of Leuven, and Tianjin Museum of Modern History. In addition, the authors have conducted interviews with many descendants of Belgian expatriates who had worked and lived in China in the modern era, and professionally and meticulously collected and sorted out the materials of their family history. Therefore, this book is of high historical value. Illustrated with a large number of rare historical images and photos, this book provides a rich basis for the imagination of travelers and readers through the ancient and modern worlds.

　　As this book goes to press, we would like to extend our special thanks to following mentors and friends for their support and assistance: Mr. Song Mingjiang, former Ambassador Extraordinary and Plenipotentiary of China to Belgium and Head of Mission to the European Union, and his wife Mrs. Zhang Youyun; Mr. Li Tongbai, former secretary-general of the Tianjin Academy of Social Sciences; Belgian scholars Mr. Charles Lagrange, Dr. Johan Mattelaer and Mr. Philip Vanhaelemeersch; Mrs. Caroline Six, from State Archives of Belgium; Mr. Dominiek Dendooven, curator of the In Flanders Fields Museum; Angela Cox Elliott and Anne Megowan, the granddaughters of Paul Splingaerd; Mr. Jean Jadot, the grandson of Belgian Engineer Jean Jadot; Mr. Dou Xilun, a collector from Binzhou, Shandong Province.

Zhang Chang

June 6, 2021

第一部分 比利时与中国

Part I: Belgium and China

黄道經緯儀

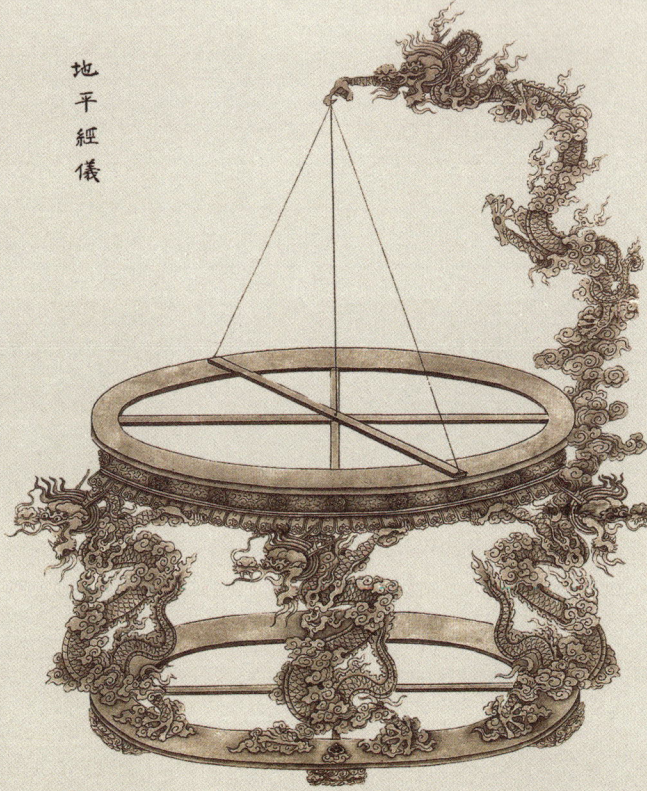

地平經儀

紀限儀

南怀仁绘制的天文仪器图纸，出自其编纂的《新制灵台仪象志》

Ferdinand Verbiest's drawings, from his work of *Xin Zhi Ling Tai Yi Xiang Zhi*

第一章　蒙着面纱的交往

Chapter 1: Veiled Interactions

比利时国旗
National flag of Belgium

比利时国徽
National emblem of Belgium

欧洲的十字路口

比利时是一个欧洲小国，全国人口只有 1152 万，但它却是一个联邦制国家，境内分为三大语言区，分别是荷兰语区、德语区和法语区，其语言分属日耳曼语和拉丁语两大语系。讲荷兰语的被称为弗拉芒人，讲法语的被称为瓦隆人，讲德语的人相对占少数。放眼欧洲乃至整个世界，如比利时这样小却十分复杂的国家，真不多见！要想搞清楚它的状况，以及它与中国的关系，有必要追溯一下它立国之前漫长纷杂的历史。

Europe at the Crossroads

Belgium is a small European country. The country's population is only 11.52 million, but it is a federal state. Its territory is divided into three major language areas respectively: Dutch, German and French. Dutch speakers are called Flemish, French speakers are called Walloons, and German speakers are a relative minority. There are few countries in Europe, and indeed in the world, as small and yet complex as Belgium! To understand Belgium and its relationship with China, it is necessary to trace the long and complicated history of the country before it was founded.

比利时位于欧洲西北部，与英国隔海相望，北与荷兰比邻，东与德国接壤，东南与卢森堡毗连，南与法国交界。地理位置十分重要，是英国与欧洲大陆之间的交通要道，历来的兵家必争之地。近代发生在那里的著名战役有1815年6月18日发生在布鲁塞尔以南的滑铁卢战役，此役终结了拿破仑帝国的短暂历史，也是拿破仑的最后一战。而第一次世界大战期间，有数百万战士在横跨伊瑟平原的堑壕战中丧生，整个地区毁于一旦。第二次世界大战中，整个二战初期最大规模的坦克战就在列日省的汉努特（Hannut, Liège）发生。

比利时西邻北海，地势由西向东逐步升高：西部的佛兰德斯平原地势平坦，河网密布，构成尼德兰地区（包括荷兰与比利时在内）便捷的内河航运网，并由河入海延伸到北海沿岸各港口；中部为渐渐升高的高原地区，土地富饶，灌溉充分，适宜农业耕作；东部为著名的阿登山脉，山高林密，风光旖旎，二战早期和后期两次经典战役均发生于此。[1]

与德国、奥地利、意大利这些单一民族国家不同，比利时可以称得上是欧洲真正的种族大熔炉，是日耳曼文化与拉丁文化的共融体。比利时人的祖先是凯尔特人和日耳曼人。公元前54年，最早居住在这一地区的凯尔特人被罗马帝国的恺撒征服，"比利时"这个名称的前身"比利其"（Belgae）就来源于恺撒对他们的称呼。公元5世纪时，属于日耳曼民族的法兰克人大举入侵西欧，他们建立起法兰克王国，[2] 其统治者是墨洛温王朝，[3] 比利时即在其领土范围内。公元8世纪，墨洛温王朝被加洛林王朝[4]所取代。这一王朝中最著名的君主是查理大帝，他出生于比利时的列日。

Belgium is located in northwestern Europe: across the sea from the United Kingdom, neighboring the Netherlands in the north, bordering Germany in the east, adjacent to Luxembourg in southeast, and sharing borders with France in the south. Its geographical location is very important. As the main transportation route between the United Kingdom and the European continent, Belgium is of significant military importance. The famous battles that took place there in modern times include the Battle of Waterloo, which occurred south of Brussels on June 18, 1815 and ended the short history of Napoleon's empire and was his last battle. During World War I, millions of soldiers were killed in trench warfare across the Flanders Plain, and the entire regions were destroyed. The largest tank battle during the Second World War took place at Hannut in the province of Liège.

Belgium is adjacent to the North Sea in the west - its terrain gradually rises from west to east: the western Flanders plain is flat with dense river network, forming convenient inland navigation network in the Netherland region (including the Netherlands and Belgium). The gradually rising plateau area in the center features rich land is suitable for agriculture. The famous Ardennes Mountains in the east is endowed with high forests and beautiful scenery where two classic battles of the World War II were fought.[1]

Unlike the mono-ethnic countries such as Germany, Austria and Italy, Belgium can be described as a true ethnic melting pot of Europe, a symbiosis of Germanic and Latin cultures. The ancestors of the Belgians are Celtic and Germanic. First in 54 BC, the first Celts living in the region was conquered by Caesar of the Roman Empire. "Belgian" (Belgae) the name of the predecessor of the "Belgium" is derived from Caesar's name for them. In the 5th century AD, the Franks, a Germanic people, invaded Western Europe and established the Kingdom of the Franks,[2] ruled by the

从中世纪开始，日耳曼人占据了现在比利时的北部地区（一般称作佛兰德斯[5]地区，与荷兰合称"尼德兰"，意思是"低地"），北部地区逐渐日耳曼化，而南部逐渐被拉丁文化所同化。北部讲荷兰语、德语而南部讲法语的语言分界线就是这样形成的。

加洛林王朝解体之后、独立建国以前，比利时长期被一些大帝国和公爵伯爵们所统治。比利时北部的佛兰德斯在很长一段时间内是法兰西王国的封邑，大约包括现在的法国东北一角（北部省）及比利时大半，也包括了今荷兰西兰省的南部。[6]佛兰德斯伯爵国曾在中古初期为法兰西王国强大的诸侯之一，在其极盛期，领土几

Merovingian dynasty,[3] within whose territory Belgium was located. In the 8th century AD, the Merovingian dynasty was replaced by the Carolingian dynasty[4]. The most famous monarch of this dynasty was Charles the Great, who was born in Liège, Belgium.

From the Middle Ages onwards, the Germanic peoples occupied the northern part of what is now Belgium (generally known as the Flanders[5] and, together with the Netherlands, the "Netherland", meaning "lowlands"), which gradually became Germanicized, while the southern part of Belgium was gradually assimilated by Latin culture. This is how the linguistic divide between Dutch and German in the north and French in the south was formed.

After the dissolution of the Carolingian dynasty and

欧洲中世纪的统治者查理大帝（公元742—814），或称为查理曼、查尔斯大帝、卡尔大帝，"曼"即大帝之意。法兰克王国加洛林王朝的第二任国王，德意志神圣罗马帝国的奠基人。他建立了囊括西欧大部分地区的庞大的查理曼帝国。查理曼在公元800年的圣诞节在罗马被教皇加冕为"罗马人的皇帝""文明的启导者"，权力达到了巅峰。在他统治期间，欧洲的文化重心从地中海希腊一带转移至欧洲莱茵河附近，因此被后世尊为"欧洲之父"。查理曼是扑克牌红心K与法国塔罗牌上的人物

The medieval European ruler Charles the Great (742 AD - 814 AD), or Charlemagne (German: Karl der Große). He was the second king of the Frankish Kingdom of Caroline and the founder of the Holy Roman Empire in Germany. He founded the vast Charlemagne Empire, which encompassed most of Western Europe. Charlemagne reached the peak of his power when he was crowned "Emperor of the Romans" and "Enlightener of Civilization" by the Pope in Rome on Christmas Day, 800 AD. During his reign, the cultural center of Europe shifted from the Mediterranean Sea around Greece to Europe around the Rhine River, and he was therefore revered as the "Father of Europe". Charlemagne is the character on the King of Hearts and the French Tarot

佛兰德斯伯爵国纹章
Coat of Arms of the Count
of Flanders

勃艮第公国徽章
Emblem of the Duchy
of Burgundy

乎囊括了整个比利时与法兰西东北部，后逐渐为法兰西国王所压制，其领土也渐渐缩小。

在 15 世纪以后，佛兰德斯与其他 16 个尼德兰地区的省份（封邑），同为勃艮第公国[7]（公元 9—15 世纪下半期）的领土，后随着勃艮第王朝的覆灭，被划入了哈布斯堡家族[8]的领地。再后来哈布斯堡家族一分为二时，佛兰德斯与其他 16 省归到了哈布斯堡家族西班牙支系之手，因此该地被称为"西属尼德兰"。

现在的比利时在历史上命运多舛，总是被欧洲列强所争夺和瓜分，甚至不幸沦为战场。除了之前提到的滑铁卢战役、一战和二战中的几次著名战役，在之前的 17 和 18 世纪，为了争夺领土和霸权，法国先后与奥地利、西班牙发生战争，战场都在如今的比利时境内，那里因此被称作"欧洲的斗鸡场"，遭受到严重的人员和财产损失。

1701—1713 年发生了西班牙王位继承战争，其后佛兰德斯与其他西属尼德兰南部 6 省（北部 10 省早已独

before the establishment of independent statehood, Belgium was ruled by a number of large empires and various dukes and counts. Flanders, in northern Belgium, was for a long time a fief of the Kingdom of France, from what is now the northeastern corner of France (the Northern Province) to most of Belgium, including the southern part of the present-day Dutch province of Zealand.[6] The Count of Flanders was one of the powerful vassals of the Kingdom of France in the early Middle Ages, and at its height, its territory encompassed almost all of Belgium and northeastern France, and then gradually subdued by the King of France, and its territory gradually shrank.

After the 15th century, Flanders was part of the Duchy of Burgundy[7] (9th - 2nd half of the 15th century), along with 16 other Netherlandish provinces (fiefs). With the fall of the Burgundian dynasty, it was transferred to the Habsburgs[8]. Later, when the Habsburgs split into two, Flanders and the other 16 provinces came under the Spanish branch of the Habsburgs, hence the name "Western Netherland."

The land that is now Belgium has had an ill-fated history - always contested and divided by the European powers and even fallen into battle grounds. In addition to the previously mentioned battles of Waterloo, World War I and World War II, in the 17th and 18th centuries, France fought wars with Austria and Spain over territory and hegemony, all on the territory of present-day Belgium. It thus became known as the "Cockpit of Europe" and suffered severe human and property losses.

After the Spanish War of Succession in 1701-1713, Flanders, along with the other six provinces in the southern part of Western Netherland (the ten northern provinces had already become independent as the Netherlandish Republic, commonly known as the Dutch Republic, De Republiek der Zeven Verenigde Nederlanden), was assigned to the Austrian branch of the Habsburg family, and was then renamed "Austrian Netherland." After the

立为尼德兰共和国，也就是俗称的荷兰共和国），被划归哈布斯堡家族奥地利支系，于是改称"奥属尼德兰"。法国大革命后，拿破仑击败欧洲的反法联盟，开始对外扩张，18世纪末比利时为法国所侵占，拿破仑战败后，南尼德兰（即比利时）与北尼德兰（即荷兰）组成尼德兰（荷兰）联合王国。1830年南尼德兰爆发独立运动，从荷兰统治下独立，并迎立了一位德国王子利奥波德作为第一任国王，开创了比利时萨克森—科堡—哥达王朝。本来比利时立国后奉行中立政策，但在两次世界大战中都被德意志帝国及纳粹德国占领，因此二战后比利时放弃中立原则，参加了北约。后来又加入欧洲经济共同体，成为创始国之一。

由于以上历史因素，比利时成为君主立宪的联邦制国家，其主要联邦机构是联邦政府和由参议院、下议院组成的两院制议会。根据语言族群而设立了三个社区，即荷兰语社区、法语社区以及德语社区；同时又设立了三个行政区，即弗拉芒区、瓦隆区和布鲁塞尔首都大区。[9]三大语区和行政区保留各自的立法和行政权力。

French Revolution, Napoleon defeated the anti-French alliance in Europe and began to expand abroad. At the end of the 18th century, Belgium was invaded and occupied by France. After Napoleon's defeat, the Southern Netherlands (Belgium) and the Northern Netherlands (Netherlands) formed the Kingdom of Netherlands. In 1830, the Southern Netherlands launched independence movement, gaining independence from the Kingdom of Netherlands, and selecting a German prince, Leopold, as its first King. Since then, the Saxe-Coburg-Gotha dynasty of Belgium was established. Originally Belgium was founded on a policy of neutrality, but was occupied by the German Empire and Nazi Germany in both world wars. After World War II, Belgium abandoned the principle of neutrality and joined the North Atlantic Treaty Organization (NATO). Later it joined the European Economic Community (EEC) as one of the founding members.

For these historical reasons, Belgium is a constitutional monarchy with a federal government and a bicameral parliament consisting of a Senate and a lower house. Three communities have been established according to language groups, namely the Dutch community, the French community and the German community. Three administrative regions were also created, namely the Flemish Region, the Walloon Region and the Brussels-Capital Region.[9] The three Communities and the Administrative Regions retain their respective legislative and executive powers.

中世纪与东方的贸易

比利时人口稠密，经济繁荣，生产力水平极高。它最出名的物产，早期是佛兰德斯的呢绒，工业革命之后是火车和其他工业产品。从很早开始，甚至早在地理大发现以前，它就融入世界经济一体化的进程中。

在中世纪，比利时基本上是以农业为基础的文明。农民以耕种土地为主要谋生手段，以纺织呢绒为副业。这造成整个帝国经济不发达，商业凋敝。即便如此，大约在9世纪，弗里斯兰（荷兰西北部的一个省）人的商船就不断往返于斯海尔德河（流经图尔奈、根特、安特卫普）、马斯河与莱茵河，并在北海沿岸进行贸易，进行贸易的主要商品之一就是佛兰德斯农民纺织的被称为"呢绒"的毛织品，其色泽鲜明，远近驰名，被当作查理曼大帝送给国王哈努恩—阿尔—拉斯希德的珍贵礼品。[10] 整个尼德兰表现出西欧其他地方不曾有的商业活力。

佛兰德斯的地理位置得天独厚，布鲁日港成为来自英国和北欧地区的商船出波罗的海南下的天然中转站，舟楫云涌。除了优越的地理位置，佛兰德斯的工业（主要是冶金）在当时也是领先的。人口的增长使这块土地生机勃勃，农民可以从单纯的耕作中解脱出来，从事纺织、冶金（主要是制铜业）等其他行业。新增的没有土地的人口，则被鼓励去围堤排涝造出新的土地。在新出现的海岸湿润的草地上，牧养着成群的绵羊，羊毛的品质尤其精良。到了10世纪，随着进出口贸易的发展，本地的羊毛已经不敷使用，佛兰德斯的纺织匠不得不依靠商人从英国进口更多的羊毛，羊毛漂染匠则可以得到商人从海外进口的肥皂和染料，于是本来在乡村就地取

Trade with the East in the Middle Ages

Belgium was densely populated, with a thriving economy and a very high level of productivity. It is best known for its early tweeds from Flanders and, after the Industrial Revolution, for its trains and other industrial products. From very early on, even before the geographical discoveries, it was assimilated into the process of world economic integration.

In the Middle Ages, Belgium was essentially an agriculture-based civilization. Peasants cultivated the land as their main means of livelihood and wove tweed as a side business. This resulted in an underdeveloped economy and a decline in commerce throughout the empire. Even so, around the 9th century, the merchant ships of the Frieslanders (a province in the northwest of the Netherlands) were constantly trading between the Scheldt River (which flows through Tournai, Ghent and Antwerp), the Maas and the Rhine, and along the North Sea coast. One of the main commodities traded was the woolen goods spun by the Flemish farmers which were known far and wide for their bright colors and were given as a precious gift by Charlemagne to the King Harun Al-Rasheed.[10] All of Netherland exhibits a commercial vitality not found elsewhere in Western Europe.

Flanders was uniquely located, with the port of Bruges serving as a natural transit point for merchant ships from England and the Nordic region heading south out of the Baltic Sea. In addition to its privileged location, Flanders was a leader in industry (mainly metallurgy) at the time. The growing population made the land vibrant, and the peasants were freed from simple farming to engage in other industries such as weaving and metallurgy (mainly copper production). The additional landless population was encouraged to create new land by enclosing dikes and draining water. On the newly emerged wet grasslands of

材的呢绒织造业迁移到便于产品销售贸易的各个港口。佛兰德斯手工作坊织成的精致呢绒，作为商船回程货物卖给欧洲大陆其他地方，商人获利丰厚、大发其财。而在 12 世纪，整个佛兰德斯成了纺织匠和漂染匠的国度，它因此发展成欧洲最富有的地区，开始了它的黄金时代。

the coast, flocks of sheep were raised, and the quality of the wool was particularly fine. By the 10th century, with the development of the import/export trade, local wool was running out and Flemish weavers had to rely on merchants to import more wool from England, while wool bleachers had access to soap and dyes imported from overseas by merchants. Consequently, the local weaving industry, which had been based in the countryside, moved to various ports where the product could be easily sold and traded. The delicate woolen fabrics woven in Flemish workshops were sold to the rest of the continent as return cargo for merchant ships, making merchants rich and prosperous. In the 12th century, all of Flanders became a country of weavers and

《伊莎贝尔王后1389年进入巴黎》。出自让·弗罗萨特所著《弗洛伊萨尔编年史》第4卷第1部分插图，由比利时布鲁日的无名画家所作，画于约1470年。由于匠人和商人的贡献，"漫长黑暗"的中世纪里，贵族们的服装异常艳丽。1389年，法兰西的查理六世在巴黎庆祝他的新王后伊莎贝尔首次到来。在公爵、领主和议员的安排下，坐在马背上的王后带着她的随扈侍女到达，仕女们坐着轿子或骑着偏鞍。画中人物穿戴着李子红的呢绒帽子和斗篷，绣花丝绸上金色的丝线闪着微光

Queen Isabelle's Arrival in Paris in 1389 – by an unknown artist from Bruges, Belgium, painted around 1470 (from the first part illustrations of Volume IV of the Froissart's Chronicles by Jean Froissart). Thanks to the contribution of artisans and merchants, the nobility's costumes were exceptionally colorful during the "long dark" Middle Ages. In 1389, Charles VI of France celebrated the first arrival of his new queen, Isabel, in Paris. Arranged by dukes, lords and councilors, the queen arrived on horseback with her retinue of ladies in sedan chairs or on partial saddles. In the painting, the figures are dressed in plum-red tweed hats and cloaks, with golden threads shimmering on embroidered silk

查理大帝棺椁上覆盖的锦缎（丝织品）。出自 Herta Lepie, Georg Minkenberg, *The Cathedral Treasury of Aachen*，第 18 页

Brocade (silk fabric) covering the coffin of Charles the Great. From Herta Lepie, Georg Minkenberg, *The Cathedral Treasury of Aachen*, p. 18

曾有人骄傲地说："世界上所有国家都要靠由弗拉芒人织成布匹的英格兰羊毛取暖。"[11] 虽有所夸大，但的确，当时北欧的毛皮、佛兰德斯的呢绒和中国的丝绸，在远程贸易商品名单上几乎居于同等重要的地位。它们共同的特点是：价格高而又运输方便。

11 世纪的时候，欧洲的商业开始进入复兴时期。造成这次复兴的有两大因素：内因是欧洲大部分地区的人口增长，外因则是十字军东征。[12] 这次复兴的两个策源地，一个是位于欧洲南部的意大利威尼斯，另一个就是位于欧洲北部的佛兰德斯海岸。关于导致这次商业复兴的两个因素，彼此之间相辅相成，难分先后。

十字军的东征结束了伊斯兰教徒对地中海的垄断，恢复了原来的海上贸易，从北海到地中海沿岸的海路热闹起来。自 12 世纪初起，因用船只为军队运送给养而暴富的大量威尼斯商人开始出现在佛兰德斯的市集。到了 13 世纪，威尼斯人、佛罗伦萨人、西班牙人、布雷特伊人、汉萨人都在佛兰德斯的布鲁日港设有各自的商行。与贸易发展密切相关的货币和信用体系也在这一地区建立起来。[13]

佛兰德斯市集上的货品基本上是来自叙利亚、埃及、拜占庭的香料和贵重物品，主要是胡椒、丝绸、珐琅器皿和象牙制品，而叙利亚的香料、丝绸则是由中国和印度的商队运来的。此时的东方已经由蒙古帝国统一，境内的商队几乎可以畅行无阻。所以，早在大航海时代到来以前，远在西欧的比利时就已经与来自中国的商人和商品联系到了一起。由此可知，全球化并不是什么新鲜的事物。几百年以前，居于世界各地的人类祖先，就曾尽力收集各国各地的信息，派出各种商团使节，探索哪

dyers, and it developed into the richest region in Europe, marking the beginning of its golden age. Someone once proudly said, "All the countries of the world are warmed by the wool of England, which is woven into cloth by the Flemish."[11] Although exaggerated, it is true that at that time the furs of Northern Europe, the tweeds of Flanders and the silks of China were almost equally important in the list of long-distance traded goods. They shared the same characteristics: high prices and easy transportation.

In the 11th century, European commerce began a period of Renaissance. Two major factors contributed to this Renaissance: the internal factor was the population growth in most of Europe, and the external factor was the Crusades.[12] The two sources of this renaissance were Venice, Italy, in southern Europe, and the Flemish coast, in northern Europe. Regarding the two factors that led to this business renaissance, they complement each other and are indistinguishable from each other.

The Crusades put an end to the Islamist monopoly on the Mediterranean and restored the earlier maritime trade, and the sea route from the North Sea to the Mediterranean coast came alive. From the beginning of the 12th century, a large number of Venetian merchants, who had become rich by carrying supplies for the army in their ships, began to appear in the marketplaces of Flanders. By the 13th century, Venetians, Florentines, Spaniards, Breteuil and Hanseatic merchants all had their own trading houses in the Flemish port of Bruges. The money and credit system, which was closely linked to the development of trade, was also established in this area.[13]

The goods in the Flanders bazaar were primarily spices and valuables from Syria, Egypt and Byzantium - mainly pepper, silk, enameled vessels and ivory products. The spices and silks from Syria were brought in by Chinese and Indian caravans. At this time, the East was already unified by the Mongol Empire, and the caravans in the territory

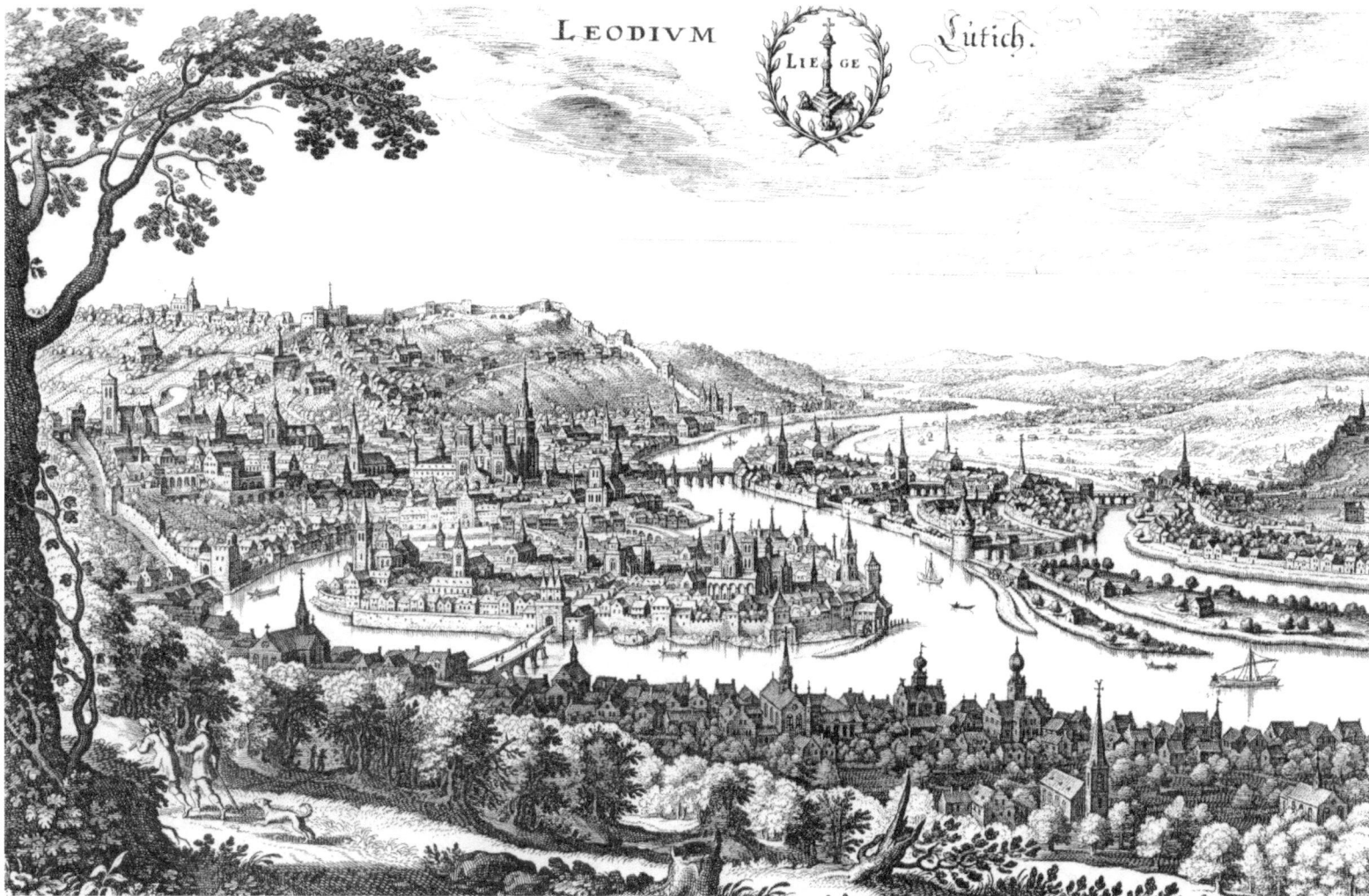

《列日》。马特乌斯·梅里安刻版，约 1647 年在法兰克福出版

Liège. Gravure by Matthäus Merian, published in Francfort circa 1647

《布鲁日的城堡》，大约画于 1672 年。收藏于格罗宁格博物馆
The Burg in Bruges, painted circa 1672 by Jan Baptist van Meunincxhove.
Collection of Groeninge museum

19 世纪的布鲁日。下载自 MonoVisions 黑白照片杂志网站
Bruges in the 19th century, downloaded from the MonoVisions website
资料来源（Source）：http://monovisions.com。

里是最好的市场，哪里可以找到满足人们各种消费欲望的商品，寻找可以跨越沙漠和山脉抵达另一端神奇国度的商路。

商业和贸易的发展带来了分工，促进了手工业的发展。由于工业的增长，收入来源稳定的佛兰德斯与布拉邦特的人们对于贸易的兴趣越来越小。它们把具有更高风险性的海上贸易交给其他地方的商人。从这一时期开始，海岸线漫长的荷兰人热衷于从事航运贸易及相关产业，于是荷兰人成为"海上马车夫"；相对处于内陆的比利时人则更愿意从事纺织、冶金等加工制造业。这种国情逐渐固定下来，并最终导致了比利时从低地国家（荷

could travel almost unimpededly. So, long before the advent of the Great Age of Navigation, Belgium, far away in Western Europe, was already connected with merchants and goods from China. Thus, globalization is nothing new: hundreds of years ago, human ancestors living all over the world did their best to collect information from all over the world, sending all kinds of merchant missions to explore where the best markets were, where to bring goods to satisfy people's various consumption desires, and how to cross deserts and mountains to reach the magical land on the other side of the trade route.

The development of commerce and trade brought about a division of labor and promoted the development of handicrafts. Due to the growth of industry, the people of

兰王国）分离出来，成为日后独立的比利时王国。

　　商业和贸易自然带来了大量的财富。除了佛兰德斯，中世纪时期这一地区还先后产生了布拉邦特、埃诺、那慕尔、卢森堡等城邦，由各个公爵、伯爵等统治。其下又统辖着大量由富有的自由人聚集的如根特、列日、布鲁日、安特卫普、伊珀尔（又译作伊普雷）等大城市。这些城市都是在这一时期创造出令人惊羡的原始财富，并从贵族手里获得了城市自主权，发展出令人自豪的城市文化。在当时的欧洲，能与之相媲美的，只有意大利的威尼斯、佛罗伦萨、米兰等大城市。时至今日，尽管

Flanders and Brabant, who had a stable source of income, became less interested in trade. They left the riskier maritime trade to merchants from other places. From this period onwards, the Dutch, who had a long coastline, were keen to engage in the shipping trade and related industries. The Dutch became known as the "Sea Coachman." The Belgians, who were relatively more inland, preferred to engage in textile, metallurgy and other processing industries. This situation was gradually fixed, and eventually led to the separation of Belgium from the Low Countries (Kingdom of the Netherlands), which became the independent Kingdom of Belgium.

曾经作为中世纪的战场，历经两次世界大战的炮火硝烟，比利时仍然保留了大量中世纪的教堂、钟楼和古堡。2000 年比利时的 32 座教堂钟楼入选联合国教科文组织的世界文化遗产名录，入选总数之多，甚至高于面积 18 倍于己的法国，其财富积累之丰可见一斑。

商业和贸易的发展还促进了民族意识的觉醒，并导致尼德兰独立运动的爆发，其最终结果是一个历史上从未存在的比利时王国的诞生。佛兰德斯地区诸城镇是 14 世纪欧洲首要的商业中心，意大利的商业银行家和放贷者在这里也拥有庞大的资本。纺织和制造业使城市财富不断增长，以商人、手工业者为基础的市民阶层力量不断壮大。当法国王后参观布鲁日时，深感震惊道："我以为自己是这里唯一的王后，可我发现，另外还有 600 个王后。"[14] 在英法战争中，因为与英国方面的贸

根特的圣尼古拉斯教堂，摄于 1890—1905 年。
收藏于美国国会图书馆

Saint Nicholas Church, Ghent, during 1890-1905.
Collection of United States Library of Congress

Commerce and trade naturally brought a great deal of wealth. In addition to Flanders, the medieval period also saw the creation of city-states such as Brabant, Hainault, Namur and Luxembourg, ruled by dukes and counts. The cities of Ghent, Liège, Bruges, Antwerp, Ypres, etc. were also under their jurisdiction which gathered a large number of wealthy freemen. All of these cities created an enviable amount of raw wealth during this period, acquired urban autonomy from the nobility, and developed a proud urban culture. In Europe at the time, the only major cities that could rival them were Italy's Venice, Florence, and Milan. To this day, despite having been a medieval battleground and having survived two world wars, Belgium still retains a large number of medieval churches, bell towers and fortresses. In 2000, 32 of Belgium's churches bell towers were included on the United Nations Educational, Scientific and Cultural Organization (UNESCO) World Heritage List, a total that is even higher than that of France, which is 17 times larger in area than Belgium.

The development of commerce and trade also contributed to the awakening of national consciousness and led to the outbreak of the Netherlandish independence movement, the end result of which was the birth of a Belgian kingdom that had never existed before in history. The towns of the Flanders region were the premier commercial centers of Europe in the 14th century, and Italian commercial bankers and moneylenders also had large capital here. The textile and manufacturing industries made

16 世纪表现金马刺战役的弗拉芒版画。画家不详

Battle of the Golden Spurs in Kortrijk in 1302, circa the 16th century, by an unknown painter

资料来源（Source）：http://www.liebaart. org/figuren/guldensp.jpg。

易往来密切，共同的经济利益使佛兰德斯的市民阶层更加倾向于英国，而由于通婚和受教育的因素，当时的佛兰德斯伯爵和贵族们则站在法国国王与贵族一边。在著名的金马刺战役中，[15] 佛兰德斯的行会民兵大败法国封建骑士。到了 16 世纪，哈布斯堡王朝为了争霸欧洲，需要更好地控制佛兰德斯地区以得到源源不绝的资金，国王们总想对尼德兰地区足以构成反抗的一切力量加以摧毁。那些极端的做法，不仅加重了手工业者、底层市民阶层的捐税负担，也触犯了当地贵族、僧侣还有上层市民阶层的利益，于是极大地刺激了尼德兰的民族意识觉醒、坚定了反抗决心。从 16 世纪到法国大革命爆发，这个阶段是欧洲从绝对君主专制向现代民族国家 [16] 过渡的历史阶段。比利时作为民族国家的诞生正是从这个阶段开始不断酝酿，直到工业革命之后瓜熟蒂落。

the city's wealth grow and the strength of the civic class based on merchants and craftsmen continued to grow. When the Queen of France visited Bruges, she was deeply shocked and remarked, "I thought I was the only queen here, but I found out that there were 600 other queens."[14] During the Anglo-French War, because of the close trade with the British side, the common economic interests made the Flemish citizen class more inclined to the British, while the Flemish counts and nobles of the time sided with the French king and nobility due to intermarriage and education. In the famous Battle of the Golden Spur,[15] the Flemish guild militia defeated the French feudal knights. By the 16th century, the Habsburgs needed to gain better control of Flanders in order to gain a steady flow of money for European domination, and the kings always wanted to destroy all the forces in the Netherland that could constitute a resistance. Those extreme measures not only increased the tax burden of craftsmen and the lower class, but also offended the interests of the local nobles, monks and the upper class, which greatly stimulated the Netherland's national consciousness and resistance determination to resist. From the 16th century to the outbreak of the French Revolution, this period was the historical transition from absolute monarchy to modern nation-state[16] in Europe. It was from this stage that Belgium was born as a nation-state, and it was only after the Industrial Revolution that it came to fruition.

蒙古帝国时期的中西交流

最早踏上向东漫漫贸易之路的除了商人，还有传教士。当然，传教士的使命并不是为了赚钱，而是为了传教和扩大教会的影响力。中世纪欧洲的教会相当于一个国家，在民族国家崛起之前，欧洲只有两大巨头——天主教会与神圣罗马帝国。在一定程度上，天主教会与其他帝制国家没有什么两样，它拥有庞大的组织机构，管辖着大片领土和众多民众，同时不断对外发动战争、吞并土地、扩张势力。除了意大利，它还在欧洲其他许多地方拥有领主权、司法裁断权，参与放贷、买卖地产、出租房屋等经济活动。教皇们也和皇帝国王们一样远交近攻，开展外交活动。

兴盛于 13 世纪的蒙古帝国是历史上版图最辽阔的国家，疆土横跨欧亚两洲。对外征战扩张几乎贯穿着蒙古帝国的整个历史。1236—1242 年蒙古帝国向欧洲发动第二次西征，[17] 蒙古大军一举击溃波兰王国和神圣罗马帝国联军，大败匈牙利王国和保加利亚第二帝国，前锋曾远达当时意大利的威尼斯共和国和巴尔干半岛。一时间被打懵的整个欧洲惶惶不安，都想弄清楚这些掠夺者的底细：他们究竟是什么人、来自哪里、他们的习俗和信仰是什么。同时，他们也想要刺探蒙古军队的动向、军情、实力等，以制定策略抵御其进犯。1243—1253 年期间，教皇英诺森四世（Innocent IV）先后派出四个外交使团，其中最有名的是由意大利传教士柏朗嘉宾（Bertrand）率领的；[18] 法国国王路易九世（Louis IX）也派出了一个由佛兰德斯传教士卢布鲁克（William of Rubruck）率领的外交代表团。几个使团的使者都带着教皇或者国王的书信，以上帝的名义乞求蒙古人停止对

Exchanges between China and the West during the Mongol Empire

The first to set out on the long trade route to the east were not only merchants, but also missionaries. Of course, the mission of missionaries was not to make money, but to preach and expand the influence of the Church. The church in medieval Europe was the equivalent of a state, and before the rise of nation-states, there were only two giants in Europe - the Catholic Church and the Holy Roman Empire. To a certain extent, the Catholic Church was no different from other imperial states in that it had a large organizational structure and governed large territories and large populations, while constantly launching wars abroad, annexing land, and expanding its power. In addition to Italy, it also had lordship and judicial discretion in many other parts of Europe, and was involved in economic activities such as lending money, buying and selling real estate, and renting houses. The popes also carried out diplomatic activities just like the emperors and kings, befriending the far.

The Mongol Empire, which flourished in the 13th century, was the most extensive state in history, spanning both Europe and Asia. From 1236 to 1242, the Mongols launched their second expedition to Europe[17] and defeated the Kingdom of Poland, the Holy Roman Empire, the Kingdom of Hungary and the Second Bulgarian Empire, reaching as far as the Italian Republic of Venice and the Balkans. The whole of Europe was on edge, trying to find out who these plunderers were, where they came from, what their customs and beliefs were. At the same time, they also want to spy on the Mongolian army's movements, military situation, strength, etc., in order to formulate strategies to resist its attack. Four diplomatic missions were sent by Pope Innocent IV between 1243 and 1253, the most famous of which was led by the Italian missionary Bertrand.[18] King

卢布鲁克
William of Rubruck

基督徒的杀戮，接受基督教信仰，并寻求一起合作攻打穆斯林的可能性。

卢布鲁克（Guillaume de Rubruquis，也写作 Willem，约 1210、1215、1220—1270、1290、1293，也译作鲁布鲁克、吕柏克），名威廉，出生于佛兰德斯王国（当时属于法国）的卢布鲁克村，以村为姓。后成为佛兰德斯方济各会[19] 会士。1248—1250 年，卢布鲁克曾随法王路易九世参加第七次十字军东侵。[20] 进军埃及失败后，于 1253 年奉命秘密前往蒙古。至于他此次的使命，是奉路易九世之命拉拢其统治者作为同盟者参与西欧各国发动的十字军东侵，还是奉教皇之命传教，同之前已随阿拉伯商人传入蒙古的伊斯兰教进行竞争，在他后来的著作中并未明确提及。据说，卢布鲁克其人，善观察，能言辞，会讲多种语言，非常适合外交和传教工作。不过，他长得很胖，所以每次他们在路上换马时，他都得去抢

卢布鲁克出使路线图。下载自美国华盛顿大学
Roadmap of Rubruck's Mission, downloaded from the University of Washington
资料来源（Source）：http://depts.washington.edu/uwch/silkroad/maps/rubruck.html。

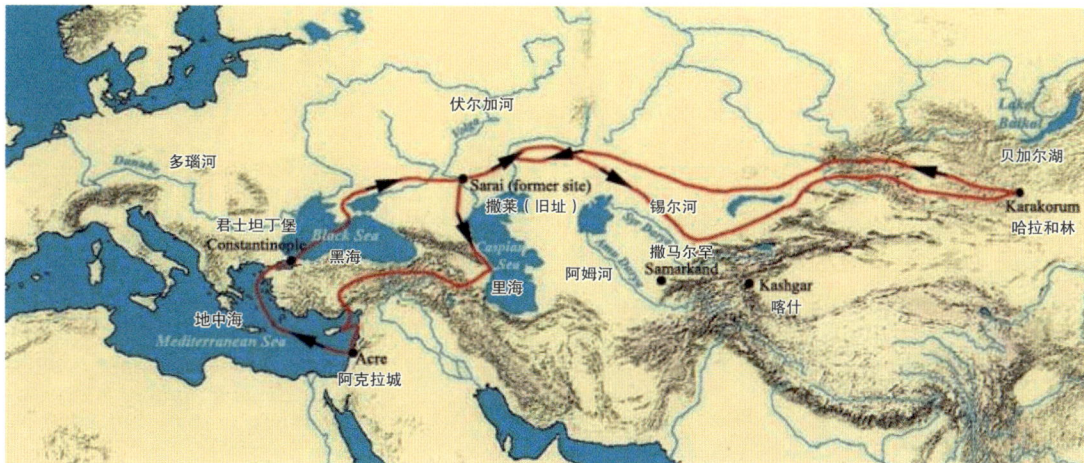

Louis IX of France also sent a diplomatic mission led by the Flemish missionary William of Rubruck. The messengers of several missions carried letters from the pope or the king, begging the Mongols in the name of God to stop the killing of Christians, to accept the Christian faith, and to seek the possibility of cooperating together in the attack on the Muslims.

William of Rubruck (Guillaume de Rubruquis, also written as Willem van Ruysbroeck, Guillaume de Rubrouck, Willielmus de Rubruquis, c. 1210 or 1215 or 1220 - 1270 or 1290 or 1293), was born in the village of Rubruck in the Kingdom of Flanders (then part of France) and took the village as his surname. He later became a Flemish Franciscan[19] missionary. From 1248 to 1250, William participated in the Seventh Crusade with King Louis IX of France.[20] After failing to advance to Egypt, he was ordered to go to Mongolia secretly in 1253. It is not clear from his later writings that whether his mission was on the orders of Louis IX to convince the rulers to participate as allies in the crusades launched by the Western European countries, or on the orders of the Pope to preach Christianity in competition with Islam, which had already been introduced to Mongolia by Arab traders. William is said to have been an observant, articulate, and multilingual man, well suited for diplomatic and missionary work. However, he was physically large - whenever the mission changed horses on the road, he had to go for the fittest one.[21]

William set out from the city of Accra (north of modern Haifa, Egypt) on the eastern shore of the Mediterranean Sea and made his way east, "carrying with me from Constantinople, according to the advice of the merchants, fruits, muscat wine and fine cookies for the first batch of (Tatar) governors, so as to make my journey easier, for it seemed to them impolite to go empty-handed".[22] After crossing the Black Sea, he arrived at the Volga in August of the same year to visit Batu Khan. Believing that he had no

那匹最健壮的马。[21]

卢布鲁克从地中海东岸阿克拉城（Accra，今埃及海法以北）出发，一路东行，"按商人的劝告，我从康（君）士坦丁堡随身携带了果品、麝香葡萄酒和精美的饼干，送给头一批（鞑靼）长官，好让我旅途方便些，因为在他们看来，空着手去是不礼貌的"[22]。渡过黑海后，于同年8月到达伏尔加河畔，谒见拔都汗。拔都认为自己无权准许他在蒙古人中传教，便派他去见蒙古大汗蒙哥。他只好继续东行，路上日趋寒冷，还不时忍受饥饿，过了咸海（Aral Sea），终于在12月到达蒙古都城附近的蒙哥冬季营地。他于1254年1月第一次觐见蒙哥汗。蒙哥待之以礼，而对皈依基督教和联盟的事却态度冷淡。4月，他随同蒙哥来到当时的蒙古都城哈拉和林（Karakorum）。7月带着蒙哥致路易九世的一封言辞非常傲慢的国书西归，于1255年回到地中海东岸。

出使蒙古的使团返回一年后，卢布鲁克用拉丁文写成了给路易九世的出使报告，即《卢布鲁克东行纪》。根据耳闻目睹，他在《东行纪》中不惜笔墨、生动具体地记述了13世纪蒙古各个部落的衣食住行、风俗习惯、法律宗教等情况，还仔细记述了所经山川湖泊、各地、各城以及沿途各民族的情况，这些记载不仅是研究中世纪历史地理及中西交通史的重要原始资料，而且为欧洲人提供了认识另一种文化的非凡见解。他说："当我发现自己在他们当中时，我真感到好像我是到了另一个世纪。"[23]

在《东行纪》中，卢布鲁克提到在蒙古庞大的疆域中有许多民族和各种宗教信仰。那里不仅有被称作鞑靼的蒙古人及中亚、西亚的各个民族的人，如亚美尼亚

right to grant William the permission to preach Christianity among the Mongols, Batu sent William to Mongol Khan. William had to continue his journey eastward, getting colder and colder and suffering from hunger from time to time, and crossed the Aral Sea, finally reaching Mongol's winter camp near the Mongol capital in December. He had his first audience with Mongol Khan in January 1254. In April he accompanied Mongol to Karakorum, then the Mongol capital, and in July he returned to the east coast of the Mediterranean in 1255 with a very arrogant letter of state from Mongol to Louis IX.

A year after the return of the Mongolian mission, William wrote his report in Latin to Louis IX, known as *The Journey of William of Rubruck to the Eastern Parts of the World*. Based on what he heard and saw, William spared no effort in his report to give a vivid and concrete account of the clothing, food, housing, customs, laws and religion of the various Mongolian tribes in the 13th century, as well as a careful account of the mountains, lakes, places and cities he passed through and the various ethnic groups along the way, which are not only important primary sources for the study of medieval history and geography and the history of East-West communication, but also provide Europeans with a remarkable insight into another remarkable culture. He wrote, "When I found myself among them, I really felt as if I had arrived in another century."[23]

In *The Journey of William of Rubruck to the Eastern Parts of the World*, William mentions that there were many ethnic groups and various religious beliefs in the vast territory of Mongolia. There were not only Mongols, called Tatars, and people of various nationalities from Central and West Asia, such as Armenians, Georgians, Bohemians, but also Russians, Poles, Hungarians, Germans, Slavs, as well as Nestorians[24] of the Christian branch, Buddhists of Uyghurs[25], and Muslims of Saracens[26], who were taken captive. William also identifies what the ancient Greeks

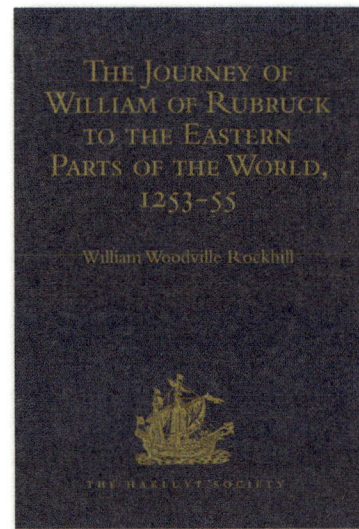

卢布鲁克撰写的出使报告《卢布鲁克东行纪》。该版图书于2010年7月28日由哈克鲁伊特协会出版

Rubruck's report on the mission – *The Journey of William of Rubruck to the Eastern Parts of the World*. Published on July 28, 2010 by Hakluyt Society

一份卢布鲁克撰写的出使报告《东行纪》的14世纪副本插图。图中上半部分是卢布鲁克和他的旅伴从法王路易九世那里接受委托。下半部分展示了两位修士的旅程。收藏于英国剑桥科珀斯克里斯蒂学院帕克图书馆

An illustration of a 14th-century copy of *Rubruck's Report on His Mission to the East*. The upper portion shows William of Rubruck and his travelling companion with Louis IX of France. The lower portion shows the two friars on their journey. Collection of Parker Library, Corpus Christi College, Cambridge, the United Kingdom

人、格鲁吉亚人、波西米亚人，还有被掳掠来的信奉基督教的罗斯人（即俄罗斯人）、波兰人、匈牙利人、日耳曼人、斯拉夫人，以及信奉基督教分支教派的聂斯脱里教徒[24]、信奉佛教的畏兀儿人[25]和信奉伊斯兰教的撒拉逊人[26]。卢布鲁克还确认了古希腊人所说的"赛里丝"（Seres，意为丝国）是当时契丹的一个组成部分："还有大契丹，我认为其民族就是古代的丝人。他们生产最好的丝绸（该民族把它称为丝），而他们是从他们的一座城市得到丝人之名。……该国土内有许多省，大部分还没有臣服于蒙古。"[27] 他见到了中国的纸币，"契丹通行的钱是一种绵纸，长宽约为一巴掌，上面印有几行字，像蒙哥印玺上的一样"。他提及中国文字及书写工具毛笔："他们使用毛刷写字，像画师用毛刷绘画。他们把几个字母写成一个字形，构成一个完整的词。"[28] 他还注意到中西医的不同，他说："（中国的）医师很熟悉草药的性能，熟练地按脉诊断；但他们不用利尿剂，也不知道检查小便。这是我亲眼所见。"[29] 这是欧洲人在中世纪对中国及其文化的最早最确切的记录了。

最让卢布鲁克大开眼界的是蒙古王朝的首都哈拉和林。13世纪中叶的哈拉和林可以说是世界的首都，云集着来自罗马教皇的传教士、南宋朝廷的使节团、波斯商人的驼马队、高丽王国的进贡者。蒙哥每年有两次要在哈拉和林的大宫殿里大宴朝臣，届时，哪怕远在两个月路程之外的贵族们，也都要赶赴他的宫廷朝觐他，并接受他的赏赐。在这座宫殿的门口，他让来自巴黎的金匠威廉（Guillaume Boucher）制作了一座巨大的可以喷出四种不同饮料、奶酒的银树喷泉，以彰显王朝的富贵威仪。"在银树的根部是四只银狮，各通有管道，喷出白色马奶。

called "Seres" (meaning silk country) as a component of the Khitan state of the time: "There is also the Great Khitan, whose people I believe to be the ancient silk people. They produced the best silk which earned them the name Silk People. There are many provinces within that land, most of which have not yet submitted to Mongolia."[27] He saw Chinese paper money - "The money prevailing in Khitan is a kind of cotton paper, about a palm's length and width, on which are printed a few lines of characters, like those on the seal of Mongol". He mentions Chinese writing and the writing instrument, the brush: "They use brushes to write, like painters using brushes to draw. They write several letters in a glyph that formed a complete word."[28] He also noted the differences between Chinese and Western medicine, saying "(Chinese) physicians are well acquainted with the properties of herbs and skilled in diagnosing by the pulse; but they do not use diuretics and do not know how to check urine. This is what I have seen with my own eyes."[29] This is the earliest and most definitive record of Europeans in the Middle Ages about China and its culture.

The most eye-opening event for William was the capital of the Mongol dynasty, Karakorum, which in the mid-13th century was just as the capital of the world, filled with missionaries from the Pope, envoys from the Southern Song court, camel caravans of Persian merchants, and tributes from the kingdom of Koryo. Twice a year, Mongkol would feast his courtiers in the great palace of Karakorum, when noblemen, despite the journey of two months, would come to his court to pay respects and receive his rewards. At the entrance of the palace, he had Guillaume Boucher, a goldsmith from Paris, create a huge fountain of silver trees that spouted four different drinks and milk wines, in order to show off the wealth and prestige of the dynasty. "Master William the Parisian had made for him a great silver tree, and at its roots are four lions of silver, each with a conduit through it, and all belching forth white milk of mares.

树内有四根管子，通到它的顶端，向下弯曲，每根上还有金蛇，蛇尾缠绕树身。一根管子流出酒，另一根流出哈喇忽迷思，即澄清的马奶，另一根流出布勒，一种用蜜做成的饮料，还有一根流出米酒，叫做特拉辛纳的。树足各有一特制的银盆，接受每根管子流出的饮料。"[30]在树的顶端四根管子之间，还有一个手拿喇叭的天使，由藏在树干腹中的仆人用管子从树心通到天使口中，吹响天使手中的喇叭，宣布宴会开始。

卢布鲁克是早于马可·波罗来到东方并对它加以描绘的人，只是由于使命和身份的不同，他本人及其著作都不及后来的马可·波罗有名。卢布鲁克之后，蒙古帝国也曾遣使往西。1289年，来自北京的使臣哈班古马来到罗马，备受欧洲欢迎。1338年，教皇本笃十二世接见了蒙古使臣阿兰公卿，典礼隆重。之后，教皇命马黎诺里回访。马黎诺里来华后，投其所好，向元朝皇帝献了一匹骏马，深受皇帝喜爱。据《元史》卷四十《顺帝本纪》中记载，马黎诺里所献的马为"佛郎国贡异马，长一丈一尺三寸，高六尺四寸，身纯黑，后二蹄皆白"。另外，在《庚申外史》一书中，亦曾提及此事："脱脱好人，不宜久在外，上遂领之。会佛郎国进天马黑色五明，其项高而下钩，置之群马中，若橐驼之在羊队也。上因叹美曰：人中有脱脱，马中有佛郎国马，皆世间杰出者也。"[31]"佛朗国进天马"一事成为当时轰动一时的大事，文人士子竞相以"天马赞""天马赋"为题赋诗作画，成为元末中西文化交流的一大盛事。

上文中所提马黎诺里所进献的马，其实是比利时特有的马种，称佛兰德斯巨马，是中世纪的战马，也是后世重型马的祖先。它体毛黑色，身躯硕大，肌肉发达，

And four conduits are led inside the tree to its tops, which are bent downward, and on each of these is also a gilded serpent, whose tail twines round the tree. And from one of these pipes flows wine; from another crocosmia, or clarified mare's milk; from another bal, a drink made with honey; and from yet another rice mead, which is called terracina. And for each liquor there is a special silver bowl at the foot of the tree to receive it."[30] At the top of the tree, between the four conduits, there was also an angel holding a trumpet. A servant hidden in the belly of the trunk used a pipe to go up through the heart of the tree to the mouth of angel and blew the trumpet in the angel's hand to announce the beginning of the feast.

William was the one who came to the East and depicted it before Marco Polo. But because of his mission and status, William himself and his writings are not as famous as the later Marco Polo. After William, the Mongol Empire also sent ambassadors to the West, and in 1289, Habban-cauma, an ambassador from Beijing, came to Rome and was welcomed in Europe. In 1338, Pope Benoit XII received the Mongol ambassador Alans with great pomp and ceremony. Afterwards, the pope ordered Giovanni da Marignolli to pay a return visit. When Marignolli came to China, he offered a stallion to the Yuan emperor, who really liked the stallion. According to the *History of Yuan Dynasty* (Volume 40), *The Records of Emperor Shun*, the horse offered by Marignolli was "a horse of foreign quality from the county of Flanders - about eleven feet three inches long and six feet four inches tall, with a pure black body and two white hind hooves". In addition, the book *Geng Shen Wai Shi* also mentioned this matter. ...[31] The "heavenly horse" from Flander county became a big cultural event at that time, featured in numerous poetry and paintings created during the end of the Yuan dynasty.

The horse offered by Marignolli mentioned above is actually a unique Belgian horse breed called the Flemish

1846 年荷兰画家 Mathieu Richard Auguste Henrion 绘制的银树喷泉

The silver tree fountain painted by the Dutch painter Mathieu Richard Auguste Henrion in 1846

资料来源（Source）：https://www.maryevans.com/search.php。

蒙古图格里克 10000 元面额纸币背面图案

The back design of 10,000-yuan bank note of Mongolian Tugrik

腿短，一般身高 163—173 厘米，体重 820—1000 公斤，堪称巨兽，偏又性情温顺。看到它，才能理解什么样的马才能驮着顶盔贯甲的重装骑士冲锋陷阵。中世纪后，重骑兵逐渐退出历史舞台，这种马也变成了耕田拉车的农畜。当时比利时尚属法国（佛郎国），所以元朝人以为是法国马。几百年后的 1890 年，钦差大臣薛福成奉命出使比利时，参观马会，也曾见到这种巨马，并详加描述："马皆肥硕膘健，有重至一千五百斤者，较常马高大倍之，皆牡马也。惟比国有此巨马，善牧者以重费养之，每岁售与各国为种，价高者可鬻至一万数千佛郎。各埠购得一二马以归，俾与牝马交，所生之子亦皆肥硕，而膘色已稍弗如；三传之后，则复同常马矣。故各国必来购种，大抵用之耕田者为多。"[32]

horse, which is a medieval war horse and the ancestor of later heavy horses. It has black hair, a large, muscular body and short legs, and is generally 163-173 cm tall and weighs 820-1,000 kg. It is only when seeing in person that one can realize how this kind of horse can carry a heavy knight in armor and charge into battle. After the Middle Ages, heavy cavalry gradually receded from the stage of history, and the horse became a farm animal for plowing the fields and pulling carts. At that time, Belgium was still part of France (Flanders), so the Yuan dynasty people thought it was a French horse. Hundreds of years later, in 1890, when Minister Xue Fucheng visited the horse fair in Belgium, he also saw this huge horse and recorded his impression. ...[32]

两位重装骑士在原野上对战。由法国画家欧仁·德拉克洛瓦绘于 1824 年。收藏于法国卢浮宫

Tow Knights Fighting in a Landscape, painted by the French painter Eugene Delacroix in 1824. Collection of the Louvre Museum, France

以书传教的金尼阁

　　蒙古帝国走向衰亡后，中欧之间的交通中断了有200多年的时间。西班牙、葡萄牙人在海上寻找到新航线之前，中西之间变得彼此隔膜和充满神秘感。在东方，中国的封建社会逐渐发展到它的顶峰，国力之强，罕有其匹，依然是万邦来朝的盛景。在欧洲，随着新航路开辟、大航海时代到来，比利时的亲兄弟、并称尼德兰的荷兰于1588年独立，发展成为航海和贸易强国，被誉为"海上马车夫"。它在世界各地建立殖民地和贸易据点，并于1655年派出使团扬帆而来，抵达北京，要求与建国不久的清朝通商。而比利时此时仍在西班牙的统治之下。

　　相比于民族国家，欧洲的基督教教会仍然拥有巨大的权力和超越国家的影响力。尽管交通不便道路阻隔，教会一直没有完全放弃向东方派遣传教士。教会不仅集中了大量的权力和财富，也垄断了知识，当时受教育程度最高的群体就是教士。教士们在教会中根据各自的能力和兴趣而各尽所能、各司其职：口才好有毅力的负责传教，有管理能力的负责处理教会日常事务，擅长理财的负责管理教产增加财富，而有天赋有才智的则撰写了大量基督教著作，他们甚至也研究其他宗教的文化，以为其所用。

　　传教士为了有效吸引和归化中国人，使用了多种方法，如向中国皇帝和官员进献礼物，给中国人治病，展现神迹等，其中使用最广、最有成效的莫过于"书籍传教"。明清之际，搭乘商船沿新航路来华传教的耶稣会[33]传教士们，摸索出了一套与卢布鲁克不同的传教方式，即利用自身所长，借助印刷书籍传授科学知识进行传教。比利时学者钟鸣旦（Nicolas Standaert）指出，由

Nicolas Trigault - Preaching through Books

After the fall of the Mongol Empire, the communication between China and Europe was interrupted for more than two hundred years. Before the Spanish and Portuguese found new routes on the sea, the East and the West became separated from each other and full of mystery. In the East, the feudal society of China gradually developed to its peak, and the power of the state was unparalleled. In Europe, with the opening of new routes and the advent of the Great Age of Navigation, the Netherlands, a relative of Belgium became independent in 1588 and developed into a seafaring and trading power, known as the "Sea Coachman." It established colonies and trading posts around the world, and in 1655 sent a mission to Beijing, asking for commerce with the soon to be established Qing dynasty. Belgium, however, was still under Spanish rule.

In contrast to nation-states, the Christian churches in Europe still possessed enormous power and influence beyond the state. The Church never completely abandoned sending missionaries to the East, despite the inaccessibility of roads. The church not only concentrated a great deal of power and wealth, but also had a monopoly on knowledge - the most educated group at the time was the clergy. The priests were each competent in their own way according to their abilities and interests: those who were eloquent and persevering were responsible for preaching, those who had managerial skills were responsible for handling the daily affairs of the church, those who were good at managing money were responsible for managing the church property and increasing wealth, while those who were gifted and talented wrote a large number of Christian works, and they even studied pagan cultures.

In order to effectively attract and convert the Chinese, missionaries used a variety of methods, such as offering gifts to Chinese emperors and officials, healing the Chinese

比利时著名画家鲁本斯（Peter Paul Rubens）所绘金尼阁画像，绘于1616—1617 年。画中金尼阁身穿中国明朝人服饰。左图藏于美国大都会美术馆，右图收藏于杜埃美术馆

The portrait of Nicolas Trigault painted by the famous Belgian painter Peter Paul Rubens in 1616-1617. In the painting, Nicolas Trigault is dressed in Chinese Ming dynasty costume. The picture on the left is in the collection of the Metropolitan Museum of Art, USA. The picture on the right is in the collection of Musée de la Chartreuse de Douai of France

于欧洲出版和印刷业的繁荣，"'书籍传教'成为在社会精英中传播基督教的主要方法"[34]。

传教士们在踏上中国国土之后很快注意到中国是一个有着悠久文明的国度，人们尊敬知识分子，热爱书籍。耶稣会士范礼安（Alessandro Valignano）说："中国各城市藏书之丰富，真是美不胜收"，"他们拥有的书籍只会多于我们欧洲，都是印出来的，论述科学以及其他主题"[35]。惊叹之余，传教士们总结出：在中国，知识分子，也就是"士"，居于社会各阶层之首，属于统治

of illnesses, and performing miracles, among which the most widespread and effective was the "preaching through books." During the Ming and Qing dynasties, the Society of Jesus[33] missionaries, who came to China by merchant ships along the New Passage, developed a different missionary method from that of William of Rubruck: namely, preaching through printing books and teaching scientific knowledge. The Belgian scholar Nicolas Standaert noted that, as a result of the European publishing and printing boom, "'preaching through books' became the main method of spreading Christianity among the social elite.[34]"

After setting foot on Chinese soil, the missionaries soon noticed that China was a country with a long civilization, a people who respected intellectuals and loved books. The Jesuit Alessandro Valignano noted, "The wealth of books in the Chinese cities is truly magnificent," "They have only more books than we have in Europe, all printed, on subjects matters of science as well as others.[35]" In their amazement, the missionaries concluded that in China, the intellectuals, or "Shi," were at the head of all social classes and belonged to the ruling class. To succeed in their missionary work in China, they had to conquer the hearts of the Shi. In order to expand their influence among the Shi, and to arouse the interest and admiration of the Chinese, they had to use European books to prove the superiority of Western culture and that the missionaries came from a culturally prosperous country. To this end, Nicolas Trigault, a Belgian Jesuit, came to China in 1613 with more than 7,000 books collected in Europe.

Nicolas Trigault (also known in Latin as Trigautius or Trigaultius, 1577-1628) was a Jesuit missionary to China. He and other early missionaries to China inherited and further developed the missionary method of Matteo Ricci[36] in China[37]. During his lifetime, he came to China twice, spending a total of 12 years, and traveled extensively in the north and south. He wrote and published extensively, and

阶级；要想在中国传教成功，就要征服士大夫们的心；而若想在士大夫阶层扩大影响力、引起中国人的兴趣和景仰，则须借助欧洲的书籍来证明西方文化的优越性，证明传教士来自于文化昌明之邦。为此，1613 年比利时籍耶稣会士金尼阁携在欧洲募集到的 7000 余部图书来到中国。

金尼阁（Nicolas Trigault，拉丁文又作 Trigautius 或 Trigaultius，1577—1628）是一位耶稣会来华传教士。他与其他早期来华传教士继承了利玛窦[36]创下的中国传教方法[37]，并进一步发扬光大。金尼阁一生中两次来华，在华时间长达 12 年，足迹遍及大江南北，著述颇丰，为耶稣会在华传教事业做出巨大贡献，并最终埋骨于杭州。

1577 年 3 月 3 日金尼阁出生在杜埃城，那时杜埃城属于佛兰德斯地区的一部分，后并入法国，因此他生前自称比利时人。1615 年他在刊印的利玛窦遗稿《基督教远征中国史》封面上即自称"Belga"（比利时人）。金尼阁曾在杜埃城耶稣会士主持的学校就读，于 1594 年获得文科硕士学位，之后不久便加入耶稣会。在赴海外传教之前，他进行了长达几年的系统学习，包括修辞学与哲学，研究语言、地理、天文、数学、医学等有助于传教的学问。这种训练使金尼阁等传教士成为那个时代的知识精英。

金尼阁第一次来华是在 1610 年，当时他在印度果阿传教。金尼阁于次年到达南京，在先于他抵华的传教士指导下学习汉语，不久应李之藻[38]之邀，前往杭州传教。[39]在赴北京汇报教务时，他发现了利玛窦的札记，将其带走整理翻译为拉丁文，并撰写了利玛窦的生平。

made great contributions to the Jesuit mission in China. He died and was buried in Hangzhou.

Born on March 3, 1577 in Douai, then part of Flanders and later annexed to France, Nicolas Trigault called himself a Belgian. In 1615, Trigault printed Matteo Ricci's posthumous manuscript *History of the Christian Expedition to China*. On its cover, Trigault referred to himself as "Belga" (Belgian). Nicolas Trigault attended a Jesuit-run school in Douai, where he received his Master of Arts degree in 1594, and soon afterwards joined the Jesuits. He studied rhetoric and philosophy, languages, geography, astronomy, mathematics, medicine, and other missionary studies for several years before going overseas, a training that made missionaries such as Nicolas Trigault the intellectual elite of his time.

Nicolas Trigault first came to China in 1610 when he was a missionary in Goa, India. He arrived in Nanjing the following year, studied Chinese under the guidance of the missionaries who had arrived before him, and was soon invited by Li Zhizao[38] to preach in Hangzhou.[39] When he went to Beijing to report on his teaching duties, he found Matteo Ricci's journals, which he later translated into Latin and wrote a biography of Ricci. In 1613, he was sent back to Europe to report on his missionary work. In 1615, he published his book *Matteo Ricci's Journal of China* (originally titled *De Christiana Expeditio ne apvd Sinas Svscepta ab Scoietate Jesv, Ex P. Matthæi Ricci ejusdem Societatis Comentarris*), which was very well received in Europe. For the first time, the book gives an accurate and faithful description of China, including appellations, geography, products, craftsmanship, court, customs, laws and institutions, as well as insights into missionary experiences throughout China. This book is of great historical value for the study of the history of the Chinese and Western Transportation in the Ming dynasty, the history of the Jesuit missions in China, and the history of the late

1613 年金尼阁奉派返回欧洲汇报教务。1615 年《利玛窦中国札记》（原书名《基督教远征中国史》，拉丁文书名为 *De Christiana Expeditio ne apvd Sinas Svscepta ab Scoietate Jesv, Ex P. Matthæi Ricci ejusdem Societatis Comentarris*）在欧洲正式出版，并获得了极大的反响。书中首次精确地、忠实地描述了中国的情况，包括名称、地理、物产、工艺技术、朝廷、风俗、法律、制度以及在中国各地传教的经历见闻等。这本书对研究明代中西交通史、耶稣会士在华传教史和明朝后期历史，都具有重要的史料价值。

在罗马，金尼阁向教皇报告了在中国传教的情形，并就具体传教事务提出了相应的要求。根据在华经验，金尼阁请求教皇准许将圣经、弥撒经、司铎日课、司铎典要等译成中文，并请求传教及举行礼拜仪式时不用拉丁文而用中文，允许在中国的神父举行弥撒仪式时不脱帽，以及准许任命中国人为神职人员。[40] 这些问题看似微小，但性质重要，影响深远。在华耶稣会士认为，要想在中国达到传教的目的，就要尊重一些特别的规则，应该入乡随俗。金尼阁以其口若悬河的游说能力和随机应变的才能在罗马教廷得到了胜利，在华传教的种种障碍被一一清扫。1616 年 1 月 15 日在教皇保禄五世出席的会议上，同意给予在中国的耶稣会请求下的特许权：允许神父们在行弥撒礼时戴帽子；允许将圣经翻译成中文文言文；允许中国籍的神父主持弥撒，允许祈祷时用中文文言文背诵。[41] 不过，在华传教士真正使用这些特许权要到 100 多年以后了。

金尼阁欧洲之行的另一大收获是募集到 7000 余册图书。[42] 在欧洲期间，他用卓越的口才四处宣传介绍中

Ming dynasty.

In Rome, Nicolas Trigault reported to the Pope on his missionary work in China and made corresponding requests regarding specific missionary matters. Based on his experience in China, he requested the Pope's permission to translate the Bible, the Mass, the daily lessons for priests, and the canons of the priesthood into Chinese, to use Chinese instead of Latin in his missions and liturgies, to allow priests in China to celebrate Mass without taking off their hats, and to allow the appointment of Chinese to the priesthood.[40] These issues may seem minor, but they are important in nature and have far-reaching implications. The Jesuits in China believed that in order to achieve missionary purposes in China, they had to respect certain special rules and should follow the customs of the country. At a meeting on January 15, 1616, in the presence of Pope Paolo V, it was agreed that the Jesuits in China would be granted the concessions they had requested: permission for priests to wear hats during Mass; permission to translate the Bible into the Chinese language; and permission for Chinese priests to preside; and permission to recite prayers in the Chinese language.[41] However, it would be more than 100 years later these concessions were actually implemented by the missionaries in China.

Another major achievement of Nicolas Trigault's trip to Europe was the collection of more than 7,000 books.[42] During his stay in Europe, he used his outstanding eloquence to promote Chinese culture and the Jesuit missionary activities in China, and received the strong support of the most powerful kings and bishops in Europe. The books he collected alone were immensely valuable. This collection included not only religious books, but also a large number of books on humanities, social sciences and natural sciences. He proudly described it as follows:

There is no one in the Jesuits who can match the

1615 年出版的《利玛窦中国札记》拉丁文第 1 版。现藏于澳门中央图书馆议事亭藏书楼
The first Latin edition of *Matteo Ricci's Journal of China* published in 1615. It's now in Biblioteca do Senado, Macao Central Library

国文化和耶稣会在华传教活动，得到欧洲最有权势的国王和主教们的大力支持，仅他募集到的书籍就价值万金。这批书里不仅有宗教类书籍，而且有大量人文社会科学与自然科学类书籍。他骄傲地夸赞道：

> 余迄今所获者，无论就数量言（重复者不计），就学术门类之繁多言，就装潢之富丽言，在耶稣会中尚无足以与此颉颃者。……以学科之门类言，除吾人图书馆所习有之人文类、哲学类、神学类、教义类及其他名著外，余所搜医学、法学、音乐类书，亦复甚多，而今日所已发明之数学书，则可谓应有尽有。余从各王公大臣所征集及在各地所收购之各项测算仪器与制造仪器之机械，种类之多，品质之精，可谓已一无所缺，若欲一一

number (not counting duplicates), the variety of academic disciplines, or the richness of the decoration of what I have acquired so far. ... In terms of disciplines, in addition to the humanities, philosophy, theology, doctrine, and other masterpieces that our libraries are accustomed to, I have found many books on medicine, law, music, and mathematics. I have collected from various princes and officials and acquired in various places many measuring instruments and the machinery of manufacturing instruments, whose quality and quantity are incomparable. This collection of books and instruments, before leaving Europe, is worth 10,000 gold coins. If we talk about their beauty - all the books are bound in red leather, with the papal seal on one side, and the titles and other

意大利工程师阿戈斯蒂诺·拉梅利（Agostino Ramelli）著作中使用绞盘打水的水井（windlass well），1588 年出版

The windlass well described in the work of Agostino Ramelli, an Italian engineer, published in 1588

《远西奇器图说录最》中使用绞盘打水的水井，1627 年出版

A well using a windlass well mechanism in the book *Yuan Xi Qi Qi Tu Shuo Lu Zui* (The Illustrations of Instruments from the Far West), published in 1627

缕述，则未免太长矣。余愿为君等一言者，即此书藏与仪器，在离欧前值一万金币。若论其精美，则所有书籍均以红皮装订，一面有教宗御玺，书名并其他花饰，均烫金。余并尽量设法，使所有书籍均为大本。[43]

后来，这批书的到来果然引起中国士人的极大反响，成为传教士进入中国文化圈的敲门砖。信教者喜不自禁，以此向教外人士炫耀，如杨廷筠[44]将此举比为玄奘西行取经；反教人士则对此深感不安，认为此举"盖欲扫灭中国贤圣教统"[45]。当然，这批书最终翻译成中文又花费了很长时间。1623年以后，这批图书终于辗转运到北京利玛窦所创建的图书馆中收藏。根据金尼阁所携图书，由传教士邓玉函（Johann Schreck）口授、王徵[46]笔述并摹绘的《远西奇器图说录最》于1627年出版，在

decorations are stamped in gold. [43]

Later, the arrival of the books did cause a great reaction among the Chinese scholars and became a doorstop for the missionaries to enter the Chinese cultural circle. Believers were overwhelmed with joy and used it to show off to laymen, as Yang Tingjun[44] compared it to Xuanzang's trip to the west to obtain scriptures, while opponents were deeply disturbed by the move, saying that it was "intended to destroy the Chinese saintly tradition."[45] Of course, it took a long time for the books to be translated into Chinese, and after 1623 they were finally transported to the library founded by Matteo Ricci in Beijing. Based on the books brought by Nicolas Trigault, the book *Yuan Xi Qi Qi Tu Shuo Lu Zui* (The Illustrations of Instruments from the Far West), dictated by the missionary Johann Schreck and written and illustrated by Wang Zheng[46], was published in

宗卡（Vittorio Zonca）作品中的旁派·塔冈尼（Pompeo Targone）磨车，1607年出版

The Pompeo Targone mill carriage described in the work of Vittorio Zonca, published in 1607

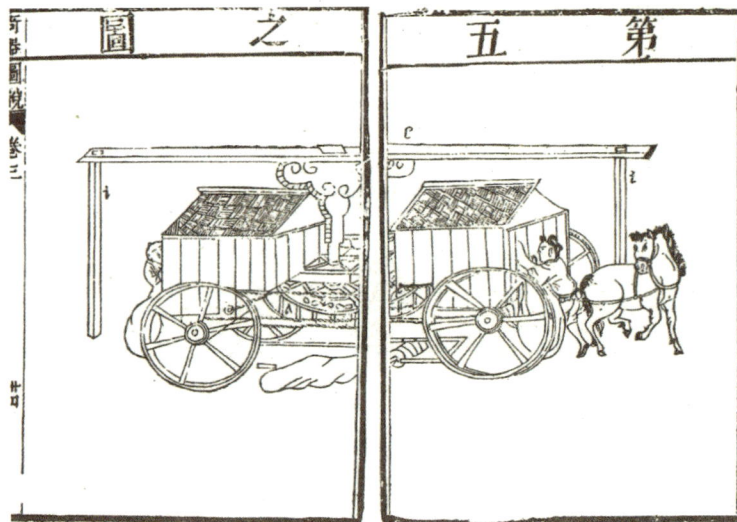

《远西奇器图说录最》中的磨车，1627年出版

The mill carriage in *Yuan Xi Qi Qi Tu Shuo Lu Zui* (The Illustrations of Instruments from the Far West), published in 1627

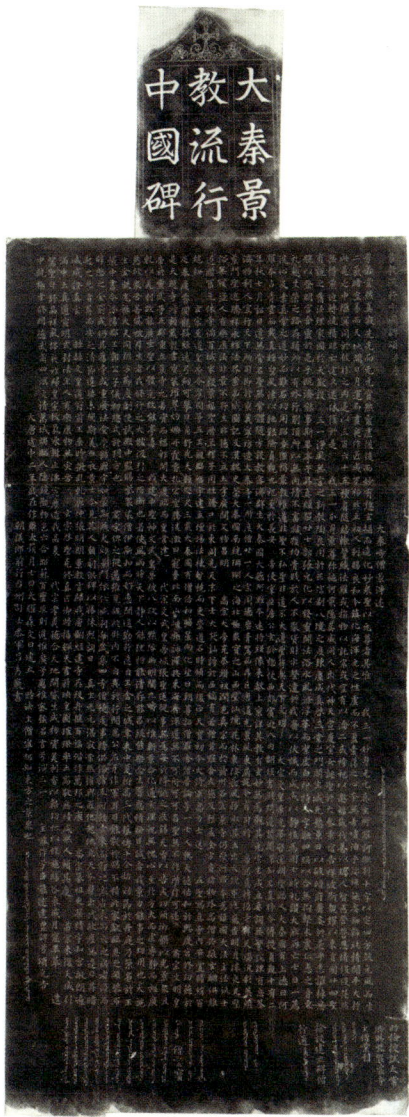

《大秦景教流行中国碑》。1623 年至 1625 年出土于陕西西安城西。现藏于西安碑林博物馆

The Nestorian Monument in China, unearthed between 1623 and 1625 in the west of Xi'an, Shaanxi Province, and is now in the Forest of Stone Steles Museum in Xi'an

当时给国人带来极大震撼，是西学东渐中的一个重要成果。李约瑟（Joseph Needham）在《中国的科学与文明》（*Science and Civilization in China*）一书中，给予这本书高度评价。

金尼阁第二次来华是在 1618 年。这一次他带着在欧洲募集到的图书和新招募的 22 名传教士，其中包括邓玉函、汤若望等明末清初著名传教士。[47] 旅程艰险，不仅有海盗劫掠，还有瘟疫蔓延，先后有 7 名传教士在途中患病逝世。这次来华，金尼阁远赴江西、浙江、河南、山西、陕西等地传教。在各地传教期间，他设立印书厂，印行了很多中文和拉丁文书籍。

相比于传教，在华耶稣会更看重金尼阁卓越的语言文字能力，后来让他专门从事翻译著述工作。在西学中传方面，他编撰了一本万年历式的历法书《推历年瞻礼法》，与张赓[48] 合作选译了部分《伊索寓言》（*Aesop's Fables*）故事，结集为《况义》印行。在中学西传方面，他首次将《大秦景教流行中国碑》[49] 的碑文译成拉丁文，还第一次将中国儒家典籍"五经"译成拉丁文《中国五经》（*Pentabiblion Sinense*），另外还编写了一本重要的汉语工具书，也是中国最早的汉语拼音方案《西儒耳目资》（*Aid to the Eyes and Ears of Western Literati*），并编译了西方第一部系统的中国史著作《中国编年史》（*Annales Regui Sinensis*）。[50] 笔耕不辍的金尼阁最终于 1629 年在杭州逝世，葬于杭州大方井耶稣会司铎公墓。

中国人因其五千年的文明史以及"天圆地方我在中央"的帝国观念，具有一种天然的文化优越感，特别是与周围其他国家相对落后的文化进行比较之后，更是如此。对于改变中国人信仰的难度，利玛窦、金尼阁等人

1627, and greatly shocked the Chinese people at that time. This book is an important achievement in the Western learning's spread to the East. Joseph Needham, in his book *Science and Civilization in China*, gave this book high praises.

Nicolas Trigault's second visit to China was in 1618. This time he brought with him the books collected in Europe and 22 newly recruited missionaries, including Johann Schreck, Johann Adam Schall von Bell, and other famous missionaries of the late Ming and early Qing dynasties.[47] The journey was treacherous, not only because of pirates and pestilence, but also because seven missionaries died of diseases on the way. In this visit to China, Nicolas Trigault went to Jiangxi, Zhejiang, Henan, Shanxi and Shaanxi to preach. During his missionary work in various places, he set up a book printing factory and printed many books in Chinese and Latin.

The Jesuits in China valued Nicolas Trigault's excellent linguistic and writing skills more than his missionary work, and later engaged him exclusively in translation and writing. In the area of Western and Chinese missions, he compiled a calendar book in the style of the almanac, *Tui Li Nian Zhan Li Fa* (Calculation of the Holiday Calendar), and collaborated with Zhang Geng[48] in the translation of some of the stories of *Aesop's Fables*, which were collected and printed in the book, *Kuang Yi*. In order to spread the Chinese learning to the West, he translated the tablet inscription of *Da Qin Jing Jiao Liu Xing Bei* (The Nestorian Monument in China)[49] into Latin for the first time. He also translated the first Chinese Confucian text, the *Pentabiblion Sinense*, into Latin, and compiled the earliest Chinese *Pinyin* program, *Aid to the Eyes and Ears of Western Literati*, which was an important Chinese linguistic tool. He also compiled the first systematic work on Chinese history in the West, *Annales Regui Sinensis*.[50] He died in 1629 in Hangzhou and was buried in the Jesuit priest's cemetery in

杭州大方井耶稣会司铎公墓。照片作者徐海松，约摄于 2020 年

Dafangjing Jesuit Priests Cemetery in Hangzhou, taken by Xu Haisong, circa 2020

有着清醒的认识，他说："中国人的骄傲还没有降低到似乎可以接受他们的任何同胞所从未信仰过的外来宗教的地步。"[51] 他们敏锐地意识到，要在中国传教，必须得到中国知识分子的认可与支持。金尼阁说，耶稣会士的态度是"把儒士派的大多数吸引到我们的观点方面来具有很大的好处，他们拥护孔夫子，所以可以对孔夫子著作中所遗留下的这种或那种不肯定的东西作出有利于我们的解释。这样一来，我们的人就可以博得儒士们的极大好感"[52]。虽然手段狡黠，这种由利玛窦开创、金尼阁等人继承发扬的在中国传教的方法，却体现了无论何时传教士都应具有的务实精神。也正因此，他们为东方和西方彼此了解搭建了一座桥梁。

Dafangjing, Hangzhou.

The Chinese have a natural sense of cultural superiority due to their 5,000-year history of civilization and the imperial concept of "Heaven is round and I am in the center," especially when compared with the relatively backward cultures of other countries around them. Matteo Ricci, Nicolas Trigault, and others had a sober understanding of the difficulty of changing the beliefs of the Chinese, noting "The pride of the Chinese has not yet been reduced to the point where they seem to accept foreign religions that no one of their countrymen has ever believed in."[51] They were keenly aware that in order to preach in China, they had to have the approved support of Chinese intellectuals. The attitude of the Jesuits, says Nicolas Trigault, was that "it would be of great advantage to draw the majority of the Confucianists to our side of the argument, who embraced Confucius and so could interpret in our favor those uncertain areas in his writings. In this way, our people could win the great favor of the Confucian scholars"[52]. Despite its cunning methods, this Chinese missionary method, pioneered by Matteo Ricci and carried on by Nicolas Trigault and others, embodies the pragmatic spirit that should always characterize intellectuals. In this way, they built a bridge for understanding between the East and the West.

康熙大帝的科学启蒙老师南怀仁

　　在金尼阁之后，另一位大名鼎鼎的比利时传教士就是康熙皇帝的科学启蒙老师——南怀仁。在那个时代，利玛窦、汤若望[53]、南怀仁，这三位是最具影响力的，他们的名字成为明末清初在华传教士的代名词。特别是南怀仁，因其作为备受康熙皇帝信任的科学启蒙老师，而使天主教的传教活动在鸦片战争以前达到了顶峰。虽然传教才是他们的目的，但在一定程度上，他们也为近代中西文化交流做出了重要贡献。

　　中世纪的基督教教会，除了权力和财富，还垄断了知识和教育。世界上所有大学制度的源头都可以追溯到欧洲，到 1400 年，欧洲已有 53 所大学。它们为世俗人

Emperor Kangxi's Scientific Enlightenment Teacher - Ferdinand Verbiest

　　After Nicolas Trigault, another famous Belgian missionary was Ferdinand Verbiest, the scientific enlightenment teacher of Emperor Kangxi. In that era, Matteo Ricci, Johann Adam Schall von Bell[53] and Ferdinand Verbiest were the three most influential, and their names became synonymous with the missionaries in China in the late Ming and early Qing dynasties. Ferdinand Verbiest, in particular, promoted the Catholic missionary activity to reach the peak before the Opium War because he was trusted by the Emperor Kangxi as a teacher of scientific enlightenment. Although missionary was their purpose, to a certain extent they also made important contributions to the

鲁汶大学为了纪念南怀仁这位伟大的校友，特别建立了南怀仁厅。在南怀仁逝世300周年的时候，中国政府向比利时鲁汶大学南怀仁基金会赠送了"天球仪"（即南怀仁设计制造的大型天文仪器之一）的模型，原件现存于故宫

The Catholic University of Leuven has created a special hall in memory of this great alumnus, Ferdinand Verbiest. On the 300th anniversary of his death, the Chinese government presented the Ferdinand Verbiest Foundation at the University of Leuven with a model of the "Celestial Sphere Instrument" (one of the large astronomical instruments designed and built by Ferdinand Verbiest), the original of which is in the collection of the Forbidden City Museum, Beijing

提供教育，为教会培养未来的服务者，为国王们提供行政官员。比利时的第一所也是最具声望的大学是鲁汶大学，创办于1425年，由重新统一了西方教会的强权人物教宗马丁五世（Martin V）下令建立，是现存最古老的天主教大学。初创时期教授主要来自巴黎大学、科隆大学和维也纳大学，并设有文学院、法学院和医学院。1432年，鲁汶大学增设神学院，后来规模逐渐扩大，学术声望也明显提高。创建200多年后，它的一位毕业生来到中国传教，并最终成为康熙皇帝的科学启蒙老师，他就是南怀仁。

南怀仁（Ferdinand Verbiest，1623—1688），1623年10月9日出生于布鲁日附近一座叫比滕（Pittem）的小镇，1640年开始在鲁汶大学学习，一年后因加入耶稣会而辍学。为了传教，1643年他再次来到鲁汶的耶稣会学院（Collegium Societatis Jesu），并重返鲁汶大学听课两年，系统学习了亚里士多德的哲学，掌握了逻辑

modern cultural exchange between China and the West.

The Christian Church in the Middle Ages, in addition to power and wealth, had a monopoly on knowledge and education. The origins of all university systems in the world can be traced back to Europe, where by 1400 there were 53 universities. They provided education for secular people, trained future servants for the church, and provided administrative officials for kings. Belgium's first and most prestigious university was KU Leuven (Katholieke Universiteit Leuven), founded in 1425 by Pope Martin V, the powerful man who reunited the Western Church, and it is the oldest surviving Catholic university. During the initial period, its professors were mainly from the University of Paris, University of Cologne and University of Vienna, and there set up the faculties of liberal arts, law and medicine. In 1432, the Faculty of Theology was added. Later, it grew in size and academic prestige. About 200 years after its creation, one of its graduates came to China to preach and eventually became the teacher of scientific enlightenment for Emperor Kangxi: Ferdinand Verbiest.

康熙皇帝（1654—1722）
Emperor Kangxi (1654–1722)

学和辩证法，以及"物理学"的一些初步概念，但他更有数学天赋。[54] 1645 年到一所耶稣会学院教授拉丁文。1652 年，受佛兰德斯教区主教派遣，赴罗马入耶稣会罗马学院，专攻神学。1655 年获神学博士学位。1656 年随传教士卫匡国（Martin Martini）[55] 来华，历尽艰险而于 1658 年到达澳门。

南怀仁本来在陕西传教，1660 年奉诏前往北京，用他的数学才能协助在钦天监负责编制历书的汤若望神父。汤若望被弹劾去职后，中国官员杨光先接掌钦天监，任职期间历法推算上频繁出错，在朝廷内部引起了很大争议，民间也传出了中国历法没有西方历法精确的说法。为了平息这场纷争，亲政不久的康熙皇帝决定举办一个公开测验来让双方一较高下。1668 年和 1669 年两次比

Ferdinand Verbiest (1623-1688), born on October 9, 1623 in Pittem, a town near Bruges, began his studies at the Catholic University of Leuven in 1640 and dropped out after a year to join the Jesuits. In 1643 he came back to the Collegium Societatis Jesu in Leuven for missionary purposes, and returned to the Catholic University of Leuven for two years to study Aristotle's philosophy. He mastered logic and dialectics, as well as some preliminary concepts of physics. However, he was especially endowed with the talent of mathematics[54]. In 1645, he went to a Jesuit college to teach Latin, and in 1652 he was sent by the bishop of Flanders to Rome to join the Jesuit College of Rome, where he specialized in theology, and received his doctorate in theology in 1655. In 1656, he came to China with the missionary Martin Martini[55], and arrived in Macau in 1658 after a long and arduous journey.

Ferdinand Verbiest, who was originally a missionary in Shaanxi, was ordered to go to Beijing in 1660 to use his mathematical skills to assist Father Johann Adam Schall von Bell, who was in charge of compiling the calendar at the Qin Tian Jian (Imperial Astronomical Bureau). After Schall's impeachment, Yang Guangxian, a Chinese official, took over the reins of the Qin Tian Jian. During his tenure, Yang made frequent errors in the calendar calculations, causing much controversy within the imperial court, and it was also circulated in the public that the Chinese calendar was not as accurate as the Western calendar. In order to quell this dispute, Emperor Kangxi, who had not long been in power, decided to hold a public test to let both sides compete. After two competitions in 1668 and 1669, both proved that the Western calendar was indeed more accurate than the old one. In March 1674, Ferdinand Verbiest was promoted to the post of Supervisor of the Qin Tian Jian with additional title of the Secretary of the Taichang Temple.

Rare in Chinese history, Emperor Kangxi is a ruler characterized with enlightened thinking and a strong

试，均证明西洋历法较旧历确实更为精准。康熙终于决定将历法天文交与南怀仁推算，并授予钦天监监副之职。1674 年 3 月升南怀仁为钦天监监正，加太常寺卿。

康熙皇帝是中国历史上并不多见的具有开明思想和强烈求知欲的最高统治者。这大概是由于他少年即位，适逢满人入关不久，内有权臣，外有三藩，在危机四伏的情况下，他必须奋发自强以稳固江山，加之他本身聪敏好学有毅力，遂对南怀仁等西方传教士所带来的西方科技产生强烈的学习欲望以图明辨是非。作为一名立志有所作为的开明君主，康熙皇帝自然不可能认同杨光先所说的"宁可使中夏无好历法，不可使中夏有西洋人"的愚顽观点。[56] 当南怀仁通过两次比试证明了自己的才能后，他很快成为康熙的私人教师和亲近之人，经常被传召到内廷讲解西方科学。在两年的时间里，南怀仁将主要天文仪器及数学仪器的使用方法教授给皇帝，此外还讲解了几何学、静力学、天文学中最有趣和最容易理解的内容。康熙皇帝也是一位资质优异的学生，他不仅聪明敏慧而且记忆力特强。南怀仁常随康熙外出，有一次遇到一只鸟，康熙问西语发何音，南怀仁以弗拉芒语告之。数年后，康熙再遇同种鸟，仍能叫出弗拉芒语的鸟名。[57]

借讲解西方科学的机会，南怀仁不失时机地"向康熙皇帝灌输天主教的初步知识"。他对于使康熙皇帝皈依天主教抱着极大的乐观："欧洲天文学给康熙皇帝留下的深刻印象以及西洋机械师给他带来的怡乐，一定会把他的目光转向科学背后的信仰。"[58] 应该说，后来康熙皇帝对欧洲传教士的宽容态度，都与对南怀仁渊博知识的赞赏和卓越贡献的肯定有很大关系。不过，实际上

desire to learn. This is probably due to his youthful reign started with both internal and external crises, a situation that forced him to strive for self-improvement in order to secure the kingdom. Coupled with his own intelligence and perseverance, Emperor Kangxi had a strong desire to learn about Western technology brought by Western missionaries such as Ferdinand Verbiest. As an enlightened Emperor who was determined to make a difference, Kangxi naturally could not agree with Yang Guangxian's ignorant view that "it would rather have no good calendar than have Westerners in China."[56] When Ferdinand Verbiest proved his knowledge and talent through the two competitions, he soon became Kangxi's personal teacher and close friend, and was often summoned to the inner court to explain Western science. For two years, Ferdinand Verbiest taught the emperor the use of the main astronomical and mathematical instruments, in addition to the most interesting and accessible aspects of geometry, statics, and astronomy. Emperor Kangxi was also a highly qualified student. He was not only intelligent and perceptive but also had a very good memory. Once he saw a bird and asked what it was pronounced in Western language. Ferdinand Verbiest told him in Flemish. A few years later, Kangxi saw the same kind of bird again and was still able to say its name in Flemish.[57]

Taking the opportunity to explain Western science, Ferdinand Verbiest lost no time in "inculcating the preliminary knowledge of Catholicism to Emperor Kangxi." He was extremely optimistic about converting Emperor Kangxi to Catholicism: "The deep impression that European astronomy left on Emperor Kangxi and the pleasure that Western mechanics brought him would surely turn his attention to the faith behind science."[58] It should be said that later Emperor Kangxi's tolerant attitude toward European missionaries was all very much related to his appreciation of Ferdinand Verbiest's profound knowledge and recognition of Verbiest's outstanding contributions. In reality, however,

精明的康熙帝与中国历朝君主一样，对宗教所持有的观点是迷信利用兼而有之。他虽然信任欣赏南怀仁，但只是把他当作一位有特殊才能的顾问专家来任用，对天主教的教义并没有产生强烈的兴趣，而"只吸收了重怀疑、重实验及尊重科学知识的精神"[59]。在根本上，他仍然是中国传统儒家思想的支持者和继承者，将其作为统治的根基，而西方科学只是他繁忙政务之外的一项兴趣爱好，甚至并未纳入皇室继承人培养的教学计划中。所以总的来说，南怀仁对康熙皇帝的传教并不成功，终其一生，清廷也并没有正式解除禁教令。

南怀仁的传教虽然成果不大，但是他以之为传教手段的科技工作却成绩斐然。首先，他将欧洲天文学应用于中国历法。南怀仁接掌钦天监后，不断精进天文历法研究，并将自己的测算方法与研究成果集结成书，于15年间出版著作十余卷。1668年出版《测验纪略》，描述天文观测的方法。1671年出版《验气说》，1672年出版《赤道南北星图》，1673年出版《仪象图》。著书立说之外，南怀仁认为仪器在天文观测和历法制定工作中具有头等重要性。因此，在主持钦天监之后，他把中国铸造工艺和欧洲机械加工工艺结合起来，历时4年时间用铜铸成六件大型天文仪器。这些设备典雅精美，不仅是观测天象的仪器，也是富于中国元素的瑰丽的艺术品，至今保存在北京古观象台上。在制造和安装观象台新仪器的同时，南怀仁将各种仪器的制造原理、安装和使用方法等，详细记述，绘图立说。他于1674年将《新制灵台仪象志》共十六卷进呈，并请镂版刊行。1678年南怀仁遵旨编撰完成能够预测未来2000年的星历表《康熙永年历法》，再根据星历表编出民历。

the shrewd Emperor Kangxi, like all Chinese monarchs, held views on religion that were both superstitious and exploitative. Although he trusted and admired Ferdinand Verbiest and appointed him only as an expert consultant, Kangxi did not take a strong interest in Catholic doctrine and "absorbed only the spirit of skepticism, experimentation and respect for scientific knowledge."[59] In essence, he was still a supporter and successor of traditional Chinese Confucianism as the foundation of his rule, while Western science was only a hobby outside his busy political duties, and was not even included in the teaching program for the training of the imperial heirs.

Although Ferdinand Verbiest's missionary work was not very fruitful, his scientific and technological achievements, which he used as a means of missionary work, were remarkable. First, he applied European astronomy to the Chinese calendar. After taking over Qin Tian Jian, he continuously refined his research on astronomy and calendar, and compiled his own calculation methods and research results into a book. Over the past 15 years, he published more than ten volumes of books. In 1668, he published *Ce Yan Ji Lue* (The Chronicle of the Test), which described the methods of astronomical observation. In 1671, he published *Yan Qi Shuo* (The Test of Qi) and in 1672 he published *Chi Dao Nan Bei Xing Tu* (The Star Chart of the North and South of the Equator). In 1673, he published *Yi Xiang Tu* (The Instrument Chart). In addition to writing books, Ferdinand Verbiest believed that instruments were of primary importance in astronomical observation and calendar making. Therefore, after presiding over the Qin Tian Jian, he combined Chinese casting techniques with European machining techniques and cast six large astronomical instruments in bronze over a period of four years. These elegant and beautiful instruments are not only instruments for observing the celestial phenomena, but also magnificent works of art rich in Chinese elements,

康熙时期的北京古天文台（许多设备由南怀仁所监造）。本图为版画，出自法国作家普雷沃
（1697—1763）于 1764 年开始出版的系列著作《中国远航》（*Voyage au Chine*）一书

Astronomical observatory in Beijing during the Kangxi period, with much of the equipment supervised by Ferdinand Verbiest. This print is from the series of works entitled *Voyage au Chine* published by Antoine Francois Prevost (1697-1763) in 1764

北京古观象台今景。照片由汤馥鳞拍摄于 2015 年 9 月 5 日
Beijing Ancient Observatory today. Photo taken by Tang Fulin on September 5, 2015

资料来源（Source）：https://commons.wikimedia.org/wiki/File:%E5%8C%97%E4%BA%AC%E5%8F%A4%E8%A7%82%E8%B1%A1%E5%8F%B0CNBJ-010-028.jpg。

　　南怀仁是一位真正的"桥梁架设者"，为了向康熙皇帝系统介绍中国以外的西方世界，他于 1669 年着手编辑《西方要纪》，介绍了欧洲社会文化、地理风俗等各个方面。5 年后，他完成了巨幅着色木版《坤舆全图》的绘制，并著《坤舆图说》、《坤舆格致略说》和《坤舆外纪》作为解说词，向中国人全方位介绍了地球五大洲的人文地理知识。《坤舆图说》后被《四库全书》收入，是《四库全书》史部地理类收录清代欧洲人的唯一一部著作。1682 年他奉命随皇帝东巡，著《鞑靼旅行记》，向欧洲人介绍中国。

　　科学技术是南怀仁传教的有力工具，这是继承利玛窦所创立的中国传教方法，南怀仁将这种方法在清朝初期发扬光大。1671 年康熙皇帝为其父母修建孝陵，建造孝陵大石牌坊须将重达十余万斤的 6 根石柱以及其他石件拖过卢沟桥，并要求不能损伤桥体。南怀仁利用物理学中的原理轻松完成，却故作神秘、假托天主信仰。⁶⁰

which are preserved to this day on the ancient observatory in Beijing. While manufacturing and installing the new instruments in the Observatory, Ferdinand Verbiest wrote down in detail the manufacturing principles, installation and usage of the various instruments, and drew up the descriptions. In 1674, he submitted a total of 16 volumes of the *Xin Zhi Ling Tai Yi Xiang Zhi* (Newly Made Spiritual Observatory Instrument and Elephant) to the government and asked for the publication. In 1678, Ferdinand Verbiest compiled the *Kang Xi Yong Nian Li Fa* (Kangxi Perpetual Calendar), which was able to predict the ephemeris for the next two thousand years, and then compiled the civil calendar according to the ephemeris.

Ferdinand Verbiest was a true bridge builder - in order to systematically introduce the Western world outside of China to Emperor Kangxi, he began editing the *Xi Fang Yao Ji* (Western Chronicle) in 1669, introducing various aspects of European society and culture, geography and customs, etc. Five years later, he completed the drawing of the huge coloring map *Great Universal Geographic Map* used for block printing, and wrote *Kun Yu Tu Shuo* (Notes on the Great Universal Geographic Map), *Kun Yu Ge Zhi Lve Shuo* (Notes on the Geographical Sketch) and *Kun Yu Wai Ji* (Additional Notes on the Great Universal Geographic Map) as commentaries, introducing Chinese people to the five continents of the earth in a comprehensive manner. *Kun Yu Tu Shuo* was later included in *The Complete Books of the Four Storehouses*, as the only work by European in its geography division of historiography during Qing dynasty. In 1682, he was ordered to accompany the emperor on eastern tour and wrote *Da Da Lv Xing Ji* (Travels in Tartary) to introduce China to the Europeans.

Science and technology were powerful tools for Ferdinand Verbiest's missionary work. Inherited this method from Matteo Ricci, Ferdinand Verbiest perfected it during the early Qing dynasty. In 1671, when Emperor Kangxi was

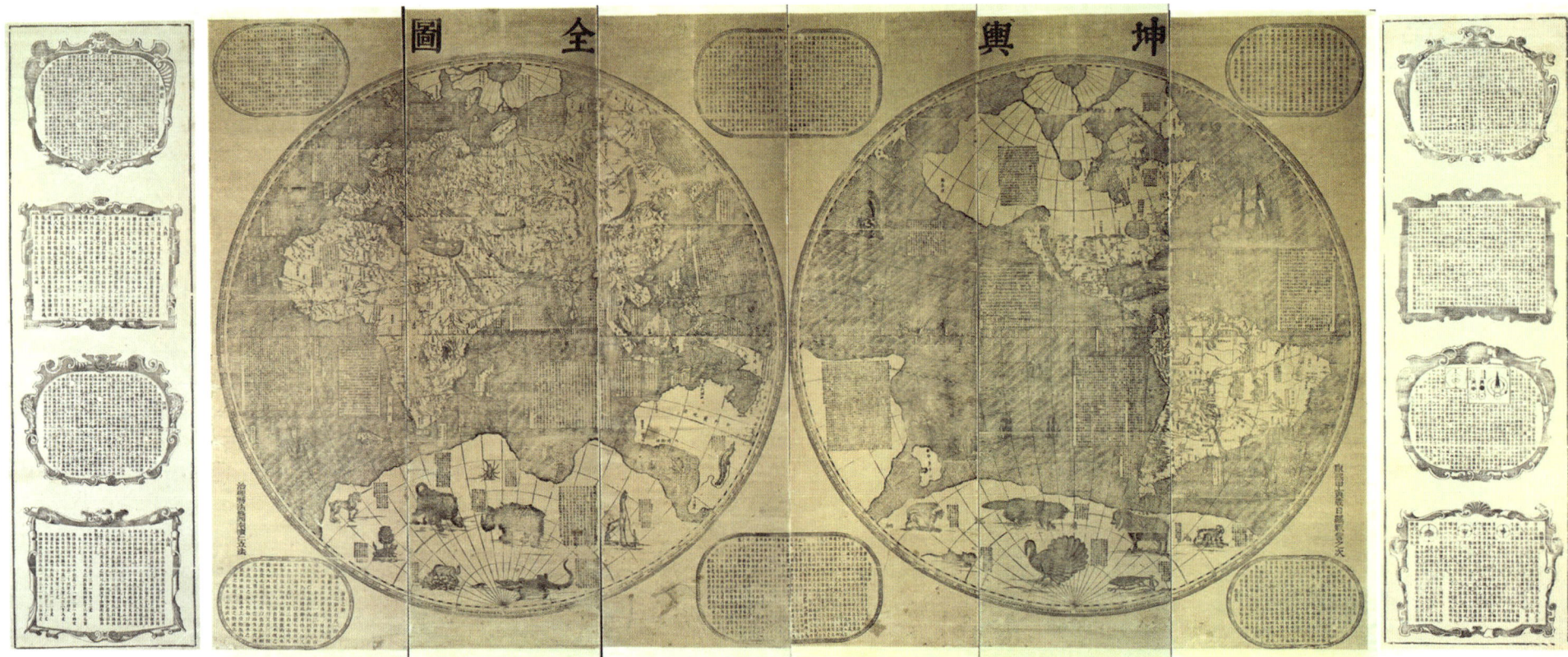

全圖 坤輿

《坤舆全图》（*Great Universal Geographic Map*），于甲寅年 (1674) 木版印制。现藏于台北"故宫博物院"

The Great Universal Geographic Map, printed in 1674 with blockprinting technique. Currently in the collection of the Taipei "National Palace Museum"

全图幅面很大，图文并茂，制作精致，设色鲜明。作者南怀仁巧妙地运用"动静之义"，论证"地圆说"；用经纬理法的科学制图方法，标识出五大洲的南北东西迄点；对世界各地的风土、人情、物产等做了全面的记述；又对全球著名的山岳高度、河流长度等做了大量的数据统计；第一次提出小西洋的概念，即印度洋水系。南怀仁在《坤舆全图》的注记文字中，宣传了自然地理方面的许多知识。他解释了因地球是球体而具有的各种自然现象，因月球环绕地球运动而引起潮汐的周期性消长，雨和云系大气中水汽凝结而成，风和公海上影响航行的季风的成因，各地不同的气候状况导致了文化的地区性差异，以及江河的起源、山岳的形成、空气的运动等等。南怀仁还批评了中国人对自然现象的迷信观念，如有关月食和地震的错误说法。《坤舆全图》是中国古代中文版世界地图的集大成者，是近代以来世界地图史上第一份比较完整的世界地图，具有里程碑的意义。

The whole map is large in size with excellent pictures and accompanying texts and exquisitely drawn with bright colors. Ferdinand Verbiest skillfully used the "meanings of movement and stillness" to demonstrate the "Idea of a Spherical Earth"; marked the south, north, east and west ends of five continents by the scientific longitude and latitude map-making method; made a comprehensive account of the local customs, practices and products all over the world; presented data for the height of mountains and length of rivers renowned in the world; put forward the concept of "Little West Ocean (i.e., the Indian Ocean)" for the first time. Ferdinand Verbiest promoted knowledge about natural geography in the annotation text of *The Great Universal Geographic Map*. He explained various natural phenomena due to the fact that the earth is round, the periodic ebb and flow of tides caused by the motion of moon around the earth, the formation of rain and cloud caused by condensation of water vapor in the atmosphere, the formation of wind and monsoon and how they affect the navigation on the open sea, regional cultural differences caused by different climate conditions, and etc. Ferdinand Verbiest also criticized the Chinese people's superstitious belief about natural phenomena, such as the incorrect understanding about lunar eclipses and earthquakes. *The Great Universal Geographic Map* is the epitome of the ancient Chinese version of the world map. It is the first relatively complete world map in the history of world maps – it therefore is of milestone significance.

之后，1673 年在平定吴三桂叛乱时，叛军盘踞山区，非大炮无法攻破。南怀仁奉旨铸造红衣大炮襄助清廷，把汤若望所铸火炮修复，并继续制造新炮。他负责监造了轻巧木炮及红衣铜炮 132 门、神威将军炮 240 门，后来又制成红衣大炮 53 门、武成永固大将军炮 61 门、神武将军炮 80 门。1681 年，南怀仁著《神武图说》，详细描述铸炮方法，次年进呈给康熙。"于每炮制成后，必在制造局内设台供天主像，自穿司铎品服，虔诚跪祷，行祝炮礼。每炮锡以教中圣人名号，令凿刻其上。"[61] 为奖赏他造炮有功，康熙皇帝封赏他为工部右侍郎职衔，后又加赏一级。工部侍郎，官至二品大员，"工部右侍郎"之上再加赏一级，用如今的话来说那就是"二品官职一品大员的待遇"了。

南怀仁还有可能是汽车的发明人，1672 年在北京制造出蒸汽动力机械装置——架设在马车上的五轮蒸汽车。该车作为给康熙皇帝的玩具，长度只有 60 厘米。

building the Xiaoling Mausoleum for his parents, six stone pillars weighing more than 100,000 pounds and other stone parts had to be dragged across the Marco Polo Bridge, and it was required that the bridge not be damaged. Ferdinand Verbiest used the principles of physics to do it easily, but pretended to be the work of God.[60] Later, in 1673, during the pacification of Wu Sangui rebellion, the rebels were entrenched in the mountains, which could not be breached without cannons. Ferdinand Verbiest was ordered to cast red cannons to assist the Qing court, repair the cannons cast by Johann Adam Schall von Bell, and continue to manufacture new cannons. He was responsible for casting 132 lightweight wooden and red copper cannons, 240 General Shen-Wei cannons, and later manufacturing 53 red cannons, 61 General Wu-Cheng-Yong-Gu cannons and 80 General Shen-Wu cannons. In 1681, Ferdinand Verbiest wrote *Shen Wu Tu Shuo* (Illustrations of the Shenwu Cannons), a detailed description of the method of casting cannons, and submitted it to Kangxi in the following year. "After each cannon was made, a platform was set up in

武成永固大将军炮，现藏于北京中国历史博物馆
General Wucheng Yonggu Cannon, now in the collection of Chinese History Museum, Beijing

由南怀仁于公元 1672 年设计的蒸汽车，本图收录于一幅 18 世纪的出版品中
Steam-propelled vehicle designed by Ferdinand Verbiest in 1672, 18th century print

比利时发行的南怀仁纪念邮票
Belgian stamps commemorating
Ferdinand Verbiest

这辆玩具机车应当是历史上第一次以蒸汽驱动交通工具的尝试，只是最终是否试验成功已无从考证了。

1688 年 1 月 28 日，南怀仁在北京逝世，享年 65 岁。南怀仁在华期间，康熙朝所发生的至关重要的三件大事——平定三藩、统一台湾和中俄签订《尼布楚条约》[62]——都与南怀仁有关。因此，康熙皇帝赐其谥号"勤敏"。明清时期客死中国的"洋员"中，南怀仁是唯一身后得到皇封谥号的。

南怀仁的继任者之一也是一位比利时耶稣会士，名叫安多（Antoine Thomas，1644—1709），1644 年出生于佛兰德斯王国的那慕尔（Namur），1660 年加入耶稣会，来华之前系统学习了数学和天文学。1677 年他申请来华传教，1682 年抵达澳门，1685 年经南怀仁推荐入京。南怀仁去世后，他协助传教士闵明我（Philippus Maria Grimaldi，1639—1712）负责钦天监的工作，被任命为钦天监副，后来还两次作为康熙皇帝的侍从，扈驾

the manufacturing bureau for the statue of God. Ferdinand Verbiest wore a priest's uniform, kneeled down and prayed, and performed the ritual of consecrating the cannon. The name of the saint of the Church was engraved on each cannon."[61] In order to reward him for his meritorious work in building the cannon, Emperor Kangxi made him the Right Assistant Minister of the Ministry of Works, and later added another level of reward.

Ferdinand Verbiest may also have been the inventor of the automobile, a steam-powered mechanical device, a five-wheeled steam car mounted on a horse-drawn cart, made in Beijing in 1672. The car was only 60cm in length and served as a toy for Emperor Kangxi. This toy locomotive should have been the first attempt at steam-powered transportation in history, except that there is no way to verify whether the experiment was ultimately successful.

Ferdinand Verbiest died in Beijing on January 28, 1688, at the age of 65. During his time in China, Ferdinand Verbiest was associated with three of the most important events of the Kangxi dynasty - the pacification of the three clans, the unification of Taiwan and the signing of the Treaty of Nerchinsk[62] between Russia and China. As a result, Emperor Kangxi gave him the posthumous title of "Qinmin." Among the "foreign officials" who died in China during the Ming and Qing dynasties, Ferdinand Verbiest was the only one who received a posthumous title from the emperor.

One of Ferdinand Verbiest's successors was also a Belgian Jesuit named Antoine Thomas (1644-1709), who was born in Namur, Flanders in 1644. He joined the Jesuits in 1660 and studied mathematics and astronomy before coming to China. In 1677, he asked for coming to China to do missionary work. He arrived in Macau in 1682 and entered the capital in 1685 on the recommendation of Ferdinand Verbiest. After Ferdinand Verbiest's death, Antoine Thomas assisted Philippus Maria Grimaldi (1639-

南怀仁故乡的比滕大教堂旁的南怀仁铜像
The bronze statue of Ferdinand Verbiest by Pittem Cathedral in his hometown

出关巡视，还曾协助绘制北京地区平面图的工作。他在1692年成功促使康熙皇帝颁布了宽容敕令（即允许天主教在中国自由传播，容许中国百姓领洗加入基督教）。应该说宽容敕令的颁布，是由南怀仁帮助铺下的路、由安多完成，这是对南怀仁一生贡献的最大褒奖。其后天主教在中国一度迅速发展，只是后来罗马教廷在"礼仪之争"问题上态度强硬，使得康熙皇帝又对天主教作出限制。至雍正、乾隆两朝，对天主教愈禁愈严。

　　由利玛窦开创的走上层路线的传教政策，其效果在南怀仁与康熙皇帝的关系上最为显著，而又随着中国封建集权达到顶峰而逐渐失去作用。康熙皇帝固然是历史上的贤明君主，西方人称之为"中国路易十四"[63]。耶稣会传教士评价康熙皇帝，说他"是人们在许多世纪中

南怀仁墓碑。他与利玛窦、汤若望葬于今北京阜成门外的滕公栅栏传教士墓地。由近代天津博物馆提供

Tombstone of Ferdinand Verbiest. He is buried with Matteo Ricci and Johann Adam Schall von Bell in the missionary cemetery of Tenggong Zhalan, outside Fuchengmen in present-day Beijing. Photo from Tianjin Museum of Modern History

1712) in managing the work of the Qin Tian Jian, and was appointed as its deputy Supervisor. Later, he also served twice as the attendant of Emperor Kangxi, escorting him on his domestic tours. He also assisted in the work of drawing the plan of the Beijing area. In 1692, he succeeded in getting Emperor Kangxi to issue the Edict of Toleration (i.e., to allow the free spread of Catholicism in China and to allow the Chinese people to be baptized into Christianity). It should be said that the promulgation of the Edict of Tolerance was the road paved with the help of Ferdinand Verbiest and completed by Antoine Thomas. It was also the greatest tribute to his life's work. In turn, Catholicism grew rapidly in China. However, the Holy See's later stricter attitude on the "Chinese Rites Controversy" led Emperor Kangxi to restrict Catholicism again. During the reign of Emperors Yongzheng and Qianlong, Catholicism became more and more strictly prohibited.

The effect of the missionary policy initiated by Matteo Ricci, which took the upper elite route, reached its peak in the relationship between Ferdinand Verbiest and Emperor Kangxi, and gradually lost its effect as China reached the peak of feudal centralization. Emperor Kangxi was certainly a historically wise monarch, known in the West as "Louis XIV of China."[63] The Jesuit missionaries said of Emperor Kangxi that he was "one of those extraordinary men one sees only in many centuries, who put no limits on his knowledge, and who never had such a love of science and art among all the monarchs of Asia." He also ordered Father Dominique Parrenin, a Jesuit, to lead a team of Chinese officials, painters, plate makers, etc. They spent five years translating an anatomical work and a medical encyclopedia into Tatar (i.e., Manchu language) to supplement the knowledge of Chinese medicine and to instruct surgeons in surgery. Kangxi even "personally revised the words and embellished the writing," "but did not change the theoretical basis."[64] From this account, we can easily see

才能见到一个的那种非凡人物之一，他对自己的求知领域不加任何限制，亚洲所有君主中从未有任何人像他这样爱好科学和艺术"。他还曾命耶稣会士巴多明神父（Dominique Parrenin）领导一个由一群中国官员、画师、制版工等组成的班子，耗时五年将一部解剖学著作和一部医学大全翻译成鞑靼语（满语），以补充中医知识的不足，并指导外科医生进行手术。他甚至"亲自修改词语，润色文笔"，"但对理论基础不做更动"⁶⁴。从这一举动，我们不难看出康熙皇帝对待西方科学是一种后来被鲁迅先生称为"拿来主义"的态度，体现了他重视学习西方先进技术和经验、放开眼界、博采众长、丰富自己的务实开放精神；但是换一个视角来看，康熙命传教士将医学著作翻译成满语而非汉语，是因为满人以异族而据有华夏，心中始终惴惴不安，相比于华夏几千年的文明史更不免自惭形秽，而自远方而来的传教士与满人皆为异族，但与华夏民族一样拥有高度文明，满人正可以将其在科学技术方面的特长"拿来"弥补满人在文化上的不足，并对这些来自西方的知识加以垄断，以稳固其对人数远超于本民族的汉族的统治。基于这个理由，康熙皇帝只让具有某些方面特长的传教士或者说技术人员服务于宫廷，却不允许他们在中国四处传教、传播科学知识。后来学者评价南怀仁等耶稣会士对中国的科学技术发展贡献有限，不应当忽略明末清初的统治者的狭隘保守、封闭知识的"愚民政策"的影响因素。

that Emperor Kangxi treated Western science in what Mr. Lu Xun later called "Give Me" doctrine, reflecting the importance he attached to learning the advanced technology and experience of the West. From another perspective, Kangxi ordered missionaries to translate medical works into Manchu rather than Chinese, because the Manchus always felt inferior and foreign when compared to the thousands of years of Chinese civilization. Since Western missionaries and Manchus were both from far away, Manchu rulers could learn from Western science and technology to make up and improve its cultural deficiencies vis-à-vis the Han Chinese and to solidify its rule over the empire. For this reason, Emperor Kangxi only allowed missionaries or technicians with certain specialties to serve the court, but did not allow them to go around China preaching and spreading scientific knowledge. Later scholars evaluated the limited contribution of Jesuits such as Ferdinand Verbiest to the development of science and technology in China and noted that one should not forget the influence of the narrow-minded and conservative policy of the rulers of the late Ming and early Qing dynasties.

柏应理画像。画家与收藏处不详
Portrait of Philippe Couplet.
Artist and collection unknown

把孔子学说介绍到欧洲的柏应理
与助手沈福宗

　　柏应理（Philippe Couplet，1623—1693），耶稣会神父，著名汉学家，对东西方文化交流做出杰出贡献。作为"桥梁建设者"，他不仅通过自己的著作，将西方宗教和哲学输入中国，更重要的是，他将中国文化系统地介绍给了欧洲诸国。

　　柏应理1623年生于安特卫普附近的梅赫伦。他自小在当地的耶稣会学校求学，学习内容包括古典文学、文法、修辞学、伦理学、自然哲学、形而上学、经院神学、实证神学、圣经等课程，学习期间曾获得那里的年度优秀学生奖。17岁那年成为耶稣会见习修士。1642—1644

Introducing the Teachings of Confucius to Europe - Philippe Couplet and His Assistant Shen Fuzong

　　Philippe Couplet (1623-1693), a Jesuit priest and renowned sinologist, made an outstanding contribution to the cultural exchange between East and West. As a bridge builder, he not only imported Western religion and philosophy into China through his writings, but more importantly, he systematically introduced Chinese culture to Europe.

　　Philippe Couplet was born in Mechlin, near Antwerp, in 1623. He studied at the local Jesuit school from an early age, including classical literature, grammar, rhetoric, ethics, natural philosophy, metaphysics, scholastic theology, positive theology, and the Bible, and was awarded the prize for outstanding student of the year during his studies there. At the age of 17, he became a Jesuits novice. From 1642 to 1644, Couplet entered the University of Leuven to study philosophy. After graduation, he taught Greek and Pedagogy in the Jesuit school.[65] In 1651, he returned to Catholic University of Leuven to study theology for two years, and in 1654, under the influence of Martin Martini, a missionary who had just returned from China, Couplet applied to go to China and was ordained to the priesthood at the same time as Ferdinand Verbiest[66]. In 1656, he left for China with Michel Borm, a missionary, and after three years of hardships, he arrived in Macao in 1659 at the age of 35. Among the eight people in the group, five died on their way.

　　During his stay in China, Couplet studied Chinese arduously, became familiar with Chinese culture, and studied Confucianism intensively in order to integrate Catholic doctrine into it. He took a Chinese name, Bo Yingli, according to the custom of the missionaries to China, and was known by the courtesy name Xinwei. He

年柏应理进入鲁汶大学学习哲学，毕业后在耶稣会的学校里教授希腊文和教理学。[65]1651年他再次来到鲁汶大学学习神学，为期两年。1654年受刚从中国回来的传教士卫匡国（Martin Martini）的影响，申请去中国，与南怀仁同时获得批准，并被祝圣为司铎。[66]1656年随传教士卜弥格（Michel Borm）来华，途中历尽艰辛困苦，历时三年方于1659年抵达澳门，同行八人，五人逝于途中。时年，柏应理35岁。

在华期间，柏应理认真学习中文，熟悉中国文化，潜心研究儒家学说，以便将天主教教理融于其中。他按照来华传教士习惯，取了一个华名——柏应理，字信末。他尊重中国文化及风俗习惯，着中国服装，以利玛窦为榜样，与中国士大夫交友，介绍西方哲学思想，通过他们扩大天主教的影响。自1660年从澳门出发到内陆，至1681年返欧的二十余年间，柏应理辗转江南各省之间传教，踪迹很广，交往亦众。

柏应理坚定维护利玛窦的中国传教方法，根据本土实际情况发展教务。为传教需要，柏应理用中文撰写了不少宗教方面的著作。1675年他在北京印行了天主教教义《四末真论》和《天主圣教百问答》。这两本书展现了柏应理极高的中文水平，系统介绍了天主教的教义和仪式，对宣传天主教起到了重要作用。尤其后者一再付梓印行，在中国天主教书籍中，发行量及印刷次数很少有超过该书的。

1681年，柏应理受耶稣会中国传教会委派回到欧洲，向罗马的教皇汇报中国传教工作。他还献上四百余卷由在华传教士编纂译著的中国文献，这批书被收入梵蒂冈图书馆，成为该馆早期汉籍藏本。在欧洲，柏应理还在

respected Chinese culture and customs and dressed in Chinese clothes. Following the example of Matteo Ricci, he made friends with Chinese scholars through whom he introduced Western philosophical ideas and expanded the influence of Catholicism in China. During the period for more than 20 years between his departure from Macau for mainland China in 1660 and his return to Europe in 1681, he moved from province to province in the south and preached. He had a wide range of contacts and missions.

Couplet firmly defended Matteo Ricci's missionary method in China and developed his teaching according to the actual situation in China. For missionary purposes, he wrote a number of religious works in Chinese. In 1675, Couplet published in Beijing the Catholic doctrine *Si Mo Zhen Lun* (The Four Last Truths) and *Tian Zhu Sheng Jiao Bai Wen Da* (The Hundred Questions and Answers of the Holy Catholic Church). These two books demonstrated his high level of Chinese language proficiency and systematically introduced Catholic doctrine and rituals, which played an important role in promoting Catholicism. Especially the latter has been printed repeatedly, and among Chinese Catholic books, few have been distributed and printed more often than this book.

In 1681, Couplet was sent back to Europe by the Jesuit Mission to China to report to the Pope in Rome on his missionary work in China. He also presented more than 400 volumes of Chinese documents compiled and translated by missionaries in China, which were included in the Vatican Library and became an early part of its Chinese collection. In Europe, he also introduced the Chinese diocese before King Louis XIV of France, the King of England, the Pope and renowned scholars, and praised Chinese culture.

In the decade from 1682 to 1692, Couplet published various Latin works on China and its culture in Europe. In 1686 he published the *Tabula Chronologica Monarchiae Sinica*, a fundamental contribution to the Western

法国国王路易十四、英格兰国王、罗马教皇及知名学者等面前，宣讲中国教区的情况，对中国文化大加赞扬。

1682—1692 年的十年间，柏应理在欧洲刊行了多种介绍中国及其文化的拉丁文著作。1686 年出版了《中华帝国年表》（*Tabula Chronologica Monarchiae Sinica*），为西人理解中国史做出了根本性的贡献。德国思想家莱布尼茨说，这本书"是很有价值的作品"，使欧洲人不得不接受这样的事实，即像伏羲和黄帝这些最早的中国人生活在《圣经》大洪水之前的时代。[67] 由柏应理、殷铎泽（Prospero Intorcetta）、鲁日满（Francois

understanding of Chinese history. Gottfried Wilhelm Leibniz, a German thinker, said that it "is a valuable work," which made Europeans accept the fact that the earliest Chinese like Fuxi (one of the earliest legendary rulers) and Huangdi (one of the Five Emperors in the ancient Chinese legendary) lived prior to the Great Flood in the *Bible*.[67] The book *Confucius Sinarum Philosophus*, which was translated and edited by 17 Jesuits, such as Philippe Couplet, Prospero Intorcetta, Francois de Rougemont and Manuel Henrique, was published in Paris in 1687. It introduced Confucian classics *The Analects of Confucius, The Doctrine of the Mean, The Creat Learning* to the Europeans.[68] Previous

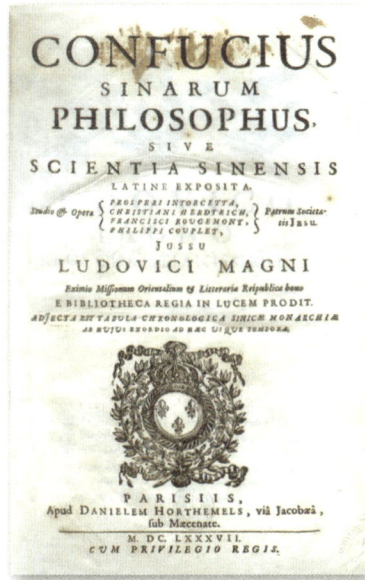

《中国贤哲孔子》一书的扉页，1687年出版于法国巴黎

Title page of *Confucius Sinarum Philosophus*, published in Paris, France, 1687

《中国贤哲孔子》一书书首印有柏应理题献给法国国王路易十四的献呈文及孔子肖像。他在献呈文中赞扬孔子："这位思想家的道德体系无比伟大，同时又朴实、敏感，从上天汲取而来的理性思考力，没有了上帝的意志，却变得如此强有力和丰富。"该书的出版在欧洲文化界造成很大影响，并且一直持续至 18 世纪，在法国思想家伏尔泰、德国思想家莱布尼茨的作品中都明确提到了自己曾阅读此书，受到了孔子思想的影响

Confucius Sinarum Philosophus has a dedication to King Louis XIV of France and a portrait of Confucius printed at the beginning of the book. He praised Confucius in the dedication: "The morality of this thinker is immensely great, yet simple and sensitive. The rational thinking ability drawn from heaven, without the will of God, has become so powerful and rich." The publication of this book had a great impact on the European cultural circle and its influence lasted until the 18th century. The French thinker Voltaire and German thinker Leibniz both explicitly mentions in their works that they had read this book and were influenced by Confucian thought de Rougemont）、恩理格（Manuel Henrique）等 17 位耶稣会士集体翻译编著的《中国贤哲孔子》（*Confucius Sinarum Philosophus*）一书于 1687 年在巴黎出版，该书主要翻译了儒家经典《论语》《中庸》《大学》。[68] 之前利玛窦、罗明坚（Michele Ruggieri）、曾德昭（Alvaro Semedohad）等传教士都向欧洲介绍过中国的儒家著作，但大多比较零散，不成系统。这本书是欧洲第一部最完备地介绍孔子及其儒家思想的著作，受到当时西方主流学界的高度重视和极力推崇。著名学者莱布尼茨、伏尔泰、孟德斯鸠等人都曾通过阅读这本书而对中国文化做出很高评价。因此，它在欧洲汉学史和中西文化交流史上具有重大意义，是早期中学西传的重要成果。另外，柏应理于 1686 年将卜弥格的《医论》（*Clavis Medica*）在欧洲刊布，这是第一部系统向欧洲介绍中医的书，可见柏氏对中国医学西传也曾做出一定贡献。

回欧洲时，柏应理带了一名年轻的中国教徒——沈福宗。沈福宗为顺治、康熙年间人，1657 年生于南京，后成为天主教徒，并与在江南传教的柏应理结识，跟随他学习拉丁文。1682 年二人到达欧洲后，沈福宗被柏应理安排在葡萄牙里斯本初级学院进修，老师为他起葡国名为弥格尔·阿方索（Michel Alphonsius），此后他在英、法等国时，人称他为弥格尔·沈（Michel Chen）或弥格尔·沈福宗（Michel Tchin Fo-Tsung），也有文献直呼其中国名沈福宗（Shin Fo-Cung）。留学为期两年，包括拉丁文、葡萄牙语、神学及哲学等课程。[69] 沈福宗于是成为 17 世纪最早到欧洲的中国留学生。柏应理赴罗马教廷述职时，教皇听说有中国教徒随行到欧洲，还特意召见了沈福宗。之后他又在罗马深造，并参与翻译

missionaries such as Matteo Ricci, Michele Ruggieri and Alvaro Semedohad introduced Chinese Confucian writings to Europe, but most of them were rather fragmentary and unsystematic. This book was the first and most complete introduction to Confucius and his ideas Confucianism in Europe, and was highly valued and highly esteemed by the mainstream Western academia at that time. Famous scholars such as Gottfried Wilhelm Leibniz, Voltaire, and Montesquieu all came to a high opinion of Chinese culture by reading this book. Therefore, it is of great significance in the history of Chinese studies in Europe and the history of cultural exchanges between China and the West. In addition, in 1686, Couplet published *Clavis Medica*, the first book that systematically introduced Chinese medicine to Europe, which shows that Couplet had also made contributions to the western transmission of Chinese medicine.

When Couplet returned to Europe, he brought with him a young Chinese convert, Shen Fuzong. Shen Fuzong, born in 1657 in Nanjing during the reign of Emperors Shunzhi and Kangxi, became a Catholic and became acquainted with Couplet. After they arrived in Europe in 1682, Shen Fuzong was arranged by Couplet to study at the Lisbon Junior College in Portugal, where his teacher gave him the Portuguese name of Michel Alphonsius. While in England and France, he was called Michel Chen or Michel Tchin Fo-Tsung. There are also documents directly call his Chinese name Shin Fo-Cung. The two-year program included courses in Latin, Portuguese, theology, and philosophy.[69] Shen thus became the first Chinese student to come to Europe in the 17th century. When Couplet went to the Holy See, the Pope, hearing that a Chinese convert was accompanying Couplet to Europe, summoned Shen to see him. Shen then furthered his studies in Rome and participated in the translation of Chinese classics, specifically the proofreading of *The Analects of Confucius*. These translations were later published in Latin in 1711.

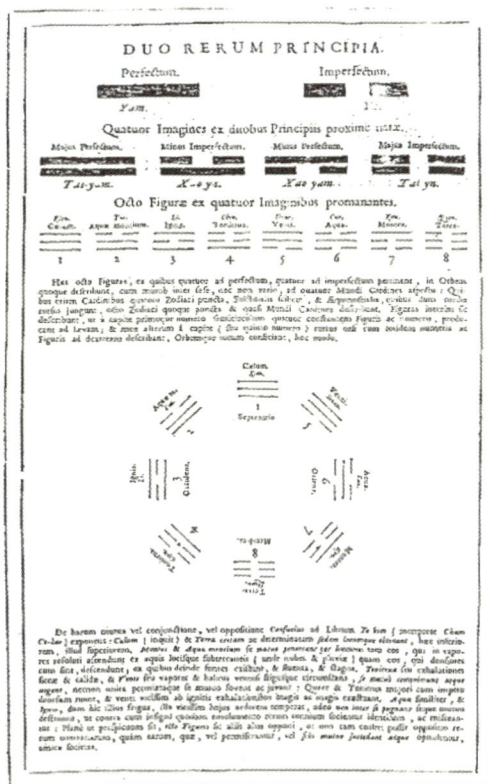

柏应理译著中的伏羲八卦次序图和伏羲八卦方位
I-ching hexagrams in Philippe Couplet's translated work

沈福宗画像。德国画家 Godfrey Kueller 绘于 1687 年。英国王室收藏

Portrait of Shen Fuzong, drawn by German painter Godfrey Kueller in 1687. British Royal collection

了中国经典的工作，具体负责《论语》的校对。这些译作后来于 1711 年用拉丁语出版。

1684 年柏应理与沈福宗应邀访问法国，在巴黎受到了法国国王路易十四（Louis XIV，le Grand Monaque，1638—1715）的接见。沈福宗是受到路易十四接见的第一个中国人，他凭借机敏的反应、出色的拉丁语和庄重得体的言谈举止给法国国王留下了极佳的印象。这次接

In 1684, Couplet and Shen were invited to visit France and were received in Paris by King Louis XIV (le Grand Monaque, 1638-1715). Shen Fuzong was the first Chinese to be received by Louis XIV, and he made a great impression on the French king with his quick response, excellent Latin and dignified manner of speech. This visit became a widely told story for a while and he captivated the Paris newspaper. In the presence of Louis XIV, he showed a statue of the saint Confucius and performed calligraphy with a brush. He

见一时传为佳话，他也成为巴黎报刊争相报道的对象。在路易十四面前，他向众人展示圣人孔子的像，用毛笔表演了书法。他还在宴会上向国王展示了筷子的用法，熟练地用拉丁语为国王边讲解边做示范动作，国王认真模仿并学会了筷子的使用，心情大悦。一时间，使用中国餐具进餐成为法国王公贵族、社会名流推崇的时尚。他们争相目睹这位能流利说出当时欧洲上流社会和学术界通用的拉丁语的博学中国学者的风采，以赞赏眼光欢迎他的到来。[70]

这位博学多才、儒雅有礼的中国学者沈福宗，掀起了所到国对中国知识探求的热潮。当时的报道称赞汉语有八万字，须费时三十年方能熟习，可见中国人记忆力之强和想象力之富，并称中国有很多学校和救济院，不见有乞丐。在回答问题时，沈福宗介绍了中国教育制度和各地书院的讲学情况，以及通过国家举办的各级考试把成绩优秀的人选拔到政府行政部门工作的方法，使法国人耳目一新。通过沈福宗的介绍，西方人对东方有了一点真正的感性认识，虽然有些认识仍不免幼稚甚至错误，但毕竟由彼此陌生向相互了解迈出了一大步。至今巴黎国家图书馆（Bibliotheque Nationale Paris）还收藏着沈福宗头戴纱帽，留着辫子的版画画像，并附有当时宴会情景的文字说明。[71]

1685 年沈福宗离开法国，应邀出访英国，受到英国国王詹姆士二世（James II）的接见。之后，沈福宗应汉学研究者海德（Thomas Hyde）邀请前往牛津大学与其他东方学学者一起做研究，助其完成《中国度量衡考》（*Epistola de Mensuris et Ponderibus Serum seu Sinensium*），这部拉丁文专著 1688 年出版于牛津。

also showed the king the use of chopsticks at the banquet, skillfully explaining them in Latin and demonstrating them to the king, who imitated them carefully and learned how to use them, much to his delight. In time, the use of Chinese cutlery became a fashion among French princes, nobles and socialites. They were eager to see this erudite Chinese scholar, who was fluent in Latin, a language common in European high society and academia at that time, and welcomed him with appreciation.[70]

This erudite, elegant and polite Chinese scholar, Shen Fuzong, set off a craze for the search for Chinese knowledge in the countries he visited. Reports at the time praised Chinese for having 80,000 words that took thirty years to master, showing the Chinese people's strong memory and rich imagination, and said that there were many schools and almshouses in China and no beggars in sight. In answer to the questions, Shen introduced the Chinese education system and the lectures of the academies around the country, as well as the method of selecting the best talents to work in the government administration through the examinations held by the state at all levels, which was refreshing to the French. Through Shen's introduction, Westerners gained some real understanding of the East, though some of which were still naive or even wrong. To this day, the Bibliotheque Nationale Paris still has a print of Shen Fuzong wearing a sarong hat and a braid, with a written description of the banquet.[71]

In 1685, Shen Fuzong left France and was invited to visit England, where he was received by King James II. Afterwards, Shen Fuzong was invited by the sinologist Thomas Hyde to Oxford University to do research with other orientalists, helping him to complete his *Epistola de Mensuris et Ponderibus Serum seu Sinensium*, a Latin monograph published in Oxford in 1688. He also had many contacts with Robert Hooke, the famous physicist and astronomer of the Royal Academy of Sciences, which

他还与英国皇家科学院著名物理学家和天文学家胡克（Robert Hooke）多有往来，使中国传统科学文化与近代科学找到了某种汇合点。[72]

1694 年海德用拉丁文发表的作品中，专门谈到沈福宗，原文如下："中国南京人沈福宗使我懂得很多中国知识，他由柏应理神父从中国带来。而近年来与同一耶稣会士在欧洲停留，并编译巴黎版的中国哲学著作。这个年青人现年三十岁，性情善良，学习极其勤奋。他为人礼貌、热情，有中国文化和哲学方面的良好教养，读过用汉文写的各种各样的书，而他在中国时就早已是懂得拉丁文的少数人之一。"[73]

柏应理和沈福宗在欧洲十年间，为东西方在科学、哲学、文化领域的沟通、交流与发展做出了不可磨灭的贡献。源于他们的努力，可称为科学门类之一的东方学，在 17 世纪的欧洲得以创建，其影响一直持续到 18 世纪，为百科全书派启蒙思想家提供了精神食粮。

法国思想家伏尔泰（Voltaire，1694—1778）在《论各民族的风俗与精神》第 143 章（*Essai sur les Moeurs et l'Esprit des Nations*, chapitre 143, Paris, 1756）中写道："欧洲王公和商人发现东方，追求的只是财富，但哲学家却在那里发现了一个全新的精神世界。"他说："中国人有完备的道德学，居于多科学问之首。"他将据元曲《赵氏孤儿》法译本（1735）改编的《中国孤儿》（*L'orphelin de la Chine*，1755）称为按孔子道德学说编成的五幕悲剧。他通过赞美中国儒家思想，来表达反对神权统治下欧洲君主政治的残暴统治，把有理性、合乎道德而开明的政治制度作为理想追求。[74]

同时期的德国思想家莱布尼茨（Gottfried Wilhelm

enabled the traditional Chinese scientific culture to find some kind of rendezvous point with modern science.[72]

In a work published in Latin in 1694, Hyde mentioned Shen Fuzong, "I have learned much about China from Shen Fuzong, a Chinese from Nanjing, who was brought from China by Father Couplet. And in recent years he has been traveling in Europe with the same Jesuit, and compiling the Paris edition of Chinese philosophical works. This young man, now thirty years old, has a good nature and is extremely diligent in his studies. He is polite and warm, well educated in Chinese culture and philosophy, and has read many books written in Chinese, while he was already one of the few who knew Latin when he was in China."[73]

During their ten-year stay in Europe, Couplet and Shen made indelible contributions to the East-West communication and exchange in the fields of science, philosophy and culture. As a result of their efforts, Orientalism, which can be called one of the scientific disciplines, was created in Europe in the 17th century. Its influence lasted until the 18th century, providing spiritual food for the Encyclopaedists.

In Chapter 143 of *Essai sur les Moeurs et l'Esprit des Nations* (Paris, 1756), the French thinker Voltaire (1694-1778) wrote "The European princes and merchants found the East, seeking only wealth; but the philosophers found there a whole new world of spirituality." He said: "The Chinese have a complete morality, above all other sciences." He called *L'orphelin de la Chine* (1755), based on the French translation of the Yuan dynasty opera *The Orphan of Zhao* (1735), a tragedy in five acts based on the moral teachings of Confucius. By celebrating Chinese Confucianism, he expressed his opposition to the brutal rule of European monarchs under the theocracy and his ideal of a rational, moral and enlightened political system.[74]

In a letter of 1687, the German thinker of the same period, Gottfried Wilhelm Leibniz (1646-1716), said that

Leibniz, 1646—1716）1687 年在一封信中说，他已细心读过"今年巴黎出版的哲学之王孔子的著作"[75]。1679 年他出版《当代中国史新论》（*Novissima Sinica Historiam Nostril Temporis Illustratura*），认为中、欧文化交流有益于双方，西方自然科学超过中国，但中国哲学和道德治理比西方优越。[76]

欧洲的哲学家以中国为例，说明人类具有不同的思想，它不是由上帝赐予的；社会体制并没有一定之规，中国编年史记载的历史之长使欧洲人原本推算的《圣经》中关于"大洪水"和人类起源的日子再也站不住脚。[77]欧洲人由此学会了自省，欧洲是世界的中心这种观点已经不再被人们相信。在民族林立的世界上，欧洲人逐渐发现自己没有中国人那般自信，但不久之后的地理大发现以及随之而来的征服与殖民，让他们重新找到了强者的感觉。

沈福宗在英国居住两年后，回到法国与柏应理重聚，然后又一起去比利时住了一段时间。最后由比利时前往荷兰，等候商船返回中国。1692 年二人搭乘荷兰商船启程，沿大西洋南下至非洲西海岸时，沈福宗突然染病，至非洲东南莫桑比克（Mozambique）附近不幸逝世，享年 35 岁。1693 年，船行至印度果阿附近时，柏应理在风暴中被船上货箱击中头部，重伤而逝，享年 70 岁。

此外，还有一些比利时传教士，他们虽然大多默默无闻，但也对中西文化交流做出了贡献。

鲁日满（Francois de Rougemont，1624—1676），生于比利时马斯特瑞特（Maestricht）的显贵世家。1641年入耶稣会，1659 年来华，被派入中国内地传教，除教难期间一度发配广州外，一直到去世，未远离江南地

he had carefully read "the works of Confucius, the king of philosophy, published this year in Paris."[75] In 1679 he published *Novissima Sinica Historiam Nostril Temporis Illustratura*, arguing that the cultural exchange between China and Europe was beneficial to both sides and that Western natural science surpassed China, but Chinese philosophy and moral governance were superior to the West. By advocating Confucian moral philosophy, Leibniz intended to express his dissatisfaction with the divided and warring lordships of Germany and hoped that an enlightened monarch like Emperor Kangxi would put an end to this state of affairs.[76]

European philosophers used the example of China to show that human beings have different ideas which were not bestowed by God. There are no set social institutions, and that the long history recorded in Chinese chronicles makes the original European projections of the date of the "Great Flood" and the origin of mankind in the *Bible* no longer tenable.[77] Europeans thus learned to reflect on themselves, and the idea that Europe was the center of the world was no longer believed. In an ethnically diverse world, Europeans gradually found themselves less confident than the Chinese, but soon the conquest and colonization that followed the geographic discoveries allowed them to rediscover their sense of power.

After living in England for two years, Shen Fuzong returned to France to reunite with Philippe Couplet, and then went to Belgium together. Finally, they left from Belgium for the Netherlands, waiting for the merchant ships to return to China. In 1692, the two of them sailed on a Dutch merchant ship and went south along the Atlantic Ocean to the west coast of Africa, when Shen suddenly fell ill and died near Mozambique in southeast Africa at the age of 35. Afterwards, when the ship was traveling near Goa, India, Couplet was hit in the head by a cargo crate on board during a storm and died of serious injuries at the age of 70.

区。著有《圣教要理》《同世编》《要理六端》《通俗圣歌集》《鞑靼中国新史》等，参与翻译《中国贤哲孔子》。

吴尔铎（Albert d'Orville，1622—1662），生于布鲁塞尔，1657 年前往中国。1661 年受耶稣会派遣，从西安出发，试图开辟一条通往罗马的陆路，以避开绕道好望角的漫长航程。他历时数月，经过西藏，翻山越岭到达尼泊尔（Nepal），最后不幸死于途中。

卫方济（Francois Noel，1651—1729）生于比利时海丝特鲁德（Hestrud），1670 年加入耶稣会，1684 年从里斯本出发前往东方传教，1687 年进入内地，主要在江南、淮安、江西一带传教。1702 年因为礼仪之争而被耶稣会派往欧洲进行申辩，后返回澳门。1708 年再次回到欧洲，在布拉格出版了《中国六经》《中国哲学》等著作为中国礼仪进行辩护。1729 年在里尔（Lille）去世。

朱耶芮（Philippe Cazier，1677—1722），生于梅嫩（Menen），1714 年到达中国。他在广州附近照顾麻风病人达八年之久。最后本人亦身患麻风病，于 1722 年病逝。

In addition, there were some other Belgian missionaries, mostly obscure, who also contributed to the cultural exchange between China and the West.

Francois de Rougemont (1624-1676) was born in Maestricht, Belgium, into a distinguished family. He joined the Society of Jesus in 1641 and came to China in 1659, where he was sent to preach in the interior of China until his death. He is the author of *Sheng Jiao Yao Li* (The Essentials of Sacred Christianity), *Tong Shi Bian* (The Companion to the World), *Yao Li Liu Duan* (The Six Ends of the Essentials), *Tong Su Sheng Ge Ji* (A Collection of Popular Hymns), and *Da Da Zhong Guo Xin Shi* (A New History of Tartar China), and participates in the translation of *Confucius Sinarum Philosophus*.

Albert d'Orville (1622-1662), born in Brussels, went to China in 1657 and was sent by the Jesuits from Xi'an in 1661 to try to open a land route to Rome to avoid the long voyage around the Cape of Good Hope. It took him several months to travel through Tibet and over the mountains to Nepal, where he unfortunately died on the way.

Francois Noel (1651-1729) was born in Hestrud, Belgium. He joined the Jesuits in 1670, set out from Lisbon in 1684 to preach in the East, and entered the mainland in 1687, preaching mainly in the areas of Jiangnan, Huai'an and Jiangxi. In 1702, he was sent by Jesuit to Europe to defend himself because of the Rites Controversy, and later returned to Macau. He returned to Europe again in 1708 and published in Prague the *Six Chinese Classics* and the *Chinese Philosophy* to defend the Chinese liturgy. He died in Lille in 1729.

Philippe Cazier (1677-1722), born in Menen, arrived in China in 1714. He spent eight years caring for leprosy patients near Guangzhou. He eventually became ill with leprosy and died in 1722.

比利时的"东印度公司"——奥斯坦德公司

17世纪时，荷兰和英国是全球两个最大的海上贸易王国。之后其他新兴势力开始挑战这两个国家的地位，希冀从远洋贸易这块大蛋糕上切下属于自己的那一份。18世纪，南部尼德兰地区（今比利时）为了发展本地区的经济，争夺对外贸易份额。1722年12月，在西北部北海沿岸港口奥斯坦德港，一家资本主要来自根特和安特卫普的富商的贸易公司正式成立。同时，股东还包括英国、荷兰、法国和其他佛兰德斯地区的商人与银行家。

奥斯坦德东印度公司开辟了一条前往几内亚、也门、印度、孟加拉地区各港口，终点为中国广州的新航线。公司船只装备日益齐全，从1724年至1732年，该公司21艘船只中大部分都定期驶往广州。公司最大股东之一乔纳斯·雅各布斯·莫雷图斯（Joannes Jacobus Moretus），是安特卫普一家印刷厂的经理，为奥斯坦德东印度公司的探险活动提供资金支持。另一位重要的投资者是阿姆斯特丹银行家保罗·雅科莫·克洛茨（Paulo Jacomo Cloots），他最初来自安特卫普。克洛茨赞助了前往广州的航海活动，并从康熙皇帝那里获得了与中国贸易的正式授权，最终在广州珠江岸边建立了自己的商行。[78]

在奥斯坦德公司与东方贸易往来的相关档案与日志中，有许多佛兰德斯商人穿梭于奥斯坦德和远东之间的记录。例如，1723—1724年，乔纳斯·德·克莱尔（Joannes de Clerck）作为第一舵手，驾驶"普里侯爵"号（Marquis de Prié）从奥斯坦德出发行至中国；不久后，他被提升为开往广州的"凯瑟琳"号（Keyzerinne）船长；1732年在奥斯坦德公司最后一次航行中国的航程

Belgium's "East India Company" - Ostend

In the 17th century, the Netherlands and Great Britain were the two largest maritime trading powers in the world. In the 18th century, the southern Netherland (today's Belgium) was competing for a share of foreign trade in order to develop its economy. In December 1722, a trading company with capital mainly from the wealthy merchants of Ghent and Antwerp was officially founded in the Northwest North Sea coastal port of Ostend. The shareholders also included British, Dutch, French and other Flemish merchants and bankers.

The Ostend East India Company opened a new route to the ports of Guinea, Yemen, India, and Bengal, ending at Guangzhou, China. The company's ships became increasingly well-equipped, and between 1724 and 1732 most of the company's 21 ships sailed regularly to Guangzhou. One of the company's largest shareholders, Joannes Jacobus Moretus, was the manager of a printing house in Antwerp that financed the Ostend East India Company's expeditions. Another important investor was Amsterdam banker Paulo Jacomo Cloots, originally from Antwerp. Cloots sponsored voyages to Guangzhou and obtained formal authorization from Emperor Kangxi to trade with China, eventually establishing his own trading house on the banks of the Pearl River in Guangzhou.[78]

There are many records of Flemish merchants travelling between Ostend and the Far East in the archives and journals relating to Ostend East India Company's trade with the East. For example, between 1723 and 1724, Joannes De Clerck sailed as first coxswain on the Marquis de Priè from Ostend to China. Soon after, he was promoted to captain of the Keyzerinne, bound for Guangzhou, and on the last voyage of the Ostend Company to China in 1732, he served as captain of the Hertogh van Lorreyn (the Duke of Lorraine). Another Flemish, Guillielmo Philippe

中，他担任"洛林公爵"号（Hertogh van Lorreynen）船长。另一位佛兰德斯人吉列尔莫·菲利普·德·布鲁尔（Guillielmo Philippe de Brouwer）第一次前往广州便是乘坐德·克莱尔船长驾驶的"凯瑟琳"号；1727年，德·布鲁尔晋升为"普里侯爵"号船长，负责广州航线。1723—1724年，佛兰德斯商人亨利·查尔斯·吉塞林克（Henri-Charles Gyselinck）从根特出发，乘"圣约瑟夫"号（Saint Joseph）前往中国，目的地也是广州。他对广州的印象记录在他写的汇报和一幅绘制珠江口虎门的水彩画中。吉塞林克形容周围的环境为"见过的最美风景"[79]。

奥斯坦德东印度公司开业后，经营的远洋贸易货物主要是丝绸、茶叶和瓷器。特别是在茶叶贸易上，它很快抢占了超过荷兰东印度公司的市场份额，获利丰厚。这严重威胁到老牌东印度公司（荷兰、英国和法国东印

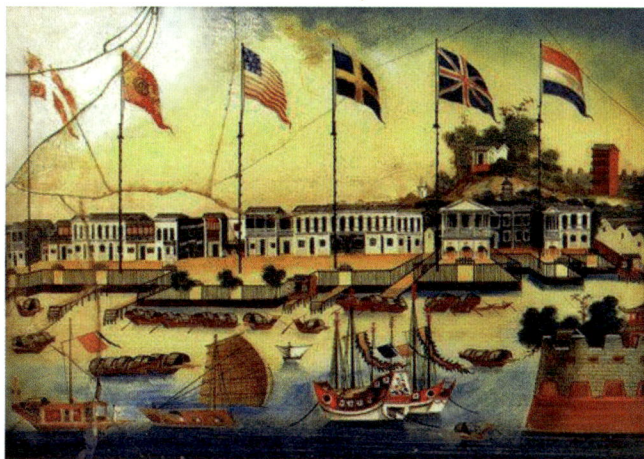

广州十三行商馆外销玻璃画，绘于18世纪末19世纪初。现藏于广州博物馆
Guangzhou Thirteen Hongs' export glass painting, painted in the late 18th and early 19th century. Now in the collection of Guangzhou Museum

de Brouwer, made his first voyage to Guangzhou on the Keyzerine, captained by Captain de Clare. In 1727, de Brouwer was promoted to captain of the Marquis de Pury and took charge of the Guangzhou route. Henri-Charles Gyselinck, a Flemish merchant, sailed from Ghent to China on the Saint Joseph during 1723 to 1724, also destined for Guangzhou. His impressions of Guangzhou were recorded in a report he wrote and in a watercolor painting of Humen at the mouth of the Pearl River. Gyselinck described the surroundings as "the most beautiful landscape ever seen"[79].

After the opening of the Ostend East India Company, the ocean-going trade goods involved mainly silk, tea and porcelain. Especially in the tea trade, it quickly seized more market share than the Dutch East India Company and profited handsomely. This seriously threatened the interests of the old East India Company (i.e., the Dutch, British and French East India Companies), who regarded it as an unwelcome intruder and united to protest to the Austrian branch of the Habsburg family, the rulers of the Belgian region at that time. In 1727, the Ostend East India Company was banned from trading with India. However, the Company did not close down completely - they switched to investing in other trading companies from countries such as Prussia and Sweden. The company existed until 1793.[80]

Making money is to spend money. Due to the development of trade with China, more and more Chinese goods entered Europe, making a strong "Chinese wind" in modern Europe. Among the goods of the ocean trade, the most profitable ones were of course the luxury goods. The influx of Chinese silk, porcelain, and lacquer ware triggered the pursuit of European royalty, nobility, and wealthy merchants, and the elegant and exotic style brought far-reaching effects to many aspects of Western society. This "Chinese style" began in the 17th century, reached its peak of popularity in the mid-18th century, and faded after the 19th century. This style is often found in interior furnishing

商船停泊在广州珠江口附近的情景。玻璃彩绘，中国画派，绘于 1786 年

Scene of merchant ships moored near the Pearl River Estuary in Guangzhou. Painting on glass, Chinese school, 1786

度公司）的利益，它们将其视为不受欢迎的不速之客，联合起来向当时比利时地区的统治者奥地利哈布斯堡王朝提出抗议。1727年奥斯坦德公司接到政府禁止其与印度通商的禁令。因为比起影响力更大的国家的利益，佛兰德斯地区的利益被牺牲掉。不过，奥斯坦德公司并没有完全关闭，它们改为向其他国外的贸易公司投资入股，如普鲁士、瑞典和其他国家，公司一直存在到1793年。[80]

赚钱之后就是花钱。由于对华贸易的发展，越来越多的中国商品进入欧洲，近代欧洲刮起了一股强劲的"中国风"。远洋贸易的商品中，利润最高的当然是奢侈品。中国的丝绸、瓷器、漆器等大量涌入，引发了欧洲王室、贵族、富商的追捧，高雅的异国风情给西方社会的许多方面带来了深远影响。这股"中国风"始于17世纪，在18世纪中叶达到流行的顶峰，19世纪之后逐渐消退，这一风格通常出现在室内陈设与装饰艺术中，同时也影响了建筑和造型艺术。

清朝时期，在康熙、雍正年间，奥斯坦德公司与中国的贸易往来将中国壁画、瓷器等商品也引进了低地国家。在当时的欧洲人眼里，能生产出这些精美器物的中国，应该是世界上最理想的国度，于是他们对中国和中国文化都充满着向往和好奇。在没有照相术的时代，画无疑是展现中国文化风俗山川景物的最形象最直观的选择。如果能将这些画直接贴到墙上作为房屋的内部装饰，无疑是最能显示财富最值得炫耀的。佛兰德斯是这类壁画装饰保存最为集中的地方，根特至少有五座宅邸留有相关遗存。一家公司文稿里曾将清朝壁纸描述为"华丽的人物画像"（pièces de Pecquin blanc orné de figures peintes）。[81]

在中国定制的"外销瓷"。盘子中间的字样为"佛兰德斯"。（私人收藏）
Chine de Commande. A luxurious Chinese export porcelain plate decorated with the word "Vlaanderen" (Flanders). Private collection

and decorative arts, and has also influenced architecture and the plastic arts.

During the Kangxi and Yongzheng periods of the Qing dynasty, the trade between the Ostend East India Company and China introduced Chinese frescoes, porcelain and other goods to the Low Countries as well. In the eyes of the Europeans at that time, China, which could produce these fine wares, was supposed to be the most desirable country in the world. Yearning and curiosity about China and Chinese culture abound. In an era without photography, paintings were undoubtedly the most visual option to show Chinese culture, customs, mountains and scenery. If these paintings could be put directly on the wall as the interior decoration of the house, it would undoubtedly be the most effective way of showing off wealth. Flanders has the highest concentration of such fresco decoration, and at least five houses in Ghent have survived. A company manuscript described Qing dynasty wallpapers as "pièces de Pecquin blanc ornè de figures peintes"[81].

In Brussels, Belgium, there are two Chinese temple (together with an octagonal pavilion) with a history of more than 100 years, which were designed and built by a group of Chinese workers in order to attract the audience during the Paris Universal Exhibition in 1900. At the time, the "Chinese style" had faded in Europe. But after seeing the two buildings, King Leopold II of Belgium was so impressed that he bought and moved them to Royal Palace of Laeken, making them the exclusive property of the Belgian royal family. When it was opened to the public in 1913, the Chinese pavilion and other buildings had been transferred to the Belgian National Museum of Commerce, where a large number of famous Chinese works of art, such as porcelain and silk, were displayed. The pavilion is still open to the public as a museum.

Foreign trade was supposed to be mutually beneficial, but rulers, unlike merchants, sometimes considered things

东印度公司的主要股东之一是布鲁塞尔的企业家让·巴蒂斯特·德佩斯特（Jean-Baptiste Depestre），他的女儿珍妮·艾格尼丝（Jeanne Agnes）嫁给了法国贵族奥布松勋爵赫克托·法利冈（Hector Falligan）。法利冈对根特库特河（Kouter）上的一座中世纪晚期建筑进行修复，将其改造为法利冈酒店。这座豪华酒店至今仍可参观，其中一间客房采用东方风格，内部装饰有中式情调图案。照片出自 *A Belgian Passage to China（1879-1930）*（Sterck & De Vreese, 2020）第 39 页

One of main shareholders in the Compagnie Impériale des Indes was Jean-Baptiste Depestre, a Brussels entrepreneur whose daughter Jeanne Agnes had married the French Nobleman Hector Falligan, Lord of Aubuisson. Falligan restored a late medieval building on the Kouter in Ghent, transforming it into the Hotel Falligan. In this mansion, which still can be visited today, one of the rooms is furnished in an oriental style, decorated with Chinese ornamentation. The photo is in the 39th page of *A Belgian Passage to China（1879-1930）*（Sterck & De Vreese, 2020）

安特卫普西南角 Hingene 的于瑟尔城堡。在 18 世纪，于瑟尔家族（d'Ursel）投入大量时间、精力和资金翻修他们的城堡，在重新装饰过程中，将几个房间都贴上了优雅的中国本土壁纸

The d'Ursel Castle in the village of Hingene, in the south-western corner of the province of Antwerp. In the course of the 18th century, the d'Ursel family invested considerable time, effort and money in renovating and redecorating their castle, several rooms of which were adorned with elegant and original Chinese wallpaper

在布鲁塞尔，还有两座拥有 100 多年历史的中式殿宇，它们是 1900 年巴黎万国博览会时期，当局为了招揽观众，雇用了一批华工精心设计并建造的新颖独特的"中国博物馆"和一座八角亭。当时"中国风"在欧洲的热度已渐渐消散，但比利时国王利奥波德二世见了之后，赞叹不已，把两座建筑买了下来，重建到了拉肯王宫的花园内，成为比利时王室的专有物。后来，这座中国馆和其他建筑物被转让给比利时国家商业博物馆。1913 年向公众开放时，馆中陈列着大量中国著名艺术品，如瓷器和丝绸。该馆现仍作为博物馆对外开放。

对外贸易本来应当是各取所需，互利互惠，但是统治者与商人不同，考虑问题有时不仅是为了利益。从 15 世纪到 17 世纪，中国经常不断地受到侵略者的攻击侵扰。虽然消灭了蒙古帝国建立了明王朝，可是中国还是不得不提防来自北方的蒙古人的骚扰，永乐皇帝朱棣也把首都由南京迁往北京，美其名曰"天子守国门"。由于集中注意力应付北方陆上敌人，中央政府对那些小事情——那些到达中国南方边陲口岸的少数欧洲商船——就只能给予微小的注意，采取对自己麻烦最少的方法来解决，那就是颁布禁海令。明王朝在之后不断被内部的农民起义和新兴的满族人打击，以致最后被打败，中国再次改朝换代。新的清朝统治者，以少数民族的身份而据有华夏，内心深处始终不安。他们不仅对汉人的反抗一直抱着警惕的态度，而且对不断叩关而来的西方人，因深恐其与汉人联手对付自己，而对其贸易要求，也是能拒绝就拒绝。

1757 年乾隆皇帝下谕，仅留粤海关一口对外通商，而且外国商人不能直接经商，只能通过代理人。清政府

for more than just profit. From the 15th to the 17th century, China was constantly attacked by invaders. Although the Mongol empire was destroyed and the Ming dynasty was established, China had to guard itself against Mongol harassment from the north, and Emperor Zhu Di moved the capital from Nanjing to Beijing in the name of "the Son of Heaven guarding the gates of the country". With its focus on land-based enemies in the north, the central government could only give minor attention to the few European merchant ships that arrived at China's southern frontier ports, and therefore took the least troublesome solution for itself, which was to issue the sea ban. The Ming dynasty was then continually struck down by internal peasant revolts and the emerging Manchus, to the point where it was finally defeated and China once again changed dynasties. The new rulers of the Qing dynasty, who had taken over China as minority, were always uneasy deep down. Not only were they wary of the Han revolt, but they also refused to trade with the Westerners for fear that they would join forces with the Han against them.

In 1757, Emperor Qianlong issued an edict that only the Guangdong Customs would be left open for foreign trade, and that foreign merchants could not do business directly, but only through agents. The Qing government appointed thirteen firms (intermediaries, middlemen who earned the difference) in Guangzhou to specialize in foreign trade, called the "Thirteen Hongs" (i.e., the monopoly institutions established by the Qing government to specialize in foreign trade). Until the Opium War, these foreign trade houses had exclusive control over China's foreign trade for 85 years. Relying on its monopoly, the Thirteen Hongs in Guangzhou brought huge income to the merchants there. The four major merchants, Pan, Wu, Lu and Ye, were known as the "four richest men in Guangzhou," whose combined wealth was more than the state treasury at the time.

布鲁塞尔的中国馆与中国亭

The China Temple in Brussels with the China Pavilion

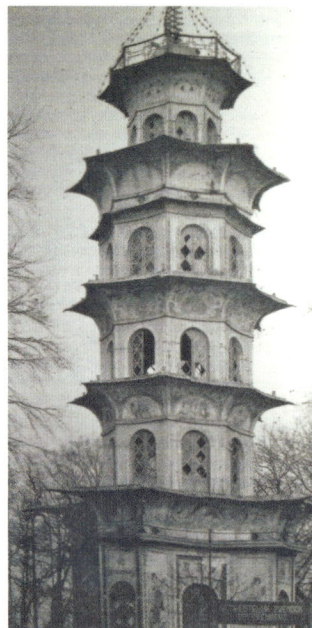

安特卫普附近博肯伯格公园内的中国塔（1800—1802）

The Chinese Tower (1800-1802) in the Boekenberg Park near Antwerp

中国塔（1780—1792）的建筑图纸（建于舍伦伯格城堡，即现在的拉肯皇家花园）

Drawings of the Chinese Pagoda (1780–1792, at Schoonenberg Castle, now the Royal Park at Laeken)

中国亭"雕梁"上的肖像，左起：柏应理、孔子、李鸿章、南怀仁

Portraits on the "carved beams" of the Chinese pavilion. From left: Philippe Couplet, Confucius, Li Hongzhang, and Ferdinand Verbiest

以上彩色照片由航鹰女士摄于 2010 年

Above color photos were taken by Ms. Hang Ying in 2010

指定广州十三家牙行（中介机构，赚差价的中间商）专做对外贸易，称之为"十三行"，即清政府制定专营对外贸易的垄断机构。直至鸦片战争为止，这个洋货行独揽中国外贸长达 85 年。依靠垄断地位，广州十三行给那里的行商们带来了巨额收入。十三行的潘、伍、卢、叶四大行商号称"广州四大富豪"，其家产总和比当时的国库收入还要多，是货真价实的"富可敌国"。

然而，对于那些不远万里踏浪而来、与中国行商打交道的外国商人来说，却不是那么愉快了。首先，所有贸易往来的规则，必须由这些中间商来制定，并从中赚取巨大利润，而且外商船只进出广州内河还须缴纳不菲的费用以及各种不定额的关税，实际征收往往是公布税则所核定税率的 5 倍。不仅如此，对于那些在华经商的外国人、外国船只和对外贸易，清政府还制定了种种章程，其中不乏苛刻的内容，比如，妇女不得带到商馆；洋人不得乘轿，只许徒步行走；洋人不得呈递禀帖，如有陈述，必须由行商转呈；在贸易季节之后，洋人不得逗留广州，必须在他们的货物卖尽和船装好之后，回国或前往澳门；等等。[82]外国商人在中国面临的最大问题，其实是赚不到钱。他们在中国购买了大量的茶叶、丝织品，而他们带来的商品，除了钟表等少数奢侈品能卖给中国富人之外，并没有什么市场。于是，他们很快找到利润丰厚的替代商品——鸦片。最早向中国输入鸦片的是荷兰人和葡萄牙人，后来英国的东印度公司把这项获利丰厚的贸易垄断在自己手中。再后来，随着工业革命和煤铁时代的到来，比利时商人找到了更加道德也更有利可图的商品——铁路。

However, it was not so pleasant for the foreign merchants who came from far and wide to deal with the Chinese merchants. First of all, all the rules of trade had to be set by these middlemen and they made huge profits. Foreign ships had to pay a lot of fees and various variable tariffs to enter and leave the inner river of Guangzhou, which were often four times higher than the approved rate of the published tax rules. In addition, for those foreigners doing business in China, the Qing government also established various harsh regulations. For example, women were not allowed in the business amenities; foreigners were not allowed to take sedan chairs and must walk on foot; foreigners were not allowed to submit request directly to the government and must go through the middlemen; foreigners were not allowed to stay in Guangzhou after the trading season and must return home or go to Macao.[82] The biggest problem faced by foreign merchants in China was actually the failure to make money. They bought a lot of tea and silk in China, and there was no market for the goods they brought, except for a few luxury items such as clocks and watches that could be sold to the rich Chinese. However, they soon found a lucrative alternative commodity - opium. The Dutch and Portuguese were the first to import opium into China, and the British East India Company later monopolized this lucrative trade for itself. Later, with the advent of the coal and iron age of the Industrial Revolution, Belgian merchants found a more ethical and profitable trade - the railroad.

注释

1 二战中发生在阿登森林的有两次重要战役。第一次发生在二战早期的 1940 年 5 月 10 日，希特勒采用"曼施坦因计划"，令德军坦克部队用 48 小时穿越阿登森林，绕过法德边境号称坚不可摧的"马奇诺防线"，直插英法联军后身，逼迫联军在敦刻尔克撤退，仅用 44 天攻陷法国。第二次发生在二战结束前，是西线最后也是最大规模的战役，一直节节败退的德国人意图发动这次战役重现 1940 年席卷英法军队的情景，而最终结果却是西线盟军获胜，德军彻底丧失反攻能力，四个月后柏林被攻陷。

2 法兰克王国（拉丁语为 Regnum Francorum，法语为 Royaumes Francs，意为"法兰克人的王国"）是 5 世纪至 9 世纪在西欧和中欧的一个王国，统治者先后为墨洛温王朝和加洛林王朝，在查理大帝统治时期国力达到顶峰。在它瓦解后，它的各部分逐渐演变为今天的法国、德国、比利时、荷兰和其他一些小国。

3 墨洛温王朝（法语为 Mérovingiens，又译梅罗文王朝或梅罗文加王朝）是公元 5 世纪由法兰克人建立的一个中世纪王朝，是统治法兰克王国的第一个王朝。墨洛温王朝奉行诸子均分制，这导致法兰克王国的土地持续分割，王朝统治衰弱，直至公元 8 世纪被加洛林王朝所取代。由墨洛温王朝引入的基督教文化一直影响着法兰克王国与其后继国家的发展。

4 加洛林王朝（法语为 les Carolingiens，旧称 Carlovingiens，中世纪拉丁语为 Karolingi，又译卡洛林王朝）是自公元 751 年后统治法兰克王国的王朝。王朝鼎盛时期为查理大帝在位期间，加洛林家族在名义上继承了古典时期的罗马帝国，也即是开创了后世所谓的神圣罗马帝国。

5 又译为弗蓝德、佛兰德勒、佛兰德斯或弗朗德伦（荷兰语为 Vlaanderen，法语为 Flandre，英语为 Flanders）是比利时西部的一个地区，人口主要是弗拉芒人，说荷兰语（又称"弗拉芒语"）。

6 现在比利时仍有两个省区以佛兰德斯为名，分别为东佛兰德斯（又译作东佛莱芒）、西佛兰德斯（又译作西佛莱芒）。

7 勃艮第公国（法语为 Bourgogne）由理查德伯爵于 9 世纪建立，包括法国中部和东部一些地区。在腓力二世（大胆者）当政时期（1363—1404），勃艮第公国的军事和政治势力有所扩展，亦获得了佛兰德、阿图瓦、弗朗什孔泰（又称勃艮第伯国）以及其他地区；腓力三世（好人）执政时（1419—1467），又获得了布洛涅伯爵领地、卢森堡以及尼德兰的一部分和皮卡第。勃艮第公国在查理公爵（大胆者）统治之下（1467—1477），势力达到顶峰，并与法国争雄。然而，1477 年查理公爵在南锡战役中被瑞士击败，公国逐渐被法国和哈布斯堡王朝瓜分。

8 哈布斯堡王朝（德语为 Habsburg），也称哈普斯堡家族（Hapsburg），是欧洲历史上最为显赫、统治地域最广的王室之一，其家族成员曾出任神圣罗马帝国皇帝和欧洲主要国家的国王、大公与公爵。16 世纪中叶分裂为奥地利和西班牙两个分支。

9 布鲁塞尔首都大区为双语区。瓦隆行政区大部分对应法语社区，但东部边疆地区为德语社区。

10 皮朗：《佛里斯兰的呢绒还是法兰德斯的呢绒？》，转引自〔比〕亨利·皮朗《中世纪欧洲经济社会史》，乐文译，上海：上海人民出版社，2014，第 25 页。

11 转引自〔美〕巴巴拉·W. 塔奇曼《远方之镜：动荡不安的 14 世纪》，邵文实译，北京：中信出版社，2016，第 80 页。

12 十字军东征（拉丁语为 Cruciata，伊斯兰世界称法兰克人的入侵时间为 1096—1291）。这是一系列在教皇的准许下的战役，由西欧的封建领主和骑士对他们认为是异教徒的国家（地中海东岸）发动持续近 200 年的宗教战争。十字军的成员还包括商人和农民。

13 〔比〕亨利·皮朗：《中世纪欧洲经济社会史》，乐文译，上海：上海人民出版社，2014，第 85 页。

14 Mollat Michel and Philippe Wolff. Ongles bleues, Jacques et Ciompi. Paris, 1970, p.25. 转引自〔美〕巴巴拉·W. 塔奇曼《远方之镜：动荡不安的 14 世纪》，邵文实译，北京：中信出版社，2016，第 80 页。

15 金马刺战役（荷兰语为 Guldensporenslag，法语为 Bataille des éperons d'or）是 1302 年 7 月 11 日发生于佛兰德斯的库特赖（Courtrai）附近的一场战役。佛兰德斯地区因为与英国贸易往来密切，经常联手对抗法国。1302 年 3 月，法国贵族在弗拉芒征收过高的赋税，遭到根特居民的强烈反抗。7 月 11 日由工匠和农民组成的装备着长矛的佛兰德斯民兵，在布满无数小溪和沟壑的库特赖附近遭遇了法国骑兵和步兵。利用地利之便，以及法军指挥官指挥失误，佛兰德斯民兵大败法军。大批法国骑士的金马刺被佛兰德斯人缴获，这场战役由此而得名。至少 1000 名贵族骑兵战死，有些同时代的记述中称超过 1 万法军战死或负伤。缴获的法国金马刺被悬挂在科尔特赖克的圣母教堂内，以纪念这次伟大的胜利。

16 现代民族的意义，不在于其与古代民族有着怎样的历史和文化的连续性，而在于现代的"民族"和民族主义形成于资本主义上升时期，故资本主义（或世界现代化过程）的开始是民族形态的分界线，在此之前，民族为古代民族，在此之后是现代民族。

17 公元 1206 年铁木真在斡难河畔建立蒙古国，国号"大蒙古国"，铁木真被尊为"成吉思汗"。蒙古建国后，成吉思汗及其子孙曾发动三次西征，将版图不断扩大，囊括欧亚大陆和北非各地，其最大疆域曾达到 3450 万平方公里，是历史上版图最辽阔的国家。1219—1221 年蒙古第一次西征，灭西辽、花剌子模、亚美尼亚、格鲁吉亚和阿塞拜疆，并越过高加索山击破钦察人各部。1236—1242 年蒙古第二次西征，先灭亡位于东欧平原的基辅罗斯，而后击溃波兰王国和神圣罗马帝国联军，大败匈牙利王国、保加利亚第二帝国，前锋远达当时意大利的威尼斯共和国的达尔马提亚、原南斯拉夫地区的拉什卡。1252—1260 年第三次西征，灭亡了木剌夷（伊斯兰教极端派的一个暗杀组织）、两河流域的阿拔斯王朝，以及叙利亚的阿尤布王朝。

18 意大利人柏朗嘉宾（Jean de Plan Carpin）是方济各会的创始人之一，是中世纪最早出使东方的使者。1245 年由法国里昂登程，出使蒙古，从西欧到中亚，于 1246 年 4 月 4 日到达伏尔加河畔的西蒙古拔都幕帐，后于 8 月 24 日抵达哈拉和林，有幸参加贵由大汗登基大典。同年 11 月 13 日启程返回，于 1247 年 11 月 24 日返回里昂。柏朗嘉宾的使命是规劝蒙古人皈依基督教和建立盟邦关系，同时刺探蒙古的风俗民情和军事情报。前一个使命没有达到目的，而后一个使命则出色完成。在他写给教廷的报告《蒙古史》中第一次对关于蒙古和中亚的许多情况进行了详细的介绍。

19 方济各会（意大利语为 Ordine Francescano）又称方济会或小兄弟会，或译法兰西斯会、佛兰西斯会。方济会提倡过清贫生活，互称"小兄弟"。方济会效忠教宗，重视学术研究和文化教育事业，反对异端，为传扬福音而到处游方。1289 年，方济各会会士孟高维诺总主教（意大利语为 Giovanni da Montecorvino，1247—1328），受罗马教廷派遣前往时值元朝统治的中国。经海路，1291 年抵达泉州，1294 年抵达大都（今北京），是最早期的来华天主教传教士。

20 1248 年，在英诺森四世的支持下，路易九世发动了第七次十字军东征。结果军队遭遇瘟疫，并被埃及击败，路易九世本人也被俘，后法国用重金将其赎回。

21 何高济译《鲁布鲁克东行纪》，北京：中华书局，2013，第 225 页。

22 何高济译《鲁布鲁克东行纪》，北京：中华书局，2013，第 180 页。

23 何高济译《鲁布鲁克东行纪》，北京：中华书局，2013，第 181 页。

24 聂斯脱里派，即唐代传入中国的景教，也就是东方亚述教会。景教起源于今日叙利亚，是从希腊正教（东正教）分裂出来的基督教教派，由叙利亚教士君士坦丁堡牧首聂斯脱里于公元 428—431 年创立，在波斯建立教会。景教被视为最早进入中国的基督教派。

25 畏兀儿人，又称西州回鹘。唐朝时期称作回鹘人。回鹘人原居于漠北，回鹘汗国时代，已有一些回鹘族部落迁居到今天山以北和河西一带。

26 撒拉逊的原来意义，系指从如今的叙利亚到沙特阿拉伯之间的沙漠牧民，广义上则指中古时代所有的阿拉伯人。

27 何高济译《鲁布鲁克东行纪》，北京：中华书局，2013，第236—237页。

28 何高济译《鲁布鲁克东行纪》，北京：中华书局，2013，第262页。

29 何高济译《鲁布鲁克东行纪》，北京：中华书局，2013，第237页。

30 何高济译《鲁布鲁克东行纪》，北京：中华书局，2013，第266页。

31 张星烺：《中国史书上关于马黎诺里使节之记载》，厦门大学国学研究院编《厦门大学国学研究院集刊》第1辑，北京：中华书局，2007，第10页。

32 薛福成：《出使四国日记》，北京：社会科学文献出版社，2007，第95页。

33 天主教主要修会之一。1534年由西班牙人圣依纳爵·罗耀拉（Ignacio de Loyola）创立于巴黎，旨在反对欧洲的宗教改革运动。耶稣会热衷于参与社会生活、积极关注现实政治而在近代欧洲产生深远影响。注重文化教育事业，是耶稣会区别于其他修会的显著标志，也是耶稣会和现实社会保持接触、施加影响的有效手段。当时耶稣会传教士的足迹遍布世界各地。

34 Nicolas Standaert (ed.). *Handbook of Christianity in China*, Volume One: 635-1800. Leiben Boston Knoll: Brill, 2001, p.600.

35 〔法〕裴化行：《利玛窦神父传》（上），管震湖译，北京：商务印书馆，1998，第68—69页。

36 利玛窦（Matteo Ricci，1552年10月6日—1610年5月11日），意大利马切拉塔人，耶稣会传教士、学者。明朝万历年间来华传教，是天主教在中国传教的最早开拓者之一，也是第一位阅读中国文学并对中国典籍进行钻研的西方学者。他通过"西方僧侣"的身份、"汉语著述"的方式传播天主教教义，并广交中国官员和社会名流，传播西方天文、数学、地理等科学技术知识，他的著述对中西文化交流做出了重要贡献。

37 利玛窦传教方法，即①学汉语，改装易服，习新礼，以利沟通，方便中国人接纳；②结交皇室贵族、士大夫等上层人士，以获得保护和提高影响力；③改编圣经故事，迎合中国人的道德观和宿命论；④注重传授西方科学知识，借此得到中国人对西方科学的关注以接受基督教信仰；⑤发展天主教徒要重质不重量。

38 李之藻（1565—1630），明代科学家。1610年入天主教。

与利玛窦交往甚深，曾随利玛窦学习西洋历算，主张西法，一生致力于介绍西方天文学、数学、逻辑学等，与利玛窦、徐光启及其他人合作翻译西学著作10余部。与徐光启、杨廷筠并称为"天主教三柱石"。

39 徐明德、计翔翔：《杰出的法国传教士金尼阁》，载许明龙主编《中西文化交流先驱——从利玛窦到郎世宁》，北京：东方出版社，1993，第86页。

40 徐宗泽：《中国天主教传教史概论》，北京：商务印书馆，2015，第142页。

41 〔美〕邓恩：《从利玛窦到汤若望：晚明的耶稣会传教士》，余三乐、石蓉译，上海：上海古籍出版社，2003，第148页。

42 徐宗泽：《中国天主教传教史概论》，北京：商务印书馆，2015，第142页。

43 1617年1月2日金尼阁书信。转引自方豪《方豪六十自定稿》（上），台北：台湾学生书局，1969，第44页。

44 杨廷筠（1557—1627），明末朝廷重要官员，中国最早的天主教徒之一，著名学者、神学家。与徐光启、李之藻并称为"天主教三柱石"，对中国天主教的初创与发展影响与贡献甚大。

45 伍玉西：《"书籍传教"：一种适应明清之际中国社会的传教方法》，《中国出版史研究》2016年第3期，第21—37页。

46 王徵（1571—1644），明代科学家，与瑞士传教士邓玉函一起编译《远西奇器图说录最》，对明末西方科学技术传入中国曾起到重要作用。

47 徐明德、计翔翔：《杰出的法国传教士金尼阁》，载许明龙主编《中西文化交流先驱——从利玛窦到郎世宁》，北京：东方出版社，1993，第92页。

48 张赓，福建泉州人，明代天主教信徒，曾任浙江平湖县教谕。

49 所谓"景教"是基督教的一个支派，是叙利亚人聂思脱里（Nestorius，约386—451）所创，故又称"聂思脱里派"，被正统天主教所排斥，后来传到波斯。公元635年（唐太宗贞观九年），景教传入中国，因景教专走上层路线，在初唐盛唐时期颇有影响。公元781年（唐建中二年）2月4日，景教传教士伊斯（Yazdhozid）在大秦寺院中立碑，因该碑正面刻着"大秦景教流行中国碑并颂"，后世称之为《大秦景教流行中国碑》。

50 徐明德、计翔翔：《杰出的法国传教士金尼阁》，载许明龙主编《中西文化交流先驱——从利玛窦到郎世宁》，北京：东方出版社，1993，第94—95页。

51 〔意〕利玛窦、〔比〕金尼阁：《利玛窦中国札记》，何高济、王遵仲、李申译，桂林：广西师范大学出版社，2001，第464页。

52 〔意〕利玛窦、〔比〕金尼阁：《利玛窦中国札记》，何高济、王遵仲、李申译，桂林：广西师范大学出版社，2001，第465页。

53 汤若望（Johann Adam Schall von Bell，1592—1666），德国科隆人，天主教耶稣会传教士。1620年（明万历四十八年）到澳门，在中国生活47年，汤若望历经明、清两朝，是继利玛窦之后最重要的来华耶稣会士之一。曾任钦天监监正，是中国历史上第一个洋监正，开创清廷任用传教士掌管钦天监的近200年传统。

54 李培德：《对南怀仁科学工作的总评价》，载魏若望主编《传教士·科学家·工程师·外交家南怀仁（1623—1688）：鲁汶国际学术研讨会论文集》，北京：社会科学文献出版社，2001，第44—56页。

55 卫匡国（Martin Martini），意大利籍耶稣会士，1643年赴中国传教，在华传教时游历名山大川，著有《中国新地图志》，1650年被派赴罗马汇报教务，抵达欧洲后在德意志、比利时等地宣讲中国传教副省的情况，备受学者欢迎，吸引了很多人来华传教。

56 席泽宗：《南怀仁对中国科学的贡献》，载魏若望主编《传教士·科学家·工程师·外交家南怀仁（1623—1688）：鲁汶国际学术研讨会论文集》，北京：社会科学文献出版社，2001，第199页。

57 阎宗临：《中西交通史》，桂林：广西师范大学出版社，2007，第100页注释①。

58 林金水：《试论南怀仁对康熙皇帝天主教政策的影响》，载魏若望主编《传教士·科学家·工程师·外交家南怀仁（1623—1688）：鲁汶国际学术研讨会论文集》，北京：社会科学文献出版社，2001，第412—413页。

59 古伟瀛：《朝廷与教会之间：中国天主教史中的南怀仁》，载魏若望主编《传教士·科学家·工程师·外交家南怀仁（1623—1688）：鲁汶国际学术研讨会论文集》，北京：社会科学文献出版社，2001，第378页。

60 Arnold H. Rowbotham. *Missionary and Mandarin-The Jesuits at the Court of China*. Berkeley, 1942, p.99, 转引自林金水《试论南怀仁对康熙皇帝天主教政策的影响》，载魏若望主编《传教士·科学家·工程师·外交家南怀仁（1623—1688）：鲁汶国际学术研讨会论文集》，北京：社会科学文献出版社，2001，第413页。

61 黄伯禄：《正教奉褒》"序"，上海：慈母堂，1894，第3页。转引自林金水《试论南怀仁对康熙皇帝天主教政策的影响》，载魏若望主编《传教士·科学家·工程师·外交家南怀仁（1623—1688）：鲁汶国际学术研讨会论文集》，北京：社会科学文献出版社，2001，第412—413页。

62 尼布楚条约的谈判和签订，南怀仁虽没有直接参与，但其中起到重要作用的两位传教士徐日昇和张诚，均是由南怀仁引荐给清廷的。

63 Brucker. *Conmunication sur L'exécution des Cartes de la Chine par les Misssiounaires du XVe siècle d'après Documents Inédits*. Paris, 1890, p. 387.

64〔法〕杜赫德：《耶稣会士中国书简集：中国回忆录》第2卷，郑德弟译，郑州：大象出版社，2001，第287页。

65 L. Pfister. *Notices Biographiques et Bibliographiques sur les Jesuites de l'ancienne Mission de Chine, 1552-1738*. Shanghai, 1932, I, p. 307.

66 与南怀仁、柏应理一起获批来华的传教士中，还有几位比利时耶稣会士，包括鲁日满、吴尔铎。

67〔美〕孟德卫：《奇异的国度：耶稣会适应政策及汉学的起源》，陈怡译，郑州：大象出版社，2010，第315页。

68〔美〕孟德卫：《奇异的国度：耶稣会适应政策及汉学的起源》，陈怡译，郑州：大象出版社，2010，第273页。

69 潘吉星：《沈福宗在17世纪欧洲的学术活动》，《北京教育学院学报》（自然科学版）2007年第3期，第1页。

70〔美〕孟德卫：《奇异的国度：耶稣会适应政策及汉学的起源》，陈怡译，郑州：大象出版社，2010，第277页。

71 转引自潘吉星《沈福宗在17世纪欧洲的学术活动》，《北京教育学院学报》（自然科学版），2007年第3期，第1—8页。

72 潘吉星：《沈福宗在17世纪欧洲的学术活动》，《北京教育学院学报》（自然科学版）2007年第3期，第5页。

73 转引自潘吉星《沈福宗在17世纪欧洲的学术活动》，《北京教育学院学报》（自然科学版）2007年第3期，第5页。

74 潘吉星：《沈福宗在17世纪欧洲的学术活动》，《北京教育学院学报》（自然科学版）2007年第3期，第3页。

75〔美〕孟德卫：《奇异的国度：耶稣会适应政策及汉学的起源》，陈怡译，郑州：大象出版社，2010，第314页。

76 潘吉星：《沈福宗在17世纪欧洲的学术活动》，《北京教育学院学报》（自然科学版）2007年第3期，第4页。

77〔英〕J. M. 罗伯茨：《欧洲史》，李腾等译，上海：东方出版中心，2015，第420页。

78 J Johan J. Mattelaer, Mathieu Torck (eds.). *A Belgian Passage to China (1870-1930)*. Uitgeverij Sterck & De Vreese, 2020, p. 35.

79 J Johan J. Mattelaer, Mathieu Torck (eds.). *A Belgian Passage to China (1870-1930)*. Uitgeverij Sterck & De Vreese, 2020, pp. 35-36.

80〔比〕让·东特：《比利时史》，南京大学外文系翻译组译，南京：江苏人民出版社，1973，第102页。

81 J Johan J. Mattelaer, Mathieu Torck (eds.). *A Belgian Passage to China (1870-1930)*. Uitgeverij Sterck & De Vreese, 2020, p. 39.

82〔美〕马士：《中华帝国对外关系史》，张汇文等译，上海：上海世纪出版集团，2006，第76—78页。

参考文献

中文文献

[1] 斌椿、张德彝. 乘槎笔记 航海述奇 [M]. 北京：商务印书馆，2016.

[2] 蔡尔康等. 李鸿章历聘欧美记 [M]. 长沙：湖南人民出版社，1986.

[3] 方豪. 方豪六十自定稿：上 [M]. 台北：台湾学生书局，1969.

[4] 郭嵩焘. 伦敦与巴黎日记 [M]. 长沙：岳麓书社，1984.

[5] 吴孟雪. 明清时期欧洲人眼中的中国 [M]. 北京：中华书局，2000.

[6] 徐宗泽. 中国天主教传教史概论 [M]. 北京：商务印书馆，2015.

[7] 薛福成. 出使四国日记 [M]. 北京：社会科学文献出版社，2007.

[8] 阎宗临. 中西交通史 [M]. 桂林：广西师范大学出版社，2007.

[9] 余三乐. 早期西方传教士与北京 [M]. 北京：北京出版社，2001.

[10]〔澳〕杰克·特纳. 香料传奇 [M]. 周子平译. 北京：生活·读书·新知三联书店，2007.

[11]〔比〕让·东特. 比利时史 [M]. 南京大学外文系翻译组译. 南京：江苏人民出版社，1973.

[12]〔比〕亨利·皮雷纳. 中世纪的城市 [M]. 陈国樑译. 北京：商务印书馆，2009.

[13]〔比〕亨利·皮朗. 中世纪欧洲经济社会史 [M]. 乐文译. 上海：上海人民出版社，2014.

[14]〔法〕杜赫德. 耶稣会士中国书简集：中国回忆录：第2卷 [M]. 郑德弟译. 郑州：大象出版社，2001.

[15]〔法〕裴化行. 利玛窦神父传：上 [M]. 管震湖译. 北京：商务印书馆，1998.

[16] 何高济译. 鲁布鲁克东行纪 [M]. 北京：中华书局，2013.

[17]〔美〕邓恩. 从利玛窦到汤若望：晚明的耶稣会传教士 [M]. 余三乐、石蓉译. 上海：上海古籍出版社，2003.

[18]〔美〕马士. 中华帝国对外关系史 [M]. 张汇文等译. 上海：上海世纪出版集团，2006.

[19]〔美〕巴巴拉·W. 塔奇曼. 远方之镜：动荡不安的14世纪 [M]. 邵文实译. 北京：中信出版社，2016.

[20]〔意〕利玛窦,〔比〕金尼阁.利玛窦中国札记 [M].何高济、王遵仲、李申译.桂林：广西师范大学出版社,2001.

[21]〔英〕J.M. 罗伯茨.欧洲史 [M].李腾等译.上海：东方出版中心,2015.

[22]〔英〕彼得·弗兰科潘.丝绸之路 [M].邵旭东等译.杭州：浙江大学出版社,2016.

[23]〔英〕尼科拉·弗莱彻.查理曼大帝的桌布 [M].李响译.北京：生活·读书·新知三联书店,2007.

[24]〔美〕孟德卫.奇异的国度：耶稣会适应政策及汉学的起源 [M].陈怡译.郑州：大象出版社,2010.

[25]〔美〕魏若望.传教士·科学家·工程师·外交家南怀仁（1623—1688）：鲁汶国际学术研讨会论文集 [C].北京：社会科学文献出版社,2001.

[26] 厦门大学国学研究院编.厦门大学国学研究院集刊：第 1 辑 [C].北京：中华书局,2007.

[27] 潘吉星.沈福宗在 17 世纪欧洲的学术活动 [J].北京教育学院学报（自然科学版）,2007（3）：1—8.

[28] 伍玉西.“书籍传教”：一种适应明清之际中国社会的传教方法 [J].中国出版史研究,2016（3）：21—37.

外文文献

[1] Barbara Emerson. *Leopold II of the Belgium, King of Colonialism* [M]. London: Bulterand Tanner Ltd. 1979.

[2] Brucker. *Conmunication sur L'exécution des Cartes de la Chine par les Misssiounaires du XVe siècle d'après Documents Inédits* [M]. Paris. 1890.

[3] Pfister, L. *Notices Biographiques et Bibliographiques sur les Jesuites de l'ancienne Mission de Chine, 1552-1738* [M]. I. Shanghai. 1932.

[4] Standaert, Nicolas ed. *Handbook of Christianity in China: Volume one: 635-1800* [M]. Leiben Boston Knoll: Brill. 2001.

[5] W.F. Vande Walle. *The History of the Relations between the Low Countries and China the Qing Era (1644-1911)* [M]. Leuven: Leuven University Press. 2003.

[6] J Johan J. Mattelaer, Mathieu Torck (eds.). *A Belgian Passage to China (1870-1930)* [M]. Uitgeverij Sterck & De Vreese, 2020.

电子文献

[1] http://www.railwaywondersoftheworld.com/belgian_railways.html.

[2] https://en.wikipedia.org/wiki/History_of_rail_transport_in_Belgium.

"中国火箭"号机车。约摄于 19 世纪 80 年代。照片由近代天津博物馆提供

"Rocket of China" Locomotive, taken circa 1880s. Photo from Tianjin Museum of Modern History

第二章 被火车头牵引的交往

Chapter 2: Interactions Led by the Locomotive

工业革命与国家独立

公元 1500—1800 年的 300 年间，西欧发生了巨变，现代历史的序幕，至此已经拉开。新航路的开辟逐渐将世界变成一个统一的广阔市场，欧洲西北部人口的不断增长扩大了消费需求，人们像越盖越高的教堂尖顶那样精进各种新技术，以这些变革为基础，西欧实现了真正的飞跃。

18 世纪中叶，比利时的工业发展经历了一个决定性的阶段。随着经济的发展，它的煤炭和冶炼工业迅速发展，工业从过去分散在农村的手工作坊向中心城市转移，企业的规模不断扩大，逐渐向工厂过渡。新式蒸汽机在 18 世纪得到推广，使产能大大提升。人们已知最古老的被使用的一台纽康门式蒸汽抽水机[1]1720年出现在马斯河岸热梅普（Jemeppe-sur-Meuse）的一家采煤企业中。[2]人们对工业发展的前途充满信心，资本家和贵族热衷于投资工业，资金源源不绝。

新技术的应用不仅体现在工业方面，也体现在农业

Industrial Revolution and National Independence

In the 300 years between 1500 and 1800 AD, Western Europe changed dramatically and the prelude to modern history had henceforth begun. The opening of new transportation routes gradually turned the world into a unified marketplace. The growing population of northwestern Europe expanded consumer demand, and many new technologies were invented with a fast speed. Based on these changes, Western Europe has made a real leap forward.

In the middle of the 18th century, Belgium went through a decisive phase in its industrial development. With the development of the economy, its coal and smelting industries had developed rapidly, and industries had shifted from handicraft workshops scattered in rural areas to centralized cities. The scale of enterprises continued to expand, gradually transitioning to major factories. New types of steam engines were popularized in the 18th century, leading to a significant increase in production capacity. The

方面。这一时期，比利时采用了新式耕犁，还引进了新的农业品种——土豆，使农业出现了显著的兴旺景象，从而养活了更多的人口。18世纪的前半期，布拉邦特省和安特卫普省的人口增长了20%，而在1755—1784年，人口增长了39%。这一时期，奥属尼德兰和列日公国的总人口大约250万，是全欧洲人口最稠密的地方，[3]而增长的人口为工厂提供了大量廉价的劳动力。

工业的发展离不开交通运输。各地方政府致力于发展交通，努力建设公路网和运河网。不到100年的时间里，比利时地区铺设的公路里程达到2850公里。人们还开凿了从梅克林到鲁汶（Louvain）的运河，与斯海尔德河流域连接起来，形成了四通八达的运河网。这些公路与运河相互交织，把西部的海港奥斯坦德和布鲁日与内陆的根特、梅克林串接到一起，建成一个庞大的货物转口轴心。[4]

经济独立与政治独立几乎总是相辅相成。一个经济繁荣富庶的比利时终于从那些老牌帝国的统治下获得政治独立，甚至过去的亲兄弟荷兰也因为发展方向不同而与它分道扬镳。从16世纪到1789年法国大革命爆发，这个阶段是欧洲从绝对君主专制向现代民族国家过渡的历史阶段。在这一阶段中，商业资本主义在尼德兰及其所在的西欧也得以进一步发展，由资本主义的生产方式所推动的全球化和现代化打破了封建割据的局面，统一了市场，催生了现代民族主义，从而建立了统一的民族国家。同时，这一时期的天主教和新教的对立，又分裂了尼德兰地区。按照马克斯·韦伯（Max Weber）的观点，新教伦理与隐藏在资本主义发展背后的某种心理驱力（即资本主义精神）之间相互契合，彼此存在着相互生成的关系，所以新教在资本

earliest used Newcomen steam pumping engine[1] appeared in 1720 in a coal mining enterprise on the banks of the Jemeppe-sur-Meuse River.[2] Fueled with confidence in the future of industry, capitalists and aristocrats were keen to invest in industry, and money started flowing in.

The application of new technologies was not only in industry, but also in agriculture. During this period, Belgium adopted a new type of plow and also introduced a new agricultural variety, the potato, which led to a remarkable boom in agriculture, providing food to a larger population. In the first half of the 18th century, the population of the provinces of Brabant and Antwerp grew by 20%, while between 1755 and 1784, it grew by 39%. With a total population of about 2.5 million, the Belgian region was the most densely populated in Europe.[3] The growing population provided a large amount of cheap labor for factories.

The development of industry cannot be achieved without transportation. The local governments were committed to developing transportation and worked to open up a network of roads and canals. In less than 100 years, 2,850 kilometers of roads were paved in the Belgian regions. Canals were also dug from Malines (or Mechelen) to Louvain to connect with the Scheldt River basin, creating a network of canals. These roads and canals were intertwined, linking the western seaports of Ostende and Bruges with the inland ports of Ghent and Mechelen, creating a vast axis of goods transit.[4]

Economic independence and political independence almost always go hand in hand. An economically prosperous and affluent Belgium finally gained political independence from the domination of those great empires. Even its former blood brother, the Netherlands, parted ways with Belgium because of their different path of development. The period from the 16th century to the outbreak of the French Revolution in 1789 was a period in the history of Europe's transition from absolute monarchy

19 世纪中期列日省的一家煤矿
A coal mine in Liège province in the middle of 19 century

19 世纪中期列日省的一家毛纺厂
A woolen mill in Liège province in the middle of 19 century

成立于 1824 年的比利时赫尔斯托的小型煤矿。约摄于 19 世纪中期
Small-scale coal mines established in 1824 in Helstow, Belgium. Taken circa in middle of 19 century

以上资料来源（Source）：http://www.delcampe.net。

主义更为发达的北部地区占优势，而天主教则在南部占优势。到 1789 年法国爆发资产阶级大革命时，在当时被并入法国的今比利时领土上也爆发了资产阶级革命性质的"布拉邦特革命"和"列日革命"。1830 年日益工业化后实力大增的资产阶级要求进行政治改革，比利时终于独立建国。

独立后，富有远见的新政府励精图治，决定抓住火车这个交通发展机遇，在全国兴建铁路网，代替运河上的水路运输，以刺激历经 10 多年的政治动荡和经济萧条之后衰弱的经济。1834 年，比利时政府批准了从工业中心蒙斯（Mons）经布鲁塞尔到安特卫普港、耗资约 1.5 亿比利时法郎的大规模铁路兴建计划。刚刚登基的国王利奥波德一世积极支持和赞助了这项计划。他希望通过控制铁路来掌控国家和议会，在这个君主立宪的国家获得更大的权力。考虑到铁路将是一个主要的经济来源，而且需要一个完整的网络，比利时政府没有像英国那样，将铁路交由私营部

to the modern nation-state. During this period, commercial capitalism also developed further in the Netherland and in the broader Western Europe. Globalization and modernization driven by the capitalist mode of production broke down feudal fragmentation, unified the market, and gave birth to modern nationalism, thus establishing a unified nation-state. At the same time, the Catholic-Protestant rivalry of this period divided the Netherland. According to Max Weber, the Protestant ethic and a certain psychological drive hidden behind the development of capitalism (i.e., the spirit of capitalism) were compatible with each other and existed in a mutually generative relationship, so that Protestantism prevailed in the more developed capitalist north, while Catholicism prevailed in the south. By the time the bourgeois revolution broke out in France in 1789, the "Brabant Revolution" and the "Liège Revolution" of a bourgeois revolutionary nature had also broken out in the territory of what is now Belgium, which was then incorporated into France. In 1830, the bourgeoisie, which

门修建，而是由政府主导铁路系统的规划设计，并使用私营部门的资金，以防止大银行对铁路的垄断。随后这一做法被其他国家所效仿。

1835 年，这条铁路线中从布鲁塞尔到梅伦的一段修建完成。这是欧洲大陆上第一条蒸汽机车客运铁路。[5] 另一条由列日到奥斯坦德铁路的完成，标志着比利时铁路的发展从一开始就已形成系统。1836 年，铁路延伸到安特卫普；1843 年，两条南北、东西交叉的主干线

邮票上的 1835 年"比利时"号火车头
Locomotive "Le Belge" 1835 on the stamp

1835 年的"比利时"号火车头是欧洲大陆上第一辆蒸汽机车头
Le Belge ("The Belgian", 1835) was the first steam locomotive built in continental Europe

以上资料来源（Source）：http://www.railwaywonderoftheworld.com。

had become increasingly industrialized and powerful, demanded political reforms, and Belgium was finally established as an independent state.

After independence, the new visionary government decided to seize the opportunity to build a railroad network throughout the country to replace the waterways on the canals in order to stimulate the weakened economy after more than 10 years of political turmoil and economic depression. In 1834, the Belgian government approved the construction of a massive railroad from the industrial center of Mons to the port of Antwerp at a cost of about 150 million Belgian francs. The newly crowned King Leopold I actively supported and sponsored this project. He wanted to gain control of the state and parliament through control of the railroad, and to gain more power in the constitutional monarchy. Considering that the railroads would be a major source of revenue and the need for a complete network, the Belgian government did not leave the construction of the railroads to the private sector, as Britain had done. Instead, the government led the planning and design of the railroad system and used private sector funds to prevent the monopoly of the big banks on the railroads. This approach was subsequently followed by other countries.

In 1835, the section of the line from Brussels to Mechelen was completed. This was the first steam locomotive passenger railroad on the European continent.[5]

全部完成。至 1900 年，比利时铁路的密度已达 170 米 / 平方公里，远高于同期英格兰 103 米 / 平方公里、德国 79 米 / 平方公里和法国 70 米 / 平方公里的密度水平。由此，比利时成为欧洲第二个、大陆第一个兴修铁路的国家，并率先形成国家铁路网。至今，比利时仍是世界上铁路网络最密集的国家。[6]

铁路的修建又进一步推动着工商业的发展，虽然 1835 年这项铁路总计划中的第一段才铺设完成，但自 1834 年开始至 1838 年，比利时的经济即已从衰退中恢

比利时铁路系统上的重要站点——安特卫普火车站。约摄于 20 世纪初

Antwerp Central Station, an important station on the Belgian National railway system. Taken circa in the early of 20 century

火车：工业革命的主要参与者。登基不久的国王利奥波德一世赞助修建了比利时第一条铁路——从布鲁塞尔到梅赫伦（Brussels-Mechelen）。1835 年 5 月 5 日他参加了这条铁路的通车典礼，这也是欧洲大陆的第一条铁路

The train: a major player in the industrial revolution. King Leopold I, soon after his accession to the throne, sponsored the construction of the first Belgian railroad (between Brussels and Mechelen), which he inaugurated on May 5, 1835. It was the first railroad in continental Europe

以上资料来源（Source）：http://www.railwaywonderoftheworld.com。

The completion of another railroad line from Liège to Ostend marked the beginning of the development of the Belgian railroad system. 1836 saw the extension of the railroad to Antwerp, and in 1843 the completion of two main lines crossing north-south and east-west. By 1900, the density of Belgian railroads had reached 170 meters per square kilometer, much higher than the density levels of 103 meters per square kilometer in England, 79 meters per square kilometer in Germany and 70 meters per square kilometer in France during the same period. As a result, Belgium became the second country in Europe and the first on the continent to build railroads and was the first to form a national railroad network. To this day, Belgium still has the most extensive railroad network in the world.[6]

The construction of the railroads gave a further impetus to the development of industry and commerce. Although the first section of this master plan was only laid in 1835, the Belgian economy had recovered from recession and made rapid progress between 1834 and 1838. From 1848

从布鲁塞尔到奥斯坦德运行着当时欧洲最强有力的火车头
The most powerful locomotive in Europe, operating
between Brussels and Ostend

to 1884, a large number of joint-stock companies were
established. In 1834, the nominal value of shares issued by
all Belgian companies amounted to 37 million, and in 1836,
to 145 million.[7] From 1848 to 1884, Belgium experienced a
decisive development in industrialization and rapidly rose to
become a capitalist power. The steam engine's exert horse-
power increased from 48,000 in 1845 to 781,000 in 1885.[8]
Many factors contributed to Belgium's rise to an industrial
power. In addition to the long tradition of handicrafts,
the industrial revolution, abundance of cheap labor and
abundant coal and iron resources, the "General Company"
established by King Willem also played a significant role in
the economic development.

复过来，并突飞猛进。1848—1884 年大量股份有限公
司在这一时期建立。1834 年，比利时所有公司发行的
股票面值计 3700 万，1836 年达 1.45 亿。[7] 1848—1884 年，
比利时的工业化出现了决定性的发展，迅速跃升为资本
主义强国。蒸汽机的输出功率从 1845 年的 48000 马力
上升到 1885 年的 781000 马力。[8] 比利时成为工业强国，
除了长期手工业传统的积累、工业革命、大量廉价的劳
动力和丰富的煤铁资源之外，国王威廉建立的"通用公
司"在经济发展中也起到了巨大作用。

1835—1913 年行驶在比利时国家铁路上的火车头
"比利时"号是比利时第一辆运行的火车头，仅 41 马力，身侧
为巨大的"弗拉芒"号，输出功率达到 2300 马力
Locomotive in the Belgian State Railways in 1835 - 1913.
"Le Belge", the first locomotive to run in that country, which
developed 41 horse-power, standing beside the monster
"Flamme Pacific", which exerts 2,300 horse-power

以上资料来源（Source）：http://www.railwaywondersoftheworld.
com/locomotive-giants4.html.

利奥波德一世（1790 年 12 月 16 日—1865 年 12 月 10 日，1831 年 7 月 21 日—1865 年 12 月 10 日在位），全名利奥波德·乔治·克里斯蒂安·弗里德里希（德语为 Leopold Georg Christian Friedrich）；出生于德国科堡，称德国萨克森－科堡－萨尔菲德公爵。1831 年 7 月 21 日成为比利时的第一位国王。他的子女包括比利时国王利奥波德二世和墨西哥王后玛丽—夏洛特。绘于约 1840 年

Leopold I (Full name: Leopold Georg Christian Friedrich) was born on December 16, 1790 and died on December 10, 1865. He reigned between July 21, 1831 and December 10, 1865. He was born in Coburg, Germany, known as the Duke of Sachsen Coburg Saalfeld. On July 21, 1831, he became the first King of Belgium. King Leopold II of Belgium and Queen Mary Charlotte of Mexico are his son and daughter. Drawn in 1840

公司董事长——国王利奥波德父子

比利时独立后，成为君主立宪制国家。议会和内阁是真正的权力所在，但利奥波德父子却并不甘心放弃影响力。他们不但利用君主的地位，更借助手中掌握的公司来游说政府投资自己所青睐的经济发展项目。这家公司就是"通用公司"，公司的最大股东和董事长就是国王本人。

这家公司的前身是"荷兰国家工业通用公司"（General Company of the Netherlands for National Industry），由荷兰（尼德兰）国王威廉一世于 1822 年 12 月 16 日成立，目的是用来发展荷兰南部（即比利时）的经济。通用公司名为公司，实际上它发挥了重要的信贷投资作用，所以也被称为世界上第一家投资银行。有别于荷兰的商业贸易和捕鱼业经济，当时比利时的工业和农业已经很发达。威廉一世尤其注重工业，通过"通用公司"对工业贷款，比利时的煤矿、钢铁、纺织等工业在欧洲大陆首屈一指。

1830 年比利时独立后，萨克森－科堡－哥达公国的王子利奥波德成为比利时第一任国王，通用公司也归属比利时国王所有。公司改名为"国家工业发展通用公司"（Société Générale pour Favoriser l'Industrie Nationale），人们习惯简称它为比利时通用公司（Société Générale de Belgique），总部设在比利时布鲁塞尔。它既经营商业银行业务，也向采矿业、冶炼业和制造业投资，成为比利时工业化的重要资本来源。1850 年前它还独享比利时的发钞权。

事实证明，比利时人在挑选国王方面颇具慧眼。利奥波德一世是一位超级外交家和政治强人。他的登基得

Chairman of the Company - King Leopold and His Son

After its independence, Belgium became a constitutional monarchy. Parliament and the cabinet were where the real power resided, but King Leopold and his son were not willing to give up their influence. They not only used their position as monarchs, but also used the company they held to lobby the government to invest in their favored economic development projects. This company is the "General Company", whose chairman and the largest shareholder are the king himself.

This company, formerly known as the General Company of the Netherlands for National Industry, was founded on December 16, 1822 by King Willem I of the Netherlands to develop the economy of the southern Netherlands (i.e., Belgium). Though named as a company, it played an important role of credit investment, hence known as the world's first investment bank. Unlike the Dutch commercial trade and fishing economy, industry and agriculture were already well developed in Belgium at that time. Willem I especially focused on industry, making industrial loans through the "General Company", which made Belgium's coal and iron, textile and other industries second to none in the European continent.

After Belgium's independence in 1830, Prince Leopold of the Duchy of Saxe-Coburg-Gotha became the first King of Belgium, and the company became the property of the King of Belgium. The company was renamed "Société Générale pour Favoriser l'Industrie Nationale" (National Industrial Development Corporation), or simply Société Générale de Belgique (Belgian General Company). Headquartered in Brussels, it was an important source of capital for Belgium's industrialization, both in terms of commercial banking and investment in mining, smelting and manufacturing. Until 1850, it was the only bank in Belgium

到了欧洲著名财团罗斯柴尔德家族和英法德奥各大强国的保证。由于良好的私人关系，通用公司与罗斯柴尔德银行巴黎分行紧密合作，开展了对比利时政府的借贷，还将一系列比利时矿业公司推向巴黎交易所上市。通用公司在比利时城镇设立了不少分行，既办理储蓄、信贷、商业票据贴现，也开办投资银行业务。19 世纪中叶的33 年中，通用银行客户数增长了 20 倍。通过吸收小额存款、发行银行券而投资于公路、铁路和运河等大型项目，核心业务是参与修建铁路网络。从 1835 年到 1850 年，其业务收入增长了近 15 倍。在 19 世纪五六十年代，通用银行又成为世界上第一家股份制上市银行。

早在独立以前，随着工业革命的进行，比利时的企业规模日趋扩大，新兴资产阶级逐渐成长壮大，他们不仅投资于本国工厂，还向从事海外贸易的公司进行投资，投资对象不只包括本国的贸易公司，还有普鲁士、瑞典和其他国家的贸易公司。安特卫普 [9] 的资本家很早就从工业资本家转向金融资本家了。而独立以后，利奥波德一世的通用公司更是发扬光大，通过操纵银行、保险公司，在国内和国外都控制了众多重工业企业。

1865 年 12 月利奥波德一世去世后，他的长子登基成为利奥波德二世，同时也继承了“通用公司”。19世纪后半期，西欧的大多数君主被迫把大部分权力让渡给选民，所以比利时议会和内阁是权力的真正场所。利奥波德父子都是旧制度下富有才智的人，他们不甘心只做“虚君”，于是通过赞助修建铁路、投资控制比利时的工业和煤炭业等方式，积极增强影响力，想要从议会获得更大的权力，比如各省、区议会的任命权或解散权、以及行政人员的任免权。[10] 但是，他们的尝试几乎毫无

with the right to issue banknotes.

The Belgians proved to be quite discerning in their choice of kings. Leopold I was a superb diplomat and political powerhouse. His accession to the throne was guaranteed by the famous European conglomerate Rothschild family and the major powers of England, France, Germany and Austria. Thanks to good personal relations, the General Company worked closely with the Paris branch of the Rothschild Bank, carried out lending to the Belgian government and also launched a series of Belgian mining companies to be listed on the Paris Exchange. General Company established many branches in towns and cities in Belgium, providing services of savings, credit, commercial paper discounting, and investment banking. In the 33 years of the mid-19th century, the number of General Company's customers grew twentytimes. It invested in large projects such as roads, railroads and canals by taking small deposits and issuing bank notes. Its core business had been the construction of the railroad network. From 1835 to 1850, its revenues increased nearly 15 times. In the 1850s and 1860s, General Bank became the world's first publicly traded bank.

Long before independence, with the industrial revolution, Belgian businesses grew in size and the new bourgeoisie grew. They invested not only in national factories but also in companies trading abroad, including both Belgian companies and those from Prussia, Sweden and other countries. Antwerp's [9] capitalists shifted from industrial to financial capitalism early on. After independence, Leopold I's General Company flourished, controlling numerous heavy industrial enterprises both at home and abroad through the control over banks and insurance companies.

After the death of Leopold I in December 1865, his eldest son ascended the throne as Leopold II and inherited the "General Company". In the second half of the 19th century, most monarchs in Western Europe were forced to cede most of their power to the electorate, so the Belgian

国王利奥波德二世（1835 年 4 月 9 日—1909 年 12 月 17 日，1865 年 12 月 17 日—1909 年 12 月 17 日在位），全名利奥波德·路易·菲利普·马里·维克多（法语为 Léopold Louis Philippe Marie Victor；荷兰语为 Leopold Lodewijk Filips Maria Victor），出生于布鲁塞尔。1865 年继承父亲利奥波德一世成为比利时国王。在位期间对内投资发展工商业，实行自由贸易政策，使比利时国家实力日益壮大。对外实行殖民侵略，1876 年组织国际非洲协会，以考察和开发非洲为名，以个人名义霸占刚果大片土地，被比利时国会授予"刚果自由邦国王"的称号。他对当地居民的残酷剥削、压迫和屠杀，遭到世界舆论的谴责，被称为"殖民主义之王"。1908 年刚果转归比利时政府管辖，成为比利时殖民地，即比属刚果（今刚果民主共和国），1960 年 2 月独立。约摄于 1900 年

King Leopold II (Full name in French: Léopold Louis Philippe Marie Victor) was born on April 9, 1835 in Brussels and died on December 17, 1909. He reigned between December 17, 1865 and December 17, 1909. ... Circa 1900

结果——旧制度在欧洲已经一去不复返。另一个让利奥波德二世非常烦恼、耿耿于怀甚至寝食难安的问题是，地处于拿破仑三世治下领土辽阔的法国和迅速崛起的奥匈帝国之间的这块国土面积实在是太小了，他将其称为"Petit pays, petits gens"（法语，意为小国寡民）。[11] 于是，在欧洲以外寻找殖民地，获得君主的威势并充盈自己的金库，成了利奥波德二世一生的重心和焦点。

比利时的议会和政府，虽然对国王在政治上丝毫不予让步，但是在国家发展的大政方针上，却是志同道合。工业革命后，比利时的生产力出现决定性的飞跃，工业产量居于世界前列。然而，它的工人工资低微，国内市场狭小，所生产的制成品和半制成品需要向海外输出，所以对外贸易是必不可少的。[12] 比利时是欧洲小国，工业实力虽然强大，但军事力量弱小。尽管如此，它的国王和政府对海外殖民扩张的关注度却并不低。在继承王

parliament and cabinet were the real seat of power. Leopold and his son, both men of great talent under the old system, were not willing to be "powerless kings", so they actively exerted their influence by sponsoring the construction of railroads, investing in the control of Belgian industry and coal, etc. They wanted to gain more power from the Parliament, such as the power to appoint or dissolve provincial and regional assemblies, and the power to appoint and dismiss administrative staff.[10] However, their attempts were almost fruitless. Another problem that troubled Leopold II was the small size of his country, located between the vast territory of France under Napoleon III and the rapidly rising Austro-Hungarian Empire, which he called "Petit pays, petits gens" (French for "small country, small population").[11] The search for colonies outside Europe, to gain the prestige of a monarch and to fill his coffers, became the focus of Leopold II's reign.

The Belgian parliament and government, while not conceding anything to the king politically, were like-minded in the general policy of national development. After the Industrial Revolution, Belgium's productivity took a decisive leap forward and its industrial output was among the highest in the world. However, because of the low wages of its workers, the small domestic market, and the production of manufactured and semi-manufactured goods needed to be exported overseas, foreign trade became essential.[12] Even though Belgium was strong in industrial strength, its military strength was weak. Despite this, its king and government were not less concerned with overseas colonial expansion. Before inheriting the throne, Leopold, as crown prince, traveled abroad to gain experience or to find countries suitable for Belgium's own colonies. From 1854 to 1865, he went to India, Egypt, and other African countries along the Mediterranean, and even set his sights on China. It was when he arrived in Shanghai in 1865 that he received the news of his father's serious illness and

位前，作为太子的利奥波德四处游历，增长见闻阅历，或者说寻找适合作为本国殖民地的土地。自 1854 年至 1865 年，他去了印度、埃及和地中海沿岸的其他非洲国家，甚至也把目光投向了中国。正是 1865 年他来到上海的时候，接到父亲病重的消息，立刻返回比利时接任国王。

后来在整个 19 世纪欧洲抢占非洲和亚洲殖民地的热潮中，他试图购买过斐济，研究过巴西的铁路，分析过租赁中国台湾的可行性，尝试过从西班牙手里买下菲律宾，皆无所获，直到他费尽心机在 1884 年的柏林会议上拿下约 200 万平方公里的刚果（相当于比利时领土面积的 76 倍），成为"刚果自由邦"的国王。在刚果，利奥波德二世成为手操生杀大权的独裁者，获利丰厚。但这仍然不能满足他的野心。1897 年，他开始将从刚果剥削来的利润投向中国铁路。在帝国主义瓜分中国的盛宴中，他觉得这个国家就像是先前的"巨大的非洲蛋糕"。他在谈及希望能够铺设的那条铁路时说："这是中国的脊柱。如果他们把这条路线交给我，我还可以从骨架上弄下一些肉来。"[13] 他还以刚果独立邦的名义在中国买下（实为永租）天津的比租界。当利奥波德派遣一个刚果国代表团（当然，所有代表都是比利时人）来到中国谈判时，负责外交事务的李鸿章故作惊讶地说："我以为非洲人都是黑皮肤，不是这样吗？"[14]

immediately returned to Belgium to take over as king.

Later, during the European rush to seize colonies in Africa and Asia throughout the 19th century, he tried to purchase Fiji, studied the railroads in Brazil, analyzed the feasibility of leasing Taiwan province of China, and tried to buy the Philippines from Spain, all to no avail. Finally, he took Congo, a territory of about 2 million square kilometers (76 times the size of Belgium), at the Congress of Berlin in 1884. In Congo, Leopold II became a dictator with the power of life and death, and profited enormously. In 1897, he began to invest the profits from Congo in Chinese railroads. In the feast of imperialist partition of China, he felt that the country was like the previous "giant African cake." "This is the backbone of China," he said of the railroad he hoped to build in China, "If they give me the route, I can still get some meat off the bones."[13] He also bought (in fact leased in perpetuity) the Belgian concession in Tianjin in the name of the independent Congolese state. When Leopold sent a delegation from the Congolese state (all the delegates were Belgians, of course) to China to negotiate, Li Hongzhang, who was in charge of foreign affairs, pretended to be surprised and said, "I thought Africans were all dark-skinned, aren't they?"[14]

开启近代中比外交的《中比通商条约》

自康熙皇帝之后清朝开始走向封闭，对不断叩关而来的西方人所提出的通商要求，一律说不。连曾经在皇帝身边服务、掌管钦天监的天主教教士，也于1724年全部被雍正皇帝逐出中国。但是闭锁的大门，挡不住工业革命之后西方列强的坚船利炮。为了结束第一次鸦片战争，清政府被迫与英国签订了条约，即《中英南京条约》（1842年8月29日）、《中英虎门条约》（1843年10月8日）。之后，清政府又分别与美国、法国签订了《中美望厦条约》（1844年7月3日）和《中法黄埔条约》（1844年10月24日）。这些条约所建立的原则，奠定了日后中国与列强之间外交和商务关系的基础，其主要内容包括割地、赔款以及开放中国市场予缔约国。

第一次鸦片战争打响后，潜在的中国市场就引起了比利时政府的极大兴趣。它的外交部部长墨伦奈尔（Felix de Meulenaere）要与清政府建立直接的联系，甚至想向中国派出远征军。1841年，墨伦奈尔派比利时驻新加坡总领事墨克西特（Augustus Moxhet）到中国南方考察，寻找商机。《中英南京条约》签订之后，议会敦促内阁尽快与清政府谈判签约，打开中国市场的大门。1845年3月，驻马尼拉总领事兰哪（J. Lannoy）奉派到中国广州，要求与中国当局谈判缔约。1845年7月，两广总督兼钦差大臣耆英与广东巡抚黄恩彤将一道二人签署的正式公文给兰哪，传达上谕，准许比利时商人依现有条约办法在中国经商。也就是说，比利时虽然没有出兵也没有签约，但是获得了英、美、法等国条约内容所许的一切权利。不过，这道公文事实上只是一道口头上的保证，一旦签署公文的这两位官员被调离，也就没有什

The Treaty that Started Modern Sino-Belgian Diplomacy - Treaty of Commerce between China and Belgium

After Emperor Kangxi, the Qing dynasty began to be closed, rejecting all the requests for trade made by the Westerners who kept knocking on the gates. Even the Catholic priests who used to serve the emperors and were in charge of the Qin Tian Jian were all expelled from China by Emperor Yongzheng in 1724. But the closed door could not stop the powerful western warships and cannons after the Industrial Revolution. In order to end the First Opium War, the Qing government was forced to sign treaties with Britain, namely Sino-British Treaty of Nanjing (August 29, 1842), Sino-British Treaty of Humen (October 8, 1843). After that, the Qing government signed treaties with America and France, respectively, Sino-U.S. Treaty of Wangxia (July 3, 1844), and Sino-French Treaty of Huangpu (October 24, 1844). The principles established by these treaties laid the foundation for future diplomatic and commercial relations between China and the great powers. Their main content, besides the cession of land and reparations as a direct result of the war, was most notably the opening of the Chinese market to the treaty nations.

Right after the First Opium War, the potential Chinese market aroused great interest of the Belgian government. Its foreign minister Felix de Meulenaere wanted to establish direct contacts with the Qing government and even wanted to send an expeditionary force to China. In 1841, Meulenaere sent Augustus Moxhet, the Belgian consul general in Singapore, to visit southern China in search of business opportunities. After the signing of the Sino-British Treaty of Nanjing, the Belgian parliament urged the cabinet to negotiate with the Qing government as soon as possible to sign treaties that would open the Chinese market. In

么效用了。当然，那时西欧与中国之间的商业主要为英国商人所控制，比利时商人还难以与其竞争中国的市场。

第一次鸦片战争爆发20年后，列强对于与中国之间的贸易状况并不满意，他们认为由于清政府的种种阻挠，中国的市场还远没有打开。而且，傲慢的北京朝廷始终拒绝承认：西方列强并不是中国的藩属，而是应该享受平等待遇的自主国家。因此，它的最高统治者始终拒绝接见任何国家的代表；把外交事务看作纯粹的商务性质，把通商限制于离北京最远的口岸——广州。总之，想与清政府直接联系，是不允许的。于是就有了第二次

第二次鸦片战争中，天津大沽炮台被英法联军占领。由19世纪著名战地摄影师菲利斯·比托摄于1860年3—11月

During the Second Opium War, the Tianjin Dagu Fortress was occupied by the British and French Allies. This photo was taken by the renowned 19th century war photographer Felice Beato between March - November, 1860

March 1845, J. Lannoy, Consul General in Manila, was sent to Guangzhou, China, to negotiate a treaty with the Chinese authorities. In July 1845, the Governor of Guangdong and Guangxi, Qiying, and the Governor of Guangdong, Huang Entong, sent an official document signed by them to J. Lannoy, conveying the imperial decree that allowed Belgian merchants to do business in China under the existing treaties. In other words, although Belgium did not send troops and did not sign a contract, it was granted all the rights allowed by the treaties with Britain, the United States and France. However, this document was in fact only a verbal guarantee, and was of little use once the two officials who signed it were transferred. Of course, at that time, the commerce between Western Europe and China was mainly controlled by British merchants, and it was difficult for Belgian merchants to compete with them for the Chinese market.

Twenty years after the First Opium War, the Western powers were not satisfied with the state of trade with China, which they believed was far from opening up its market due to all the obstructions of the Qing government. Moreover, the arrogant Beijing court always refused to recognize that the Western powers were autonomous states that should enjoy equal treatment. Thus, its supreme rulers consistently refused to receive representatives of any country, treating foreign affairs as purely commercial in nature, and limiting commerce to Guangzhou, the farthest seaport from Beijing. In short, trying to make direct contact with the Qing government was not allowed. Thus came the Second Opium War and the subsequent Treaty of Tianjin (1858)[15] and Treaty of Beijing (1860)[16]. The Western powers were finally able to impose their will on China.

In 1863, Belgium sent a delegation led by Louis Bols to China and negotiated three articles with Xue Huan, Minister of the Premier's Office of the Qing dynasty, in Shanghai. But the treaty was not ratified due to the refusal

of the Belgian government. In August 1865, the Belgian government again sent Auguste T'Kint de Roodenbeke to China[17] and negotiated the Treaty of Friendship, Commerce and Navigation between China and Belgium (hereafter referred to as "Treaty of Commerce between China and Belgium") with Qing officials Dong Xun, the right Assistant Minister of Revenue Department and official of Ministry of Foreign Affairs, and Chong Hou, the Assistant Minister of War Department and Minister of Three-port Commerce in November 2, 1865. In October 1866, the treaty signed by the two monarchs (Emperor Tongzhi and Leopold II) was exchanged in Shanghai between Auguste T'Kint de Roodenbeke and Guo Baiyin, the Governor of Jiangsu and Zhejiang.

The Treaty of Commerce between China and Belgium consists of 47 articles. The main contents are: ① To send envoys to each other's capital, and to allow the Belgian imperial commissioner and his entourage to travel to and from various places in the interior of China; ② The Belgian state shall set up consulates in all Chinese ports of commerce and enjoy the most favored nation treatment; ③ Belgian nationals may travel to various places in the interior of China with passports; Belgian merchants may live and do business in the ports of commerce agreed upon by each country, and are allowed to rent houses and build houses, warehouses, churches, hospitals, cemeteries, etc;

鸦片战争，以及为结束战争签订的《天津条约》（1858 年）[15] 和《北京条约》（1860 年）[16]。西方列强终于能够把它们的意图强加在中国身上了。

1863 年，比利时派出包礼士（Louis Bols）使团来华，在上海与清总理衙门大臣薛焕议定条约共 3 款，因比国政府拒绝，未交换批准。1865 年 8 月，比利时政府再派金德（也译作金得俄，或金德俄固斯德，Auguste T'Kint de Roodenbeke）来华，[17]1865 年 11 月 2 日，在北京与清户部右侍郎、总理衙门大臣董恂，兵部侍郎、三口通商大臣崇厚议定《中比通商条约》。1866 年 10 月，金德与江浙总督郭柏荫在上海互换经两国君主（同治皇帝与利奥波德二世）签署了的条约。

《中比通商条约》共 47 款，主要内容为以下几个方面。①互派使臣驻扎彼国京城，比国钦差大臣与随员，皆可往来中国内地各处。②比国在中国各通商港口设立领事，享受最惠国之待遇。③比国侨民持护照可前往中国内地各处游历；各国议定的通商口岸，比国商民可以居住、经商，听其租赁房屋及建造房屋、栈房、教堂、医院、墓地等。④对比国天主教传教士，中国地方官务必厚待保护，不准查禁惩治中国人崇信天主教。⑤比国侨民有被华民违例相欺，由地方官审办；华民有被比民违例相欺，由比国官员查办；比民之间有互控事件，由比国官员处理；比民如在各地方犯有大小等罪，均照比国律例办理；遇有比国人与各国人有争执之事，中国官员不必过问。⑥比国商民起卸货物按所订税则输纳税饷，按船吨额纳船钞，150 吨以上，每吨纳钞银 4 钱；150 吨整及 150 吨以下，每吨纳钞银 1 钱。⑦中国地方官应保护比国商船。⑧中国今后所有施于别国之利益，比国无不一体均沾实惠。

与同时期列强与清政府签订的《天津条约》和《北京条约》等一系列条约相比，除了没有战争赔款以外，《中比通商条约》的内容基本相同。比利时借此约攫取一系列在华特权。

④ The Chinese magistrates must treat and protect the Catholic missionaries from Belgium; they must not prohibit Catholicism or punish Chinese Catholics for their beliefs; ⑤ If Belgian nationals' rights were violated by Chinese people, the local officials shall investigate and handle the case. If the Chinese people's rights were violated by Belgian nationals, the officials of Belgium shall investigate and handle the case; ⑥ The merchants of Belgium shall pay the tax according to the tax rules; ⑦ The local officials of China shall protect the merchant ships of Belgium; ⑧ All the benefits that China will give to other countries in the future will be given to Belgium as well.

Compared with the Treaty of Tianjin and the Treaty of Beijing signed between other powers and the Qing government during the same period, the content of the Treaty of Commerce between China and Belgium is essentially the same, except for the absence of war reparations. By this treaty, Belgium seized a series of privileges in China.

清朝时期比利时的驻华使节们[18]

金德（1816—1878），1866 年 12 月 26 日—1870 年 9 月 1 日在任。比利时外交官。1864 年被委派为首任驻华公使。1865 年 11 月 2 日代表比利时政府在北京签订《中比通商条约》，1866 年 8 月 1 日签订《日比通商条约》。1868 年 12 月被利奥波德二世任命为比利时驻中国和日本特命全权公使。1872 年因健康问题回到欧洲并退休。[19]

罗淑亚（1830—1879），1871 年—1872 年 7 月 26 日在任，为法国驻华公使，代办比利时驻华公使。

热福礼，1872 年 7 月 26 日—1874 年 5 月 18 日在任，为法国驻华公使，代办比利时驻华公使。

谢维斯，1874 年 5 月 18 日—1878 年 4 月 27 日在任，原为比利时驻印度领事，1874 年被比利时外交部指派来华，与清政府建立直接关系。

谢武伯，1878 年 4 月 27 日—1881 年 5 月 26 日暂时代理。

诺丹福，1881 年 5 月 26 日—1884 年 2 月 13 日在任。

米师丽，1884 年 2 月 13 日—1885 年 5 月 18 日暂时代理；1887 年 4 月 29 日—1888 年 11 月 19 日暂时代理；1890 年 9 月 10 日—1891 年 6 月 2 日暂时代理；1892 年 10 月 20 日—1893 年 11 月 21 日暂时代理；1896 年 4 月 22 日—1896 年 9 月 18 日暂时代理。

维礼用（1839—1906），1885 年 5 月 18 日—1887 年 4 月 29 日在任；1888 年 11 月 19 日—1890 年 9 月 10 日在任。比利时外交官，1884 年 11 月 25 日被任命为驻华全权公使，1885 年到任，1890 年离任。1903 年任驻意大利特命全权公使。

Belgian Envoys to China during the Qing Dynasty[18]

Auguste T'Kint de Roodenbeke (1816-1878), tenure in China: December 26, 1866 - September 1, 1870. He was a Belgian diplomat. In 1864, he was appointed the first Minister to China. On November 2, 1865, he signed the Treaty of Commerce between China and Belgium in Beijing on behalf of the Belgian government, and on August 1, 1866, he signed the Treaty of Commerce between Japan and Belgium. In December 1868, he was appointed the Belgian Minister Extraordinary and Plenipotentiary to China and Japan by Leopold II. In 1872, he returned to Europe for health reasons and retired.[19]

Louis Jules Émilien de Rochechouart (1830-1879), tenure in China: 1871- July 26, 1872, French Minister to China, acting as the Belgian Minister to China.

F.L.H. de Geofroy, tenure in China: July 26, 1872 - May 18, 1874, French Minister to China, acting as the Belgian Minister to China.

Edmond Serruys, tenure in China: May 18, 1874 - April 27, 1878. He was originally a Belgian consul in India. He was appointed by the Belgian Ministry of Foreign Affairs to China in 1874 to establish direct relations with the Qing government.

Hubert Serruys, tenure in China: April 27, 1878 - May 26, 1881.

Count Hector de Noidans-Calf, tenure in China: May 26, 1881 - February 13, 1884.

Charles Michel, tenure in hina: February 13, 1884 - May 18, 1885; April 29, 1887 - November 19, 1888; September 10, 1890 - June 2, 1891; October 20, 1892 - November 21, 1893; April 22, 1896 - September 18, 1896.

Léon Verhaeghe de Naeyer (1839-1906), tenure in China: May 18, 1885 - April 29, 1887; November 19, 1888 - September 10, 1890. He was a Belgian diplomat. He was appointed Minister Plenipotentiary to China on November 25, 1884. He took up his post in 1885 and left

贾尔牒。摄于 1920 年

E.de Cartier de Marchienne. Taken in 1920

姚世登。法国外交周刊"*La Revue Diplomatique*" 1904 年刊登的肖像

Maurice Joostens, published in *La Revue Diplomatique* in 1904

陆弥业，1891 年 6 月 2 日—1892 年 10 月 20 日暂时代理；1893 年 11 月 21 日—1896 年 5 月 8 日（在任期间去世）。

费葛，1896 年 9 月 18 日—1899 年 4 月 21 日在任。

贾尔牒（1871—1946），1899 年 4 月 21 日—1900 年 5 月 9 日暂时代理；1902 年 1 月—1902 年 8 月暂时代理；1910 年 10 月 18 日—1911 年在任。比利时外交官，曾在巴西、日本、中国和法国担任临时代办。后在美国、中国、英国、古巴、海地和多米尼加共和国担任比利时的特命全权大使。在华任公使时，中国变更国体，重新递交国书。

姚士登（1862—1910），比利时外交家，专职起草条约。1900 年 5 月 6 日—1902 年 1 月在任；1902 年

in 1890. He was appointed Minister Extraordinary and Plenipotentiary to Italy in 1903.

H.G. Loumyer, tenure in China: June 2, 1891 - October 20, 1892; November 21, 1893 - May 8, 1896 (Death).

Baron Carl de Vinck de Deux Orp, tenure in China: September 18, 1896 - April 21, 1899.

E. de Cartier de Marchienne (1871-1946), tenure in China: April 21, 1899 - May 9, 1900; January 1902 - August 1902; October 18, 1910 - 1911. He was a Belgian diplomat who served as charge d'affaires in Brazil, Japan, China and France. Later, he was appointed the Belgian Ambassador Extraordinary and Plenipotentiary to the United States, China, the United Kingdom, Cuba, Haiti and the Dominican Republic. When serving as Minister to China, China changed its state system and he resubmitted

10 月—1904 年 7 月 25 日在任。1900—1901 年代表比利时驻扎中华及暹罗任便宜行事全权大臣,任内签署《辛丑和约》,为八国联军之役善后。1904—1910 年任比利时驻西班牙特命全权公使,任内签署《阿尔赫西拉斯会议决议书》,为第一次摩洛哥危机善后。曾代表国王签署《比属刚果制诰》令比利时吞并刚果自由邦,为比利时国王利奥波德二世最信赖的外交家。外交生涯以在北京那一年最闻名,成功开辟天津比租界,而且和议期间他的外交活动令欧洲大国开始留意到比利时的商人与传教士在华的存在。清朝授双龙宝星一等三品。

葛飞业,1902 年 8 月—1902 年 10 月暂时代理;1904 年 7 月 25 日—1905 年 11 月 21 日在任。

博来尔,1905 年 11 月 21 日—1906 年 7 月 28 日在任;1909 年 9 月 13 日—1910 年 10 月 18 日暂时代理。

柯霓雅,1906 年 7 月 28 日—1908 年 5 月 30 日在任;1908 年 10 月 6 日—1909 年 8 月 10 日在任。

德勒高尼,1908 年 5 月 30 日—1908 年 10 月 6 日暂时代理;1909 年 8 月 10 日—1909 年 9 月 13 日在任。

its credentials.

Maurice Joostens (1862-1910), with the Chinese name of Yao Shideng, was a Belgian diplomat, specializing in drafting treaties. His tenure in China: May 6, 1900 - January 1902; October 1902 - July 25, 1904. During his tenure as Belgian imperial envoy and Minister Plenipotentiary (1900-1901) to China and Siam, he signed the Boxer Protocol in the aftermath of the invasion of the Eight-Power Allied Forces. When he served as the Belgian Minister Plenipotentiary to Spain (1904-1910), he signed the Resolution of Algeciras Conference to resolve the First Moroccan Crisis, and signed the Belgian Congo Imperial Edict in the name of the King to make the Belgium annex the Congo Free State. He was the most trusted diplomat of King Leopold II. He was best known for his diplomacy during the year in Beijing, when he successfully established the Belgian concession in Tianjin. Moreover, his diplomatic activities during the peace negotiation made European powers start to notice the presence of the Belgian businessmen and missionaries in China. The Emperor of Qing dynasty awarded him the first-class medal with double dragons and jewels.

Baron E.de Gaiffier D'Hestroy, tenure in China: August 1902 - October 1902; July 25, 1904 - November 21, 1905.

E.de Prelle de la Nieppe, tenure in China: November 21, 1905 - July 28, 1906; September 13, 1909 - October 18, 1910.

Baron A. Grenier, tenure in China: July 28, 1906 - May 30, 1908; October 6, 1908 - August 10, 1909.

Adhémar Delcoigne, tenure in China: May 30, 1908 - October 6, 1908; August 10, 1909 - September 13, 1909.

斌椿在欧洲拍摄的名片照，约摄于1866年。斌椿，满族，曾在山西和江西做知县一类的低级官员。60多岁时已经赋闲在家。经文祥和恒祺介绍，中国海关总税务司赫德聘请他做文案（中文秘书）。1866年，海关总税务司赫德见中国政府没有外派大使领事等，中国发生的许多情况外国政府基本一无所知，任凭本国外交官随意解释发挥，就想带同文馆的学生出访学习，帮助中国打开外交局面。按照外交惯例，这个国家代表团本应该由朝廷大臣率领，但是当时官员们对出国考察都不愿去，也不敢去。只有63岁的斌椿报名应征。亲朋故旧以"云风险涛"相劝止，甚至有人以苏武被扣匈奴相告诫，但他决心亲自一试。最终，负责带领这支国家使团的只是一位小小的知县。尽管如此，斌椿一行在欧洲所到之处都受到了高规格接待，他成为政府官员中赴西欧考察的"东土西来第一人"。约摄于1866年

Bin Chun's business card photo taken in Europe, taken circa 1866. Bin Chun, of Manchu nationality, once served as county magistrate or other low-level official in Shanxi and Jiangxi. ... Bin Chun and his delegation received high-level reception wherever they went in Europe, becoming the "first person from the East to Western Europe" among government officials.

First Visit to Belgium by the Bin Chun Mission

Modern diplomacy began in the West, and before the two Opium Wars, the conservative and arrogant Qing government knew almost nothing about foreign affairs. The Qing government always kept to the "defense of the barbarians" and the Chinese emperor wanted to be as far away from the barbarians as possible, preferably ignoring them, and refused to establish diplomatic relations with other countries on an equal footing. After the First Opium War, although the Treaty of Nanking was signed and the Western powers were finally given the right to set up consulates in some Chinese cities, it was still part of the Qing government's established policy to ignore foreign representatives and to avoid sending envoys to foreign countries. It was not until after the Second Opium War that the powers gained not only a range of economic benefits, but also the diplomatic power to station ministers in Beijing. The Qing government also had to consider setting up a government department (Ministry of Foreign Affairs) to deal with foreign affairs and even to send envoys overseas. This was the beginning of modern Chinese diplomacy.

首次到访比利时的斌椿使团

近代外交由西方开始，在两次鸦片战争之前，保守自大的清政府对外交事务几乎一无所知。清政府一直谨守"夷夏之防"，中国皇帝希望离那些蛮夷越远越好，最好谁都不要见谁，拒绝在平等的基础上与其他国家建立外交关系。第一次鸦片战争结束后，虽然签订了《南京条约》，西方列强也终于获得了在中国一些城市设立领事馆的权力，但是对外国代表不理睬的政策仍然是清政府既定方针的一部分，对于向外国派驻使节的事情则更是竭力回避。直到第二次鸦片战争后，列强不仅获得

张德彝（1847—1918），清末外交官。1866年随斌椿使团出国，游历了法国、英国、比利时、荷兰等多个欧洲国家。后来还多次以翻译的身份出访海外，累计在国外工作27年。他还出版了很多著作，介绍外国风物，首译电报、自行车、螺丝等至今沿用的科技名词，首次介绍蒸汽机、升降机、缝纫机、收割机、管道煤气、标点符号，乃至巧克力等。约摄于19世纪60年代

Zhang Deyi (1847-1918) was a diplomat in the late Qing dynasty. Accompanying the Bin Chun mission in 1866, Zhang traveled to multiple European countries including France, Great Britain, Belgium, and Netherlands. Taken circa in 1860s

一系列经济利益，也获得了派公使常驻北京的外交权力。清政府也不得不考虑设置政府部门（总理各国事务衙门）专门处理外交事务乃至向海外派出使节的问题。中国近代外交由此开始。

在正式派驻使节之前，清政府于1866年派出第一支官方使团赴欧洲考察学习，名为"斌椿使团"。这支访问团游历了法国、英国、比利时、荷兰、汉萨同盟[20]、丹麦、瑞典、芬兰、俄国、普鲁士等10个国家，历时4个月。使团所到之处，都受到了各国政府极高规格的接待。"斌椿使团"的欧洲之行，实现了中国与欧洲各国交往的历史性突破。

高楼耸立的城市、风驰电掣的火车、富丽堂皇的宫殿、现代化的工厂、心旷神怡的风景，令使团成员大开眼界、目不暇接。不仅是文化的差异，更多的，则是来自工业革命所带来的强大生产力的冲击，使团成员们仿佛从古代一下子迈进了现代世界。斌椿与随员张德彝分别撰写了考察报告《乘槎笔记》和《航海述奇》，以日记形式记录下一路所见所闻，第一次向国人展现了工业革命后欧洲各方面的技术进步，这也是中国人第一次开始认识了解比利时这个国家。之后，陆续有一些清政府驻外大使、钦差大臣等出访欧洲，如驻外使节郭嵩焘、薛福成和钦差大臣李鸿章等，中国官方终于开始"睁眼看世界"。透过这些官方出访者的记录，国人从中了解了五彩斑斓的外部世界，被激起强烈的好奇心和进取心。国人对比利时有了更多了解，这为日后比利时的在华投资奠定了基础。

在《乘槎笔记》中，斌椿首次对比利时的历史和概括作了简明扼要的介绍：

Before the official posting of envoys, the Qing government sent the first official mission to Europe in 1866, called the "Bin Chun Mission." This mission traveled to 10 countries including France, England, Belgium, the Netherlands, Hanseatic League[20], Denmark, Sweden, Finland, Russia and Prussia for 4 months. Everywhere the mission went, it was received by the governments of each country with the highest standards. The European tour of "Bin Chun Mission" realized a historic breakthrough in the interaction between China and European countries.

The cities with towering buildings, the trains, the palaces, the modern factories, and the landscapes were an eye-opening experience for the members of the delegation. Not only the cultural differences, but also the impact of the powerful productivity brought by the Industrial Revolution, made the delegation members feel as if they had stepped into the modern world from the ancient times at once. Bin Chun and his attendant Zhang Deyi wrote the reports of the expedition respectively: *Cheng Cha Bi Ji* (Notes on the Raft) and *Hang Hai Shu Qi* (Description of the Curious Experiences during the Voyage), recording what they saw and heard along the way in the form of diary, showing to the Chinese people for the first time the technological progress in various aspects of Europe after the Industrial Revolution. It was also the first time that the Chinese people began to know and understand the country of Belgium. After that, other Qing government officials such as diplomatic envoy Guo Songtao, Xue Fucheng and imperial envoy Li Hongzhang, visited Europe. Through the records of these official visitors, Chinese people learned about the colorful outside world and were inspired by a strong sense of curiosity and initiative. This increased understanding of Belgium laid the foundation for future Belgian investments in China.

In the *Notes on the Raft*, Bin Chun gave a brief introduction to Belgium and its history for the first time:

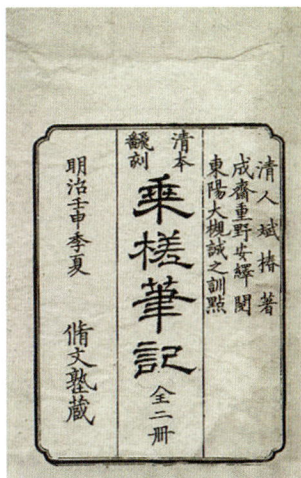

1872年日本出版的《乘槎笔记》
Notes on the Raft published in Japan in 1872

比利时北距荷兰，南接法境，长约六百里，广三百里。本为荷地。明时，隶西班牙。康熙五十三年，为奥地利亚藩属。后为法王拿破仑兼并。嘉庆十九年，复归荷。荷俗尚耶稣教，因与西班牙构兵数十年。比地毗法界，从天主教，与荷不相能。道光十一年拒战久，法人助之。荷师退，乃自立国。[21]

作为首次到访比利时的中国使团，斌椿、张德彝等使团成员得到了国王利奥波德二世的热情接见。"午初，乘双马车行十五里，至地名腊魁营（即 Laeken Palace，引者注），系国王之避暑宫也。有锦衣护兵，列队而迎。兵见明（即张德彝，引者注）等，皆举枪向鼻，肃步而来。下车入宫，厅设乐器，击大鼓，吹大号，声音错杂，非丝非竹，长角双铙，别成曲调。俄而大臣四员，迎入内庭，谒见其王，年约二十余（实年31岁，引者注），浓眉隆准，碧目乌须。西俗，男子二十留须，过五旬则薙（音tì，引者注）去。……王言：'为世子时，曾到上邦之广东、上海，原拟游历京师，一览中华之胜。因途次接先王凶讯，旋急回国，三年后乃即位（此处有误，利奥波德二世于父丧7日后即位，引者注），于今二载余矣。自即位后，始与中华和约。今贵国钦派大臣，辱临敝邦，实寡人之幸也。'"[22] "午刻，国王及妃约入宫。王英武过人，三年前曾至中国粤东，中国大臣相待甚挚。问予海舶颠簸能惯否？予答以风涛颇惯，王、妃均喜。知予不克久留，嘱就近游览。"[23]

近代西方外交向来务实。斌椿使团受到高规格的接待，自然出于商业利益的考虑。斌椿使团拜见比利时首相时，首相说：

敝邑僻处海外，乃蕞尔小国也，田地苦瘠，土产无多，

1865 年布鲁塞尔的皮埃尔·卡戈里斯证券交易所
Pierre Chargois Stock Exchange in Brussels, 1865
资料来源（Source）：http://journal.scherptediepte.eu/。

Belgium is about 600 li (1 li equals 500 meters) long and 300 li wide with Netherlands in the north and France in the south. It was originally a Netherlands territory. In the Ming dynasty, it was affiliated to Spain. In the 53rd year of Emperor Kangxi, it became a vassal state of Austria. Later, it was annexed by the French King of Napoleon. In the 19th year of Emperor Jiaqing, it returned to the Netherlands. People of the Netherlands believed in Jesus and had been fighting with Spain for decades. Belgium is adjacent to France, which is Catholic and therefore not friendly towards the Netherlands. In the 11th year of Emperor Daoguang, Belgium had been at war for a long time, and thus France offered help. The Netherlands later retreated, and Belgium founded its own independent country.[21]

As the first Chinese mission to Belgium, Bin Chun, Zhang Deyi and other members of the mission were warmly received by King Leopold II. ...

所恃者居民远涉重洋，往来贸易。今大皇帝钦使荣临敝邑，实国之光。嗣后通商日久，两国之友谊愈笃。寡君不嗜军旅之事，亦无侵占疆土之谋，可终无干戈之动也。[24]（大意是，比利时是海外的一个小国，土地贫瘠、物产不丰，只能依赖于远洋贸易。如今大清皇帝派遣使节光临，实在是我国的荣幸。以后随着通商往来，一定会加深两国的友谊。我国君主不喜欢军事，也没有侵占别国领土的图谋，两国之间必然不会发生战争。）

此话说得半真半假——比利时不是没有侵占中国领土的野心，而是没有这个实力去与列强相争、瓜分清统治下的中国这个大蛋糕——但是目的很明确，就是想要从通商贸易中获取高额利润。在列强加紧对中国进行侵略，清政府受到步步紧逼的情势下，这样的话听上去还是蛮动听的。后来清政府把修建中国第一条正式铁路卢汉（京汉）铁路的大订单授予比利时，其实就是被这样的话语所打动。

斌椿使团短期造访欧洲诸国之后10年，清政府才姗姗来迟地向英国派出了首位大使郭嵩焘，他同时也兼任驻法大使。郭嵩焘（1818—1891），中国职业外交家的先驱，近代洋务思想家，近代最早主张向西方学习的人物之一。1876年年底出使英国兼使法，为中国遣使驻欧之始。出使期间，他认真考察西方制度和历史文化，认为"西洋国政一公之于臣民，其君不以为私"，而"中国秦汉以来二千余年，适得其反"；反对"严夷夏之大防"，主张开放；反对视西方诸国为"夷狄"，主张把它们当作一个个独立的文明国家来看待。使欧期间，他还多方游历考察，于1878年来到比利时，参观了布鲁塞尔的大教堂、博物院、织纱局和议会等处。日记里记载道：

1865年坐落于布鲁塞尔的比利时王宫
Laeken Palace, Brussels, antique print, 1865
资料来源（Source）：http://www.antiquemapsandprints.com/belgium-laeken-palace-brussels-antique-print-1865-94102-p.asp。

Modern western diplomacy has always been pragmatic. The Bin Chun mission received a high-level reception, naturally for the reason of commercial interests. When the Bin Chun mission visited the Belgian Prime Minister, the Prime Minister said:

Belgium was a small country, with poor land and little production, and could only rely on ocean-going trade. Now the emperor of the Qing dynasty has sent an envoy to visit Belgium, which is really an honor for our country. The friendship between the two countries will definitely be deepened with the trade exchanges in the future. Our sovereign is not fond of military and has no intention to invade other countries' territories, so there will certainly be no war between our two countries.[24]

This statement is only half-true - Belgium is not

比利时北境与荷兰气象无异。过汪非尔（Anvers,安特卫普）海口，有巨溪通海，惟见舟樯林立海汊。再过抹仃伦（Mechelen梅克琳），则地势逶迤高下，不若荷兰之平衍。晚至比利时博里克塞来（Bruxelles布鲁塞尔）都城。是日大风，寒甚。游历穷日夜，困倦殊甚。

初八日，礼拜。遍历博里克塞来（布鲁塞尔）都城。衢道广阔，市肆繁盛，屋宇皆穷极雕镂，西洋名比利时都城为小巴黎也。所见礼拜堂五六处，其名洛登类得非勒（Sainte Gudule），为礼拜堂之最巨者。往视，男女参错，鸣铙诵经。旋过比利时国王类沃布里第一（利奥波德一世）铜表，当都城最高处，俯视廛肆如覆盂。表高十余丈，园〔围〕丈许，铸类沃布里第一立像其上。表中空，可缘而至其颠。一千八百三十一年比利时始立国，造立王像，以志勋伐。续至妙西因罗亚尔博物院（今为比利时皇家美术馆 Musées Royaux des Beaux-Arts de Belgique），所见凡四种：一油画，一禽兽体骨，一矿产，一书籍。即油画一院，加多荷兰两画馆数倍。物产、书籍各为一院。院内上下二十余厅，所陈设不减英、法博物院也。

又至费尔尼织纱局，专织妇女领、袖及后帔，专织纱为之，为人物花卉，工细绝伦。手内〔帕〕一方，长不逾尺，直（值）一百法兰（郎）者。后帔有直三千法兰者。其局女工四十余人，云别有一厂千数百人。通行西洋诸国，以织纱惟比人为之最工，他国不能及也。

又至议政院，与王宫正相对。中间一大花园，景地绝胜。右为上议院，左为下议院，并起自一千八百三十一年。（上议院六十九人，下议院百四十人。视荷兰加增一倍之多。）下议院中座（开会堂时国

without ambition to invade Chinese territory. Rather it did not possess the strength to compete with the powers to divide the large cake of China under the rule of the Qing government. But its intention was clear - to obtain high profits from trade. In the situation where the foreign powers were intensifying their aggression against China and the Qing government was being pressured, such words sounded quite appealing. The Qing government was in fact impressed by such words that it awarded Belgium a large contract to build the first official railroad in China, the Lu-Han (Beijing-Hankou) Railway.

Ten years after the short visit of the Bin Chun Mission to European countries, the Qing government belatedly sent Guo Songtao, China's first ambassador, to England (concurrently ambassador to France). Guo Songtao (1818-1891) was a pioneer of Chinese professional diplomats, a modern foreign affairs thinker, and one of the earliest modern advocates of learning from the West. In the end of 1876, he served as the ambassador to Britain and France concurrently, symbolizing the beginging of sending Chinese ambassador to Europe. During this visit, he carefully studied the Western system and historical culture, finding that "Western politics are a matter of public interest to their subjects, not the private matter of their ruler", while "for over two thousand years since the Qin and Han dynasties in China, it's exactly opposite"; opposing "being strictly on guard against barbarians" and advocating for opening-up; and proposing regarding Western countries as the independent civilized countries rather than "barbarians". During his mission, Guo traveled extensively and visited Belgium in 1878, where he visited the cathedral, the museum, the yarn bureau and the parliament in Brussels.

...

In 1886, the Qing dynasty sent Liu Ruifen as Minister to England, France, Italy and Belgium, a position later taken over by Xue Fucheng in 1890. The first thing that

1881 年《Le Tour Monde》杂志上刊载的漫画《布鲁塞尔街上的商贩》
Vendors on the streets of Brussels published in the *Le Tour Monde* in 1881

郭嵩焘。摄于 19 世纪 70—90 年代
Guo Songtao. Taken in 1870s or 1890s

王坐其处）上立类沃布里（利奥波德一世）石像。上议院中座上绘比利时国神，其旁环立九女神，则所分九部也。又于九部地方，各系以事，以明其国家本务如此：或农，或猎，或制造，或医，或画学，或商，皆寓重视民事之本意。两议院并有会议座次，有客厅，有燕息厅，有诸科房（若中国之六科），规模颇极壮丽。而下议院每厅皆有油画，详叙荷兰、西班牙战绩，拿破仑与奥、英相持战迹，所以记比利时与荷兰分合之由及后立国之原始；又有西班牙与土耳其战迹，则或比利时前属西班牙事迹也。画皆巨幅峥嵘，鬼神下降，刿目怵心。[25]

1886 年起，清朝开始向比利时派驻钦差大臣，由刘瑞芬出任驻英、法、意、比四国公使。1890 年薛福成接任四国公使。薛福成走马上任后第一件例行公事，是向所在国的元首递交国书，拜会外交部和各国公使。他不卑不亢，举止不凡，各国都表示热烈欢迎。光绪十六年（1890 年）四月二十六日，薛福成向比利时国王利奥波德二世递交国书。国书云：

大清国大皇帝，问大比国大君主好。贵国与中国换约以来，夙称和睦。兹特简二品顶戴、候补三品京堂薛福成为钦差出使大臣，前往贵国都城通问，并令亲赍国书，以表真心和好之据。朕稔知该大臣老成练达，公正和平，办理交涉事件，必能悉臻妥协。朕恭膺天命，寅绍丕基，中外一家，罔有歧视。嗣后愿与贵国益敦友谊，长享升平，朕有厚望焉。[26]（大意为：大清国皇帝问比利时君主好。两国自换约以来，和睦相处。现在特派二品顶戴候补三品京堂官薛福成为钦差大臣，前往贵国首都拜会，并令他亲往递交国书，作为表达我国与贵国友好的依据。我深知该大臣为人稳重老练、通达事理、公

Xue Fucheng did after he took office was to present his credentials to the heads of state and to visit foreign ministries and the ministers. Xue was unassuming and had an uncommon demeanor, and all the host countries expressed their warm welcome. On April 26, 1890, Xue Fucheng presented a letter of credentials to King Leopold II of Belgium. The letter read:

The emperor of the Qing dynasty sends greetings to the Belgian monarch. Since the exchange of treaties, the two countries have been living in harmony. Now, I am sending Xue Fucheng as the imperial envoy to your capital to pay you a visit and to deliver a letter expressing our friendship with your country. I am well aware that Minister Xue is experienced, understanding, fair and upright, and able to handle things calmly. Authorized to handle foreign affairs, he is able to do so in a considerate and proper manner. I am obedient to the mandate of Heaven, respectful of my ancestral heritage, and regard Chinese and foreign people as one family without any discrimination. In the future, I would like to promote friendship and prosperity with your country, for which I have high hope.[26]

Xue Fucheng read the eulogy to King Leopold II. The words of the ode read:

I understand and appreciate that the Belgian monarch has visited our country before and is very friendly to our government, and that your monarch has made Belgium stronger and stronger in both domestic and foreign affairs through his outstanding achievements and knowledge. I present to you today a letter of credence, which I invite you to read as a proof of the friendship between our two countries. I hope that you will understand the feelings of our emperor, and that

平正直、处事平和，让他办理外交事务，一定能做到周到完善、稳妥恰当。我顺应天命，敬承祖业，视中外人民为一家，没有任何歧视。以后愿与贵国促进友谊、共享繁荣，对此我有深深的期望。）

薛福成向国王宣读颂辞。颂辞云：

大清国钦差大臣薛福成，钦承简命，出使贵国，恭惟大比国大君主前曾游历中华，与我中朝最称亲睦，勋猷学识，超越寻常，内政外交，蒸蒸日上。使臣亲奉国书，上呈尊览，以为永敦和好之据。惟冀大君主体中国大皇帝之意，益笃邦交，互求裨益，使臣不胜欣忭之至。[27]

（大意为：大清国钦差大臣薛福成，秉承皇帝命令，出使贵国，我了解并赞赏比利时君主以前曾来我国的游览考察，对我们政府非常友好，贵国君主政绩卓著、学识丰富，使比利时无论内政还是外交都日益强盛。我今天奉上国书，请您阅览，作为我们两国友谊的证明。谨希望您了解我国皇帝的心意，促进两国往来，取长补短，我不胜感激欣喜。）

利奥波德二世致答辞。答辞云：

蒙贵大臣来递大清国大皇帝国书，不胜钦感。本君主前经游历中华，见其风俗政治，知为教化最先之国；而人民繁盛，物产殷富，实甲于地球。今虽事隔二十余年，本君主追念前游，未尝不神往也。敝国以局外立邦，丁口稠密，借可勤求制造。如中国有采办军械事件，深愿效劳，敝国亦可渐习中国之教化，以补其不及。烦贵大臣转奏大皇帝，表我此心，实于两国互有裨益。[28]（大意为：感谢你亲来递交国书。我曾经前往中国游历，见识了那里的风土民俗和政治治理，了解到中国是在社会管理方面非常先进的国家；而且人口众多、物产丰富，

比利时司法宫（明信片）。布鲁塞尔上诉法院和最高法院的所在地。1860 年由建筑师 Joseph Poelaert 设计建造，是 19 世纪世界上最大的建筑

The Belgian Palace of Justice (postcard), home of the Brussels Court of Appeal and the Supreme Court

you will promote the exchange of ideas between the two countries, so that they may complement each other's strengths and weaknesses.[27]

Leopold II gave a reply. The reply read:

Thank you for coming in person to present the letter of credence. I once traveled to China and saw the customs and political governance there, and learned that China is a very advanced country in terms of social management; it is also one of the most populous countries in the world and rich in products. Although it has been more than 20 years since then, I still can't help but think about my previous visit. We have always

位居世界前列。虽然至今已时隔 20 多年，想到之前的游历历程，我还是不禁神往。我国向来奉行中立、置身事外，人口密集，努力发展工业制造。将来中国如需采买军火，我们非常愿意效劳。我们也愿意学习中国的社会管理方法，来弥补我们的不足。请您转达给贵国皇帝，表达我们这番心意。）

4 月 28 日，利奥波德二世设宴会宴请薛福成。宴毕，王与其弟携手同行，导宾入别室，饮加非（咖啡）、皮酒（啤酒）之属，皆立而饮之，宾主任意。比利时外交部副部长郎贝尔芒（也译作郎白蒙，Lang Belmont）与薛福成纵谈天下大局，说道：

中国教化最好，民物最殷，但能参用西法，便可立致富强。方今外交之道，既不能免。非谓谋国当自忘其本，即如日本之自改服式，我西人亦非笑之。中西政俗，要在集所长而去所短耳，愿贵大臣留意焉。[29]（大意为，中国的社会管理制度是最好的，人民物产丰富，只要能参照引进西方制度，便可以迅速变得富强。当今世界，必须对外进行交往。不是说要抛弃本国的立国根本制度，而是像日本那样进行自我改革，我们是不会加以嘲笑的。中西之间的政治习俗，要取长补短，希望您能留意考察。）

之后，在任期间，薛福成果然集中精力考察欧洲的社会得失。通过对议院、工厂的考察，他悟出：欧美国家之所以先进，中国之所以落后，其根本在于制度的不同。诚如比利时外交部副部长郎贝尔芒所说，应“集所长而去所短”。

been a neutral and densely populated country that has worked hard to develop industrial manufacturing. If China needs to buy arms in the future, we are more than willing to help. We are also willing to learn Chinese social management methods to make up for our shortcomings. Please convey this to your emperor as a token of our appreciation.[28]

On April 28, Leopold II hosted a banquet for Xue Fucheng. After the banquet, the king and his brother guided the guests into a separate room, where they drank coffee and beer. The Belgian Vice-Minister of Foreign Affairs, Lang Belmont, talked with Xue Fucheng about world affairs and said:

China has the best system of social management, and it is populous and rich in goods. As long as it can learn from and import Western system, China can become rich and strong quickly. In today's world, it is necessary to engage with the outside world. It does not mean to abandon the fundamental system of one's country, but to reform as Japan did. No one will laugh at you. The political customs between the East and the West can complement each other's strengths and weaknesses. We hope you will look into this seriously.[29]

After that, during his term of office, Xue Fucheng concentrated on studying the social strengths and weaknesses of Europe. Through the investigation of parliament and factories, he realized that the fundamental reason why Europe and America were advanced and China was lagging behind was the difference between the systems.

清朝派驻比利时的使节们 [30]

1885 年起，清朝开始向比利时派驻钦差大臣。首任钦差大臣名为许景澄，于 1885 年 12 月 16 日正式上任，初时，驻比国钦差大臣一职为兼职，自 1902 年杨兆鋆上任起改为专使。

许景澄 1885 年 7 月 14 日—1887 年 6 月 23 日（兼）

许景澄（1845—1900），清末外交官，同治年间进士，1880 年开始外交生涯。曾被清政府任命为驻法、德、奥、荷 4 国公使。1890 年改任驻俄、德、奥、荷 4 国公使。曾写《外国师船表》，上疏清廷，建议加强海防。1892 年，沙俄出兵侵占中国新疆帕米尔地区，他曾作为中方谈判代表，据理驳斥沙俄侵略行径。1897 年，出任总理各国事务衙门大臣兼工部左侍郎，并兼任中东铁路公司督办。中东铁路由沙俄兴建，许景澄往来于圣彼得堡、哈尔滨之间，为签订协议奔波。义和团运动期间，以团民滥杀无辜、攻击外国使团为由，上书慈禧太后："攻

许景澄。摄于 19 世纪 80—90 年代

Xu Jingcheng. Taken in 1880s or 1890s

Envoys of the Qing Dynasty to Belgium [30]

Since 1885, the Qing government started to send imperial envoys to Belgium. The first minister was Xu Jingcheng, who officially took office on December 16, 1885. At the beginning, the post of minister to Belgium was a concurrent position, but it was changed to an exclusive envoy starting in 1902 when Yang Zhaojun took office.

Xu Jingcheng (1845-1900)

Tenure in Belgium: July 14, 1885 - June 23, 1887 (concurrent post)

Xu Jingcheng, a diplomat in the late Qing dynasty, passed the highest imperial examination during the Emperor Tongzhi period and began his diplomatic career in 1880. He was appointed Minister to France, Germany, Austria and the Netherlands by the Qing government. In 1890, he had a new appointment as Minister to Russia, Germany, Austria and the Netherlands. He wrote and submitted to the emperor the *Chart of Foreign Vessels*, recommending the strengthening coastal defense. In 1892, Tsarist Russia sent troops to occupy Pamir region in Xinjiang. As a Chinese negotiator, he reasoned against the aggression of Tsarist Russia. In 1897, he concurrently served as the minister of the Ministry of Foreign Affairs, assistant minister of the Ministry of Public Works and supervisor of Chinese Eastern Railway Company. The Chinese Eastern Railway was built by Tsarist Russia. Xu Jingcheng traveled between St. Petersburg and Harbin to sign the agreement. During the Boxer Rebellion, because the Boxers killed the innocent people and attacked the foreign missions, he pleaded to Empress Dowager Cixi: "There is no precedent both in China and aboard to kill the foreign diplomatic envoys" but was punished for "indulging in pure fabrication and sowing discord." He was executed in Beijing on July 28 of the same year at the age of 55. He is the author of *Posthumous Manuscript of Xu Wensu*, *Compilation of Manuscripts of Xu Wensu* and *Envoy's Letter*.

刘瑞芬。约摄于 19 世纪 80—90 年代

Liu Ruifeng. Taken in 1880s or 1890s

薛福成。摄于 1894 年前

Xue Fucheng. Taken before 1894

杀使臣，中外皆无成案"，被定为"任意妄奏，语多离间"的罪名，于同年 7 月 28 日在北京处死，时年 55 岁。著有《许文肃公遗稿》《许文肃公外集》《出使函稿》。

刘瑞芬 1887 年 6 月 23 日—1889 年 3 月 31 日（兼）

刘瑞芬（1827—1892），清末外交官员、藏书家。以诸生入李鸿章幕府。1885 年受命出使英、俄等国，后改任驻英、法、意、比等国。出使期间，为维护国家领土主权力争奔走。1889 年被召回国任广东巡抚。

薛福成 1889 年 5 月 15 日—1894 年 7 月 11 日（兼）

薛福成（1838—1894），清末外交官，洋务运动的主要领导者之一，资本主义工商业的发起者。1890 年被派为出使英、法、意、比大臣。在驻欧使节任内，薛福成走访了欧洲许多国家，考察欧洲的工业发展，详细地研究了欧洲的政治、军事、教育、法律、财经等制度。他认为西方富强已百倍于中国，中国应不懈地师法西方，建立活跃的私人公司，并具体提出"求新法以致

Liu Ruifeng (1827-1892)

Tenure in Belgium: June 23, 1887 - March 31, 1889 (concurrent post)

Liu Ruifen was a diplomat and renowned book collector in the late Qing dynasty. He followed Li Hongzhang throughout his life. In 1885, he was sent on a diplomatic mission to Britain, Russia and other countries, and then was stationed in Britain, France, Italy, Belgium and other countries. During his mission, he strived to safeguard national territorial sovereignty. In 1889, he was recalled to serve as the Governor of Guangdong.

Xue Fucheng (1838-1894)

Tenure in Belgium: May 15, 1889 - July 11, 1894 (concurrent post)

Xue Fucheng was a diplomat in the late Qing dynasty, one of the main leaders of the Westernization Movement and the initiator of capitalist industry and commerce. In 1890, he was appointed Minister to Britain, France, Italy and Belgium. During his tenure in Europe, Xue Fucheng visited many European countries, investigated their industrial development, and studied their political, military, educational, legal, financial and other systems in details. He believed that the West was already a hundred times richer and stronger than China. He suggested that China should unremittingly learn from the West and establish active private companies, and specifically put forward 21 plans of Westernization, such as "seeking new ways to achieve prosperity and strength," "selecting able and virtuous person to hold the official position," "making machines to develop the manufacturing industry."

Gong Zhaoai

Tenure in Belgium: July 11, 1894 - April 19, 1897 (concurrent post)

Luo Fenglu (1850-1903)

Tenure in Belgium: April 19, 1897 - May 26, 1902

富强""选贤能以任庶事""造机器以便制造"等21条洋务计划。

龚照瑗 1894年7月11日—1897年4月19日（兼）

罗丰禄 1897年4月19日—1902年5月26日（兼）

罗丰禄（1850—1903），毕业于福州船政学堂，1877年赴英国留学，之后先后兼任清朝驻英公使馆翻译、驻德国公使馆翻译。1880年2月回国，入幕于北洋大臣李鸿章，兼任李鸿章的英文秘书和外交顾问。1883年5月，罗丰禄调升水师营务处道员，后协同北洋水师提督丁汝昌及林泰曾等起草《北洋海军章程》。1896年春，李鸿章奉命作为头等专使参加俄皇尼古拉二世加冕典礼，罗丰禄以翻译身份随同出访，并参加《中俄密约》的谈判。随后罗丰禄又随李鸿章继续前往德、荷、比、法、英、美等国访问。1896年11月23日，罗丰禄以二品顶戴记名海关道赏四品京卿出任驻英公使兼驻意、比公使，1902年卸任。

杨兆鋆 1902年12月12日—1906年6月17日

杨兆鋆（1854—？）首任清政府出使比利时钦差大臣，首位参加世博会的中国官员。1884年随许景澄公使出洋。1902年任清政府出使比利时钦差大臣。1904年被任命为派驻比利时列日世博会的钦差大臣兼监督。1904年，与曾出使法、俄、英的大臣孙宝琦、胡惟德、张德彝等联名上书奏请变法，"以激励人心，植立国本"。

李盛铎 1906年6月17日—1909年10月18日

李盛铎（1859—1934），中国近代著名政治家、收藏家，1905年，作为清廷五大臣之一，出使东洋西洋各国考察政治，以为立宪之预备。考察结束后，1906年李盛铎到任驻比利时公使，1909年卸任。

(concurrent post)

Luo Fenglu, graduated from Foochow Shipbuilding Institution, went to England to study in 1877. Later, he served as the interpreter of the Legation in Britain and in Germany. He returned to China in February 1880 and worked for Li Hongzhang, the Minister of Beiyang. He also served as Li Hongzhang's English secretary and diplomatic adviser. In May 1883, Luo Fenglu was promoted to be a local governor of the Navy Bureau, and then worked with Ding Ruchang, the commander of Beiyang Fleet and Lin Taizeng to draft the Articles of Beiyang Fleet. In the spring of 1896, Li Hongzhang received orders to attend the coronation ceremony of Russian Emperor Nicholas II as the first-class envoy. Luo Fenglu accompanied Li as an interpreter and participated in the negotiation of the Sino-Russian Secret Treaty. Soon afterwards, Luo Fenglu followed Li Hongzhang to visit Germany, Netherlands, Belgium, France, Britain, the United States and other countries. On November 23, 1896, Luo Fenglu took up the post of Minister to Britain and Minister to Italy and Belgium, and resigned in 1902.

Yang Zhaoyun (1854-?)

Tenure in Belgium: December 12, 1902 - June 17, 1906

Yang Zhaoyun was the first envoy of the Qing government to Belgium and the first Chinese official to participate in the World Expo. He went abroad with Xu Jingcheng in 1884. In 1902, he was appointed the imperial envoy to Belgium. In 1904, he was appointed imperial envoy and supervisor of the World Expo in Liège, Belgium. In 1904, Yang, together with Sun Baoqi, Hu Weide and Zhang Deyi, who had been sent to France, Russia and Britain, jointly submitted a written statement to plead the Qing government for reforms, "so as to inspire people and establish the foundation of the country."

Li Shengduo (1859-1934)

罗丰禄。摄于19世纪80—90年代
Luo Fenglu. Taken in 1880s or 1890s

杨兆鋆。摄于20世纪初
Yang Zhaoyun. Taken in the early of 20 century

杨枢 1909 年 10 月 18 日—1911 年 3 月 30 日

杨枢（1844—1917），清末著名回族外交家。曾在广州帮助张之洞创办洋务企业。1891—1902 年，出任清政府驻日本长崎领事。1903 年接替蔡钧出任驻日公使，1909—1910 年出任驻比利时公使。在担任驻日公使期间，多次和日本政府交涉，扩大接受中国留学生的名额和专业，在留学生中开展爱国主义教育。

李国杰 1911 年 3 月 30 日—1911 年 10 月 10 日

李国杰（1881—1939），晚清重臣李鸿章的长孙，李经述的长子，承袭了李鸿章一等侯爵的爵位。1910 年他受命出任驻比利时公使。辛亥革命后，民国政府让他继续留任比利时，1914 年回国。

Tenure in Belgium: June 17, 1906 - October 18, 1909

Li Shengduo was a famous politician and collector in modern China. In 1905, as one of the five Ministers of the Qing dynasty, he was sent to investigate politics in Eastern and Western countries to prepare for the constitution. After the inspection, Li Shengduo became Minister to Belgium in 1906 and resigned in 1909.

Yang Shu (1844-1917)

Tenure in Belgium: October 18, 1909 - March 30, 1911

Yang Shu was a famous diplomat of Hui nationality in the late Qing dynasty. He helped Zhang Zhidong to establish a Westernization enterprise in Guangzhou. From 1891 to 1902, he served as the consul of the Qing government in Nagasaki, Japan. He succeeded Cai Jun as Minister to Japan in 1903 and took the post as Minister to Belgium from 1909 to 1910. During his tenure as Minister to Japan, he negotiated with the Japanese government many times to accept more Chinese students to study in Japan. He also advocated for patriotic education among Chinese overseas students.

Li Guojie (1881-1939)

Tenure in Belgium: March 30, 1911 - October 10, 1911

Li Guojie, the eldest son of Li Jingshu and the eldest grandson of Li Hongzhang, an important Minister of the late Qing dynasty, inherited the title of first-class Marquis of Li Hongzhang. In 1910, he was appointed as Minister to Belgium. After the Revolution of 1911, the government of the Republic of China allowed him to stay in Belgium and he returned to China in 1914.

杨枢。摄于 19 世纪末 20 世纪初

Yang Shu. Taken in the end of 19 century to the early of 20 century

李盛铎。约摄于 20 世纪初

Li Shengduo. Taken in the early of 20 century

李国杰。出自《中国名人录》第 3 版，上海《密勒氏评论报》，1925，第 465 页

Li Guojie. The photo is from the third editition of Who's Who in China, *Millard's Review* of Shanghai, 1925, p. 465

1896 年李鸿章访比

19 世纪下半叶，旨在"自强"的洋务运动开始。李鸿章是晚清重臣，也是洋务运动的领袖。与其他保守僵化的封建官吏不同，李鸿章是愿意了解世界、接触西人且非常具有能力的官员。李鸿章与外国人打交道，从 1862 年他麾下的淮军进驻上海与常胜军会剿太平军开始。在这一过程中，李鸿章与几位外国将领以及英法驻军司令和驻沪领事等经常往来，商议各种事项，建立起良好的关系。后来，李鸿章移督直隶坐镇天津，负责北方的洋务活动，逐渐成为清政府的首席外交顾问和主要外交代表，参与了清末几乎所有外交政策的制定和执行。而派驻比利时驻节的几位大使，都得到了李鸿章的全力支持，甚至如薛福成、刘瑞芬本身就出自李鸿章的幕府。

对于李鸿章在中国的权势地位，比利时人也多有了解。1890 年利奥波德二世为薛福成举办国宴之后，外交部副部长郎贝尔芒曾对薛福成说："方今地球各国名相，以比土马克（俾斯麦）为第一。而中国之李中堂，亦当在二三之间，闻其所注意经营，亦伟人也。"[31] 比利时为了开拓中国市场，一直试图与李鸿章建立直接关系，说服李鸿章引进比利时的资金和技术，修建铁路。因此，在 1896 年李鸿章访问欧美七国时，对李鸿章极尽热情地招待。

当时，由于在中日战争中的失败，李鸿章被罢免了直隶总督兼北洋大臣，投闲京师。不过，慈禧太后并没有对他弃之不顾。1896 年 2 月，借恭贺俄国尼古拉二世（Tsar Nicholas II）加冕之机，清廷决定让李鸿章以"钦差头等出使大臣"的名义前往俄国致贺，并游历欧美诸国进行外交访问。李鸿章此行主要有三项使命：第一，

Li Hongzhang's Visit to Belgium in 1896

In the second half of the 19th century, the Self-Strengthening Movement began in China. Li Hongzhang was an important official of the late Qing dynasty and the leader of the Self-Strengthening Movement. Unlike other conservative and rigid feudal officials, Li Hongzhang was a very competent official who was willing to learn about the world and reach out to Westerners. Li's dealings with foreigners began in 1862 when the Huai Army under his command moved into Shanghai to fight the Taiping Army with the Ever Victorious Army. In this process, Li Hongzhang often corresponded and discussed various matters with several foreign generals, as well as the British and French garrison commanders and consuls in Shanghai, therefore establishing good relations. Later, Li Hongzhang moved to Tianjin to govern Zhili. He was also responsible for foreign affairs activities in the north, and gradually became the chief diplomatic adviser and the main diplomatic representative of the Qing government, participating in the formulation and implementation of almost all foreign policies in the late Qing dynasty. Several of the ambassadors sent to Belgium had the full support of Li Hongzhang, and even Xue Fucheng and Liu Ruifen came from Li Hongzhang's staff.

The Belgians were well aware of Li Hongzhang's power in China. After the state banquet hosted by Leopold II for Xue Fucheng in 1890, Vice Minister of Foreign Affairs Lang Belmont said to Xue: "The most famous minister in the world today is Otto Eduard Leopold von Bismarck. And China's Minister Li is also a great man."[31] Belgium had been trying to establish direct relations with Li Hongzhang in order to develop the Chinese market and convince him to introduce Belgian capital and technology to build railroads. Therefore, during Li Hongzhang's visit to seven countries in Europe and America in 1896, he was treated with extreme

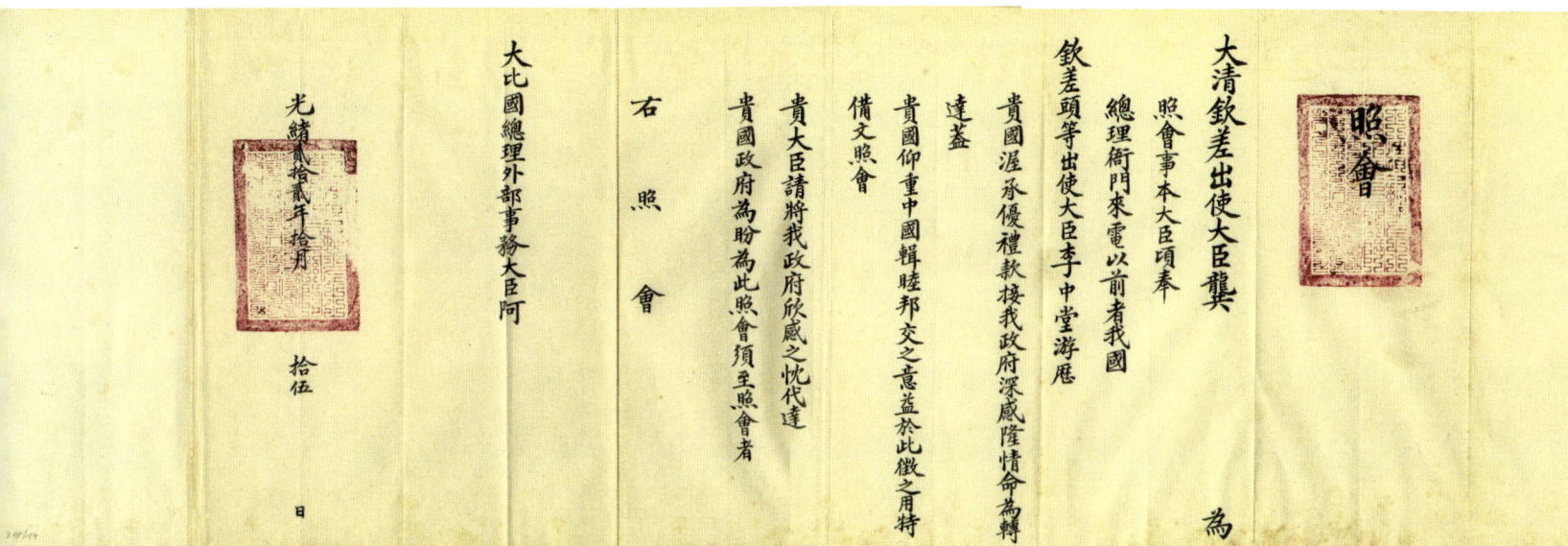

出使大臣李鸿章的外交照会。收藏于比利时外交部档案馆

Diplomatic Note from the Imperial Envoy Li Hongzhang. In the Archives of the Ministry of Foreign Affairs of Belgium

联络俄国，签署《中俄密约》以共同抵御日本对中国的进一步侵略；第二，对俄、德、法三国在夺回辽东半岛过程中提供的帮助以及美、英两国在中日战争中提供的支持表示感谢；第三，与各国商讨提高关税的问题。以上这三项任务，环顾当时清政府的众多官员确实找不出第二个人能完成。

1896 年 3 月 1 日，李鸿章向光绪皇帝陛辞出京。先由天津乘海船至上海，专乘法国邮轮出海，正式开始环

hospitality in Belgium.

At that time, due to the defeat in the first Sino-Japanese War, Li Hongzhang was dismissed from his post as Governor of Zhili and Minister of Beiyang and was living in Beijing. In February 1896, on the occasion of the coronation of Tsar Nicholas II of Russia, the Qing court decided to send Li Hongzhang to Russia in the name of "First Imperial Envoy" to attend the ceremony and make diplomatic visits to Europe and America. Li Hongzhang's trip had three main missions: first, to contact Russia and sign the Sino-Russian Secret Treaty to jointly defend against further Japanese

球访问。经过一个多月的海上航程，于 4 月 27 日抵达黑海港口敖德萨（Odessa），转乘火车于 4 月 30 日抵达俄国首都圣彼得堡（St. Petersburg），开始首站访问，参加俄皇的加冕典礼。之后，李鸿章前往欧洲其他国家访问。7 月 8 日，李鸿章一行来到比利时首都布鲁塞尔。在这里，李鸿章觐见了比利时国王利奥波尔德二世，并秘密商谈卢汉铁路的修筑问题。

李鸿章一行到达布鲁塞尔当天，受到御前大臣某男爵及其他文武官员的迎接，皇家军队整齐肃立于车站两侧，纷纷行礼。李鸿章下了火车直接被请上皇家马车，由军队夹道护送，直到国王为他安排入住的酒店。比利时报纸争相报道李鸿章访比盛况，并配以绘图再现当时李鸿章与比方大臣在街市上被民众围观的热闹场面。据报纸记载，李中堂在比利时期间，国王为他准备的行馆多达 21 个房间，且其中家具器皿华丽精美，不亚于琼台瑶岛。[32]

负责接待的男爵对李鸿章说："王为世子时，本爵随侍至华；既至北京，惊接先王噩耗，仓卒言归。今王闻中堂莅止，辄忆前尘。而以本爵曾诣贵国之故，饬令奉迓行旌。"[33]（大意为，我们的国王登基前，我跟随他到过中国，还未到北京的时候，突然收到老国王逝世的噩耗，不得不仓促返回。如今国王听说您到访敝国，回忆起上次到中国的经历，就特意派了我这个去过中国的大臣来负责接待您。）李鸿章听了之后对比王的热情周到深表感谢。

到达比利时的第二天（7 月 9 日），男爵又随御用马车迎接李鸿章到王宫觐见利奥波德二世。李鸿章出生于 1823 年，访问比利时时已是 73 岁高龄的老人了。利

aggression towards China; second, to express gratitude to Russia, Germany and France for their help in retaking the Liaodong Peninsula and to the United States and Britain for their support in the Sino-Japanese War; third, to discuss with various countries the issue of increasing tariffs. These three tasks could not be accomplished by any other official of the Qing government at that time.

On March 1, 1896, Li Hongzhang departed from the capital after bidding farewell to Emperor Guangxu. He first travelled from Tianjin to Shanghai by sea ship, and then kicked off the world tour boarding a French cruise ship. After a month of sea voyage, he arrived in Odessa, the port of the Black Sea, on April 27. He then transferred by train to St. Petersburg, the capital of Russia, on April 30, to attend the coronation of the Russian Emperor. Afterwards, Li Hongzhang went to visit other European countries, and on July 8, Li and his party arrived in Brussels, the capital of Belgium. Here, Li Hongzhang had an audience with King Leopold II of Belgium and secretly negotiated the construction of the Marco Polo Bridge-Hankou Railway.

On the day of his arrival in Brussels, Li Hongzhang and his party were greeted by a Baron of the Imperial court and other civil and military officials, with the Royal Army standing and saluting neatly and solemnly on both sides of the station. Li Hongzhang was invited to the royal carriage directly after getting off the train, and was escorted by the army until he checked into the hotel arranged by the king. The Belgian newspapers reported the visit of Li Hongzhang, with drawings reproducing the lively scene of Li Hongzhang and the Belgian officials in the market surrounded by people. According to the newspaper, during Li's stay in Belgium, the king prepared 21 rooms for him, and the furniture and utensils were magnificent.[32]

The baron in charge of the reception said to Li Hongzhang: "I followed our king to China before his accession to the throne. But before I reached Beijing, I

李鸿章访问布鲁塞尔盛况。比利时画家绘制铜版画。
由查尔斯·拉格朗日先生提供

The visit of Li Hongzhang to Brussels (copper plate etching made by Belgian painters). By courtesy of Mr. Charles Lagrange

布鲁塞尔 Bellevue 酒店店徽
Bellevue Hotel logo

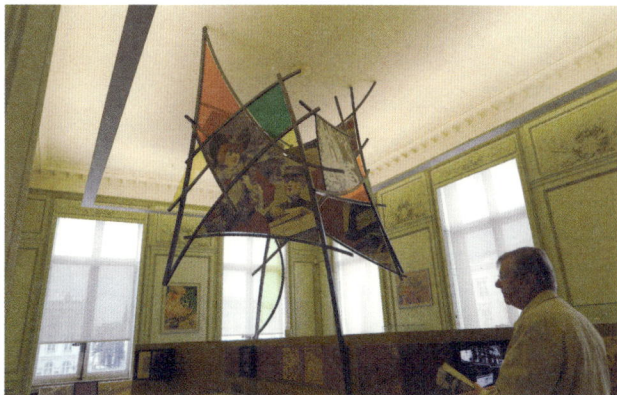

李鸿章曾经下榻的房间。航鹰女士摄于 2015 年

The room where Li Hongzhang stayed. Photo taken by Ms. Hang Ying in 2015

以上两张图片为李鸿章在布鲁塞尔下榻的 Bellevue 酒店，如今成为博物馆。
航鹰女士摄于 2015 年

The Hotel Bellevue, where Li Hongzhang stayed in Brussels, is now BELvue Museum. Photos taken by Ms. Hang Ying in 2015

比利时报纸关于李鸿章到访的相关报道。收藏于比利时外交部档案馆
Coverage of Li Hongzhang's visit in Belgian newspapers. In the Archives of the Ministry of Foreign Affairs of Belgium

建于 17 世纪的布鲁塞尔市政厅
Brussels City Hall, built in the 17th century

奥波德二世国王虽说比李鸿章小 12 岁，也已是一大把白胡子年过六旬的老人了。远隔万里的东西方两位互相倾慕已久的铁腕人物会面，大有相见恨晚的感慨。李鸿章通过翻译对比王说："比利时与中国交谊甚笃。"比王回答："余为白兰鹏公之岁，曾至贵国。今中堂复

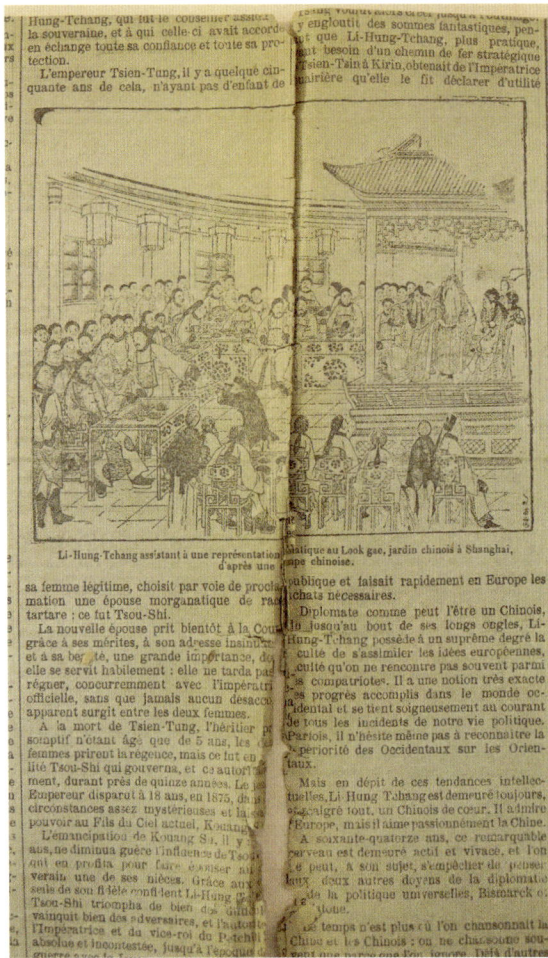

suddenly heard the sad news of the old king's death and had to return in haste. Now when the king heard that you were visiting our country, he recalled his last visit to China and sent me, someone who had been to China, to receive you."[33] After hearing this, Li Hongzhang thanked the King for his hospitality and thoughtfulness.

比利时王宫外景。航鹰女士摄于 2015 年
Exterior view of the Royal Palace of Belgium. Photo taken by Ms. Hang Ying in 2015

辱临敝国，彼此深知情势，此后益加亲密，可预卜也。"[34]（大意为，我还是佛兰德斯公爵的时候，到过贵国。现在您光临敝国，我们彼此加深了解，今后两国关系一定会更加紧密。）

随后，李鸿章在布鲁塞尔市市长的陪同下参观了市政厅。在那里，拿惯了毛笔的他生平第一次使用硬笔写下了"李鸿章来游"几个字，虽然因用不惯硬笔而字迹欠佳，但仍可谓"力透纸背"。

当晚，国王设宴款待李鸿章及其随员，作陪的还有比利时大臣及其夫人、各国使节及其随员等。在宴会上发生了一桩很有意思的事情：李鸿章酒足饭饱之后犯了烟瘾，侍从立刻递上烟卷。西欧王宫贵族礼仪森严，在国宴的餐桌上不得吸烟。一众宾客面面相觑，礼仪官们更是大惊失色。利奥波德二世不愿意在众目睽睽之下，

The day after his arrival in Belgium (July 9), Li was greeted by the royal carriage to meet with Leopold II at the Royal Palace. Li Hongzhang was born in 1823 and was already 73 years old when he visited Belgium. King Leopold II, although younger than Li by 12 years, was also an old man more than sixties. Li Hongzhang said to King Leopold II through an interpreter: "Belgium and China have a deep friendship." The Belgian King replied: "When I was the Duke of Flanders, I visited your country once. Now that you have come to my country, we have a better understanding of each other, and our relations will certainly become closer in the future."[34]

Afterwards, Li Hongzhang visited the city hall, accompanied by the mayor of Brussels. There, for the first time in his life, he wrote the words "Li Hongzhang came to visit" with a hard pen. Although his handwriting was not good due to his inability to use a hard pen, it was still "strong and penetrating."

李鸿章对烟草持开放态度，吸中国水烟，也抽外国的烟卷和雪茄。摄于 1896 年。照片为 74 岁（虚岁）的李鸿章

Li Hongzhang was open to tobacco and smoked Chinese hookah as well as foreign rolls and cigars. Taken in 1896. He was at the age of 74 (nominal age) in this picture

凸显李鸿章的失宜令其尴尬，立刻下令让侍从给宴会上的所有男客上烟。这些欧洲的王族显贵大臣使节们从来没有得到过国王如此的招待，一个个在国宴餐桌上喷云吐雾，乐开了怀。李鸿章仍在一旁怡然自得地抽着香烟，浑然不觉王宫禁地空前绝后的破例待遇皆拜他所赐。国王对李鸿章的尊重可谓至矣。[35]

第三天（7 月 10 日），李鸿章应邀前往埃诺省参观

That night, the king hosted a banquet for Li Hongzhang and his entourage, accompanied by Belgian ministers and their wives, foreign ambassadors and their entourage. A very interesting episode happened at the banquet: Li Hongzhang wanted to smoke after the meal and his attendant immediately handed him a cigarette. The Western European royal court has very strict etiquette by which smoking is prohibited in state banquets. The guests looked at each other in dismay, and the ceremonial officers were shocked. Leopold II did not want to embarrass Li Hongzhang in the public and he immediately ordered the attendants to serve cigarettes to all male guests at the banquet. These European royals, ministers and ambassadors had never received such hospitality from the king before, and they were all puffing away at the state banquet table. Li Hongzhang remained on the sidelines smoking cigarettes, unaware of the unprecedented exceptions in the royal palace thanks to him. The king had shown Li Hongzhang the ultimate respect.[35]

On the third day (July 10), Li Hongzhang was invited to visit the military exercises of the Belgian army in Hainaut province. The army drilled various skills for Li Hongzhang and demonstrated the attack and defense drills of battalion and battery soldiers. Li Hongzhang watched in admiration. In the following days, Li Hongzhang went to Liège to tour the Belgian steel and glass companies, and tried to understand the advanced technology of Western industrial countries.

In Belgium, Li Hongzhang also visited the John Cockerill Company and was impressed by the speed and power of the weapons it manufactured. The manager of the company wanted to choose a new cannon of the highest quality to give to Li Hongzhang as a gift. Li Hongzhang declined gratefully and told him, "I am grateful for the generous gift, but unfortunately our luggage is too heavy, and there is no rule that imperial envoys on mission should receive weapons from others. If your company wants to

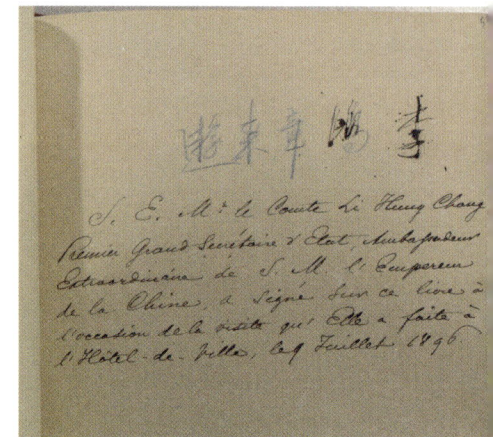

李鸿章的钢笔题字。收藏于 Bellevue 酒店博物馆

Li Hongzhang's pen inscription. Collection of the BELvue Museum

利奥波德二世宴请李鸿章的大厅。约摄于19世纪末。由查尔斯·拉格朗日先生提供

Leopold II's banquet hall for Li Hongzhang. Taken circa in the end of 19 century. By courtesy of Mr. Charles Lagrange

比国陆军的军事演习。军队为李鸿章操练各种技艺，并展示了营兵与炮台兵的攻防演练。李鸿章观后赞叹不已。随后几日，李鸿章不辞劳苦赴列日考察比利时钢铁厂和玻璃公司，努力了解西方工业国家的先进技术。

李鸿章在比利时还参观了克革列（Cockerill，也译作考科里尔）枪炮公司的产品，对这些武器的速度之快威力之大赞不绝口。克革列公司经理见状欲选一尊上等新炮赠予李鸿章。李鸿章辞谢道："猥承厚赐，不第行李重滞已也，奉使之大臣无受人军器之礼。贵公司果爱吾华，莫妙于进呈朝廷，斯为得体。"[36]（大意为，承蒙厚赐，可惜我们的行礼不堪重负，况且向来也没有出使大臣受人武器的规矩。贵公司如果想对我的国家示好，不如进呈给朝廷，更为得体。）于是公司经理向国王请示，特派公使护送火炮到中国，进献给朝廷。

比利时在欧洲仅是一小国，尤其军事实力不能与列强相比。但是自第一次鸦片战争之后，比利时商人、政

show favor to my country, it would be more appropriate to present it to the imperial court."[36] The manager of the company then asked the king to send an official to escort the cannon to China and present it to the court.

Belgium is only a small country in Europe, its military power could not compete with other great powers. But since the First Opium War, Belgian merchants, the government and the king had been thinking about opening up the Chinese market. The signing of the Treaty of Commerce did not bring about real gains. The original itinerary of Li Hongzhang's tour of Europe and America did not include Belgium. After hearing about Li Hongzhang's upcoming visit to Europe, Leopold II hurriedly sent an envoy to invite Li. Belgium not only gave Li Hongzhang very high courtesy but also sent a special envoy to present cannons to the Qing court. Many people thought it was due to the personal charm of Li Hongzhang. Today, it looks more like how a large company treats its VIP customers.

Li Hongzhang's world tour crossed three oceans and covered four continents. He was the first person among

钢铁厂老板格雷纳夫妇与李鸿章合影。摄于1896 年。由查尔斯·拉格朗日先生提供

Mr. and Mrs. Greiner, owners of Cockerill Steel Plant, with Li Hongzhang. Taken in 1896. By courtesy of Mr. Charles Lagrange

府及国王一直心心念念打开中国市场。此后虽然签订了通商条约，但其实并无收获。此次李鸿章出访欧美七国，比利时本不在行程之中。利奥波德二世得知李鸿章来访欧洲的消息后，赶紧派出驻华使节邀请李鸿章。比利时给予李鸿章极高的礼遇，并以特派大臣不远万里赠献大炮，时人以为是仰赖李鸿章的个人魅力，今日看来，更像是一个大公司对待 VIP 顾客的做法。

李鸿章此次环球访问，跨越三大洋，遍访四大洲，是清朝大臣中第一个做环球访问的人。他以清廷头等钦差大臣的身份周游列国，所到之处皆受到热情接待，被待以上宾之礼。前面提到，欧美的近代外交是务实外交，以商业利益为优先考虑。欧美诸国给予李鸿章异乎寻常的礼遇，自然是希望能从他的手里接到大笔订单。果然，后来终于有了中比之间的第一次合作——京汉铁路。

the Qing ministers to embark on a round-the-world visit. He traveled around the world in his capacity as the special imperial envoy of the Qing court, and was warmly received and treated as an esteemed guest everywhere he went. As mentioned earlier, modern diplomacy in Europe and the United States is characterized with pragmatism, with commercial interests as a priority. Li Hongzhang was treated with extraordinary courtesy in Europe and the United States, who hoped to receive large commercial orders from him in return. Sure enough, then came the first cooperation between China and Belgium - the Beijing-Hankou railroad.

列日玻璃艺术博物馆的明信片

The postcard in the Liège Museum of Glass Art

列日玻璃艺术博物馆收藏的古老玻璃艺术品

Old glass artworks in the collection of the Liège Museum of Glass Art

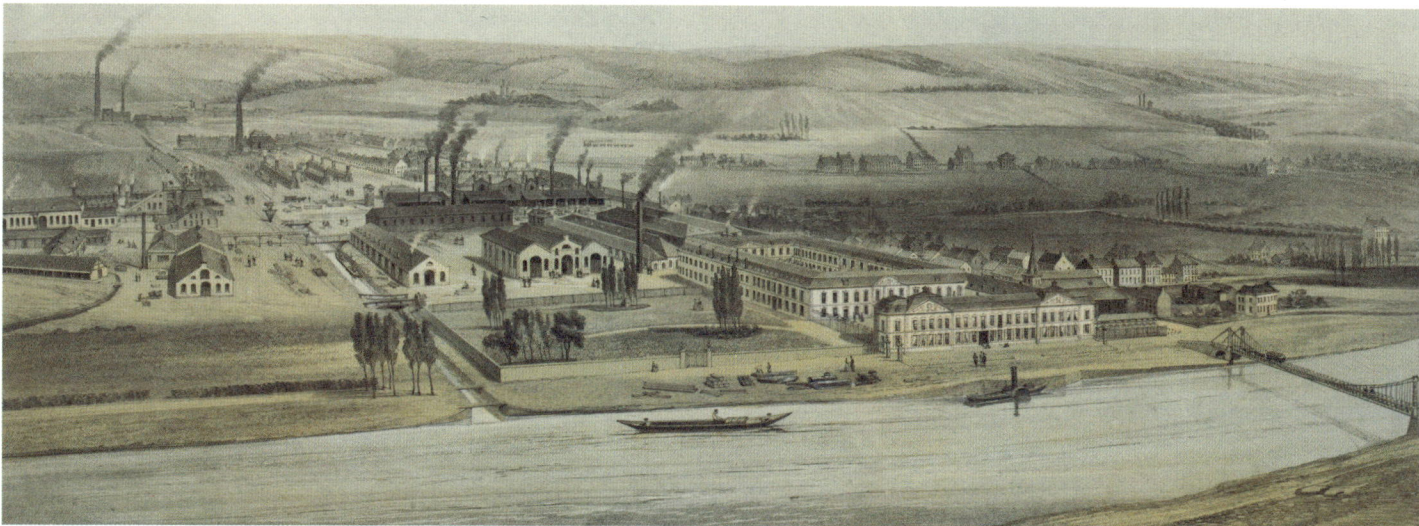

李鸿章参观的列日省克革列钢铁厂

Cockerill Steel Plant in Liège visited by Li Hongzhang

资料来源 （Source）：http://wawmagazine.be/fr/ville/seraing。

1876 年开通的吴淞铁路。出自雪珥《绝版恭亲王》（人民出版社，2010）

Wusong Railway opened in 1876. From Xue Er's *Jue Ban Gong Qin Wang* (the Out-of-Print Book of Prince Gong, published by People's Publishing House, 2010)

中比之间的第一次合作——京汉铁路

贯通南北的京汉铁路是 20 世纪初中国最重要的工业项目之一，至今仍然是中国铁路网的大动脉。从 1895 年年底清政府开始决议兴建卢汉（卢沟桥—汉口）铁路，到 1906 年 4 月 1 日全线竣工通车，历时近 10 年，全线完成后即改称京汉（北京—汉口）铁路。而在此之前，关于是否修筑铁路，清政府的态度曾经历了一个漫长而艰难的转变过程。

煤炭和钢铁在第二次工业革命中占据重要的地位，而铁路则是煤铁工业的综合。铁路既是煤铁工业相结合的产物，又促进了二者的发展。洋务运动开始后，李鸿章等洋务派官员都意识到，开发矿藏，举办实业，均需

The First Cooperation between China and Belgium - Beijing-Hankou Railroad

The Beijing-Hankou Railway, which runs from north to south, was one of the most important industrial projects in China at the beginning of the 20th century and is still the main artery of China's railroad network. It took nearly 10 years from the end of 1895, when the Qing government decided to build the Lu-Han (Marco Polo Bridge-Hankou) Railway, to April 1, 1906, when the whole line was completed and opened to traffic. It was later renamed the Beijing-Hankou Railway. Prior to that, the attitude of the Qing government towards whether to build a railroad or not had gone through a long and difficult transition.

While coal and steel occupied an important place in

唐廷枢（1832—1892）中国近代史上著名的洋行买办，民族资本家，清末洋务运动的代表人物之一。创办中国第一家民用企业轮船招商局、第一家煤矿开平矿务局、中国民族保险历史上第一家较具规模的保险公司仁济和保险公司，主持修建第一条铁路唐胥铁路（唐山—胥各庄），钻探出第一口油井，铺设了中国第一条电报线

Tang Tingshu (1832-1892) was a famous comprador of foreign companies in modern Chinese history, a national capitalist and one of the representative figures of the Self-Strengthening Movement in the late Qing dynasty

恭亲王奕䜣。摄于 1866 年 11 月 2 日

Prince Gong (Yixin). Taken in November 2, 1866

要便利的运输以降低成本。1863 年，英国铁路工程师斯蒂芬森（Sir M. Stephenson）曾向中国提出了第一个铁路建设方案，劝清政府有计划地修建铁路。他甚至还未经实地考察直接在地图上设计了几条干线。[37] 然而，清政府是不可能采纳他的设计的。一方面出于极端守旧的落后观念，顽固派认为隆隆的火车声会破坏地气，打扰地下的亡灵。为此，清政府于 1877 年将一年前怡和洋行在上海与吴淞之间建成的轻便铁路以 28.5 万两的代价收回拆毁。[38] 另一方面，一些始终对列强侵略持警惕心理的中国官员认识到，铁路的修建与列强的入侵和对中国资源的掠夺紧密相连。因此，不管外国公使、领事们如何千方百计地劝说，总是以一种消极抵抗的态度对待。但是，洋务派官员并非认识不到铁路的长处。1874 年，李鸿章曾向恭亲王奕䜣力陈铁路之利，恭亲王虽表赞同，却认为慑于保守势力的强大压力，连最高统治者"两宫亦不能定此大计"。[39]

1870 年李鸿章移督直隶，开始汲汲以开矿为发展实业的主要目标之一。1876 年，唐廷枢奉李鸿章之命，勘探开发唐山附近的开平煤矿，曾建议为降低煤炭的运

the second industrial revolution, railroads were a synthesis of the coal and iron industries. While a product of the combination of coal and iron industries, the railroad promoted the development of both industries. After the Westernization Movement began, Li Hongzhang and other Westernization officials realized that it needed convenient transportation to reduce costs in mining natural resources and developing industries. In 1863, Sir M. Stephenson, a British railroad engineer, proposed the first railroad construction plan to China, urging the Qing government to build railroads in a planned manner. He even designed several trunk lines directly on the map without fieldwork.[37] However, it was impossible for the Qing government to adopt his design. On the one hand, out of the extremely old-fashioned and backward concept, the hard-headed conservative faction in the Qing government believed that the rumbling trains shook and destroyed the earth's atmosphere, disturbing the spirits of the dead underground. For this reason, in 1877, the Qing government took back the light railroad built by Jardine Matheson between Shanghai and Wusong a year earlier and demolished it for 285,000 taels.[38] On the other hand, some Chinese officials, who were always wary of the invasion of the foreign powers, realized that the construction of the railroad was closely linked to the invasion of foreign powers and the plundering of Chinese resources. Therefore, no matter how much foreign diplomats and consuls tried to persuade them, they always treated it with an attitude of passive resistance. However, it was not that the Westernization officials did not recognize the advantages of the railroads: in 1874, Li Hongzhang argued the benefits of the railroads to Prince Yixin, who, although agreed, nonetheless thought that "even the supreme ruler of the Qing court could not easily decide on this great plan" because of the strong pressure of the conservative faction.[39]

In 1870, Li Hongzhang's authority of governor moved to Zhili and started to develop mining as one of the main

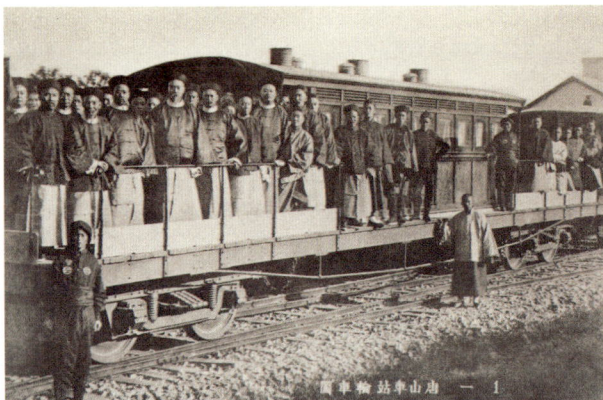

1888 年 10 月 9 日李鸿章率官员、绅商等视察刚建成的唐津铁路

On October 9, 1888, Li Hongzhang inspected the newly completed Tangshan-Tianjin Railway in the company of officials and merchants

1881 年唐胥铁路建成初期使用骡马牵引矿车场景

Mule and horse-drawn ore cars at the beginning of the Tang-Xu Railway in 1881

英籍工程师金达站在"中国火箭"号（又称龙号）列车旁留影。约摄于 19 世纪 80 年代

British engineer C. W. Kinder standing next to the "Rocket of China" train. Taken circa in 1880s

输成本修筑铁路。1877 年中国首任驻英、法大臣郭嵩焘也曾致书李鸿章，详加陈述铁路之利，李鸿章颇为所动。但鉴于同年吴淞铁路被拆毁的前车之鉴，唐廷枢改为建议先修建马拉车小铁路一条。[40]

当时情势下，只能满足于开挖一条从唐山到胥各庄的长 11 公里的轨道，即唐胥铁路，其后再连接一条运河。在 1881 年李鸿章给清廷的奏折里，这条轨道被含混地称作"马路"，[41] 以免引人注目。李鸿章此时似乎想借开平煤矿的运煤铁路做个试验，所以他让唐廷枢继续修建"马路"。唐廷枢同时令英国工程师金达（C. W. Kinder）秘密研制一个火车头，即"中国火箭"号，甚至深谋远虑地在修建轨道通过的桥梁时，将它们建造得特别坚固，以便火车将来可以在上面行驶。1881 年"中国火箭"号终于造成。1882 年它载着一批官员以每小时 13.5 公里的速度走完了唐胥铁路全程，证实了机车

goals of industrial development. In 1876, Tang Tingshu was ordered by Li Hongzhang to explore and develop the Kaiping coal mine near Tangshan. Tang suggested building a railroad to reduce the cost of coal transportation. In 1877, Guo Songtao, the first Chinese ambassador to the United Kingdom and France, also wrote to Li Hongzhang, detailing the benefits of the railroad. Li Hongzhang was quite impressed. However, in view of the previous experience of the Wusong Railway being demolished, Tang Tingshu instead suggested building a small railroad with horse-drawn carriages first.[40]

The situation was such that it was necessary to settle for an 11-kilometer-long track from Tangshan to Xugezhuang, known as the Tang-Xu Railway, followed by a canal connection. In Li Hongzhang's memo to the Qing court in 1881, the track was vaguely referred to as a "horse road"[41] to avoid attention. Li Hongzhang seemed to have wanted to use the coal railroad in Kaiping as an experiment at this time, so he asked Tang Tingshu to continue the

比骡马劲头更大、速度更快，于是李鸿章决定许可将轨道改成铁路。这条铁路继续秘密地运行了 5 年之久。李鸿章把他的赌注压在这条路线上，以它的成功来证明他的办法是正确的。关于这条铁路他一直没有上奏。很多人猜测，慈禧太后是赞赏这样的改革措施的，而李鸿章正是有把握知道太后会支持他，才会大胆进行开平铁路的建设。1883 年，开平矿务局已拥有 3 辆客车和由"中国火箭号"牵引的 50 辆运煤火车。[42]

李鸿章一直在等待时机成熟，将大规模建造铁路的计划付诸实施。但比李鸿章更着急的是欧美列强。无论是从输出商品还是从输出资本的角度，铁路修建都是当时最理想的手段。有了铁路，中国广袤的腹地与沿海、沿江通商口岸将连接在一起，运输距离大大缩短，中国市场将进一步打开。列强不仅可以更方便地倾销它们的商品（火车和铁轨本身就是大宗商品），廉价榨取中国的农、矿产品，还能通过向清政府贷款把它们国内过剩的资本输入中国。而在世界潮流的裹挟之下，在列强的枪炮威胁之下，即便是清政府中的顽固派，亦无法阻挡时代的车轮。

1884—1885 年中法战争期间，法国利用清政府急于谋和的机会，强迫后者于 1885 年 6 月签订的《中法新约》中做出中国日后建筑铁路须向法国厂商商办的承诺，且这一条约受益者不独是法国一国。在战争中，因调兵运械均不畅达，清政府日益认识到铁路的重要性。1887 年，李鸿章见时机已基本成熟，遂通过醇亲王奕譞提出修建津通（天津—通州）铁路及其支线的计划。1888 年，又由总理海军衙门向光绪皇帝提出奏折，申述修建铁路的重要性与紧迫性。1889 年清政府最终肯定了修建铁

慈禧太后。摄于 1903 年
Empress Dowager Cixi.
Taken circa in 1903

construction of the "horse road". At the same time, Tang had the British engineer C. W. Kinder secretly develop a locomotive, named the "Rocket of China." Even when building the bridge through which the tracks passed, they deliberately built it sturdy enough for supporting trains in the future. In 1881, the "Rocket of China" was finally completed. In 1882 it carried a group of officials through the entire length of the Tang-Xu Railway at a speed of 13.5 kilometers per hour, confirming that locomotives were more powerful and faster than mules and horses. Li Hongzhang then decided to give permission to convert the track into a railroad which continued to run secretly for five years. Li Hongzhang put his bets on this route to prove his approach right by its success. He didn't report this railway to the imperial court. Many speculated that Empress Dowager Cixi appreciated such a Western reform measure, and it was with the certainty of knowing that the Empress would support him that Li Hongzhang boldly proceeded with the construction of the Kaiping Railway. By 1883, the Kaiping Mining Bureau already had three passenger trains and 50 coal trains drawn by the "Rocket of China."[42]

Li Hongzhang had been waiting for the right time to put into practice the plan of large-scale construction of railroads. But the Western powers were more anxious than Li Hongzhang. Whether from the point of view of exporting goods or exporting capital, the construction of railroads was the most ideal means at that time. With the railroad, China's vast hinterland and coastal and river ports of commerce would be linked together and, in turn, the transport distance would be greatly shortened, and the Chinese market would be further opened. The Western powers could not only dump their goods (trains and tracks were commodities in their own right) and cheaply exploit China's agricultural and mining products, but also import their excess domestic capital into China through loans to the Qing government. Even the stubborn faction of the Qing government could not

盛宣怀（1844—1916）清末著名官办商人，洋务派代表人物，被誉为"中国实业之父""中国商父""中国高等教育之父"。创办中国第一个民用股份制企业轮船招商局、第一个电报局中国电报总局、第一个内河小火轮公司、第一家银行中国通商银行，主持修筑中国第一条铁路干线京汉铁路，建立中国第一家钢铁联合企业汉冶萍公司，创办中国第一所大学北洋大学堂（今天津大学）和第一所高等师范学堂南洋公学（今交通大学），创建第一个勘矿公司，建立第一座公共图书馆，创办中国红十字会。盛宣怀一生经历传奇，成就不凡，创办了许多开时代先河的事业，涉及轮船、电报、铁路、钢铁、银行、纺织、教育诸多领域，影响巨大

Sheng Xuanhuai (1844-1916) was a famous government-sanctioned businessman in the late Qing dynasty and a representative figure of the Self-Strengthening Movement. He was known as "the father of Chinese industry," "the father of Chinese business" and "the father of Chinese higher education"

路"为自强要策""即可毅然兴办"[43]。但津通铁路的修建计划进展极不顺利、障碍重重。清政府决定接受张之洞的建议，罢建津通，改建卢汉铁路，并任命津关道盛宣怀为督办大臣。

卢汉铁路是一条贯通南北的铁路交通干线，"南连湘粤，西通川陕，东达长江"，无论是铁路本身的修建工程，还是深入中国腹地的极佳地理位置，都将带来巨大的直接或间接利益，还能进一步带动本国的工业、航运业发展。清政府的官员们自然希望能够"权自我操"。但是，对于当时的中国来说，洋务事业刚刚起步，一无充足资金，二无技术，三无人才。因此，与列强合作、引进资金技术和专业人才是必然的。借款筑路的消息一经传出，美、英、法、德、比等国的公司派代表蜂拥来华，竞相兜揽。到底向哪个国家借款成了张之洞、李鸿

stop the wheel of the times under the threat of the guns of the great powers and the tide of the time.

During the Sino-French War of 1884-1885, France took advantage of the Qing government's eagerness for peace to press the latter to make a commitment to French manufacturers for future railroad construction in the Sino-French New Treaty signed in June 1885. And France was not the only beneficiary of this treaty. During the war, the Qing government became increasingly aware of the importance of railroads because of the lack of access for the transfer of troops and weapons. In 1887, Li Hongzhang, seeing that the time was ripe, proposed the construction of the Jin-Tong (Tianjin-Tongzhou) Railway and its branch lines through Prince Chun (Yixuan), and in 1888, the Navy Department submitted a memo to Emperor Guangxu, explaining the importance and urgency of building a railroad. In 1889, the Qing government finally affirmed that the construction of railroads was "an important policy for self-improvement" and "could be done with determination".[43] However, the plan to build the Jin-Tong Railway was not developed smoothly and there were many obstacles. The Qing government decided to accept Zhang Zhidong's proposal to stop the construction of Jin-Tong and to instead build the Lu-Han Railway. Sheng Xuanhuai, Tianjin Customs Commissioner, was appointed as the supervising official of the project.

The Lu-Han Railway was a railroad line that ran from north to south China - "south to Hunan and Guangdong, west to Sichuan and Shaanxi, and east to the Yangtze River." Both the construction of the railroad itself and its excellent geographical location deep into the Chinese hinterland would bring huge direct or indirect benefits, and could further drive the development of the country's industrial manufacturing and shipping industry. The Qing government officials naturally wanted to be able to exert full control of the railway. However, for China at that time,

张之洞（1837—1909），晚清名臣、清代洋务派主要代表人物，曾任两广、湖广、两江总督，与曾国藩、李鸿章、左宗棠并称"晚清中兴四大名臣"。教育方面，创办了自强学堂（今武汉大学前身）、三江师范学堂（今南京大学前身）、湖北农务学堂、湖北武昌蒙养院、湖北工艺学堂、慈恩学堂（南皮县第一中学）、广雅书院等。政治上主张"中学为体，西学为用"。工业上创办汉阳铁厂、大冶铁矿、湖北枪炮厂，倡议修建汉京铁路。他认为，卢汉铁路是"干路之枢纽，枝路之始基，而中国大利之萃也"。在中国腹地修建铁路，以便内地土产得以畅流，"苟有铁路，则机器可入，笨货可出"。铁路之利，以通土货厚民生为最大，征兵、转饷次之，两者相辅相成。照片约摄于 20 世纪初

Zhang Zhidong (1837-1909) was a famous official of the late Qing dynasty, the main representative of the Self-Strengthening faction of the Qing dynasty, and one of the "Four Famous Ministers of the Late Qing Dynasty," together with Zeng Guofan, Li Hongzhang and Zuo Zongtang. Taken circa in the early of 20 century

章、盛宣怀等人最大的难题。经过多方谈判，最终，比利时在这场竞争中脱颖而出。为什么是这个欧洲小国摘得了果实呢？

张之洞对比利时素有好感，1891 年他创办汉阳铁厂时期，曾雇用比利时的技术专家，并派遣了 40 名中国工匠到列日克革列钢铁厂学炼钢铁，也订购过比利时工厂的材料，效果很好。张之洞认为，其他国家胃口太大，多次利用战争压迫清政府割地赔款，而比利时是个小国，煤铁资源丰富，铁路技术成熟，最主要是他们国小兵弱，于中国素无大志，比较让人放心。出于同样的理由，李鸿章、盛宣怀等人也倾向于与比利时合作，再加上访比时得到利奥波德二世的高规格接待，好感素在，也表示赞同。

1897 年 3 月 17 日，比利时驻汉口领事法朗基与张之洞面商筑造卢汉铁路事宜，除了借款 2000 万两（约合 450 万英镑）、利息 5 厘之外，还要求"工程均用比

the Self-Strengthening Movement had just started, with no sufficient funds, no technology, and no talents. Therefore, cooperation with the foreign powers, and the introduction of capital and technology and professional talent were inevitable. Once the news of the Qing government needing to borrow money to build railroads spread, the United States, Britain, France, Germany, Belgium and other countries sent representatives flocking to China, competing to be the lender. From which country to borrow the money became Zhang Zhidong, Li Hongzhang, Sheng Xuanhuai and other relevant Qing officials' biggest problem. After many negotiations, finally, Belgium came out on top in this competition. Why did this small European country win?

Zhang Zhidong had a fondness for Belgium - when he founded the Hanyang Iron Works in 1891, he employed Belgian technical experts and sent 40 Chinese craftsmen to Cockerill Steel Plant in Liège to learn how to make steel. He also purchased materials from the Belgian factory, which worked very well. Zhang Zhidong believed that other Western countries were too greedy, repeatedly using war to pressure the Qing government to cede land and make reparations. In comparison, Belgium was a small country, rich in coal and iron resources and advanced in railroad technology. Primarily, it was small and relatively weak, with no great ambitions in China. For the same reason, Li Hongzhang, Sheng Xuanhuai and others were also inclined to cooperate with Belgium. In addition, the high-profile reception that Li Hongzhang received during his visit to Belgium further solidified the positive impression of Belgium.

On March 17, 1897, Émile Francqui, the Belgian consul in Hankou, met with Zhang Zhidong to discuss the construction of the Lu-Han Railway. In addition to the loan of 20 million taels (about 4.5 million pounds) with an interest rate of 5%, Francqui also requested that "all construction work be done by Belgian workers" and that "all

匠", 路料"自造外均买比物"。后来，比利时利用德国侵占胶州湾事件，一再增提苛刻条件，要求提高利息。经过曲折的谈判，清政府最终与比利时人达成了协议。1898年6月26日，《卢汉铁路比国借款续订详细合同》和《卢汉铁路行车合同》正式签订，清政府向以利奥波德二世为大股东的比利时通用公司借款1.125亿法郎。然而，这条名为"中国国有"的铁路，不单铁路要由比利时银团代雇工程师负责监造，而且筑成之后，"由比公司选派妥人，将该路代为调度经理，行车生利"[44]，卢汉铁路实际上完全控制在比利时通用公司手中。比利时通用公司中，原有俄国和法国的股份，所以卢汉铁路借款成功，也被俄国和法国看作是共同的外交胜利，且是在"没有费一枪一弹并且没有任何不必要的吵闹或骚扰下取得的"[45]。被排除在外的英、美、日等国自不甘心，于是，卢汉铁路借款标志着帝国主义列强争夺中国铁路投资利益的全面展开。

京汉铁路长达1214公里，沿途设有125个站点。其南段要跨越崎岖不平的乡间地带，北段需要穿越极为稠密的河网，其中包括越过黄河，这就要求在冲积河床上修建一座3公里长的桥梁。工程任务极其艰巨。1898年通用公司邀请曾在比利时列日省和卢森堡省从事铁路修建工作的工程师让·沙多（Jean Jadot），来中国指挥京汉铁路的修建工程。1899年1月铁路总公司督办盛宣怀与沙多签订了合同，规定聘期至少以四年为限，此限可由比国公司延至六年，薪水每年10万法郎。

让·沙多接受这项工程的时候，卢沟桥至保定之间的铁路已经完成。在他的指挥下，5000名工人同时从保定和武汉相向施工，平均每天铺设铁路1公里。修建

materials for the project be purchased from Belgians." Later, Belgium took advantage of the German invasion of Jiaozhou Bay, and repeatedly added harsh conditions including demanding higher interest rates. After difficult negotiations, the Qing government finally reached an agreement with the Belgians. On June 26, 1898, the "Detailed Contract for the Renewal of the Loan from Belgium for the Lu-Han Railway" and the "Lu-Han Railway Operation Contract" were formally signed, with the Qing government borrowing 112.5 million Belgians francs from the Belgian General Company, of which Leopold II was the major shareholder. However, this railroad, so-called "state-owned by China," was not only supervised by the engineers hired by the Belgian syndicate, but also, after it was built, "the Belgian company would choose the right person to manage the road and make profits from the operation."[44] In fact, the Lu-Han Railway was completely controlled by the Belgian General Company. As Russia and France were both shareholders of the Belgian General Company, the successful loan program to the Lu-Han Railway was regarded as a joint diplomatic victory by Russia and France, achieved "without a single shot being fired."[45] The excluded countries, such as the United Kingdom, the United States and Japan, were not willing to give up. The loan of the Lu-Han Railway marked the beginning of a full-scale competition among the imperialist powers for Chinese railroad investment interests.

The Beijing-Hankou Railway is 1,214 kilometers long and has 125 stations along its route. The southern section had to cross rugged countryside and the northern section had to cross an extremely dense network of rivers, including the Yellow River. This required the construction of a 3 km long bridge over the alluvial riverbed. In 1898, the General Company invited Jean Jadot, an engineer who had been engaged in railroad construction in the Belgian provinces of Liège and Luxembourg, to come to China to supervise the construction of the Beijing-Hankou Railway. In January

1898 年发行的京汉铁路股票

Beijing–Hankou Railway Stock Certificate issued in 1898

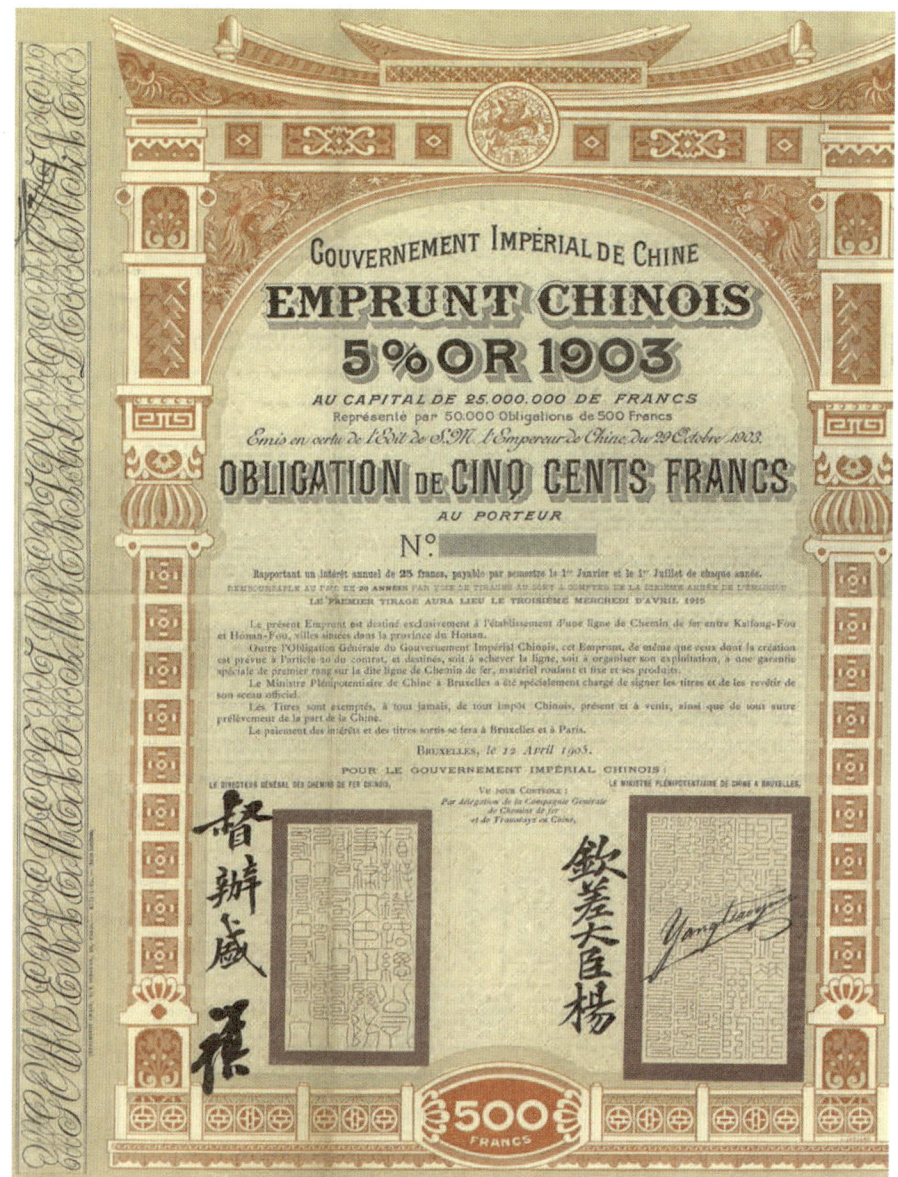

1903 年发行的京汉铁路股票

Beijing–Hankou Railway Stock Certificate issued in 1903

铁路期间，让·沙多克服了许多困难和挑战，尤其是义和团运动期间，他带领自己的团队为保护铁路付出了很多努力。沙多在中国出色的工作赢得了国王利奥波德二世的赏识，1906年京汉铁路竣工后，回到比利时的沙多被任命为通用公司在刚果的经理，1913年接任通用公司总裁。[46]

卢汉铁路于1899年开工，1905年9月建成，当年11月12日举行了通车仪式。1906年北京至卢沟桥段完成，至此全线贯通，改称京汉铁路。这条南北铁路干线建成后，极大地推动了北方社会商品经济和沿线工业的发展，促进了文化交流与传播，加快了中国近代化进程。1908年清政府还清借款，1909年购回京汉线的主权。[47]

1899, Sheng Xuanhuai, the director of the Chinese Imperial Railway, signed a contract with Jadot, stipulating that the appointment would be for a minimum of four years, and can be extendable up to six years by the Belgian company, with an annual salary of 100,000 Belgian francs.

The railroad between Marco Polo Bridge and Baoding was already completed when Jean Jadot took on this project. Under his command, 5,000 workers worked simultaneously from Baoding and Wuhan in opposite directions, laying an average of 1 km of railroad per day. During the construction of the railroad, Jean Jadot overcame many challenges, especially during the Boxer Rebellion, when he led his team to protect the railroad. Jean Jadot's outstanding work in China won the appreciation of King Leopold II. After the completion of the Beijing-Hankou Railway in 1906, Jean Jadot returned to Belgium and was appointed manager of the General Company in Congo. In 1913, he took over as President of the General Company.[46]

The construction of the Lu-Han Railway began in 1899 and was completed in September 1905, with an opening ceremony held on November 12 of that year. 1906 saw the completion of the Beijing-Marco Polo Bridge section, and the entire line was then opened and renamed the Beijing-Hankou Railway. After the completion of this north-south railroad line, it greatly promoted the development of the northern commerce and industries along the line, enhanced cultural exchange and accelerated the process of modernization in China. In 1908, the Qing government repaid the loan and bought back the sovereignty of the Beijing-Hankou Railway in 1909.[47]

北京城墙处的铁轨。1900 年后不久，为使京汉铁路线穿过城墙抵达终点站，城墙被炸出了
两处开口。由比利时工程师沙多之孙 Jean Jadot 先生提供

Railway tracks at the Beijing city wall. Shortly after 1900, two openings were blown out of
the city walls to allow the Beijing-Hankou railway line to pass through to its final destination.
By courtesy of Jean Jadot, the grandson of Belgian Engineer Jean Jadot

1901 年铁轨穿过北京天安门广场附近的城墙。由比利时工程师
沙多之孙 Jean Jadot 先生提供

The railway track passes through the city wall near Tiananmen
Square in Beijing in 1901. By courtesy of Jean Jadot, the
grandson of Belgian Engineer Jean Jadot

黄河附近的隧道。摄于 20 世纪的第一个十年（图片来自布鲁塞尔皇家档案馆）

Tunnel near the Yellow River . Taken in 1910s (Royal Archives Brussels)

长江河畔汉口江岸终点站。摄于 20 世纪的第一个十年（中国滨州窦希仑收藏）

The river terminal in Hankou on the banks of the Yangzi River. Taken in 1910s (Dou Xilun Collection, Binzhou, China)

修建京汉铁路黄河大桥。摄于 20 世纪初（照片由比利时铁路公司某位职员拍摄，中国滨州窦希仑收藏）

Construction of the bridge over the Yellow River for the Beijing-Hankou railway. Taken in the early of 20 century (Picture taken by an unknown Belgian member of staff at the railway company. Dou Xilun Collection, Binzhou, China)

让·沙多（Jean Jadot，1862—1932）比利时工程师、实业家。曾任京汉铁路总工程师、比利时通用公司总经理。毕业于鲁汶大学。曾任比利时卢森堡省铁路总工程师，后在埃及修筑铁路。1896年年底应聘来华，修筑京汉铁路，在华工作8年。1899年初沙多到达天津，"候旨进京"。他很喜欢这座城市，后来介绍弟弟兰伯特·沙多（Lambert Jadot）于1904年在天津比商电车电灯公司任工程师

Jean Jadot (1862-1932) was a Belgian engineer and industrialist. He was the chief engineer of the Beijing-Hankou railroad and the general manager of the Belgian General Company. ...

清政府授予沙多的双龙宝星勋章
The Double Dragon Star Medal awarded to Jean Jadot by the Qing government

中华民国政府授予沙多的嘉禾勋章
Order of Golden Grain awarded to Jean Jadot by the government of the Republic of China

沙多与清政府官员
Jean Jadot and Qing government officials

沙多与中国铁路建设人员
Jean Jadot and Chinese railroad construction workers

以上照片由比利时工程师沙多之孙 Jean Jadot 先生提供
By courtesy of Jean Jadot, the grandson of Belgian Engineer Jean Jadot

慈禧太后视察京汉铁路北京段。摄于 1902 年

Empress Dowager Cixi inspected the Beijing section of the Beijing-Hankou railroad. Taken in 1902

《辛丑条约》签订后，慈禧太后由西安返回北京，途中乘坐沙多为其准备的专列，并赐沙多双龙宝星勋章。摄于 1902 年

After the signing of the Boxer Protocol, Empress Dowager Cixi returned to Beijing from Xi'an on a special train prepared for her by Jean Jadot, to whom she awarded the Double Dragon Star Medal. Taken in 1902

以上照片由比利时工程师沙多之孙 Jean Jadot 先生提供

By courtesy of Jean Jadot, the grandson of Belgian Engineer Jean Jadot

林辅臣与黄河第一桥

黄河是世界第五大长河，中国第二长河，全长约5464公里，流域面积752443平方公里。位于黄河上游的兰州，是甘肃省省会，西部地区重要的中心城市之一。黄河在这里从西向东穿城而过，兰州黄河大桥闻名全国，有"天下黄河第一桥"之称，是兰州市标志性建筑之一。这座铁桥的谋划建设与一位比利时籍的中国官员"林大人"有着重要关系。

林辅臣（1842—1906），比利时籍清政府洋员，第一任肃州（即嘉峪关，今属甘肃省酒泉市）常关税务官，人称"林大人"。他最为人所知的是，充当中比之间的合作项目联络人，为在甘肃引进西方科学技术做出重要贡献。他娶了一位中国夫人，在中国度过了41年的生命旅途。

林辅臣1842年出生于比利时布鲁塞尔郊区，刚出生即成为弃儿，先后被两个家庭收养。巧合的是，这一年也是第一次鸦片战争中国战败后被迫打开国门的那年。21岁时，林辅臣到布鲁塞尔某教会当杂工，1865年8月跟随四位天主教传教士来华。林辅臣有极高的语言天赋，在来华途中就向轮船上的中国人学会了日常用语。到中国后他先是在崇礼县（今河北省境内）给神父做助手，日常工作包括打杂、采购、联络等等，有机会常与当地村民聊天，汉语更加流利，几个月以后就能充当翻译。

1868年，26岁的林辅臣离开崇礼，到北京的普鲁士（德国）公使馆工作，往返于使馆与天津港之间，负责监督物资运输。林辅臣因工作之便在京津两地结识了很多外国人，其中就有著名的德国地质学家李希霍芬

Paul Splingaerd and the First Bridge over the Yellow River

The Yellow River is the fifth longest river in the world and the second longest river in China, with a total length of about 5,464 km and a basin area of about 752,443 square kilometers. Lanzhou, located in the upper reaches of the Yellow River, is the capital of Gansu Province and one of the important central cities in the western region of China. The Yellow River runs from west to east through the city, and the Lanzhou Yellow River Bridge, known nationwide as the "First Bridge over the Yellow River," is one of the landmarks of Lanzhou. The planning and construction of this iron bridge had an important relationship with a Chinese official of Belgian origin, known as "Lin Da Ren" (Lord Lin).

Paul Splingaerd (Chinese name: Lin Fuchen, 1842-1906), a Qing government official of Belgian origin, was the first tax official of Suzhou (i.e., Jiayuguan, now Jiuquan City, Gansu Province), known as "Lord Lin." He was best known for acting as a liaison between China and Belgium for cooperation projects and making important contributions to the introduction of Western science and technology to Gansu. He married a Chinese wife and spent 41 years of his life in China.

Born in 1842 in the suburbs of Brussels, Belgium, Paul Splingaerd was an abandoned child at birth and later adopted by two families. His birth year was coincidentally the year when China was forced to open its doors after its defeat in the First Opium War. At the age of 21, he worked as a handyman in a church in Brussels and followed four Catholic missionaries to China in August 1865. Splingaerd had a great talent for languages and learned to speak everyday Chinese from the Chinese people on the ships on his way to China. After arriving in China, he first worked as an assistant to the priest in Chongli County (in present-

青年时代的林辅臣。约摄于19世纪60年代。照片由林辅臣家族提供
Paul Splingaerd in his youth. Taken in 1860s. Photos from Paul Splingaerd's family archives

（Ferdinand von Richthofen），也就是第一个提出"丝绸之路"概念的人。李希霍芬当时刚刚来到中国，正好急需一个精通中国语言和文化的人做翻译，便将林辅臣雇为自己的管家兼助手，协助进行地理、地质考察工作。林辅臣跟随李希霍芬在 1868—1872 年的 4 年间进行了 7 次考察活动，足迹遍及当时中国的 11 个行省（当时共 18 个）。得益于这一系列的考察活动，林辅臣变成了彻头彻尾的"中国通"，为他日后进入清政府服务打下了重要的基础。对当地官员礼节性拜访过程中，李希霍芬有个惊人的发现。原来清政府为了防止偏袒及裙带关系，会派遣高级官员去管理其籍贯之外的地区，致使官员在辖区内很难与当地人进行语言上的交流。让李希

day Hebei Province), where his daily duties included miscellaneous work such as chores, purchasing, liaison, and etc. He often had the opportunity to chat with the local villagers and improved his Chinese, and after a few months he was able to act as an interpreter.

In 1868, at the age of 26, Paul Splingaerd left Chongli Mongolia to work for the Prussian (German) Legation in Beijing whose job was to supervise the transportation of the goods between the legation and Tianjin Port. As a result of his work, he met many foreigners in Beijing and Tianjin, among them the famous German geologist Ferdinand von Richthofen (better known in English as Baron von Richthofen), who was the first person to propose the concept of the Silk Road. At that time, Baron von Richthofen had just arrived in China and was in urgent need of a person who was proficient in Chinese language and

李希霍芬（1833—1905），德国旅行家、地理学家。在他的著作中，第一次将起始于中国，连接亚洲、非洲和欧洲的古代陆上商业贸易路线命名为"丝绸之路"。1861 年首次来华。后来他再度来华，在中国内地进行了 7 次考察旅行，走遍了大半个中国。回国后，李希霍芬出版了《中国：亲身旅行和据此所作研究的成果》（*China: Ergebnisse eigner Reisen und darauf gegründeter Studien*）一书，共三大卷和一部地图集。在这本书中，作者不仅涉及地理，还涉及各地的水陆交通、经济状况、历史文化等等

Ferdinand von Richthofen (1833-1905) was a German traveler and geographer. In his writings, he named the ancient road trade route that began in China and connected Asia, Africa and Europe as "Silk Road" for the first time. Later he came back to China and made seven study trips in the interior of China, covering half of the country. After his return to China, Richthofen published *China: Ergebnisse eigner Reisen und darauf gegrünchendeter Studien*, a book in three volumes and an atlas. In this book, the author deals not only with geography, but also with land and water transportation, economic conditions, history and culture, etc

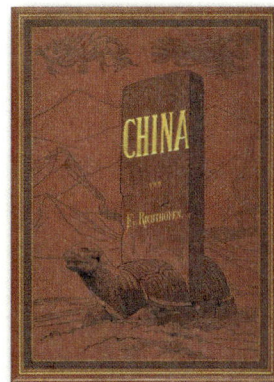

林辅臣随李希霍芬探险时照片。摄于 19 世纪 60—70 年代

Paul Splingaerd and Ferdinand von Richthofen. Taken in 1860s or 1870s

身着清朝服饰、留着辫子的洋大人林辅臣。肃州不属于沿海或沿江通商口岸，1881 年所设的税务机构应为常关，隶属北洋通商大臣管理，不属海关管辖。所以照片中的"林大人"着清政府官服，而非海关税务司穿的西装。他说："当我与中国官员一起工作时，他们不能在我身上占上风，因为我也是清朝官员。我努力与所有人保持良好关系，无论他们是大人物还是小官吏，还包括普通民众。这样，一切就能运行顺利。"照片摄于 19 世纪 80—90 年代。由林辅臣家族提供

Paul Splingaerd, dressed in Qing dynasty costume with braids, said "When I work with Chinese officials, they cannot get the upper hand on me because I am also a Qing Dynasty official. I try to maintain good relations with everyone, whether they are big or small officials, and also the general public. That way, everything runs smoothly." Taken in 1880s or 1890s. Photo from Paul Splingaerd's family archives

霍芬大为吃惊的是，由于每个地区的方言不同，有几次保罗被叫去承担中国的高级官员与其当地下属之间的翻译工作。[48]

1881 年，清政府与沙俄签订归还新疆伊犁地区的《中俄伊犁条约》，规定准许俄商在肃州（今酒泉）贸易，由俄国运入该处的货物，按旧例减税三分之一。条约签订前，在蒙古地区（包括今内蒙古自治区和蒙古国）贩运茶叶的俄国商人屡屡偷税漏税，原本由津海关派扦子手（检查员）赴张家口、恰克图两处查验，但是路途遥远、耗费较大。所以条约签订后，清政府决定于肃州设

culture as a translator, so he hired Paul Splingaerd as his housekeeper and assistant to assist him in his geographic and geological expeditions. Paul Splingaerd followed Baron von Richthofen on seven expeditions during the four years from 1868 to 1872, covering 11 provinces (out of 18 in total) in China at that time. Thanks to this series of study tours, Paul Splingaerd became a complete China expert, which laid an important foundation for his future service in the Qing government. During his courtesy visits to local officials, von Richhofen made a surprising discovery. It turned out that in order to prevent favoritism and nepotism, the Qing government would send high-ranking officials to administer areas outside their places of origin, making it difficult for the officials to communicate with the locals in their jurisdictions in terms of dialect. To von Richthofen's surprise, Splingaerd was called upon on several occasions to interpret between senior Chinese officials and their local subordinates because of the different dialects spoken in each region.[48]

In 1881, the Qing government and the tsarist Russia signed the Sino-Russian Ili Treaty pertaining to the return of the Xinjiang Ili region to China. The treaty provided that Russian merchants were allowed to trade in Suzhou (present-day Jiuquan) and the goods shipped there from Russia would enjoy the reduction of taxes by one third according to the old rules. Before the signing of the treaty, in the Mongolian region (including today's Inner Mongolia and Outer Mongolia) Russian tea merchants had repeatedly evaded taxes. Tianjin Customs originally sent inspectors to Kalgan and Kiakhta for inspection, but the journey was long and costly. Therefore, after the treaty was signed, the Qing government set up a customs office in Suzhou to check and collect taxes from Russian merchants nearby. But this customs office was not under the new customs office headed by Sir Robert Hart, but under the management of Li Hongzhang, the Minister of Beiyang. Li Hongzhang had

立海关，就近向俄国商人检查征税。但是这个海关并不隶属于由赫德（Robert Hart）掌管的海关新关，而是归属北洋大臣李鸿章管理。李鸿章为寻觅税务官的人选很伤脑筋，无意中从李希霍芬发表在《华北先锋》上的科学文章里发现了斯普林格尔德（Splingaerd）这个名字。当年李希霍芬到中国各地进行广泛地质勘查时，林辅臣曾陪同他前往总理衙门办理手续。可能在李鸿章会见李希霍芬时，就注意到地质学家的比利时助手既能说一口

肃州海关衙门。摄于19世纪80—90年代。以上照片由林辅臣家族提供
Suzhou Customs Office. Taken in 1880s or 1890s. Photos from Paul Splingaerd's family archives

a hard time finding a qualified tax collector. Accidentally he found the name of Splingaerd in a scientific article published by von Richthofen in the journal of *Hua Bei Xian Feng* (North China Herald). Before von Richthofen went to various parts of China for extensive geological investigations, Splingaerd accompanied him to the Ministry of Foreign Affairs for formalities. Probably when Li Hongzhang met with von Richthofen, he noticed that the geologist's Belgian assistant was both fluent in Chinese and knowledgeable about the northwest region. Since Li also wanted the new Suzhou tax collector to survey the local mineral deposits, Splingaerd became the perfect candidate for the post. In 1882, Splingaerd was appointed by the Qing government as the first tax collector of Suzhou.[49]

During his 14-year tenure in Jiuquan, from 1882 to 1896, Paul Splingaerd was highly appreciated by the court for his impartiality in enforcing the law and establishing industries. He also set up a pharmacy and clinic in the customs office, using his knowledge of Western medicine acquired from missionaries in his early years to treat local people and administer cowpox to children, who was well received by the people. A picture of the umbrella given to "Lin Da Ren" (Lord Lin) by the locals is still kept in the home of Splingaerd's descendants.

Around 1895, Leopold II hired Paul Splingaerd to participate in the Sino-Belgian negotiations on financing, equipment and technology for the construction of the Lu-Han Railway. For his outstanding performance in the negotiations, Leopold II awarded him Knight of the Order of the Crown in 1898. In 1905, at the age of 63, Splingaerd was appointed by the Qing government as the commander of a brigade and led an expedition to Xinjiang. After returning from Xinjiang, Splingaerd stopped by Lanzhou to visit his old friend Peng Yingjia, the Governor of Lanzhou. This visit became the beginning of the venture to help Gansu building industries by Splingaerd and his eldest son,

流利的汉语又很了解西北地区的情况，而且李鸿章希望新的肃州税务官也能够勘查一下本地的矿藏。如此一来，林辅臣便是这一职位的不二人选。1882年林辅臣被清政府任命为第一任肃州地区税务官。[49]

从1882年到1896年，林辅臣在酒泉任职14年其间他秉公执法、兴办实业，深得朝廷赏识。他还在海关衙门内设了药铺和诊所，利用自己早年跟传教士习得的西医知识为百姓治病，为儿童接种牛痘，因此深受百姓爱戴。林氏后裔的家中至今保留着当年百姓赠给林大人的万民伞的照片。

1895年左右，利奥波德二世聘请林辅臣参加中比关于卢汉铁路修筑项目的融资、设备和技术等方面的谈判。由于在谈判中的出色表现，利奥波德二世于1898年授予他王冠骑士勋章。1905年，年届63岁的林辅臣被清政府任命为协统（旅长），率军远征新疆。自新疆返回后，林辅臣去了兰州，拜访老朋友兰州道彭英甲。这一拜访成了林辅臣及其长子林阿德协助甘肃举办实业的开端。

彼时，1900年八国联军入侵，清朝的最高统治者慈禧太后带着光绪皇帝仓皇西逃。《辛丑条约》议定后，慈禧太后坐火车回京，终于认识到改革的重要性。于清朝的最后10年，开始了号称"新政"的变法自强。时任兰州道的彭英甲正在筹备举办实业，但是甘肃地处偏远，经济文化比较落后，要想推行"新政"，必须"借材异地"，借助外国人才。这个现成的顾问就是长期在酒泉地方任税务官的林辅臣。

1905年，在兰州负责新政的彭英甲，得陕甘总督升允同意，与林辅臣反复商讨，确定了一系列引进比利时技术、开发实业的洋务项目，由林辅臣赴比利时招聘相

Alphonse Splingaerd.

At that time, when the Eight-Power Allied Forces invaded in 1900, Empress Dowager Cixi, the supreme ruler of the Qing dynasty, fled west with Emperor Guangxu. After the Boxer Protocol was signed, Empress Dowager Cixi returned to Beijing by train and finally realized the importance of reform. In the last decade of the Qing dynasty, she started the "New Deal" reform for strengthening China. Peng Yingjia, then Governor of Lanzhou, was preparing to build industries. But Gansu is located in a remote region, economically and culturally backward. To implement the "New Deal", it was necessary to have the help of foreign talents. This ready-made advisor was the long-time Jiuquan local tax official, Paul Splingaerd.

In 1905, Peng Yingjia, who was in charge of implementing the "New Deal" reform in Lanzhou, worked with Paul Splingaerd to draw up a series of plans to import Belgian technology and develop industrial projects. Splingaerd went to Belgium to recruit relevant technical personnel. These plans included: (1) restoring the Lanzhou Weaving Bureau founded by Zuo Zongtang; (2) developing the Yumen oil field; opening a factory to manufacture foreign wax and foreign soap; (3) introducing good seeds of sugar beet and grape, and planting them on a large scale to produce sugar and wine; (4) building the Lanzhou Yellow River Bridge.

With the good wishes for Sino-Belgian cooperation and expanding bilateral trade, Splingaerd returned to Belgium in January 1906. His work was extremely efficient and soon recruited three engineers and technicians. He embarked on the trip returning to China in May 1906. Unfortunately, he fell ill on the way and died near Xi'an. He was buried, dressed in the official uniform of the Qing court, in the Catholic cemetery in Beijing. Before he died, he entrusted his unfinished plans for the development of Gansu to his eldest son, Alphonse, and asked him to accompany the three

林氏家族收藏的林辅臣一品官服。备受清政府信任和赏识的林辅臣最后官至一品，在晚清政府所雇用的洋员中是绝无仅有的。以上照片由林辅臣家族提供

Splingaerd's first-rank official uniforms collected by his family. Photos from Paul Splingaerd's family archives

比利时国王利奥波德二世授予林辅臣的王冠骑士勋章

Knight of the Order of the Crown awarded by King Leopold II of Belgium to Paul Splingaerd

林辅臣完成酒泉的任期后与全家在上海团聚时的合影，约摄于 1896 年。林辅臣和凯瑟琳生了 12 个子女。女儿苏珊娜到上海上学后不久，死于霍乱，所以照片中只有 11 个孩子。照片背景：为感谢林辅臣在酒泉任职期间的业绩和对公共卫生方面的贡献，当地人们赠予他多面锦旗。右边仆人身后的圆形"万民伞"是当地市民赠给林辅臣的礼物。当清朝高官离任出城的时候，由仆人走在前面举万民伞表示百姓的挽留之情。后排为罗莎、雷米、玛丽、克莱拉、林阿德。前排坐着的为保丽娜、安娜、凯瑟琳（林辅臣夫人）、林辅臣、凯瑟琳（女儿）、露西。坐在地板上的为特蕾泽和让巴蒂斯特

Photo of the Splingaerd family was taken in Shanghai around 1896 after the family was reunited upon completion of Paul's assignment in Jiuquan (Suzhou). Paul and Catherine had twelve children. Daughter Suzanne died of cholera in Shanghai shortly after beginning school there, so only eleven are in this photo. The background: the banners presented to Paul in recognition of his service in Jiuquan and his medical contributions. The round "parade parasol" behind the servant at the right bore tributes from the citizens. It was held up by a servant ahead of the mandarin when riding through a city. The people: back row: Rosa, Remy, Marie, Clara, Alphonse. seated: Pauline, Anna, Catherine (mother), Paul, Catherine (daughter), Lucie. on floor: Therese and Jean-Baptiste

以上照片由林辅臣家族提供

Photos from Paul Splingaerd's family archives

黄河第一桥。约摄于 1909 年

The First Bridge over the Yellow River. Circa 1909

以上两张照片为兰州黄河铁桥，后改名为"中山桥"。约摄于 2010 年

Above two photos were Lanzhou Yellow River iron bridge, later renamed "Zhongshan Bridge." Circa 2010

建成开通的兰州黄河铁桥。约摄于 1909 年

The completed and opened Lanzhou Yellow River Iron Bridge. Circa 1909

以上照片由林辅臣家族提供

Photos from Paul Splingaerd's family archives

林阿德（Alphonse Splingaerd，1877—1943），林辅臣长子，曾任比利时驻华使馆参赞，恰逢义和团运动时包围各国使馆，因表现勇敢，获得俄、比、英、法四个国家的嘉奖。后遵父遗命，1906年辞职赴甘肃继续其父未完事业，长期驻兰州，协助彭英甲从比利时购买机器设备、聘请工匠，先后恢复织呢局、创办官办金厂铜厂、创办洋蜡胰子厂，为彭英甲创办的矿务学堂、农林堂担任英文教员，为甘肃工业、教育现代化的开始奠定了基础。后回天津居住，并成为天津比商电车电灯公司（CTET）董事会董事。约摄于义和团运动之后

Alphonse Splingaerd (1877-1943), eldest son of Paul Splingaerd. Former Counsellor of the Belgian Embassy in China. In his tenure, the Boxer attacked the foreign legation in Beijing and his heroic actions were recognized with medals from the Russian, Belgian, British and French governments. In 1906, he resigned and went to Gansu to continue his father's unfinished business ... Later, he settled in Tianjin and became board member of Belgian Tianjin Tramway and Electric Lighting Company (CTET). Taken after the Boxer Rebellion

关技术人员。项目包括：一，恢复左宗棠所创立的兰州织呢局；二，开发玉门油田；开工厂，制造洋蜡、洋胰子；三，引进甜菜、葡萄良种，试验后大面积种植，以生产糖和葡萄酒；四，修建兰州黄河大桥；等等。

带着中比合作、打通两国贸易通道的美好愿望，林辅臣于1906年1月回到比利时。他的工作极富效率，很快就招募到三位工程技术人员，于1906年5月一起返回中国。但不幸的是，他于途中染病，在西安附近去世，后着清朝官服葬于北京天主教会公墓。临终前，他将未竟的开发甘肃的计划托付给长子林阿德，嘱其将三位比利时工程师送往兰州交给彭英甲。

后来，兰州黄河铁桥项目交与天津的一家德国洋行建造。1906年10月28日签订合同后，工程全面展开。黄河铁桥所用的钢桁架构件、水泥及各种器材、机具、设备等，全部由泰来洋行从德国购置，经海运到天津，再由京奉铁路运至丰台火车站，转经京汉铁路运至新乡火车站，再用马车由新乡运输至西安，由西安再到兰州。

Belgian engineers to Lanzhou to Peng Yingjia.

Later, Lanzhou Yellow River iron bridge project was handed over to a German company in Tianjin to build. After the signing of the contract on October 28, 1906, the project was in full swing. The steel truss components, cement and related equipment, machinery, and other materials were all imported from Germany by Telge & Schroeter. These materials arrived at Tianjin by sea, later by the Beijing-Fengtian Railway to Fengtai Railway Station, and then by the Beijing-Hankou Railway to Xinxiang Railway Station. Afterwards, they were transported by carriage from Xinxiang to Xi'an, and then to Lanzhou. Transportation of the materials and equipment itself lasted 21 months. The total weight of the building materials amounted to 2,281,500 jin (1 jin equals 0.45kg). The Iron bridge construction crew included foreign craftsmen and Chinese workers, totaling 69 people. The Yellow River iron bridge project officially started on May 9, 1908 and completed on July 26, 1909. It was open for traffic on August 25, ending the long history of the absence of a permanent bridge on the upper streams of the Yellow River. This was also the first successful cooperation between Gansu local government

路途遥遥，仅运送物料即历时 21 个月，转运建材总重达 228.15 万斤。铁桥工程的施工人员，有德商招募来到兰州的洋匠、华工共计 69 人。人员和建材全部到齐后，黄河铁桥工程于 1908 年 5 月 9 日正式开工，1909 年 7 月 26 日竣工，8 月 25 日开通，一举结束了黄河上游千百年来没有永久性桥梁通行的历史。这也是甘肃地方政府与西方人在自主、自愿前提下的第一次成功合作。

林辅臣是晚清政府雇用的一大批洋员的杰出代表。自 1861 年洋务运动开始以来，清政府为了"师夷长技以制夷"，雇用了大量"洋顾问"。最著名的，当属以赫德为首的海关中的洋员。仅 1875 年，海关就有洋员 408 人。洋务运动中的各项事业，包括购买舰船火炮、组建近代海军、开筑矿山铁路、设立现代化工厂、开办同文馆、遣派幼童留美、参加世界博览会，以及协办外交和对外派驻使节等等，几乎无处没有海关洋员的参与。这些洋员当中，既有不少真正掌握并认真向中国传播西方先进科学技术、成绩卓著者，也有很多平庸之辈，甚至滥竽充数、招摇撞骗之徒。他们中很多人长期在中国生活，受到中华文化的影响。有学者指出，这些人开始经历了一个"杂交"的过程，变成了"在中国的西方人"（Westerner-in-China），而不再是"单一纯粹的西方人"了。[50] 他们为近代中西文化的碰撞交流做出了杰出的贡献，历史不应忘记他们。

and Westerners under the premise of autonomy and mutual willingness.

Paul Splingaerd was an outstanding representative of a large number of foreign officials employed by the government of the late Qing dynasty. Since the beginning of the Self-Strengthening Movement in 1861, the Qing government employed a large number of foreign advisors in order to "master the skills of the barbarians to control the barbarians." The most famous ones were those working in the customs office headed by Sir Robert Hart. In 1875 alone, there were 408 foreign employees in the customs. The various undertakings of the Self-Strengthening Movement, including the purchase of ships and guns, the formation of a modern navy, the opening of mines and railroads, the establishment of modern factories, the opening of the Tongwen Guan (The School of Combined Learning), the dispatch of young children to study in the United States, participation in the World Exposition, as well as dispatching diplomatic envoys abroad, etc., almost all involved the participation and contribution of these foreign staff members. Among these foreigners, there were many who had really mastered and seriously spread advanced Western science and technology to China and had achieved great success. But of course, there was also no shortage of mediocre, even indiscriminate, fraudulent people. Many of them lived in China for a long time and were influenced by Chinese culture. Some scholars point out that these people underwent a process of "hybridization" at the beginning and became "Westerner-in-China" instead of "pure Westerners."[50] They had made outstanding contributions to the modern cultural exchange between East and West, and history should not forget them.

兰州当地为林辅臣制作的纪念雕像，雕像底座上有他在酒泉任职时的详细功绩介绍

A statue of Paul Splingaerd in Lanzhou, with a detailed description of his achievements in Jiuquan on the base of the statue

林辅臣比利时家乡为他立的纪念像

A memorial statue of Paul Splingaerd in his hometown in Belgium

以上照片由林辅臣家族提供

Photos from Paul Splingaerd's family archives

林氏家族后裔出席布鲁塞尔展览开幕式。摄于 2017 年 4 月

Splingaerd family descendants at the exhibition opening in Brussels.Taken in April 2017

注释

1 纽康门（Newcommen，1663—1729），又译牛珂门，英国机械师，其发明的蒸汽机是最早的蒸汽机之一。

2 〔比〕让·东特：《比利时史》，南京大学外文系法文翻译组译，南京：江苏人民出版社，1973，第 109 页。

3 〔比〕让·东特：《比利时史》，南京大学外文系法文翻译组译，南京：江苏人民出版社，1973，第 107 页。

4 〔比〕让·东特：《比利时史》，南京大学外文系法文翻译组译，南京：江苏人民出版社，1973，第 101—102 页。

5 1814 年 7 月 25 日，英国人乔治·斯蒂芬孙自己动手制作的第一台蒸汽机车运行成功。1822 年 5 月 23 日，欧洲也是世界第一条铁路在英国开始修建。

6 https://www.railwaywondersoftheworld.com/belgian_railways.html.

7 〔比〕让·东特：《比利时史》，南京大学外文系法文翻译组译，南京：江苏人民出版社，1973，第 128 页。

8 〔比〕让·东特：《比利时史》，南京大学外文系法文翻译组译，南京：江苏人民出版社，1973，第 130 页。

9 安特卫普位于比利时西北部斯海尔德河畔，是比利时最大港口和重要工业城市、欧洲人口最密集的地区。16 世纪成为欧洲最富有的商业城市。

10 〔比〕让·东特：《比利时史》，南京大学外文系法文翻译组译，南京：江苏人民出版社，1973，第 127 页。

11 〔美〕亚当·霍赫希尔德：《利奥波德国王的鬼魂：贪婪、恐惧、英雄主义与比利时的非洲殖民地》，扈喜林译，北京：社会科学文献出版社，2018，第 36 页。

12 这里所谓的"自由贸易"是指历史上西方列强在晚期重商主义思想政策指导下，通过武力征服、侵占、收购、扩张等方式把不发达国家、民族和地区变成自己的商品市场、原料产地、投资场所，以及廉价劳动力和雇佣兵的来源地。与早期重商主义那种一味用暴力手段掠夺金银的积累方式相比，晚期的重商主义转向注重商品交换的"贸易平衡论"，即主张大力发展能在国外大量销售的商品生产，为此可以扩大对外国原料的购买，征收低关税，允许货币输出，但要求保持输入超过输出，通过调节商品运动来达到货币积累的目的。

13 转引自〔美〕亚当·霍赫希尔德《利奥波德国王的鬼魂：贪婪、恐惧、英雄主义与比利时的非洲殖民地》，扈喜林译，北京：社会科学文献出版社，2018，第 222 页。

14 转引自〔美〕亚当·霍赫希尔德《利奥波德国王的鬼魂：贪婪、恐惧、英雄主义与比利时的非洲殖民地》，扈喜林译，北京：社会科学文献出版社，2018，第 222 页。

15 即《中英天津条约》、《中美天津条约》和《中法天津条约》。

16 即《中英北京条约》、《中法北京条约》和《中俄北京条约》。

17 金得俄使团随员中有彼时尚为太子的利奥波德二世。使团从广东到达上海后，太子接到国王重病的消息，立即赶回比利时，未能到达北京参与最后的签约。1865 年 12 月利奥波德二世登基。

18 故宫博物院明清档案部、福建师范大学历史系合编《清季中外使领年表》，北京：中华书局，1985，第 47—48 页。

19 Charles Terlinden, "T'Kint, Auguste-Pierre-Joseph," *Biographie Nationale de Belgique*, Vol. 25 (Brussels, 1932), pp. 368–371.

20 汉萨同盟是德意志北部城市之间形成的商业、政治联盟。汉萨（Hanse）一词，德文意为"公所"或者"会馆"。13 世纪逐渐形成，14 世纪达到兴盛，加盟城市最多达到 160 个。1367 年成立以吕贝克城为首的领导机构，有汉堡、科隆、不来梅等大城市的富商、贵族参加。拥有武装和金库。斌椿使团抵达汉堡，时为汉萨同盟成员。

21 斌椿：《乘槎笔记》，北京：商务印书馆，2016，第 39—40 页。

22 张德彝：《航海述奇》，北京：商务印书馆，2016，第 106 页。

23 斌椿：《乘槎笔记》，北京：商务印书馆，2016，第 40 页。

24 张德彝：《航海述奇》，北京：商务印书馆，2016，第 104—105 页。

25 郭嵩焘：《伦敦与巴黎日记》，长沙：岳麓书社，1984，第 646 页。

26 薛福成：《出使四国日记》，北京：社会科学文献出版社，2007，第 94 页。

27 薛福成：《出使四国日记》，北京：社会科学文献出版社，2007，第 94 页。

28 薛福成：《出使四国日记》，北京：社会科学文献出版社，2007，第 94 页。

29 薛福成：《出使四国日记》，北京：社会科学文献出版社，2007，第 97 页。

30 故宫博物院明清档案部、福建师范大学历史系合编《清季中外使领年表》，北京：中华书局，1985，第 15—16 页。

31 薛福成：《出使四国日记》，北京：社会科学文献出版社，2007，第 97 页。

32 蔡尔康等：《李鸿章历聘欧美记》，长沙：岳麓书社，1986，第 79 页。

33 蔡尔康等：《李鸿章历聘欧美记》，长沙：岳麓书社，

34 蔡尔康等：《李鸿章历聘欧美记》，长沙：岳麓书社，1986，第 78 页。

35 蔡尔康等：《李鸿章历聘欧美记》，长沙：岳麓书社，1986，第 79 页。

36 蔡尔康等：《李鸿章历聘欧美记》，长沙：岳麓书社，1986，第 79 页。

37 《工程师》杂志，1864 年 6 月 3 日，转引自宓汝成《帝国主义与中国铁路：1847—1949》，北京：经济管理出版社，2007，第 23—24 页。

38 〔美〕马士：《中华帝国对外关系史》第 3 卷，张汇文等译，上海：上海世纪出版集团，2006，第 83 页。

39 李守孔：《李鸿章传》，台北：台湾学生书局，1978，第 162—163 页。

40 熊性美等：《开平煤矿矿权史料》，天津：南开大学出版社，2004，第 8 页。

41 熊性美等：《开平煤矿矿权史料》，天津：南开大学出版社，2004，第 16 页。

42 熊性美等：《开平煤矿矿权史料》，天津：南开大学出版社，2004，第 20—22 页。

43 上谕，光绪十五年四月初六日，《德宗实录》第 269 卷，第 5—6 页，转引自宓汝成《帝国主义与中国铁路：1847—1949》，北京：经济管理出版社，2007，第 46 页。

44 王铁崖编《中外旧约章汇编》第 1 册，北京：生活·读书·新知三联书店，1982，第 773—782 页。

45 〔英〕菲利浦·约瑟夫：《列强对华外交：1894—1900》，胡滨译，北京：商务印书馆，1959，第 353 页。

46 J Johan J. Mattelaer, Mathieu Torck (eds.). *A Belgian Passage to China (1870–1930)*. Uitgeverij Sterck & De Vreese, 2020, pp.104–106.

47 潘越：《中国近代留学比利时研究（1903—1949）》，博士学位论文，暨南大学，2012，第 12 页。

48 Anne Splingaerd Megowan. *The Belgian Mandarin: Paul Splingaerd*. Xlibris, 2008, p.60.

49 Anne Splingaerd Megowan. *The Belgian Mandarin: Paul Splingaerd*. Xlibris, 2008, p.86.

50 〔美〕柯文：《在中国发现历史》，林同奇译，北京：中华书局，2002，第 5—6 页。

参考文献

中文文献

[1] 斌椿 . 乘槎笔记 [M]. 北京 : 商务印书馆 , 2016.

[2] 蔡尔康等 . 李鸿章历聘欧美记 [M]. 长沙 : 湖南人民出版社 , 1982.

[3] 宓汝成 . 帝国主义与中国铁路 : 1847—1949 [M]. 北京 : 经济管理出版社 , 2007.

[4] 故宫博物院明清档案部、福建师范大学历史系合编 . 清季中外使领年表 [M]. 北京 : 中华书局 , 1985.

[5] 郭嵩焘 . 伦敦与巴黎日记 [M]. 长沙 : 岳麓书社 , 1984.

[6] 李守孔 . 李鸿章传 [M]. 台北 : 台湾学生书局 , 1978.

[7] 王铁崖编 . 中外旧约章汇编 [M]. 北京 : 生活·读书·新知三联书店 , 1982.

[8] 熊性美等主编 . 开滦煤矿矿权史料 [M]. 天津 : 南开大学出版社 , 2004.

[9] 薛福成 . 出使四国日记 [M]. 北京 : 社会科学文献出版社 , 2007.

[10] 张德彝 . 航海述奇 [M]. 北京 : 商务印书馆 , 2016.

[11]〔比〕让·东特 . 比利时史 [M]. 南京大学外文系法文翻译组译 . 南京 : 江苏人民出版社 , 1973.

[12]〔美〕柯文 . 在中国发现历史 [M]. 林同奇译 . 北京 : 中华书局 , 2002.

[13]〔美〕马士 . 中华帝国对外关系史 : 第 3 卷 [M]. 张汇文等译 . 上海 : 上海世纪出版集团 , 2006.

[14]〔美〕亚当·霍赫希尔德 . 利奥波德国王的鬼魂 : 贪婪、恐惧、英雄主义与比利时的非洲殖民地 [M]. 扈喜林译 . 北京 : 社会科学文献出版社 , 2018.

[15]〔英〕菲利浦·约瑟夫 . 列强对华外交 : 1894—1900 [M]. 胡滨译 . 北京 : 商务印书馆 , 1959.

外文文献

[1] Anne Splingaerd Megowan. *The Belgian Mandarin: Paul Splingaerd* [M]. Xlibris, 2008.

[2] Terlinden. *Charles and "T'Kint, Auguste-Pierre-Joseph". Biographie Nationale de Belgique* [M]. Vol. 25. Brussels, 1932.

电子文献

[1] https://en.wikipedia.org/wiki/History_of_rail_transport_in_Belgium.

[2] http://www.railwaywondersoftheworld.com/belgian_railways.html.

[3] https://www.splingaerd.net.

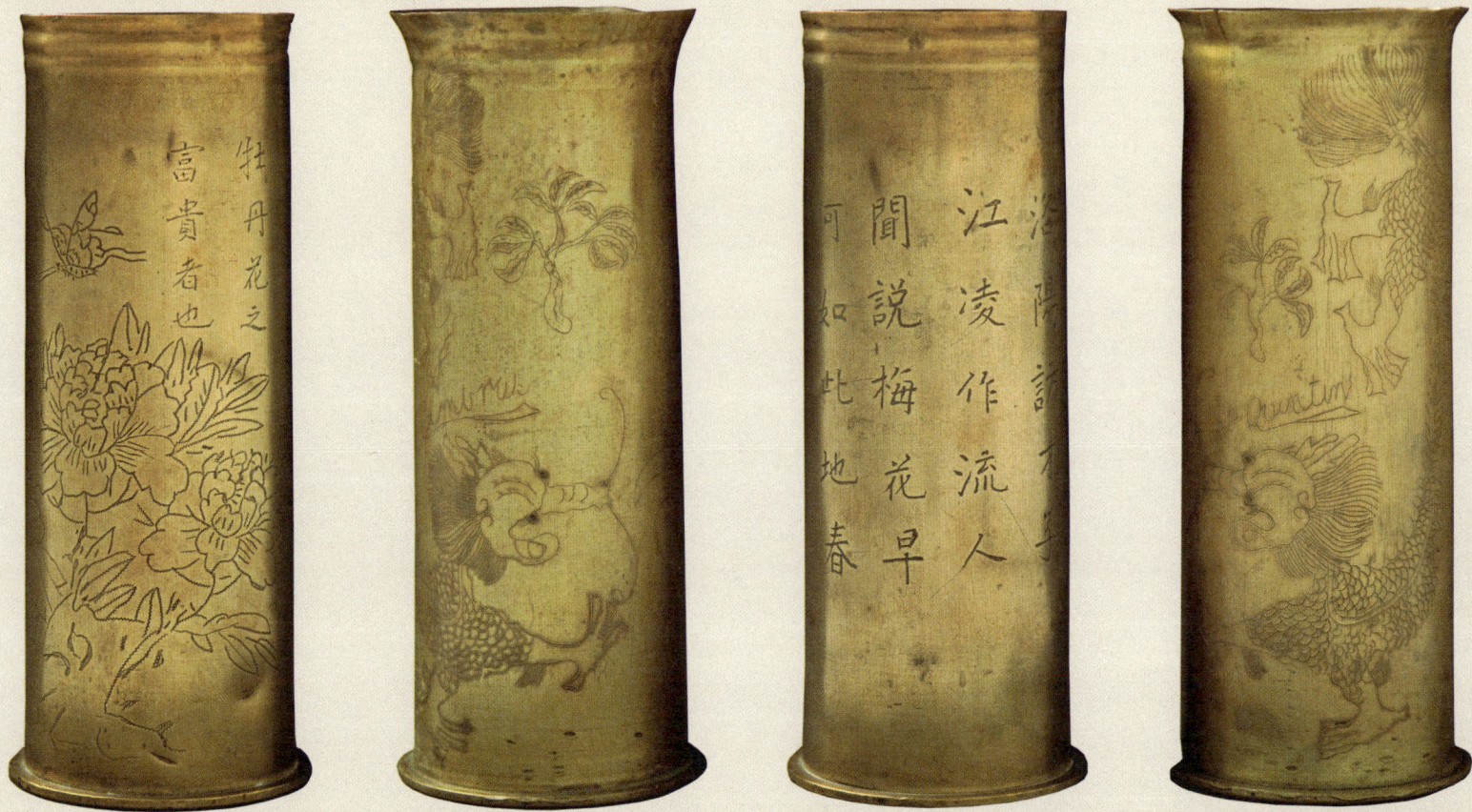

伊珀尔市佛兰德斯战地博物馆中还有一组极其独特的展品，是一战时期中国劳工留下的空炮弹壳，每个大约20厘米高，表面或有诗文或有极富中国传统元素的刻绘。这些便是劳工们闲暇时间思念家乡之际，用钉子之类的尖锐工具雕刻上去的。其中一个弹壳上赫然刻着孟浩然的《洛中访袁拾遗不遇》："洛阳访才子，江岭作流人。闻说梅花早，何如北地春。"由此可见当时在欧洲战场华工中也有一些是受过教育、具有良好文化素养的。炮弹经他们的敏感之心与灵巧之手转化为别致的艺术品，既是对历史的见证也表达了对和平的希冀

Another unique exhibit at the Flanders Field Museum in Ypres is a collection of empty shells left behind by Chinese laborers during World War I. Each shell is about 20 centimeters high and has either poetic inscriptions or engravings of traditional Chinese elements. This shows that some of the Chinese workers in the battlefields of Europe were educated and cultured. The shells were transformed by their sensitive hearts and dexterous hands into charming works of art, which both bear witness to history and express the hope for peace

第三章 日益密切的交往

Chapter 3: Increasingly Close Contacts

近代中国留比教育

由于历史与地缘的关系，比利时教育常常被附属于法国教育，在世界教育史上易被忽视。实际上，比利时不仅很早就开始实行义务教育（6岁至14岁），而且拥有历史悠久、体系完善、布局合理的高等教育。19世纪初，比利时所属的尼德兰王国的国王威廉一世（英语为 William I，法语为 Guillaume I）为开展扫盲运动，初步建立了初等至高等教育体系，至1930年比利时全国教育普及率已高达96%。比利时的国土面积一定程度上限制了其教育规模的发展，使其在某些大型技术开发领域较为薄弱。但比利时的教育整体较发达，且教学方向上理论与实践并重，学费较其他欧洲国家略低，十分符合当时中国亟待培养新式人才的需求。

清末中比之间交往愈发频繁，1887年张之洞在汉阳铁厂创办初期经由盛宣怀推荐聘请了比利时矿业专家白乃富（Emile Braive），后升任铁厂总管。白乃富向

Studying Overseas in Belgium and Modern Chinese Education

Due to its history and geography, Belgian education has often been subordinated to French education and thus easily overlooked in the history of education worldwide. In fact, Belgium has a long history of compulsory education (from 6 to 14 years old) and a well-established and well-organized higher education system. In the early 19th century, King William I of the Kingdom of the Netherlands, which consisted of Belgium, preliminarily established a primary to higher education system in order to launch a literacy campaign. By 1930, Belgium's national literacy rate had reached 96%. The size of the country limited the development of education to a certain extent, and it was weak in certain technological development areas. But its education was the more developed, which educational approach focused on both theoretical and practical knowledge-building, and tuition fees were slightly lower than those of other European countries. This was very much in line with the urgent need to train new talents in China at

克革列钢铁厂是一家比利时钢铁制造公司，总部位于列日省瑟兰，由英国实业家约翰·考科里尔于1825年创建

Cockerill Steel Plant was a Belgian iron and steel manufacturing company based at Seraing, Liège Province. It was founded in 1825 by English-born industrialist John Cockerill

资料来源（Source）：http://connaitrelawallonie.wallonie.be/sites/wallonie/files/styles/large_colorbox/public/photos/1827-00-00_hauts_fourneaux_cockerill.jpg?itok=fhC8RGu4。

张之洞建议派40名中国工匠赴比利时列日省的克革列钢铁厂学炼钢铁，张之洞询问时任驻俄公使的许景澄了解实情后欣然应允。克革列厂包建过俄国的钢铁厂，该厂也正是1896年李鸿章出访比利时所参观的钢铁厂。1892年，这批最早赴比实习的中国工人抵达比利时，他们虽算不上正式的留学生，但为其后长达一个多世纪的中国学生赴比留学揭开了序幕。

近代留比教育正式开始于1903年端方上书。1903—1911年，由于国内近代化建设的需要及"实业

that time.

At the end of the Qing dynasty, the interaction between China and Belgium became more and more frequent. In 1887, through the recommendation of Sheng Xuanhuai, Zhang Zhidong hired a Belgian mining expert, Emile Braive, who was later promoted to be the general manager of the Hanyang Ironworks. Braive suggested that Zhang Zhidong send 40 Chinese craftsmen to learn steel making at the Cockerill Steel Plant in Liège, Belgium. After consulting with Xu Jingcheng, then Minister to Russia, Zhang Zhidong agreed. Cockerill Steel Plant had built a steel plant in Russia, and this was also the steel plant that visited by Li Hongzhang during his visit to Belgium in 1896. In 1892, the first Chinese workers to go to Belgium for internship arrived in Belgium. Although they were not official students studying abroad, they opened the door to a century-long history of Chinese students studying in Belgium.

The phenomenon of Chinese students studying in Belgium in modern era officially began in 1903 with the petition of Duan Fang. From 1903 to 1911, the first wave of studying abroad emerged due to the need for domestic modernization and the rise of the idea of "industry for national salvation," and gradually declined in the turbulent times at the beginning of the Republic period, and basically came to a standstill during the First World War. The Second wave occurred from 1919 to 1937, driven by the "May Fourth," "Work-Study" and "Return Reparation; Support Education" movements. It again declined during the second Sino-Japanese War and the Second World War and never recovered.

In 1903, Duan Fang, acting Viceroy of Hu-Guang at that time, submitted a petition to the Qing court to send Chinese students to study in Belgium. In the *Petition to Send Students to Study in Belgium*, he pointed out that:

The country of Belgium is located in the western part

托忒克·端方（1861—1911），满洲正白旗人，清末大臣，金石学家，收藏家，中国新式教育的创始人之一。曾任代理湖广总督、两江总督、直隶总督、北洋大臣。在代任两江总督期间，在南京鼓楼创办了暨南学堂。在任湖北、湖南巡抚期间，命令各道、府开办师范学院。我国最早的几个官办公共图书馆，如江南图书馆、湖北省图书馆、湖南图书馆、京师图书馆等馆的创立，他出力甚多。镇压保路运动中被起义新军杀害[1]

Duan Fang (1861-1911) was an official of the late Qing dynasty. A scholar and a collector, he was one of the founders of modern Chinese education[1]

救国"思潮的兴起出现第一次留学高潮，至民初时局动荡逐渐式微，一战期间基本陷入停滞状态。受"五四""勤工俭学""退庚兴学"运动的推动，留学比利时于1919—1937年出现第二次高潮，在抗日战争及二战的冲击下再次转颓，难以恢复。

1903年时任代理湖广总督的端方上疏清廷，请派学生赴比游学。在《奏派学生前赴比国游学折》中他指出：

比利时国在欧洲西部，其教育、工业、技术、制造、矿业，各有专修学校，他如商业则有高等专门学校，农业则有高等农会，矿业及其余工业又有实业工所。故其工艺，则机械最精；矿产则煤铁最富。其铁路通法国巴黎，长六千余里；路矿之学，尤为他国所推许……

比国实业较精，学费较省，诚能多派学生前往肄习。他日学成而归，上足以备任用，下足以裕资生，实于大局不无裨益。[2]

端方为官期间派遣多批留比生，大力推动官费生留比事业的发展，1904年之后兴起的留比热潮端方功不可没。意外的是，端方本希望为清政府培养更多可用之才，不想他从湖北派去的留学生后来大都加入同盟会，参加了辛亥革命。1905年年初留比进步学生邀请孙中

of Europe. It has specialized schools for education, industry, technology, manufacturing, and mining. There are advanced schools for commerce and associations for agriculture, mining, and other industrial sectors. Belgium's technology is the best in sophisticated machinery; its natural resources are rich in coal and iron. Its railroads are more than 6,000 li long, connected to Paris, France. Belgium's research in mining and railway is especially appreciated by other countries ...

While Belgium's industry is more advanced than other countries, its schools' tuition fees are less expensive. So we can send more students to study there. In the future, when they return from their studies, they will be ready to serve our country and to educate more students. This will be beneficial to the overall situation.[2]

During his tenure as a government official, Duan Fang sent many groups of students to study in Belgium and actively promoted these trips to be funded by the government. He deserved the credit for making possible the waves of Chinese students studying in Belgium after 1904. Unexpectedly, Duan Fang hoped to train more talents for the Qing government, but most of the foreign students he sent from Hubei later joined the Tung Meng Hui (the Chinese Revolutionary League) and participated in the 1911 Revolution. In early 1905, the progressive Chinese students studying in Belgium invited Dr. Sun Yat-sen (Sun Zhongshan) to visit Belgium and raised 3,000 francs for his travel expenses. Sun stayed at a student's home in Brussels for three days and talked with Shi Qing, He Zhicai, Hu Bingke and other students about the domestic political situation and revolutionary strategies. More than thirty students took the oath to join the Tung Meng Hui, and Brussels later became the headquarter of the European branch of the organization. What had taken place in Belgium set the precedent for Sun Yat-sen's formal establishment of

孙中山（1866—1925）
Sun Yat-sen

前排左起：魏宸组、孙中山、胡秉柯。史青（1886—？）、胡秉柯（1882—1914）、魏宸组（1885—1942）皆为湖北进步青年，1903年被公费派赴比留学，1905年加入欧洲中国同盟会，成为首批骨干成员，并负责欧洲支部执行小组工作。中华民国成立后三人均在南京临时政府任要职

Front row from left: Wei Chenzu, Sun Yat-sen, Hu Bingke

以上图片来源（Source）：孙中山故居纪念馆网站，http://www.sunyat-sen.org。

山访比，并为其筹措 3000 法郎的路费。孙中山住在布鲁塞尔一位学生家中三天，与史青、贺之才、胡秉柯等留比生大谈国内政局与革命方略，一拍即合，留比生前后共有 30 多位学生宣誓加入同盟会，布鲁塞尔后来也成为同盟会欧洲支部的所在地。以留比生为核心的欧洲同盟会为 1905 年 8 月孙中山在日本东京正式成立中国同盟会开启先声。

清末西洋留学生以官费为主，截至 1911 年，官费留欧学生约 1000 人，留比学生人数仅次于留英，与法、德相当 。[3] 他们中的近八成学习路、矿、钢铁等工科，少数习政法、商科 。[4] 晚清的路矿人才多出自比国，留比人数仅次于留日人数。从专业上看，多为机电、土木工程、矿冶等专业。出资派遣他们的四川、云南、湖南、湖北、江苏等省，也是基于本省铁路、矿产的发展需要。

the Tung Meng Hui in Tokyo, Japan in August 1905.

In the late Qing dynasty, students studying abroad were mainly supported by government. By 1911, there were more than 1,000 government-funded students studying in Europe. The number of students studying in Belgium was second only to that in Great Britain and comparable to France and Germany.[3] Nearly 80% of the students in Belgium studied engineering subjects such as railways, mines, iron and steel, while others studied politics, law and commerce.[4] Most of the railway and mining talents in the late Qing dynasty studied in Belgium. The provinces, such as Sichuan, Yunnan, Hunan, Hubei and Jiangsu, that financed their studies, were based on the development needs of railroads and minerals in these regions. These students mostly obtained the engineer title in Belgium and entered various railway departments after returning to China. For example, the father of the famous writer Han Suyin (who

李石曾（1881—1973），民国时期著名教育家，故宫博物院创办人之一，与张静江、蔡元培、吴稚晖并称为"国民党四大元老"。1902 年随驻法公使孙宝琦赴法国留学，1906 年经张静江介绍加入同盟会巴黎分会。1920 年在北京创办中法大学，任校董，同年得到孙中山和广州政府支持在法国建立里昂中法大学。1973 年 9 月病逝于台湾[5]

Li Shizeng (1881-1973), a famous educator in the Republic of China, one of the founders of the National Palace Museum[5]

这批留学生在比利时多获得工程师称号，回国后进入铁路各部门。如著名作家韩素音（本身也是留比生），在她的自传小说里提到她的父亲是四川都督锡良派往比国的首批学生，学成后回国在铁路部门工作。归国留比生一般进入到利用比利时资金和技术修建的陇海、京汉铁路上工作。由于他们大多为一线技术骨干，而非专家学者，鲜有著述存世，所以逐渐湮没于历史长河，较少为学者所关注。

民国期间留比教育分为三个阶段，第一阶段由 1912 年至一战结束，第二阶段由 1919 年至 1927 年南京国民政府成立，第三阶段由 1928 年至二战结束。民国初年政权更迭频繁，社会动荡，政府财力较清末更是左支右绌，再加上北洋政府遏制革命派留学生，导致这一时期官费生人数渐次萎缩，自费生人数开始增长。1914 年一战爆发，比利时在战争初期就被德军占领，国内战火频仍，满目疮痍，校舍被毁，学费难酬，交通阻绝，留比生们或冒险回国，或转学法、英，少数滞留本地，学业难以为继。但随着战争结束，由于比利时自身教育积淀深厚，政府重视教育恢复工作，加上国际多方援助，比利时教育很快复兴，大学也陆续复课。

was also a student in Belgium herself), mentioned in her autobiographical novel, was one of the first students sent to Belgium by Xiliang, the governor of Sichuan. He returned to work in the railroad sector after completing his studies. The students who returned from Belgium generally worked on the Longhai (Lianyungang-Lanzhou) and Beijing-Hankou railroads, which were built with Belgian funds and technology. Since most of them were front-line technicians rather than experts and scholars, they have not received much scholarly attention.

There were three phases of Chinese students studying in Belgium during the Republican period: the first phases from 1912 to the end of World War I, the second phases from 1919 to 1927 when the Nanjing National Government was established, and the third phases from 1928 to the end of World War II. In the early years of the Republic of China, there were frequent regime changes and social unrest, and the government's financial resources were even more limited than those of the late Qing dynasty. Due to limited financial support and the Beiyang government's hampering of revolutionary students, the number of government-funded students gradually shrank during this period, and that of self-funded students began to increase. When World War I broke out in 1914, Belgium was occupied by the Germans at the beginning of the war. The students in Belgium either ventured back to China or transferred to France or England. After the war ended, education in Belgium soon recovered and universities resumed classes one after another.

In 1920s, there was a significant decrease in the number of government-funded students studying in Belgium. In 1919, when the May Fourth Movement was in full swing in China, a large number of young people of progressive ideas and modest backgrounds studied in Europe at their own expense and started a wave of work-study movement. The earliest "work-study movement" can be traced back to the "Association for Students Studying in France" established

耶洛（Jules Hiernaux，1881—1944），沙洛瓦劳动大学校长，与中方教育界人士合办中比大学，接收了大量勤工俭学生

Jules Hiernaux (1881-1944), president of the University of Charleroi

20 世纪 20 年代官费留比生大幅减少，1919 年正值国内五四运动如火如荼开展，大批思想进步出身寒微的有志青年自费留学欧洲，掀起一股勤工俭学的风潮。"勤工俭学运动"最早可追溯到 1912 年李石曾等建立的"留法学生会"，其宗旨为"勤于作工，俭以求学，以进劳动者之智识"，该会得到蔡元培大力支持。由于法比临近，语言相通，也有部分学生被介绍到比利时留学（1920 年前后介绍 150 余人留比）。[6] 旅欧学潮兴起后各地纷纷建立"俭学会"，组织者在当地开办各类法语预备班，为学生留法留比做准备，后来在沙洛瓦劳动大学留学的聂荣臻即是重庆留法勤工俭学预备学校的学生。

20 世纪 20 年代很多俭学生留法受挫转而留比，且都选择了价格低廉工科发达的沙洛瓦劳动大学。勤工俭学运动引起了欧洲的关注，国内同时开展"退庚兴学"运动，[7] 在争取赔款的过程中，1921 年建立里昂中法大学，其后沙洛瓦劳动大学校长耶洛（Jules Hiernaux）与中方教育界人士合办中比大学，接收了大量勤工俭学生。学生学费生活费除做工赚取外，还可求助于公教。

by Li Shizeng and others in 1912 with the aim of "working diligently to learn on a work-study basis in order to improve the one's knowledge." The association was strongly supported by Cai Yuanpei. Due to the close proximity and the common language between France and Belgium, some students were introduced to Belgium to study (more than 150 students around 1920).[6] After the rise of the number of Chinese students studying in Europe, Work-Study Societies were established everywhere. The organizers set up various French preparatory classes locally to prepare students for studying in France. Nie Rongzhen, who later studied at the University of Charleroi, was a student of French work-study preparatory school in Chongqing.

In the 1920s, many work-study students went to Belgium and enrolled in the University of Charleroi, which was known for an advanced engineering program and low tuitions. The work-study movement attracted much attention in Europe. At the same time in China, the "Use the Boxer Indemnities for Education" campaign was launched.[7] In the process of fighting for indemnity, the Lyon Sino-French University was established in 1921. Jules Hiernaux, the president of the University of Charleroi, founded the Sino-Belgian University in cooperation with Chinese educators, which accepted a large number of work-study students.

Belgium has four world-renowned comprehensive higher education institutions: Katholieke Universiteit Leuven, Université libre de Bruxelles, Université de Liège and Université de Gand. These four universities were also where the early publicly funded Chinese students concentrated in Belgium. Other work-study students attended the University of Charleroi, where tuition fees were lower.

Father Vincent Lebbe, who was a priest in Tianjin, was the advising priest for Chinese Catholic students (mainly work-study students) in Belgium from 1920 to 1927. He was very concerned about the study and daily life of the Chinese

蔡元培（1868—1940），民国时期革命家、教育家、政治家。民主进步人士，中华民国首任教育总长，1916—1927 年任北京大学校长，革新北大开"学术"与"自由"之风。1920—1930 年，蔡元培同时兼任中法大学校长。1928—1940 年专任中央研究院院长，1933 年，蔡元培倡议创建国立中央博物院，并兼任第一届理事会代理事长。1940 年 3 月 5 日病逝于香港[8]

Cai Yuanpei (1868-1940) was a revolutionary, educator and politician in the Republic of China. He was the president of Beijing University from 1916 to 1927[8]

比利时有四所世界著名的综合性高等学府：天主教鲁汶大学（Katholieke Universiteit Leuven）、布鲁塞尔自由大学（Université libre de Bruxelles）、国立列日大学（Université de Liège）和根特大学（Université de Gand）。这四所大学也是早期中国公费留比生的集中地。其他勤工俭学的留比生多就读于学费较低的沙洛瓦劳动大学（Université du Travail à Charleroi）。

曾在天津担任司铎的神父雷鸣远（Vincent Lebbe）于 1920—1927 年在比利时担任中国天主教学生（以勤工俭学生为主）的辅导司铎，他十分关心中国学生的学

students. He often gave lectures, sold handicrafts, etc. to raise money for the students, guided them to set up the Chinese Catholic Youth Association, and organized various activities for the students. He got along very well with them as if they were family members. Some students who had received his help still spent time with him when Lebbe was confined to bed by sickness in his later years.[9] In the 1920s, there were about 460 students studying in Belgium,[10] mainly at the University of Charleroi and University of Leuven. Although engineering students were still the mainstream, the number of students studying humanities increased steadily. The Chinese students' majors were more diversified than in the late Qing dynasty.

20 世纪 20 年代的沙洛瓦劳动大学
University of Charleroi in the 1920s

沙洛瓦劳动大学
University of Charleroi
资料来源（Source）：https://upload.wikimedia.org/wikipedia/commons/b/bc/Charleroi_-_Universit%C3%A9_du_Travail_-_boulevard_Roulier_01.jpg。

习与生活，常常到各处演讲，售卖工艺品等为学生筹款，指导他们成立留欧中国公教青年会，组织学生开展各种活动，与学生相处得如同亲人一般，直至雷鸣远晚年卧病在床，依然有他帮助过的留比生陪在身边。[9] 20 世纪20 年代留比学生约 460 人，[10] 主要集中在沙洛瓦劳动大学和天主教鲁汶大学，虽然工科学生依然占主流，但学文人数有所增加，专业较清末更多元化。

1927 年南京国民政府成立，国内政局趋于稳定，政府出台相关政策鼓励留学。此时庚子赔款也有了新的进展，同年年底中比庚款委员会成立。这一时期庚款成为公费生主要经济来源，自费生也大多申请了庚款补助。据统计，1929—1938 年，受资助的中国留比生人数约150 人。[11] 留学事业延续 20 年代的蓬勃发展，学生所学专业更加百花齐放，特别在艺术领域涌现了一批人才，如女高音歌唱家郎毓秀、雕塑家张充仁、画家吴作人等。全面抗战开始后，南京政府限制留学，留比生原籍地区陆续沦陷，国内经济来源断绝，无力负担学业。1939年二战爆发后留比生更是大批离开比利时，或绕道回国或退至法国，鲜有继续完成学业者。

自 1903 年以来，约 40 年的留比教育成功培养了一大批杰出人才，为中国的近代化、现代化建设以及文学艺术等领域的发展做出了卓越的贡献。留比生是中比两国友好交往的桥梁，也是中比友谊的象征，他们为中国留学史、中比关系史画上了浓墨重彩的一笔。

In 1927, when the Nanjing national government was established and the domestic political situation became more stable, the Chinese government introduced relevant policies to encourage studying abroad. With the establishment of the Sino-Belgian Boxer Indemnity Committee later that same year, the Boxer Indemnity scholarship became the main financial source for publicly funded students, and most of the self-funded students also applied for Boxer Indemnity subsidies. According to statistics, between 1929 and 1938, no more than 150 Chinese students were sponsored to study in Belgium[11]. The study abroad program continued to flourish just as in the 1920s, and the students' fields of study blossomed, especially in the field of art, where a number of talents emerged, such as soprano Lang Yuxiu, sculptor Zhang Chongren, and painter Wu Zuoren. After the breakout of Second Sino-Japanese War in full scale, the Nanjing government prohibited students from studying overseas. With their hometowns consecutively falling into Japanese occupation, Chinese students in Belgium lost their financial support from home and most were unable to continue their studies. After the outbreak of World War II in 1939, a large number of students left Belgium and either returned home or retreated to France, and few of them continued their studies.

The forty years of education in Belgium since 1903 had successfully cultivated a large number of outstanding talents who made remarkable contributions to the development of China's modernization as well as literature and art. The students are the bridge of friendly exchanges between China and Belgium and the symbol of Sino-Belgian friendship, and they have painted a colorful picture for the history of Chinese studying abroad and Sino-Belgian relations.

雷鸣远（1877—1940），天主教遣使会神父

Father Vincent Lebbe (1877-1940)

曾在比利时求学的中国名人

1. 开国元帅聂荣臻

聂荣臻（1899—1992），中华人民共和国开国元帅，中国人民解放军创建人之一。1919年赴法勤工俭学，并积极投身旅法学生运动。1921—1923年，聂荣臻怀着"实业救国"的理想，到比利时沙洛瓦劳动大学化学系求学。1922年8月，聂荣臻加入旅欧中国少年共产党（后称中国社会主义青年团旅欧支部），次年初加入中国共产党。1924年到苏联学习，1925年回国。在国外度过的5年多时间里，聂荣臻的世界观发生了根本转变，由"实业救国论"者转变为以天下为己任的社会革命论者，并成为一位职业革命家。

1927年，先后参加南昌起义，领导广州起义，然后在上海、天津、香港等地坚持秘密斗争。1931年前往江西中央革命根据地。1934年率红一军团参加长征。抗日战争时期，先后任八路军第115师副师长、政治委员。与林彪共同指挥了平型关战役，取得全国抗战以来

聂荣臻留学期间与同学合影，左二为聂荣臻
Nie Rongzhen (the second from the left) with his classmates during his study abroad

Famous Chinese Who Have Studied in Belgium

1. Founding Marshal Nie Rongzhen

Nie Rongzhen (1899-1992) was a founding marshal of the People's Republic of China and one of the founders of the Chinese People's Liberation Army. In 1919, he went to France to work and study, and actively participated in the student movement in France. From 1921 to 1923, with the ideal of "saving the country through industry," Nie Rongzhen went to Belgium to study in the chemistry department of the University of Charleroi. In August 1922, Nie joined the Chinese Young Communist Party in Europe (later called the European branch of the Chinese Socialist Youth League) and joined the Chinese Communist Party at the beginning of the following year. He went to Soviet Union for study in 1924 and returned in 1925. During the period of more than five years he spent abroad, Nie's worldview underwent a fundamental transformation from that of an "industrialist" to a social revolutionary and he later became a professional revolutionary.

In 1927, he participated in the Nanchang Uprising and led the Guangzhou Uprising, then persisted in the secret struggle against the Nationalists in various places including Shanghai, Tianjin and Hong Kong. In 1931, he went to the Central Revolutionary Base in Jiangxi, and in 1934, he led the First Red Division in the Long March. During the Second Sino-Japanese War, he served as deputy commander and political committee member of the 115th Division of the Eighth Route Army. Together with Lin Biao, he commanded his division in the Battle of Pingxingguan, which was the first major victory since the beginning of the Second Sino-Japanese War, shattering the myth that the Japanese were "invincible" and winning praise and acclaim from international public opinion for the Chinese Communist Party and the Eighth Route Army. In the Civil War between the Communists and Nationalists that followed, he took part in

大学图书馆，右二为聂荣臻
University Library, with Nie Rongzhen second from the right

美术大师吴作人
Master Artist Wu Zuoren

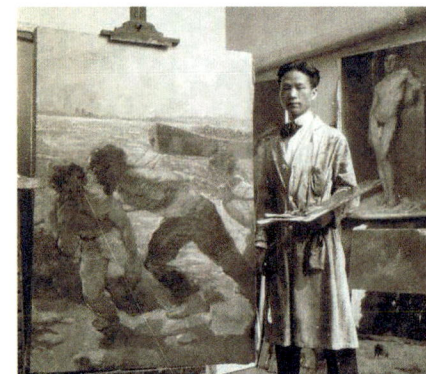

留比期间的吴作人与其作品《纤夫》
Wu Zuoren and his work *Burlak* during his study in Belgium

第一个大胜利，打破了日军"不可战胜"的神话，为中国共产党和八路军赢得了国际舆论的称赞和好评。解放战争中，参与指挥平津战役。

新中国成立后，曾任中央军委秘书长兼中国人民解放军代总参谋长、国防委员会副主席、中央军委副主席。20世纪50年代中期，聂荣臻被中共中央确定为具体领导和组织新中国科技工作的负责人，领导研制成功"两弹一星"，为中国国防科技事业和军队现代化做出了杰出贡献。1992年5月14日去世。[12]

2. 美术大师吴作人

吴作人（1908—1997），年轻时就读于多所美术院校，师从徐悲鸿先生，1930年赴欧洲深造，先入巴黎高等美术学校，后考入比利时布鲁塞尔皇家美术学院白思天院长画室学习，在学院获金奖和桂冠生荣誉。1932年与比籍女子李娜（Célina）结婚，1935年回国。

吴作人一生创作了大量美术作品，素描、油画造诣深厚，晚年专攻国画，融会中西艺术。他于20世纪50年代任中央美术学院院长，80年代当选中国美术家协会主席，1984年获法国政府"艺术与文学最高勋章"，1986年获比利时"王冠级荣誉勋章"。[13]

the command of the Peking-Tianjin Campaign.

After the founding of the People's Republic of China, he served as Secretary General of the Central Military Commission and Acting Chief of General Staff of the Chinese People's Liberation Army, Vice Chairman of the National Defense Commission and Vice Chairman of the Central Military Commission. In the mid-1950s, Nie Rongzhen was put by the CPC Central Committee in charge of leading and organizing the scientific and technological development of New China. He led the successful research and development of "two bombs and one satellite," making outstanding contributions to China's national defense science and technology and military modernization. He died on May 14, 1992.[12]

2. Art Master Wu Zuoren

Wu Zuoren (1908-1997) studied at several art schools as a young man, under the tutelage of Mr. Xu Beihong. He then went to Europe in 1930 to further his studies, first at the École des Beaux-Arts in Paris (Paris School of Fine Arts), and then at the studio of A. Bastien, the Director of the Royal Academy of Fine Arts in Brussels, where he won the Gold Medal and the honor of Laureate. He married Célina, a Belgian woman, in 1932 and returned to China in 1935.

During his lifetime, Wu Zuoren produced a large number of works of art, with profound attainments in

吴作人与妻子李娜在布鲁塞尔寓所的院子里
Wu Zuoren and his wife, Célina, in the courtyard of their Brussels apartment

drawing and oil painting. In his later years, he specialized in Chinese painting, blending Chinese and Western art. He was elected president of the Central Academy of Fine Arts in the 1950s and chairman of the Chinese Artists Association in the 1980s. He was awarded the French government's "Highest Order of Arts and Letters" in 1984 and the Belgian "Order of Merit of the Crown" in 1986.[13]

3. The biologist Tong Dizhou

Tong Dizhou (1902-1979) was a member (academician) of the Chinese Academy of Sciences, Director of the Institute of Marine Biology at the Chinese Academy of Sciences, and Vice President of the Chinese Academy of Sciences. He studied at the Université libre de Bruxelles from 1930 to 1934 and received his Ph.D. During his study in Belgium, he wrote an open letter to Chinese overseas students after the September 18th Incident, organized and established the Association of Chinese Overseas Students in Belgium, and led them to the Japanese Embassy in Belgium to protest against Japan's invasion to China.[14] Through his research on amphibians and fishes, he revealed the phenomenon of embryonic development polarity. And

生物学家童第周
The biologist Tong Dizhou

3. 生物学家童第周

童第周（1902—1979），曾任中国科学院学部委员（院士）、中国科学院海洋生物研究所所长、中国科学院副院长。1930—1934年于比利时布鲁塞尔自由大学留学，获博士学位。在留比期间，他曾在九一八事变后写了告中国留学生公开信，组织成立中国留学生留比总会，并带领留学生到日本驻比利时使馆抗议日本侵略中国。[14]童第周通过对两栖类和鱼类的研究，揭示了胚胎发育的极性现象；通过研究文昌鱼的个体发育和分类地位，在对核质关系的研究中取得重大成果；1963年首次完成鱼类的核移植研究，为20世纪七八十年代国内完成鱼类异种间克隆和成年鲫鱼体细胞克隆打下基础。

童第周在比利时做科学实验
Tong Dizhou conducting scientific experiments in Belgium

4. 雕塑名家张充仁

张充仁（1907—1998)，著名雕塑家、画家，曾因为邓小平同志和密特朗总统（François Mitterrand，1916—1996）塑像而闻名。1931年留学比利时，1935年毕业于比利时布鲁塞尔皇家美术学院，获比利时国王亚尔培金质奖。1936年回国，1977年当选为上海第五届政协委员。[15]

1934年，经陆徵祥和鲁汶大学戈赛神父（Léon Gosset）介绍，张充仁结识比利时漫画家埃尔热（Hergé，1907—1983)，他们两人建立了长达半个世纪的友谊。40年后埃尔热在给张充仁的信中写道："是你让我继马可·波罗之后认识了中国，认识了她的文明、她的思想、她的艺术和艺术家。"由张充仁提供素材，埃尔热在其名著《丁丁历险记》中增写了《蓝莲花》和《丁丁在西藏》，故事中"张"的原型就是张充仁。

through the study of individual development and taxonomic status of amphioxus, he made significant achievements in the study of cell nucleus and cytoplasm interaction. In 1963, he completed the first study of cell nucleus transplantation in fishes, which laid the foundation for the completion of interspecific cloning of fishes and somatic cell cloning of adult crucian carp in China in the 1970s and 1980s.

4. Famous sculptor Zhang Chongren

Zhang Chongren (1907-1998), a famous sculptor and painter, was famous for the statues of Comrade Deng Xiaoping and President François Mitterrand (1916-1996). He studied in Belgium in 1931 and graduated from the Royal Academy of Fine Arts in Brussels, Belgium in 1935. He won the gold medal of Belgian King Albert Award. Zhang returned to China in 1936 and was elected to a member of the Fifth Chinese People's Political Consultative Conference (CPPCC) of Shanghai in 1977.[15]

In 1934, Zhang Chongren was introduced to the Belgian cartoonist Hergé (1907-1983) by Lu Zhengxiang

雕塑名家张充仁
Famous sculptor Zhang Chongren

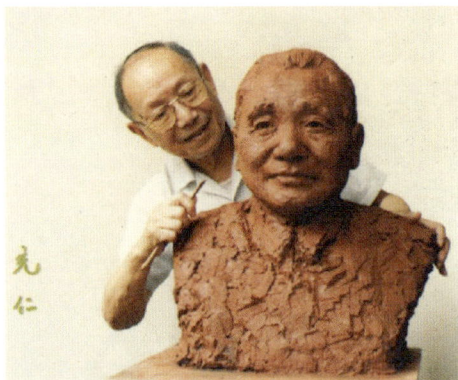

20世纪80年代张充仁为邓小平塑像
Zhang Chongren making the statue of Deng Xiaoping in 1980s

1988年张充仁为密特朗塑像
Zhang Chongren making the statue of Mitterrand in 1988

1985 年应法国国家艺术收藏馆之请，张充仁特为自己雕塑了一只手模，与毕加索、罗丹的手模，一同为该馆永久收藏，全球艺术家获此殊荣者仅此三人。

and Father Léon Gosset of the University of Leuven, and they established a friendship that lasted half a century. In a letter to Zhang Chongren 40 years later, Hergé wrote: "It was you who made me aware of China after Marco Polo, of her civilization, her ideas, her art and artists." Hergé added *The Blue Lotus* and *Tintin in Tibet* to his famous series *The Adventures of Tintin*, in which the character of "Zhang" was based on Zhang Chongren.

In 1985, at the request of the Centre National Des Arts Plastiques (CNAP), Zhang Chongren specially sculpted a hand model for himself, which, together with the hand models of Pablo Picasso and Auguste Rodin, is in the permanent collection of the museum, the only three artists in the world to receive this honor.

青年时代的埃尔热与张充仁
Hergé and Zhang Chongren in their youth

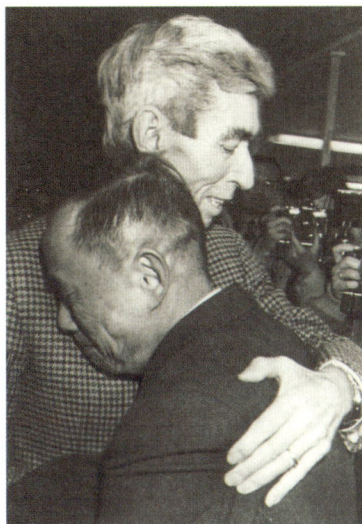

比利时媒体上关于二人重逢的报道（埃尔热与张充仁在第二次世界大战期间失去联系，直到 1981 年重逢）
Report on the reunion of the two friends in Belgian media (Hergé and Zhang Chongren lost contact during World War II until they were reunited in 1981)

张充仁自塑手模
Zhang Chongren's self-molded hand model

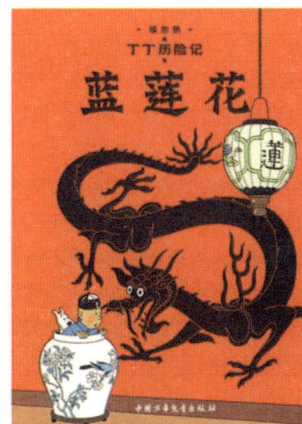

中文版《蓝莲花》封面
Cover of the Chinese version of *Blue Lotus*

中文版《丁丁在西藏》封面
Cover of the Chinese edition of *Tintin in Tibet*

表3–1 根据周棉主编《中国留学生大辞典》（南京大学出版社，1999）整理的其他留比名人

Chart3-1 Other famous Chinese who studied in Belgium - compiled in the *Dictionary of Chinese Overseas Students* (Nanjing University Press, 1999) edited by Zhou Mian

姓 名 Name	留比时间 Time While Studying in Belgium	所在学校 School/University	主要事迹 Main Achievements
英千里 Ying Qianli (1901—1969)	1913—1914	比利时北部 天主教会中学 Catholic High School in Northern Belgium	1911年于天津南开中学读书，1913年随雷鸣远赴比留学。1924年回国协助父亲英敛之筹办辅仁大学。1946年任北平教育局长、教育部社会教育司司长。1948年后赴台湾执教于辅仁大学、台湾大学等。致力哲学、逻辑学研究，精通多种语言，编写《英汉字典》等教科书，其子英若诚曾任中华人民共和国文化部副部长 In 1911, he studied at Nankai Middle School in Tianjin, and in 1913, he went to Belgium to study with Father Vincent Lebbe. In 1924, he returned to China to help his father, Ying Lianzhi, to found Fu Jen Catholic University. In 1946, he became the Director of the Bureau of Education in Peking and the Director of the Department of Social Education in the Ministry of Education. After 1948, he went to Taiwan to teach at Fu Jen Catholic University and National Taiwan University. He devoted himself to the study of philosophy and logic, was proficient in many languages, and wrote textbooks such as the *English-Chinese Dictionary*. His son, Ying Ruocheng, was vice minister of the Ministry of Cultural Affairs in the People's Republic of China
刘伯坚 Liu Bojian (1895—1935)	1920—1923	沙洛瓦劳动大学 University of Charleroi	1922年与赵世炎、周恩来等人建立"旅欧少共"，后更名为"旅欧共青团"，同年任首届中共旅比支部书记。1923年任第三届中共旅欧总支部书记 In 1922, Liu, together Zhao Shiyan and Zhou Enlai, founded the "Young Communist Party in Europe," which later changed its name to "Communist Youth League in Europe." In the same year he became the first secretary of the branch of the Communist Party of China in Belgium. In 1923, he became the third secretary of the general branch of the CPC in Europe
何长工 He Changgong (1900—1987)	1923—1924	沙洛瓦劳动大学 University of Charleroi	无产阶级革命家、军事家、教育家，1922年赴法留学加入少共和中共。1927年参加秋收起义，后促成朱毛会师。曾任抗日军政大学总校教育长、代校长，东北军政大学代校长，第三、四届全国政协常委，第五届全国政协副主席 A proletarian revolutionary, militarist and educator, he studied in France in 1922 and joined the Chinese Communist Party. In 1927, he participated in the Autumn Harvest Uprising and later facilitated the armies of Zhu De and Mao Zedong to join forces. He formerly served as Education Director and Acting President of Chinese People's Anti-Japanese Military and Political College, as well as Acting President of Northeast Military and Political College. He was a member of the Standing Committee of the Third and Fourth National Committee of the Chinese People's Political Consultative Conference (CPPCC) and Vice Chairman of the Fifth CPPCC

姓 名 Name	留比时间 Time While Studying in Belgium	所在学校 School/University	主要事迹 Main Achievements
生宝堂 Sheng Baotang (1901—1937)	？—1929	鲁汶大学 Catholic University of Leuven	1937 年 6 月任天津《益世报》总经理，8 月被日军抓捕杀害 In June 1937, he became the general manager of the Tianjin *Yishi Newspaper*. He was later arrested and murdered by the Japanese occupation authority in August
熊庆来 Xiong Qinglai (1893—1969)	1930—1934	布鲁塞尔大学 University of Brussels	1930 年任清华大学数学系主任，并创办数学研究部，是中国第一个数学研究机构。1957 年在巴黎出版关于亚纯函数论的著作，同年 6 月回国任中国科学院数学研究所函数论研究室主任。曾任第三届全国政协委员、第四届政协常委。编写多种教科书，培养了多位数学家 In 1930, he became the head of the Department of Mathematics of Qinghua University and founded the Department of Mathematical Research, the first mathematical research institution in China. In 1957, he published the book on meromorphic function in Paris. In June of the same year, he returned to China and served as the director of the Research Office of Function Theory at the Institute of Mathematics, Chinese Academy of Sciences. He was a member of the Third National Committee of the Chinese People's Political Consultative Conference (CPPCC) and a member of the Standing Committee of the Fourth CPPCC. He has written many textbooks and trained several mathematicians
韩素音 Han Suyin (1917—2012)	1935—1938	布鲁塞尔大学 医学院 School of Medicine, University of Brussels	原名周月宾，著名作家，著有《目的地重庆》、《瑰宝》（改编成好莱坞电影《生死恋》），自传体小说《伤残的树》《凋谢的花朵》等。致力于用英语、法语向全世界介绍中国，出版《毛泽东传》《周恩来的世纪》等 Formerly known as Zhou Yuebin, Han was a famous writer, author of *Destination Chongqing*, *The Jewel* (adapted into the Hollywood movie *Life is a Many-Splendored Thing*), and the autobiographical novels *The Wounded Tree* and *The Withered Flower*. She devoted herself to introducing China to the world in English and French, and has published *The Biography of Mao Zedong* and *The Century of Zhou Enlai*
郎毓秀 Lang Yuxiu (1918—2012)	1937—1941	比利时皇家 音乐学院 Royal Conservatory of Belgium	摄影家郎静山之女，"中国四大女高音"之一，音乐教育家。任首三届全国人大代表，第五、六、七届全国政协委员，四川音乐协会副主席。2001 年获首届"中国音乐金钟奖"终身荣誉勋章 She is the daughter of photographer Lang Jingshan, one of the "Four Great Sopranos of China" and a music educator. She was a deputy of the first three National People's Congresses, the member of the fifth, sixth and seventh National Committee of the Chinese People's Political Consultative Conference (CPPCC), and the vice chairman of the Sichuan Music Association. She was awarded the lifetime honorary medal of the first "China Music Golden Bell Award" in 2001

一战后中国劳工与比利时的重建

第一次世界大战是 20 世纪最重大的事件之一。虽然中国并未派兵，但以派遣劳工的形式参与了第一次世界大战，并且有相当多的中国劳工来到比利时参与了它的战后重建。第一次世界大战对中比两国的影响都远远超出了战争的范畴，在国际和国内重新塑造了这两个国家的未来。在国际上，中比两国因在当时国力弱小而备受列强欺凌。在各自国内，比利时在战后实现了普选制，通过了一些重大的社会法令，如八小时工作制、累进税、老年人义务保险等；而在中国则爆发了影响深远的"五四运动"。

第一次世界大战的爆发是欧洲列强利益冲突不可调和的产物。当工业化国家付诸武力解决矛盾时，它们能迸发出巨大的杀伤力和破坏力，使这场战争成为零和游戏。前面提及，比利时地处欧洲西部要冲，是古往今来兵家必争之地。当比利时邻近的法、德、英等大国之间的对立日益加剧并有极大可能爆发剧烈冲突的时候，比利时国内舆论却因 1830 年独立时获得列强保证成为永久中立国，而产生一种安全感和对国际紧张局势漠不关心的态度。尽管比利时曾经修筑了一些巨大的防线，如 1859 年将安特卫普变成一个坚固的要塞，1887—1892 年建成列日和那慕尔要塞，但是全国民众普遍反对加强军事建设，军队人数也较少，完全没有对即将到来的军事入侵做好准备。

然而，在 1914 年德国人计划发动的西线战役中，德国五个集团军必须跨过比利时边境，横扫比利时西部平原和东部山区，深入法国北部和东北部，迂回包围巴黎，进而摧毁整个法国。为此，德国人毫不犹豫地背信

Chinese Laborers and the Reconstruction of Belgium after World War I

The First World War was one of the most significant events of the 20th century. Although China did not send troops to the war, it participated in the First World War by sending laborers - a significant number of Chinese laborers came to Belgium to participate in its post-war reconstruction. The impact of World War I on both China and Belgium went far beyond the war, reshaping the future of both countries internationally and domestically. Internationally, both China and Belgium were bullied by the powers because of their weakness at the time. At home, Belgium achieved universal suffrage after the war and passed major social legislation, such as the eight-hour work day, progressive taxation and compulsory insurance for the elderly, while in China, the May Fourth Movement had a profound impact.

The outbreak of World War I was a product of the irreconcilable conflicting interests of the European powers. When the industrialized countries resorted to force to resolve their conflicts, they were able to burst forth with great lethality and destructive power, making the war a zero-sum game. As mentioned earlier, Belgium is located in the western part of Europe, which had been the most important strategic location in warfare throughout the ages. While Belgium's neighbors, France, Germany, Britain, and other major powers, were increasingly antagonistic towards each other and had a high potential for violent conflict, Belgian public opinion nonetheless had a sense of security and indifference to international tensions because of the permanent neutrality guaranteed by the Great Powers at its independence in 1830. Belgium had built some enormous defenses, such as turning Antwerp into a strong fortress in 1859 and the fortresses of Liège and Namur in 1887-1892. However, the nation was generally opposed to increasing

阿尔贝一世（Albert I，1875—1934，1909—1934 年在位），利奥波德一世之孙、利奥波德二世之侄。1909 年继承比利时王位。第一次世界大战期间，保持中立，拒绝德皇通过比境的最后通牒，并领导陆军进行抵抗。在整个第一次世界大战期间，阿尔贝一世与比利时人民并肩作战。战后全力投入重建工作。在一次登山事故中丧生

Albert I (1875-1934, reigned 1909-1934), grandson of Leopold I and nephew of Leopold II, succeeded to the Belgian throne in 1909

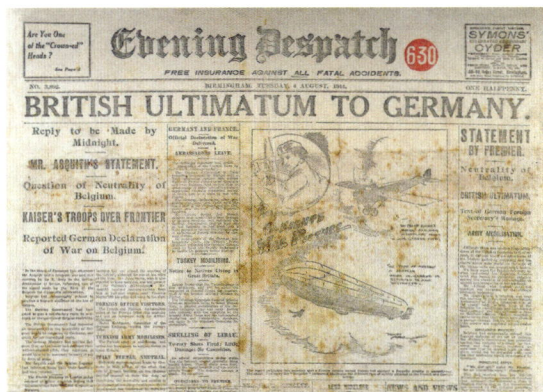

1914 年 8 月 4 日，英国向德国宣战时的《伯明翰晚报》的头版。英国向德国发出最后通牒，要求其离开比利时

The front page of the *Birmingham Evening Dispatch* on August 4, 1914, when Britain declared war on Germany. Britain issued an ultimatum to Germany, demanding its withdrawal from Belgium

一战中比利时废墟
The ruins of Belgium in World War I

弃义。比利时国王阿尔贝一世（Albert I）保持中立，拒绝了德国借道比境偷袭法国的要求，并于德军入侵后率领比利时军队采取积极防御措施。在 1914 年的英国报纸上，英国向德国发布最后通牒："如果比利时受到攻击，英国必须兑现尽全力保护比利时的诺言，这是攸关英国荣誉的生死问题。"[16] 由此，本与冲突无关的比利时沦为大国角斗的战场，各国士兵及平民数百万人丧生于此。比利时士兵死亡人数约 41000 人，占成年男性人口的 2%，整个地区毁于一旦。

对于比利时人民所遭受的苦难，中国人民给予了深切同情和无私帮助。1918 年 4 月，比利时伊丽莎白王后写信给时任民国政府外交总长陆徵祥的夫人、比利时人博斐·培德（Berthe Bovy），述说了比利时战争孤儿和寡妇的困境。陆徵祥夫妇立即捐出了 2 万比利时法郎的善款，用于帮助遭受战争重创的比利时妇女儿童。1919 年 8 月，陆徵祥率中国代表团出席巴黎和会期间，代表民国总统徐世昌个人，向正在重建的比利时捐赠了 5 万比利时法郎。阿尔贝一世国王表达了诚挚的谢意："你们的总统是最慷慨的人，比利时人民是多么幸运啊！"[17]

military construction and Belgium, had a relatively small army, and was completely unprepared for an impending military invasion.

In the planned German campaign on the Western Front in 1914, five German army groups had to cross the Belgian border, hoping to sweep across the plains of western Belgium and the mountains of the east, penetrate deep into northern and northeastern France, encircle Paris in a roundabout way, and thus destroy all of France. To do so, the Germans did not hesitate to renege on their previous guarantee of Belgium's neutrality. King Albert I of Belgium remained neutral and refused the German request to sneak into France by way of Belgium. He then led the Belgian army to take active defensive measures after the German invasion. In a British newspaper in 1914, Britain issued an ultimatum to Germany: "It is a matter of life and death for British honor that Britain must keep her promise to do all she can to protect Belgium if it is attacked."[16] As a result, Belgium, which had nothing to do with the conflict, became a battleground for great power rivalries, in which millions of soldiers and civilians from all countries lost their lives. Some 41,000 Belgian soldiers died, or 2 percent of the adult male population, and the entire region was destroyed.

The Chinese people have given deep sympathy and selfless help to the suffering of the Belgian people. In April 1918, Queen Elizabeth of Belgium wrote to Berthe Bovy, the wife of Lu Zhengxiang, then Foreign Minister of the Republic of China, about the plight of Belgian war orphans and widows. Mr. and Mrs. Lu Zhengxiang immediately donated 20,000 Belgian francs to help Belgian women and children who had been hard hit by the war. In August 1919, while attending the Paris Peace Conference with the Chinese delegation, Lu donated another 50,000 Belgian francs to Belgium, which was being rebuilt, on behalf of the President of the Republic of China, Xu Shichang. King Albert I expressed his sincere gratitude: "Your President

陆徵祥（1871—1949），中国第一代职业外交家，出生于虔诚的基督教新教家庭，毕业于广方言馆和同文馆。1892 年在驻俄使馆任翻译、参赞，驻俄期间娶一位比利时女士为妻。此后即一直在外交界服务。1911 年辛亥革命后，应总统袁世凯电命，从驻俄大使任所返国出任民国第一任外交总长，推动中国现代外交机构改革，培养了不少杰出的民国外交官，为中国这一"弱国"争取到较多利权，奠定了中国外交现代化的基础。一战爆发后，被迫签署中日"二十一条"，成为千夫所指的"卖国贼"。一战结束后，曾代表中华民国率代表团赴法国参加巴黎和会，在民众压力下最终没有签字

1926 年，依照亡妻遗愿，为洗刷签署"二十一条"的污点，陆徵祥辞去公职，在比利时布鲁日的圣安德诺修道院出家，以自己的余生忏悔罪过。抗日战争爆发后，他创办报纸，在欧洲各地发表演讲，介绍中国军民浴血奋战的情况，呼吁欧洲各国人民支持中国抗战。二战中，他利用传教的方式反抗纳粹对比利时的占领，一度还上了盖世太保的"黑名单"。最终，他看到了世界反法西斯战争的胜利，并为"在有生之年得见祖国一雪前耻"而狂喜不已。1949 年 1 月 15 日，病逝于比利时，葬于圣安德诺修道院[18]

Lu Zhengxiang (1871-1949), the first generation of Chinese diplomats, was born in a devout Protestant family. After graduating from Guang Fang Yan Guan and Tongwen Guan, Lu served as an interpreter and counsellor at the Embassy in Russia in 1892. He married a Belgian woman while in Russia. After the 1911 Revolution, he was appointed by President Yuan Shikai to return from his post as ambassador to Russia to serve as the first Foreign Minister of the Republic of China. He promoted the reform of China's modern diplomatic institutions, trained many outstanding diplomats of the Republic of China, and gained more rights for China on the world stage. These achievements laid the foundation for the modernization of Chinese diplomacy. After the outbreak of World War I, he was forced to sign the Twenty-One Demands to China by Japan and was denounced as a traitor by his countrymen. After the end of World War I, he led a delegation to France to attend the Paris Peace Conference on behalf of the Republic of China. At the end, Lu did not sign the treaty due to public pressure.
In 1926, in accordance with his late wife's wishes and in order to clear the stain of signing the Twenty-One Demands, Lu resigned from his public office and became a monk at the St. Andrew's Monastery in Bruges, Belgium, committing to spend the rest of his life repenting of his sins. After the outbreak of the Second Sino-Japanese War, he founded a newspaper and gave speeches all over Europe, introducing the bloodshed of Chinese soldiers and civilians and calling on the people of Europe to support China's war effort. During World War II, he used his missionary work to resist the Nazi occupation of Belgium and was once on the Gestapo's "blacklist." He died in Belgium on January 15, 1949, after a long illness, and was buried in St. Andrew's Monastery[18]

博斐·培德（Berthe Bovy, 1855—1926）出身比利时贵族家庭，父亲是比利时国王的侍从武官、陆军上校。旅俄期间，在沙皇宫廷舞会上结识在清朝驻俄使馆任参赞的陆徵祥。1899 年 2 月 12 日，培德女士与小自己 16 岁的陆徵祥，排除种族、家庭、年龄、宗教和来自清朝使馆的种种障碍，在俄国圣彼得堡的圣加利纳大教堂举行了天主教婚礼。婚后，培德一直追随陆徵祥在欧洲的外交界活动，利用自己的贵族身份和社交手腕为陆徵祥在欧洲外交界打开局面，助其成为著名外交家。受夫人影响，陆徵祥从虔诚的新教徒改入天主教。民国初年，培德随陆徵祥回到中国，曾给中国外交人员讲述西方外交礼仪。后来民国大总统袁世凯任命培德为总统府礼官处女礼官长，负责在总统府招待各国使节夫人。后来因不满陆徵祥受袁世凯胁迫签订"二十一条"，愤而辞职。培德夫人品德高尚，刚直好义，对陆徵祥签署"二十一条"始终耿耿于怀，不能原谅，于去世前嘱陆徵祥去修道院隐修忏悔

Berthe Bovy (1855-1926) was born into a Belgian noble family. Her father was a military attaché to the King of Belgium and a colonel in the army. On February 12, 1899, Berthe Bovy married Lu Zhengxiang, 16 years younger than Berthe Bovy, in a Catholic ceremony at St. Gallina Cathedral in St. Petersburg, Russia, despite all the obstacles of race, family, age, and religion. After the marriage, Berthe followed Lu Zhengxiang in the diplomatic circles of Europe, using her noble status and social skills to help him get into the European diplomatic circles and later became a famous diplomat. Under the influence of his wife, Lu Zhengxiang converted from a devout Protestant to a Catholic. In the early years of the Republic of China, Berthe returned to China with Lu Zhengxiang and gave lectures on Western diplomatic etiquette to Chinese diplomats. Later, Yuan Shikai, the president of the Republic of China, appointed Bovy as the head of the presidential protocol department, responsible for entertaining the wives of envoys in the presidential palace. Later, she resigned for being outraged by Lu Zhengxiang's signing of Twenty-one Demands under Yuan Shikai's coercion. Berthe, a woman of high moral character and righteousness, always held a grudge against Lu Zhengxiang for signing the Twenty-one Demands and could not forgive him. She requested him to go to a convent for penance before she died

陆徵祥
Lu Zhengxiang

1919 年 1 月陆徵祥出席巴黎和会
Lu Zhengxiang attending the Paris Peace Conference in January 1919

1899 年康有为为陆徵祥夫人培德所书对联
Couplet written by Kang Youwei for Berthe Bovy, the wife of Lu Zhengxiang in 1899

陆徵祥外交生涯所获勋章
Medals received by Lu Zhengxiang during his diplomatic career

以上照片由比利时圣安德诺修道院陆徵祥图书资料馆提供
Photos from the library of Lu Zhengxiang in St. Andrew's Monastery

徐世昌（1855—1939），天津人，清末民初著名政治人物，中华民国大总统。25岁中举人，31岁中进士。1895年辅佐袁世凯"小站练兵"，为袁世凯幕僚心腹。1889年34岁时授翰林院编修，1905年任军机大臣。袁世凯称帝时，沉默远离。1915年任北洋政府国务卿，1918年10月当选民国大总统。1922年退隐，1939年在天津去世。徐世昌国学功底深厚，一生不但著书立说，还是书法家、画家、收藏家，收藏古籍8万卷，编纂《清儒学案》《宋元学案》等30余种，有"文治总统""总统诗人"之美誉

Xu Shichang (1855-1939), a native of Tianjin, was a famous political figure in the late Qing dynasty and the early Republic of China. At the age of 25, he passed the imperial examination at the provincial level and became a successful candidate in the highest imperial examinations at 31. In 1895, he assisted Yuan Shikai in training troops at Xiaozhan and was a member of Yuan's inner circle. At age 34, in 1889, he was appointed as the editor of the Hanlin Academy and became the Minister of Military Affairs in 1905. He served as the Secretary of State of the Beiyang Government in 1915 and was elected President of the Republic of China in October 1918. He retired in 1922 and died in Tianjin in 1939. Xu Shichang, with his profound knowledge of Chinese studies, was not only a writer, but also a calligrapher, painter, and collector. He collected 80,000 volumes of ancient books and compiled more than 30 books such as *Qing Ru Xue An* (Studies of Qing Confucianism) and *Song Yuan Xue An* (Cases of Song and Yuan Studies), enjoying the reputation of "President of Cultural Governance" and "Poet President"

徐世昌在津故居今景。航鹰女士摄于 2021 年

Present view of Xu Shichang's former residence in Tianjin. Taken by Ms. Hang Ying in 2021

比利时国王阿尔贝一世与王后伊丽莎白合影

King Albert I of Belgium with Queen Elisabeth

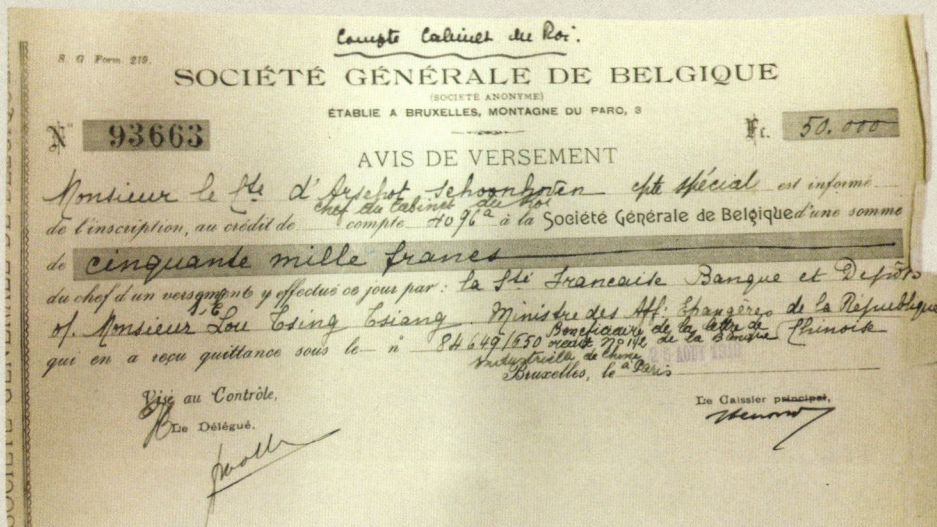

徐世昌总统的捐款支票

President Xu Shichang's donation check

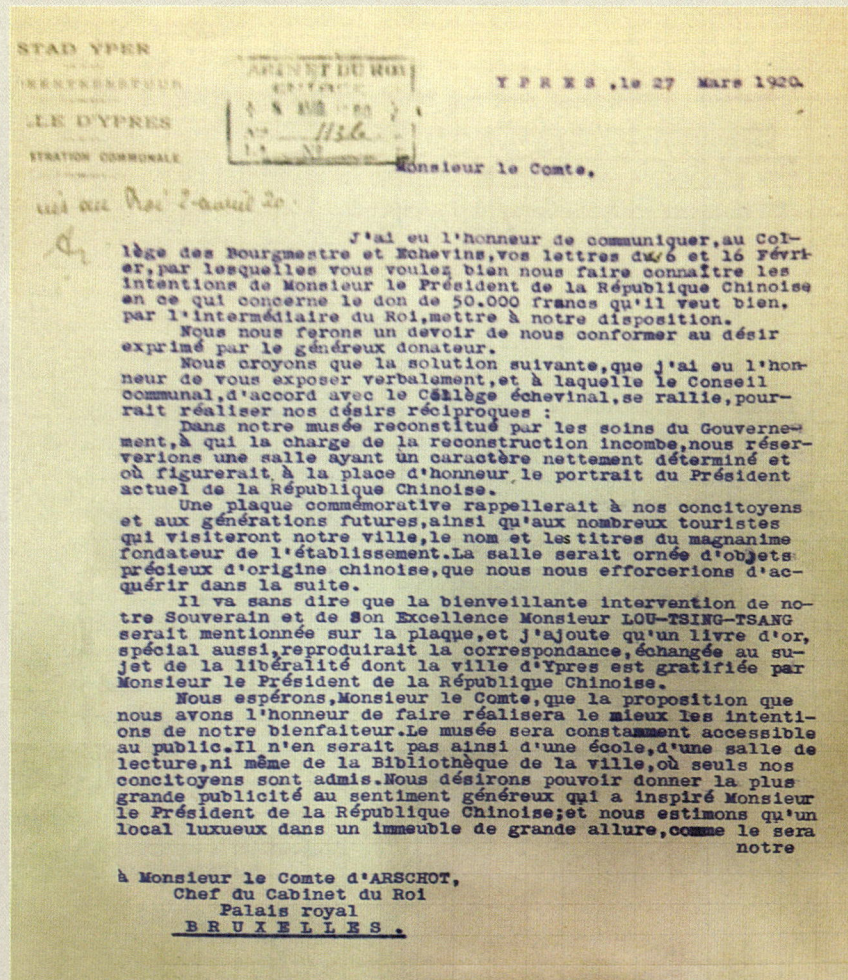

比利时王室写给徐世昌总统的感谢信

Letter of thanks from the Belgian royal family to President Xu Shichang

以上由比利时外交部档案馆提供

Provided by the Archives of the Ministry of
Foreign Affairs of Belgium

对一战后比利时重建做出更大贡献的，则是中国劳工。1914 年大战爆发后，北洋政府即宣布中立。但也有国内政治家鼓动袁世凯参战，如果押宝押在胜利一方的话，不但可以提高中国的国际地位，还可借机收回一部分中国以前被列强攫取的特权和领土，特别是收回被日本强取的山东。起初，在日本的反对下，英、法、俄等盟国也并不希望中国加入战斗并获得平等地位。但随着战争机器对士兵和劳动力的不断绞杀，法国、英国和俄国政府都不得不与中国政府签订输入劳工的长期合同。法国政府和英国政府在 1916—1920 年雇用了 14 万或 15 万中国劳工，俄国则在 1915—1917 年雇用了 5 万中国劳工。首批受雇于法国的中国劳工团队在 1916 年 8 月来到法国，而中国劳工的第一个英国派遣队则在被派往法国之后于 1917 年 4 月在普利茅斯（Plymouth）登陆，其后在英国当局管理下的中国劳工达到了 9.5 万人，在法国管理下的有 4.4 万人。这些中国劳工大部分都来自山东农村的贫困家庭。[19]

中国工人的报酬，按照当时欧洲标准来说，相当低廉——大约只有欧洲人的 1/2。不过，对贫苦的中国人来说，欧洲的工资约合国内工资的 4 倍，差强人意。合同为 3 到 5 年，每天工作 8 小时（不包括午餐休息以及其他间歇），每周可休息半天（或每两周休息一天），节假日（包括中国新年）休息，另外，每个月还会有 10 墨西哥元（5.5 美元）付给劳工在中国最亲近的亲属。[20] 中国劳工去往欧洲的旅途充满危险，极易成为德国潜艇的目标。1917 年 2 月，法国"阿索斯"号轮船在地中海遭到了鱼雷的攻击，造成船上 540 名中国劳工遇难。[21] 此事也成为北洋政府向德国和奥匈帝国宣战的直接理

is the most generous man! How lucky the Belgian people are!"[17]

An even greater contribution to the reconstruction of Belgium after World War I was made by Chinese laborers. After the outbreak of the Great War in 1914, the Beiyang government declared its neutrality. But there were also domestic politicians who encouraged Yuan Shikai to enter the war. If China ended up betting on the winning side, it would not only improve China's international status, but also provide the opportunity to recover some of the privileges and territories that previously seized by the powers, especially Shandong, which had been occupied by Japan. At first, over Japan's objections, the British, French, Russian and other allies did not want China to join the war and gain equal status either. But as the war machine continued to consume soldiers and laborers, the French, British, and Russian governments were forced to enter into long-term contracts with the Chinese government for the importation of labor. The French and British governments hired 140,000 or 150,000 Chinese laborers between 1916 and 1920, and Russia hired 50,000 Chinese laborers between 1915 and 1917. The first group of Chinese laborers employed by France arrived in August 1916, while the first dispatch of Chinese laborers to Great Britain landed in Plymouth in April 1917, bringing the number of Chinese laborers to 95,000 under British authority and 44,000 under French authority. Most of these Chinese laborers came from poor families in rural Shandong.[19]

Chinese workers were paid, by European standards at the time, quite cheaply - about 1/2 of what Europeans were paid. However, the compensation for going all the way to Europe was about 4 times the domestic wage for poor Chinese. The contract lasted about three to five years, with an eight-hour workday (not including lunch breaks and other breaks), a half-day break each week (or one day off every two weeks), holidays (including Chinese New

一战中的中国劳工
A Chinese laborer during World War I
图片来源（Source）：©Héritiers de René Matton, Proven。

协约国士兵为中国劳工点烟

Allied soldiers lit cigarettes for Chinese laborers

由。见《中华民国政府对德奥两国宣战布告》（1917年8月14日）：

我中华民国政府，前以德国施行潜水艇计划，违背国际公法，危害中立国人民生命财产，曾于本年二月九日向德政府提出抗议，并声明万一抗议无效，不得已将与德国断绝外交关系等语。不意抗议之后，其潜水艇计划曾不少变，中立国之船只，交战国之商船，横被轰毁，日增其数。我国人民之被害者，亦复甚众。……中外共愤，询谋佥同，遂于三月十四日向德政府宣告断绝外交关系。……乃自绝交以后，历时五月，潜艇之攻击如故，非特德国而已，即与德国取同一政策之奥国，亦始终未改其度。既背公法，复伤害吾人民，我政府责善之深心，至是实已绝望。爰自中华民国六年八月十四日上午十时起，对德国、奥国宣告立于战争地位……[22]

战场上运送炮弹的中国劳工

Chinese laborers carrying artillery shells on the battlefield

以上资料来源（Source）：http://new.qq.com/omn/20210825/。

Year), and a monthly payment of 10 Mexican dollars (5.50 U.S. dollars) to the laborer's closest relatives in China.[20] The journey of Chinese laborers to Europe was full of danger and the ships they boarded could be easily targeted by German submarines. In February 1917, the French ship *Athos* was torpedoed in the Mediterranean Sea, killing 540 Chinese laborers on board.[21] This incident also became the direct reason for the Beiyang government to declare war on Germany and Austria-Hungary. As stated in "Declaration of War against Germany and Austria by the Government of the Republic of China" (August 14, 1917):

On the 9th day of the 2nd month of this year (February 9, 1917) the Government of the Republic addressed a protest to the German Government against the policy of submarine warfare inaugurated by Germany, which was considered by this Government as contrary to International Law, and imperiled neutral lives and property, and declared therein that in case the protest should be ineffectual this Government would be constrained, much to its regret, to sever diplomatic relations with Germany. Contrary to our expectations, however, no modification was made in Germany's submarine policy after the lodging of our protest. On the contrary, the number of neutral vessels and belligerent merchantmen destroyed in an arbitrary and illegal manner was daily increasing and the lives of our citizens lost were numerous. … Both here, as well as in the friendly states, the cause of indignation was the same, and among the people of this country there could be found no difference of opinion. This government, therefore, notified the German Government on the 14th day of the 3rd month of the severance of diplomatic relations. … Nevertheless, during the five months following the severance of diplomatic relations, the submarine attacks have continued exactly as before.

抵达欧洲后，劳工们有的被送往冶金、化工和兵工厂等企业工作，有的则前往战场服务。尽管合同上规定，中国劳工原则上不应该参与"军事活动"，但北洋政府对德宣战后，中国劳工几乎全部被送往佛兰德斯和伊泽尔河（Yser）前线。在那里，他们主要负责挖战壕、运送伤员、补给等体力劳动，虽然没有直接参与战争，但他们的工作依然繁重且极具危险性。频繁的炮火轰炸后，常常有很多劳工牺牲。战争结束后，军队撤离了，留下的中国劳工帮助当地人继续清理战场的废墟，搬运安葬尸体，修建桥梁、公路、铁路。战后工作的危险程度一点不亚于战时，他们在搬运埋在土地里未爆炸的弹药时稍有疏忽便可能伤亡，战场上腐烂的尸体滋生的细菌也可能导致他们染上瘟疫。

欧洲战场上的中国劳工是一群吃苦耐劳、技术过硬、聪明睿智的人。一战结束几十年后，比利时人仍会这样描述："他们是最顽强的工人，有着高超的技能和智慧。""他们永远值得我们怀念、感激和尊重，正是他们帮助我们重建家园。"[23]

战场上的中国劳工。照片收藏于比利时弗兰德斯战地博物馆
Chinese laborers on the battlefield. Collection of the Flanders Fields Museum

It is Germany alone, but Austria-Hungary as well, which has adopted and pursued this policy without abatement. Not only has International Law been thereby violated, but also our part of bringing about a better state is now shattered. Therefore, it is hereby declared, that a state of war exists between China on the one hand and Germany and Austria-Hungary on the other commencing from ten o'clock of this, the 14th day of the 8th month of the 6th year of the Republic of China ... [22]

Upon arrival in Europe, the laborers were sent to work in metallurgical, chemical, and arsenal enterprises, while others served on the battlefield. Although the contracts stipulated that Chinese laborers should be in principle not to participate in "military activities," after the Beiyang government declared war on Germany, almost all Chinese laborers were sent to the Flanders and Yser fronts. There, they were mainly responsible for manual labor such as digging trenches, transporting the wounded, and supplying. Although they were not directly involved in the war, their work was still laborious and extremely dangerous. Frequent artillery bombardments often resulted in the killing of many laborers. After the war, the army withdrew and the Chinese laborers stayed to help the locals continue to clear the ruins of the battlefield, carry and bury bodies, and build bridges, roads and railroads. The post-war work was no less dangerous than during the war, as they could be killed or injured if they were negligent in carrying unexploded ammunition buried in the ground. They could be infected with the plague due to bacteria from the decaying bodies on the battlefield.

The Chinese laborers on the battlefields of Europe were a hard-working, skilled, smart group of men. Decades after the end of World War I, Belgians would still describe them this way: "They were the most tenacious workers, with

战争间歇休息的中国劳工。照片收藏于比利时弗兰德斯战地博物馆
Chinese laborers taking a break during the war. Collection of the Flanders Fields Museum

在欧洲，佛兰德斯红罂粟被看成"缅怀之花"。第一次世界大战中，比利时的佛兰德斯大地成了西线主战场，成百万士兵（包括下级军官）倒在这里。1915年10月8日，加拿大医生约翰·麦克雷（John McCrae）在目睹了战友的死亡后，写下诗歌《在佛兰德斯战场》用于纪念为保卫祖国而献身的战士，他的诗歌蕴含着作者反对战争和向往和平的精神和理念

In Europe, the Flanders red poppy is seen as the "flower of remembrance." Flanders became the main battleground on the Western Front, where millions of soldiers (including junior officers) perished. On October 8, 1915, after witnessing the deaths of his comrades, Canadian doctor John McCrae wrote the poem *In Flanders Fields* to honor the memory of those who died defending their country. His poem embodies the author's spirit and philosophy of opposing war and yearning for peace

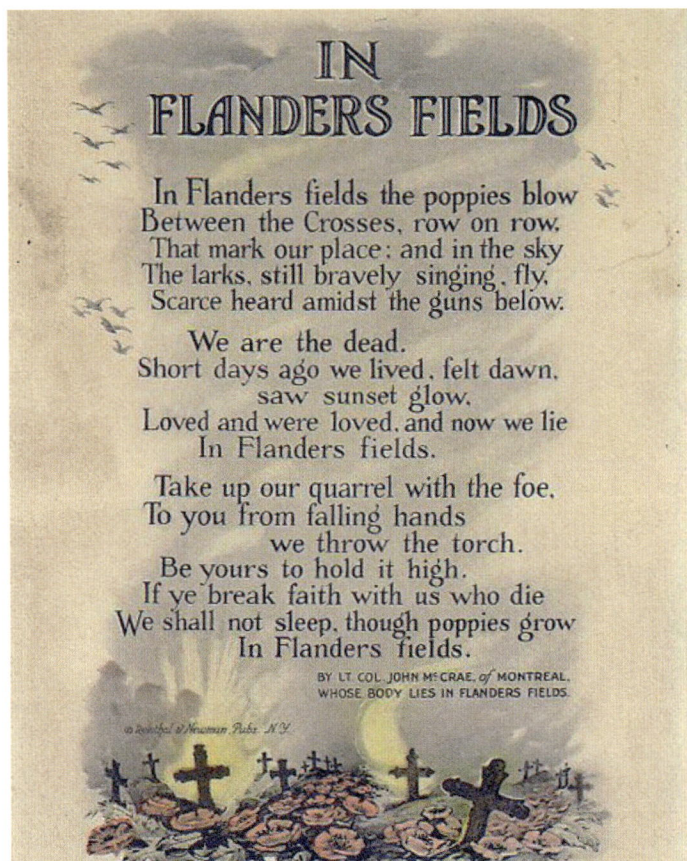

IN FLANDERS FIELDS

In Flanders fields the poppies blow
Between the Crosses, row on row,
That mark our place: and in the sky
The larks, still bravely singing, fly,
Scarce heard amidst the guns below.

We are the dead.
Short days ago we lived, felt dawn,
saw sunset glow,
Loved and were loved, and now we lie
In Flanders fields.

Take up our quarrel with the foe,
To you from falling hands
we throw the torch.
Be yours to hold it high.
If ye break faith with us who die
We shall not sleep, though poppies grow
In Flanders fields.

BY LT. COL. JOHN McCRAE, of MONTREAL,
WHOSE BODY LIES IN FLANDERS FIELDS.

© Reinthal & Newman Pubs. N.Y.

《在佛兰德斯战场》

在佛兰德斯战场，罂粟花随风飘荡
一行又一行，绽放在殇者的十字架之间，
那是我们的疆域。而天空
云雀依然在勇敢地歌唱，展翅
歌声湮没在连天的烽火里

此刻，我们已然罹难。倏忽之前，
我还一起生活着，感受晨曦，仰望落日
我们爱过，一如我们曾被爱过。
而今，我们长眠在佛兰德斯战场……

继续战斗吧
请你从我们低垂的手中接过火炬，
让它的光辉，照亮血色的疆场
若你背弃了与逝者的盟约
我们将永不瞑目。纵使罂粟花依旧绽放
在佛兰德斯战场……

描绘一战的经典诗作《在佛兰德斯战场》，由参战加拿大人约翰·麦克雷创作于第二次伊珀尔战役期间

The classic World War I poem, *In Flanders Fields* was written by Canadian war veteran John McCrae during the Second Battle of Ypres

伊珀尔（Ypres, 又译作伊普雷）是位于比利时佛兰德斯大区西部的古老城镇，自罗马帝国时期已经存在。第一次世界大战期间，伊珀尔这座城市饱受炮火洗礼长达 4 年之久，协约国军队同德军于 1914 年、1915 年和 1917 年进行了三次战役。第一次伊珀尔战役被称作"大兵之战"[24]，英、法、比联军士兵顶住了德军的正面进攻，战争进入阵地战阶段，最终德军伤亡 13 万，协约国军队损失 10 余万人。[25] 第二次伊珀尔战役，德军的作战目的是试验其秘密武器——氯气，这是战争史上首次大规模使用生化武器，造成联军 1.5 万人中毒，其中 5000 人死亡。此役德军伤亡 4 万，联军损失 7 万人。[26] 描绘一战的经典诗作《在佛兰德斯战场》，即诞生于此次战役。第三次伊珀尔战役由英法联军发动，并掌握了制空权，联军伤亡 30.8 万人，德军损失约 27 万人。[27] 除了

great skill and wisdom." "They will always be remembered, appreciated and respected. It was they who helped us rebuild our homes."[23]

Ypres is an ancient town located in the western part of the Flanders region of Belgium and has existed since the Roman Empire. During the First World War, the city of Ypres was under fire for four years, with three battles fought between the Allied forces and the German army in 1914, 1915 and 1917. The first Battle of Ypres, known as the "Soldiers' Battle"[24] saw British, French, and Belgian soldiers hold off the German frontal assault, that ended with 130,000 German casualties and over 100,000 Allied losses.[25] During the second Battle of Ypres, the German army's combat objective was to test its secret weapon - chlorine gas. This was the first large-scale use of biochemical weapons in the history of warfare, resulting in the poisoning of 15,000 Allied troops, of which 5,000 died. The battle resulted in 40,000 German casualties and 70,000 Allied losses.[26] The

伊珀尔的市政厅和布匹礼堂。与华工有关的历史资料及物品大部分收藏于伊珀尔的"佛兰德斯战地博物馆"，该博物馆即坐落于布匹礼堂。它修建于 13 世纪，一战中被炮火摧毁，仅剩一层，战后中国劳工最早参与了重建工作。这里的展品包括当时拍摄的华工工作、娱乐、生活的影像资料，印有华工姓名、编号的铭牌，还有一些其他的随身物品。展品中有一本曾经在欧洲做华工的中国人的日记，写于中日战争时期，他们将自己在欧洲战场上的经历和经验记录下来，希望能够帮助到当时正在被日本侵略的中国。还有当时一位比利时神父的演讲稿，里面有很多涉及华工的故事。这两件展品彼此对照，使人们既能看到中国人眼中的比利时，又能看到比利时人眼中的中国，历史便在对照中被多次阐述，以更多视角呈现在今人面前

The Town Hall and Cloth Hall, Ypres. In Flanders Fields Museum in Ypres, where most of the historical materials and objects related to the Chinese workers are housed, is located in the Cloth Hall. Built in the 13th century, it was destroyed by artillery fire in World War I with only one floor remained. Chinese laborers were the first to participate in its reconstruction after the war. The exhibits here include video footage and photographs of Chinese workers at work or engaging in recreation and other activities. The exhibits also contain Chinese workers' name tags and other accompanying items. There is also a speech script by a Belgian priest at that time, which contains many stories involving Chinese workers

士兵的伤亡，那里因战争死亡的平民人口将近 50 万，整座城市几乎变为一片废墟。100 多年前也正是在这片土地上，数以万计的中国劳工搬运尸体，清理炸弹，并在废墟上重建了一座城市。民国时期天津有一条路被命名为"一坡城路"（伊珀尔旧译，今河南路），即是纪念一战后伊珀尔城的重生。

第一次世界大战期间，一共有 86 位华工长眠于佛兰德斯地区。比利时至今完好保存了他们的墓地，墓碑由华工们自己刻写，墓碑样式统一，顶部刻有悼词"流芳百世""虽死犹生""鞠躬尽瘁""勇往直前"四者之一，下面依次刻有姓名、籍贯、劳工编码、死亡日期。86 位劳工分别就地安葬于佛兰德斯地区 16 个公墓。[28]

埃尔弗丁厄（斯蒂恩杰斯莫伦大街），瓜利亚公墓：4 座。

伊珀尔（茨瓦恩霍夫路），新爱尔兰农场公墓：7 座。

科姆梅尔（莫伦大街），克莱恩—维尔大街英国公墓：1 座。

科特赖克（米恩斯路），古市立公墓：8 座。

马赫伦 - 莱厄河（多普斯大街），国家军事公墓：1 座。

波珀灵厄（博舍尔普路），利森托克军事公墓：35 座。

波珀灵厄（德肯·德·博兰），波珀灵厄新军事公墓：1 座。

波珀灵厄（德肯·德·博兰），波珀灵厄旧军事公墓：1 座。

普罗芬（鲁斯布吕赫大街），门町厄姆公墓：8 座。

雷尼格尔斯特（巴尔朱大街），雷尼格尔斯特新

classic poem depicting World War I, *In Flanders Fields*, was born from this battle. The third Battle of Ypres was waged by the British and French allied forces, who took control of the air. The battle ended with 308,000 Allied casualties and German losses of about 270,000.[27] In addition to the casualties of soldiers, nearly 500,000 civilians died in the war, and the whole city laid in ruins. It was on this same land that tens of thousands of Chinese laborers carried bodies, cleared bombs, and rebuilt a city on its ruins more than 100 years ago. During the Republican era, a road in Tianjin was named "Yi Po Cheng Road" (the old translation of Ypres, now Henan Road) to commemorate the rebirth of Ypres after World War I.

During the First World War, a total of 86 Chinese workers were buried in the Flanders region. Their graves are still intact in Belgium. The tombstones were engraved by the workers themselves in a uniform style: the top of the tombstone is engraved with one of the four idioms of "to be remembered for a hundred years," "to be alive despite death," "to have done one's best," or "moving forward with courage." The name, ancestral hometown, labor code, and the date of death were engraved below in order. The 86 workers were buried in 16 cemeteries in Flanders. Below is the list of cemeteries and the number of Chinese workers buried in each.[28]

Elverdinge (Steentjesmolenstraat), Gwalia Cemetery: 4.
Ypres (Zwaanhofweg), New Irish Farm Cemetery: 7.

Kemmel (Molenstraat), Klein-Vierstraat British Cemetery: 1.

Courtrai (Meenseweg), ancient Cimetière communal: 8.
Machelen-aan-de-Leie (Dorpsstraat), Cimetiére national militaire: 1.

Poperinge (Boescheepseweg), Lijssenthoek Military Cemetery: 35.

Poperinge (Deken De Bolaan), Poperinghe New Military Cemetery: 1.

利森托克公墓里天津同乡的墓碑
Tombstone of a fellow Tianjin resident in Lijssenthoek Military Cemetery

以上照片由刘悦先生摄于 2017 年
Photos taken by Mr. Liu Yue in 2017

军事公墓：7 座。

鲁斯布吕赫－哈灵厄（纳赫塔戈尔大街），哈灵厄（班达厄姆）军事公墓：4 座。

弗拉默廷厄（泽弗科特大街），布兰德霍克新军事公墓 3 号：1 座。

维斯桃特（波珀灵厄大街），维斯桃特英军公墓：3 座。

威斯特莱特伦（莱韦里克大街），多津厄姆公墓：3 座。

韦弗尔海姆（科尔特路），凯泽尔贝格军事公墓：1 座。

韦茨哈特（沃尔梅泽尔大街），克罗纳特教堂公墓：1 座。

北洋政府派劳工到欧洲战场，"把参战视为列席和会的入场券"[29]。终于，根据中国劳工在战争中对协约国方所做出的贡献，中国代表参加了 1919 年凡尔赛和会。然而，北洋政府希望提高中国国际地位、与列强平起平坐的愿望却没能实现。1920 年中国劳工开始被送返回国，然而很多在法国监管下的中国劳工直到 1922 年才得以回国。大约有 6000 名劳工死于疾病、敌人的攻击或者恶劣的医疗条件，他们被埋葬在了法国和比利时接壤的两座军人公墓中。[30]

Poperinge (Deken De Bolaan), Poperinghe Old Military Cemetery: 1.

Proven (Roesbruggestraat), Mendinghem Cemetery: 8;

Reningelst (Baljuwstraat), Reninghelst New Military Cemetery: 7.

Rosebrugge-Haringe (Nachtegaalstraat), Haringhe (Bandaghem) Military Cemetery: 4.

Vlamertinge (Zevekotestraat), Brandhoek New Military Cemetery No.3: 1.

Westouter (Poperinge straat), Westoutre British Military Cemetery: 3.

Westvleteren (Leeuwerikstraat), Dozinghem Cemetery: 3.

Wevelgem (Korteweg), Kezelberg Military Cemetery: 1.

Wijtschate (Voormezelestraat), Croonaert Chapel Cemetery: 1.

The Beiyang government sent laborers to the battlefields of Europe as a ticket to the Peace Conference.[29] Eventually, due to the contribution of Chinese laborers to the Allied Powers, Chinese delegates participated in the Versailles Peace Conference in 1919. However, the Beiyang government's desire to improve China's international standing and to be on an equal footing with the Great Powers was not realized. In 1920, Chinese laborers began to be repatriated to China, although many of those in French custody were not able to return until 1922. About 6,000 of them died from disease, enemy attacks or poor medical conditions and were buried in two military cemeteries on the border between France and Belgium.[30]

废除《中比通商条约》

在近代中国，殖民主义、帝国主义通过不平等条约，攫取了种种侵略特权，给中国人民带来了深重苦难。近代历史上，中国的各种政治势力、各种社会力量都前赴后继、锲而不舍地为修订和废除不平等条约而努力、斗争。一战后的巴黎和会（1919年）上，中国第一次全面提出修改不平等条约的要求。1926年顾维钧代表北京政府主持废除《中比通商条约》，开近代中国废约之先河，是北洋外交史中最为光彩的一笔。而作为另一当事方，比利时由最先的拒不接受甚至提交国际法庭诉讼，到后来转而追随正义，尊重中国的民族自决权利而放弃不平等条约，亦以实际行动支持了中国人民争取平等的废约运动。

1865年11月，清政府与比利时签订《中比通商条约》和《通商章程：海关税则》。从此，比利时获得了公使驻京、领事裁判权和片面最惠国待遇等与列强一样的种种特权（除割地赔款外）。1900年八国联军入侵中国，比利时趁机在天津设立了比利时租界。1926年4月，鉴于条约即将期满，当时的北京政府通知比方，决定终止旧约，以便在平等互惠基础上举行缔结新约的谈判。但比利时方面坚持要求中方保证在新约生效前，旧条约继续有效，双方难以调和。

彼时，中国国内舆论对此次中比条约修订极为关注，"期为中国外交划一新纪元"[31]，全国民众一致主张取消。天津《大公报》著论，提出"民族兴亡存废之关键，全在此类恶约之能否废除"；"如不宣布失效，或另订过渡办法，则恶例一开，其他所有不平等条约，均可引为先例，完全丧失恢复独立自由之机会"[32]，号召全国民

Abolition of the Treaty of Commerce between China and Belgium

In modern China, colonialists and imperialists seized all kinds of privileges through unequal treaties, which brought great suffering to the Chinese people. In modern history, various political forces and social forces in China had been striving and struggling for the revision and abolition of unequal treaties. At the Paris Peace Conference (1919) after World War I, China made a formal request to amend the unequal treaties for the first time. In 1926, Gu Weijun, on behalf of the Beijing government, took charge of the abolition of the Sino-Belgian Treaty of Commerce, the first treaty abrogation in modern China and the most glorious achievement in the history of Beiyang diplomacy. As the other party, Belgium at first refused to accept China's request or even submitted to international court for adjudication, but later chose to respect China's right to national self-determination and renounce the unequal treaty. Belgium's action practically supported Chinese people's movement of abolishing unequal treaties in pursuit of equality.

In November 1865, the Qing government signed the *Treaty of Commerce between Belgium and China* and the *Regulations of Commerce: Customs Tariff*. Since then, Belgium had obtained the same privileges as other great powers, such as the privilege of stationing its minister in Beijing, consular jurisdiction, and unilateral most-favored-nation treatment (except ceding territory and paying indemnities). When the Eight-Power Allied Forces invaded China in 1900, Belgium also took the opportunity to claim the Tianjin concession from the Qing government. In April 1926, in view of the imminent expiration of the treaty, then Beijing government informed the Belgian side that it had decided to terminate the old treaty in order to negotiate for a new treaty on the basis of equality and reciprocity.

顾维钧（1888—1985），中国近代史上最卓越的外交家之一，北洋政府和国民党政府时期外交界的领袖人物。1904 年入美国哥伦比亚大学，专攻国际法及外交，获博士学位。1912 年回国，任袁世凯总统英文秘书。1919 年和 1921 年作为中国代表团成员出席巴黎和会和华盛顿会议。在巴黎和会上，就山东的主权问题据理力争，以出色的辩论才能阐述中国对山东有不容争辩的主权，维护了国家民族权益。1922—1926 年先后任北洋政府的外交总长、财政总长、代理国务总理等职，后任国民政府驻法国、英国大使等职。1945 年 6 月，参加《联合国宪章》起草工作，并代表中国在《联合国宪章》上签字，其后任国民党政府驻联合国首席代表、驻美大使。1956—1967 年，历任海牙国际法庭法官、国际法院副院长等职。退休后定居美国，以 17 年时间完成口述回忆录《顾维钧回忆录》，记述了 50 多年从事外交工作的经历。1985 年在美国纽约逝世

Gu Weijun (1888-1985) was one of the most outstanding diplomats in modern Chinese history and a leading figure in diplomacy during the Beiyang government and the Nationalist government periods. In 1904, he entered Columbia University, where he specialized in international law and diplomacy and received his doctorate. He returned to China in 1912 and served as the English secretary to President Yuan Shikai. In 1919 and 1921, he attended the Paris Peace Conference and the Washington Conference as a member of the Chinese delegation. From 1922 to 1926, he served as Foreign Minister, Finance Minister and Acting State Premier of the Beiyang Government, and later as Ambassador of the Government of the Republic of China to France and Britain. In June 1945, he participated in the drafting of the Charter of the United Nations and signed it on behalf of China. He later served as the chief representative of the Nationalist government to the United Nations and Ambassador to the United States. From 1956 to 1967, he served as a judge of the International Court of Justice in The Hague, Vice-President of the International Court of Justice. After retirement, he settled in the United States and completed his oral memoir *Gu Weijun's Memoirs* in 17 years, recording his experience in diplomatic work for more than 50 years. He died in 1985 in New York City, USA

众急起监督政府，不能妥协。此论一出，京、津、沪商界、学界乃至各派系军阀，纷纷致电外交部，要求即刻宣布比约失效。与此同时，布鲁塞尔的中国留学生与旅比各界华侨多次集会，并赴比利时外交部示威，沿途散发法文传单，宣传中国人民的合理诉求。[33]

时任代理国务总理的顾维钧，认为不能让比利时这样无限制地拖延下去，建议中比双方在旧条约期满后先商定一个临时协定，但比方采取与其他列强同进同退的策略，要求继续行使治外法权和领事裁判权，毫无谈判诚意。比利时方面拒不接受中国的提议，反而宣布终止谈判，将争议提交海牙国际法庭。面对僵局，顾维钧指

However, the Belgian side insisted that the Chinese side guarantee that the old treaty would remain in force until the new one came into force, and the two sides had difficulty in reconciling the different positions.

At that time, Chinese public opinion was extremely concerned about the amendment of the Sino-Belgian Treaty, "hoping to bring an epoch-making influence in China diplomacy"[31], and the whole country unanimously supported its abolition. The Tianjin *Ta Kung Pao newspaper* published an article, argued that "the key to the survival of the nation lies in the abolition of such bad treaties" and that "if the treaty is not declared null and void, or if another transitional arrangement is made, then once the bad example is set, all other unequal treaties can be cited as precedents and the opportunity to regain independence and freedom will be completely lost."[32] It called on the public to urgently monitor the government to not to compromise. As soon as this rhetoric came out, the business and academic circles in Beijing, Tianjin, Shanghai and even the warlords of various factions called the Ministry of Foreign Affairs and demanded that the treaty be declared null and void immediately. At the same time, Chinese students in Brussels and overseas Chinese from all walks of life gathered several times and went to the Belgian Foreign Ministry to demonstrate, distributing leaflets in French along the way to publicize the reasonable demands of the Chinese people.[33]

Gu Weijun, then acting Premier, thought that Belgium should not be allowed to drag on indefinitely and suggested that the two sides should first agree on a provisional agreement after the expiration of the old treaty. But the Belgian side adopted the strategy of acting in concert with the other powers, demanding the continued exercise of extraterritoriality and consular jurisdiction without any sincerity in the negotiations. The Belgian side refused to accept the Chinese proposal and instead announced the termination of the negotiations and submitted the dispute to

出，中国不能屈服于比利时的无理立场，除终止中比旧约外别无选择。

1926 年 11 月 6 日，在顾维钧的主持下，北京政府自主宣布了终止中比条约的声明，并将废约照会送交比使馆。照会宣布：由于比利时政府现在所持之态度，"中国政府以为除宣布一八六五年中比条约终止外，别无他途"[34]。此举开创了中国政府单方面废除不平等条约的先例，"充分体现了国民外交及其力量，以及政府交涉与国民外交的结合"，说明"充分发挥民众的反帝热情，是废除不平等条约的基本条件和保证"[35]。主持此事的顾维钧称：

正式废除 1865 年中比条约是中国外交史上的一个里程碑。因为这是中国政府第一次在面对另一缔约国公开、正式反对的情况下宣布彻底废除旧的不平等条约的。中国有必要这样做，不仅因为中国根据情况变迁原则在国际法面前有充分理由，而且因为中国有必要开创一个先例，证明中国决心行动起来，以结束一个世纪以来不平等条约给中国人民带来的灾难。[36]

中比条约废除后，整个欧洲大陆亦为之震动。之后，受国际局势和中国国内北伐战争的影响，列强改变对华政策，比利时失去有力支持。尤其是，比利时国内主张和平、反对与中国决裂的倾向扩大。爱好和平的比利时民众并无诉诸强力之意，认为中比之间只有商业关系，不必注重政治见解，没必要为列强充当把持不平等条约的傀儡。

在各种因素的影响下，比利时的态度发生改变。1927 年中比双方重新回到谈判桌。顾维钧向比利时驻华公使华洛思（Maire de Warzeed Hermalle）表示，彼

the Permanent Court of International Justice in The Hague. Faced with the deadlock, Gu Weijun pointed out that China could not give in to Belgium's unreasonable position and had no choice but to terminate the old Sino-Belgian Treaty.

On November 6, 1926, under the auspices of Gu Weijun, the Beijing government announced the termination of the Sino-Belgian Treaty and sent a note of abrogation to the Belgian legation declaring that, due to the attitude of the Belgian government, "the Chinese government believes that there is no other way than to declare the termination of the Sino-Belgian Treaty of 1865"[34]. This action set a precedent for the unilateral abrogation of an unequal treaty by the Chinese government, and "fully reflected national diplomacy and its strength," which showed that "giving full play to the anti-imperialist enthusiasm of the people is the basic condition and guarantee for the abrogation of unequal treaties"[35]. Gu Weijun, who presided over the matter, stated:

The formal abrogation of the Sino-Belgian Treaty of 1865 is a milestone in China's diplomatic history. This is because it is the first time that the Chinese government has announced the complete abrogation of an old unequal treaty in the face of open and formal opposition from another contracting party. It is necessary for China to do so, not only because it has good reasons before international law based on the principle of changed circumstances, but because it is necessary for China to set a precedent that would demonstrate its determination to act in order to put an end to the disaster that a century of unequal treaties have brought to the Chinese people.[36]

After the abrogation of the Sino-Belgian Treaty, the whole European continent was also shaken by it. Later, influenced by the international situation and the war of the Northern Expedition in China, the powers changed their

此如能和平解决，"足开中比间之新纪元，而两国人民，亦将益趋亲睦"[37]。比利时公使则同意："为表证其始终未变之调和精神起见，决定在不久即将开始之会商时期以内，中止在海牙国际永久法庭之诉讼。……愿以平等及互相尊重领土主权为基础，缔结新约。"[38] 在 1 月 17 日的会商中，比方承诺无条件归还天津比租界，对中国表达善意。[39] 之后中比谈判时断时续，直至 1931 年 1 月 15 日，比利时正式将天津租界交还中国。

　　废除《中比通商条约》，对于中比关系有着重要意义和深远影响。比利时首先抛弃领事裁判权，使其在中国民众心目中的印象发生了变化，并对中国的废约斗争产生了积极影响。当时舆论认为，"比独不徘徊瞻顾，毅然交还租界，此次又首先放弃不合现代精神之领判权，实与中国人以无穷之好印象"[40]。1927 年时任比利时外交总长的温德威尔（Emile Vandervelde）发表文章说，

顾维钧在天津的故居。航鹰女士摄于 2023 年
Gu Weijun's former residence in Tianjin. Taken by Ms. Hang Ying in 2023

policy towards China and Belgium lost its strong support. In particular, the Belgian domestic support for advocating peace and opposing a break with China expanded. The peace-loving Belgian public did not want to resort to force and believed that there were only commercial relations between China and Belgium, and that there was no need to act as a puppet for the great powers to uphold unequal treaties.

Under the influence of various factors, Belgium's attitude changed, and in 1927 the two sides returned to the negotiating table. Gu Weijun told Belgian Minister Maire de Warzeed Hermalle that a peaceful settlement would "open up a new era between China and Belgium, and the two peoples would become closer"[37]. For his part, the Belgian Minister agreed: "In testimony to its unchanging spirit of conciliation, it has been decided to suspend the proceedings before the International Permanent Court of Justice in The Hague for the period of the forthcoming conference. ... is willing to conclude a new treaty on the basis of equality and mutual respect for territorial sovereignty."[38] At the meeting on January 17, the Belgians promised to return the Tianjin concession unconditionally and expressed goodwill to China.[39] The Sino-Belgian negotiations continued intermittently until January 15, 1931, when Belgium formally returned the Tianjin concession to China.

The abrogation of the Sino-Belgian Treaty of Commerce had a significant and far-reaching impact on Sino-Belgian relations. Belgium was the first to abandon its consular jurisdiction, which changed its image among the Chinese public and had a positive impact on China's struggle for the abrogation of the treaty. The public opinion at that time was that "Belgium's determination to surrender its concession without hesitation and to be the first to give up its consular jurisdiction made an infinitely good impression on the Chinese"[40]. Giving up privileges in China, said Emile Vandervelde, Belgian Foreign Minister,

放弃在华特权，"作为精神上之价值，较物质上之重要，实超越无穷"；因为区区一块"既非富饶，又不广大"的租界而被中国列入帝国主义列强之内，实在得不偿失；比利时从自身历史出发，注重"民族自决权利为最要"的原则；"以弹丸之邦，既无政治野心，又无军事实力，除正义外，自不能大有作为"，但放弃特权此举对列强来说，意味着宣告"不平等条约治外法权及侵占华人主权之土地等，均已成过去之物"。温德威尔希望，待他日中国完全脱离外国侵占之后，"或尚有人能忆及1927年时，曾有比利时小国，首先予以援助"[41]。

in an article in 1927, "has a spiritual value that is infinitely more important than the material one." It was not worth the cost to be named by China as an imperialist merely for the sake of the concession that was "neither rich nor broad." Belgium, from its own history, focused on the principle that "the right of self-determination of peoples is of paramount importance." As a small country with neither political ambition nor military power, Belgium could not do much except for justice. Its renunciation of privileges meant to the great powers that "unequal treaties of extraterritoriality and the usurpation of Chinese sovereign lands were things of the past." Vandervelde hoped that in the future, when China was completely free from foreign occupation, "some Chinese might recall that in 1927 a small country, Belgium, had been the first to offer assistance"[41].

民国时期的中国和比利时外交代表们

1912年1月1日中华民国成立，1913年10月6日比利时外交部承认中华民国北洋政府，双方建立公使级外交关系。北洋政府向比利时派驻外交代表，于首都布鲁塞尔设立中华民国驻比利时王国公使馆，并派驻公使（其间派驻代办、一等秘书、二等秘书兼任）。1928年11月22日，随着国民革命军北伐接近尾声，比利时外交部承认中华民国国民政府。1937年6月1日，建立大使级外交关系。公使馆升格为中华民国驻比利时王国大使馆，并派驻大使。1940年5月德军占领比利时，中国停闭使馆，召回大使。比利时政府流亡伦敦后，中国于1941年5月30日，任命驻荷兰全权公使兼代驻比利时大使馆馆务。

中国驻比利时外交代表们

李国杰，1912年，原清政府驻比钦差大臣，二等公使。民国成立后，改任外交代表。

吴尔昌，1912年11月任命，1913年11月14日离任。临时代办。

王广圻，1912年12月29日任命，1913年11月14日到任，1913年12月27日离职。特命全权公使，民国时期职业外交官。毕业于北京同文馆。曾任驻荷兰使馆随员、海牙第二次和平会议中国全权专使处三等参赞、中俄修改陆路通商条约参赞和留俄学务监督。1912年12月任驻比利时特命全权公使。1915年9月，任驻意大利特命全权公使。1919年，任罗马万国农会第五次大会全权代表，被选为副会长，并任中国与波斯订约全权代表。1920年12月，任驻荷兰特命全权公使。

Chinese and Belgian Diplomatic Representatives during the Republican Era

After the establishment of the Republic of China in January 1, 1912, on October 6, 1913, Belgium recognized the Beiyang government, with which it established diplomatic relations at the ministerial level. The Chinese government started sending diplomatic representatives overseas. The Legation of the Republic of China to the Kingdom of Belgium was thereafter established in Brussels, and Chinese government started sending ministers (including sending Chargé d'Affaires, First Secretary and Second Secretary during the period). On November 22, 1928, as the Northern Expedition of the National Revolutionary Army came to an end, the Belgian Ministry of Foreign Affairs recognized the Government of the Republic of China. On June 1, 1937, diplomatic relations were established at the ambassadorial level. The Legation was upgraded to the Embassy of the Republic of China to the Kingdom of Belgium with an Ambassador. When the German army occupied Belgium in May 1940, the Chinese Embassy was closed and the ambassador was recalled. After the Belgian government went into exile in London, China appointed a Minister Plenipotentiary in the Netherlands on May 30, 1941 to be in charge of the embassy affairs in Belgium.

Chinese Diplomatic Representatives in Belgium

Li Guojie, 1912, Former Imperial Envoy of the Qing Government to Belgium. After the establishment of the Republic of China, he was reappointed as a diplomatic representative.

Wu Erchang, November 1912 - November 14, 1913, Temporary Chargè d'affaires.

Wang Guangqi, appointed on December 29, 1912; in office November 14, 1913 - December 27, 1913,

1921 年 9 月，华盛顿会议前夕，曾与其他八位驻欧外交公使联名致电国内，呼吁息争，一致对外。1924 年任日内瓦国际禁烟公会第二全权代表，发出中国声音。[42]

章祖申，1913 年 12 月 27 日任命，同日到任，1914 年 4 月 20 日卸职。代办。

汪荣宝，1914 年 2 月 19 日任命，1914 年 4 月 20 日到任，1919 年 1 月 5 日免离。特命全权公使。民国时期法政学家、职业外交官。曾在清朝任官，后辞职入南洋公学，与黄炎培、邵力子、李叔同、谢无量等人成为同学，后赴日本早稻田大学与庆应私塾留学。回国后参与君主立宪，起草中国近代第一部完整的宪法草案。1914 年 2 月 19 日被袁世凯任命为驻比利时公使，开启了职业外交官生涯。一年后，又被袁世凯召回国起草宪法，当袁世凯谈及政府体制之事时，他说"愿公为华盛顿，不愿公为拿破仑"，反对袁世凯称帝。1918 年奉命与顾维钧、王正廷、颜惠庆出席巴黎和会。1919 年 4 月赴任中国首任瑞士大使。1922 年 6 月被委派为驻日公使，

汪荣宝
Wang Rongbao

Minister Extraordinary and Plenipotentiary. He was a professional diplomat in the Republic of China era. He graduated from Tongwen Guan (The School of Combined Learning) and once served as an attaché of the Chinese Embassy in the Netherlands, the third counsellor of the Chinese Plenipotentiary Office of the Second Hague Peace Conference, the counsellor in charge of the revision of the Sino-Russian land-route trade treaty, and the supervisor of affairs on studying abroad in Russia. He was appointed the Minister Extraordinary and Plenipotentiary to Belgium in December 1912. In September 1915, he was appointed the Minister Extraordinary and Plenipotentiary to Italy. In 1919, he was elected the Plenipotentiary and the vice president of the Fifth Congress of the International Institute of Agriculture in Rome, and the Plenipotentiary of concluding the treaty between China and Persia. In December 1920, he was appointed the Minister Extraordinary and Plenipotentiary to the Netherlands. In September 1921, on the eve of the Washington Conference, he and eight other Chinese diplomatic ministers stationed in Europe sent a joint announcement, calling for suspending domestic disputes and uniting against external enemies. In 1924, he served as the second Plenipotentiary of the Geneva International Opium Convention and expressed the Chinese voice.[42]

Zhang Zushen, December 27, 1913 - April 20, 1914, Chargè d'affaires.

Wang Rongbao, appointed on February 19, 1914, in office April 20, 1914 - January 5, 1919. Minister Extraordinary and Plenipotentiary. He was a legal scholar, political scientist and a professional diplomat in the Republican period. He served as an official in the Qing dynasty, then resigned and joined the Nanyang Public School, where he became a classmate of Huang Yanpei, Shao Lizi, Li Shutong and Xie Wuliang. He later went to Japan to study at Waseda University. After returning to

民国第一届内阁阁员合影。前排左起：教育总长蔡元培、工商次长王正廷、海军总长刘冠雄、代外交总长胡惟德、内阁总理唐绍仪。后排左起：农林总长宋教仁、交通总长施肇基、陆军总长段祺瑞、司法总长王宠惠、外交次长魏宸组

A group photo of the members of the first cabinet of the Republic of China. Front row from left: Cai Yuanpei, Chief of Education; Wang Zhengting, Undersecretary of Commerce and Industry; Liu Guanxiong, Chief of Navy; Hu Weide, Acting Chief of Foreign Affairs; Tang Shaoyi, Premier of the Cabinet. Back row from left: Song Jiaoren, General Secretary of Agriculture and Forestry; Shi Zhaoji, General Secretary of Transportation; Duan Qirui, General Secretary of the Army General; Wang Chonghui, Secretary of Justice; Wei Chenzu, Undersecretary of Foreign Affairs

长达 8 年之久，"九一八事变"前回国。在日期间，敦促日本以庚子赔款在中国举办各种文化教育事业及给予留学生补助，并安排商务印书馆赴日搜集国内散佚的宋、元、明古籍 46 种重新出版为《辑印古书》。1930 年协助签署《中日关税协定》，收回关税自主权。[43]

魏宸组，1919 年 1 月 5 日任命，1919 年 2 月 20 日到任，1921 年 8 月 2 日免离。特命全权公使。民国时期职业外交官。1903 年由清政府选派赴比利时留学，并加入同盟会。回国后入外务部任主事。与汪精卫、

China, he participated in the drafting of the first complete constitution in modern China, and was appointed by Yuan Shikai as Minister to Belgium on February 19, 1914, starting his career as a professional diplomat. A year later, he was called back by Yuan Shikai to draft the constitution. When Yuan Shikai asked him about the government system, Wang said "I would like you to be George Washington rather than Napoleon Bonaparte," and opposed Yuan proclaiming himself emperor. In 1918, he was appointed to attend the Paris Peace Conference with Gu Weijun, Wang Zhengting and Yan Huiqing, and in April 1919, he became the first Chinese ambassador to Switzerland. In June 1922, he was appointed Minister to Japan for eight years and returned to China before the September 18 Incident in 1931. During his time in Japan, Wang urged Japan to use the Boxer Indemnity to sponsor cultural and educational activities in China and provide subsidies to Chinese overseas students. He arranged the Commercial Press to collect 46 kinds of lost ancient books of Song, Yuan and Ming dynasties in Japan and republished them in a volume entitled *Compilation of Ancient Books*. In 1930, he assisted in signing the Sino-Japanese Tariff Agreement and recovered the right of tariff autonomy.[43]

Wei Chenzu, appointed on January 5, 1919, in office February 20, 1919 - August 2, 1921, Minister Extraordinary and Plenipotentiary. He was a career diplomat in the Republican period. In 1903, he was sent by the Qing government to study in Belgium and joined the Tung Meng Hui. After returning to China, he was put in charge of foreign affairs. He organized Anti-Qing activities with Wang Jingwei and Li Shizeng and served as the leader of the Beijing-Tianjin Tung Meng Hui. When the Revolution of 1911 broke out, he took the opportunity to convert Yuan Shikai by instilling the idea of republicanism into him, and promoted the north-south peace negotiation.

1905年初孙中山在布鲁塞尔与留欧学生合影（前排左二为史青，中排左二为魏宸组，左三为孙中山）

Sun Yat-sen with students studying in Brussels in early 1905 (Shi Qing is second from left in the front row, Wei Chenzu is second from left in the middle row, and Sun Yat-sen is third from left)

李石曾等组织反清活动，任京津同盟会领导人。辛亥革命爆发后，他趁机策反袁世凯，向其灌输共和理念，促成南北议和，被袁委为议和代表参赞，随唐绍仪南下上海促成共和。1912年1月中华民国成立后出任第一任临时政府外交次长，借鉴西方外交轨仪，开启了中国外交发言人制度之先河。1912年11月被委任为中国驻荷兰公使。1919年1月任驻比公使，其间与时任外交总长陆徵祥、驻美公使顾维钧、南方政府外交部长王正廷、驻法公使施肇基组成中国代表团，出席巴黎和会，最终五人拒绝在和约上签字。1925年辞职回国。1937年被国民政府委任为驻波兰公使。第二次世界大战爆发后回国。[44]

He was then appointed by Yuan as the representative of peace negotiation, and went to Shanghai with Tang Shaoyi to promote the republic system. After the founding of the Republic of China in January 1912, he became the first Undersecretary for Foreign Affairs of the Provisional Government. Drawing on Western diplomatic practices, he started the first Chinese diplomatic spokesman system. In November 1912, he was appointed as Chinese Minister to the Netherlands. In January 1919, he was appointed Minister to Belgium, during which time he formed a Chinese delegation with then Foreign Minister Lu Zhengxiang, Minister to the United States Gu Weijun, Minister of Foreign Affairs Wang Zhengting of the Southern Government, and Minister to France Shi Zhaoji to attend the Paris Peace Conference, where the five eventually refused to sign the peace treaty. He resigned and returned to China in 1925. In 1937, he was appointed by the Nationalist Government as Minister to Poland and returned to China after the outbreak of World War II.[44]

Wang Jingqi, appointed on August 2, 1921, in office November 20, 1921 - March 29, 1929. Minister Extraordinary and Plenipotentiary. He was a career Diplomat in the Republican Era. Wang studied politics in France in 1900 and returned to China in 1903 to work as secretary of the Beijing-Hankou Railway Company. He went to study in France again in 1908. After graduation in 1910, Wang studied international law at Oxford University, England and returned to China in 1912. At the beginning of 1914, he was appointed the researcher of the Association of Constitutional Law of Ministry of Foreign Affairs. In 1917, he became the Second Secretary of the Embassy in Italy. In December 1918, Wang went to France as a counsellor of the Chinese delegation to the Paris Peace Conference. In January 1920, he returned to China and was appointed as a member of

《北洋画报》1443 期上刊载的新任瑞典兼挪威公使王景岐夫妇乘船赴任时合影，摄于 1936 年

A photo of the newly appointed Minister to Sweden and Norway, Wang Jingqi and his wife on their trip to the new post. Published in *Beiyang Pictorial* No.1443, photo taken in 1936

王景岐，1921 年 8 月 2 日任命，1921 年 11 月 20 日到任，1929 年 3 月 29 日免离。特命全权公使。民国时期职业外交官。1900 年，赴法国研习政治。1903 年回国任京汉铁路秘书。1908 年再度留学法国。1910 年毕业转入英国牛津大学专攻国际法。1912 年归国任北京政府农林部编纂。1914 年初任外交部宪法研究会调查员。1917 年任驻意大利使馆二等秘书。1918 年 12 月，赴法国任出席巴黎和会中国代表团参事。1920 年 1 月返国任外交部和约研究会会员、司法部法权讨论会会员；同年任商订中德通商条约谈判代表，取消德国在华特权。1921 年 8 月任驻比利时全权公使。借《中比通商条约》到期，积极推动、协助交涉改订新约，启动北洋政府的"修约运动"。[45] 1926—1928 年作为全权代表出席国联第七、八、九届大会。1924 年与中国国内人士合作在上海成立"中华国民拒毒会"，1928 年支持妻子在比利时发起成立"海外拒毒后援会"，任国联禁烟顾问委员会委员兼驻万国红十字会代表。1929 年 1 月 25 日在国际联盟禁烟顾问委员会会议上提议并确定，将林则徐"6·3"焚烧鸦片日定为国际禁烟日。1929 年获赠比利时鲁汶大学名誉博士学位。后历任华北政治委员会顾问、中华民国拒毒会主席、外交部条约委员会副委员长。1936 年 5 月任驻瑞典兼驻挪威全权公使；1938 年 10 月改任驻波兰全权大使；二战爆发后移居瑞士。1941 年 8 月 25 日病逝于日内瓦。[46]

罗怀，1928 年 10 月 26 日任命，二等秘书暂代馆务，1929 年 3 月 31 日到任，1930 年 7 月 31 日移交。暂代馆务。

傅秉常，1929 年 2 月 28 日任命，未到任，1933 年

Peace Treaty Research of the Ministry of Foreign Affairs and the Extraterritoriality Commission of the Ministry of Justice. In the same year, he served as a negotiator for the negotiation of the Sino-German Trade Treaty and abolished Germany's privileges in China. In August 1921, he was appointed Minister Plenipotentiary in Belgium. Taking advantage of the expiration of the Sino-Belgian Treaty of Commerce, he actively promoted and assisted in negotiating for a new treaty. He initiated the "Treaty Amendment Movement" of the Beiyang government.[45] From 1926 to 1928, he attended the seventh, eighth and ninth Assembly of the League of Nations as plenipotentiary. In 1924, he worked with domestic groups to establish the "Chinese National Anti-Opium Association" in Shanghai. In 1928, he supported his wife to establish the "Overseas Anti-Opium Support Association" in Belgium. He served as a member of the Anti-Opium Advisory Committee of the League of Nations and a representative to the World Red Cross Society. On January 25, 1929, he proposed to set the date of "June 3," when Lin Zexu, the politician, litterateur and national hero of late Qing dynasty, burned confiscated opium, as the International No-Opium Day at the meeting of the Anti-Opium Advisory Committee. His proposal was passed eventually. In 1929, he received an honorary doctorate from the University of Leuven in Belgium. He was appointed Minister Plenipotentiary to Sweden and Norway in May 1936, and Ambassador Plenipotentiary to Poland in October 1938; he moved to Switzerland after the outbreak of World War II and later died in Geneva on August 25, 1941.[46]

Luo Huai, appointed on October 26, 1928, in office March 31, 1929 - July 31, 1930, Second Secretary.

Fu Bingchang, appointed on February 28, 1929. Never assumed office. Relieved from position on May 20, 1933, Minister Extraordinary and Plenipotentiary.

5月20日免。特命全权公使。

谢寿康，1930年2月17日任命，1930年7月31日到任，1933年5月31日离任。一等秘书代办使事。民国时期职业外交官。1912年作为官费留学生赴比利时留学，在布鲁塞尔自由大学攻读政治经济学。1914年转学至法国巴黎法政学校学习，后获经济学硕士学位。1919年与李石曾、吴稚晖等人组织成立中法教育会。1923年入比利时布鲁塞尔大学深造，获经济学博士学位。后获选为比利时皇家文学研究院院士，成为华人获欧洲国家院士第一人。1928年返回中国任国立中央大学文学院院长。1930年任驻比利时公使馆代办。1933年回国后任立法院立法委员。1935年出任国立戏剧学校教授。1937年任驻瑞士公使馆代办。1942年改任驻罗马教廷公使，成为中国首任驻教廷公使。1946年当选比利时法语皇家学会（L'Académie royale de langue et de littérature françaises de Belgique）会员。1947年被聘为法国知识分子联合会名誉会长。1949年参与发起成立国际戏剧协会，同年前往美国，被聘为哥伦比亚大学助理戏剧教授。1973年逝世。著有法文版《法国战时公债》《东方与西方》《中国思想与种族问题》，英文版《蝴蝶梦及其他民间故事》等，均在法国、比利时、美国、瑞士印刷发行。[47]

张乃燕，1933年5月20日任命，1933年12月19日到任，1935年7月1日免离。全权公使。民国时期教育家、外交官、历史学家。1913年赴欧留学，先后在英国伯明翰大学、伦敦大学、帝国理工学院学习，后到瑞士，1919年获日内瓦大学化学哲学博士学位。1919年回国后，历任北京大学、北京高等师范学校

Xie Shoukang, appointed on February 17, 1930, in office July 31, 1930 - May 31, 1933, First Secretary. He was a career diplomat in the Republican period. In 1912, he went to Belgium as a government-funded student and studied political economy at the Universitè libre de Bruxelles. In 1914, he transferred to the I'Ecole des Sciences Politiques in Paris, France, where he received a master's degree in economics. In 1919, he, together with Li Shizeng and Wu Zhihui and others, organized and established the Sino-French Education Association. In 1923, he enrolled in the University of Brussels, Belgium, where he received a doctorate in economics. Later, he was awarded the membership of the Royal Academy of Literature of Belgium, becoming the first Chinese person to be awarded the membership of a European country. In 1928, he returned to China and became Dean of the Faculty of Arts of the National Central University, and in 1930, he became Chargè d'affaires of the Chinese Legation in Belgium. He again returned to China in 1933 and was appointed a member of the legislature. In 1935, he was appointed a professor of the National Drama School. In 1937, he served as Chargè d'affaires of the Chinese Legation in Switzerland, and in 1942, he became the first Chinese Minister to the Holy See. In 1946, he was elected a member of the L'Acadèmie royale de langue et de littèrature françaises de Belgique. He participated in the founding of the International Theatre Association in 1949 and later appointed assistant professor of drama at Columbia University in the United States. He passed away in 1973. He had written French versions of *French War Bonds*, *East and West*, *Chinese Thought and Race Issues*, and English versions of *A Butterfly's Dream & Other Chinese Tales*, all of which had been printed and distributed in France, Belgium, the United States, and Switzerland.[47]

Zhang Naiyan, appointed on May 20, 1933, in office

谢寿康
Xie Shoukang

张乃燕
Zhang Naiyan

《凌其翰回忆录》
Memoirs of Ling Qihan

（1923 年改名北京师范大学）、浙江省立工业专门学校、上海光华大学、国立广东大学（1926 年改名中山大学）化学教授、校长，同时任国民政府教育行政委员会委员。1927 年 6 月出任改组后的国立中央大学校长。1932 年任全国建设委员会副委员长。1933 年任驻比利时特命全权公使。1935 年辞职返国。著有《欧洲大战史》《世界大战全史》《芸庐历史丛书》《欧战中之军用化学》《药用有机砒化物》《有机染化学》等著作。[48]

凌其翰，1934 年 12 月 1 日到任，1935 年 9 月 1 日移交，暂代馆务。民国时期和新中国外交官。早年就读于震旦大学，1927 年毕业后留学比利时，先后获鲁汶大学政治外交系硕士学位、布鲁塞尔大学海事立法硕士、法学博士学位。1931 年回国，曾任《申报》国际评论员并任教于东吴大学法学院，后任外交部国际司科长、专门委员、礼宾司司长、驻法国大使馆公使等。1949 年 10 月与驻法使馆部分外交官一同通电起义，支持新成立的中华人民共和国。次年回国后任外交部专门委员，1956 年加入中国共产党。曾任外交部法律顾问、外交学院教授、欧美同学会名誉副会长等。他还是第二至四届全国政协委员，第五至七届全国政协常委，民革中央常委会顾问、中央监察委员会常委。1992 年去世。著有著作《我的外交官生涯》。[49]

朱鹤翔，1935 年 4 月 25 日任命，1935 年 9 月 1 日到任，1937 年 7 月 16 日免离。特命全权公使。

钱 泰，1937 年 7 月 23 日—1940 年 8 月 18 日；1943 年 4 月 12 日—1944 年 8 月 18 日两次任特命全权大使。民国时期职业外交家，著名法学家，在国际法等领域卓有成就。早年参加科举，为 1906 年丙午科优贡。

December 19, 1933 - July 1, 1935, Minister Extraordinary and Plenipotentiary. He was an educator, diplomat and historian during the Republican period. In 1913, Zhang went to Europe to study at the University of Birmingham, the University of London and the Imperial College of Science and Technology, and then went to Switzerland, where he received a doctorate of philosophy of chemistry from the University of Geneva in 1919. After returning to China in 1919, he had successively held the posts of professor of chemistry and president at Peking University, Beijing Higher Normal School (renamed Beijing Normal University in 1923), Zhejiang Provincial Industrial College, Kwang Hua University of Shanghai, and National Guangdong University (renamed Sun Yat-sen University in 1926). He also served as a member of the Education Administration Committee of the National Government. In June 1927, he started serving as the president of the reorganized National Central University. In 1932, he was appointed as the Vice Chairman of the National Construction Commission. In 1933, Zhang was appointed the Minister Extraordinary and Plenipotentiary in Belgium. He resigned and returned to China in 1935. He is the author of *The History of the Great War in Europe*, *The Complete History of the World War*, *Yunlu History Series*, *Military Chemistry in the European War*, *Organic Arsenic for Medicinal Use*, *Organic Dyeing Chemistry* and other works.[48]

Ling Qihan, in office December 1, 1934 - September 1, 1935, temporarily in charge of embassy affairs. He was a diplomat in the Republican period and the People's Republic of China. He studied at Aurora University in his early years and went to Belgium for further study after graduation in 1927, where he received a master's degree in political and diplomatic affairs from KU Leuven and a master's degree in maritime legislation and a doctorate in law from the University of Brussels. After

钱泰
Qian Tai

1914 年毕业于法国巴黎大学，获法学博士学位。回国后历任北洋政府条约司司长和国民政府外交部国际司司长。1934 年至 1937 年 7 月任中华民国驻西班牙全权公使。1937 年 6 月至 1940 年 8 月任中华民国驻比利时全权大使。1941 年 10 月至 1942 年 12 月任国民政府外交部常务次长。1943 年 8 月至 1944 年 9 月任中华民国驻挪威全权大使。1944 年任中华民国驻法国全权大使，至 1949 年。著有《中国不平等条约之缘起及其废除之经过》《钱泰法学文集》。[50]

金问泗，1941 年 7 月 7 日—1943 年 4 月 12 日驻荷兰全权公使兼代驻比利时大使馆馆务，1944 年 9 月 18 日—1945 年 3 月 19 日驻荷兰兼驻比利时全权大使，1945 年 3 月 19 日改专任驻比利时全权大使，1955 年 6 月 18 日离职。民国职业外交家、关税专家。1915 年获北洋大学法学学士学位。1916 年参加北京政府首次外交官领事官考试进入外交部。1917 年任驻美国使馆

returning to China in 1931, he served as an international commentator for *Shen Bao* and taught at the Law School of Soochow University, and then he served as head of the International Department of the Ministry of Foreign Affairs, special commissioner, director of the Protocol Department, Minister of the Embassy in France, etc. In October 1949, he joined some diplomats in the Embassy of the Republic of China in France in support of the newly established People's Republic of China. He served as a senior specialist of the Ministry of Foreign Affairs after returning to China the following year. He joined the Communist Party of China in 1956 and served as a legal advisor to the Ministry of Foreign Affairs, a professor at the Foreign Affairs College, and honorary vice president of the Overseas-educated Scholars Association of China. He was also a member of the 2nd to 4th National Committee of the Chinese People's Political Consultative Conference (CPPCC), a standing committee member of the 5th to 7th CPPCC National Committee, an advisor to the Central Standing Committee of the Revolutionary Committee, and a standing committee member of the Central Supervisory Committee. He passed away in 1922, and authored his memoir *My Career as a Diplomat*.[49]

Zhu Hexiang, appointed on April 25, 1935, in office September 1, 1935 - July 16, 1937, Minister Extraordinary and Plenipotentiary.

Qian Tai, in office July 23, 1937 - August 18, 1940 and April 12, 1943 - August 18, 1944, Twice as Minister Extraordinary and Plenipotentiary. He was a professional diplomat during the Republican period, a renowned jurist, and an accomplished scholar in the field of international law. He participated in the imperial examination in his young and was enrolled in the Imperial College in 1906. In 1914, Qian Tai graduated from the University of Paris, France, with a doctorate in law. He served as Minister Plenipotentiary of the Republic of China to Spain from

学习员，同时入哥伦比亚大学学习，获法学硕士学位。第一次世界大战结束后，他先后参加了巴黎和会、华盛顿会议以及国际联盟的多次会议，并先后出任驻荷兰、比利时、卢森堡、波兰、挪威、捷克等国公使、大使。1947年作为中国代表团首席代表参与起草《关税贸易总协定》（General Agreement on Tariffs and Trade）的基本条文，被称为"中国接触关贸总协定第一人"。同时，与各缔约国展开平等协商，并在《关贸总协定》之《最后议定书》上签字，为当时的中国政府和人民争取到较大的国际政治、经济利益。有《从巴黎和会到国联》、《外交工作的回忆》和《金问泗日记》等著作出版。[51]

中国代表团团长金问泗代表中国在协议上签字

Jin Wensi, head of the Chinese delegation, signing the agreement on behalf of China

1934 to July 1937, as Ambassador Plenipotentiary of the Republic of China to Belgium from June 1937 to August 1940, and as Executive Undersecretary of the Ministry of Foreign Affairs of the Nationalist Government from October 1941 to December 1942. He also served as Ambassador Plenipotentiary of the Republic of China to Norway from August 1943 to September 1944, and Ambassador Plenipotentiary of the Republic of China to France from 1944 to 1949. He is the author of *The Origin of China's Unequal Treaties and Their Abolition* and *Qian Tai's Legal Writings*.[50]

Jin Wensi, July 7, 1941 - April 12, 1943, Minister Plenipotentiary to the Netherlands and Chargè d'affaires of the Embassy in Belgium; September 18, 1944 - March 19, 1945, Ambassador Plenipotentiary to the Netherlands and to Belgium; March 19, 1945 - June 18, 1955, Ambassador Plenipotentiary to Belgium. He was a diplomat and tariff expert in the Republic of China. Jin Wensi received his bachelor's degree in law from Beiyang University in 1915. He took the first examination for diplomats and consuls in Beijing and entered the Ministry of Foreign Affairs in 1916, and became an intern at the Chinese Embassy to the United States in 1917. He studied law at Columbia University, where he received his Master's degree in law (LLM). After the First World War, he participated in the Paris Peace Conference, the Washington Conference and many meetings of the League of Nations, and served as minister and ambassador to the Netherlands, Belgium, Luxembourg, Poland, Norway and Czechoslovakia, etc. In 1947, he participated in the drafting of the General Agreement on Tariffs and Trade as the chief representative of the Chinese delegation. He is the author of *From the Paris Peace Conference to the League of Nations*, *Memories of Diplomatic Work* and *Jin Wensi's Diary*.[51]

比利时驻中国外交代表们

贾尔牒（Emile de Cartier de Marchienne），1913年11月17日—1917年8月6日在任。特命全权公使，因中国变更国体，1913年重新递交国书。

麦叶（M. Paul May），1917年8月1日—1920年。特命全权公使。

艾维滋（Robert Everts），1920年6月18日—1924年。特命全权公使。

华洛思（Maire de Warzée Hermalle），1924年11月16日—1931年。特命全权公使。任内去世。

葛拉夫（Egbert Graeffe），1931年3月20日—1933年4月15日。参事、临时代办。

纪佑穆（Baron Jules Guillaume），1933年4月15日—1937年9月，特命全权公使。1937年9月6日—1944年，特命全权大使。

戴尔福（Jacques Delaux de Fenffe），1944年12月17日—1947年12月。特命全权大使。又译"德尔福"。

魏里（Max Wery），1947年12月—1948年8月，参事、临时代办。

赖恺（Le Ghait），1948年7月28日—1949年，特命全权大使。

The Belgian diplomatic representatives in China

Emile de Cartier de Marchienne, November 17, 1913 - August 6, 1917, Minister Extraordinary and Plenipotentiary.

M. Paul May, August 1, 1917 - 1920, Minister Extraordinary and Plenipotentiary.

Robert Everts, June 18, 1920 - 1924, Minister Extraordinary and Plenipotentiary.

Maire de Warzèe Hermalle, November 16, 1924 - 1931, Minister Extraordinary and Plenipotentiary.

Egbert Graeffe, March 20, 1931 - April 15, 1933, counselor; chargè d'affaires ad interim.

Baron Jules Guillaume, April 15, 1933 - September 1937, Minister Extraordinary and Plenipotentiary; September 6, 1937 - 1944, Ambassador Extraordinary and Plenipotentiary.

Jacques Delaux de Fenffe, December 17, 1944 - December 1947, Ambassador Extraordinary and Plenipotentiary.

Max Wery, December 1947 - August 1948, counselor; chargè d'affaires ad interim.

Le Ghait, July 28, 1948 - 1949, Ambassador Extraordinary and Plenipotentiary.

"盖世太保枪口下的中国女人"

提起钱秀玲，有着诸多不同的叫法："中国小女孩""盖世太保枪口下的中国女人""中国的女'辛德勒'""比利时的中国母亲""国家英雄"，这其中饱含着比利时人对这位二战女英雄的无限敬意。她在二战时期从纳粹魔掌下拯救出近百名比利时人。这段非凡历史，使她永远为大家所铭记、怀念。

1912年3月12日钱秀玲出生在江苏宜兴一个开明的乡绅家庭。她的父母善于经商，在祖辈微薄家业的基础上，苦心经营，从事纺织、布匹等轻工行业，逐渐成为当地小有名气的富豪之家。钱秀玲从小长相娟秀靓丽，聪慧过人，成绩优良，是当地有名的才女。和一般大家闺秀很不同，她爱打篮球，喜爱化学。学生时代起，即立志科学报国，最大的理想是去法国居里原子能实验室学习，立志要成为居里夫人那样的科学家。

1929年夏天，年仅17岁的钱秀玲随同哥哥一起到比利时留学，入读世界闻名的鲁汶大学化学系。仅仅5年之后，她便获得了化学博士学位，成为当时获鲁汶大学博士学位的唯一中国女人。

在学期间，钱秀玲不仅学业优秀，还在鲁汶大学邂逅了此生挚爱——同校医学系比自己大4岁、具有俄罗斯和希腊两种血统的格列高利·德·佩令吉。1935年，她与佩令吉结为伉俪，相濡以沫地生活了60年。

婚后不久，1937年卢沟桥事变爆发，日本发动了全面侵华战争。很快，二战也在欧洲爆发。怀抱科学梦想矢志不渝的钱秀玲来到已经沦陷的巴黎，想要找寻约里奥·居里主持的原子能研究所。可惜，研究所为逃脱纳粹魔掌，已迁往美国。面对人去楼空的大楼，钱秀玲

钱秀玲（1912—2008）
Qian Xiuling (1912-2008)

钱秀玲到比利时后的第一张照片
Qian Xiuling's first photo after arriving in Belgium

"The Chinese Woman at the Gunpoint of the Gestapo"

Qian Xiuling is known by many different names: "the little Chinese girl," "the Chinese woman at the gunpoint of the Gestapo," "China's female 'Schindler'," "Belgium's Chinese mother," "national hero," all of which embody the infinite respect of Belgians for this heroine of World War II. She saved nearly 100 Belgians from the clutches of the Nazis during World War II. This remarkable history makes her forever remembered and missed by everyone.

On March 12, 1912, Qian Xiuling was born into a wealthy and enlightened country squire family in Yixing, Jiangsu Province. Qian grew up to be a beautiful and intelligent girl with excellent grades and was a famous local talent. She was very different from ordinary ladies at the time: she was good at sports and loved to study chemistry. As a student, she aspired to serve her country with scientific knowledge. Her greatest dream was to study at the Curie Atomic Energy Laboratory in France, aspiring to become a scientist like Madame Curie.

In the summer of 1929, at the age of 17, Qian Xiuling went to Belgium with her brother to study in the chemistry department of the world-renowned Catholic University of Leuven. Just five years later, she received her doctorate in chemistry, becoming the only Chinese woman to receive a doctorate from KU Leuven at that time.

During her studies, Qian Xiuling not only excelled in her studies, but also met the love of her life at the medical school of University of Leuven. Grègoire de Perlinghi, of both Russian and Greek descent, was four years older than her. In 1935, she married Perlinghi and they lived together for 60 years.

After her marriage, the Marco Polo Bridge Incident broke out in 1937 and Japan launched a full-scale war against China. Soon after, World War II also broke out in

美丽又东方风韵十足的钱秀玲与高大帅气又绅士的佩令吉

The beautiful Qian Xiuling with oriental charm and the tall, handsome and gentlemanly Perlinghi

黯然神伤，返回比利时。此后，为躲避战火，她与丈夫一起，搬到距布鲁塞尔170多公里外的偏远小镇艾尔伯蒙，开了一家诊所。

1940年5月德军占领比利时。在钱秀玲居住的小镇，一个参加抵抗活动的青年，因炸毁德军军列通过的铁路而被抓，旋即被宣判绞刑。中华传统文化所孕育的正义感使钱秀玲对抵抗运动的英雄充满同情，希望能设法营救。偶然间，她从报纸上看到冯·法尔肯豪森（Alexander von Falkenhausen）这个名字，立刻想起这位德军驻比利时和法国北部战区最高行政长官，正是出国留学时堂兄钱卓伦提起的挚友。

亚历山大·冯·法尔肯豪森 1878 年生于德国北部一个贵族家庭。1897 年毕业于德国陆军参谋大学。1900

Europe. Qian Xiuling, with her dream of science in her heart, came to Paris to look for the Institute of Atomic Energy, previously headed by Joliot-Curie. Unfortunately, the institute had already moved to the United States to escape the clutches of the Nazis. Saddened by the sight of empty building, Qian Xiuling returned to Belgium. Afterwards, to escape the war, she moved with her husband to Herbeumont, a remote town more than 170 kilometers away from Brussels, and opened a clinic.

In May 1940, the German army occupied Belgium. In the town where Qian Xiuling lived, a young man who had participated in the resistance was arrested for blowing up the railroad through which the German trains were passing and was immediately sentenced to death by hanging. The sense of justice nurtured by traditional Chinese culture prompted Qian Xiuling to sympathize with the heroes of the resistance movement and to try to rescue him. By chance, she read the name Alexander von Falkenhausen, the top commander of the German war zone in Belgium and northern France, in the newspaper and immediately remembered that he was a close friend of her cousin Qian Zhuolun when he was studying abroad.

Alexander von Falkenhausen was born in 1878 to an aristocratic family in northern Germany. After graduating from the German Army Staff University in 1897, he joined the Eight-Power Allied Forces in 1900 and travelled to China and came back to China in 1935 as a military advisor to Chiang Kai-shek and was actively involved in the top-secret planning of China to counter the impending Japanese invasion. He was forced by Nazi Germany to resign as an advisor in 1938. After the outbreak of World War II, von Falkenhausen was recalled to active service as an army general on the Western Front until May 1940, when he was appointed military governor of Belgium.

When General von Falkenhausen was a military advisor in China, he and Qian Xiuling's cousin, Nationalist

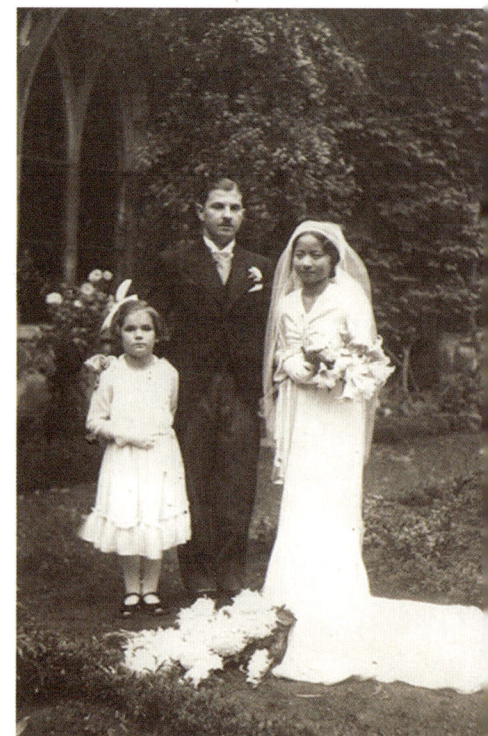

1935 年 10 月 27 日，佩令吉与钱秀玲结为伉俪

On October 27, 1935, Perlinghi and Qian Xiuling were married

年参加八国联军到过中国。1935年再次来华担任蒋介石的军事顾问，积极参与中国的最高机密筹划，为应对日本侵华出谋划策。1838年纳粹德国强迫冯·法尔肯豪森辞去中国顾问职务。二战爆发后，冯·法尔肯豪森被召回现役，在西部战线担任陆军将军，1940年5月他被任命为比利时军事总督。

冯·法尔肯豪森将军在华担任军事顾问时，与钱秀玲的堂兄、国民党中将钱卓伦（历任国民党国防部第一厅厅长、国民党国防部参谋总长办公室主任等职）互相赏识，最终结为莫逆之交。对堂妹疼爱有加的钱卓伦曾对钱秀玲说，要是遇上难事，可以找冯·法尔肯豪森将军帮忙。钱卓伦后来还多次给钱秀玲写信说，冯·法尔肯豪森与那些德国纳粹不同，为人正直，极富正义感，对中国和中国人感情很深。

救人如救火，钱秀玲带着堂兄的信，立刻赶到布鲁塞尔，设法找到冯·法尔肯豪森将军，恳求他从人道主义考虑，免除那位比利时青年的死刑。法尔肯豪森将军欣然同意帮忙，不但将那位青年的死刑改成了苦役，而且，另一名同名的死刑犯也因此获救。此后，钱秀玲的救人事迹不胫而走，成为比利时人民心中的英雄。比利时各地被押人员的家属纷纷向她求助，她有求必应，在将军的帮助下，从纳粹枪口下救出了一批批无辜的比利时人和犹太人。

1944年6月8日，也就是盟军在诺曼底登陆后的第2天，在艾尔伯蒙附近的艾克兴市，反法西斯抵抗组织击毙了3名盖世太保军官。半小时后，几百名盖世太保包围了小镇，逮捕了96个年轻力壮的男人。盖世太保宣布：36小时之内，必须交出枪杀盖世太保军官的游

亚历山大·冯·法尔肯豪森将军

General Alexander von Falkenhausen

钱卓伦将军

General Qian Zhuolun

Lieutenant General Qian Zhuolun, became close friends. Qian Zhuolun once told Qian Xiuling that she could ask General von Falkenhausen for help if she encountered any difficulties. Qian Zhuolun also wrote to Qian Xiuling several times later, saying that unlike the German Nazis, Von Falkenhausen was a man of integrity, with a strong sense of justice and a deep affection for China and the Chinese people.

With a letter from her cousin, Qian Xiuling immediately went to Brussels and managed to find General von Falkenhausen and pleaded with him to spare the death sentence of the young Belgian man on humanitarian grounds. General Falkenhausen readily agreed to help, and not only was the youth's death sentence commuted to hard labor, but another condemned man with the same name was also saved. Thereafter, Qian Xiuling's rescue story widely spread, and she became a hero in the hearts of the Belgian people. Families of detainees from all over Belgium came to her for help, and she answered every request, saving a large number of innocent Belgians and Jews from the Nazis with the help of General von Falkenhausen.

被钱秀玲营救出来的 90 多名人质，从纳粹集中营释放后合影

A group photo of the more than 90 hostages rescued by Qian Xiuling after their release from the Nazi concentration camp

Nous avons interviewé

Madame Perlinghi, de Herbeumont, qui pendant l'occupation sauva la vie à tant de patriotes belges

Elle rentre d'un séjour de quatre mois en Chine

战后比利时报纸刊登了采访钱秀玲夫人的报道

After the war, Belgian newspapers published an interview with Mrs. Qian Xiuling

击队员，否则，每隔半小时枪毙 15 个人，直到交出袭击者为止。钱秀玲接到求援后，又在冯·法尔肯豪森将军的帮助下救出了这 96 名比利时人。他们被押解到德国的集中营去干苦力，直到二战结束。战后，比利时政府特授予钱秀玲"国家英雄"勋章，并将艾克兴市的一条街命名为"钱秀玲女士之路"。钱秀玲成了家喻户晓的英雄人物。[52]

事情并未就此结束。1944 年暗杀希特勒的"7·20"事件失败之后，冯·法尔肯豪森将军被盖世太保逮捕，关进了集中营。1948 年 2 月，冯·法尔肯豪森以比利时头号战犯的身份被押回布鲁塞尔，接受军事法庭的审判。钱秀玲再次挺身而出，她本着一颗公正而善良的心，不畏舆论压力，不惧众人唾骂，为这名虽有过也有功的德国将军四处奔走呼号，向社会大胆陈述自己的观点：

"我在大战期间为比利时人民做了一点事情，得到政府

On June 8, 1944, the 2nd day after the Allied landings in Normandy, the anti-fascist resistance killed three Gestapo officers in the city of Écaussines, near the town of Herbeumont. Half an hour later, several hundred Gestapo officers surrounded the town and arrested 96 young men. The Gestapo announced that within 36 hours, the guerrillas who shot the Gestapo officers must be handed over, or else 15 innocent men would be shot every half hour until the attackers were handed over. Qian Xiuling received a plea for help and rescued the 96 Belgians with the help of General von Falkenhausen. They were taken to German concentration camps to do hard labor until the end of World War II. After the war, the Belgian government awarded Qian Xiuling the "National Hero" medal and named a street in the town of Écaussines the "Ms. Qian Xiuling Road (Rue Perlinghi)." Qian Xiuling became a household name and a heroic figure.[52]

The story did not end there. After the failed assassination of Hitler on July 20, 1944, General von Falkenhausen was

比利时政府授予钱秀玲的"国家英雄"的勋章

The "National Hero" medal awarded to Qian Xiuling by the Belgian government

以钱秀玲名字命名的街道

The street named after Qian Xiuling

2004 年 3 月 7 日，中国驻比利时大使关呈远（左）夫妇为二战华人女英雄钱秀玲女士（中）送来生日贺卡和花篮，祝贺她 92 岁生日

On March 7, 2004, Chinese Ambassador to Belgium Mr. Guan Chengyuan (left) and his wife sent a birthday card and flower basket to Ms. Qian Xiuling (center) to congratulate her on her 92nd birthday

授予的国家勋章。如果说，这是我个人努力的结果，那么这个结果恰恰是冯·法尔肯豪森将军给的，是他冒着生命危险，做出极大努力的结果。如果没有他的努力和帮助，我将一事无成！"

1951 年 3 月，冯·法尔肯豪森终于等来了法庭的审判。在法庭上，钱秀玲以证人的身份，向法官出示当年被冯·法尔肯豪森赦免死刑者的联名信，并请来许多被营救过的人出庭作证。最终，冯·法尔肯豪森虽然被判处有期徒刑 12 年，但于 3 周后被释放回德国，直到 1966 年去世，享年 88 岁。[53]

战后，应早年导师之邀，钱秀玲进入联合国核能科学研究所工作了 5 年，圆了她的科学家之梦。20 世纪 60 年代，她捐款创办了比利时第一所中文学校——中山小学，并出任第一任董事长和校长。1990 年，她又在比利时华侨华人中发起赞助国王慈善基金的活动，获得媒体对中国移民的好评。2008 年 8 月 1 日这位曾为中比两国友谊做出杰出贡献的老人在布鲁塞尔走完自己 96 年的人生旅途，比利时政府特地为她举办了隆重的葬礼。[54]

arrested by the Gestapo and imprisoned in a concentration camp. In February 1948, he was taken back to Brussels as the number one war criminal in Belgium to be tried by a military court. Qian Xiuling once again stood up, this time for the German general. She courageously stated her own views to the society: "I have done some small things for the Belgian people during the war and have been awarded the National Medal by the government. If this was considered an achievement, then it was only made possible by General von Falkenhausen, who risked his life and made great efforts. Without his efforts and help, I would have accomplished nothing!"

In March 1951, Von Falkenhausen finally waited for the court trial. In the courtroom, Qian Xiuling, as a witness, presented the judge with a joint letter from those who had been pardoned by Von Falkenhausen and invited many people who had been rescued to testify in court. Eventually, Von Falkenhausen was sentenced to 12 years in prison, but was released to Germany three weeks later, where he remained until his death in 1966 at the age of 88.[53]

After the war, at the invitation of her early mentor, Qian Xiuling joined the United Nations Institute of Nuclear Energy for five years, fulfilling her dream of becoming a scientist. In the 1960s she donated money to found the first Chinese school in Belgium, Zhongshan Primary School, and became its first chairman and principal. On August 1, 2008, Ms. Qian Xiuling, who had made outstanding contributions to the friendship between China and Belgium, finished her 96 years of life in Brussels, and the Belgian government held a grand funeral for her.[54]

注释

1《清史稿·卷四百六十九·列传二百五十六》。

2《约章成案汇览》乙编，卷32，下，转引自陈学恂、田正平编《中国近代教育史资料汇编：留学教育》，上海：上海教育出版社，2007，第284—285页。

3 王奇生：《中国留学生的历史轨迹：1872—1949》，武汉：湖北教育出版社，1992，第57页。

4 潘越：《中国近代留学比利时研究（1903—1949）》，博士学位论文，暨南大学，2012，第37页。

5 见《中国大百科全书数据库》"李煜瀛"词条，来源：http://h.bkzx.cn/item/%E6%9D%8E%E7%85%9C%E7%80%9B?from=216458 "中国大百科全书数据库"。

6《中比教育运动导言》，《中法教育界》1928年12期，第13页，转引自潘越《中国近代留学比利时研究（1903—1949）》，博士学位论文，暨南大学，2012，第69页。

7 1901年清政府与列强签订《辛丑条约》，向英、美、法、德、意等国赔款，其中比利时获得8484345两关银，加上利息，共有18519216.30两关银。赔款由1902年开始，分38年分期偿付。1904年开始，国内教育界、政界开始动员各国退还庚款用于教育事业。1908年美国率先同意退还部分庚款。经过中比双方人士共同努力，最终于1925年和1927年分别达成了第一次、第二次中比庚款退还换文。比国庚款大部用于实业，小部分（5%）用于文化教育事业。

8 见周天度《蔡元培传》，北京：人民出版社，1984。

9 赵雅博：《雷鸣远神父传》，台中：天主教耀汉小兄弟会，1990，第320—358页。

10 潘越：《中国近代留学比利时研究（1903—1949）》，博士学位论文，暨南大学，2012，第47页。

11 潘越：《中国近代留学比利时研究（1903—1949）》，博士学位论文，暨南大学，2012，第59页。

12 周棉主编《中国留学生大辞典》，南京：南京大学出版社，1999，第324页。

13 周棉主编《中国留学生大辞典》，南京：南京大学出版社，1999，第175页。

14 周棉主编《中国留学生大辞典》，南京：南京大学出版社，1999，第411页。

15 周棉主编《中国留学生大辞典》，南京：南京大学出版社，1999，第218页。

16 1914年8月4日《伯明翰晚报》头版。

17 比利时驻华大使馆、《使馆商社贸易快讯》杂志社编《走进比利时》，北京：世界在线外交传媒集团，2004，第144页。

18 台湾中研院台湾史研究所档案馆，https://archives.ith.sinica.edu.tw/news_con.php?no=285。

19〔法〕多米尼克·马亚尔、曲辰：《第一次世界大战期间在法国的中国劳工》，《国际观察》2009年第2期，第74页；〔比〕Dominiek Dendooven & Piet Chielens. La Cinq Premiere Continents Guerre au Front Mondiale, Editions Racine, 2008, pp.136–144。

20〔法〕多米尼克·马亚尔、曲辰：《第一次世界大战期间在法国的中国劳工》，《国际观察》2009年第2期，第74—75页；比利时驻华大使馆、《使馆商社贸易快讯》杂志社编《走进比利时》，北京：世界在线外交传媒集团，2004，第141页。

21〔法〕多米尼克·马亚尔、曲辰：《第一次世界大战期间在法国的中国劳工》，《国际观察》2009年第2期，第74页。

22 国家图书馆藏历史档案文献丛刊《外交文牍》影印本第1册，北京：全国图书馆文献缩微复制中心，2004，第193—195页。

23 比利时驻华大使馆、《使馆商社贸易快讯》杂志社编《走进比利时》，北京：世界在线外交传媒集团，2004，第140页。

24〔英〕李德·哈特：《第一次世界大战战史》，林光余译，上海：上海人民出版社，2010，第124页。

25〔美〕梅尔：《一战秘史：鲜为人知的1914—1918》，何卫宁译，北京：新华出版社，2013，第155页。

26〔美〕梅尔：《一战秘史：鲜为人知的1914—1918》，何卫宁译，北京：新华出版社，2013，第196—198页。

27 第一次世界大战中，除了传统的大炮之外，飞机、潜艇和毒气这些新式武器投入到战场上，并造成了大量人员伤亡。飞机从战争开始时仅用于侦察到战争后期直接轰炸敌方阵地，贯穿于整场战争。

28 Benedicte Vaerman, Sara Vantournhout, Nicolas Standaert.《中国之路：在比利时寻找中国踪迹》，布鲁塞尔：比利时王国外交部、对外贸易与发展协会，2009，第74页。

29 见 Stephen G. Craft. Angling for an Invitation to Paris: China's Entry into the First World War. The International History Review, XVI, Toranto, 1994。

30〔法〕多米尼克·马亚尔、曲辰：《第一次世界大战期间在法国的中国劳工》，《国际观察》2009年第2期，第73页。

31 政之：《比法日三国修订商约问题》，《大公报》1926年9月7日论评。

32《不平等条约能否废除视此一周间民众之努力如何》，《大公报》1926年10月21日。

33《政府宣布中比条约失效之经过》，《国闻周报》第3卷第44期，1926；《修约延宕》，《国闻周报》第3卷第43期，1926。

34《外交部致比使照会》，《顺天时报》1926年11月7日，转引自李育民《中国废约史》，北京：中华书局，2005，第593页。

35 李育民：《中国废约史》，北京：中华书局，2005，第594—595页。

36《顾维钧回忆录》第1分册，中国社会科学院近代史研究所译，北京：中华书局，1983，第357—358页。

37《中比修约明日开议》，《晨报》1927年1月16日，转引自李育民《中国废约史》，北京：中华书局，2005，第601页。

38 中国第二历史档案馆《中华民国史档案资料汇编》第3辑《外交》，南京：江苏古籍出版社，1991，第982页。

39 唐启华：《被"废除不平等条约"遮蔽的北洋修约史（1912~1928）》，北京：社会科学文献出版社，2010，第382页。

40《比国首先抛弃领判权》，《晨报》1927年3月15日，转引自李育民《中国废约史》，北京：中华书局，2005，第603页。

41《比外长发表对于中国问题之文章》，《北益报》1927年5月30日，转引自李育民《中国废约史》，北京：中华书局，2005，第604页。

42 龙锋：《王广圻早期外交经历自述稿》，《民国档案》2011年第1期，第24—30页；徐友春主编《民国人物大辞典》，石家庄：河北人民出版社，1991，第167页。

43 沈慧瑛：《近代外交家汪荣宝》，《中国档案报》2014年5月30日，第4版；徐友春主编《民国人物大辞典》，石家庄：河北人民出版社，1991，第726页。

44《湖北省志·人物》，武汉：湖北人民出版社，2000，第155页。

45 从五卅惨案到北伐战争结束（1925—1928），全国反帝情绪高涨，国民政府高举"废约"旗帜，北洋政府也向列强提出《修约照会》，进行了一连串的修约交涉。

46 徐友春主编《民国人物大辞典》，石家庄：河北人民出版社，1991，第153页。

47 徐友春主编《民国人物大辞典》，石家庄：河北人民出版社，

参考文献

1991，第2725页；唐玉清：《中法文化交流中的谢寿康》，《现代传记研究》第5辑，上海：商务印书馆，2015，第138—144页。

48 参见宁路霞、张文嘉《民国才子张乃燕》，上海：上海科学技术文献出版社，2011。

49 参见凌其翰《我的外交官生涯》，北京：中国文史出版社，1993。

50 林吕建主编《浙江民国人物大辞典》，杭州：浙江大学出版社，2013，第508页。

51 参见金问泗《从巴黎和会到国联》，台北：传记文学出版社，1967；金问泗：《外交工作的回忆》，台北：传记文学出版社，1987。

52 参见Benedicte Vaerman, Sara Vantournhout, Nicolas Standaert《中国之路：在比利时寻找中国踪迹》，布鲁塞尔：比利时王国外交部、对外贸易与发展协会，2009，第82—83页；比利时驻华大使馆：《走进比利时——比利时王国与中华人民共和国建交40周年特刊》，2011，第145—146页。

53 参见傅宝真《德籍军事顾问与抗战前的中德合作及对军事的贡献》，台北：台湾民生出版，1998。

54 参见Benedicte Vaerman, Sara Vantournhout, Nicolas Standaert《中国之路：在比利时寻找中国踪迹》，布鲁塞尔：比利时王国外交部、对外贸易与发展协会，2009，第82—83页；比利时驻华大使馆：《走进比利时——比利时王国与中华人民共和国建交40周年特刊》，2011，第145—146页。

中文文献

[1] Benedicte Vaerman, Sara Vantournhout, Nicolas Standaert. 中国之路：在比利时寻找中国踪迹 [M]. 布鲁塞尔：比利时王国外交部、对外贸易与发展协会，2009.

[2] 比利时驻华大使馆、"使馆商社贸易快讯"杂志社编. 走进比利时 [M]. 北京：世界在线外交传媒集团，2004.

[3] 比利时驻华大使馆. 走进比利时——比利时王国与中华人民共和国建交40周年特刊 [M]. 2011.

[4] 陈学恂、田正平. 中国近代教育史资料汇编：留学教育 [M]. 上海：上海教育出版社，2007.

[5] 端方. 端忠敏公奏稿 [M]. 台北：文海出版社，1967.

[6] 傅宝真. 德籍军事顾问与抗战前的中德合作及对军事的贡献 [M]. 台北：台湾民生出版，1998.

[7] 谷牧回忆录 [M]. 北京：中央文献出版社，2009.

[8] 顾维钧回忆录 [M]. 北京：中华书局，1985.

[9] 国家图书馆藏历史档案文献丛刊 "外交文牍" 影印本：第1册 [M]. 北京：全国图书馆文献缩微复制中心，2004.

[10] 湖北省志·人物 [M]. 武汉：湖北人民出版社，2000.

[11] 金问泗. 从巴黎和会到国联 [M]. 台北：传记文学出版社，1967.

[12] 金问泗. 外交工作的回忆 [M]. 台北：传记文学出版社，1987.

[13] 李育民. 中国废约史 [M]. 北京：中华书局，2005.

[14] 林吕建主编. 浙江民国人物大辞典 [M]. 杭州：浙江大学出版社，2013.

[15] 凌其翰. 我的外交官生涯 [M]. 北京：中国文史出版社，1993.

[16] 宁路霞、张文嘉. 民国才子张乃燕 [M]. 上海：上海科学技术文献出版社，2011.

[17] 唐启华. 被 "废除不平等条约" 遮蔽的北洋修约史（1912~1928）[M]. 北京：社会科学文献出版社，2010.

[18] 王奇生. 中国留学生的历史轨迹：1872—1949 [M]. 武汉：湖北教育出版社，1992.

[19] 徐友春主编. 民国人物大辞典 [M]. 石家庄：河北人民出版社，1991.

[20] 张建国. 中国劳工与第一次世界大战 [M]. 济南：山东大学出版社，2009.

[21] 中国第二历史档案馆编. 中华民国史档案资料汇编 [M]. 第3辑外交，南京：江苏古籍出版社，1991.

[22] 周天度. 蔡元培传 [M]. 北京：人民出版社，1984.

[23] 赵雅博. 雷鸣远神父传 [M]. 台中：天主教耀汉小兄弟会，1990.

[24] 中国大百科全书（网络版本）[DB]. http://h.bkzx.cn.

[25] 周棉主编. 中国留学生大辞典 [M]. 南京：南京大学出版社，1999.

[26] 顾维钧回忆录：第1分册 [M]. 中国社会科学院近代史研究所译，北京：中华书局，1983.

[27] 〔美〕傅高义. 邓小平时代 [M]. 冯克利译. 北京：生活·读书·新知三联书店，2013.

[28] 〔美〕梅尔. 一战秘史：鲜为人知的1914—1918[M]. 何卫宁译. 北京：新华出版社，2013.

[29] 〔英〕李德·哈特. 第一次世界大战战史 [M]. 林光余译. 上海：上海人民出版社，2010.

[30] 杨正润. 现代传记研究：第5辑 [C]. 上海：商务印书馆，2015.

[31] 〔法〕多米尼克·马亚尔、曲辰. 第一次世界大战期间在法国的中国劳工 [J]. 国际观察.2009（2）：73—79.

[32] 谷牧. 关于访问欧洲五国的情况报告 [J]. 党的文献.2009（1）.

[33] 龙锋. 王广圻早期外交经历自述稿 [J]. 民国档案.2011（1）.

[34] 潘越. 中国近代留学比利时研究（1903—1949）[D]. 博士学位论文，暨南大学，2012.

[35] 沈慧瑛. 近代外交家汪荣宝 [J]. 中国档案报.2014.5.30.（总第2615期）：第4版.

第二部分 比利时与天津

Part II: Belgium and Tianjin

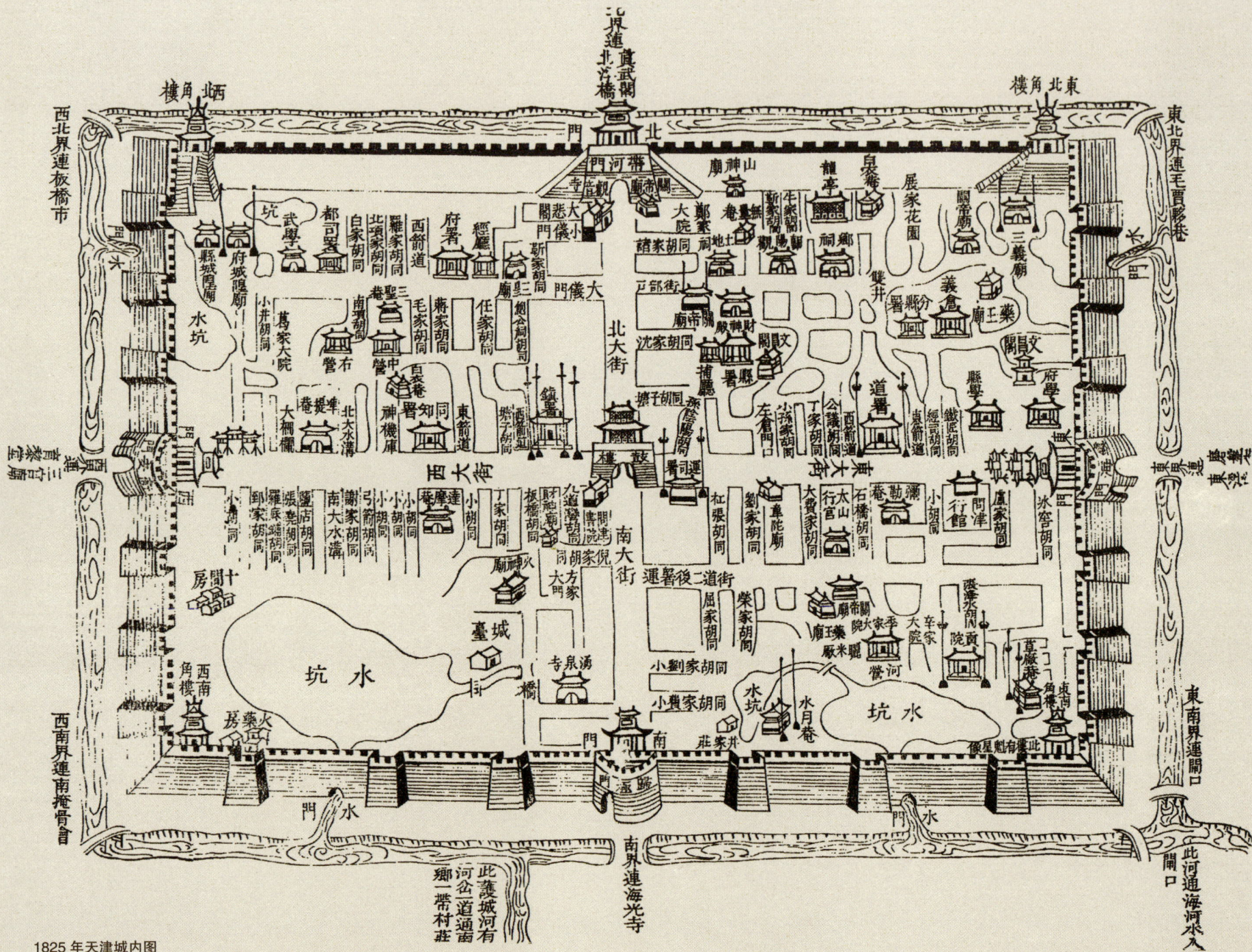

1825 年天津城内图

A map of the city of Tianjin in 1825

第四章 比利时在旧天津的遗迹

Chapter 4: The Traces of Belgium in Old Tianjin

为什么是天津？

工业革命后，海外殖民地对于欧洲资本家变得日益重要，因为它意味着廉价的原材料供应地和广阔的产品倾销市场。对于欧洲大陆上率先完成工业革命的比利时来说，国内市场狭窄，立国时间不长，国力也不强大，在海外拥有殖民地是发展外向型经济所亟须的。中国广阔的市场一直是国王利奥波德父子所垂涎的。第一次鸦片战争之后，比利时人意识到，他们可以借助列强的势力，在战争中渔翁得利，利用英法美三国所签订的条约，"利益均沾"，从而直接进入中国市场。1845 年，比利时驻马尼拉领事兰哪（J. Lannoy）前往广州与两广总督耆英谈判，要求通商，并得到允许。然而，这只是一份协议而非条约，并不能切实保证比利时在中国沿海地区的商业活动。[1] 尽管在开放中国市场方面，比利时屡遭挫折，但受到国王支持的政客们却没有放弃争取中国市场向其商人及产品开放的野心。

Why Tianjin?

After the Industrial Revolution, overseas colonies became increasingly important to European capitalists because they meant a cheap supply of raw materials and a wide market for the dumping of their products. For Belgium, the first to complete the Industrial Revolution on the European continent, its domestic market was small, thus having colonies overseas was much needed to develop an outward-looking economy. The vast market of China had always been coveted by King Leopold and his son. After the First Opium War, the Belgians realized that they could take advantage of the treaties signed by Britain, France, and the United States with China to "share the benefits" and thus gain direct access to the Chinese market. In 1845, J. Lannoy, the Belgian consul in Manila, went to Guangzhou to negotiate with the Governor of Guangdong and Guangxi, Qiying, for permission to open up to trade. However, this was an agreement rather than a treaty and did not effectively guarantee Belgian commercial activities in the coastal areas of China.[1] Despite repeated setbacks, the politicians

咸丰皇帝
Emperor Xianfeng

第一次鸦片战争之后的十几年来，五口通商没能打开中国的市场，列强与中国直接对话的愿望也没有达成，直到 1858 年签订的《天津条约》才明确规定了外国使节常驻北京。原因在于，与西方国家签订的不平等条约是中国在战败压力之下被迫接受的，所以从条约签订的一开始，清政府内部就不打算要认真遵守这些条约。由于已经领教了英国人的"船坚炮利"，他们不敢明里违背条约，只能暗地阻止条约履行，或者如另一派朝臣所坚持的——以"信守"条约来阻止列强的进一步行动。于是，英、法、美、俄四国为了扩大在华权益，而挑起了第二次鸦片战争。1857 年 12 月，广州陷落之后，年轻的咸丰皇帝仍然无视外国人要求，认为南方的战事仅是地方性事件。为了打破清政府的大国迷梦，四个国

supported by the king did not give up their ambition to open up the Chinese market to their merchants and products.

For more than a decade after the First Opium War, the five ports of commerce failed to open China's market, and the desire of the powers to engage in direct dialogue with China was not achieved until the Treaty of Tianjin, signed in 1858, which explicitly provided for the permanent presence of foreign envoys in Beijing. The reason for this was that the unequal treaties with Western countries were forced upon China under the pressure of military defeat. Therefore, from the very beginning of the treaties, the Qing government had no intention to seriously comply with them. Having already learned of the British's "strength of battleships", they dared not violate the treaties openly, but could only prevent the fulfillment secretly. Thus, Britain, France, the United States and Russia provoked the Second Opium War to expand their rights and interests in China. In December 1857, after the fall of Guangzhou, the young Emperor Xianfeng still ignored the foreigners' demands and considered the war in the south as a local event only. To break the Qing government's dream of greatness, the four countries decided to shift the scope of the war to the north. In April 1858, the British, French and American ministers led their ships north to join the Russians who had arrived at the mouth of Tianjin's Dagu in advance, ready to launch further military operations. Tianjin was therefore the real battleground of the Second Opium War.

The land of Tianjin, from its birth, has formed its unique geographical position as "the key to the river and the sea." The importance of Tianjin lies in that it is an important port for urban and rural goods distribution and military food transit in the north. From the Qin, Han and the Three Kingdoms to the Tang, Song and Ming dynasties, in order to defend against the invasion and harassment from ethnic minorities such as the Huns and Khitan, Chinese rulers all stationed massive forces in the north, and even spent a lot of

1655 年荷兰东印度公司使团访华，经过天津城

In 1655, a delegation of the Dutch East India Company visited China and passed through the city of Tianjin

1793 年为招待马戛尔尼使团而在天津搭建的戏台

The theater stage built in Tianjin in 1793 to entertain the Lord Macartney delegation

家决定把战事范围转移到北方。1858 年 4 月，英、法、美三国公使率舰船北上，与先期到达天津大沽口的俄国公使及其舰船会合，准备展开进一步的军事行动。天津，才是第二次鸦片战争的真正战场。

天津这片土地，从诞生之日起，就形成了其"河海要冲"的得天独厚的地理位置。天津的重要性在于，它是北方城乡物资集散和军粮转运的重要港口。自秦、汉、三国至唐、宋、明等朝代，为防御来自匈奴、契丹等少数民族的侵扰，均在北方屯以重兵，甚至不惜耗费大量人力物力修筑长城、运河。因此，天津虽不是古代兵家必争的军事要塞，却是北方最重要的水路运输枢纽，承担着军粮转运和仓储等后勤保障任务。特别是明清以来，两个王朝均定都北京，天津更成为首都的门户和出海口。

在近代史上，由于这种拱卫京师、物资集散的特殊地位，"威胁天津，压服北京"就成了列强的战略方针。

manpower and resources to build the Great Wall and canals. Although Tianjin was not a military fortress in ancient times, it was the most important waterway transportation hub in the north, undertaking logistics tasks such as military food transfer and storage. Especially since the Ming and Qing dynasties, both dynasties established their capitals in Beijing, and Tianjin became the gateway to the capital and an outlet to the sea.

In modern history, due to this special position of defending the capital and distributing materials, "threatening Tianjin to subdue Beijing" became the strategic policy of the western powers. Since 1840, Tianjin had been the preferred target of the powers in their wars against China. Before the First Opium War, British diplomats and merchants suggested that while blockading the coastal towns of southern China, "a few small ships should be sent to Tanggu, the seaport of Beijing, to show our strength."[2] During the Second Opium War, the British and French Allied Forces attacked Dagu Forts at the mouth of the Hai

自 1840 年之后，天津一直是列强发动侵华战争的首选目标。在第一次鸦片战争发动前，英国外交官和商人们曾建议，在封锁中国南方沿海城镇的同时，"又要派遣几只小船去塘沽，这是北京的海口，在进行交涉中，这便可以表示我们的力量"[2]。第二次鸦片战争期间，英法联军三次进攻大沽炮台，两次打到天津城，并于 1860 年占领天津城，进逼北京，最终逼迫清政府与英法两国签订了《北京条约》，其中特别规定了将天津开放为通商口岸。

在第二次鸦片战争中，也想要分一杯羹的利奥波德一世曾向法国皇帝拿破仑三世提议比利时参与战争，但这个想法遭到了比利时议会的否定。[3] 参与攫取海外殖民地，必须要有强大的军力，而比利时向来托庇于大国保护，其议会并不热心发展军备。退而求其次，彼时尚为王储的利奥波德二世力劝参议院在中国要占有一席之地。于是，议会于 1861 年通过了一笔 25000 法郎的贷款，用于在上海设立领事馆。此举的目的是，以此为基地派驻外交官，与清政府谈判，获得"最惠国待遇"。1864 年利奥波德二世甚至亲自动身前往远东，进行了近六个月的旅行，以寻找机会在中国获取一块殖民地。但是清政府此时尚不会对比利时这样的欧洲小国低头。

中日甲午之战后，帝国主义掀起瓜分中国的狂潮，欧洲列强在中国几乎都有自己的势力范围。但在当时，像比利时这样的小国，尚难以同英、法、俄等欧洲大国竞争，甚至无力与有教皇支持的意大利相争。曾有人清醒地看到，"在中国，我们是装备不良的新来者，对手均凶猛残暴、不讲道德，并且大部分国家都已经长期驻扎在中国，占领了无限资源，背靠精英军队。这些都是我们没有的东西"[4]。

River three times, reached Tianjin twice, finally occupied it in 1860 and threaten Beijing, forcing the Qing government to sign the Treaty of Beijing with the Britain and France. The treaty specifically stipulated the opening of Tianjin as a port of commerce.

During the Second Opium War, Leopold I proposed to the French Emperor Napoleon III that Belgium participate in the war, but the idea was rejected by the Belgian Parliament.[3] To participate in the seizure of overseas colonies, it was necessary to have a strong military force. Belgium had always taken refuge in the protection of the great powers, and its parliament was not keen on developing armaments. Leopold II, who was then crown prince, urged the Senate to take an interest in China, and in 1861 a loan of 25,000 francs was approved for the establishment of a consulate in Shanghai. The purpose of this move was to use this as a base to station diplomats and negotiate with the Qing government to obtain "most favored nation status." In 1864, Leopold II even set out on a six-month trip to the Far East in search of an opportunity to acquire a colony in China. But the Qing government would not yet bow to a small European country like Belgium.

After the Sino-Japanese War, the imperialists set off a frenzy to carve up China, and almost all the European powers at the time had their own spheres of influence in China. But at that time, it was difficult for a small country like Belgium to compete with the great European powers such as Great Britain, France and Russia, and it was even unable to compete with Italy, which had the support of the Pope. Someone soberingly observed that "In China we are ill-equipped newcomers, while our competitors are all fierce and brutal and immoral. Most of the countries are already permanently stationed in China, occupying unlimited resources and backed by elite armies. These are the things we don't have."[4]

"殖民主义之王" 利奥波德二世在中国谋夺租界的历次尝试

1856 年，法国和英国出兵中国，引发了第二次鸦片战争。利奥波德王子想要派遣一支比利时军队参与战争，希望能在长江口占领一座岛屿。然而，比利时政府否决了这一计划。[5]

1864 年，利奥波德王子周游中国。他计划将台湾岛变为殖民地，但由于父亲利奥波德一世即将去世，只得匆忙返回比利时。[6]

1872 年，一位比利时军火商受王室所托，尝试前往中国建立租界地，但比利时政府再次对其进行阻挠。

1897 年，为了避开比利时政府的反对，利奥波德二世决定借助他个人的殖民地——刚果自由邦来实现他对中国的野心，派遣刚果外交使团赴京。这一次，他仍未能在中国占领一片区域，但他的努力带来了一定程度的商业成功——获得与中国铁路公司共同修建京汉铁路的特许权，并将这个重要的项目委托给一位比利时工程师让·沙多。

1898 年，比利时借承建京汉铁路的机会，买下汉口日租界东北火车站一带的民地 3.6 万余平方米，随后以预备比国铁路工人赁住为词，强硬要求总理衙门将该地辟为比租界。湖广总督张之洞坚决反对，指出比国工人可由铁路公司代借房屋。比利时索要租界未果。[7]

1898 年，利奥波德二世派遣两个使团前往甘肃，其中一个使团的目的是在甘肃的西北寻找据点，因使团内部冲突中止。[8]

1901—1902 年，义和团运动后，比利时给予财政援助，帮助八国联军镇压中国人民的反抗。为了表示感谢，

The Various Attempts by Leopold II – the "King of Colonialism" – to Seize the Concessions in China

In 1856, France and Britain sent troops to China, starting the Second Opium War. Prince Leopold wanted to send a Belgian army to participate in the war, hoping to capture an island at the mouth of the Yangtze River. However, the Belgian government vetoed his plan.[5]

In 1864, Prince Leopold traveled in extensively inside China. He planned to colonize the island of Taiwan but had to return to Belgium in a hurry because his father, Leopold I, was about to die.[6]

In 1872, a Belgian arms dealer was commissioned by the royal family to try to go to China to establish a concession. But once again, the Belgian government obstructed this plan.

In 1897, in order to avoid the opposition of the Belgian government, Leopold II decided to use his personal colony, the Congo Free State, to realize his ambitions for China, by sending a Congolese diplomatic mission to Beijing. This time, he still failed to occupy a territory in China, but his efforts brought a certain degree of commercial success - a concession to build the Beijing-Hankou railroad with the Chinese railroad company and entrusting this important project to another Belgian engineer, Jean Jadot.

In 1898, Belgium took the opportunity of constructing the Beijing-Hankou railroad to buy 36,000 square meters of land in the northeast railway station of the Japanese concession in Hankou, and then demanded the Ministry of Foreign Affairs to turn the land into a Belgian concession on the pretext that it was prepared for the Belgian railroad workers to live there. Zhang Zhidong, the Governor of Hu-Guang, strongly opposed this and pointed out that the Belgian workers could be housed by the railroad company.

Belgians who had been in interior maintaining stations of Belgian built RR. They were smuggled out at night during Boxer uprising, aided by friendly Chinese.

义和团运动期间比利时铁路职工及其家属在天津合影。照片下文字说明，他们是被友好的中国人在晚上偷偷救出来的。图片出自华盛顿大学图书馆

Belgian railroad workers and their families in Tianjin during the Boxer Rebellion. Photo from the library of Washington University

八国联军同意比利时在天津设立租界。

1902 年，比利时先斩后奏，再次企图开辟汉口比租界。但这一行动遭到比利时国内的一片反对，德国也表示抗议。后由湖广总督张之洞主持，于 1906 年收回汉口租界。[9]

1900 年义和团运动爆发，这给比利时带来了一次绝好的机会。义和团攻击了卢汉铁路，拆毁铁轨，推倒电

Belgium was unsuccessful in demanding the concession.[7]

In 1898, Leopold II sent two delegations to Gansu, one of which was intended to find a foothold in northwestern Gansu. The mission was suspended due to internal conflicts within the delegation.[8]

In 1901-1902, after the Boxer Rebellion, Belgium gave financial assistance to help the Eight-Power Allied Forces to put down the resistance of Chinese people. As a token of appreciation, the Eight-Power Allied Forces agreed to the

报线杆，杀死了6名比利时工人，还在中国北方杀害了多名比利时籍传教士。利奥波德二世立即抓住这个机会。他先是打算派遣一支约790人组成的远征队来华，名义上是为了保护比利时在华商业利益和人员安全，实为借出兵出力获得列强承认以谋取设立租界。但是1839年的《伦敦条约》[10]中要求比利时严守中立原则，列强由此反对比利时军队驻扎中国。因此，比利时远征军被解散了。[11]后来他匿名捐款资助一批比利时志愿兵（时称"义勇队"）前往中国，参与八国联军保护北京使馆侨民及镇压义和团运动的行动（这笔捐款虽为匿名，但数目高达300万法郎，如此巨额捐助只有可能来自国王本人）。[12]联军占领津、京后，在国王的支持下，头脑精明、手腕灵活的比利时驻华公使姚士登（Maurice Joostens）向北京的外国使团提出，要求在天津开辟租界。在联军与清政府议和期间，姚士登的外交活动令欧洲大国不得不注

义和团运动后列强瓜分中国的漫画明信片

A cartoon post depicting the powers dividing China after the Boxer Rebellion

establishment of a Belgian concession in Tianjin.

In 1902, Belgium again attempted to open a Belgian concession in Hankou. However, this action was met with a wave of domestic opposition; Germany also protested. Later, Zhang Zhidong, the Governor of Hu-Guang, presided over the repossession of the Hankou concession in 1906.[9]

The outbreak of the Boxer Rebellion in 1900 presented Belgium with a great opportunity. The Boxers attacked the Lu-Han Railway, tearing up the tracks, knocking down telegraph poles, killing six Belgian workers and a few Belgian missionaries in northern China. Leopold II immediately seized this opportunity. He first planned to send a 790-men expeditionary team to China in name of protecting Belgian commercial interests and personnel; this was actually intended to gain recognition from the other powers for the establishment of a concession by contributing troops. However, the Treaty of London[10] of 1839 required Belgium to adhere strictly to the principle of neutrality, and the other powers thus opposed the presence of Belgian troops in China. As a result, the Belgian Expeditionary Force was disbanded.[11] Later, Leopold II made an anonymous donation to finance a group of Belgian volunteers (then called the "Voluntary Corps") to go to China and join the Eight-Power Allied Forces in protecting the expatriates of the legation in Beijing and suppressing the Boxer Rebellion (this donation, although anonymous, amounted to 3 million francs, a sum that could only come from the King himself).[12] After the occupation of Tianjin and Beijing by the Allied Forces, the shrewd Belgian Minister in China, Maurice Joostens (Chinese name Yao Shideng), with the support of the king, proposed to the foreign mission in Beijing to establish a concession in Tianjin. During the peace negotiations between the Allied Forces and the Qing government, Joostens's diplomatic activities forced the European powers to pay attention to the interests of Belgian merchants and missionaries in China. In this way, Belgium,

《辛丑条约》签订后合影。1901 年 9 月 7 日，外国列强的全权代表们与中国政府在西班牙公使馆签订《辛丑条约》。从左至右坐着的人物为：克罗伯（Knobel）（荷兰）、小村寿太郎（Komura Jutarō）（日本）、萨尔瓦葛（Marquis Salvago）（意大利）、姚士登（比利时）、齐干（Baron van Wahlborn）（奥匈帝国）、葛络干（de Cologan y Cologan）（西班牙）、格尔思（von Giers）（俄国）、穆默（Mumm von Schwarzenstein）（德国）、萨道义（Ernest Satow）（英国）、柔克义（Rockhill）（美国）、鲍渥（Beau）（法国），联芳、李鸿章、奕劻

The signature of the Boxer Protocol between the plenipotentiaries of the foreign powers and the Chinese government at the Spanish Legation in Beijing on 7 September 1901. From left to right are seated: Mr. Knobel (The Netherlands), Mr. Komura Jutarō (Japan), Marquis Salvago Raggi (Italy), Mr. Joostens (Belgium), Baron von Wahlborn (Austrian-Hungarian Empire), Mr. de Cologan y Cologan (Spain), Mr. von Giers (Russian Empire), Mr. Mumm von Schwarzenstein (German Empire), Sir Ernest Satow (Great Britain), Mr. Rockhill (USA), Mr. Beau (French Republic), Lien Fang (China), Li Hongzhang (China), Yi Kuang (China)

意到比利时商人与传教士在华的利益。这样，比利时虽未参加联军，但也凭借高超的外交技巧，获得参加列强瓜分中国这场盛宴的入场券。

　　借由联军入侵，利奥波德二世统治下的比利时终于达成在中国拥有一块殖民地的夙愿。和议期间，姚士登先是授权下属、比利时驻津领事梅禄德（Chevalier de Mellotte）于 1900 年 11 月 7 日，向列强驻津领事团发出通告，宣布"本日奉北京公使训令"，占领"德租界下方对岸，沿白河至世昌洋行（E. Meyer & Co.）油栈下方约五十米地点"，"以为比国通商市场"；"禁止上列地域内一切财产之买卖、让渡与转移，但占领前经过正当手续，凡是以中国人以外之欧洲人名义之地契，认为有效并尊重之"[13]。通告发出还未得到明确回复时，又于 1901 年 3 月 21 日，以比利时驻北京公使的名义通知八国联军占领天津后组成的临时政府委员会，允许其

although not participating in the Allied Forces, was able to gain admission to the feast of the partition of China by the powers, thanks to its excellent diplomatic skills.

　　With the invasion of the Allied Forces, Belgium under Leopold II finally achieved its long-cherished dream of having a colony in China. During the peace negotiations, Maurice Joostens first authorized his subordinate, the Belgian consul in Tianjin, Chevalier de Mellotte, to issue a notice to the consular corps of the powers in Tianjin on November 7, 1900, announcing that "on this day, by order of the Minister in Beijing," Belgium would occupy "the opposite bank of the river from German concession, along the White River to a point about fifty meters below the oil depot of E. Meyer & Co." as "a commercial market in Belgium." And "the sale, transfer and disposal of all property in the above-mentioned area are prohibited. Before the occupation, the deeds in the name of Europeans other than Chinese are considered valid and respected."[13] When the notice did not receive a clear reply, on March

在一定条件下，"在划定的比利时租界内行使治安监督"[14]，意即再次宣示比利时对天津租界的占有权。彼时，八国联军攻陷京津，慈禧太后和光绪皇帝西逃，东南互保[15]，清政府的政权岌岌可危。那种形势下，许多在华外国人都预计，"中国将被列强瓜分，会出现多年的无政府状态"[16]。所以比利时当时是向列强而非清政府，提出在天津设立租界的要求，如同它在非洲攫取到的刚果殖民地一样，无须征得当地人的准许。而湖北在张之洞的管辖下参加东南互保，得到列强应允的"互保"，比利时没有借口要求在汉口设立租界。

之后，比利时驻津领事嘎德斯（W. Henri Ketels）与天津河间道张莲芬开始进行交涉。1902年2月6日嘎德斯与张莲芬、津海关道唐绍仪、直隶候补道钱鏐签订《天津比国租界合同》，在俄租界之南划定比租界，范围北起俄租界，南至小孙庄，东穿大直沽村，西临海河，约占地747.5亩。同时，还规定，如果日后比租界商务兴旺，可以开辟由比租界到京山铁路的通道，作为比租界的预备租界，这片土地不得卖与别国。因界内原有世昌、信义、顺全隆等洋行，占地191亩，故比利时能支配的土地仅556.5亩。[17]划为比租界的土地，由比利时支付4.5万两白银用于收购界内原住户所有土地，之后比租界管理方按照各国租界的先例，每亩每年向清政府交地租1000文钱。比租界名义上仍为中国领土，但比利时驻津领事馆对该地区拥有管辖权和领事裁判权。天津这块土地上，又出现了一片界内中国居民反而受外国政府统治的外国人居住区——比利时租界。

八国联军占领天津时，海河西岸已有英国、法国、日本、德国四国的租界，所以后来的比利时只能与俄国、

21, 1901, the Belgian Minister in Beijing notified the Provisional Government Committee formed after the occupation of Tianjin by the Eight-Power Allied Forces that it was allowed, under certain conditions, to "exercise the supervision of the security in the Belgian concessions."[14] This in fact meant another declaration of Belgian possession of the Tianjin concession. At that time, the Eight-Power Allied Forces had captured the capital and Tianjin, and the Empress Dowager Cixi and the Emperor Guangxu had fled to the west and the southeast China signed the agreement of mutual protection.[15] In that situation, many foreigners in China expected that "China would be divided up by the powers and there would be anarchy for many years."[16] So Belgium asked the powers, not the Qing government, to set up a concession in Tianjin, just as it had done with the Congo colony in Africa, without the permission of the locals. And since Hubei Province was under the jurisdiction of Zhang Zhidong and had been promised "Mutual Protection in Southeast China" by the powers, Belgium had no excuse to ask for a concession in Hankou.

After that, W. Henri Ketels, the Belgian Consul in Tianjin, started to negotiate with Zhang Lianfen, the Tianjin Hejian Daotai (local magistrate). On February 6, 1902, Ketels signed the "Tianjin Belgian Concession Contract" with Zhang Lianfen, Tang Shaoyi, the Tianjin Customs Daotai, and Qian Rong, the Zhili Alternate Daotai, which delineated the Belgian concession to be in the south of the Russian concession, with the following four boundaries: from the Russian concession in the north to Xiaosunzhuang in the south, through Dazhigu Village in the east, and adjacent to the Hai River in the west. The total acreage was about 747.5 mu. At the same time, it was also stipulated that if the commerce in the Belgian concession would flourish in the future, a passage from the Belgian concession to the Beijing-Shanhaiguan Railway could be opened as an addition to the Belgian concession. This land could not be

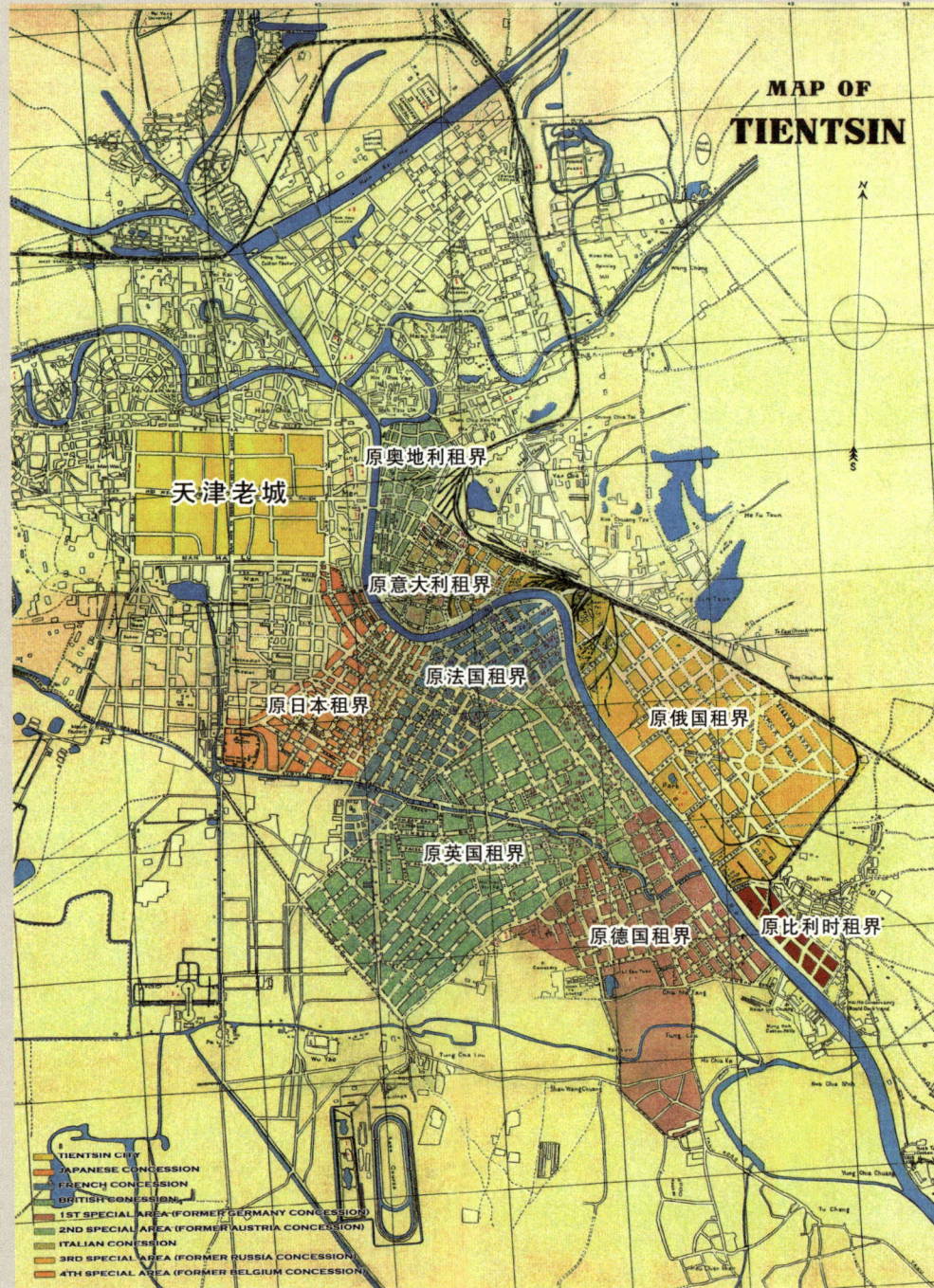

MAP OF
TIENTSIN

天津老城

原奥地利租界

原意大利租界

原法国租界

原日本租界

原俄国租界

原英国租界

原德国租界

原比利时租界

TIENTSIN CITY
JAPANESE CONCESSION
FRENCH CONCESSION
BRITISH CONCESSION
1ST SPECIAL AREA (FORMER GERMANY CONCESSION)
2ND SPECIAL AREA (FORMER AUSTRIA CONCESSION)
ITALIAN CONCESSION
3RD SPECIAL AREA (FORMER RUSSIA CONCESSION)
4TH SPECIAL AREA (FORMER BELGIUM CONCESSION)

地图上红色区域为原天津比租界

The red area on the map is the former
Tianjin Belgian concession

意大利、奥匈帝国在海河东岸划定租界。在天津拥有一块租界，俨然成为比利时跻身世界强国行列的标志之一。而对天津来说，先后有9个国家在天津城外强设租界，其总面积达到原来老城区的8倍多，这使它成为帝国主义列强瓜分中国的一个缩影。与此同时，这里也成为东西方文明冲突、融合的最初场所。随着城市的成长，天津逐渐从一个小军镇发展为一个中外各国人民的聚居处，领风气之先的繁华大都市，中国北方的政治、经济、军事和外交中心。

sold to other countries. Within the boundary, the Messrs. H. Meyers & Co., Mandl & Co., H. and Meyerink & Co., Wm. had taken up an area of 191 mu, thus the land at the disposal of Belgium was only 556.5 mu.[17] Belgium paid 45,000 taels of silver for the acquisition of all the land of the original residents within the boundary of the land designated as the Belgian concession. Thereafter, Belgian concession authority, in accordance with the precedent of other foreign concessions, paid an annual rent of 1,000 copper coins per mu to the Qing government. The Belgian concession nominally remained Chinese territory, but the Belgian Consulate in Tianjin had jurisdiction and consular authority over the area. In this piece of land in Tianjin, another area of foreign settlement emerged where the Chinese residents within the boundary were instead subject to the rule of foreign governments - the Belgian concession.

When the Eight-Power Allied Forces occupied Tianjin, there were already four foreign concessions on the west bank of the Hai River: Britain, France, Japan and Germany. Belgium hence could only establish a concession with Russia, Italy and Austria-Hungary on the east bank of the Hai River. Having a concession in Tianjin became one of the symbols that Belgium was among the world powers. As for Tianjin, nine countries had forcibly set up concessions outside the city, with the total area reaching more than eight times that of the original old city, which made it a microcosm of the imperialist powers' division of China. At the same time, it also became the first place where East and West civilizations clashed and merged. With the growth of the city, Tianjin gradually developed from a small military town to a prosperous metropolis where people from China and abroad cohabited as well as the political, economic, military, and diplomatic center of northern China.

今因

大比國欲按照舊日與
大清國所立通商條約第十二款大意擬在天津河東地
方租地一段以為比國人通商市場是以
大清國欽差北洋大臣李　派委天津河間道張
大清國欽差全權大臣姚　派委直隸候補道錢
大比國欽差全權大臣姚　派委駐津領事官嘎　公同
會議所允條款如下

一　比國租地一段在河東俄國租界以下從世昌洋
　　行煤油棧地邊起沿河向東以一千一百六十八
　　密達中國七百零一弓為止從河邊向裏以四
　　百五十密達中國二百七十弓為止其寬廣四
　　至皆於圖內載明界內所有地畝民房由租界委
　　員代為購買立契與駐津領事官收執比國商
　　民即可在租界以內修築房屋鋪面教堂學堂醫
　　院墳園及作何生理悉聽比國高民自便

二　界內地畝已經租界委員與領事官查看共約地

六百數十畝內除洋商信義行順全隆地一百數
十畝下餘之地約五百畝以上分作三等一為莊
基地一為平地一為水坑地議明比國總出銀四
萬五千兩由租界委員會同本地紳衿酌定價值
按戶發給統俟奉
旨允准畫過合同一面交欵界內有民間已蓋
之屋仍准民間暫為居住俟用地時在六簡月以
前知會遷讓其拆屋費統於知會遷讓屋時由領事
官會同地方官公平議給價值不令民間喫虧其
屋料仍歸民間自用此刻先將屋數查明存一清
冊以後不得再行添蓋界內如有坟地每棺給遷

費銀四兩

十一　以上所議各條先緒華文法文各二分由勘界
　　委員領事官畫押分存即由勘界委員鈔錄合同
　　詳請
　　北洋大臣　核定具奏俟奉到
　　外務部　核准復奏　光緒二十七年十一月初五日奉
　　　　　　　　　　　　西歷一千九百零二年十二月十五號奉
諭旨　允准後再補繕華文法文各六分彼此畫押蓋印交
　　換分執為憑
十二　此件已奏請
十三　所有界內之地已經租界委員與領事官會同
　　勘丈立有界牌為准內有世昌洋行信義洋行順
　　全隆洋行各地通計共地七百四十七畝半

硃批　依議欽此

大清國光緒二十七年十二月二十八日
天津河間道張道琴
直隸候補道唐紹儀
直隸候補道錢縣鑾

大比國一千九百零二年二月　六　號駐津領事官嘎德斯

196

《天津比国租界合同》。文件收藏
于比利时外交部档案馆

The Tianjin Belgian Concession Contract. Document preserved in the archives of the Belgian Ministry of Foreign Affairs

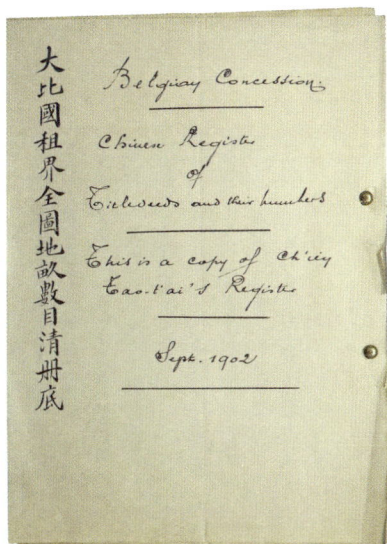

比租界地亩数目清册。文件收藏于比利时外交部档案馆

Inventory of the number of acres of land in the Belgian concession. Document are kept in the archives of the Belgian Ministry of Foreign Affairs

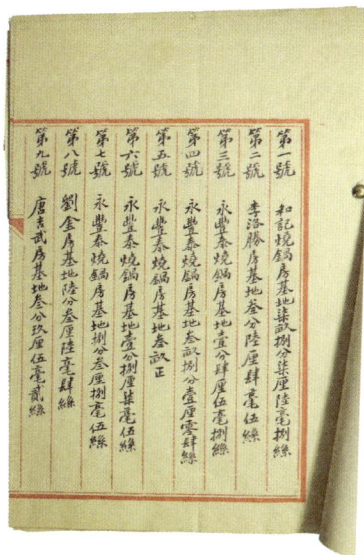

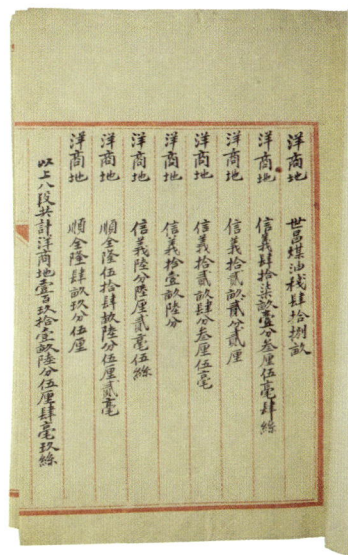

股票上的租界

　　比利时看中的这块租界，位于海河东岸的大直沽。关于天津的起源有这样的说法："先有大直沽，后有天津卫。""沽"的意思是指买或者卖。任何人群聚落乃至城市都是起源于交换和买卖的场所，交换和买卖越兴旺，村庄也就越来越大。大直沽这个海河边上的小村子逐渐形成了后来的天津。

　　虽然历史悠久，但随着天津城的发展，大直沽不再处于中心位置，相距繁荣的天津老城和已经建设较为完善的海河西岸各国租界较远。从交通条件来说，附近河面上没有桥梁，并不方便。所以，从比租界开辟直到交还中国的几十年间，比利时政府和商人都没有对租界进

The Underdeveloped Concession

　　The concession that interested Belgium was located in Dazhigu on the east bank of the Hai River. There is a saying about the origin of Tianjin: "First there was Dazhigu, then there was Tianjin Wei." The word "Gu" means to buy or sell. Any settlement or even a city originates from a place of exchange and trading. The more exchange and trading flourished, the bigger the settlement became. Dazhigu, a small village by the Hai River, gradually evolved to what became Tianjin.

　　With the development of Tianjin, Dazhigu was no longer in the center of the city. It was far away from the prosperous old city of Tianjin and the more well-constructed concessions on the west bank of the Hai River. In terms of transportation, there was no bridge over the

天津比租界的规划示意图。蓝线圈出的为原世昌、信义、顺全隆洋行所占地块。文件收藏于比利时外交部档案馆

Schematic plan of the Belgian concession in Tianjin. The land marked by blue line was occupied by Meyer & Co., Mandl & Co., H., and Meyerink & Co., Wm. The document is kept in the archives of the Belgian Ministry of Foreign Affairs

行大规模的开发建设。租界内只有原来的中国住户，人口 1100 多人，[18] 没有外国居民，连比利时驻津领事馆也设在英租界内的华比银行（今解放北路 104 号中国建设银行天津分行）。

在比租界工部局的早期发展计划，原本是要利用比租界优越的地理位置——拥有 1170 米的海河沿河地带[19] 和经过其北部边界的京奉铁路支线（为俄租界与比租界分界线），将比租界打造成工厂区和仓储货运区。计划包括：重修河坝码头以供海河内航行的轮船停泊；将现有京奉铁路支线延长，使这条支线沿着河坝马路横穿比

nearby river, which was not convenient. Therefore, from the establishment of the Belgian concession to the handover to China decades later, the Belgian government and businesses did not carry out large-scale development and construction of the concession. There were only the original Chinese residents who lived in the concession, with a population of 1,100[18]. There were no foreign residents; even the Belgian Consulate in Tianjin was located in the British concession in the Sino-Belgian Bank (present-day China Construction Bank Tianjin Branch, No. 104 North Jiefang Road).

The early development plan of the Municipal Council in the Belgian concession was to take advantage of the

No 4 Année 1908

Travaux de remblaiement dans la partie amont de la Concession belge.

No 13 Année 1911.

Le "bund belge" (partie aval en construction)

1910 年比租界工部局加固修缮了比租界的海河河坝。照片摄于 1911 年，收藏于比利时外交部档案馆

In 1910, the Municipal Council of the Belgian concession reinforced and repaired the dam of the Hai River in the Belgian concession. The photo was taken in 1911 and is kept in the archives of the Belgian Ministry of Foreign Affairs

租界。这样一来，比租界就能提供天津各国租界中最为便利的航运条件——货运者可以将货物从轮船上卸下后直接由前门运进仓库，然后从后门通过铁路转运出去。[20] 对于发展工业来说，交通运输是基础设施建设中最重要的一项。天津的外国租界中，除了俄租界内有京奉铁路天津站，其他任何租界都不具备比租界这一优势。

比租界还具有另一优势，即地势较高。这样，开发土地就不必像其他租界那样，需要把大大小小的水坑、荒地排干积水，晒干土地，然后再从海河抽取水底河沙填充垫平土地。在比租界，只须垫高不超过 18 英寸（约 46 厘米），就可以满足修筑道路与铺设下水道的要求。[21]

然而，比利时国会一直在是否发展天津比租界上犹豫不决，毕竟与列强相比，其领土、人口、军力都不占优。经过多年反复讨论，在比租界设立 10 年后的 1912 年年底，比政府决定将租界的经营权转售给一家私营公

superior location of the Belgian concession, with 1,170 meters of river frontage along the Hai River[19] and the Beijing-Fengtian Railway spur line passing through its northern boundary (the boundary between the Russian concession and the Belgian concession), to develop it into a factory and freight storage region. The plan included to rebuild the river dam wharf for ships navigating in the Hai River and to extend the existing Beijing-Fengtian Railway line to make it run across the Belgian concession along the river dam road. In this way, the Belgian concession could provide the most convenient shipping services among the Tianjin concessions - freighters could unload their goods from the ships and take them directly from the front gate into the warehouses, and then transfer them out by rail from the back gate.[20] Transportation was one of the most important infrastructural foundations for the development of industry. Among the foreign concessions in Tianjin, no other concessions had this advantage over the Belgian concession, except for the Russian concession in which

司——比租界股份有限公司（Belgian Concession Land Co. Ltd.）来进行开发建设。[22] 比租界收入主要来源于土地税和房捐（房产税）。[23] 原本只有大直沽村原住民的一部分房捐收入，最多不过 1000 两。比租界股份有限公司接手后，将界内土地划分为三等，沿河一带为一等，每亩地价 3000 元；海河与大直沽之间地带为二等，每亩地价 2000 元；大直沽村附近为三等，每亩 1500 元。

由于比租界的地利优势，英、法、美、日等国的资本家纷纷到比租界购买土地。但是，他们中大多数也并

海河边的比利时挖泥船正在作业，抽取水底淤泥到河岸上以垫平土地、修整河岸。照片摄于 1911 年，收藏于比利时外交部档案馆

A Belgian dredger at the river, extracting silt from the bottom of the water to the riverbank in order to level the land and repair the riverbank. The photo was taken in 1911 and is kept in the archives of the Belgian Ministry of Foreign Affairs

the Tianjin Station of the Beijing-Fengtian Railway was located.

The Belgian concession had another advantage: the higher terrain. As a result, it was not necessary to drain the puddles and wastelands, dry the land, and then fill the land with sand from the Hai River, as was the case in the other concessions. In the case of the Belgian concession, it was only necessary to raise the land by no more than 18 inches (about 46 cm) to meet the requirements of building roads and laying sewers.[21]

However, the Belgian Parliament was hesitant to develop the Belgian concession in Tianjin, because, after all, Belgium was not superior in terms of territory, population, or military power compared to other powers. After years of repeated discussions, at the end of 1912, ten years after the establishment of the Belgian concession, the Belgian government decided to resell the operation of the concession to a private company, Belgian Concession Land Co. Ltd. (BCL).[22] The main source of revenue for the Belgian concession was the land tax and property tax,[23] originally only from a portion of the property taxes paid by the native Dazhigu villagers, which was no more than 1,000 taels. After the BCL took over, the land within the boundary was divided into three classes: the area along the river was the first class, with a price of 3,000 yuan per mu; the area between the Hai River and Dazhigu was the second class, with a price of 2,000 yuan per mu; and the area near Dazhigu Village was the third class, with a price of 1,500 yuan per mu.

Due to the geographical advantage of the Belgian concession, capitalists from Britain, France, the United States, Japan, and other countries went there to buy land. However, most of them did not carry out construction until 1930, when the Belgian concession was officially returned to China, there were only a few lumber warehouses owned by the Boyd & Co. and Chinese merchants. Although

SOCIETE ANONYME DE LA CONCESSION BELGE DE TIENTSIN.

———————

SOCIETE ANONYME DE LA CONCESSION BELGE DE TIENTSIN.

———————

Le capital social est fixé à Frs: I.335.000.- représenté par 2670 actions de 500 francs chacune.

Il se divise en : Actions d'apport Frs: 700.000.-
            "   de capital   "   635.000.-

LES ACTIONS D'APPORT : Frs: 700.000.- sont réparties comme suit :

200 actions entièrement libérées (Frs: I00.000.-) à Mr. Detring pour le terrain Bielfeld (5 I/2 Hectares)

I200 actions entièrement libérées (Frs: 600.000.-) au Groupe composé des "Comptoirs en Chine" S.A. en liq.; du Baron Ed. Empain et du Crédit Général de Belgique (40 Hectares)   De ses Frs: 600.000.- en actions ce Groupe ristourne Frs: I00.000.- aux souscripteurs.

LES ACTIONS DE CAPITAL : Frs: 635.000.- ont été souscrites par les personnes designées ci-dessous :

M. Warocqué	Frs: 80.000.-
Société Générale de Belgique	" 80.000.-
Banque d'Outremer	" 80.000.-
Banque de Bruxelles	" 50.000.-
Baron Léon Lambert	" 50.000.-
F.M. Philippson & C°	" 50.000.-
M. Edouard Thys	" 50.000.-
M. Ernest Solvay	" 60.000.-
Mme Alfred Solvay	" 30.000.-
Baron Auguste Goffinet	Frs: 25.000.-
Baron Constant Goffinet	" 25.000.-
M. Michel Orban	" 15.000.-
Chevalier de Wouters d'Oplinter	" 10.000.-
M. Jean Cassel	" 10.000.-
M. Jules Collin	" 10.000.-
M. Arthur Bemelmans	" 5.000.-
M. Firmin Lambeau	" 5.000.-
Total des souscriptions	635.000.-

Sur ces souscriptions un premier versement de 25 % a été effectué.

x
x   x

ADMINISTRATION. Le Conseil comprendra 8 à 15 membres et il y aura de 4 à 8 commissaires.

Le Ier Conseil sera composé de Mr. Warocqué comme président et d'un ministrateur désigné par chacune des parties suivantes :
Société Générale de Belgique
Banque d'Outremer
Banque de Bruxelles
Baron Léon Lambert
F.M. Philippson & C°
M. Edouard Thys
M. Ernest Solvay
Baron Auguste Goffinet
Sont nommés Commissaires pour la première fois :
MM. Arthur Bemelmans, Jean Cassel, Jules Collin et Michel Orban.

比利时天津租界股份有限公司招股说明书。以上文件收藏于比利时外交部档案馆
Share prospectus of the Belgian Tianjin Concession Public Limited Company.
Documents are kept in the archives of the Belgian Ministry of Foreign Affairs

没有进行建设，直到1930年比租界正式交还中国之时，界内仅有英国和记洋行以及华商设立的几个木栈而已。尽管比利时商人在天津开设有不少工商企业，包括实力雄厚的义品放款公司、天津比商电车电灯公司[24]、华比银行等，却由于深知内情（比租界股份有限公司缺少建设资金），均未在该租界进行投资。而计划中的其他财政来源，包括土地税、房捐、车捐、码头捐、过境税、碇泊费、营业执照费、警捐、卫生捐等，全部也只是画饼。后来，随着一战的爆发，比利时本土成为主战场，全部可用资源都投入到抵抗德国侵略，租界只经历了短暂的发展就再次陷于停顿。在短暂的开发中，比租界工部局进行了沿河马路的修建工程，还售出一块180亩的土地（1923年），给英国和记洋行开办蛋厂，获得地价银54万元。[25]因为没有进行充分开发，比租界被称为"股票租界"，属于各国在华租界中极不发达的一类。[26]

虽然长期以来只存在于股票上，但既然有了这么一块租界，除了建设外，还得进行管理。比利时政府仿照其他外国在华租界的管理办法，实行西方的城市自治制度，即把租界的行政管理权全部或部分移交给本国侨民选举产生的董事会。但是这个董事会必须接受比利时驻华公使的直接监督和比利时外交部的间接监督，按月呈报一切办理情况，并由比利时驻津领事担任董事长。在这一点上，比租界的行政权力设置形式，更接近于法租界的"领事独裁"式体制，而非英租界的"侨民自治"式体制。天津比租界第一任董事长是驻津领事嘎德斯，嘎德斯奉调回国后，由其后历任驻津领事接任。

担任比租界董事会董事，必须具备两个条件：一，必须是侨居在天津的比利时人，[27]熟悉中国国情，但不

Belgian merchants had established many industrial and commercial enterprises in Tianjin, including the powerful CFEO, Compagnie de Tramways & D'eclairage de Tientsin (CTET)[24], and the Sino-Belgian Bank, they did not invest in the concession because they knew that the BCL lacked funds for infrastructure construction. The other planned financial sources, including land tax, real estate tax, vehicle tax, harbor tax, transit tax, anchorage fee, business license fee, policing fee, sanitation fee, etc., all fell through. Later, with the outbreak of World War I, Belgium itself became the main battlefield, and all available national resources were devoted to resisting the German invasion. The concession experienced only a short period of development before coming to a halt. During the short period of development, the Municipal Council of the Belgian concession carried out the construction of a road along the river, and sold a 180-mu piece of land (in 1923) to the Boyd & Co. to start an egg factory, for a price of 540,000 silver yuan.[25] Because it was not fully developed, the Belgian concession was called the "Stock Concession", and deemed one of the underdeveloped concessions in China.[26]

Although lacking in construction, the Belgian concession nonetheless had to be managed. The Belgian government, modeled on the management of other foreign concessions in China, implemented the Western system of municipal autonomy, i.e., transferring the administration of the concessions, in whole or in part, to a board of directors elected by its own expatriates. However, this board must be under the direct supervision of the Belgian Minister in China and the indirect supervision of the Belgian Ministry of Foreign Affairs and submit monthly reports. The Belgian Consul in Tianjin would serve as the chairman of the board. In this regard, the form of administrative power set up in the Belgian concession was closer to the "consular dictatorship" system of the French concession than to the "autonomy of the expatriates" system of the British concession. The first

早期的比租界工部局（位于大直沽），摄于1911年
The early days of the Municipal Council of the Belgian concession (located in Dazhigu), photo taken in 1911

chairman of the Tianjin concession was W. Henri Ketels, the consul in Tianjin, who was transferred back to Belgium and was succeeded by subsequent consuls in Tianjin.

To be a member of the Board of Directors of the Belgian concession, one must have two conditions: first, he must be a Belgian living in Tianjin (not necessarily in the Belgian concession),[27] familiar with Chinese conditions; second, he must have property of more than 20,000 taels of silver. Initially, the provisional board was composed of four Belgians living in Tianjin appointed by the Belgian government, and four others as assistants. Later, when the provisional board became a formal body, the four assistants became deputy directors. The Board of Directors of the Belgian concession had directors and deputy directors, which was different from other concession Boards. Those who served on the Board of Directors included Robert Devos, in charge of the Sino-Belgian Bank, G. Guillard, the general manager of Compagnie de Tramways & D'eclairage de Tientsin (CTET), J. O'neill (French), the manager of CFEO, Martin, the manager of CTET, Docquier Alexander,

限定必须居住在比租界；二，必须拥有财产白银2万两以上。最初，临时董事会由比利时政府任命4名侨居天津的比利时人组成，另派4人作为助理。后来，临时董事会成为正式机构，这4名助理便成为副董事。比利时租界董事会设董事和副董事，这是它与其他租界董事会的不同之处。先后担任董事的有华比银行负责人罗伯特·德福斯（Robert Devos）、天津比商电车电灯公司总经理马洒（G. Guillard）、义品放款公司经理欧爱叶（J. O'neill，法国人）等人，天津比商电车电灯公司经理马丁（Martin）、开滦矿务局总工程师窦根

后期的比租界工部局
The later days of the Municipal Council of the Belgian concession

以上照片收藏于比利时外交部档案馆
Photos are kept in the archives of the Belgian Ministry of Foreign Affairs

（Docquier Alexander）、耀华玻璃公司经理纳森（E. J. Nathan，英国人）等也先后担任过天津比租界董事会董事。[28]

租界里日常进行行政管理的是工部局。比租界工部局直接隶属于租界董事会，但是也必须接受比利时驻津领事的领导。工部局下设警务、捐务、工程3个处，并设有华人翻译官1人。由于比利时在津侨民人数较少，以上3个处的负责人都是由比国驻津领事馆人员兼任。所以，比租界工部局实际上是由驻津领事领导的市政管理部门。[29]

the chief engineer of the Kailuan Mining Administration, and E. J. Nathan, the manager of the Yaohua Mechanical Glass Company.[28]

The day-to-day administration of the concession was carried out by the Municipal Council, which was directly under the Board of Directors of the concession while also supervised by the Belgian Consul in Tianjin. Under the Municipal Council, there were three divisions: Police Dept., Revenues Office, Engineering Dept., and one Chinese interpreter. Due to the small number of Belgian expatriates in Tianjin, the heads of the above three divisions were all held concurrently by staff of Belgian consulate in Tianjin.

比租界巡捕房的巡捕们。照片收藏于比利时外交部档案馆

The constables of the Belgian Concession Patrol. Photos are kept in the archives of the Belgian Ministry of Foreign Affairs

比租界的警察旧时称"巡捕"。他们负责管理租界内的治安，由工部局警务处领导。警务处长即巡捕官，由比利时驻津领事馆秘书兼翻译兼任。下设中国籍巡捕长一名，巡捕长以下雇有中国籍巡捕多人。[30]

比租界还曾先后于1915年、1916年和1921年三次企图扩张租界，均因遭到中国居民的强烈抵制，加之欧战爆发比利时政府无暇东顾，未能得逞。1915年，比租界当局以重金贿赂大直沽乡长，意图将大直沽村未被划入比租界的土地占有，遭到当地农民的反对，被迫中止。1916年，比利时驻津领事趁法国制造"老西开事件"之机，借口维持治安，派巡捕设岗于大直沽村全村路口，企图强占该村，当地居民奋起将站岗的巡捕驱除村外，并联名向直隶省请愿交涉。比利时领事慑于民威罢休。最后一次，1921年，比利时领事又以加宽海河为由，要求比租界的地界向外延伸33米，并擅自派工部局翻译到居民区划线，作为占地拆房的标志，被愤怒的居民痛打后赶跑，比利时扩张租界的企图再次破产。[31]

1926年中国政府要求废除《中比通商条约》，并收回天津比租界。由于中国对收回天津比租界的声音强烈，同时租界亦面临财政危机，比利时政府终于想明白："所得租界，既非富饶，又不广大"，而"因此区区主权之故，竟被中国列入帝国主义国家列强之内"，实在得不偿失。比利时政府决定，"抛弃此种主权，不啻表明一反从前所为，今后但专信赖中国人民之睦谊，决不再参加武力对华或干涉中国之政策"[32]。

1927年1月17日，比利时驻华公使洛恩（Léon le Maire de Warzee d'Hermalle）宣布，比利时愿意将天津比租界交还中国，以示友好。[33]1929年8月31日，中比

Therefore, the Municipal Council of the Belgian concession was in fact a municipal administration department headed by the consul in Tianjin.[29]

The police officers in the Belgian concession were called "constables." They were responsible for managing the security in the concession and were led by the Police Department of the Municipal Council. The position of the head of the police department, namely the inspector, was held concurrently by the secretary of the Belgian Consulate in Tianjin, who was also the interpreter. There was a Chinese chief constable and under him many Chinese constables were employed.[30]

The Belgian concession also made three attempts to expand the concession in 1915, 1916 and 1921, all of which were strongly resisted by the Chinese residents. In addition, due to the outbreak of the European war, the Belgian government had no time to worry about the problems in the Far East. Its attempt to expand the concession therefore failed. In 1915, the Belgian concession authorities bribed the village chief of Dazhigu with a large sum of money in order to take possession of the land in Dazhigu village that was not included in the Belgian concession, but the local farmers objected, and the scheme did not materialize. In 1916, using the "Lao Xi Kai Incident" created by France as an excuse for maintaining law and order, the Belgian Consul in Tianjin sent policemen to set up posts at the intersections of the village, attempting to forcefully occupy the village. The local residents rose up and drove the police away from the village. The Belgian consul gave up in fear of the people. The last time, in 1921, the Belgian Consul demanded to extend the boundary of the Belgian concession by 33 meters outward on the grounds of widening the Hai River and sent an interpreter from the Municipal Council to the residential area without authorization to draw a line as a sign of demolition of houses on the land. He fled after being beaten up by the angry residents. Belgium's attempt to

两国签订了交还天津比租界的约章，规定该租界的行政管理权，以及所有租界公产，移交中国政府；而比租界工部局所背负的 93800 余两白银债务（包括利息）由中国政府偿还。1931 年 3 月，两国政府正式举行交接典礼，天津比租界改为天津特别行政区第四区（特四区）。[34]

1931 年中比两国政府在天津原比租界工部局前举行比租界交接典礼。照片第一排中央戴高礼帽者为中国政府代表王正廷。照片由近代天津博物馆提供

The Chinese and Belgian governments held the ceremony on the handover of the Belgian concession of Tianjin in 1931. The center in the first row in a top hat is Wang Zhengting, the representative of Chinese government. Photo from Tianjin Museum of Modern History

expand its concessions failed again.[31]

In 1926, the Chinese government demanded the abrogation of the Sino-Belgian Treaty of Commerce and the recovery of the Belgian concession in Tianjin. As the Chinese voice was strong for the recovery of the Tianjin concession and the concession was facing a financial crisis, the Belgian government finally realized that "the concession is neither rich nor extensive" and "for the reason of its mere sovereignty, Belgium is deemed by China as one of the imperialist powers." The gains did not make up for the losses. The Belgian government decided that "by abandoning such sovereignty, the Belgian government is showing its goodwill to the Chinese people and the commitment to not to take part in any policy of force against or intervention in China in the future."[32]

On January 17, 1927, Belgian Minister Léon le Maire de Warzee d'Hermalle announced that Belgium was willing to hand over the Belgian concession of Tianjin to China as a sign of friendship.[33] On August 31, 1929, the Chinese and Belgian governments signed a treaty on the handover of the Belgian concession of Tianjin, stipulating that the administration of the concession, as well as all the public property of the concession, would be handed over to the Chinese government, and that the 93,800 taels of silver debt (including interest) incurred by the Municipal Council of the Belgian concession would be repaid by the Chinese government. In March 1931, the two governments held a formal handover ceremony, and the Tianjin concession was transformed into the Fourth District of Tianjin Special Administrative Region (Special District IV).[34]

华比银行

被迫开放成为通商口岸后，随着对外贸易和工商业的发展，天津很快成为北方最大的经济中心和国际化港口城市，亚洲最大的原材料出口中心之一。在中国北方，天津拥有最优越的港口，不仅将直隶、河南、山东、山西、陕西、甘肃、东三省以及内外蒙地方出产的物品输出于海内外，而且这些地方所需要的物资也需要通过天津港来进口，于是天津港很快成为洋货输入大户，很多货品都从原产国直接进口。因此，天津与比利时之间的贸易往来也大大增强。20世纪初，在天津的主要货物输入国中，比利时居于第5位，仅次于日本、英国、美国和德国，输入货品主要为铁道材料这种大宗高值商品。[35]

有了京汉铁路的第一次成功合作，比利时国王利奥波德二世对中国的投资热情更加高涨。在国内，由于议会对王权的限制，国王除了自己手中的钱，其实没有多少可支配的权力。有一次，当利奥波德二世和表亲德国皇帝威廉二世（Kaiser Wilhelm II）在柏林观看一场游行时，他感慨道："除了金钱之外，我们这些国王真的一无所有了！"[36] 而金钱在一定程度上是可以转化为权力的。所以利奥波德二世通过担任投资公司的董事长，在海外到处抢夺殖民地掠夺资源，进行资本输出。在中国，为了与列强竞争谋夺修筑铁路开采矿山的各种利权，他于1902年3月发起创办了华比银行（英文为Sino-Belgian Bank，法文为Banque Sino-Belge、Banque Belge pour L'Étranger）。华比银行的母公司正是由利奥波德二世担任董事长的比利时通用公司，总部设在布鲁塞尔。该行最初注册资本仅有100万法郎，以后增至5000万法郎。据1930年6月该行报告，资本总额已达2亿法郎，

Sino-Belgian Bank

Forced to open as a port of commerce, Tianjin quickly became the largest economic center and international port city in northern China, and one of the largest export centers of raw materials in Asia, as foreign trade and industry and commerce developed. Tianjin had the most advanced port in northern China, not only exporting goods produced in Zhili, Henan, Shandong, Shanxi, Shaanxi, Gansu, the three Eastern provinces and Inner and Outer Mongolia abroad, but also importing materials needed in these places through the port of Tianjin. It soon became a major importer of foreign goods, many of which were imported directly from their countries of origin. As a result, trade between Tianjin and Belgium also greatly increased. In the early 20th century, Belgium ranked 5th among the major exporters of goods to Tianjin, after Japan, the United Kingdom, the United States and Germany, and exported to China mainly high value goods such as railway materials.[35]

With the first successful cooperation on the Beijing-Hankou railroad, King Leopold II of Belgium became even more enthusiastic about investing in China. At home, the king did not really have much power at his disposal except for the money in his own hands, due to the parliamentary restrictions on royal power. Once, when Leopold II and his cousin Kaiser Wilhelm II of Germany were watching a parade in Berlin, he lamented, "We kings really have nothing left but money!"[36] However, money can, to some extent, be translated into power. Leopold II did so by serving as chairman of an investment company, grabbing colonies overseas to plunder resources and exporting capital. In China, in order to compete with the great powers for the right to build railroads and extract mines, he launched the Sino-Belgian Bank (French: Banque Sino-Belge, Banque Belge pour L'Étranger) in March 1902. The parent company of Sino-Belgian Bank was the Belgian General Company,

华比银行北侧。位于和平区解放北路 104 号，重点保护等级历史风貌建筑，现为中国建设银行。建于 1921 年，占地面积约 2400 ㎡，建筑面积约 3000 ㎡，为简约的现代主义风格建筑。照片收藏于比利时外交部档案馆

The north side of Sino-Belgian Bank. Located at No.104 North Jiefang Road, Heping District, this key protection grade historical style building is now the China Construction Bank. Built in 1921, it covers an area of about 2,400m², with a construction area of about 3,000m², and is a simple modernist style building. The photo is kept in the archives of the Belgian Ministry of Foreign Affairs

华比银行东侧
The east side of Sino-Belgian Bank

其中未缴资本 5290 万法郎。[37] 几年后在上海、天津、汉口等地开设分行。华比银行成为最早在中国开设的外国银行之一。

比利时是一个欧洲小国，与列强在中国竞争路矿利权本来并无胜算。众所周知，资本主义银行在殖民地的活动离不开本国政府的实力保证和直接支持。19 世纪 90 年代以后进入中国的一批日、俄、法、德银行，就是具体的例证。日本横滨正金银行、俄国华俄道胜银行、法国法兰西银行、东方汇理银行以及德国德华银行，在其成长过程中，都得到了各自政府"特殊的鼓励"和"积极的帮助"。[38] 比利时虽然弱小，国王利奥波德父子却

chaired by Leopold II and headquartered in Brussels. The bank's initial registered capital was only 1 million francs, which was later increased to 50 million francs. In June 1930, the bank reported that its capital had reached 200 million francs, of which 52.9 million francs were outstanding.[37] A few years later, branches were opened in Shanghai, Tianjin and Hankou. Sino-Belgian Bank became one of the first foreign banks to open in China.

Belgium was a small European country that originally had no chance to compete with the powers in China for the right to build railroads and extract mines. It was well known that the activities of capitalist banks in the colonies could not be carried out without the strength and direct support of their own governments. The Japanese, Russian, French and German banks that entered China after the

华比银行二楼办公室。照片保存于比利时外交部档案馆
Sino-Belgian Bank Office on the second floor. The photo is kept
in the archives of the Belgian Ministry of Foreign Affairs

是一对擅长交际应酬、在列强缝隙中求生存的生意人、外交家。他们背靠英、法，联系欧洲大陆上的主要财团，巧妙利用国际金融市场，周转和组织国际资本，先是入股 1895 年在中国成立的华俄道胜银行，后来又组成具有银行团性质的辛迪加，来参与对华贷款业务的竞争，如有 1910 年的英比辛迪加、1911 年的英法比辛迪加、1913 年的奥比辛迪加，还有俄比银团和非正式的比法俄日四国银行团的实际存在。[39] 1911 年，天津出现了一个以华比、东方汇理、华俄道胜和横滨正金四银行为代表的临时凑合起来的四国银行团，它们为应对天津市的金融恐慌向天津商会提供 100 万两的贷款。[40] 1913 年 4 月 26 日北洋政府与英、法、德、俄、日五国银行团签订了善后借款合同，借款总额 2500 万英镑，年息 5 厘，

1890s were concrete examples of this. Yokohama Specie Bank, Russo-Asiatic Bank, Bank of France, Banque de l'Indochine and Deutsch-Asiatische Bank all received "special encouragement" and "active help" from their respective governments in their growth process.[38] Although Belgium was weak, King Leopold and his son were a pair of businessmen and diplomats who were good at socializing and surviving in the gap between the powers. With the backing of Britain and France and major financial consortia on the European continent, they skillfully used the international financial market, first taking a stake in the Russo-Asiatic Bank established in China in 1895, and later forming a banking syndicate to compete for loans to China, such as the British-Belgian syndicate in 1910, the British-French-Belgian syndicate in 1911, the Austrian-Hungarian-Belgian syndicate in 1913, and the Russian-Belgian syndicate.[39] In 1911, a temporary four-nation banking

按 84% 实交。银行团各方采取了公开发行债票的方式，每国各募集 500 万英镑。最后在发行中，比利时承购了 1388880 英镑，成为实际的债权方之一。[41]

关于华比银行的资本来源还有一种说法。1900 年八国联军入侵后，列强向清政府要求战争赔款，并成立了一个赔偿委员会。因比利时在义和团运动中也有人员伤亡和财产损失，遂位列其中。随着《辛丑条约》签字，比利时获赔 8607750 法郎，占列强赔款总数的 1.8%。有学者认为，比利时用这笔赔款于 1902 年成立了"华比银行"。[42] 笔者认为，战争赔款一般包含着对伤亡人员的抚恤、对财产损失的赔偿以及出兵海外的军费支出，然后是惩罚性的赔款。战争赔款扣除前几项支出后，所剩余的惩罚性赔款才能被政府作为收入来支配，且条约中规定，赔款自 1902 年 1 月 1 日起至 1940 年，分 39 年付清，不是也不可能一次性结清。而一所银行的设立应当是筹谋已久，不会是"等米下锅"。所以，华比银行的资金应当主要来自比利时通用公司，而非庚子赔款。但其后清政府向比利时驻北京公使馆支付的庚子赔款则是汇入了华比银行的账户中。[43]

华比银行天津分行成立于 1906 年，行址位于原英租界维多利亚路（今解放北路）——天津著名的金融街。20 世纪初，天津共开设有 7 家外国银行的分行，包括汇丰银行（1890）、麦加利银行（即渣打银行，1896）、横滨正金银行（1899）、华俄道胜银行（1897）、德华银行（1890）、华比银行（1906）和花旗银行（约1902—1908）。由于华比银行成立的主要目的是在华投资铁路、房地产、有轨电车等，所以华比银行在津初设分行时，普通商业方面的业务较少。各个银行的营业额

syndicate, represented by Sino-Belgian Bank, Banque de l'Indochine, Russo-Asiatic Bank and Yokohama Specie Bank, emerged in Tianjin to make a loan of one million taels to the Tianjin Chamber of Commerce in order to relieve the financial panic in the city.[40] On April 26, 1913, the Beiyang government signed a loan contract with the five-nation banking group of Britain, France, Germany, Russia, and Japan, with a total loan amount of 25 million pounds sterling at an interest rate of 5% per annum, which was paid at 84%. The banking group parties adopted a public issue of debt notes, with each country raising 5 million pounds. In the final issue, Belgium bought 1,388,880 pounds, and became one of the actual creditors.[41]

There is another theory about the source of the capital of the Sino-Belgian Bank: after the invasion of the Eight-Power Allied Forces in 1900, the powers demanded war reparations from the Qing government and founded a compensation committee. Belgium was included in this committee because it had also suffered casualties and property damages during the Boxer Rebellion. With the signing of the Boxers Protocol, Belgium was awarded 8,607,750 francs, accounting for 1.8% of the total reparations made to the powers. Some scholars believed that Belgium used the reparations to establish the "Sino-Belgian Bank" in 1902.[42] According to the authors of this book, war reparations generally consisted of compensations for casualties and property damage, military expenditures for troops abroad, followed by punitive reparations. After the war reparations were deducted, only the remaining punitive reparations could be disposed of by the government as income. The treaty also stipulated that the reparations would be paid in 39 years from January 1, 1902 to 1940 and could not have been settled in one lump sum. The establishment of a bank like Sino-Belgian Bank must have been planned for a long time. Therefore, the capital of the Sino-Belgian Bank should have come mainly from the

华比银行一楼营业大厅。照片保存于比利时外交部档案馆
Sino-Belgian Bank business lobby on the first floor. The photo is kept in the archives of the Belgian Ministry of Foreign Affairs

属于秘而不宣的商业机密，那么最为直观的用以判断其业务发展程度的，就是柜台营业员的数量多寡，以 1906 年 7 月的一次统计为例：

横滨正金银行：15 人

汇丰银行：7 人

华俄道胜银行：7 人

麦加利银行：7 人

德华银行：7 人

华比银行：2 人[44]

除了外籍雇员，各外国银行还通过买办与中国商人进行交易。各国银行中，这些人多则十几人，少则数人。

把以上这些人员都加起来的话，横滨正金银行显然是居于第一位的，而华比银行与在津的其他外国银行的

Belgian General Company, not from the Boxer Protocol reparations. However, the Boxer Protocol reparations paid by Qing government to the Belgian Legation in Beijing were remitted into the account of Sino-Belgian Bank.[43]

The Tianjin branch of the Sino-Belgian Bank was established in 1906, and its premises were located on Victoria Road (now North Jiefang Road), the former British concession - the famous financial street of Tianjin. In the early 20th century, seven branches of foreign banks were opened in Tianjin, including HSBC (1890), Chartered Bank of India, Australia and China (1896), Yokohama Specie Bank (1899), Russo-Asiatic Bank (1897), Deutsch-Asiatische Bank (1890), Sino-Belgian Bank (1906), and Citibank (c. 1902-1908). Since the main purpose of the establishment of the Sino-Belgian Bank was to invest in railroads, real estate, trams, etc., its regular commercial business was relatively small when its branch first opened in Tianjin. The turnover of each bank was a business secret, so the most intuitive way to judge the extent of its business operation was the number of counter clerks.

Yokohama Specie Bank: 15

HSBC: 7

Russo-Asiatic Bank: 7

Chartered Bank of India, Australia and China: 7

Deutsch-Asiatische Bank: 7

Sino-Belgian Bank: 2 [44]

In addition to foreign employees, foreign banks also dealt with Chinese merchants through compradors. There were more than a dozen of compradors in some foreign banks and less than a few people in others.

When adding up all of these employees, Yokohama Specie Bank was clearly in first place, and the difference in scale of operation between Sino-Belgian Bank and other foreign banks in Tianjin was very obvious. This was mainly because each country had different political aims and economic privileges in China. Japan was the

营业规模差距非常明显。这主要是由于各国对华的政治目的和经济权利各不相同。日本距中国最近，日本人希望更多地向中国加以多方面的渗透，达到控制和占领中国的目的；其在华侨民人口尤其是在天津的侨民，也是各国中最多的，因而它的银行业务量大、经营范围广、雇员也就更多。而比利时远在欧洲西部，在华的侨民人口较少，其在华主要是商业利益，华比银行除经营存款、放款、汇兑等一般银行业务外，更专注于承揽大宗长期贷款，特别是对中国铁路的投资和经营，我国历次所借由比利时承建铁路的贷款，如京汉铁路、陇海铁路，均由该行经理。华比银行初设时的业务范围窄，雇员自然也就少。

1913 年华比银行与英国国外银行合并，遂变更名称为 "Banque Belge pour l'Etranger. S.A."，中文名称不变。这意味着该行业务已经跨出中国境外。到了 20 世纪 20 年代，华比银行大幅扩张版图，在中国汉口、德国科隆、

华比银行营业大厅。照片保存于比利时外交部档案馆
Sino-Belgian Bank business lobby. The photo is kept in the archives of the Belgian Ministry of Foreign Affairs

geographically closest to China, and the Japanese wished to penetrate more into China in many aspects to achieve the purpose of controlling and occupying China. Its population of expatriates in China, especially in Tianjin, was also the largest among all countries. Therefore, its banking business was higher in volume, business scope was more extensive, and its employees were larger in size. Belgium, on the other hand, was far away in Europe and had a smaller population of expatriates in China, and its main interest in China was commercial. In addition to general banking business such as deposits, money lending, and exchange, the Sino-Belgian Bank was more focused on contracting large long-term loans, especially for investment in and operation of Chinese railroads. China's multiple loans for railways contracted with Belgium, such as Beijing-Hankou railway and Longhai railway, were all serviced by the Sino-Belgian Bank. When the Bank was first established, the scope of business was narrow and the number of employees was naturally small.

In 1913, Sino-Belgian Bank merged with British Foreign Bank and changed its name to "Banque Belge pour l'Etranger. S.A." with the same Chinese name. This meant that the bank's business had crossed over to outside China. By the 1920s, the bank expanded significantly, opening branches or offices in Hankou, China; Cologne, Germany; New York, USA; Paris, France; Bucharest and Braila, Romania; Manchester, UK; and Constantinople, Turkey, becoming the most important bank in the Belgian overseas banking system. In Austria-Hungary, Romania, Yugoslavia, Poland, Bulgaria, Czechoslovakia and other Central and Eastern European countries, it had numerous partner banks. It has also expanded its industrial investment areas, particularly in the tobacco sector, holding several specialized companies. In the 1930s, due to the overwhelming volume of business and the world economic crisis, its branches were converted into locally registered companies, while its operations in China were still headquartered in Brussels,

华比银行天津分行发行的钞票。收藏于布鲁塞尔
BNP 银行关于华比银行的档案资料中

Banknotes issued by Sino-Belgian Bank Tianjin
Branch. Preserved in BNP Bank of Brussels
archival material on Sino-Belgian Bank

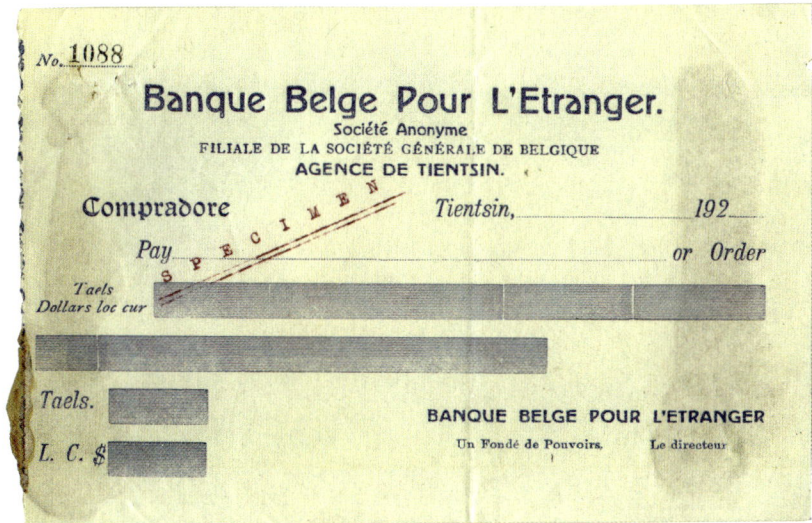

1922 年天津华比银行的支票。收藏于布鲁塞尔 BNP 银行关于华比银行的档案资料中

Checks from the Sino-Belgian Bank of Tianjin, 1922. Preserved in BNP Bank of Brussels archival material on Sino-Belgian Bank

美国纽约、法国巴黎、罗马尼亚布加勒斯特和布雷拉、英国曼彻斯特、土耳其君士坦丁堡，相继设分行或办事处，成为比利时海外银行系统中最重要的银行。在奥匈、罗马尼亚、南斯拉夫、波兰、保加利亚、捷克斯洛伐克等中东欧国家，华比银行拥有众多同盟银行。它的工业投资领域也不断扩大，特别是在烟草领域，持有多家专业公司。20 世纪 30 年代，由于业务量过于巨大以及世界经济危机的影响，其属下各地分行陆续改为当地注册公司，而在中国的业务，总部仍然设在布鲁塞尔，但改法文名称为 Banque Belge pour l'Étranger (Extrême-Orient)。1935 年华比银行在香港新设分行，之后又在埃及开罗和亚历山大港开设分行。[45]

20 世纪 20 年代，随着比利时在华投资扩大和贸易增长，华比银行天津分行的业务也越来越兴盛。华比银行天津分行先后有两位华人买办（旧称华账房）：李致堂（1906—1935 年任职）和魏采章（1935—1941 年任职）。李致堂曾在中国旧的银钱业任职；魏采章曾在东三省官银号就职，后任河北省银行经理，与东三省的军阀政客交往颇多。他们利用自己的关系，广拉客户。清朝灭亡、民国建立以后，天津的旧外国租界中居住着许多中国富商、资本家、北洋军阀、政客和清朝遗老遗少。华比银行吸收了他们的大量存款，资金变得更加雄厚。[46] 1908 年华比银行在天津开始发行纸币，还于 1921 年修建了银行大楼。

1941 年 12 月珍珠港事件后，日本向英美等国家宣战。12 月 8 日这一天，日本军队占领了英美等国在天津的重要机构，如工部局、银行以及洋行等。虽然当时的比利时国土已经被德国占领，但在伦敦的比利时流亡

but under the French name Banque Belge pour l'Étranger (Extrême-Orient). In 1935, a new branch of the bank was opened in Hong Kong. The Sino-Belgian Bank later opened branches in Cairo and Alexandria, Egypt.[45]

In the 1920s, as Belgian investments in China expanded and trade grew, so did the business of the Tianjin branch of the bank. The branch had two Chinese compradors (formerly known as Chinese accountants): Li Zhitang (served from 1906 to 1935) and Wei Caizhang (served from 1935 to 1941). Li Zhitang had worked in the old Chinese financial industry; Wei Caizhang had worked in the official bank of the three Northeastern provinces and later became the manager of the Hebei Provincial Bank and had a lot of contacts with warlords and politicians in the three Northeastern provinces. Li and Wei used their connections to attract customers. After the fall of the Qing dynasty and the establishment of the Republic of China, many rich Chinese merchants, capitalists, Beiyang warlords, politicians and Qing dynasty holdovers were living in the old foreign concessions in Tianjin. Sino-Belgian Bank absorbed a large amount of their deposits and became more capitalized.[46] In 1908, the bank started issuing banknotes in Tianjin and built a bank building in 1921.

After the attack on Pearl Harbor in December 1941, Japan declared war on Britain and the U.S. On December 8, Japanese troops occupied important institutions of Britain and the U.S. in Tianjin, such as the Municipal Councils, banks and foreign firms. Although the Belgian territory was already occupied by Germany at that time, the Belgian government-in-exile in London insisted on resisting the Japanese and German invasion, so the Sino-Belgian Bank bore the brunt of the takeover by the Japanese. Two Belgians, Leopold Pander Sr. and Lucien Pétiaux, the bank manager and chief accountant respectively, and their families were expelled from the bank, and all the family assets, including cars, pianos, carpets, refrigerators,

日本人强迫所有敌国侨民都必须戴上红色袖标，用黑色字写上他们的国籍。潘德尔每天必须带着袖标和通行证出门，袖标上的"白"代表"白耳义"，这是日本人对比利时国名的早期翻译。保存于潘德尔后代手中

The Japanese occupation authorities forced all enemy aliens to wear red armbands with their nationality written in black. The armband is from the descendants of Pander

政府坚持抵抗日本和德国的侵略，所以华比银行首先被日军接管。原来在银行大楼工作和居住的银行经理潘德尔（Leopold Pander Sr.）和总会计师佩西奥（Lucien Pétiaux）两个比利时人及其家属被赶出银行，所有家产，包括汽车、钢琴、地毯、冰箱、家具等都被日本人征用。之后，佩西奥屈从于日本人的压力，被征招到天津电车公司工作。而潘德尔由于拒绝为日本人工作，一家人于1943年3月被送往山东潍县集中营[47]关押，直到日本战败投降。[48]

2019年7月12日天津《今晚报》上刊载了一篇文章记录华比银行经理潘德尔及其雇员在天津的冒险：

1941年12月8日，星期一，早上还不到七点。一阵急促的敲门声和叫嚷声，惊醒了潘德尔和佩西奥，当他们衣着不整地下楼时，看到的是一队手持步枪且上着刺刀的日本兵。日本兵领头人宣布以天皇的名义接管整栋建筑，并命令他们将金库的钥匙以及所有备用钥匙交

furniture, etc., were requisitioned by the Japanese. Later, Pétiaux succumbed to Japanese pressure and was conscripted to work for CTET. Pander, on the other hand, refused to work for the Japanese - he and his family were sent to Wei County concentration camp in Shandong Province[47] in March 1943, where they were held until Japan's defeat and surrender.[48]

An article about the adventures of bank manager Leopold Pander and his employees in Tianjin, as published in a supplement to the Tianjin *Tonight Evening Newspaper* on July 12, 2019.

It was not yet seven o'clock in the morning on Monday, December 8, 1941. A loud knocking and shouting at the door woke up Pander and Pétiaux. When they came downstairs barely dressed, they saw a group of Japanese soldiers with rifles and bayonets. The leader of the Japanese soldiers announced that he was taking over the entire building in the name of the Japanese Emperor and ordered them to hand over the keys to the

给日本人。利奥波德（潘德尔之子，引者注）说："事后很多年，爸爸才告诉我们，在此之前爸爸已经和相关人员口头达成一致，就说我们没有金库备用钥匙，这就是比利时银行的最大特色。日本人相信了，拿走了金库的钥匙，并贴上封条，留下卫兵在门口站岗。"

......

华比银行的地下室金库存放的都是金条，大小不一，放在靠着水泥墙的架子上。有许多金条是属于客户的——这些金条如果落入日本人之手，就是有去无回。

潘德尔、佩西奥以及中方买办魏采章，三人经过一番周密的计划，决定实施一个大胆的行动。中方买办魏采章，字允楼，辽宁营口人。他有着丰富的商务经验和灵活的头脑。他受过良好的教育，1919 年从北京大学经济系毕业后进入东三省官银号，"九一八"事变后来到天津，在河北省银行任职。从 1935 年至 1941 年，魏采章任华比银行中方买办。因魏采章在东北有广泛的人脉，所以很多奉系军阀和政客将黄金都存在华比银行。在 1941 年地址簿的华比银行条目上，可以看到三人的名字。

这一天，在银行关门很久后的寂静深夜，三人蹑手蹑脚地进入地下室金库。魏采章用了特殊技术揭下日本兵粘贴的封条。接着，三人用备用钥匙打开金库大门。为避免发出声响，他们将一块厚厚的帆布铺在地下室过道上，然后将属于客户的金条一一取出，放于其上——行动必须尽可能快、尽可能轻。然后，帆布被他们拖到一楼，魏采章又将封条恢复为原来状态。他们三人不敢停顿，连夜把金条分散藏起来。潘德尔后来告知家人，金条大都藏在厕所的水箱中。

vault and all spare keys. Leopold (the son of Pander, note by the authors) said: "It was many years afterwards that Dad told us that he had, prior to the Japanese raid, verbally agreed with other bank employees that they would all say there were no spare keys to the vault. The Japanese believed it, took the key to the vault and put a seal on it, leaving guards standing by the door."

......

The basement vault of the Sino-Belgian Bank was stocked with gold bars, of various sizes, on shelves against the concrete wall. There were many gold bars that belonged to customers; if they fell into the hands of the Japanese, it would be impossible to get them back.

Pander, Pétiaux and the Chinese comprador Wei Caizhang, after some careful planning, decided to carry out a bold action. Wei Caizhang, the Chinese comprador, was a native of Yingkou, Liaoning Province. He had rich business experience and a shrewd mind. He was well educated, and after graduating from the Department of Economics of Beijing University in 1919, he joined the official bank of the three Northeastern provinces and came to Tianjin after the 'September 18' Incident to work at the Bank of Hebei Province. From 1935 to 1941, Wei served as the Chinese comprador of the Sino-Belgian Bank. Because of his extensive connections in the Northeast provinces, many Fengtian clique warlords and politicians kept their gold in the Sino-Belgian Bank. The names of the three men can be seen on the Sino-Belgian Bank entry in the 1941 telephone book.

One day, in the dead of night, long after the bank had closed, the three men crept into the basement vault. Wei Caizhang used a special technique to remove the seal affixed by the Japanese soldiers. Then, the trio used a spare key to open the vault door. To avoid

BANQUE BELGE POUR L'ETRANGER
(EXTREME-ORIENT), S.A.
Filiale de la Société Générale de Belgique
(Formerly Banque Sino-Belge).

華 比 銀 行 *Hua-pi-yin-hang*
86, Victoria Road.

Phone 31825 Manager
  ,,   31770 Sub-Manager
  ,,   31204 General Office
  ,,   31203 Compradore
  ,,   31290 Compradore Office
Tel. Address : "Sinobe"
Head Office : Brussels.
Branch Offices : Shanghai, Hongkong, Hankow.

Pander, L., *Manager.* 潘德尔 (经理)
Pétiaux, L., *Accountant.* 佩西奥(会计师)
Thomas, J., *Sub-Accountant.*
Wei, T. C., *Compradore.* 魏采章(买办)

1941 年电话簿黄页上的华比银行条目
The Sino-Belgian Bank entry in the 1941 telephone book

但是，这大量金条不能留在银行的公寓内，否则早晚会被日本人发现。于是，他们暗地里谨慎地通知金条的所有者。这些金条的主人听到这个消息时，都不相信自己的耳朵。他们原以为自己在华比银行的东西早已落入日本人之手。没过多久，客户们拿到了属于他们的财产。考虑到当时的特殊情况，双方不能留下确认收据，否则就会被日本人抓到把柄，但银行和客户都明白诚信的意义。

三年过去了，到了 1945 年 10 月，华比银行在抗战胜利后重新营业。让潘德尔一直很忐忑的问题，就是客户能确认他们三年前收到东西了吗？空口无凭，客户回来索要怎么办？这也正是潘德尔在回津的飞机上"低头不语，若有所思"的原因。但是他的担心多余了。几乎

making noise, they spread a thick piece of canvas on the basement aisle and then took out the gold bars belonging to their clients and placed them on it one by one - moving as quickly and lightly as possible. They then dragged the canvas to the first floor, and Wei Caizhang restored the seal to its original state. The three of them did not dare to pause and hid the gold bars in various places overnight. Pander later informed his family that the gold bars were mostly hidden in the water tank of the toilet.

However, this large amount of gold bars could not be left in the bank's apartment, otherwise it would be discovered by the Japanese sooner or later. So, they secretly and discreetly informed the owners of the gold bars. When the owners heard the news, they did not believe their ears. They originally thought that what they had in the bank had fallen into the hands of the Japanese long ago. It did not take long for the customers to get the property that belonged to them. Considering the special circumstances at that time, neither party could leave confirmation receipts, fearing later being caught by the Japanese. But both the bank and the customers understood the significance of honesty and trust.

Three years passed, and by October 1945, the Sino-Belgian Bank reopened after the war ended. The question that kept Pander worried was whether the customers would confirm that they had received their property three years ago. What if the customer claim that they had not? But his fears were unnecessary. Almost all the original customers who were notified came to the bank to confirm that they had received their items, and at the same time gave the bank high praise. Neither the bank nor the customer had broken trust ... Pander and their daring venture were a complete success!

所有接到通知的原客户，均到华比银行来确认他们收到了东西，同时对银行予以极高的赞誉。银行和客户双方都没有失信……潘德尔他们那次大胆的冒险才算完全成功！

二战结束后，由于佩西奥曾为日本人工作，难以回到欧洲，只能像德、意、日等轴心国侨民那样，远赴南美洲定居。魏采章又回到华比银行工作，直到 20 世纪 50 年代后调往中国银行，1973 年过世，享年 79 岁。潘德尔回到天津后不久，即调任上海华比银行经理，1946 年 5 月离开天津，1949 年转任香港华比银行经理。1952 年 5 月，潘德尔回到比利时继续在银行工作，作为私人银行顾问，他一直工作到生命的最后时刻。

中华人民共和国成立后，华比银行曾被批准为经营外汇的指定银行，经营外汇业务。后来，因为在华外商企业纷纷歇业，该行业务清淡，遂于 1956 年秋申请停业清理（实际上已停业），1976 年 2 月 27 日正式停业，只保留在香港的分行。

After the end of World War II, it was difficult for Pétiaux to return to Europe because he had worked for the Japanese and had to go as far as South America, like the German, Italian, Japanese and other Axis expatriates. Wei Caizhang returned to work for the Sino-Belgian Bank until he was transferred to the Bank of China after the 1950s. He died in 1973 at the age of 79. Pander was transferred to the manager position of the Sino-Belgian Bank in Shanghai and left Tianjin in May 1946. In May 1952, Pander returned to Belgium to continue his work at the bank, working as a private banking consultant until the end of his life.

After the establishment of the People's Republic of China, Sino-Belgian Bank was approved as a designated bank for foreign exchange operations. Later, because of the closure of foreign enterprises in China, the bank's business was sluggish. As a result, it filed for closure and liquidation in the autumn of 1956 (already ceased operations by that time), and officially ceased operations on February 27, 1976, retaining only the branch in Hong Kong.

在天津市区行驶的有轨电车

A tram operating in downtown Tianjin

天津比商电车电灯公司

1900 年后，天津共有八国租界，随着租界的设立、扩张和发展，人口日盛，交通问题也随之而来。各国租界和天津老城修建了大量道路，传统的马车、轿子、人力车等交通工具已不能满足人们迅捷出行的需要。与此同时，世界范围内的交通革命也在各地上演。1879 年，使用电力带动轨道车辆的有轨电车，由德国工程师西门子（Ernst Werner von Siemens）在柏林的博览会上首先展出。此后有轨电车在 20 世纪初的欧洲、美洲、大洋洲和亚洲的一些城市风行一时。对于这种新鲜事物，天津的外国侨民们马上意识到其中商机无限，遂成立了天津比商电车电灯公司（英语为 Tientsin Electric Tramways & Lighting Co. Ltd.，法语为 Compagnie de

Compagnie de Tramways et d'Eclairage de Tientsin (CTET)

With the establishment, expansion and development of the Tianjin concessions after 1900, the transportation became increasingly problematic. The traditional means of transportation, such as horse-drawn carriages, sedan chairs and rickshaws, could no longer meet the needs of people to travel more quickly. At the same time, a worldwide transportation revolution was taking place. In 1879, the tram, which used electric power to drive rail cars, was first exhibited by German engineer Ernst Werner von Siemens at a fair in Berlin. Thereafter, trams became popular in some cities in Europe, America, Oceania and Asia in the early 20th century. The foreigners in Tianjin immediately realized the business opportunities and established the Compagnie de Tramways et d'Eclairage de Tientsin (CTET), investing, constructing and running the trams in Tianjin.

When the Eight-Power Allied Forces occupied Tianjin in 1900 to suppress the Boxer Rebellion, a military Provisional Government was established to rule Tianjin, known in Chinese as the "Tianjin Du Tong Ya Men." During the two-year period of its administration of Tianjin, there was a fierce fight among foreigners in Tianjin over the franchise of the Tianjin tramway, the winner of which was a Belgian company, the Compagnie de Tramways et d'Eclairage de Tientsin (CTET).

In August 1900, shortly after the establishment of the Provisional Government, two Europeans immediately applied for the establishment of a tramway between the city and the concessions.[49] Almost at the same time, the Provisional Government received a letter from the Japanese consul in Tianjin, claiming that the Chinese government had agreed to grant a Japanese company a tax exemption for trams between the old city of Tianjin and the concessions. It further asked the Provisional Government to confirm this

Tramways et d'Éclairage de Tientsin），投资兴建和运营天津的有轨电车。

1900 年八国联军镇压义和团运动时占领天津，成立了一个军政府性质的临时政府来统治天津，其中文名称为"天津都统衙门"。在都统衙门管理天津的两年期间，在津外国侨民围绕天津电车的专营权展开了一场激烈争夺，最后的赢家是一家比利时公司——"天津电车电灯公司"。

1900 年 8 月，都统衙门刚刚成立不久，立即有两位欧洲人就在城区与各租界之间建立有轨电车向都统衙门提出申请。[49]几乎与此同时，都统衙门还收到了驻津日本领事的信件，声称中国政府已经同意，授予一家日本公司关于往返天津老城区与各租界的有轨电车免税权，要求都统衙门确认这一免税要求，[50]还要求都统衙门不要再授予其他国家这种免税权。[51]对于列强内部的争权夺利，都统衙门本来不想干预这件事。[52]奈何争议双方都向都统衙门提出诉求，作为当时天津地方的最高权力机构，都统衙门不得不下令让提出要求的几方自行商议。[53]几番扯皮后，来自欧洲的侨民联合起来，1901 年 5 月底，长期担任津海关税务司和李鸿章洋务顾问的德籍侨民德璀琳（Gustav Detring）与其他在津居住多年的欧洲侨民，筹组了"天津电车电灯公司"董事会，德璀琳任董事长，向都统衙门重申免税修建电车的申请。[54]这样一个由欧洲多国侨民组成的公司，自然能得到都统衙门中占据绝对优势的欧洲国家代表的支持。到 6 月中旬，争夺终于有了结果，都统衙门表示原则上同意将其管辖范围内天津城区部分（不包括租界）的特许经营权授予"有轨电车公司"。[55]

request[50] and to refrain from granting such a tax exemption to other countries.[51] The Provisional Government did not want to interfere with the internal struggle for power and profit among the foreign countries.[52] However, both sides of the dispute made claims to the Provisional Government, the highest authority in Tianjin at the time. It ordered the parties making the claims to negotiate on their own.[53] At the end of May 1901, Gustav Detring, a German expatriate who had long served as commissioner of Tianjin Customs and advisor to Li Hongzhang on foreign affairs, and other European expatriates who had lived in Tianjin for many years, organized the "Tientsin Tramways & Lighting Co. Ltd." The board of directors of the Electric Traction & Lighting Syndicate, of which Detring was the chairman, reiterated the application to the Provisional Government for a tax exemption for the construction of trams.[54] Such a company, composed of European expatriates, was naturally supported by the overwhelmingly dominant representatives of European countries in the Provisional Government. By the middle of June, the competition finally came to an end, and the Provisional Government agreed in principle to grant a concession to the "tramway company" for the part of Tianjin within its jurisdiction (but not for the concessions area).[55]

However, although this was a lucrative project, it required massive investment. Although Detring and several other expatriates in China obtained the support of the Provisional Government, they did not have enough financial resources to fund this project. Detring had to entrust E. Meyer & Co.[56] to secure financing of the project. E. Meyer & Co. then contacted a European conglomerate and transferred its rights to the "Société internationale de Belgique Orientale", also known as the "Société Orientale",[57] led by King Leopold II of Belgium and composed of a consortium of French, Russian and Belgian companies. It had more than 400 shareholders, including almost all the

不过，这虽是一项"钱"途无量的项目，也是一项投资巨大的项目。德璀琳等几位在华侨民虽有能力获得都统衙门的支持，却没有足够的财力来支撑这项投资。果然在之后资本筹措的过程中出现了困难。德璀琳只得委托世昌洋行（E. Meyer & Co.）[56]来代理这个投资项目。于是世昌洋行又联系了欧洲的大财团，将公司权利转让给"比利时东方国际公司"，又称"东方辛迪加"。[57]"东方辛迪加"，由比利时国王利奥波德二世牵头组织，由法、俄、比等多国财团组成，其股东有 400 多个，几乎囊括了欧洲大陆几个主要国家的大公司、大银行，如比利时的通用公司、新海外银行、布鲁塞尔银行、国际银行，法国的巴黎银行、国家贴现银行、奥托曼银行、巴黎第二银行以及几家大公司，德国的贴现公司和德意志银行所代表的一个银行和企业集团，奥匈帝国的维也纳银行同盟和匈牙利商业银行，俄国的华俄道胜银行、圣彼得堡国际商业银行，瑞士的瑞士信贷银行、联合银行及金融联合银行，荷兰的阿姆斯特丹银行，意大利的意大利信贷银行、意大利商业银行等。[58]"东方辛迪加"的在华代表是比利时领事埃米尔·法郎基。它还曾投资于中国香港和新加坡的电车建设中，但没能跻身于汉城的电车建设项目。义和团运动中，它侵占了中国第一家机械化开采的开平煤矿。

1902 年，都统衙门将天津政权移交给中国政府后，这项特许经营权也要求中方予以承认和继承。接下来，开办公司的具体事宜由世昌洋行承办。1902 年 6 月 14 日，比利时海外银行与东方国际公司成立了天津电车电灯股份有限公司，总公司设在比利时布鲁塞尔，注册资金为625 万法郎（当时约合 25 万英镑、中国银圆 250 万元），

major companies and banks in continental Europe such as the Belgian General Company, Banque Belge pour l'Etranger, Banque Bruxell Lambert, International Bank, Banque Nationale de Paris (BNP), Comptoir National d'Escompte de Paris (CNEP), Ottoman Bank, the Second Bank of Paris and several large corporations, including a bank and enterprise group represented by German Disconto Gesellsehaft and Deutsche Bank, Vienna Banking Union and Hungarian Commercial Bank of Austria Hungary Empire, Russo-Asiatic Bank and St. Petersburg International Commercial Bank of Russia, Credit Suisse, UBS and Financial Union Bank of Switzerland, Amsterdam Bank of the Netherlands, UniCredit and Banca Intesa of Italy, etc.[58] The representative of the "Société Orientale" in China was the Belgian Consul Émile Francqui. It also invested in the construction of trams in Hong Kong and Singapore. During the Boxer Rebellion, it also seized the Kaiping coal mine, the first mechanized mine in China.

In 1902, after the transfer of power from the Provisional Government to China authorities, the Chinese side was asked to recognize and inherit this concession. And then the specific matters of establishing company were handled by E. Meyer & Co. On June 14, 1902, the Banque d'Outremer and "Société Orientale" established the Compagnie de Tramways et d'Eclairage de Tientsin (Tientsin Tramway and Lighting Company), headquartered in Brussels, Belgium. The company's registered capital was 6,250,000 francs (about 250,000 pounds sterling and 2.5 million Chinese silver dollars). It issued a total of 12,500 shares of 500 francs and 2,000 founders' shares.[59]

On April 26, 1904, representatives of the Chinese and Belgian sides signed the *Agreement for the Concession for the Electric Tramways and Lighting of Tientsin* in Tianjin. After the agreement was approved by Yuan Shikai, the Viceroy of Zhili and Minister of the Beiyang, the operating entity was named "Tianjin Belgian Electric

共发行面值 500 法郎的股票 12500 份，还有 2000 份创始人股权。[59]

1904 年 4 月 26 日，中国与比利时双方代表在天津签订了《天津电车电灯公司合同》。合同签订后，经直隶总督兼北洋大臣袁世凯批准生效，经营机构取名为"天津比商电车电灯公司"，又称"比商天津电车电灯公司"。合同规定，由比商经营，自电车行驶之日起专利 50 年（即自 1906 年起），期满无条件归还中国；营业范围以天津老城的鼓楼为圆点，半径 6 英里内的电车、电灯事业，由比公司专权承办；未经直隶总督批准，公司不得出售或转让给其他公司或机构组织；电车行驶之日起，20 年后地方政府可以作价买回全盘电灯和车路，如到期不买，须等 7 年方可再买，以后均以 7 年为一期，地方政府如欲购买，须于 1 年前预先通知该公司；合同中还具体规划了几条行车线路；如若发生任何争端，比利时领事和公司股东代表都不能介入，所有争议都通过地方政府仲裁解决；最后，合同要求成立一个地方委员会，由具有影响力的中国市民和外籍人士组成，与天津比商电车电灯公司的经理共同商讨涉及当地利益的问题。[60]

尽管合同规定的这个委员会从未对天津比商电车电灯公司的经营产生过任何重要影响，但这不失为一个获得城市精英支持、掌控舆论的好方法。按照中比签订的合同规定，天津比商电车电灯公司的委员会由中比各 3 人组成；华人委员在清末由直隶总督委派，民国后由直隶省长委派，天津设市后由天津市长指派；比方委员 3 人由公司自行物色。委员会初期有华比银行总经理、开滦煤矿总经理等人。后期，天津电车电灯公司的委员会除了林阿德（Alphonse Splingaerd）之外，其余多为天

Tramway and Lighting Company" (Hereafter referred to as the "Company"). The agreement stipulated that the company would be operated by the Belgian merchants for 50 years from the date of operation of the tramway (i.e., from 1906), and would be returned to China unconditionally at the end of the term. The scope of business would be the tramway and electric lighting business within the radius of 6 miles of the Drum Tower in the old city of Tianjin. The company could not sell or transfer to other companies or organizations without the approval of the Governor of Zhili. The local government could buy back all the electric lights and tramway after 20 years from the date of operation of the trams. If the government didn't buy them back at the expiration date, it must wait for 7 years before it could buy again. All subsequent periods would be in 7-year increments. If the local government wanted to buy back, it must notify the company one year in advance. The agreement also specified several traffic routes. In case of any disputes, neither the Belgian consul nor the representatives of the company's shareholders could intervene; all disputes were to be settled through arbitration by the local government. Finally, the agreement called for the establishment of a local committee composed of influential Chinese citizens and foreigners to discuss issues of local interest with the manager of the company.[60]

Although this committee, as stipulated in the agreement, never had any significant influence on the operation of the company, it was an effective way to gain the support of the city's elites and to influence public opinion. According to the agreement signed between China and Belgium, the Compagnie de Tramways et d'Eclairage de Tientsin's committee was composed of three Chinese and three Belgian members each. The Chinese members were appointed by the Viceroy of Zhili in the late Qing dynasty, by the Governor of Zhili after the Republic of China, and by the Mayor of Tianjin after the establishment of the

AGREEMENT

for the

CONCESSION FOR THE ELECTRIC TRAMWAYS

AND LIGHTING OF TIENTSIN.

Concession for the Electric Tramways and Lighting of Tientsin.

1. His Excellency the Viceroy Yuan Shih Kai, Governor General of Chihli, hereby grants to Mr. E. Heyl of E. Meyer & Co., the charter for the installation of the electric Tramways and Lighting at Tientsin. For all roads on which the tramway will run plans will be submitted for the approval of H.E. the Viceroy.

2. Mr. E. Heyl shall form a public Company to take over this concession; said Company is hereby consented to by the Chinese Authorities, with an initial capital of £ 250 000.–.– under the name of "Tientsin Tramway and Lighting Company", or "Compagnie de Tramways et d'Eclairage de Tientsin".

3. H.E. the Viceroy Yuan Shih Kai grants to said Company the monopoly for the building and working of tramways and electric lighting in Tientsin, within a circle having a radius of six lis measured from the Drum Tower in the centre of the walled city, for a term of fifty years.

4. It is provided that the Company so organized shall not sell or transfer its business or advantages to any party or parties whomsoever without the consent of H.E. the Viceroy of Chihli.

5. The tramway is intended to be laid in the beginning as follows:
A. From the place called Chakou along the Bund to the North East and thence to the North West corner of the city:
B. Around the City from the North West corner, to the South West corner, from the South West to the South East, and from the South East to the North East corner:
C. From the North Gate to Hsiku;
D. From the North West corner of the City to the junction of the Mudwall and the Grand Canal, near the Tientsin Native City Water Works Pumping House.

For these roads indicated on annexed map, work may be started at once. In case of further extensions, a supplementary map must be made, which shall be submitted to H.E. the Viceroy, whose consent shall be obtained before beginning work.

《天津电车电灯公司合同》，收藏于比利时外交部档案馆

Agreement for the Concession for the Electric Tramways and Lighting of Tientsin，preserved in the archives of the Belgian Ministry of Foreign Affairs

COMPAGNIE DE TRAMWAYS ET D'ÉCLAIRAGE
de Tientsin
SOCIÉTÉ ANONYME

SIÈGE SOCIAL:
48, Rue de Namur

Adresse Télégraphique
TSINTRAM BRUXELLES

TÉLÉPHONE 4431

N° 2142

Prière de rappeler dans la réponse
le numéro de cette lettre

Bruxelles, le 16 décembre 1905.

MINISTÈRE
DES AFFAIRES ÉTRANGÈRES
17. DÉC. 05 INDIC. GÉN. N° 47,392

LITT: E   N° 4360/20

Monsieur le Baron,

Nous avons l'honneur de vous accuser la réception de
votre lettre du 13 décembre nous communiquant la réponse
que notre Ministre à Vienne a faite à votre lettre du 23
novembre concernant l'augmentation de la participation autri-
chienne à la construction du pont de Tung Fu Chiao à Tientsin.

Nous vous remercions de votre intervention en cette cir-
constance et vous prions d'agréer l'expression de notre haute
considération.

COMPAGNIE
DE
TRAMWAYS & D'ÉCLAIRAGE DE TIENTSIN

A Monsieur le Baron de Favereau,
Ministre des Affaires Étrangères,
Bruxelles.

CONSULAT DE BELGIQUE
À
TIENTSIN

N°: 21/4.

Objet.
Tramway électrique de
Tientsin.

TIENTSIN, le 25 Janvier 1904

19 — 2 - 04

Monsieur le Baron: 7123
Litt: E 4360-20

Il y a quelques jours, le vice-roi
du Chihli, Yuan-Chih-Kai écrivant à Tong
+ Tsai Taotai, ses délégués dans l'affaire
du Tramway et l'éclairage électriques de
la cité de Tientsin, une lettre dont voici
un résumé :

J'ai reçu une communication d'un
nommé Mu qui m'a proposé de constituer
une société Chinoise pour l'éclairage électrique
de la cité. Avant de donner suite à ses
propositions, il y a lieu d'examiner s'il

Son Excellence
Monsieur le Baron de Favereau
Ministre des Affaires Étrangères
Bruxelles

Je me permets d'espérer qu'il aura dit
vrai; quoi qu'il en soit, je puis assurer
Votre Excellence que, dans la limite de
mes moyens, je n'ai rien épargné pour
la faire réussir.

Veuillez agréer, Monsieur le Baron,
les assurances de mon dévouement le plus
respectueux.

Ketels.

《天津电车电灯公司合同》签订后，驻津领事嘎德斯向比利时外交部的汇报。收藏于比利时外交部档案馆

After the *Agreement for the Concession for the Electric Tramways and Lighting of Tientsin* was signed, the consul in Tianjin, Henri Ketels, reported to the Belgian Ministry of Foreign Affairs. Preserved in the archives of the Belgian Ministry of Foreign Affairs

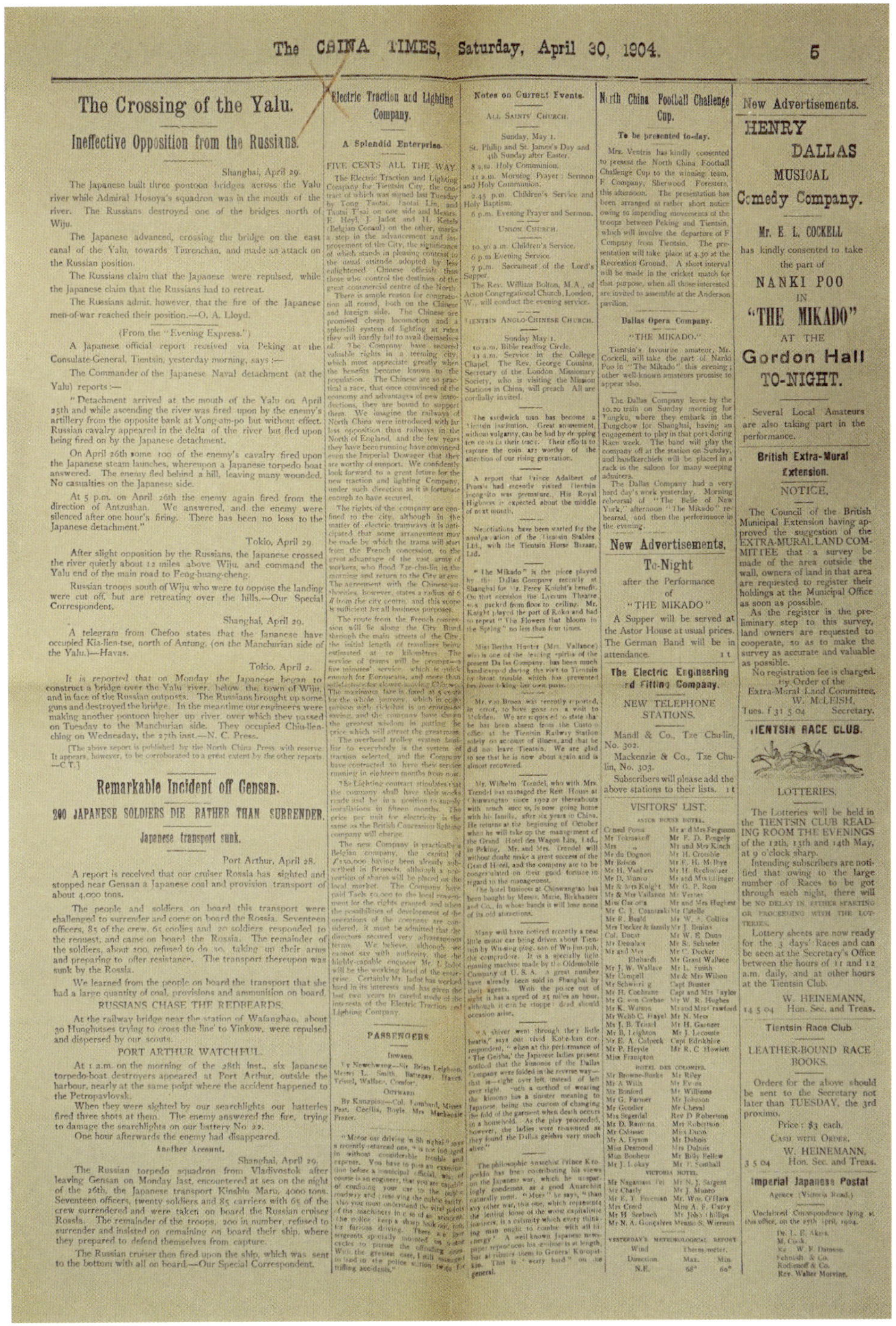

The CHINA TIMES, Saturday, April 30, 1904. 5

The Crossing of the Yalu.

Ineffective Opposition from the Russians.

Shanghai, April 29.

The Japanese built three pontoon bridges across the Yalu river while Admiral Hosoya's squadron was in the mouth of the river. The Russians destroyed one of the bridges north of Wiju.

The Japanese advanced, crossing the bridge on the east canal of the Yalu, towards Tiurenchan, and made an attack on the Russian position.

The Russians claim that the Japanese were repulsed, while the Japanese claim that the Russians had to retreat.

The Russians admit, however, that the fire of the Japanese men-of-war reached their position.—O. A. Lloyd.

(From the "Evening Express.")

A Japanese official report received via Peking at the Consulate-General, Tientsin, yesterday morning, says:—

The Commander of the Japanese Naval detachment (at the Yalu) reports:—

"Detachment arrived at the mouth of the Yalu on April 25th and while ascending the river was fired upon by the enemy's artillery from the opposite bank at Yong-am-po but without effect. Russian cavalry appeared in the delta of the river but fled upon being fired on by the Japanese detachment.

On April 26th some 100 of the enemy's cavalry fired upon the Japanese steam launches, whereupon a Japanese torpedo boat answered. The enemy fled behind a hill, leaving many wounded. No casualties on the Japanese side.

At 5 p.m. on April 26th the enemy again fired from the direction of Antzushan. We answered, and the enemy were silenced after one hour's firing. There has been no loss to the Japanese detachment."

Tokio, April 29.

After slight opposition by the Russians, the Japanese crossed the river quietly about 12 miles above Wiju, and command the Yalu end of the main road to Feng-huang-cheng.

Russian troops south of Wiju who were to oppose the landing were cut off, but are retreating over the hills.—Our Special Correspondent.

Shanghai, April 29.

A telegram from Chefoo states that the Japanese have occupied Kia-lien-tse, north of Antung, (on the Manchurian side of the Yalu.)—Havas.

Tokio, April 2.

It is reported that on Monday the Japanese began to construct a bridge over the Yalu river, below the town of Wiju, and in face of the Russian outposts. The Russians brought up some guns and destroyed the bridge. In the meantime our engineers were making another pontoon higher up river, over which they passed on Tuesday to the Manchurian side. They occupied Chiu-lien-ching on Wednesday, the 27th inst.—N. C. Press.

[The above report is published by the North China Press with reserve. It appears, however, to be corroborated to a great extent by the other reports.—C. T.]

Remarkable Incident off Gensan.

200 JAPANESE SOLDIERS DIE RATHER THAN SURRENDER.

Japanese transport sunk.

Port Arthur, April 28.

A report is received that our cruiser Rossia has sighted and stopped near Gensan a Japanese coal and provision transport of about 4,000 tons.

The people and soldiers on board this transport were challenged to surrender and come on board the Rossia. Seventeen officers, 85 of the crew, 65 coolies and 20 soldiers responded to the request, and came on board the Rossia. The remainder of the soldiers, about 200, refused to do so, taking up their arms and preparing to offer resistance. The transport thereupon was sunk by the Rossia.

We learned from the people on board the transport that she had a large quantity of coal, provisions and ammunition on board.

RUSSIANS CHASE THE REDBEARDS.

At the railway bridge near the station of Wafanghao, about 30 Hunghutses trying to cross the line to Yinkow, were repulsed and dispersed by our scouts.

PORT ARTHUR WATCHFUL.

At 1 a.m. on the morning of the 28th inst., six Japanese torpedo-boat destroyers appeared at Port Arthur, outside the harbour, nearly at the same point where the accident happened to the Petropavlovsk.

When they were sighted by our searchlights our batteries fired three shots at them. The enemy answered the fire, trying to damage the searchlights on our battery No 22.

One hour afterwards the enemy had disappeared.

Another Account.

Shanghai, April 29.

The Russian torpedo squadron from Vladivostok after leaving Gensan on Monday last, encountered at sea on the night of the 26th, the Japanese transport Kinshiu Maru, 4000 tons. Seventeen officers, twenty soldiers and 85 carriers with 65 of the crew surrendered and were taken on board the Russian cruiser Rossia. The remainder of the troops, 200 in number, refused to surrender and insisted on remaining on board their ship, where they prepared to defend themselves from capture.

The Russian cruiser then fired upon the ship, which was sent to the bottom with all on board.—Our Special Correspondent.

Electric Traction and Lighting Company.

A Splendid Enterprise.

FIVE CENTS ALL THE WAY.

The Electric Traction and Lighting Company for Tientsin City, the contract of which was signed last Tuesday by Tong Taotai, Taotai Lin, and Taotai T'sai on one side and Messrs. E. Heyl, J. Jadot and H. Ketels (Belgian Consul) on the other, marks a step in the advancement and improvement of the City, the significance of which stands in pleasing contrast to the usual attitude adopted by less enlightened Chinese officials than those who control the destinies of the great commercial centre of the North.

There is ample reason for congratulation all round, both on the Chinese and foreign side. The Chinese are promised cheap locomotion and a splendid system of lighting at rates they will hardly fail to avail themselves of. The Company have secured valuable rights in a teeming city, which must appreciate greatly when the benefits become known to the population. The Chinese are so practical a race, that once convinced of the economy and advantages of new introductions, they are bound to support them. We imagine the railways of North China were introduced with far less opposition than railways in the North of England and the few years they have been running have convinced even the Imperial Dowager that they are worthy of support. We confidently look forward to a great future for the new traction and lighting Company, under such direction as it is fortunate enough to have secured.

The rights of the company are confined to the city, although in the matter of electric tramways it is anticipated that some arrangement may be made by which the trams will start from the French concession, to the great advantage of the vast army of workers, who flood Tze-chu-lin in the morning and return to the City at eve. The agreement with the Chinese authorities, however, states a radius of 6 li from the city centre, and this scope is sufficient for all business purposes.

The route from the French concession will lie along the City Bund through the main streets of the City, the initial length of tramlines being estimated at 10 kilomètres. The service of trams will be prompt—a five minutes' service, which is quick enough for Europeans, and more than satisfactory for slower-moving Chinese. The maximum fare is fixed at 5 cents for the whole journey, which in comparison with rickshas is an enormous saving, and the company have shown the greatest wisdom in putting the price which will attract the great mass.

The overhead trolley system familiar to everybody is the system of traction selected, and the Company have contracted to have their service running in eighteen months from now.

The Lighting contract stipulates that the company shall have their works made and be in a position to supply installations in fifteen months. The price per unit for electricity is the same as the British Concession lighting company will charge.

The new Company is practically a Belgian company, the capital of £250,000 having been already subscribed in Brussels, although a proportion of shares will be placed on the local market. The Company have paid Tacls 50,000 to the local government for the rights granted and when the possibilities of development of the operations of the company are considered, it must be admitted that the directors secured very advantageous terms. We believe, although we cannot say with authority, that the highly-capable engineer Mr. J. Jadot will be the working head of the enterprise. Certainly Mr. Jadot has worked hard in its interests and has given the last two years to careful study of the interests of the Electric Traction and Lighting Company.

PASSENGERS

INWARD.

By Newchwang.—Sir Brian Leighton, Messrs L. Smith, Battegay, Haert, Trüsel, Wallace, Comfort.

OUTWARD.

By Kaiping.—Col. Lombard, Misses Peat, Cecilia, Boyle, Mrs Mackenzie Frazer.

"Motor car driving in Shanghai" says a recently-returned one, "is not indulged in without considerable trouble and expense. You have to pass an examination before a municipal official, who, of course is an engineer, that you are capable of confining your car to the public roadway and preserving the public safety. Also you must understand the vital points of the machinery in case of an accident. The police keep a sharp look-out, too, for furious driving. There are four sergeants specially mounted on motor cycles to pursue the offending ones. With the greatest care, I still managed to land in the police station twice for trifling accidents."

Notes on Current Events.

ALL SAINTS' CHURCH.

Sunday, May 1.

St. Philip and St. James's Day and 4th Sunday after Easter.

8 a.m. Holy Communion.

11 a.m. Morning Prayer: Sermon and Holy Communion.

2.45 p.m. Children's Service and Holy Baptism.

6 p.m. Evening Prayer and Sermon.

UNION CHURCH.

10.30 a.m. Children's Service.

6 p.m. Evening Service.

7 p.m. Sacrament of the Lord's Supper.

The Rev. William Bolton, M.A., of Acton Congregational Church, London, W., will conduct the evening service.

TIENTSIN ANGLO-CHINESE CHURCH.

Sunday May 1.

10 a.m. Bible reading Circle.

11 a.m. Service in the College Chapel. The Rev. George Cousins, Secretary of the London Missionary Society, who is visiting the Mission Stations in China, will preach. All are cordially invited.

The sandwich man has become a Tientsin institution. Great amusement, without vulgarity, can be had by dropping ten cents in their tract. Their efforts to capture the coin are worthy of the attention of our rising generation.

A report that Prince Adalbert of Prussia had recently visited Tientsin incognito was premature. His Royal Highness is expected about the middle of next month.

Negotiations have been started for the amalgamation of the Tientsin Stables Ltd., with the Tientsin Horse Bazaar, Ltd.

"The Mikado" is the piece played by the Dallas Company recently at Shanghai for Mr. Percy Knight's benefit. On that occasion the Lyceum Theatre was packed from floor to ceiling. Mr. Knight played the part of Koko and had to repeat "The Flowers that bloom in the Spring" no less than four times.

Miss Bertha Hunter (Mrs. Vallance) who is one of the leading spirits of the present Dallas Company, has been much handicapped during the visit to Tientsin by throat trouble which has prevented her from taking her own parts.

Mr. von Broen was recently reported, in error, to have gone on a visit to Mukden. We are requested to state that he has been absent from the Customs office at the Tientsin Railway Station solely on account of illness, and that he did not leave Tientsin. We are glad to see that he is now about again and is almost recovered.

Mr. Wilhelm Trendel, who with Mrs. Trendel has managed the Rest House at Chinwangtao since 1902 or thereabouts with much success, is now going home with his family, after six years in China. He returns at the beginning of October when he will take up the management of the Grand Hotel des Wagon Lits, Ltd., in Peking. Mr. and Mrs. Trendel will without doubt make a great success of the Grand Hotel, and the company are to be congratulated on their good fortune in regard to the management.

The hotel business at Chinwangtao has been bought by Messrs. Marie, Birkhauser and Co., in whose hands it will lose none of its old attractions.

Many will have noticed recently a neat little motor car being driven about Tientsin by Wu-sing-ping, son of Wu-jim-pah, the compradore. It is a specially light running machine made by the Oldsmobile Company of U. S. A. A great number have already been sold in Shanghai by their agents. With the power out of sight it has a speed of 25 miles an hour, although it can be stopped dead should occasion arise.

"A shiver went through their little hearts," says our vivid Kobe-kan correspondent, "when at the performance of 'The Geisha,' the Japanese ladies present noticed that the kimonos of the Dallas Company were folded in the reverse way—that is—right over left instead of left over right. Such a method of wearing the kimono has a sinister meaning to Japanese being the custom of changing the fold of the garment when death occurs in a household. As the play proceeded, however, the ladies were reassured as they found the Dallas geishas very much alive."

The philosophic anarchist Prince Kropotkin has been contributing his views on the Japanese war, which he unsparingly condemns, as a good Anarchist naturally must. "More" he says, "than any other war, this one, which represents the letting loose of the worst capitalistic instincts, is a calamity which every thinking man ought to combat with all his energy." A well known Japanese newspaper reproduces his sentiments at length, but attributes them to General Kuropatkin. This is "very hard" on the general.

North China Football Challenge Cup.

To be presented to-day.

Mrs. Ventris has kindly consented to present the North China Football Challenge Cup to the winning team, F Company, Sherwood Foresters, this afternoon. The presentation has been arranged at rather short notice owing to impending movements of the troops between Peking and Tientsin, which will involve the departure of F Company from Tientsin. The presentation will take place at 4.30 at the Recreation Ground. A short interval will be made in the cricket match for that purpose, when all those interested are invited to assemble at the Anderson pavilion.

Dallas Opera Company.

"THE MIKADO."

Tientsin's favourite amateur, Mr. Cockell, will take the part of Nanki Poo in "The Mikado" this evening; other well-known amateurs promise to appear also.

The Dallas Company leave by the 10.20 train on Sunday morning for Tongku, where they embark in the Tungchow for Shanghai, having an engagement to play in that port during Race week. The band will play the company off at the station on Sunday, and handkerchiefs will be placed in a rack in the saloon for many weeping admirers.

The Dallas Company had a very hard day's work yesterday. Morning rehearsal of "The Belle of New York," afternoon "The Mikado" rehearsal, and then the performance in the evening.

New Advertisements.

To-Night

after the Performance

of

"THE MIKADO"

A Supper will be served at the Astor House at usual prices. The German Band will be in attendance. 1 t

The Electric Engineering and Fitting Company.

NEW TELEPHONE STATIONS.

Mandl & Co., Tze Chu-lin, No. 302.

Mackenzie & Co., Tze Chu-lin, No. 303.

Subscribers will please add the above stations to their lists. 1 t

VISITORS' LIST.

ASTOR HOUSE HOTEL.

Colonel Pons	Mr and Mrs Ferguson
Mr Tokmakoff	Mr F. D. Pengely
Mrs "	Mr and Mrs Kinch
Mr du Dognon	Mr H. Crombie
Mr Brison	Mr F. H. McIlrye
Mr H. Vanlaers	Mr H. Rechnitzer
Mr D. Munro	Mr and Mrs Gillinger
Mr & Mrs Knight	Mr G. P. Ross
Mr & Mrs Vallance	Mr Vernet
Miss Garcia	Mr and Mrs Hughes
Mr C. J. Constanski	Mr Catelle
Mr R. Bauld	Mr W. A. Collins
Mrs Decker & family	Mr J. Benin
Col. Ducat	Mr W. E. Dunn
Mr Desalais	Mr S. Schaefer
Mr and Mrs Ehrhardt	Mr C. Decker
	Mr Grant Wallace
Mr J. W. Wallace	Mr L. Smith
Mr Campell	Mr & Mrs Wilson
Mr Schwering	Capt Bruster
Mr H. Cochrane	Capt and Mrs Taylor
Mr G. von Corbae	Mr W. R. Hughes
Mr K. Watson	Mr and Mrs Crawford
Mr Webb C. Hayel	Mr N. Mess
Mr J. B. Trinel	Mr H. Gaetner
Mr B. Leighton	Mr J. Lecomte
Mr E. A. Colpeck	Capt Edrikhine
Mr P. Heyde	Mr R. C. Howlett
Miss Frampton	

HOTEL DES COLONIES.

Mr Browne-Burke	Mr Riley
Mr A. Wills	Mr Evans
Mr Bonford	Mr Williams
Mr G. Farmer	Mr Johnson
Mr Goodier	Mr Cheval
Mrs Segerdal	Rev D Robertson
Mr D. Ramona	Mrs Robertson
Mr Calasac	Miss Dunn
Mr A. Dyson	Mr Dubois
Miss Desmond	Mrs Dubois
Miss Bonheur	Mr Billy Fellow
Mr J. Lokay	Mr T. Southall

VICTORIA HOTEL.

Mr Nagamasa Pei	Mr N. J. Sargent
Mr Charly	Mr J. Munro
Mr E. T. Freeman	Mr. Wm. O'Hara
Mrs Creed	Miss A. F. Carey
Mr H. Seebach	Mr John Phillips
Mr N. A. Gonçalves	Menno S. Wiersum

YESTERDAY'S METEOROLOGICAL REPORT

Wind Direction	Thermometer Max.	Thermometer Min.
N.E.	68°	60°

New Advertisements.

HENRY DALLAS MUSICAL Comedy Company.

Mr. E. L. COCKELL

has kindly consented to take the part of

NANKI POO

IN

"THE MIKADO"

AT THE

Gordon Hall

TO-NIGHT.

Several Local Amateurs are also taking part in the performance.

British Extra-Mural Extension.

NOTICE.

The Council of the British Municipal Extension having approved the suggestion of the EXTRA-MURAL LAND COMMITTEE that a survey be made of the area outside the wall, owners of land in that area are requested to register their holdings at the Municipal Office as soon as possible.

As the register is the preliminary step to this survey, land owners are requested to cooperate, so as to make the survey as accurate and valuable as possible.

No registration fee is charged.

By Order of the Extra-Mural Land Committee,

W. McLEISH,

Tues. f 31 5 04 Secretary.

TIENTSIN RACE CLUB.

LOTTERIES.

The Lotteries will be held in the TIENTSIN CLUB READING ROOM THE EVENINGS of the 12th, 13th and 14th May, at 9 o'clock sharp.

Intending subscribers are notified that owing to the large number of Races to be got through each night, there will be NO DELAY IN EITHER STARTING OR PROCEEDING WITH THE LOTTERIES.

Lottery sheets are now ready for the 3 days' Races and can be seen at the Secretary's Office between the hours of 11 and 12 a.m. daily, and at other hours at the Tientsin Club.

W. HEINEMANN,

14 5 04 Hon. Sec. and Treas.

Tientsin Race Club

LEATHER-BOUND RACE BOOKS.

Orders for the above should be sent to the Secretary not later than TUESDAY, the 3rd proximo.

Price: $3 each.

CASH WITH ORDER.

W. HEINEMANN,

3 5 04 Hon. Sec. and Treas.

Imperial Japanese Postal

Agency (Victoria Road.)

Unclaimed Correspondence lying at this office, on the 27th April, 1904.

Dr. L. E. Akers.
M. Cook.
Kr. W. F. Dawson.
Schmidt & Co.
Rodionoff & Co.
Rev. Walter Morvine.

天津第一家外文报纸《中国时报》1904 年 4 月 30 日对中比双方签订合同的报道。收藏于比利时外交部档案馆

The first foreign language newspaper in Tianjin, *China Times*, reported the signing of the agreement between China and Belgium on April 30, 1904. Preserved in the archives of the Belgian Ministry of Foreign Affairs

津地方名流，如南开大学校长张伯苓等。

天津公司设有两个部门：管理部和工程部。管理部设有总经理、副经理、秘书、华务主任、会计。工程部员工包括发电厂（300余人）、外线管理部（约60人）、电车部（1200余人）、修理部（150余人）、电灯部（约60人）、电表修理部（40余人），总计1800多人，可谓规模庞大。[61]为了便于在天津推行电车电灯这样的新鲜事物，公司聘用华人作为"华经理"。第一任华经理是天津本地人刘中和。他会讲英语，曾任京奉铁路局督办的洋文秘书，又与天津警察厅长关系亲近，[62]是一个熟悉各方关系、头脑灵活的合适人选。

按合同规定，以天津老城中心鼓楼为圆点、半径6英里（约9.66公里）之圆周内的营业范围内，包括原日、英、法、意、比、奥租界及天津老城，但后来日、英、法三国租界当局不愿将此经营权让与比商，所以比商电灯不能在此三租界内营业，但其电车仍在法、日两租界营业。比利时公司原计划修建一条长1850米的电车轨道，从法租界延伸到英国菜市场，然后沿着码头扩展至德国租界边缘。但英国人认为这项计划过于宏大，他们不愿意将轨道延伸至市场之外。这种态度就意味着要将电车线路一分为二，也因此不能扩展到位于英租界以南的德租界。德国人意外地成为"受害者"，无法享受到电车带来的交通便利。[63]1927年公司营业范围扩大至原俄租界。

电车运行需要直流电，电灯照明需要交流电。为了电力供应，必须保证水源充足，天津比商电车电灯公司先是在前临海河、后凭金钟河的望海楼后金家窑村购买了一块土地，用以修建发电厂，其后，又在海河东浮桥

municipality. The three Belgian members were appointed by the company itself. In the initial period, members included the general manager of Sino-Belgian Bank and the general manager of Kailuan Mining Administration. Later, in addition to Alphonse Splingaerd, members of the committee were mostly local celebrities, such as Zhang Boling, the president of Nankai University.

The company had two departments in Tianjin: Management Department and Engineering Department. The management department had a general manager, a deputy manager, a secretary, a director of Chinese affairs and an accountant. The engineering department consisted of the power plant (more than 300 people), external line management department (about 60 people), tram department (more than 1,200 people), repair department (more than 150 people), electric lighting department (about 60 people), and meter repair department (more than 40 people), totaling more than 1,800 employees.[61] To promote the tramway and electric lighting in Tianjin, the company hired Chinese people as "Chinese managers." The first Chinese manager was Liu Zhonghe, a native of Tianjin. Fluent in English, Liu was the foreign language secretary to the director of the Beijing-Fengtian Railway Bureau. Being close to the Tianjin police chief[62], he was a suitable candidate who had wide local connections and a shrewd mind.

According to the agreement, the business area within a circle of 6 miles radius of the Drum Tower, the center of old city of Tianjin, included the former Japanese, British, French, Italian, Belgian and Austrian concessions and the Old City of Tianjin. But later the Japanese, British and French concession authorities were unwilling to cede this operation to the Belgian company, CTET therefore could not operate electric lighting business within these three concessions, though its trams still operated in French and Japanese. CTET originally planned to build a 1,850-meter tramway that would extend from the French concession to

"天津比商电车电灯公司"股票。由德璀琳后代德义信先生提供

Stocks issued by Compagnie de Tramways et d'Eclairage de Tientsin.
By courtesy of Mr. Bruce Eason, the descendant of Gustav Detring

天津比商电车电灯公司大楼设在原意租界三马路（今河北区进步道29号），建于1904年。原为天津比商电车电灯股份有限公司总部办公楼，1937年日军接管后，称为华北电力公司天津分公司。1945年南京国民政府接管后，称为冀北电力有限公司天津分公司。1949年后由人民政府电力部门使用。该楼砖木结构，两层带地下室。建筑造型规整，典雅大方。现为天津电力科技博物馆

The building of Compagnie de Tramways & D'eclairage de Tientsin (CTET) was built in 1904 at Sanma Road, the former Italian concession (now No.29 Jinbu Road, Hebei District). It was originally CTET's headquarter. After being taken over by Japanese army in 1937, it was called the Tianjin Branch of North China Electric Power Company. In 1945 when it was handed over to Nanjing National Government, it was renamed the Tianjin Branch of Northern Hebei Provincial Electric Power Company. After 1949, it was used by the Power Department of government of New China. The building of brick-wood structure has two floors and a basement with neat and elegant architectural style. Now it is the Tianjin Electric Power Science and Technology Museum

东口沿河马路处（今河北区）购置楼房一处，作为公司办事处。还在天津老城西南角的南开中学北侧购买了另一块土地，修建电车的车库及修理厂。公司开办之初，所有电灯以及一切应需的机件器材皆由比利时企业提供，唯有电车车辆和发电厂的所有电气设备是由德国西门子舒克特公司（Siemens Schuckert）提供，并由其公司工程师负责监督安装。[64] 后期随着经营开展，修车厂设备完备，除钢轮外，全部车辆皆可自行制造。厂内共分为机务段、机工班、电工班、驾车班、铆工班、木工班、钳工班、铁工班、油工班、检车班、洗车班等部门。[65]

天津比商电车电灯公司成立后，首先开始架设线路，推销电灯电力。用于照明的煤气和电力早在19世纪80年代即已开始在天津的租界出现。1888年，世昌洋行在他们的压羊毛机上加装了一台发电机，并在荷兰领事馆内装了一盏1000 cd/m² 的电灯。之后英租界内在1889—1890年冬季的夜间开始使用煤气照明。[66] 义和团

the British vegetable market and then along the docks to the edge of the German concession. However, the British considered this plan too ambitious and they were reluctant to extend the track beyond the market. This meant the tram line could not be extended to the German concession, which was located south of the British concession. The Germans were unexpectedly "victimized" by the lack of access to the trams.[63] In 1927 the company extended its operations to the former Russian concession.

Direct current is needed for tram operation, and alternating current is needed for electric lighting. To supply electricity, it was necessary to ensure sufficient water supply, so CTET first purchased a piece of land in the village of Jinjiayao, which was in front of Hai River and behind Jinzhong River, to build a power plant. Later, it also purchased a building at the east entrance of the East Pontoon Bridge over the Hai River (present-day Hebei District) as its office. Another piece of land was also purchased in the north side of Nankai Middle School (located at the southwest corner of the old city of Tianjin) to build a depot and repair shop for the trams. At the beginning, all

远景为天津比商电车电灯公司的住宅、办公室和车间，近景为电线杆架设的为电车供电的电线网络。照片摄于 1905—1906 年

In the background: residences, offices, and workshops of CTET. Close-up: power line network for the tramway. Photo taken in 1905-1906

天津比商电车电灯公司办公室和车间今景。刘悦先生摄于 2004 年

Present view of office and depot of CTET. Photos taken by Mr. Liu Yue in 2004

天津比商电车电灯公司员工安装电灯

CTET employees installing electric lights

以上旧照出自比利时根特大学档案馆保存的天津比商电车电灯公司工程师内恩斯相册

Old photos are from the photo album of François Nuyens, an engineer of CTET, kept in the archives of Ghent University in Belgium

车辆段车间内景。摄于 1905—1906 年

Interior view of the tram depot. The photo
was taken in 1905-1906

安装设备。摄于 1905—1906 年

Installation of equipment. The photo was taken in 1905-1906

以上照片出自比利时根特大学档案馆保存的天津比商电车电灯公司工程师内恩斯相册

Photos are from the photo album of François Nuyens, an engineer of CTET, kept in
the archives of Ghent University in Belgium

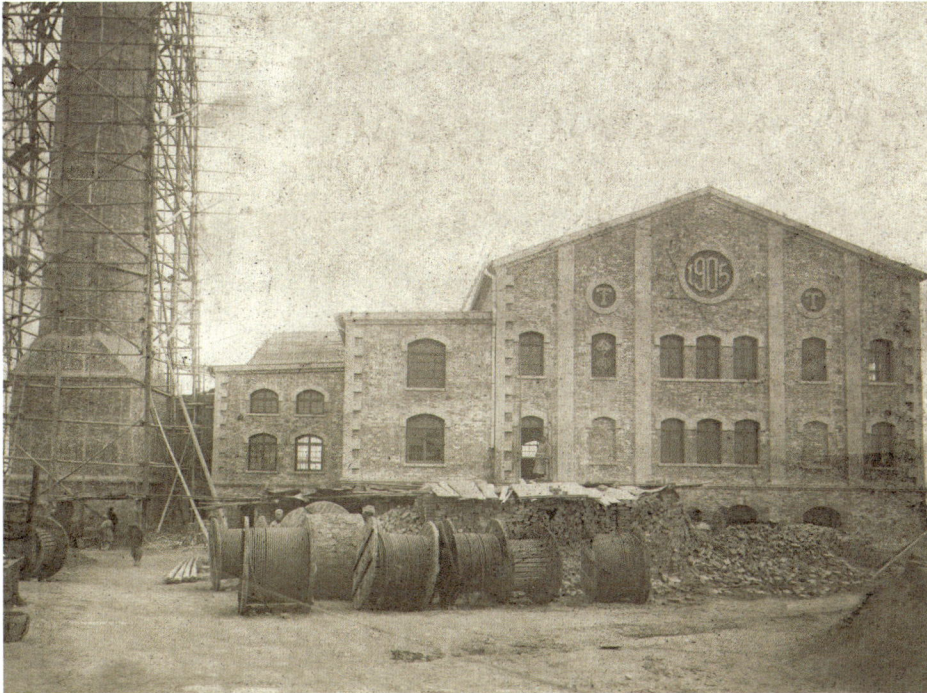

发电厂。摄于 1905—1906 年

The power plant. The photo was taken in 1905-1906

发电厂机器装配。摄于 1906 年

Machine assembly of power plant. The photo was taken in 1906

以上照片出自比利时根特大学档案馆保存的天津比商电车电灯公司工程师内恩斯相册

Photos are from the photo album of François Nuyens, an engineer of CTET, kept in the archives of Ghent University in Belgium

运动之后，八国联军对天津进行管理的临时政府做出决议，要求城区街道两侧交错每隔100步要安装一盏路灯，安装和维护费用由沿街房主承担。[67] 于是，老城区开始出现了电灯照明。而且，在天津临时政府与天津比商电车电灯公司达成协议时，临时政府委员会提出将专营权授予该公司的若干条件之一，就是公司要为电车经过的马路以及其他道路提供电力路灯照明，而且规定了电费不得高于成本价。[68]

不过，当时天津人对电灯照明的优点还没有充分认识，既怕着火又怕触电，加之对洋人怀有戒心，大都采取观望态度，不愿安装。该公司华人经理刘中和负责营销，策划先从商店入手，采取"先尝后买"的营销策略，由该公司派人与位于繁华热闹地区的商店联系，免费安装，并在商店门面牌匾上装饰一些大灯泡，待夜晚电灯一亮，照耀如同白昼。远近市民基于好奇心理，往来参观，络绎不绝，商店业务随之大增。于是，凡未安装电灯的商店也纷纷要求安装电灯，公司的电灯业务由此开展起来。随后，居民住户的电灯安装业务也开展起来。仅商家和住户的电表押金即积累成为一笔巨额资金，存入华比银行，滚动生息，足以支付员工工资。[69] 当时天津市区除了英、日、法三个租界有自己的发电设备，以及德租界借用英租界电力之外，其余奥匈、意、俄、比四国租界和全部华界的电灯电力，均由天津比商电车电灯公司包办。[70] 这为公司的发展打下了第一根坚固的桩基。

1905年，电车轨道铺设工程开工，到1905年9月，3公里长的线路修建完毕。1906年2月16日围城路线和北大关至岔口的线路都开始试运行，共有18辆电车低速行驶，以使中国人适应这种新的交通方式，第一

the electric lights, machinery and equipment were provided by Belgian companies, except for the electrical equipment for the tram cars and the power plant, which was provided by Siemens Schuckert of Germany, whose engineers were responsible for supervising the installation.[64] Later, with the development of the business, the garage was fully equipped and all trolley cars, except for steel wheels, could be manufactured by CTET itself. The plant was divided into the following departments: locomotive depot, mechanic section, electrician class, driving class, riveter class, carpentry class, clamp class, ironworker class, oiler class, car inspection class, car wash class, etc.[65]

After the establishment of CTET, the company first began to set up electric power lines to market electric light and power. Gas and electricity for lighting began to appear in the Tianjin concessions as early as the 1880s. In 1888, E. Meyer & Co. added a generator to their wool press and installed a $1,000 \text{ cd/m}^2$ electric lamp in the Dutch Consulate. Later, gas lighting began to be used in the British concession at night during the winter of 1889-1890.[66] After the Boxer Rebellion, the Provisional Government of Tianjin, which was administered by the Eight-Power Allied Forces, made a resolution to install a streetlight every 100 steps on both sides of the city streets, with the installation and maintenance costs borne by the owners of the houses along the streets.[67] As a result, electric lighting began to appear in the old city. Moreover, when the Provisional Government reached an agreement with Compagnie de Tramways & D'eclairage de Tientsin (CTET), the Provisional Government Committee proposed that one of the conditions for the granting of the agreement was that the company should provide electric streetlights for the roads on which the trams traveled and the electricity fees should not be higher than the cost.[68]

However, at that time, Tianjin people were not fully aware of the advantages of electric lighting. Afraid of

天津比商电车电灯公司经理兰伯特·沙多。经其兄京汉铁路总工程师让·沙多推荐，来天津比商电车电灯公司任工程师

Lambert Jadot, manager of CTET. Upon the recommendation of his brother Jean Jadot, chief engineer of Beijing-Hankou Railway, he was appointed as the engineer of CTET

天共载客约 10000 名。[71]1906 年 2 月 27 日下午 3 点举行正式开通仪式。[72]公司总经理兰伯特·沙多（Lambert Jadot）[73]与代表总督袁世凯的津海关道梁敦彦携其长子和女儿、北洋洋务总管蔡绍基等地方官员，以及中外地方名流参加了开通仪式。天津第一条有轨电车路线也是中国第一条公交线路——单轨"白牌"电车正式开始运营。1907 年"白牌"电车改为复线。

对于马路上新出现的快速交通工具，人们不得不需要提高安全意识以适应新事物。电车正式运行半个月之后的 3 月 3 日，一个 6 岁女孩成为新电车系统的首位受害者。司机辩解说，在事故当天他接到指示，说要首次使用电车驱动电机的并联挡位，目的是提高车速。在公

electric fire and shock and wary of foreigners, most of them took a wait-and-see attitude and were reluctant to install electric lights. The company's Chinese manager Liu Zhonghe was responsible for marketing; he adopted the marketing strategy of "try before you buy." The company sent people to contact the stores located in busy commercial areas to offer free installation of decorative light bulbs on the store front plaque. At night, when the light bulbs were lit, they were shining as bright as day. People, out of curiosity, came to see from near and far, thus increasing the store's business stream. As a result, stores that had not installed electric lights also requested to install them. The company's electric lighting business was thus launched. Subsequently, the business of installing electric lights in households also started. The deposits from merchants and

围城线路和北大关至岔口两条线路的电车试运行。摄于 1906 年 1 月。出自比利时根特大学档案馆保存的天津比商电车电灯公司工程师内恩斯相册

Trial runs of trams on circle Line. Photo was taken in January 1906, from the photo album of François Nuyens, an engineer of CTET, kept in the archives of Ghent University in Belgium

CHINA TIMES, Wednesday, February 28, 190[6]

Tientsin Electric Tramways.

Formal Opening.

Yesterday afternoon at 3 o'clock the formal opening of the Tientsin Electric Tramways took place. Immense interest was taken in the ceremony by the native population of Tientsin City, who thronged all the approaches to the Viceroy's Bridge where the inaugural proceedings were conducted.

The tramway has been open to the public for some days and has proved extremely popular. The Tramway Company has proceeded by degrees in initiating the public service, being anxious to accustom the people to the novelty of the fast-moving electrically propelled cars in their crowded thoroughfares. The system now open extends all round the Native City, the track running along the four Maloos or boulevards. It will be extended by degrees from each of the four corners formed by these broad and handsome roads.

It had been proposed to extend the tramway system from the City through the Japanese Concession to the settlement station, but the Japanese authorities has previously made arrangements with a Japanese contractor to construct an electric tramway system for the Concession, and the Tientsin Electric Tramway Co., we understand, were unable to come to terms with the Japanese authorities and the contractor, and so this part of the scheme fell through. In default of this it has now been decided to make electric tramway communication with the Settlement Station by building a new steel bridge over the river in conjunction with the Austrian authorities (the Austrian Concession being badly in need of a proper, permanent and convenient bridge), and over this bridge the trams will pass, the track being extended through the Austrian, Italian, and Russian Concessions to the railway station. This will be a more direct route than that proposed through the Japanese Concession, and the existence of the new tramway route will no doubt be a great factor in attracting residents to those at present thinly populated districts (so far as Europeans are concerned) of Tientsin, while no doubt the Chinese population also will increase in these Concessions owing to the convenience provided by the new trams.

It is also in contemplation to extend the tramway system to the Native City railway station and to various suburban villages, which—though not many Europeans may be aware of the fact—hitherto have enjoyed a primitive form of horse traction tramway, which has been very largely patronised by the teeming population of the City and its suburbs, notwithstanding the slow (walking) pace of these trams. Incidentally we may mention another fact which many Europeans who live in the Settlements are probably not aware of—there is a very large camel traffic between the City and the country beyond. Most people know, and those who have been there have seen, that there is a great camel traffic from Peking; but not so many of the Europeans in Tientsin are aware of the existence of a very considerable camel traffic so near at hand as in and around the Native City.

Among those who took part in yesterday's formal inaugural proceedings were representatives of the Viceroy and the City Government—H.E. Liang, the Customs Taotai, accompanied by his eldest son and daughter, who had their first ride in an electric tramcar; H. E. Tsa Taotai, head of the Viceroy's Foreign Bureau, and a director of the Tramway Co.; Dr. Mark, head of the Public Works Department and also a director of the Tramway Co., Liu Taotai, the Viceroy's Secretary, Yen Taotai, Dr. Watt, keeper of the Peiyang Hospital, Col. Munthe, Aide-de-Camp to the Viceroy, Mr. L. Jadot, Engineer-in-Chief to the Tramway Co., Mr. H. J. Vermeulen, Secretary to the Co., M. Disière, the new Belgian Consul in Tientsin, etc. The party were driven in an electric tramcar over that part of the route which is open for traffic and inspected the car-sheds, repairing shop, power station, and offices, in one of which refreshments were provided and success to the new undertaking was cordially drunk. That the system will be successful seems highly probable, to judge from the excellence of equipment, management, and working of the tramways and their popularity with the natives of Tientsin City. There are few if any places in the Far East where a new electric tramway system has been better installed or more successfully inaugurated than in Tientsin.

天津第一家外文报纸《中国时报》1906 年 2 月 28 日对电车正式开通仪式的报道："天津成功地安装并启用了新的电动有轨电车，在远东几乎没有任何地方可与之相比。"

The first foreign language newspaper in Tianjin, *China Times*, reported on the official opening ceremony of the tram on February 28, 1906

有轨电车行驶在奥匈租界。
摄于 1907 年

A tram car running in the Austro-Hungarian concession. Photo was taken in 1907

电车调度员毛伟汉
Mao Wai Han, a tram controller

天津比商电车电灯公司开通时的中比职员合影。摄于1906 年

A group photo of Chinese and Belgian employees at the opening of CTET. The photo was taken in 1906

以上照片出自比利时根特大学档案馆保存的天津比商电车电灯公司工程师内恩斯相册

Photos are from the photo album of François Nuyens, an engineer of CTET, kept in the archives of Ghent University in Belgium

电车司机
The tram driver

为电车过海河而修建的平开式铁桥——金汤桥，桥址上原为一座木船搭建的浮桥，称为东浮桥。摄于 1906 年，出自比利时根特大学档案馆保存的天津比商电车电灯公司工程师内恩斯相册

Jintang Bridge, a level-opening iron bridge built for trams to cross the Hai River. The photo was taken in 1906, from the photo album of François Nuyens, an engineer of CTET, kept in the archives of Ghent University in Belgium

司经理的斡旋之下，这名司机免于被绞刑处死，但仍需要接受竹棍鞭打 50 次的惩罚，还要坐 3 年牢。事故发生后，电车司机士气有所下降，西门子教官也拒绝在街上对司机进行培训，担心受到进一步处罚。后来，经过一番运作得以在发生类似悲剧时免于受到刑罚，主要是通过重金拉拢警察并向受害者或其亲属提供慷慨赔偿的政策。但困难不止于此，电车在长达几个月的时间里还遇到了黄包车协会秘密组织的激烈抵制活动。[74]

天津的市民对电车与当初对电灯一样，十分反感，一则因为仇洋心理，二则害怕乘车触电，三则担心票价

residents alone became a large sum of revenue, which was deposited in the Sino-Belgian Bank. The rolling interest was sufficient to pay the salaries of employees.[69] At that time, except for the British, Japanese and French concessions, which had their own power generation facilities, and the German concession, which borrowed electricity from the British concessions, the rest of the concessions (e.g., Austro-Hungarian, Italian, Russian and Belgian concessions) and all of the Chinese-controlled regions were undertaken by CTET.[70] This laid the first solid foundation for the development of the company.

In 1905, the construction of the tram tracks started and by September 1905, the 3 km long line was completed. On February 16, 1906, both the circle route and the line from Beidaguan to Chakou began the trial run with 18 trams running at low speed to acclimatize the Chinese to this new mode of transportation, carrying a total of about 10,000 passengers on the first day.[71] The official opening ceremony was held at 3:00 pm on February 27, 1906.[72] Lambert Jadot[73], General Manager of the company, together with Liang Dunyan, a local official representing Zhili Viceroy Yuan Shikai and his eldest son and daughter, and Cai Shaoji, the Foreign Affairs official of the Beiyang government, as well as local and foreign celebrities, attended the opening ceremony. The first tram line in Tianjin (also the first public transportation line in China), the single-track "White" tram, started to operate, and in 1907 the "White" tram became a double line.

With the new and fast means of transportation on the road, people had to be more safety conscious to adapt to the new thing. On March 3, half a month after the official operation of the tram, a 6-year-old girl became the first victim of the new tram system. The driver argued that on the day of the accident he had been instructed to use the parallel notches of the tram's drive motor for the first time, with the aim of increasing the speed of the tram car. Through

刚刚建成的东浮桥（后名金汤桥）。摄于 1906 年

The newly-built East Pontoon Bridge (now Jin Tang Bridge). Photo taken in 1906

昂贵，对于那些猎奇乘车者竟投以蔑视的眼光，所以"只闻城间铃铛响，不见人影登车来"。后来，公司华经理采取降低票价的办法：一开始票价极低，绕城一周，一等车厢只收一个小铜元，二等车厢只收半个铜元（当时铜元分大铜元、小铜元和半个铜元三种），让人们逐渐感受到现代交通工具的便利，于是乘客日多。票价也随之提高，按段收费，每段 3 个小铜元，超过一段即增收 1 个铜元。[75]

为了把线路延伸到对岸的奥、意、俄三国租界，并最终接驳位于海河东岸的火车站，天津比商电车电灯公司于 1906 年 10 月兴建了金汤桥。施工费的 50% 由天津比商电车电灯公司支付，其余部分由天津地方政府及奥、意、俄三国平均分担。[76] 之后，天津比商电车电灯公司除了最早的围城线路"白牌"（1906 年），又陆

the mediation of the company manager, the driver was saved from execution by hanging, but still had to undergo 50 lashes with bamboo sticks and three years in prison. After the accident, the morale of the tram drivers dropped significantly, and Siemens instructors refused to train drivers on the street for fear of further punishment. Later, some maneuvering was able to spare them from penalties in the event of similar tragedies, largely through bribing the police and offering generous compensation to victims or their relatives. But the difficulties did not stop there - the tram also encountered a fierce boycott organized in secret by the association of rickshaw operators over a period of several months.[74]

The people of Tianjin initially were as averse to the tram as they were to the electric light because of their hatred of foreigners, the fear of being electrocuted, and the high fares. They treated those who were riding the tram with contempt. Therefore, "Bells are ringing in the city, but no one is seen boarding the tram." Later, the Chinese manager of the company lowered the fare: it cost only one small copper dollar for the first-class carriage and half a copper dollar for the second-class carriage (at that time, there were three kinds of copper dollars: big copper dollar, small copper dollar and half a copper dollar) to travel around the city in the circle line. This made people gradually experience the convenience of modern transportation - so there were more passengers day by day. The fares were also subsequently increased: charged by sections with 3 small copper dollars per section, and one additional copper dollar if the ride exceeded one section.[75]

To extend the tram line to the Austrian, Italian and Russian concessions on the other side of the river and eventually to connect to the railway station on the east bank of the Hai River, CTET built the Jintang Bridge in October 1906. Fifty percent of the construction cost was paid by the company, while the rest was shared equally

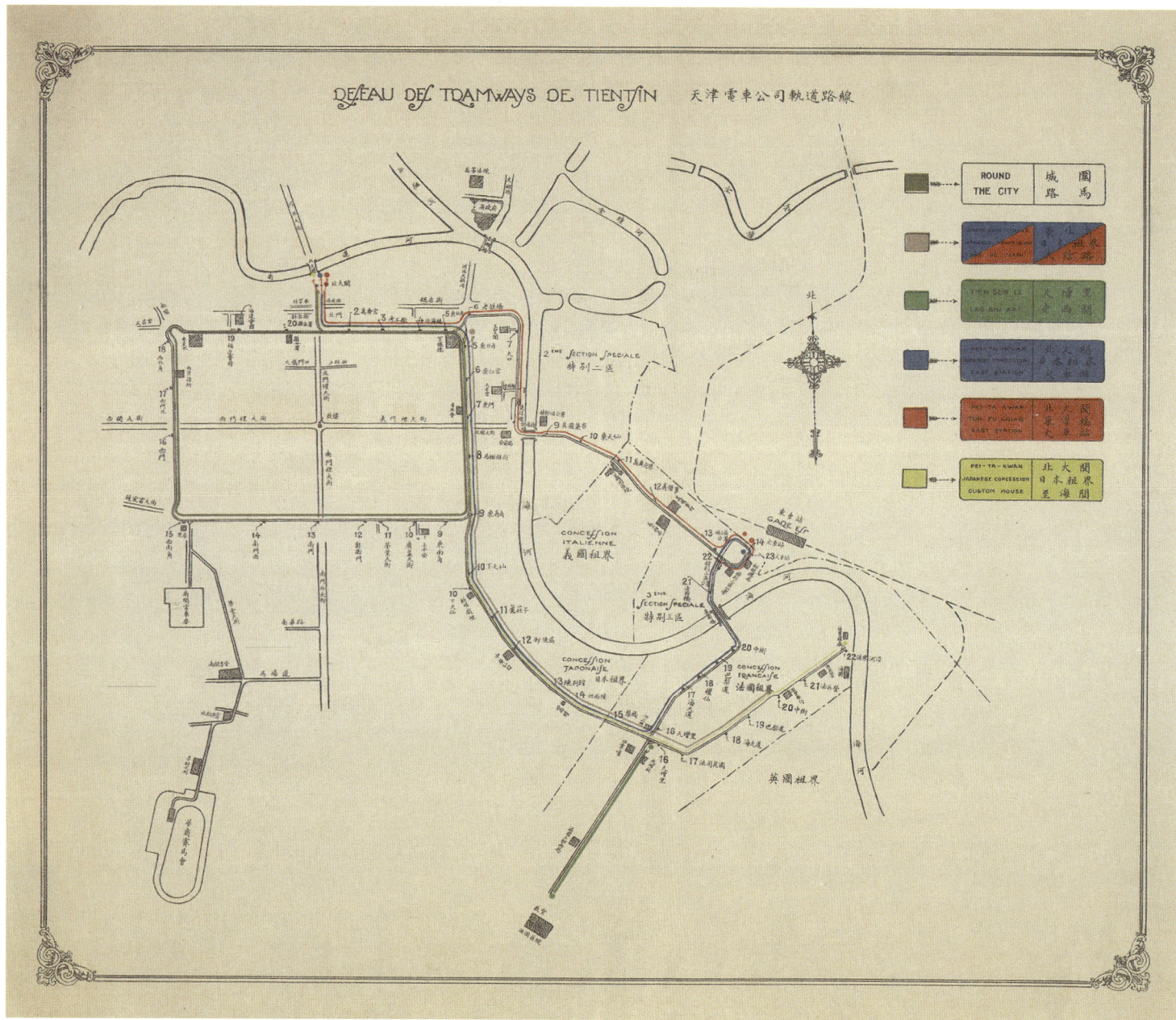

天津电车路线图。出自比利时根特大学档案馆
Tianjin tram route map. Kept in the archives of Ghent University in Belgium

天津比商电车电灯公司车库，
约摄于 2004 年

CTET depot, circa 2004

天津比商电车电灯公司职员公
寓，天津人称为"比国大院"，
约摄于 2004 年

The apartment building of the
CTET staff, which is referred to
as the "Belgian Compound" by
Tianjin people, circa 2004

天津比商电车电灯公司中比员工合影。摄于 1908 年，出自比利时根特
大学档案馆保存的电车公司工程师内恩斯相册

Photo of the Chinese and Belgian employees of CTET. The photo
was taken in 1908, from the photo album of François Nuyens, an
engineer of CTET, kept in the archives of Ghent University in Belgium

电车公司中国调度员与比利时工程师内恩斯合影。摄于1908年，出自比利时根特大学档案馆保存的电车公司工程师内恩斯相册

Photo of the Chinese controller of the CTET with the Belgian engineer Nuyens. The photo was taken in 1908, from the photo album of François Nuyens, an engineer of CTET, kept in the archives of Ghent University in Belgium

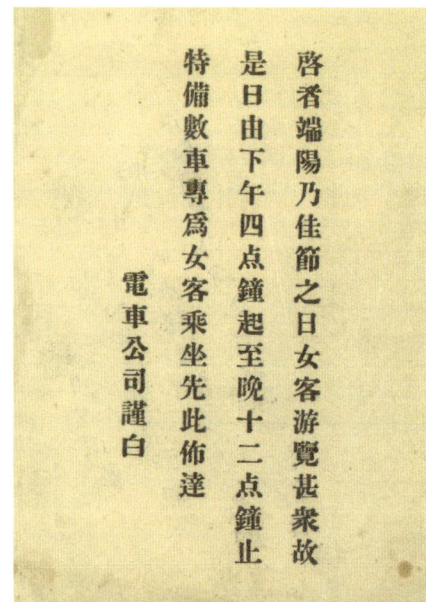

1906—1908年，端午节为女性乘客提供专车的告示

Notice of the special tram for female passengers during the Dragon Boat Festival, during 1906-1908

天津有轨电车票价表。出自比利时根特大学档案馆保存的电车公司工程师内恩斯日记

The tram fares in Tianjin, from the diary of François Nuyens, an engineer of CTET, kept in the archives of Ghent University in Belgium

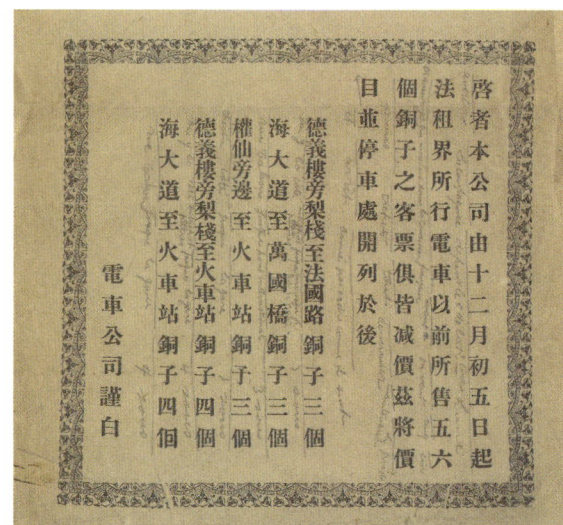

续开辟了"红牌"（1908年）、"黄牌"（1908年）、"蓝牌"（1908年）、"绿牌"（1918年）和"花牌"（1927年）5条电车线路，总长度21.68公里，形成了贯穿天津城商业繁华街区及日、法、意、奥、俄等国租界的四通八达的交通网络。[77] 电车运行两年后，"中国人已经非常熟悉不同颜色的电车目的地标牌，也能够区分不同线路的信号灯。乘客们对各种票价了如指掌"。不过，电车速度不能太快，由于市民的交通安全意识还不足，"注意力不集中，司机必须安全驾驶，才能避免发生事故"[78]。

随着老城区和租界区的商贸发展和天津城市人口的激增，电车的运客量也大幅增长。据档案记载，到民国初年，天津比商电车电灯公司就收回了之前的全部投资。1927年，公司共有130辆电车，每年运送乘客900万人次。[79] 到1940年，据该公司统计，全年乘客总数为81837000人次，按当时天津全市人口200万计算，则每人每年乘坐电车平均达到40次以上，票价收入之巨，可想而知。[80] 该公司每天把收入款项悉数存入华比银行，每周汇往比利时首都2000~3000英镑。据档案记载，从1916年至1928年的13年期间，该公司靠经营电车电灯两项，共获利25729800银元。截至1942年被日本军队强制接管，共获利至少达五六千万之巨。[81]

1927年1月17日，比利时驻华公使洛恩宣布，比利时愿意将天津比租界交还中国，同时比利时财团在天津的电车业也全部交还，但电车电灯公司最终并没有实际交回。1937年电车线路被入侵的日本人征用。1941年太平洋战争爆发，日本军队开始干涉公司行政。1943年年底，日方辞退所有不愿为其服务的比利时员

among the local government of Tianjin and Austria, Italy and Russia.[76] After that, CTET opened, in addition to the earliest "White" (1906) line, "Red" (1908), "Yellow" (1908), "Blue" (1908), "Green" (1918) and "Flower" (1927) lines, with a total length of 21.68 kilometers, forming a well-connected transportation network that ran through the busy commercial districts of Tianjin Old City as well as Japanese, French, Italian, Austrian and Russian concessions.[77] After two years of operation, "the Chinese were already familiar with the different colored destination signs of the trams and could distinguish the signals of the different lines. Passengers knew the various fares like the back of their hands." However, the trams should not go too fast because the public still lacked the awareness of road safety. The drivers thus must operate the tram safely in order to avoid accidents[78].

With the development of commerce and trade in the old city and the concession area, and the surge in the population of Tianjin, the number of passengers carried by the trams also increased significantly. According to the records, by the early years of the Republic of China, CTET had recovered all its previous investments, and in 1927, the company had 130 trams carrying 9 million passengers a year.[79] By 1940, according to the company's statistics, the total number of passengers for the year was 81,837,000, which, based on a population of 2 million in Tianjin at that time, meant that each person took the tram more than 40 times a year on average, and the revenue from fares was huge.[80] The company deposited all its income into the Sino-Belgian Bank every day and remitted 2,000 to 3,000 pounds per week to the Belgian capital. According to the records, the company made a total profit of 25,729,800 silver dollars from the operation of the trams and electric lights during the 13 years from 1916 to 1928. By 1942, when it was taken over by the Japanese army, the total profit was at least 50-60 million.[81]

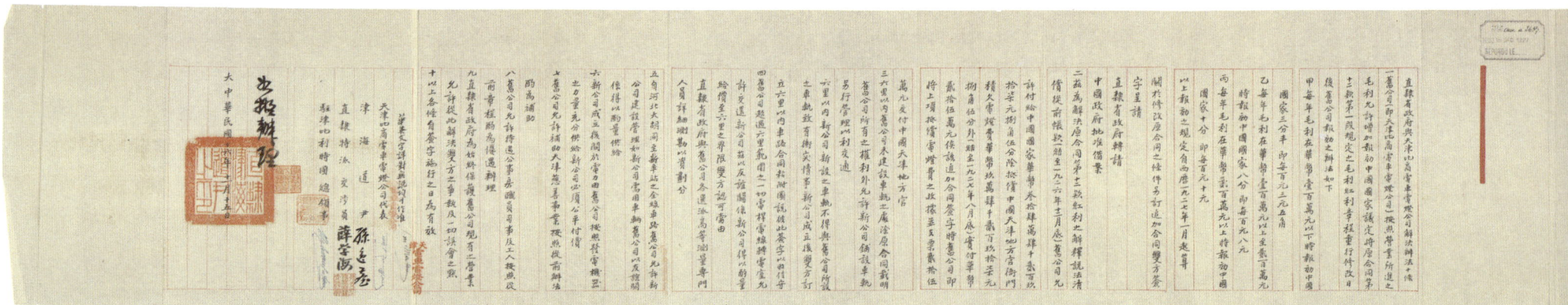

民国时期直隶省政府与天津比商电车电灯公司的条款。现藏于比利时外交部档案馆

Terms and Conditions of the Zhili Provincial Government and the Compagnie de Tramways et d'Eclairage de Tientsin during the Republic of China. Now in the archives of the Belgian Ministry of Foreign Affairs

工，并将他们作为敌国侨民送进山东潍县集中营关押，用武力强行接收了天津比商电车电灯股份有限公司的产业，电力部由华北电业公司接管，电车部由满铁株式会社接管，后又将其归入日本人经营的"天津交通公司"。1945 年，日本投降后，民国政府出面接收。1949 年 1 月 15 日，天津解放，天津比商电车电灯股份有限公司更名为"天津市公共汽车公司"。[82]

On January 17, 1927, Belgian Minister Léon le Maire de Warzee d'Hermalle announced that Belgium was willing to return the Belgian concession in Tianjin to China, but the tramway was not actually returned in the end. In 1937 the tramway was requisitioned by the invading Japanese. In 1941 the Pacific War broke out and the Japanese army began to interfere with the company's management. At the end of 1943, the Japanese dismissed all Belgian employees who did not want to serve them and sent them to Wei County concentration camp in Shandong Province as enemy aliens, and forcibly took over the properties of CTET. The department of electricity was taken over by North China Electric Power Company, and the tram department fell into the hands of the South Manchuria Railways Co., and then was merged into the "Tianjin Transportation Company" operated by the Japanese. After the surrender of Japan in 1945, the Republic of China government took over the company, and on January 15, 1949, Tianjin was liberated and the company was renamed as "Tianjin Municipal Bus Company."[82]

成立之初，公司还组织了消防队，日常进行消防演练。出自比利时根特大学档案馆保存的电车公司工程师内恩斯相册

At the beginning of its establishment, the company also organized a fire department and conducted routine fire drills. From the photo album of François Nuyens, an engineer of CTET, kept in the archives of Ghent University in Belgium

电车电灯公司员工检修电车线路。出自比利时根特大学档案馆保存的电车公司工程师内恩斯相册

CTET employees inspecting tram lines. From the photo album of François Nuyens, an engineer of CTET, kept in the archives of Ghent University in Belgium

明信片上的有轨电车。电车分为机车、拖车和工程车 3 种，均由比利时制造。机车是电车的车头，内装电动机，拖车即为机车后面拖曳的车厢，两者均可载客。工程车则为修理电车轨道故障的车辆。截至 1949 年，共有机车 86 辆、拖车 86 辆、工程车 1 辆

Trams on postcards. Tram has three parts: locomotive, trailer, and engineering vehicle, all of which are manufactured in Belgium. A locomotive is the tram head, equipped with an electric motor inside, and a trailer is the carriage dragged behind the locomotive, both of which can carry passengers. Engineering vehicle is mainly for repairing vehicles with defective tramways. As of 1949, there were a total of 86 locomotives, 86 trailers, and 1 engineering vehicle

行驶在天津老城东北角的电车。摄于 1907 年，由近代天津博物馆刘悦先生提供

A tramcar running in the northeast corner of the old city of Tianjin. The photo was taken in 1907, by courtesy of Mr. Liu Yue, Tianjin Museum of Modern History

20 世纪上半叶天津的有轨电车

Tram car in Tianjin in the first half of the 20th century

以上照片由近代天津博物馆刘悦先生提供

By courtesy of Mr. Liu Yue, Tianjin Museum of Modern History

天津比商义品放款公司

天津虽然早在 1860 年即已开辟为通商口岸，但在最初的几十年里，由于来华各国侨民和公司不多，且缺乏雄厚的资金，各租界内并未进行大规模的建筑活动。直到 20 世纪初义和团运动以后，八个国家根据《辛丑条约》拥有在天津驻军的权力。有了军队的保护，各国租界掀起了建设高潮，西方房地产商纷纷进驻开发租界地区，成立了如先农（美国）、义品等房地产开发公司，同时期一批外籍建筑师及工程技术人员主导的建筑师事务所，如乐利工程司（瑞士、英国）、景明工程司（英国）、永和工程司（法国）、同和工程司（英国）、永固工程司（英国）、盖苓美术建筑事务所（奥地利）等，也相继而来，为天津带来了国际上先进的建筑思潮、建筑技术以及系统的施工管理方法，与本地传统建筑风格在碰撞与融合中不断发展，开创了天津近代建筑的繁荣局面，形成中国近代建筑史上"世界建筑博览会"的独特景观。

天津比商义品放款公司（Crédit Foncier d'Extrême-Orient，一般简称为 CFEO）是近代天津规模最大的房地产公司之一。创办人欧艾叶（Jean O'Neill），于庚子事变后来到天津，了解到本地的天主教会借由《辛丑条约》签订的关系，大量侵占中国地产，激起民怨，于是向罗马教廷汇报，建议教皇限令教会应专心传教，房地产方面的事务责成专业的财团公司负责。得到教廷赞同后，欧艾叶前往比利时，于 1907 年 8 月 3 日在布鲁塞尔登记成立天津法比兴业银行（Société Franco-Belge de Tientsin），之后又在法国巴黎也设立了办公室，以代天津法国教会开发土地为由，在比利时和法国发行公司

Crédit Foncier d'Extreme-Orient (CFEO)

Although Tianjin was opened as a port of commerce as early as 1860, no large-scale construction activities were carried out in the first decades in the various concessions due to the small number of expatriates and companies from various countries coming to China and the lack of strong capital. It was not until after the Boxer Rebellion in the early 20th century that eight countries were given the right to station troops in Tianjin under the Boxers Protocol. With the protection of the military, the construction frenzy was set off in the concessions, and Western real estate developers moved in to develop the concessions, establishing real estate development companies such as Tientsin Land Investment Co. Ltd (American) and Crédit Foncier d'Extrême-Orient, etc. During the same period, several architecture firms led by foreign architects and engineering technicians came to Tianjin, including Loup & Young (Swiss, British), Hemmings & Berkley (British), Hunke & Muller (French), Kidner Wm & Kidner James (British), Cook & Anderson (British), Yuen Fu Building and Engineering Co. (Austrian). They brought the internationally advanced architectural thinking, building technology and systematic construction management methods to Tianjin. Their integration and intersection with local traditional architecture style formed Tianjin's unique landscape of "World Architecture Fair" in the history of modern Chinese architecture.

Crédit Foncier d'Extrême-Orient (commonly referred to as CFEO) was one of the largest real estate companies in modern Tianjin. Jean O'Neill, the founder of the company, came to Tianjin after the Boxer Rebellion and realized that the local Catholic Church, by virtue of the signing of the Boxer Protocol, had appropriated a large amount of Chinese real estate and aroused public discontent. After receiving the approval of the Holy See, O'Neill went to Belgium and registered the Société Franco-Belge de Tientsin in Brussels

天津比商义品公司大楼旧景
The old view of office building of CFEO

债券和股票。最终法比兴业银行总公司的董事会由 6 名法国人、6 名比利时人构成。欧艾叶于 1907 年在天津设立分公司和董事会，这也是义品公司最主要的分支机构，他自己出任天津董事会的董事长和总经理。天津分公司以分期付款的方式接收了天主教首善堂[83]和崇德堂[84]的 14 公顷土地，由此奠定公司发展的第一块基石。1910 年公司更名为"远东地产信贷银行"（Crédit Foncier d'Extrême-Orient Société Anonyme），中文名仪品放款银行。后因避清帝"溥仪"名讳，改为"义品放款银行"，又称"义品房地产公司"[85]。

义品公司创立初期发展迅猛，公司注册时资本为 415 万法郎，1910 年即达到 1000 万法郎，1929 年则增长到 7000 万法郎，[86]经营区域更是遍及中国沿海沿江较为发达的城市。1909 年在上海法租界购置地产并设立分

on August 3, 1907, and later set up an office in Paris, France. Under the pretext of developing land on behalf of the French Church in Tianjin, it issued corporate bonds and shares in Belgium and France. Eventually the board of directors of the Société Franco-Belge de Tientsin consisted of six French and six Belgians. O'Neill set up a branch and board of directors in Tianjin in 1907, the most important branch of CFEO of which he served as the chairman and general manager. The Tianjin branch took over the 14 hectares of land from the Congregation of Priests of the Mission[83] and Jesuit Mission[84] by paying in installments, thus laying the first cornerstone of the company's future development. In 1910, the company was renamed "Crédit Foncier d'Extrême-Orient Société Anonyme" (Far Eastern Real Estate Credit Bank). The bank's Chinese name was "Yipin Credit Bank", also known as "Yipin Real Estate Company[85]".

The company's capital was 4.15 million francs at the time of registration, but it quickly reached 10 million francs in 1910 and grew to 70 million francs in 1929.[86] In 1909, the company purchased property in the French concession in Shanghai and set up a branch office, and in the same year, built a brick factory in Bailitai and Xikai, Tianjin. It set up branches in Hankou and Hong Kong in 1911, and in Beijing and Jinan in 1915 and 1918 respectively. It also built a brick factory in Shanghai in 1919.[87] Since 1927, due to political turmoil and stricter regulations, the company decided to reduce its business in the concessions, especially in Tianjin and Shanghai, and shifted its focus to Hong Kong, which was a British colony at the time, and the adjacent Southeast Asia area.[88] In 1928, the company opened its seventh branch in Singapore and started to expand its business in Malaysia. In the late 1920s and early 1930s, the Great Depression, which spread throughout the capitalist world, hit the company's business hard, but it was still able to make a profit from its real estate business in Hong Kong.[89]

中国工人在义品公司的建筑工地
Chinese workers at the construction site of CFEO

在建房屋
Building under construction

施工工地
Construction site

以上照片保存于比利时外交部档案馆
Photos are preserved in the archives of
the Belgian Ministry of Foreign Affairs

公司，同年在天津八里台和西开成立义品砖窑厂。1911年在汉口、香港设分公司，1915年、1918年分别在北京、济南设分公司，1919年在上海成立砖窑厂。[87]1927年起，由于政局动荡、审查趋严，公司决定缩减在租界区的业务，尤其是天津和上海，把经营重心转向时为英国殖民地的香港及邻近的东南亚地区。[88]1928年在新加坡开设第七家分公司，并开始在马来西亚拓展业务。20世纪20年代末30年代初，蔓延整个资本主义世界的经济大萧条对义品公司业务造成严重冲击，但其仍能依靠香港地区的房地产业务赢利。[89]

然而，随着抗日战争的爆发，义品公司终于开始走向末路。1937年"卢沟桥事变"爆发，北京、天津、

However, with the outbreak of the war, CFEO finally came to an end. 1937 saw the outbreak of the "Marco Polo Bridge Incident" and the occupation of Beijing, Tianjin and Shanghai by Japan. In 1940, the occupation of Belgium by Germany completely disconnected CFEO branches from its headquarters. From 1942 to1943, Japan took over the business of the British and Italian concessions in China's interior. In 1942, the branches in Hong Kong and Singapore were also taken over by the Japanese, and the properties and office buildings were forcibly occupied. After the surrender of Japan, CFEO regained ownership of its real estate, but it struggled to operate due to the subsequent outbreak of the Chinese Civil War. After the founding of the People's Republic, a new land management system was implemented, which further restricted the business development of CFEO.

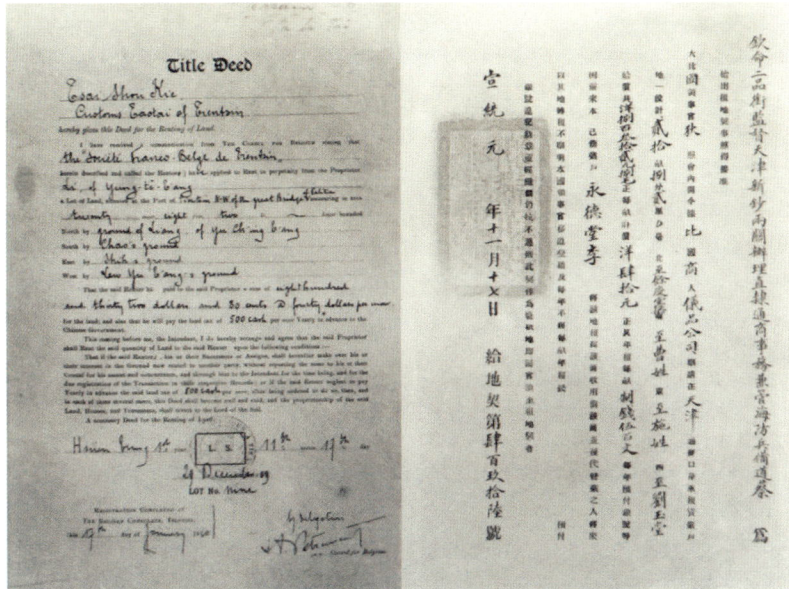

义品公司地契（1909 年）

Land deed of CFEO

义品公司银行票据

CFEO document

义品公司股票

CFEO company stock

以上文件收藏于比利时外交部档案馆

Documents are preserved in the archives
of the Belgian Ministry of Foreign Affairs

上海相继被日本占领。1940 年比利时被德国占领,自此义品公司各分公司与总部彻底失联。1942—1943 年日本接管了中国内陆的英、意租界的业务。1942 年香港和新加坡的分公司也被日军接管,房产及办公楼被强占。日本投降后义品公司虽收回了房地产所有权,但由于随后中国内战爆发,经营十分艰难。新中国成立后实行了新的土地管理制度,进一步限制了义品公司的业务发展。1955 年后,所有外资公司被迫迁出中国大陆地区,义品公司退到香港、新加坡,内陆各分公司逐渐清盘。[90]

义品公司的经营宗旨是"所有的活动都与创造价值有关,发展电气照明、电话、电报与供水管道,生产和供应建筑材料,有关动产与不动产的所有操作,包括出售、交换、租赁、经营或资产变现,所有事业都以抵押贷款的方式经营"[91]。简单来说,就是只要有利润,与房子有关的任何经营项目都可以做。秉承这一宗旨,义品公司的经营范围十分广泛,除以房地产出租及抵押放款为主业,还兼营多种副业。

公司内部设有放款部、房产经理部(经租部)、建筑工程部、挂旗部等四大部门。放款部的业务是以房地产或地产为抵押物进行贷款,并规定作为抵押品的房地产必须坐落在租界内,且放款额度不得超过产业价值的1/3,这条规定确保了公司的资金安全和丰厚回报。经租部除经营公司所有的房地产以外,也管理抵押借款的房产,代为出租和修缮。建筑工程部主要承担本公司的修缮和建筑工程,同时承揽代客设计建造等。挂旗部最具租界时代特色:由于常年军阀混战给天津市带来极大灾祸,一些有产业的中国人常常托庇于洋人势力,或者直接迁往租界居住,或者有租界以外房产的则向义品公

After 1955, all foreign companies were forced to move out of mainland China, and CFEO retreated to Hong Kong and Singapore.[90]

CFEO's business motto was to engage in "all activities related to the creation of value, the development of electrical lighting, telephone, telegraph and water pipelines, the production and supply of building materials, all operations related to movable and immovable property, including the sale, exchange, lease, operation or liquidation of assets."[91] In short, it means that any operation related to real estate can be done as long as there is profit. Adhering to this tenet, CFEO had a wide range of operations: in addition to its main business of real estate leasing and mortgage lending, it also ran a variety of sideline businesses.

There were four major departments within the company, including the Lending Department, the Property Management Department, the Construction and Engineering Department, and the Flag Hanging Department. The business of the Lending Department was to lend money against real estate or property, and it was stipulated that the real estate used as collateral must be located within the concessions area and that the amount of money lent must not exceed 1/3 of the value of the property, which ensured the safety of the company's capital and a good return. In addition to managing the real estate owned by the company, the Leasing Department also managed the properties for which mortgage loans were made. The Construction department mainly undertook repair and construction work for the company, and also design and construction on behalf of clients. The flag hanging department was the most unique. Because of the civil wars between warlords, some Chinese who had properties often took refuge in the concessions area. They also applied to CFEO for foreign protection of properties located outside of the concessions. The flag hanging department would send engineers to estimate the property value and charge 5% to 10% of the

司申请保护，由挂旗部派工程师估价产值，按5%至10%收取挂牌费，制作木牌钉在房产门前，并发给比国国旗一面，在战乱时悬挂出来，如蒙受损失，可由公司报请法、比两国领事馆，由公司予以赔偿。[92]

除此之外，义品公司旗下还有一些附属机构。第一次世界大战结束后，借由法国和比利时成为战胜国，义品公司接收了旧奥匈租界内奥地利人的房产，在此

value of the property for putting up a wooden sign at the property's front entrance, along with a Belgian national flag to hang during war times. If the property suffered any damage, CFEO would report to the consulates of France and Belgium and compensate for the damages.[92]

CFEO also had several subsidiaries. After the end of the First World War, when France and Belgium became the victorious countries, CFEO took over the Austrian properties in the old Austro-Hungarian concession and

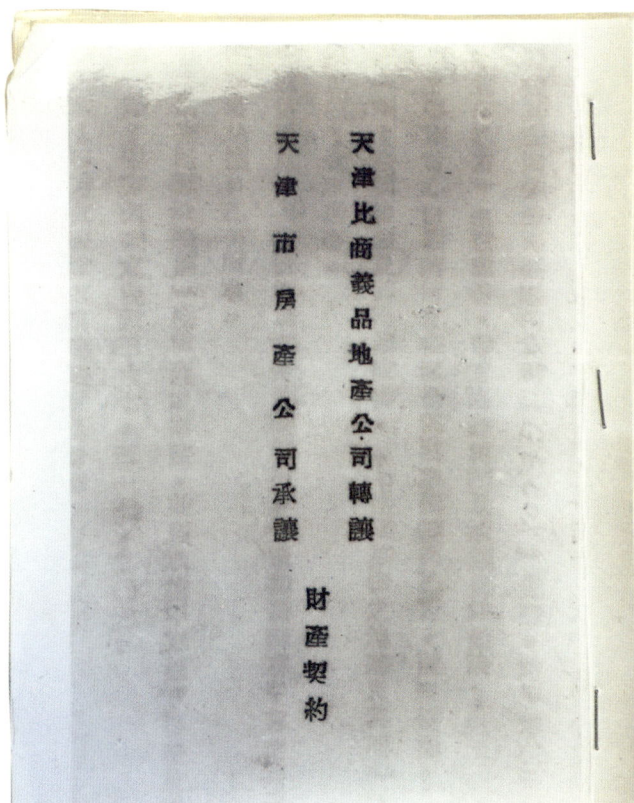

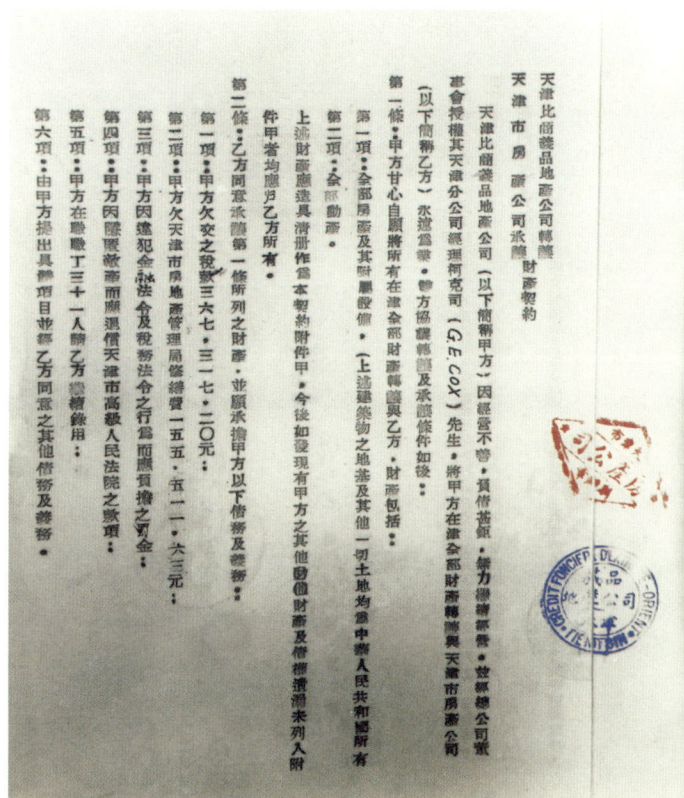

天津市房產公司承讓

天津比商義品地產公司轉讓

財產契約

天津比商義品地產公司轉讓天津市房產公司承讓財產契約

天津比商義品地產公司轉讓与天津市房产公司的契约书。收藏于比利时外交部档案馆

Deed of Assignment between CFEO and Tianjin Municipal Real Estate Company. Preserved in the archives of the Belgian Ministry of Foreign Affairs

基础上成立了中法义隆房产公司。为了运输建筑材料，义品公司又在塘沽成立了中法义兴轮船公司，往返于塘沽和金汤桥之间，除运送本公司货料之外，还接受客货运输。义品公司还开办了一个机器砖窑，天津人称之为"比国大砖窑"，所烧砖瓦除了供应本公司建筑需要外，还供应天津比商电车电灯公司、华比银行建造楼房厂舍，以及开平煤矿等其他各地比利时商行承建的工程所需材料。后来义品公司还设立了制作三层板的粘板公司。[93]

由于欧洲财团的支持，天津比商义品公司发展迅猛。公司的股东中，包括法国东方汇理银行和比利时华比银行，这两家银行在天津法租界均设有分公司。它们不仅直接给予义品公司资金支持，而且将其办公大楼交由义品公司工程部设计建造，成为义品公司进行业务扩张的强大后援，使义品公司几乎垄断了法租界的房地产业。至20世纪20年代初，义品公司已拥有天津法租界1/3的土地，[94]其设计并建造的建筑大部分位于法租界和英租界，少量在奥租界。这些建筑物大多数至今仍保存完好。

1949年新中国成立后，土地归国家和劳动者集体所有。新的土地制度限制了地产交易，为偿还债务及解决外交问题，天津比商义品公司将房地产全部移交中国政府，1956年全面清盘。

established Société Fonciére Franco-Chinoise de Tientsin. In order to transport construction materials, CFEO also founded Etablissements de Tungku in Tanggu, which carried cargo and passengers between Tanggu and Jintang Bridge. CFEO also built Manufacture Céramique de Tientsin which was named "big Belgian brick factory" by Tianjin people. In addition to meeting the parent company's construction needs, the factory supplied bricks and tiles to CTET and Sino-Belgian Bank for their respective construction needs, and materials for projects undertaken by Belgian trading firms in other places, such as Kaiping Coal Mine. CFEO later established a three-ply adhesive board company.[93]

Thanks to the support of the European consortium, CFEO grew rapidly. Among the shareholders of the company were Banque de l'Indochine and the Sino-Belgian Bank, both of which had branches in the French concession in Tianjin. They not only gave CFEO direct financial support, but also entrusted their office buildings to CFEO's engineering department for design and construction, which enabled CFEO to almost monopolize the real estate industry in the French concession. By the early 1920s, CFEO had already owned 1/3 of the land in the French concession of Tianjin,[94] and most of the buildings it designed and built were located in the French and British concessions, with a few in the Austrian concession (most of these buildings are still intact today).

After the establishment of People's Republic in 1949, land came under the collective ownership of the state and laborers. The new land system restricted real estate transactions, and in order to pay off debts and resolve diplomatic issues, CFEO handed over all of its real estate to the Chinese government and was fully liquidated in 1956.

义品公司设计建造的主要建筑

义品公司的房地产项目种类繁多，涵盖了金融商业建筑、行政办公建筑与居住建筑等，其风格均能体现出建筑的功能性和时代性特征。义品公司的建筑以砖、石两种材料为主，色彩统一，比例协调，在设计时十分重视与街道环境的整体性，对法租界大法国路（今解放北路解放桥至营口道段）街道风格的形成起了很大作用。法租界内的重要公共建筑也均为义品公司设计建造，包括工部局大楼、警察局大楼、领事馆等行政办公设施，以及法国俱乐部一期等。[95]

Major Buildings Designed and Constructed by CFEO

CFEO had a wide range of real estate projects, covering financial and commercial buildings, administrative office buildings and residential buildings. The style of the buildings reflects the functionality and period characteristics of the time. CFEO buildings were mainly made of brick and stone, with uniform color scheme and proportions, and their designs attached great importance to the integrity of the street environment, which played a great role in the formation of the street style along Rue de France (the present-day section from Jiefang Bridge to Yingkou Road on North Jiefang Road) in the French concession. The important public buildings in the French concession were also designed and built by CFEO, including the French Municipal Council building, the Police Department building, the Consulate and other administrative office facilities, as well as the first phase of the French Club. [95]

义品公司大楼图纸、旧景。大楼位于天津市和平区大沽路与彰德道交口北侧，建于1933年，占地面积约3131 ㎡，建筑面积约4910 ㎡，折中主义风格建筑，天津文物保护单位，重点保护等级历史风貌建筑。收藏于比利时外交部档案馆

The drawing and old view of CFEO Company Building. The building is located in the north side of the intersection of Dagu Road and Zhangde Road in Heping District, Tianjin, completed in 1933. It covers an area of about 3131m², with a construction area of about 4190 m², in the eclecticism style. Tianjin cultural relics protection unit, key protection grade historical style building. Preserved in the archives of the Belgian Ministry of Foreign Affairs

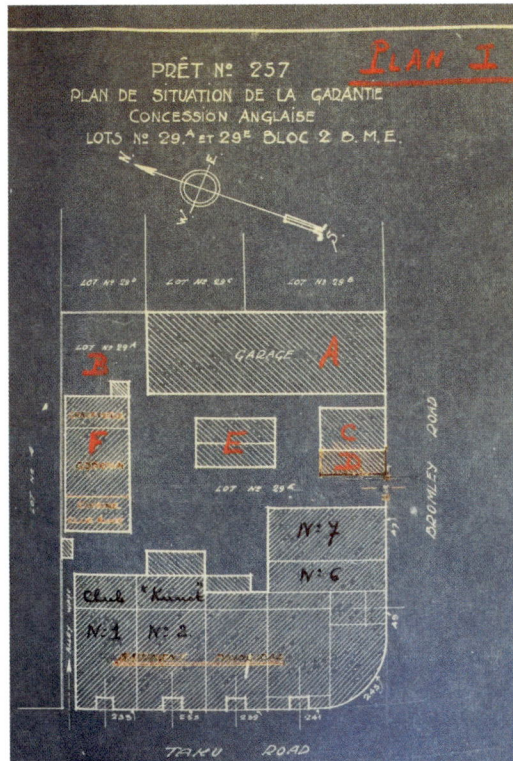

法国公议局　French Municipal Council

以上黑白照片保存于比利时外交部档案馆。彩色照片由航鹰女士摄于 2003 年

The black-and-white photos are preserved in the archives of the Belgian Ministry of Foreign Affairs. Above color photos were taken by Ms. Hang Ying in 2003

法国公议局今景、旧景。原法国公议局是法租界董事会行使行政职能的执行机构。位于和平区承德道 12 号（原法租界克雷孟梭广场旁的领事馆路）。1929—1931 年建成，占地面积约 2700 ㎡，建筑面积约 3700 ㎡，新古典主义风格建筑。《津京泰晤士报》报道了竣工典礼盛况，并赞扬公议局大楼是："天津最好的办公建筑之一……正立面是美丽的爱奥尼柱式，室内全部采用法国摩登风格。"该建筑是全国重点文物保护单位，特殊保护等级历史风貌建筑，也是天津现存各租界行政管理机构建筑中艺术水准最高、保存最完好的一个

Present and old views of the French Municipal Council. The former French Municipal Council was the executive body of the Board of Directors of the French concession in the exercise of its administrative functions. It is located at No.12 Chengde Road, Heping District. Built between 1929 and 1931, it covers an area of about 2,700 square meters, with a construction area of about 3,700 square meters, in the neoclassical style. ...

法国公议局后部及内景。以上照片收藏于比利时外交部档案馆

The back and interior scenes of the French Municipal Council. Photos are preserved in the archives of the Belgian Ministry of Foreign Affairs

法国工部局（警察局与消防队）

French Municipal Council (Police and Fire Department)

法国工部局（警察局与消防队）
今景、旧景
Old and present views of the French Municipal Council (Police and Fire Department)

法国工部局图纸（图片来自《天津历史风貌建筑》，2010）。法国工部局位于天津市解放北路34—36号，特殊保护等级历史风貌建筑，建于1934年，占地面积约4500 ㎡，建筑面积约5600 ㎡，四层混合结构楼房，立面造型采用古典三段式构图，屋顶采用法国19世纪末流行的孟莎式

Drawings of the French Municipal Council (Photo from Historic Architecture in Tianjin, 2010). The former French Municipal Council is located at No.34-36, North Jiefang Road, Tianjin, a special protection grade historical style building. Built in 1934, it covers an area of about 4,500 square meters, with a construction area of about 5,600 square meters...

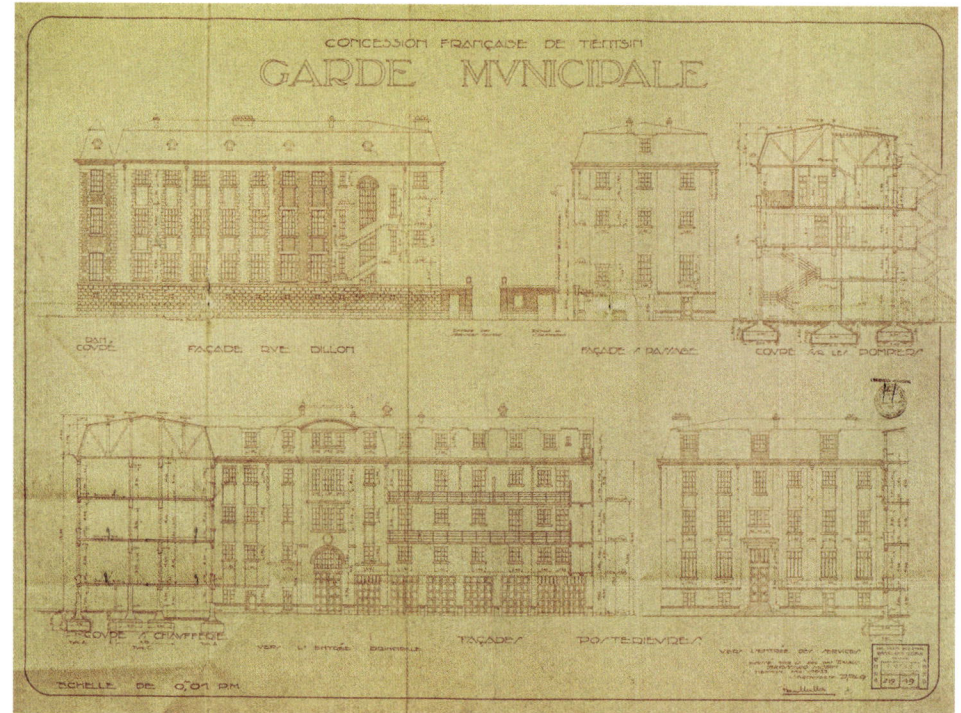

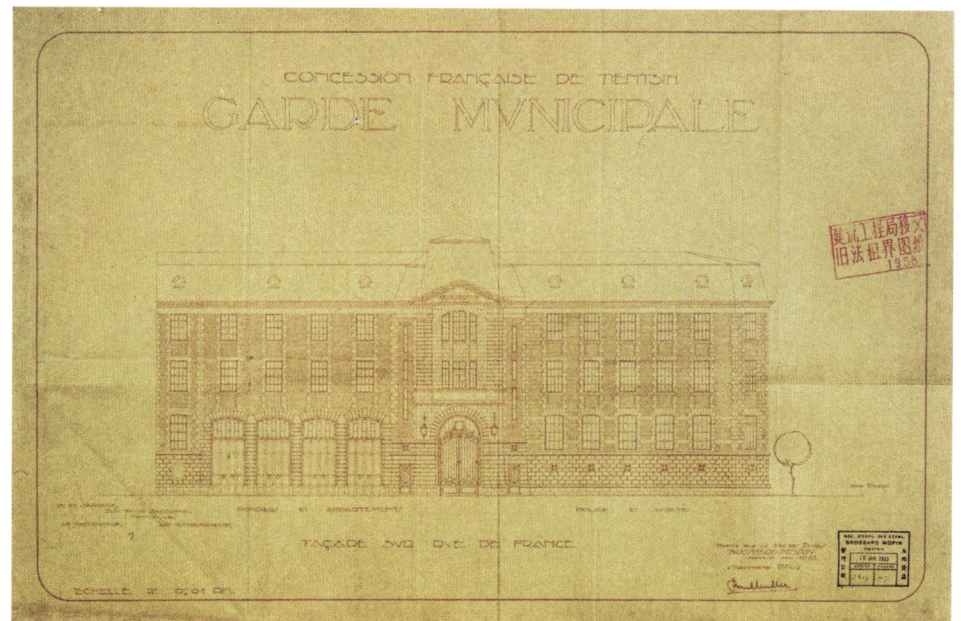

法国东方汇理银行天津分行　Tianjin branch of Banque de l'Indochine

法国东方汇理银行天津分行，旧景由刘悦先生提供，今景由航鹰女士摄于2003年。位于天津市和平区解放北路77—79号，重点保护等级历史风貌建筑。1912年建成，占地面积1200㎡，建筑面积约3500㎡，砖木结构三层楼房，具有西洋古典主义建筑特征。法国东方汇理银行于1875年创办，总部位于巴黎，天津分行于1907年开业，1957年停业

Old and present scenes of the Tianjin branch of Banque de l'Indochine, the old one provided by Mr. Liu Yue and the new one taken by Ms. Hang Ying in 2003. The Tianjin branch of the former Banque de l'Indochine is located at No.77-79 North Jiefang Road, Heping District, Tianjin, a key conservation grade historical building. Built in 1912, it covers an area of 1,200 square meters, with a construction area of about 3,500 square meters, a three-story brick and wood building with the characteristics of Western classical architecture...

朝鲜银行　Korea Building

朝鲜银行大楼今景，由航鹰女士摄于2003年。位于天津市和平区解放北路97—101号，特殊保护等级历史风貌建筑，建于1918年，占地面积约1100㎡，建筑面积约3500㎡，混合结构三层楼房，为仿希腊古典复兴建筑风格。曾为乌利文洋行（Laroche & Cie, P.）。朝鲜银行于1911年成立，总行位于朝鲜京城（今首尔特别市），天津分行于1918年开业，1950年停业

Bank of Korea Building (present-day view), taken by Ms. Hang Ying in 2003. The former Bank of Korea Building is located at No.97-101 North Jiefang Road, Heping District, Tianjin.Built in 1918, it covers an area of about 1,100m² with construction area of about 3,500m². This three-story building is In the style of Greek Classical Revival architecture...

法国俱乐部　French Club

法国俱乐部坐落于今解放北路29号。由法国公议局出资于1931年兴建，东接合江路，南抵哈尔滨道，西沿解放北路，北临滨江道，占地7260m²，建筑面积2941m²，为半地下室一层砖混结构，建筑式样基本为现代主义风格。正门建于临街转角处，竖向退线逐层内收，内装镂空花饰金属门，正门两侧设附壁灯柱。外檐简明，局部装饰。内设酒吧、剧场、舞厅、台球厅、地球厅、休息室等；一楼内部为八角形大厅，屋顶中央设有彩色玻璃窗；后院原有小花园、广场和露天舞台等，是侨民休闲娱乐社交的场所，因当时法国商会也设置于此，所以这里也是法国商人聚会的场所。曾为天津青年宫，现为天津金融博物馆

The French Club is located in No. 29 North Jiefang Road. It was built in 1931 with the investment of the French Council, with Hejiang road in the east, Harbin Road in the south, North Jiefang Road in the west and Binjiang Road in the north. It covers an area of 7,260 square meters, and the floor space is up to 2,941 square meters. It adopts masonry-concrete structure and has one ground floor with a partly-exposed basement, forming a Modernism style. The front door faces the corner of the street. The interior metal door decorates with hollow-out flowers, and wall lamps are set on both sides of the front door. The outer eave is partly decorated with simple design. Inside the club there are bar, theatre, ballroom, billiard hall, grounder hall, lounge, and etc. The interior of the first floor is an octagonal hall with stained glass windows in the center of the roof. The backyard originally has a small garden, a square and an open stage. It is a place for foreign residents to relax, entertain and socialize. Since the French Chamber of Commerce was located here at that time, the French businessmen would also gather here. It was once Tianjin Youth Club and now Tianjin Museum of Finance

以上照片收藏于比利时外交部档案馆

Photos are preserved in the archives of the Belgian Ministry of Foreign Affairs

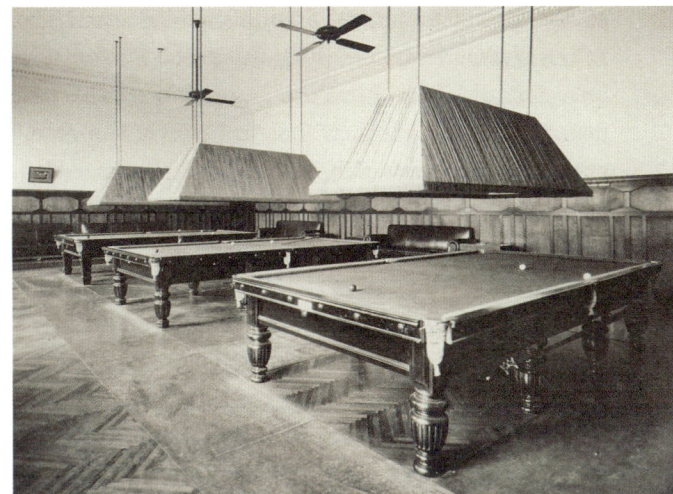
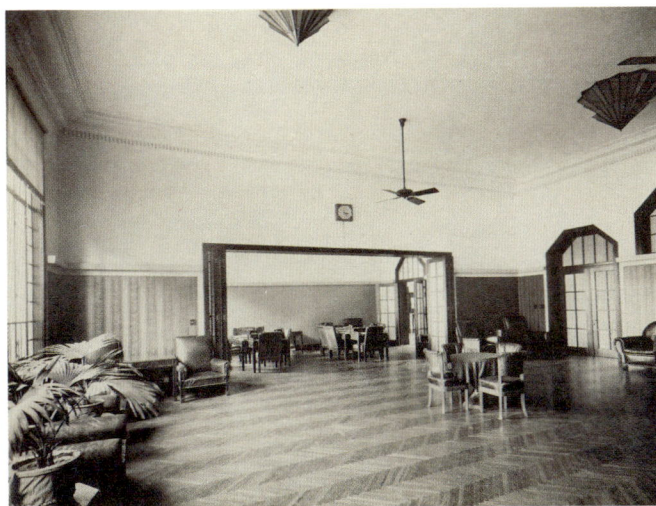

法国俱乐部内景、外景。以上照片收藏于比利时外交部档案馆

The Interior and exterior scenes of the French Club. Photos are preserved in the archives of the Belgian Ministry of Foreign Affairs

百福大楼
Belfran Building

百福大楼旧景、今景。今景由航鹰女士摄于2023年。百福大楼位于和平区解放北路和张自忠路交口处解放北路1—5号，建于1927年，重点保护等级历史风貌建筑。"百福"是由法文名称"Belfran"音译而来，是"Belgique"（比利时）和"France"（法国）两个词合成而来。百福大楼张自忠路一侧朝向海河，外观仿轮船造型而建，作为集商业、办公、公寓式住宅于一体的综合性大楼使用。现在的屋顶塔楼及桅杆为2008—2009年政府按照原设计图纸整修还原所建

Old and present views of Belfran Building. The present one was taken by Ms. Hang Ying in 2023. Built in 1927, Belfran Building is located at No.1-5, North Jiefang Road, at the intersection of North Jiefang Road and Zhangzizhong Road in Heping District. The name "Baifu" is derived from the French name "Belfran", which is a combination of Belgium and France...

2009年百福大楼整修时发现的竣工铭牌

Construction completion plaque found during the renovation of the Belfran Building in 2009

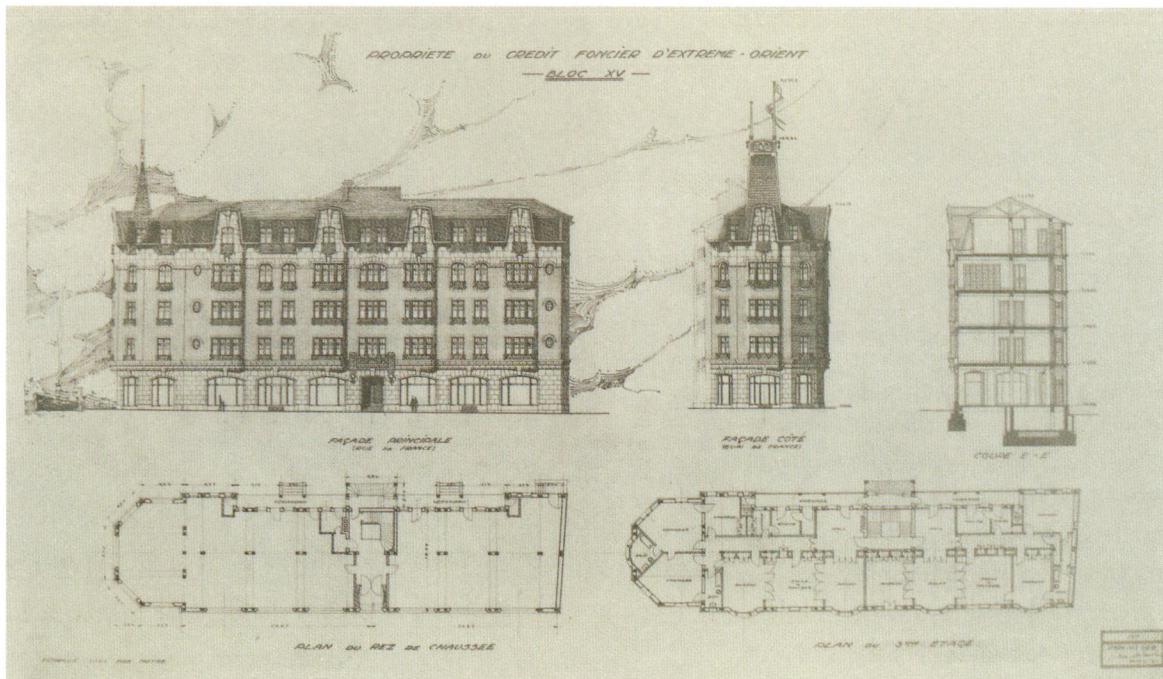

百福大楼设计图纸

Belfran Building design drawings

以上图纸和旧照收藏于比利时外交部档案馆

The above drawings and old photos are preserved in the archives of the Belgian Ministry of Foreign Affairs

百福大楼外景、内景。以上照片收藏于比利时
外交部档案馆

The exterior and interior scenes of the Belfran
Building. Photos are preserved in the archives
of the Belgian Ministry of Foreign Affairs

大陆银行仓库　Continental Bank Warehouse

大陆银行仓库旧景、今景。今景由航鹰女士摄于 2004 年。位于和平区张自忠路 223 号，特殊保护等级历史风貌建筑，建于 1925 年，建筑面积约 7700 ㎡。大陆银行存放商货使用，内部设有壁垒森严的金库，至今仍在使用

Old and present scenes of Continental Bank Warehouse. The present one was taken by Ms. Hang Ying in 2004. Located at No.223 Zhangzizhong Road, Heping District, this special protection grade historical style building was built in 1925 with a construction area of about 7,700m². It was used by the Continental Bank for storing commercial goods and had a well-barricaded vault inside, which is still in use today

北疆博物院北楼　North Building of the Beijiang

北疆博物院北楼。北疆博物院位于河西区马场道 117—119 号，天津外国语大学内，重点保护等级历史风貌建筑。该博物院由法国天主教耶稣教会桑志华（Emile Licent，1876—1952）神父创立，是我国最早、藏品最丰富的博物院，收藏了几十万件化石。桑志华给博物馆起名为 Musée Hoangho Paiho，即"黄河白白河博物馆"，中文名是"北疆博物院"。

博物院分为博物馆（北楼）和实验馆（南楼），北楼建于 1922 年，楼分三层为砖混结构，占地面积 300 ㎡，由义品地产公司的比利时建筑师比奈（J. B. Binet）设计监造

North Building of the Beijiang ("Northern Territory") Museum. The Beijiang Museum is located at No.117-119 Machang Road, Hexi District, inside the Tianjin Foreign Studies University, a key conservation grade historical style building. Founded by Father Emile Licent (1876-1952), a French Catholic Jesuit, the museum is the earliest museum in China, with a collection of hundreds of thousands of fossils. The museum was named Musée Hoangho Paiho, or "Yellow River and White River Museum," and in Chinese, "Northern Territory Museum."

The museum is divided into the museum (North Building) and the laboratory (South Building). The North Building, with three floors of brick and concrete structure, was built in 1922, covering an area of 300 square meters, designed and supervised by the Belgian architect J. B. Binet of CFEO

以上旧照片收藏于比利时外交部档案馆。今景由刘悦先生摄于 2015 年

The above old photos are preserved in the archives of the Belgian Ministry of Foreign Affairs. The present one was taken by Mr. Liu Yue in 2015

建设中的北疆博物院

Beijiang Museum under construction

大清邮政津局　Qing Dynasty Postal Office of Tianjin

大清邮政津局旧景、今景。今景由刘悦先生摄于 2023 年。位于和平区解放北路 103—111 号，特殊保护等级历史风貌建筑，现为天津邮政博物馆。占地面积约 1000 ㎡，建筑面积约 2500 ㎡。前身为天津海关书信馆，建于 1878 年，1897 年改为大清邮政津局，中华民国成立后改称直隶邮务管理局，1915 年 8 月迁出，后成为义品公司房产

Old and present scene of the Qing Dynasty Postal Office of Tianjin. The present one was taken by Mr. Liu Yue in 2023. Located at No.103-111 North Jiefang Road, Heping District, the special protection grade historical style building is now the Tianjin Postal Museum. It covers an area of about 1,000 square meters, with a construction area of about 2,500 square meters...

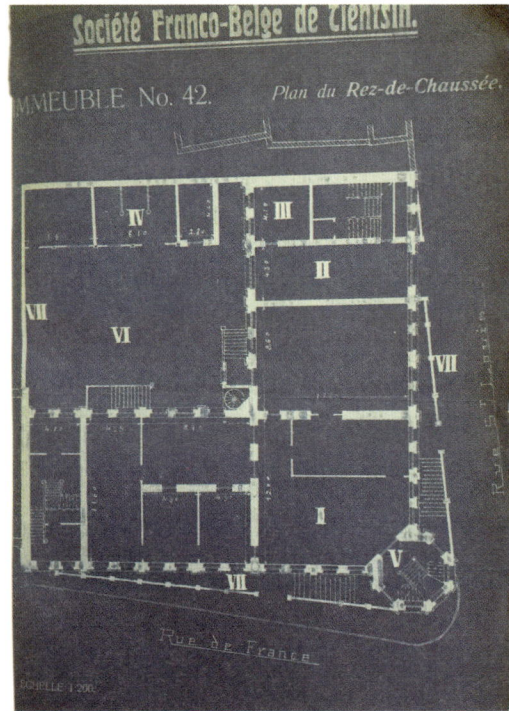

大清邮政津局设计图纸。收藏于比利时外交部档案馆

Design drawings of Qing Dynasty Postal Office of Tianjin. Drawings are preserved in the archives of the Belgian Ministry of Foreign Affairs

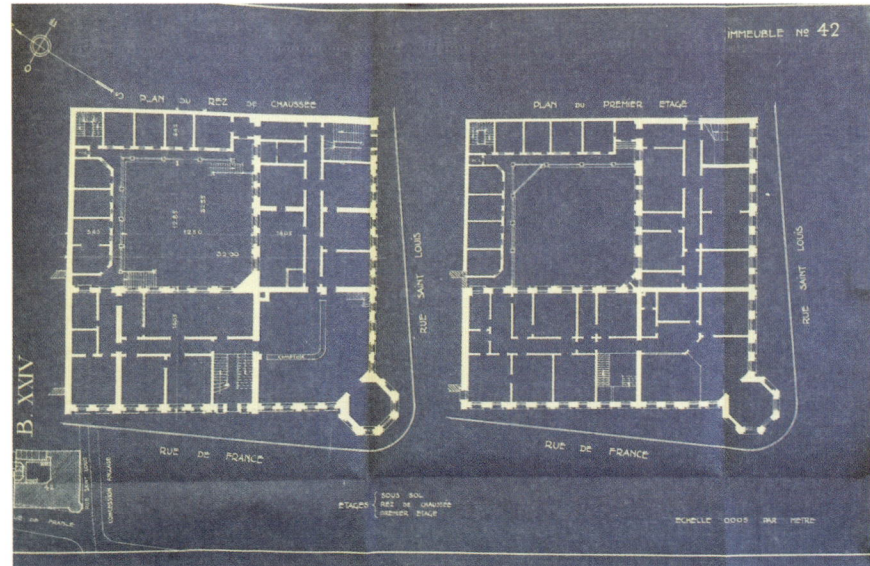

青年沃卡特在绘图桌边，约 1910 年
Young Volckaert at the drawing table,
c. 1910

义品公司中的比利时建筑设计师沃卡特

义品公司在全国各地开发了数以百计的房地产物业，它在各地分公司均设有工程部，从西方聘请年富力强的专业建筑设计师，再搭配中国的绘图员合作完成设计。公司档案显示，1907—1959 年先后有 32 名外国建筑设计师来到中国，[96] 他们流动于天津、北京、上海、汉口、香港等地工作，其中以在天津的为最多。这些建筑师均毕业于西方专业院校，既熟悉欧洲古典的建筑风格，又掌握着当时最前沿的艺术风尚，而且每个人都有独树一帜的个人设计风格。再加上义品公司丰厚的财力支持，他们可以得心应手地在中国进行自己的艺术实践，把西方现代建筑的钢筋混凝土结构引进中国，并与中国传统元素相结合，留下了大量经典的建筑作品。

义品公司还雇用了中国员工辅助设计师们。第一批是从聘用 35 名绘图员开始。一位公司负责人写道："在时间和耐心的帮助下，我们可以培养出一些非常熟练的人，这些（中国人）一丝不苟且很有耐心。他们通常都是优秀的绘图员，我知道他们中一些人，只要你给他们一个简单的草图，他们就能绘出任何蓝图。"[97] 然而在图纸上只能看到少数中国绘图员的名字，如北疆博物院设计图纸上有 3 名中国人的名字。

古斯塔夫·沃卡特（Gustave Volckaert，1888—1978），比利时建筑师，中文名叫华立慧。1888 年 9 月 18 日出生于根特，父亲是位木匠。在父亲的教导下，沃卡特从小就培养了对技术精益求精追求的精神。后来，他白天在 Van Herrewege & De Wilde 建筑公司打工，晚上在学校学习，完成了根特皇家美术学院（l'Académie royale des Beaux-Arts de Gand）8 年的建筑课程及根特

A Belgian Architect at CFEO - Gustave Volckaert

CFEO developed hundreds of real estate properties throughout the country, and it had engineering departments in each of its branches, hiring professional architects from the West and working with Chinese draftsmen to complete the designs. According to the company's records, 32 foreign architects came to China between 1907 and 1959,[96] working in Tianjin, Beijing, Shanghai, Hankou and Hong Kong, with the largest number in Tianjin. All these architects graduated from Western professional colleges and universities and were familiar with both the classical European architectural style and the most cutting-edge artistic trend of the time. Each of them also had a unique personal design style. Coupled with the generous financial support of CFEO, they were able to practice their craft in China with ease, introducing the reinforced concrete structures of Western modern architecture into China and combining them with traditional Chinese elements, leaving behind many classic architectural works.

CFEO also employed Chinese staff to assist the designers. Starting with the hiring of 35 draftsmen, a company executive wrote: "With the help of time and patience, we can produce some very skilled people, and these [Chinese] are meticulous and very patient. They are usually excellent draftsmen, and I know some of them who will produce any blueprint if you give them a simple sketch."[97] Yet only a few Chinese draftsmen's names can be seen on the drawings, such as the three Chinese names on the design drawings for The Musée Hoangho Paiho (Museum of Natural History).

Gustave Volckaert (1888-1978), a Belgian architect (Chinese name: Hua Lihui), was born in Ghent on September 18, 1888, His father was a carpenter. Under his father's tutelage, Volckaert cultivated the pursuit of technical

工业学院（l'École Industrielle de Gand）4年的工业设计课程。从1909年起，他在巴黎和布鲁塞尔的几个著名建筑师事务所实习。[98]

1914年5月26日，26岁的沃卡特在义品公司布鲁塞尔总部签下了3年的合同。当年6月10日他乘火车沿西伯利亚大铁路于10天后抵达天津。从1914年至1919年，沃卡特主要是在天津从事建筑活动，1915年北京分公司开业后也负责了一部分北京的工作，包括北京比利时公使馆的修缮。1919年他返回比利时结婚。婚礼后又与义品公司签订新一期合同，再度来到天津工作。沃卡特夫妇的蜜月旅行是从根特去天津的环球旅行途中度过的。他们乘船过大西洋到达美国，越太平洋又取道夏威夷。一路上美国各式现代建筑尽收眼底，为他的建筑理念注入了新鲜血液。[99]

沃卡特在天津的第二段任期为1919—1922年。在一战结束后的这段时间里，沃卡特作为工程部的主管承建了义品公司大部分建筑项目，包括北京、天津的华比银行大楼，中法俱乐部大堂（北京），陆徵祥家族墓地等。1921年，沃卡特的妻子产下一子，她既思念根特的亲友又对中国动荡的时局感到不安，于是1922年沃卡特一家返回了比利时。义品公司档案关于此事记载道："（沃卡特的离开）对于公司是切实的损失，他工作的勤恳努力与专业的技术知识使我们的项目成果更加完善，为工程部带来了良好声誉。"[100]

回到根特的沃卡特一直在岳父的建筑公司工作，但20世纪30年代初受到经济危机波及而失业。1934年2月，沃卡特再度加入义品公司，愉悦地回到天津。1934年5月1日至1937年3月15日是沃卡特在天津的第三段任期。

excellence from an early age. Later, he worked part-time at the construction company Van Herrewege & De Wilde during the day and studied at school at night, completing an eight-year architecture course at the Royal Academy of Fine Arts in Ghent (l'Académie royale des Beaux-Arts de Gand) and a four-year industrial design course at the Ghent Technical College (l'École Industrielle de Gand). From 1909 onwards, he interned at several prestigious architects' offices in Paris and Brussels.[98]

On May 26, 1914, at the age of 26, Volckaert signed a three-year contract at the Brussels headquarters of CFEO. On June 10 of the same year, he boarded the Trans-Siberian Railway and arrived in Tianjin 10 days later. From 1914 to 1919, he worked mainly in Tianjin, and he was also responsible for some of the work in Beijing, including the renovation of the Belgian Legation in Beijing. In 1919 he returned to Belgium to get married. After the wedding, he signed a new contract with the CFEO and returned to work in Tianjin again. The Volckaerts spent their honeymoon on their way from Ghent to Tianjin. They crossed the Atlantic Ocean to the United States, then crossed the Pacific Ocean by way of Hawaii. On their way, Volckaert was able to see all kinds of modern architecture in the United States, which gave fresh blood to his architectural ideas.[99]

Volckaert's second term in Tianjin lasted from 1919 to 1922. In the period after the end of World War I, as head of the engineering department, Volckaert was responsible for most of the construction projects of CFEO, including the Sino-Belgian Bank building in Beijing and Tianjin, the lobby of the Sino-French Club (Beijing), the Lu family cemetery, etc. In 1921, his wife gave birth to a son. Missing family and friends in Ghent and feeling uneasy about the turbulent times in China, the family returned to Belgium in 1922. The archives of the company stated, "(Volckaert's departure) was a real loss to the company, as his hard work and technical expertise had improved the results of our

陆徵祥家族墓地旧景
Old view of Lu Zhengxiang family cemetery

华比银行天津分行大楼今景。该楼建于 1921 年，由比利时义品公司设计并监理，同年华比银行天津分行迁入。由于天津比租界地处偏远，比利时并未将其领事馆设在该国租界内，20 世纪 40 年代反而在天津英租界租用该楼二楼作领事馆之用，以和各国保持经常联系。除了比利时领事馆，美商德士古石油公司也曾租用该楼层作为办公用房。该楼现由中国建设银行使用。由航鹰女士摄于 2003 年

The building of the former Sino-Belgian Bank Tianjin Branch. The building was built in 1921, designed and supervised by the Belgian company Crédit Foncier d'Extrême-Orient (CFEO). The building is now used by the China Construction Bank. Taken by Ms. Hang Ying in 2003

华比银行大楼设计图

Design drawings of Sino-Belgian Bank building

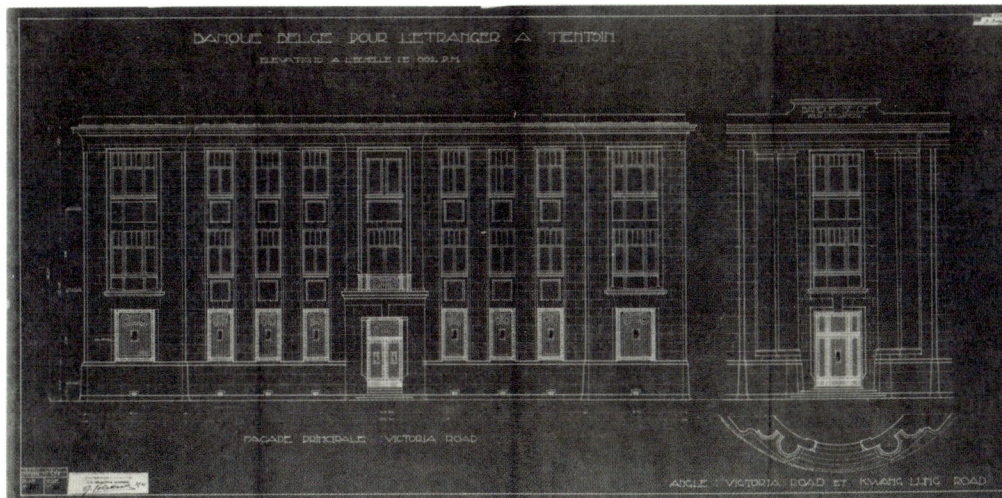

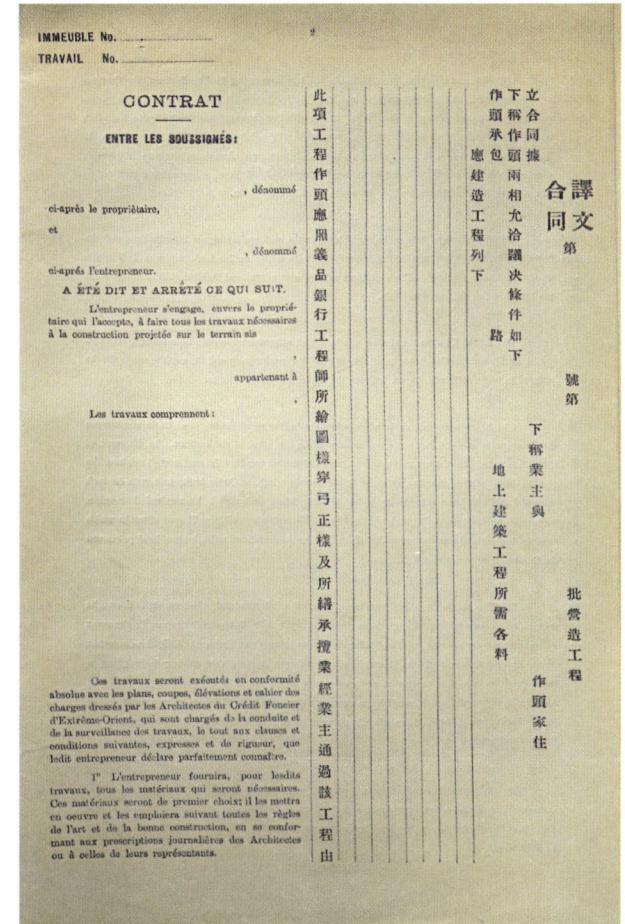

义品公司与华比银行签订的建筑合同

Construction contract signed between CFEO and Sino-Belgian Bank

以上图纸和文件收藏于比利时外交部档案馆

The above drawings and documents are preserved in the archives of the Belgian Ministry of Foreign Affairs

位于华比银行二楼的比利时领事馆内景。
收藏于比利时外交部档案馆

Interior view of the Belgian Consulate on
the second floor of Sino-Belgian Bank.
Photos are preserved in the archives of
the Belgian Ministry of Foreign Affairs

张叔诚旧宅位于成都道 118 号，为一般保护等级历史风貌建筑，建于 1936 年，由比利时建筑师沃卡特设计。独立式住宅，原为二层砖木结构楼房，后加盖三层，主入口出挑宽大雨篷。外檐为清水砖墙，局部为混水抹灰装饰，平屋顶，檐部出挑。建筑装饰简洁，正立面窗间凸出竖向线条，使建筑给人以挺拔感。摄于 2003 年

Zhang Shucheng's old residence, located at No.118 Chengdu Road, is a general protection grade historical style building. It was built in 1936 and designed by Belgian architect Gustave Volckaert. ... Taken in 2003

张叔诚（1898—1995）著名实业家、收藏家、鉴赏家。开平矿务局督办张翼之子。毕生致力于文物收藏，精于鉴赏。新中国成立后，将所藏字画、玉器、铜器、古砚珍贵文物四百余件捐献国家，其中《雪景寒林图》被誉为"宋代画中无上神品"，现藏于天津博物馆

Zhang Shucheng (1898-1995) was a famous industrialist, collector and connoisseur. He was the son of Zhang Yi, the supervisor of Kaiping Mining Administration. He devoted his life to collecting cultural relics and was a connoisseur. After the founding of the People's Republic of China, he donated more than 400 pieces of his collection of paintings, jades, bronzes and ancient inkstones to the state, among which the *Snow Scene and Cold Forest* was hailed as "the most divine painting of the Song dynasty" and is now in the Tianjin Museum

这段时期中国国内政局不稳，项目投资锐减。沃卡特主要负责本公司旗下或第三方房地产的维护整修工作，新建项目较少。其中较为出色的两个建筑是伦敦路（今成都道 47 号）的房产和张叔诚旧居（今成都道 118 号）。

1937 年的复活节沃卡特回到根特，比利时的经济状况非但没有好转反而恶化，他只好与义品公司签下第四期合同，再度返津，没想到这一次被战争困在中国长达 8 年之久。日本人占领下的租界管控愈发严格，又遭逢 1939 年天津洪水，沃卡特一家避难于比利时驻京使馆。1944—1945 年被日军抓捕关在上海附近的集中营，后逃到比属刚果。日本投降以后，沃卡特回到天津帮助修缮、重建战争中被损毁的建筑，直至 1946 年返回比利时度假。1947—1954 年沃卡特到香港负责香港分公司的工作。[101]

projects and brought the engineering department into good standing."[100]

Back in Ghent, Volckaert worked for his father-in-law's construction company, but lost his job in the early 1930s due to the economic crisis. He returned to Tianjin in February 1934 and rejoined CFEO. From May 1, 1934 to March 15, 1937 was the third period of Volckaert's tenure in Tianjin. During this period of political instability in China and a sharp decline in investment in projects, Volckaert was primarily responsible for the maintenance and refurbishment of the company's properties or those of third parties, with few new projects. Two of the more notable buildings were the property on London Road (now No. 47 Chengdu Road) and the former residence of Zhang Shucheng (now No. 118 Chengdu Road).

At Easter 1937, Volckaert returned to Ghent, but the economic situation in Belgium worsened instead of improving, so he had to sign a fourth contract with the CFEO and returned to Tianjin again, not expecting to be trapped by the war in China for eight years. The increasingly strict control of concessions under Japanese occupation, coupled with the flood in 1939, led Volckaert and his family to take refuge in the Belgian Legation in Beijing. From 1944 to 1945, the Volckaerts were arrested by the Japanese and imprisoned in a concentration camp near Shanghai before escaping to the Belgian Congo. After the surrender of Japan, he returned to Tianjin to help repair and rebuild the buildings destroyed during the war until 1946, when he returned to Belgium for a vacation, and from 1947 to 1954 he oversaw CFEO's Hong Kong branch.[101]

义品公司职员聚会，后排左一为义品公司在华最后一任总经理乔治·考克斯。照片摄于1940年4月29日。由林辅臣曾外孙女安芝拉提供

Gathering of CFEO employees. Back row, first from left, George Cox, the last general manager of CFEO. Photo taken on April 29, 1940, courtesy of Angela Cox Elliott, great-granddaughter of Paul Splingaerd

义品公司职员聚会，前排左四为义品公司在华最后一任总经理乔治·考克斯。照片摄于1950年8月29日。由林辅臣曾外孙女安芝拉提供

A gathering of the employees of CFEO, with George Cox, fourth from the left in the front row. Photo taken on August 29, 1950, courtesy of Angela Cox Elliott, great-granddaughter of Paul Splingaerd

义品公司职员聚会，前排左四为义品公司在华最后一任总经理乔治·考克斯。照片摄于1951年11月3日。由林辅臣曾外孙女安芝拉提供

A gathering of CFEO employees, with George Cox, fourth from the left in the front row. Photo taken on November 3, 1951, courtesy of Angela Cox Elliott, great-granddaughter of Paul Splingaerd

"天津人"雷鸣远

穿中国服装的"天津人"雷鸣远
Vincent Lebbe, a "Tianjiner" in Chinese costume

雷鸣远，原名腓特烈·雷博（Fréderic-Vincent Lebbe），天主教遣使会神父。1877年出生于比利时根特，年轻时曾在巴黎修道院做修士。1901年被比利时教会派往中国传教。1906年来津任天主教天津教区总铎。1915年在津创办《益世报》。1916年，天津爆发"老西开事件"，他站在中国人民一方反对扩展法租界，受到法国当局迫害达10年之久。在此期间被遣返欧洲，后又被派到河北传教，于1928年创建了耀汉小兄弟会和德来小妹妹会。他热爱中国，于1927年改入中国籍，自称"天津人"。天津历史上曾经有一条"雷鸣远路"（今南大道）以表纪念。

雷鸣远一生充满传奇经历。他在西方传教士中特立独行，把自己里里外外完全"本土化""中国化"了，有人说"他是爱中国爱疯了的一位天主教的传教士"[102]。雷鸣远于义和团运动后的第二年来到中国，尽管他对天主教徒在义和团运动中所受的灾难有所了解，仍是秉持开放包容、没有任何歧视和偏见的心态来到中国。他在给家人的信中写道："希望全世界都有我们的文明，那是一种心胸狭窄的思想。我们西方现在的文明并不是文明本身，它仅仅是适合于现在西方的民族而已。"[103]无疑，这种观念无论在当时还是当今都是令人赞佩的。一路行来，雷鸣远在天津逗留期间，亲眼见到八国联军的横行霸道、烧杀抢掠，令他的心完全站到了中国人一边。[104]为了与中国人交流，雷鸣远努力学习中国文化，读中国的儒家经典书籍，能说一口流利标准的中国话，用毛笔写漂亮的行书。初到中国时，他看到男人都留长辫。为了尽快融入中国，他写信给妹妹蜜嘉，让她剪下金发长

"Tianjiner" Vincent Lebbe

Born in 1877 in Ghent, Belgium, Fréderic-Vincent Lebbe (Chinese name: Lei Mingyuan), a Catholic priest, was sent to China by the Belgian Church as a missionary in 1901 and became dean of the Catholic Diocese of Tianjin in 1906, and later founded the *Yishi Newspaper* in 1915. In 1916, the "Lao Xi Kai Incident" broke out in Tianjin, and he stood on the side of the Chinese people against the extension of the French concession and was persecuted by the French authorities for 10 years. During this period, he was repatriated to Europe, and then sent to Hebei Province as a missionary, where he founded the Little Brothers of St. John the Baptist and the Little Sisters of St. Theresa of the Child Jesus in 1928. He loved China and became a Chinese citizen in 1927, calling himself a "Tianjiner." In the history of Tianjin, there was a "Lei Mingyuan Road" (now South Avenue) in his honor.

Vincent Lebbe's life was full of legendary experiences. He was a maverick among Western missionaries, and he completely "localized" and "Sinicized" himself inside and out, and someone once said that "he was a Catholic missionary who loved China like crazy."[102] Lebbe came to China the year after the Boxer Rebellion, but despite his knowledge of the disasters suffered by Catholics during the Boxer Rebellion, he came to China with an open and tolerant mind, without any discrimination or prejudice. In a letter to his family, he wrote: "It would be a narrow-minded thought to wish the whole world to have our civilization. Our present civilization in the West is not a civilization in itself; it is merely suited to the peoples of the West now."[103] Undoubtedly, this concept was admirable both then and today. Along the way, during his stay in Tianjin, Lebbe saw with his own eyes the bullying, burning and looting of the Eight-Power Allied Forces, which made his heart completely on the side of the Chinese.[104] To communicate

雷鸣远（前排右一）与家人在布鲁塞尔，后排中间
站立者为他的妹妹蜜嘉

Vincent Lebbe (front row, far right) with his family
in Brussels, with his sister Mica standing in the
middle of the back row

辫"捐赠"给他。妹妹毅然将发辫剪下寄往中国，他把
辫子安到帽子后边，成为一段"学习中国"的佳话。[105]

比之利玛窦的传教方法，雷鸣远更进了一步。雷鸣
远提倡爱国，鼓励教友在社会中发展力量，起到领导作
用。他说："中国的信友有权利并且也应该成为爱国者，
与欧美教友一般无二。"[106] 雷鸣远来华的时代，正值列
强争相瓜分中国，宗教很容易与政治混为一谈。身处海
外的传教士在本国军队的保护之下，不免将其本国利益
看成教会利益。[107] 虽然身受法国教会的领导和庇护，但
是正直的雷鸣远却用实际行动，坚决抵制将法国或者教
会的利益凌驾于中国人民权益之上的行为。

1906 年，雷鸣远被任命为天津总堂本堂神父，主持
教务。初到望海楼教堂，他便将教堂内外的法国国旗一

with the Chinese, he worked hard to learn Chinese culture,
read Chinese Confucian classics, speak fluent and standard
Chinese, and write beautiful cursive script with a brush.
When he first arrived in China, he saw that all men had long
braids. He wrote to his sister, Mica, asking her to cut off her
long blond hair and "donate" it to him so as to fit in with the
Chinese people as soon as possible. Mica cut off her braid
and sent it to China, and Lebbe put it on the back of his
hat.[105]

Lebbe went one step further than Matteo Ricci's
missionary approach. He advocated patriotism and
encouraged the church members to become a force in
society and to take a leadership role. He said, "The faithful
in China have the right and should be patriots in the same
way as the faithful in Europe and America."[106] Lebbe came
to China at a time when the powers were competing to
carve up China, and religion could easily be confused with
politics. Missionaries abroad, under the protection of their
own armies, could not help but see the interests of their
own country as the interests of the Church.[107] Despite being
under the management and protection of the French Church,
the upright Lebbe resolutely resisted, with his own actions,
the behavior of putting the interests of France or the Church
above the rights and interests of the Chinese people.

In 1906, Lebbe was appointed to the director in
Tianjin. When he first arrived at Wanghailou Church, he
removed all the French flags inside and outside the church
and replaced them with the dragon flag representing the
Qing government. Afterwards, he actively participated in
local charitable activities in Tianjin to influence the gentry,
such as raising funds to fight against natural disasters and
participating in the founding of the Tianjin Red Cross
Society. He also worked hard to promote education by
founding the Chengzheng Elementary School and the
Zhenshu Girls' School in the Wanghailou Church, enrolling
students from both inside and outside the Church. After

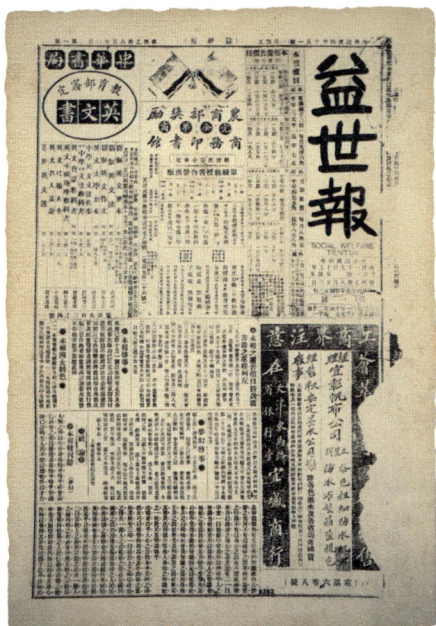

《益世报》是罗马天主教教会在华出版的中文日报，创办后不久成为天津最有名的报纸之一。1915年10月10日创刊于天津，由雷鸣远和中国教徒刘守荣创办并主持。20世纪30~40年代，《益世报》持守自由主义倾向，在反对国民党的腐败统治和抵抗帝国主义国家的侵略方面，《益世报》的立场是鲜明的，成为国内反抗日本侵略最激烈的大报。1949年新中国成立前夕停刊

Founded in Tianjin on October 10, 1915, by Vincent Lebbe and Liu Shourong, a Chinese convert, *Yishi Newspaper* was a Chinese daily newspaper published by the Roman Catholic Church in China. Soon after its founding, it became one of the most influential newspapers in Tianjin. In the 1930s and 1940s, *Yishi Newspaper* held a liberal stance against the corrupt rule of the Kuomintang government and the aggression of the imperialist countries and became the most fierce newspaper in China against Japanese aggression. It ceased publication on the eve of liberation in 1949

以上照片由近代天津博物馆提供
Photos from Tianjin Museum of Modern History

律摘下，换上代表清朝的龙旗。之后，他一边积极参加天津地方的慈善活动以影响士绅阶层，如募捐抗灾和筹款参与创办天津红十字会；一边努力兴学，在望海楼教堂内创办了诚正小学、贞淑女学，招收教内外学生入学。辛亥革命后，关心中国政治的雷鸣远又创办了共和法政研究所，聘请专职教师和当时的社会名流来讲授现代政治学、社会学和法学，讲授者积极，听众亦踊跃。1915年，雷鸣远联合几位天主教教友，广泛募捐筹款，创办了启

the 1911 Revolution, Lebbe, who was concerned about Chinese politics, founded the Institute of Law and Politics and hired full-time teachers and social celebrities to teach modern political science, sociology and law. The lectures attracted many enthusiastic participants. In 1915, Lebbe collaborated with several Catholic parishioners to raise funds and founded the *Yishi Newspaper*, for which he served as the chairman of the board. On October 10 of that year, the newspaper was officially launched, with the mission of justice, truth and patriotism. Because of its

发民智的《益世报》，他自任董事长。当年 10 月 10 日，《益世报》正式出版发行，其宗旨是正义、真理与爱国。由于该报消息准确、言论独立，受到教内外民众的欢迎，订阅者踊跃。

令雷鸣远完全站到中国人民一方从而在中国传教史上留名的，是他在"老西开事件"中的作为。1916 年 10 月 20 日爆发了法国派兵强占天津法租界外土地的事件。事件中，雷鸣远利用《益世报》大力呼吁、报道和支持天津人民的反抗，并因此受到法国天主教会的报复。事件肇始于 1912 年天主教设立直隶海滨代牧区，主教府设在天津三岔河口的望海楼教堂。而首任主教杜保禄（Paul-Marie Dumond，法国遣使会会士）认为望海楼教堂地处天津旧市区，不利于今后扩展，于是在紧邻天津法租界西南面的老西开地区购买了一片洼地兴建新的主教座堂。1913 年 8 月，西开教堂动土兴建，1916 年竣工建成。这一时期，这一地区形成一大片以西开教堂为核心，包括教堂、学校、医院的天主教社区。这里不仅成为天津天主教会的中心，也成为许多社会底层的天津天主教徒聚集居住区。

1915 年 5 月 9 日，袁世凯为推动帝制，接受日本提出的"二十一条"，给予日本种种特权。法国等列强乃随之心动，进而化为行动。1915 年 9 月，天津法租界工部局在老西开地区散发传单，要求当地中国居民向租界当局纳税，即事实上将老西开地区并入法租界管理。天津人民闻之大哗，坚决不承认。同月，天津的一批绅商组织成立了"维持国权国土会"抗议。1916 年 6 月，法租界工部局在老西开地区安插涂有法国三色旗的木标，设置界牌，表示此地已划入法租界。10 月 17 日法

accurate information and independent voice, the newspaper was well received by people inside and outside the Church, and subscriptions were numerous.

What made Lebbe's name in the history of Chinese missions was his role in the "Lao Xi Kai Incident," which took place on October 20, 1916, when French troops forcibly occupied land outside the French concession in Tianjin. During the incident, Lebbe used the *Yishi Newspaper* to report and support the resistance of the people of Tianjin and was subsequently retaliated by the French Catholic Church. The incident started in 1912 when the Catholic Church established the Apostolic Vicariate of Coastal Zhili, with the bishop's residence in the church of Wanghailou. The first bishop, Paul-Marie Dumond (a French lazarist), considering that the location of the church in the old downtown area of Tianjin was not conducive to future expansion, purchased a piece of land in the old Xikai area, to the southwest of the French concession in Tianjin, to build a new cathedral. In August 1913, the construction of Xikai Church broke the ground and it was completed in 1916. During this period, a large Catholic community was formed in this area with the Xikai Church as the core, including churches, schools and hospitals. This area became the center of the Catholic Church in Tianjinas as well as a residential area for many Tianjin Catholics from the lower social strata.

On May 9, 1915, Yuan Shikai, hoping to return to the old dynastic system, accepted the 21 Demands proposed by Japan and granted Japan various privileges. The French and other powers were also tempted to seize more privileges and interests from China. In September 1915, the Police Department of the French concession in Tianjin distributed leaflets in the old Xikai area, demanding the local Chinese residents to pay taxes to the concession authorities, which in effect annexed the old Xikai area to the French concession. The people of Tianjin were in an uproar and refused

抗战中日租界《益世报》牌楼跟前的路障哨卡

A roadblock post in front of the *Yishi Newspaper* decorated archway in the Japanese concession during the Anti-Japanese War

1918年的天津西开教堂。西开教堂初建时，这里还是一片苇塘，地势较墙子河低四五尺。因地势低洼，每逢大雨，堂前堂后便水漫金山

The St. Joseph Cathedral in Tianjin in 1918. When it was build, this area was still a reed pond, four or five feet lower than the Qiangzi River. Because it lied in low-lying area, whenever heavy rain came, both front and back of the hall were flooded with water.

租界工部局向直隶省发出最后通牒，限中国在48小时内撤走老西开地区的中国警察，随后又将驻守其间的中国警察缴械拘禁。这一事件立即引起天津市民大规模抗议活动。10月21日，"维持国权国土会"发动数千人举行向直隶省政府的示威请愿活动。10月23日，天津商会决议，抵制法国银行所发行的纸币，抵制法国货，请政府致电法国政府更换公使。10月25日，8000余名各界人士举行公民大会，决议通电全国与法国断绝贸易，中国货不售予法国等。法汉学校以及老西开内的中小学学生也都宣布罢课。11月12日，法租界内义品公司和义善实业铁厂的华人首先罢工，之后其他公司、洋行、

to recognize it. In the same month, a group of Tianjin merchants organized the "Association for the Preservation of National Sovereignty and Territory" to protest. In June 1916, the Police Department placed wooden signs painted with the French tricolor flag in the Old Xikai area and set up boundary signs, indicating that the area had been incorporated into the French concession. On October 17, it issued an ultimatum to the Zhili provincial government, which demanded the withdrawal of the Chinese police from the old Xikai area within 48 hours. The French then disarmed and detained the Chinese police stationed there. This incident immediately led to a massive protest by the citizens of Tianjin. On October 21, the "Association for the Preservation of National Sovereignty and Territory" mobilized thousands of people to demonstrate and petition the Zhili provincial government. On October 23, the Tianjin Chamber of Commerce decided to boycott the banknotes issued by French banks and French goods and requested the Chinese government to demand the French government to replace its Minister. On October 25, more than 8,000 people from all walks of life held a Citizens' Assembly and resolved to cut off trade with France. On November 12, the Chinese in the French concession went on strike first at CFEO and Yishan Industrial Iron Works, followed by Chinese workers, porters, rickshaw workers, maids and employees of other foreign companies and factories. The Citizens' Assembly also collected donations of more than 40,000 yuan to finance the strike, which lasted for four months and paralyzed the French concession. At the same time, the Chinese residents and merchants living in the French concession also started a movement to move out of the concession and the Chinese authorties "reduced 30 percent of rent for all mover".[108] As French merchants in China suffered heavy losses and France was fully enmeshed in the First World War, the French government agreed to maintain the status quo for the time being and recalled

工厂的中国工人、夫役、人力车工人、女佣工、职员群起罢工。公民大会还举办义演募集捐款超过4万元作为罢工经费，使罢工持续了4个月之久，法租界陷于瘫痪。同时，居住在法租界内的中国居民、商人也掀起迁居华界的运动，华界为迁居者租金"一律减价三成"[108]。由于在华法国商人损失惨重，而法国正全力投入第一次世界大战，无力干预东方事务，1916年年底，法国提出暂时维持现状的要求，孔狄（Alexandre Conty）公使被召回国，老西开事件落幕。

在此次事件中，雷鸣远坚持他来华后的一贯立场，选择站在中国人民一边。当主教开始筹划想要在老西开地区建新的教堂时，他即痛陈利害，表示反对。法国籍主教不得不背着雷鸣远勾结法国领事偷偷买地。雷鸣远发现阴谋之后，立刻找来《益世报》经理刘俊卿，要他提醒天津警察局长加派岗哨。[109]他还向天津士绅建议，在法租界组织华人大罢工。罢工组织得力，效果显著，是天津有史以来的第一次罢工，这也成为后来五四运动的一场预演。他还在其创办的《益世报》上连续报道天津市民反对法国人扩展天津法租界的正义行动，并在《益世报》上登出致法国驻北京公使的公开信，吁请其放弃妄想。法国驻津领事被触到痛处，向法国籍主教杜保禄抗议雷鸣远的作为。于是杜主教命雷鸣远不许再就老西开问题向中国人发言，更禁止他在《益世报》上发表文章。雷鸣远虽然迫于压力答应下来，但无法违背自己的良心，甘愿接受被降职调往外地的惩罚。[110]1920年又被遣送回欧洲，此后遭受长达十几年的排挤迫害。

1916年6月雷鸣远刊登在《益世报》上的致法国驻华公使孔狄的公开信[111]：

Minister Alexandre Conty back to France. The Lao Xi Kai Incident thus came to an end.

In this incident, Lebbe stood by the Chinese people. When the bishop began to plan for a new church in the old Xikai area, he spoke out against it. The French bishop had to buy the land in collusion with the French consul behind Lebbe's back. When Lebbe discovered the conspiracy, he immediately called Liu Junqing, the manager of *Yishi Newspaper*, and asked him to remind the Tianjin police chief to post more policemen.[109] He also suggested the Tianjin gentry organizing a general strike in the French concession. The strike was well organized and effective, and it was the first strike in the history of Tianjin, which became a rehearsal of the May Fourth Movement (1919). He also continuously reported in *Yishi* the actions of Tianjin citizens against France's attempted expansion of its concession in Tianjin. He also published in *Yishi* an open letter to the French Minister in Beijing, calling on him to give up his delusions. Angered by Lebbe's actions, the French consul in Tianjin complained to the French bishop Paul-Marie Dumond, who ordered Lebbe to stop speaking in public on the issue of Lao Xi Kai. Although Lebbe was forced to stop, he could not go against his conscience and willingly accepted the punishment of being demoted and transferred to a different region.[110] In 1920, he was sent back to Europe and was persecuted for more than ten years.

Vincent Lebbe's open letter to Alexandre Conty, the French Minister to China, published in *Yishi Newspaper* in June 1916[111]:

Your Excellency the Minister:
......
The French Minister (here should be Consul, note by the authors) in Tianjin wishes to extend the French concession ... but should try to do so through legal channels, not under the opposition of the Chinese

公使阁下：

······

在天津的法国公使（此处应为领事，引者注）先生希望扩展法国租界······但应循合法的途径去设法进行此事，并不是在中国政府反对之下，而仍然去执行。此外中国在无力抵抗下，只有接受这更坏的处境。

我总看不出来法国从扩展领土所能获得的利益······

公使先生，您知道吗？为攫取老西开的这小小一块土地，对法国引起多大的仇恨吗？其影响所遭受的损失是无法估计的。

布尔乔（Bourgeois）领事先生尚未成为业主之前，竟要行使业主的权利。他曾三次到这里树立分划界线的桩子，而未能抑止中国警察的抵抗。第四次他带着武装

Government. Moreover, China, being powerless to resist, can only accept the worse situation.

I don't see the benefit that France would gain from expanding its territory ...

Are you aware, Mr. Minister? How much hatred has been aroused against France for the seizure of this small piece of land in Lao Xi Kai? The losses suffered by its effects are incalculable.

Mr. Bourgeois, the consul, wished to exercise the rights of a property owner before he became one. He came here three times to erect the stakes of the demarcation line and failed to repress the resistance of the Chinese police. The fourth time he appeared with armed police, and while he was speaking to the Director of the Foreign Office (of the Chinese side), the French police erected the boundary stones by force. This

雷鸣远在广东会馆戏台上（今戏剧博物馆）演讲（照片为玻璃底板）。由近代天津博物馆提供

Vincent Lebbe giving a speech on the stage of the Cantonese Guild Hall (now the Drama Museum). Photo from Tianjin Museum of Modern History

警察出现，他跟（中方）外事厅主任交谈时（法国警察）以武力树立了界桩。这种交谈完全使人想到像恶狼与羔羊的交涉（公使先生，请原谅我这种比喻，否则没有别的方式来形容这种情况）。

当我晚间回到教堂时，我看见地上插了柱架，上面悬挂三色旗，我于是悲从中来，热泪盈眶。

是否可以让法国的国旗遭受公正的仇恨呢？是否可以让法国旗遮盖武力的侵略而反对正义呢？

……

在基督内最敬重您的
雷鸣远

尽管在天主教会内遭受不公正的待遇，雷鸣远却毫不改变自己的初衷。他是一位实干家，身体力行，常常深入到华北民间走访，甚至到偏远的农村地区。天主教中国教区一向由西洋人担任主教，洋主教凌驾于中国神职人员之上。雷鸣远则提出"中国归中国人，中国人归基督"的口号，积极推动教廷任命中国籍主教。[112]他于1920年、1926年两度赴罗马晋谒教皇本笃十五世，说服教皇同意中国主教本土化，终获成功。[113]1927年雷鸣远改入中国籍。

1931年"九一八事变"之后，雷鸣远振臂号召教友和青年学生参加抗日活动。全面抗战开始后，他告诉年轻的修士们："现在抗战开始了，我们要停止一切与救国直接无关的日常工作，一心从事抗战，不把日本鬼子驱逐出去，誓不生还！"[114]他主动组织医疗队，随军队转战华北、华中前线，救治伤员无数。他还在《益世报》上发表社论号召抗日救国，其中有很多脍炙人口的警

conversation was entirely reminiscent of a negotiation between a wolf and a lamb (please forgive me for this analogy, Mr. Minister, otherwise there is no other way to describe this situation).

When I came back to the church in the evening, I saw column frames standing on the floor with the tricolor flag hanging on them, and I was overcome with sorrow and tears.

Is it acceptable to subject the flag of France to hatred of justice? Is it acceptable to make the French flag cover up forceful aggression against justice?

......

The one who honors you most in Christ
Vincent Lebbe

Despite the injustice he suffered within the Catholic Church, Lebbe was unchanged in his original intentions. He was a practical man, who often visited the people of northern China, even in remote rural areas. The Catholic diocese of China had always been headed by a Western bishop, who was above the Chinese clergy. Lebbe proposed the slogan "China to the Chinese and the Chinese to Christ" and actively promoted the appointment of Chinese bishops by the Holy See.[112] In 1920 and 1926, he went to Rome to visit Pope Benedict XV and persuaded him to agree to the localization of Chinese bishops, which was successful.[113] In 1927, Vincent Lebbe converted to Chinese citizenship.

After the "September 18 Incident" in 1931, Lebbe called on the laity and young students to join the anti-Japanese activities. When the war began, he told his young brothers, "Now that the war has begun, we must stop all our daily work that is not directly related to saving the country and concentrate on the war, and we will not live until the Japanese are expelled!"[114] He took the initiative to organize a medical team and accompanied the army to the front lines in North and Central China, saving and

雷鸣远设计修建的河北省安国教堂，富于中西合璧风格

Vincent Lebbe designed and built the Anguo Church in Hebei Province

在欧洲期间，雷鸣远四处筹款，先后资助数百名中国学生赴比利时留学

During his time in Europe, Lebbe raised money to sponsor hundreds of Chinese students to study in Belgium

以上照片由近代天津博物馆提供

Photos from Tianjin Museum of Modern History

句：“以必死之心，求再生之路！”“用我们的头颅和热血，同日本作殊死战！”“牺牲一切，拯救中华！”“最后的胜利一定是我们的！”[115]1938 年 3 月在山西洪洞，雷鸣远遇见朱德。朱德曾赴德国、法国留学，而比利时人大多讲法语，两人相谈甚欢。朱德拿出 100 元法币，请雷神父举行一台弥撒追悼阵亡将士，《晋察冀边区日报》以红字头题版面刊发了朱德率其政治部成员出席了在马牧教堂举行的追悼活动。因为他的救护队救过不少八路军伤员，朱德多次给雷鸣远捎话：“只要有事，您便写信给我，我一定要给您帮助的。”[116]1940 年 6 月 24 日雷鸣远因积劳成疾，在重庆病重逝世。

treating countless wounded soldiers. He also published an editorial in the *Yishi* Newspaper calling for anti-Japanese salvation, which contained many popular aphorisms: "With a heart of certain death, seek the road to rebirth!" "With our heads and hot blood, we will fight Japan to the death!" "Sacrifice everything to save China!" "The final victory must be ours!"[115] In March 1938 in Hongdong, Shanxi Province, Lebbe met Zhu De, who had studied in Germany and France. The two had a good conversation. Zhu De gave Lebbe one hundred French dollars and asked him to hold a mass in memory of the fallen soldiers. The *Jinchaji Border Area Daily* published in red character headlines that Zhu De led members of his political department to attend the memorial service at Mamu Church. Because Lebbe's rescue team had saved many of the Eighth Route Army wounded, Zhu De repeatedly sent a message to him: "If there is anything I can help you with, please write to me."[116] On June 24, 1940, Vincent Lebbe became seriously ill and died in Chongqing.

鲁汶大学学生宿舍区。以上照片由近代天津博物馆提供
KU Leuven student dorm area. Photos from Tianjin Museum of Modern History

林辅臣着清朝官服照

Paul Splingaerd in Qing
dynasty official uniform

一个比利时家族在天津

两次鸦片战争之后，随着越来越多的城镇被开辟为通商口岸，大批西方侨民来到中国。侨民来华的这个时代，既是带给中华民族耻辱的时代，也是中华民族由故步自封转而奋起自强、近代中国由闭关自守走向对外开放并由传统农业社会向现代工业社会转变的时代。虽然侨民来华的目的也许一开始仅仅是谋生，但他们通过其在华活动参与和影响了中国的现代化进程，刺激和促进了中国社会在许多方面的变革，这使他们成为近代中西文化交流的桥梁与纽带。

林辅臣是一位成功的近代来华西方侨民。他出身寒微，1842 年生于比利时布鲁塞尔郊区，刚出生即成为弃儿，先后被两个家族收养。年纪轻轻来到中国，他梦想着在这里成就一番事业。为此，他刻苦工作，努力学习中文，很快成为"中国通"。他为人谦逊正直，与中外官员商人打交道能不卑不亢，秉公执法，深受地方百姓爱戴，获得当时中国最有权势的大臣之一李鸿章的信任和倚重，被任命为刚开关的肃州海关税务司（关长），并为晚清时期甘肃省所进行的各项现代化事业出谋划策、鞠躬尽瘁。[117]

林辅臣不仅在中国奠定了一生事业发展的基础，人生中最重要也最美好的时光都是在此度过的。在内蒙古，他娶了一位由教会抚养长大的中国姑娘凯瑟琳·李（Catherine Li）为妻，在中国开枝散叶，两人共生育 3 子 9 女，组成了一个幸福的侨民大家庭，成为众多近代来华侨民的成功典范。

结束了在肃州海关的任期，备受李鸿章赏识信任的林辅臣被推荐到开平煤矿，掌管矿务工作，由此他们这

A Belgian Family in Tianjin

After the two Opium Wars, as more and more towns were opened as ports of commerce, many Western expatriates came to China. They came to China in an era that brought shame to the Chinese nation, but also one when the Chinese nation was transformed from an arrogant and self-isolating nation to a self-strengthening nation. Although their purpose of coming to China might have been to make a living, the expatriates participated in and influenced the modernization of China through their activities in China, stimulating and promoting the transformation of Chinese society in many aspects, which made them a bridge and link between Chinese and Western cultures in modern times.

Paul Splingaerd was a successful Western expatriate to China in the modern era. Born in 1842 in the suburbs of Brussels, Belgium, he was an outcast at birth and was adopted by two families. Coming to China at a young age, he dreamed of making a career here. To this end, he worked hard, studied Chinese, and soon became a "China Hand." He was a humble and upright person, dealing with Chinese and foreign officials and businessmen with dignity and impartiality. He was loved by local people, and won the trust of Li Hongzhang, one of the most powerful ministers in China at that time. He was appointed as the commissioner of newly established Suzhou Customs and later made important contributions to the modernization of Gansu Province by advising on and participating in various projects.[117]

Not only did Splingaerd lay the foundation for a lifetime career in China, but the most important and best years of his life were spent here. In Inner Mongolia, he married a Chinese girl (Catherine Li) who was raised by the church and started a family in China. Together they had 3 sons and 9 daughters, forming a large and happy expatriate family that became a model of success for many modern-

林辅臣夫人（Catherine Li, 1846—1918）山西人，出身基督教家庭，为逃避对基督徒的迫害，由山西逃往内蒙古。幼时父亲去世母亲再嫁，因继父与基督教会关系密切，入教会学堂学习成为教师。后经神父介绍，与林辅臣结婚

Mrs. Splingaerd (Catherine Li, 1846-1918), a native of Shanxi, came from a Christian family that fled to Inner Mongolia to escape the persecution of Christians. She was introduced by a priest and married Paul Splingaerd

个大家族在天津安了家。因为比利时在天津的商业影响，更由于李鸿章等中国大臣的赏识，林辅臣一家在天津的欧美侨民中，拥有比较大的影响力，也积累了巨大的财富。1906 年林辅臣去世后，他在甘肃的事业由长子林阿德继承，协助彭英甲举办实业，后回天津成为天津电车电灯公司（法语简称 CTET）的董事；次子雷米曾在开平煤矿任高级职员；三子林子香先在京汉铁路工作，后在 CTET 供职；林辅臣的一个女儿也在 CTET 工作，担任总会计师。他的前四个女儿都加入了教会，成为修女，在中国、后来到欧美从事慈善事业。林辅臣的三个儿子都娶了兰州张氏家族的女儿，其他五个女儿大多嫁给在华西方侨民。子孙一代也多有在天津工作居住，就职于各个比利时洋行，如义品房地产公司。除此以外，林氏家族后人中也不乏与中国人通婚者，成为一个在中

day expatriates to China.

After his term at Suzhou Customs, Paul Splingaerd, who was highly appreciated and trusted by Li Hongzhang, was recommended to take charge of the mining work at Kaiping Coal Mine, and thus the family made their home in Tianjin. Because of the Belgian commercial influence in Tianjin, and even more so because of the appreciation of Li Hongzhang and other Chinese ministers, the Splingaerd family had a relatively large influence among the European and American expatriates in Tianjin, and also accumulated great wealth. After his death in 1906, his business in Gansu Province was continued by his eldest son, Alphonse, who assisted Peng Yingjia in organizing industries and later returned to Tianjin to become the director of the Belgian company Tianjin Tramways and Electric Lighting Company (CTET). The second son, Remy, worked as a senior staff in Kaiping Coal Mine; the third son, Jean-Baptiste Splingaerd, worked first for the Beijing-Hankou Railway and then for CTET. One of Splingaerd's daughters also worked for CTET as a chief accountant. His first four daughters all joined the Church, became nuns, and engaged in charitable work in China and later in Europe and the United States. Three of Splingaerd's sons married daughters of the Zhang family in Lanzhou, and most of the other five daughters married Western expatriates in China. Many of the children and grandchildren also worked and lived in Tianjin, working for various Belgian companies, such as the CFEO. In addition, many of the descendants of the Splingaerd family intermarried with the Chinese, making it a large family that has spread its branches in China.

The above basic information about the descendants of the family is based on the Splingaerd family tree compiled by the descendants of the Splingaerd family.[118]

The outbreak of the Second World War was a turning point in the fate of the Splingaerd family. After the Japanese occupied Northern China, they forcibly occupied many

林辅臣夫人在女儿凯瑟琳的婚礼上

Mrs. Splingaerd at her daughter Catherine's wedding to Louis Castaigne

林辅臣夫人（居中坐者），女儿露西（后排右立者），女婿帕特诺斯特（后排左立者），前排地上坐着他们的三个孩子。林辅臣在西安去世后，在生命的最后几年，林辅臣夫人与她的女儿露西、女婿阿尔波特·帕特诺斯特一家住在天津，并去世于此。1918年她被葬于北京，与林辅臣合葬

Mrs. Splingaerd (center), spent the last few years of her life in Tianjin, with her daughter Lucie (Back row right standing) and son-in-law, Albert Paternoster (Back row left standing) and their family. She was buried in 1918 next to Paul

林辅臣夫妇在北京天主教会的墓地

The tombstones of Mr. and Mrs. Splingaerd in the Catholic Church cemetery in Beijing

以上照片由林辅臣家族提供

Photos from Paul Splingaerd's family archives

林阿德夫妇（1879—1934）及其三个女儿
Alphonse and Anna Colette Zhang and their three daughters

林阿德（Alphonse Splingaerd，1877—1943），林辅臣长子。1877 年 10 月生于内蒙古归化城（今呼和浩特市）。曾任比利时驻华使馆参赞，恰逢义和团运动时包围各国使馆，因表现勇敢，获得俄、比、英、法四个国家的嘉奖。后遵父遗命，辞职赴甘肃继续其父未完事业，为甘肃近代工业化之肇始。后回天津居住，并成为天津比商电车电灯公司（CTET）董事会董事。1900 年与兰州张氏之女结婚，育有六个子女。张氏去世后，与另一中国女子吴玉明（音译）结婚，育有一子。1943 年去世于天津

Alphonse Splingaerd (1877-1943), the eldest son of Paul Splingaerd, was born in October 1877 in the city of Guihua in Inner Mongolia (now Hohhot). He was the counsellor of the Belgian Legation in China, and was commended by the Russian, Belgian, British and French embassies for his bravery during the Boxer Rebellion. Later, following his father's order, he resigned and went to Gansu Province to continue his father's unfinished business, the beginning of modern industrialization in Gansu Province. After returning to live in Tianjin, he became a member of the Board of Directors of the Belgian Tianjin Tram and Electric Lighting Company (CTET). In 1900, he married one of the daughters of Lanzhou's Zhang family. They had six children together. After Zhang passed away, he married another Chinese woman, Marie Theresa Wu, and had one son together. He died in 1943 in Tianjin

林亚纳夫妇
Remy Splingaerd and his wife

雷米·斯普林格尔德（Remy Splingaerd，1879—1931，中文名为"林亚纳"），林辅臣次子。曾在开平煤矿任高级主管，后又受雇于河北临城矿业和河南矿业等地，退休后居于北京，1931 年去世

Remy Splingaerd (1879-1931, Chinese name: Lin Yana) was the second son of Paul Splingaerd. He worked as a senior supervisor in Kaiping Coal Mine. Later, he worked for Lincheng Mining Company in Hebei Province and the Henan Provincial Mining Company. After retiring, he lived in Beijing and died in 1931

雷米·斯普林格尔德一家，八个女儿和一个儿子，唯一男孩为 Joe Splingaerd。照片摄于 1925 年
The family of Remy Splingaerd, with 8 daughters and 1 son. Photo taken in 1925

以上照片由林辅臣家族提供
Photos from Paul Splingaerd's family archives

林子香（Jean-Baptiste Splingaerd，1888—1948），林辅臣三子。1888 年 12 月生于甘肃肃州（今酒泉）。年轻时在比利时圣博尼费斯学院（Saint-Boniface College）接受教育。回到中国后，于 1911—1913 年受雇于中国海关，1913—1928 年在北京的中国铁路公司任职，1929—1946 年为天津比商电车电灯公司（CTET）中国业务经理。由于语言便利、文化熟悉，林子香在公司与中国顾客和中国职员之间架起沟通桥梁，使公司保持了长期稳定的运营，是后期天津比商电车电灯公司最重要的高级职员。二战后中国政府收回电车电灯公司，林子香被解雇。1948 年，林子香病逝，夫妇合葬于北京栅栏墓地。没有后代

Jean-Baptiste Splingaerd, (1888-1948; Chinese name Lin Zixiang) was born in December 1888 in Suzhou (present day Jiuquan), Gansu Province, the third son of Paul Splingaerd. As a young man, he received his education at Saint-Boniface College in Belgium. After returning to China, he was employed by the Chinese Customs from 1911 to 1913, by the Chinese Railway Company in Beijing from 1913 to 1928, and was the manager of CTET from 1929 to 1946. Bilingual and familiar with both cultures, Jean-Baptiste bridged the gap between the company and its Chinese customers and staff, keeping the company in stable operation for a long time and was the most important senior staff member of CTET in its later years. After the Chinese government took back the company after World War II, Jean-Baptiste was dismissed from his position. He died in 1948. He and his wife were buried together in Beijing Zhalan Cemetery. They had no descendants

以上照片由林辅臣家族提供

Photos from Paul Splingaerd's family archives

林子香印
Seal of Jean-Baptiste Splingaerd

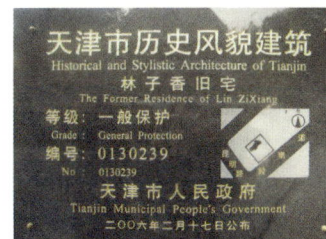

林子香在津旧居，今睦南道 114 号。由刘悦先生摄于 2003 年
Jean-Baptiste's former residence in Tianjin, now No.114 Munan Road. Taken by Mr. Liu Yue in 2003

林辅臣的三个儿媳，都来自兰州张家。从左至右为菲洛梅妮，安娜和玛丽·张（兰州张家），摄于雷米与安娜在北京的家中，照片由在巴黎的安娜的孙女莫妮克·比塞尔提供

Paul Splingaerd's three daughter-in-laws, all from the Zhang family in Lanzhou. L-R: Philomene, Anna, and Marie Zhang of Lanzhou, at Remy and Anna's home in Beijing. (Photo courtesy of Anna's granddaughter, Monique Biesel in Paris)

林辅臣年长的四个女儿后来成为法国天主教会的修女（左起下蹲者为安娜，中间端坐者为玛丽，后排站立者为克拉拉和罗莎）

The four oldest daughters of Paul Splingaerd, who all became nuns in French Catholic church

玛丽·斯普林格尔德（Mary Splingaerd，1874—1933），林辅臣长女，1874年3月生于今张家口，当时林辅臣在此经商。1897年10月28日前往法国泽西岛的一所教会作见习修女。在巴黎的修道院见习一年后，于1900年3月25日回到上海，正式成为修女。她的一生都在上海的一处修道院度过，1933年去世。照片摄于1898年她在法国泽西作见习修女时

Mary Splingaerd (1874-1933) is the eldest. She was born at Kalgan (Zhangjiakou-Hebei-China) during the time her father was a businessman, on March 9, 1874. She came as a postulant for the Dames Auxiliatrices Jersey (France) on October 28, 1897. She spent a year in Paris before returning to Shanghai, where she took her first vows on March 25, 1900. She spent all her life in a convent in Shanghai. She died in 1933. Pictured in Jersey in 1898 during her novitiate

克拉拉·斯普林格尔德（Clara Splingaerd，1875—1951），双胞胎姐妹之一，1875年10月出生于内蒙古首府归化城（今呼和浩特老城）。1899年赴法国泽西岛作见习修女，之后在巴黎待了一年。1901年她回到上海成为正式修女。1903—1914年她在上海教会的孤儿院和幼儿园担任监督或院长。1914年她前往旧金山，去服务那里的华人社区，直到1951年去世

Clara Splingaerd (1875-1951), one of Paul Splingaerd's twin daughers. Born in October 1875 in Guihua, the capital of Inner Mongolia (present day Hohhot), she was a postulant in Jersey (France) in 1899 and afterwards spent a year in Paris. Returning to Shanghai in 1901, she became a nun and supervised the orphanage and kindergarten of the Shanghai church. She moved to San Francisco in 1914 to served the Chinese community there until her death in 1951

以上照片由林辅臣家族提供

Photos from Paul Splingaerd's family archives

罗莎·斯普林格尔德（Rosa Splingaerd，1875—1968），双胞胎姐妹之一，1875 年 10 月出生于内蒙古首府归化城（今呼和浩特老城）。1897 年她来到法国泽西岛作见习修女，之后她在巴黎待了两年时间，1900 年回到上海，与姐妹们待在同一所修道院。1902—1951 年，她在国际租界和法租界的教会里，与天主教徒们一起工作，担任教会学校的绘画教师，并负责其他工作。1951 年她和妹妹安娜去往法国。1968 年去世于法国埃松省埃皮奈

Rosa Splingaerd (1875-1968), one of the twins. She was born in Guihua city, the provincial capital of Inner Mongolia (the old city of Huhhot nowadays), in October 1875. She was as a postulant in Jersey, France in 1897 and afterwards spent two years in Paris. Returning to Shanghai in 1900, she entered the same convent as her sister. Between 1902 and 1951, she worked as an art teacher and other jobs in church schools. In 1951, she and her sister, Anna, went to France. She died there in 1968

露西·斯普林格尔德（Lucie Splingaerd，1885—1983）林辅臣第五女，1885 年生于甘肃肃州（今酒泉）。曾任天津比商电车电灯公司（CTET）总会计师。1934 年返回欧洲

Lucie Splingaerd (1885-1983), Paul Splingaerd's fifth daughter. She was born in Suzhou in 1885, Guansu Province (present day Jiuquan) and served as the chief accountant at CTET. She returned to Europe in 1934

安娜·斯普林格尔德（Anna Splingaerd，1881—1971），1881 年出生于今内蒙古首府呼和浩特市，那时她的父亲林辅臣还是一个商人。与她的姐妹们一样，安娜于 1905 年加入上海的教会作见习修女。1917 年在上海安娜正式成为修女，一直到 1951 年，她在教会里充当音乐老师。1951 年，她与罗莎一起去往法国。1971 年去世于法国埃皮奈

Anna Splingaerd (1881-1971) was born in 1881 in Hohhot, Inner Mongolia. Following her older sisters' path, she became a postulant in Shanghai in 1905 and later a nun in 1917. In the church, she worked as a music teacher until 1951, when she and her sister Rosa went to France. She died in Epinay, France in 1971

林辅臣的其他五个女儿和小儿子

Paul Splingaerd's other five daughters and youngest son

林辅臣次子雷米的儿子 Joe 的婚礼。照片摄于 1942 年天津圣路易斯教堂。当时林氏家族在津的重要成员均出席了婚礼，包括林阿德（后排居中者）、林子香（林阿德左边）、林义方（后排右一）等

The wedding photo of Joe Splingaerd (Remy Splingaerd's second son) and Mary Anderson taken in Tianjin's St. Louis Church in 1942. Attendees included many members of the Splingaerd family in Tianjin such as Alphonse Splingaerd (back row in the middle), Jean-Baptiste Splingaerd (to the left of Alphonse) and Paul Joseph Splingaerd (the right side of the back row)

林义方（Paul Joseph Splingaerd，1902—1969），林辅臣长孙、林阿德长子，1902年生于北京。年轻时在比利时接受教育，后回到中国，就职于天津比商电车电灯公司（CTET）。1950年移民美国

Paul Joseph Splingaerd (1902-1969), oldest grandson of Paul Splingaerd and oldest son of Alphonse Splingaerd. Born in 1902 in Beijing, he was educated in Belgium. He later returned to Tianjin and was employed by CTET. In 1950 he immigrated to the United States

林阿德之女菲洛米娜（Philomène Splingaerd）一家。摄于20世纪50年代。女婿乔治·考克斯（George E. Cox）（右一）是义品公司在华最后一任总经理。太平洋战争爆发后，其全家被日本人送往山东潍县集中营关押

The family of Philomène Splingaerd, Alphonse Bernard Splingaerd's daughter, with husband George Cox

林阿德之外孙女、考克斯之女安芝拉·艾利奥特（Angela Cox Elliott，1943年出生于山东潍县集中营。照片中穿黑衣者）与安妮·梅戈文，2005年寻访曾外祖父林辅臣夫妇在北京栅栏天主教墓地的坟墓

Angela Cox Elliott, granddaughter of Alphonse Splingaerd, Philomène Splingaerd and George Cox's daughter, and Anne Megowan. She was born in the Wei County concentration camp in 1943. In 2005, she (dressed in black) visited the Beijing Shilar Catholic Cemetery to look for the tombs of her grandparents

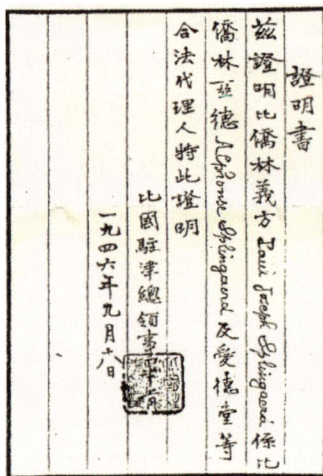

林义方证明书

Letter of authorization

Marie（Mary）Splingaerd（1915—2004），林辅臣次子（Remy François Xavier Splingaerd）之四女，1915年生于中国。曾在天津比商电车电灯公司（CTET）任中文、日文翻译，后在比利时布鲁塞尔作进出口商

Marie（Mary）Splingaerd（1915-2004），Remy François Xavier Splingaerd's fourth daughter. Born in 1915 in China, she worked as Chinese and Japanese interpreter at CTET. Later she worked as an importer and exporter in Brussels, Belgium

以上照片由林辅臣家族提供

Photos from Paul Splingaerd's family archives

国开枝散叶的庞大家族。

以上家族后代基本情况，系根据林氏后代整理的林氏家谱。[118]

第二次世界大战爆发是林氏家族命运的一个转折点。日本人占领华北后，强占了许多比利时的产业，林氏后人不得不与日本人周旋以委屈保全。太平洋战争爆发后，与英美籍男士通婚的天津林氏后人，都被送往了山东潍县集中营关押。二战结束后，林氏后代陆续迁居其他国家。新中国成立后，20世纪50年代，欧美籍的侨民都被驱逐出境。林氏后代现散居世界各地。

比利时在津侨民虽然不多，但是在领事馆的组织下，比较和睦团结，也参加了一些天津当地的慈善公益活动。例如，辛亥革命时期，天津本地士绅筹办红十字会。在比利时籍天主教天津教区主教雷鸣远牵头组织下，比利时驻津领事馆、华比银行、天津比商电车电灯公司及在津比商洋行认捐了1000元现洋（当时一袋面粉价值一元上下，所以1000元现洋是一笔不小的数目）。由此，天津的红十字会创办成功。

Belgian properties, and the Splingaerd descendants had to cooperate with the Japanese to survive. After the outbreak of the Pacific War, the descendants of the Splingaerd family in Tianjin, who had intermarried with British and American men, were all taken into the Wei County concentration camp in Shandong Province. After the end of World War II, Splingaerd descendants moved to other countries one after another. After the founding of the People's Republic, the European and American expatriates were deported in the 1950s. Splingaerd descendants are now scattered all over the world.

Although there were not many Belgian expatriates in Tianjin, they were still relatively harmonious and united under the organization of the consulate, and they also participated in some local charity activities in Tianjin. For example, when Tianjin local gentry were preparing to set up the Red Cross during the Revolution in 1911, the Belgian consulate in Tianjin, Sino-Belgian Bank, CTET and other Belgian firms donated 1,000 silver dollars led by Vincent Lebbe, the Belgian bishop of Tianjin Catholic diocese. At the time, a bag of wheat flour cost one silver dollar, thus 1,000 silver dollars was a significant amount. Thanks to the donation, Tianjin Red Cross Society was successfully established.

注释

1 Johan Mattelaer en Mathieu Torck (eds.). *A Belgian Passage to China (1879-1930)*. Uitgeverij Sterck & De Vreese, 2020, p.64.

2 来新夏主编《天津近代史》，天津：南开大学出版社，1987，第 17 页。

3 Johan Mattelaer en Mathieu Torck (eds.). *A Belgian Passage to China (1879-1930)*. Published by Sterck & De Vreese, 2020, p.64.

4 Johan Mattelaer en Mathieu Torck (eds.). *A Belgian Passage to China (1879-1930)*. Published by Sterck & De Vreese, 2020, p.71.

5 Johan Mattelaer en Mathieu Torck (eds.). *A Belgian Passage to China (1879-1930)*. Published by Sterck & De Vreese, 2020, p.72.

6 Johan Mattelaer en Mathieu Torck (eds.). *A Belgian Passage to China (1879-1930)*. Published by Sterck & De Vreese, 2020, p.72.

7 侯祖畲修，吕寅东等纂《夏口县志》第 11 卷，第 20 页，转引自费成康《中国租界史》，上海：上海社会科学院出版社，1991，第 261 页。

8 Koen De Ridder. The First Diplomatic Contacts between Belgium and China, Its Background and Consequences for Politics, Trade and Mission Activity. Leuven Chinese Studies IX. Belgium: Leuven University Press, 2001, p.45.

9 赵尔巽等撰《清史稿》第 158 卷，北京：中华书局，1977，第 4666 页。

10 1839 年 4 月 19 日，英国、法国、奥地利、俄国、普鲁士和荷兰在伦敦签署的条约，保证比利时的独立与中立。

11 Johan Mattelaer en Mathieu Torck (eds.). *A Belgian Passage to China (1879-1930)*. Published by Sterck & De Vreese, 2020, p.75.

12 Barbara Emerson. *Leopold II of the Belgium, King of Colonialism*. Great Britain: Bulterand Tanner, 1979, p.224.

13 天津市地方志编修委员会编著《天津通志·附志·租界》，天津：天津社会科学院出版社，1996，第 58 页。

14 1901 年 3 月 25 日第 123 次会议第 6 项，刘海岩等编《八国联军占领实录——天津临时政府会议纪要》，天津：天津社会科学院出版社，2004，第 226 页。

15 1900 年 6 月 21 日清政府以光绪皇帝名义向英、美、法、德、俄、奥匈、日、意、西、荷、比等 11 个国家宣战。当宣战诏书下达至各地方，邮政大臣盛宣怀领头联络各地督抚，不要服从这一命令。而李鸿章时任两广总督，闻此讯，复电朝廷："此乱命也，粤不奉诏。"两江总督刘坤一、湖广总督张之洞、两广总督李鸿章、闽浙总督许应骙、四川总督奎俊、铁路大臣盛宣怀、山东巡抚袁世凯、浙江巡抚刘树棠、安徽巡抚王之春和广东巡抚德寿，即与各参战国达成协议，拒绝支持义

和团，保护辖区内外国侨民生命财产，史称东南互保。

16 熊性美、阎光华编《开滦煤矿矿权史料》，天津：南开大学出版社，2004，第 74 页。

17 天津市地方志编修委员会编著《天津通志·附志·租界》，天津：天津社会科学院出版社，1996，第 59 页。

18 〔日〕中国驻屯军司令部：《二十世纪初的天津概括》，侯振彤译，内部发行，1986，第 19 页。

19 〔英〕雷穆森：《天津租界史：插图本》，许逸凡、赵地译，天津：天津人民出版社，2008，第 318 页。

20 〔英〕雷穆森：《天津租界史：插图本》，许逸凡、赵地译，天津：天津人民出版社，2008，第 319 页。

21 〔英〕雷穆森：《天津租界史：插图本》，许逸凡、赵地译，天津：天津人民出版社，2008，第 318—319 页。

22 宋蕴璞编《天津志略》，天津：协成印刷局，1931，第 12 页，转引自费成康《中国租界史》，上海：上海社会科学院出版社，1991，第 265 页。

23 天津市地方志编修委员会编著《天津通志·附志·租界》，天津：天津社会科学院出版社，1996，第 129 页。

24 天津比商电车电灯公司，又称比商天津电车电灯公司、天津电车电灯股份有限公司，其法文名称为 the Compagnie de Tramways et d'Eclairage de Tientsin，直译为"天津电车电灯公司"。1901 年 5 月天津德籍侨民德璀琳（Gustav Detring）联合其他在津居住多年的欧洲侨民发起组织"天津电车电灯公司"董事会，获得免税修建电车的获得特许经营权。此项经营权后来被转让给于 1902 年 6 月 14 日在比利时布鲁塞尔成立的天津电车电灯股份有限公司。1904 年 4 月 26 日该公司代表与中国政府代表在天津签订《天津电车电灯公司合同》，获准投资经营天津第一条有轨电车路线也是中国第一条公交线路。

25 天津市地方志编修委员会编著《天津通志·附志·租界》，天津：天津社会科学院出版社，1996，第 174 页。

26 天津市地方志编修委员会编著《天津通志·附志·租界》，天津：天津社会科学院出版社，1996，第 174 页；宋蕴璞编《天津志略》，天津：协成印刷局，1931，第 12 页，转引自费成康《中国租界史》，上海：上海社会科学院出版社，1991，第 265 页。

27 也包括一些拥有比利时和其他国家国籍的双重国籍拥有者。

28 天津市地方志编修委员会编著《天津通志·附志·租界》，天津：天津社会科学院出版社，1996，第 86 页。

29 天津市地方志编修委员会编著《天津通志·附志·租界》，

天津：天津社会科学院出版社，1996，第 100 页。

30 天津市地方志编修委员会编著《天津通志·附志·租界》，天津：天津社会科学院出版社，1996，第 111 页。

31 天津市地方志编修委员会编著《天津通志·附志·租界》，天津：天津社会科学院出版社，1996，第 60 页。

32 《比外长发表对于中国问题之文章》，《北益报》1927 年 5 月 30 日，转引自李育民《中国废约史》，北京：中华书局，2005，第 604 页。

33 唐启华：《被"废除不平等条约"遮蔽的北洋修约史：1912~1928》，北京：社会科学文献出版社，2010，第 382 页。

34 李育民：《中国废约史》，北京：中华书局，2005，第 841 页。

35 〔日〕中国驻屯军司令部：《二十世纪初的天津概括》，侯振彤译，内部发行，1986，第 240 页。

36 Ludwig Bauer, *Leopold the Unloved: King of the Belgians and of Wealth* (Boston: Little, Brown, and Co., 1935), p.169.

37 吴筹中、吴中英：《华比银行及其发行的钞票》，《中国钱币》1993 年第 4 期，第 41 页；John E. Sandrock. *Foreign Banks in China, Part II-Imperial Chinese Issues (1900-1911)*, p.9, http://www.thecurrencycollector.com/pdfs/Foreign_Banks_in_China_Part-II.pdf.

38 汪敬虞：《十九世纪外国在华金融活动中的银行与洋行》，《历史研究》1994 年第 1 期，第 112—136 页。

39 汪敬虞：《外国在华金融活动中的银行与银行团（1895—1927）》，《历史研究》1995 年第 3 期，第 111—132 页。

40 《天津商会档案汇编》（1903—1911），第 633 页，转引自汪敬虞《外国在华金融活动中的银行与银行团（1895—1927）》，《历史研究》1995 年第 3 期，第 126 页。

41 《民国外债档案史料》第 4 卷，第 438 页，转引自吴景平《关于近代中国外债史研究对象的若干思考》，《历史研究》1997 年第 4 期，第 53—73 页。

42 杨公素：《晚清外交史》，北京：北京大学出版社，1991，第 113 页。

43 Johan Mattelaer en Mathieu Torck (eds.). *A Belgian Passage to China (1879-1930)*. Published by Sterck & De Vreese, 2020, p.77.

44 （日）中国驻屯军司令部：《二十世纪初的天津概括》，侯振彤译，内部发行，1986，第 207—208 页。

45 比利时外交银行档案，p.2, https://www.avae-vvba.be/5-banque-belge-pour-letranger.

46 根据李焕章、刘嘉琛《天津外商银行简介》一文（见寿充一等编《外商银行在中国》，北京：中国文史出版社，1996）编辑而成；李晓春：《近代中国外商银行买办群体分析》，硕士学位论文，安徽师范大学，2006，第6、10页。

47 山东潍县集中营，是二战时期日本人在中国建立的最大集中营，由美国长老会的乐道院改建而成。从1943年到1945年，这里先后关押过2000多名欧美在华侨民，其中一半是英国人，还有200多名比利时人，潘德尔一家就在其中。

48 www.weihsien-paintings.org

49 1900年8月6日第4次会议第9项，载刘海岩等编《八国联军占领实录——天津临时政府会议纪要》，天津：天津社会科学院出版社，2004，第8页。

50 1900年8月8日第5次会议第3项，载刘海岩等编《八国联军占领实录——天津临时政府会议纪要》，天津：天津社会科学院出版社，2004，第8页。

51 1900年11月30日第76次会议第2项，载刘海岩等编《八国联军占领实录——天津临时政府会议纪要》，天津：天津社会科学院出版社，2004，第101页。

52 1900年12月3日第77次会议第2项，载刘海岩等编《八国联军占领实录——天津临时政府会议纪要》，天津：天津社会科学院出版社，2004，第102页。

53 1901年1月2日第89次会议第3项，载刘海岩等编《八国联军占领实录——天津临时政府会议纪要》，天津：天津社会科学院出版社，2004，第127页。

54 1901年6月12日第156次会议第6项，载刘海岩等编《八国联军占领实录——天津临时政府会议纪要》，天津：天津社会科学院出版社，2004，第315页。

55 1901年6月14日第157次会议第6项，载刘海岩等编《八国联军占领实录——天津临时政府会议纪要》，天津：天津社会科学院出版社，2004，第318—319页。

56 世昌洋行（E. Meyer & Co.）是一家老牌专做对华贸易的洋行。1866年爱德华·梅耶（H. C. Eduard Meyer，1841—1926）与其兄弟约翰内斯·梅耶（W. D. Johannes Meyer）在香港创办公司。1873年在天津创办"世昌洋行"，并注册了"金龙牌"和"恒记"两个商标，以这两个品牌从事了大量的进出口贸易。世昌洋行位于旧俄租界哈尔滨路（今河东区三纬路）。

57 1902年7月25日第320次会议第6项，载刘海岩等编《八国联军占领实录——天津临时政府会议纪要》，天津：天津社会科学院出版社，2004，第751页。

58 熊性美、阎光华编《开滦煤矿矿权史料》，天津：南开大学出版社，2004，第157—158页。

59 1902年7月18日第317次会议第2项，载刘海岩等编《八国联军占领实录——天津临时政府会议纪要》，天津：天津社会科学院出版社，2004，第742页。

60 天津比商电车电灯公司合约，以及合约签订后驻津领事嘎德斯向比利时外交部部长的汇报。现藏于比利时外交部档案馆。

61 萧祝文：《天津比商电车电灯公司》，载天津市政协文史资料研究委员会编《天津的洋行与买办》，天津：天津人民出版社，1987，第342页。

62 萧祝文：《天津比商电车电灯公司》，载天津市政协文史资料研究委员会编《天津的洋行与买办》，天津：天津人民出版社，1987，第342页。

63 Johan Mattelaer en Mathieu Torck (eds.). *A Belgian Passage to China (1870-1930)*. Published by Sterck & De Vreese, 2020, pp.149-150.

64 Johan Mattelaer en Mathieu Torck (eds.). *A Belgian Passage to China (1870-1930)*. Published by Sterck & De Vreese, 2020, pp.151-152.

65 《天津比商电车电灯公司情况调查》（1949年4月16日），载天津市档案馆编：《近代以来天津城市化进程实录》，天津：天津人民出版社，2005，第192页。

66 〔英〕雷穆森：《天津租界史：插图本》，许逸凡、赵地译，天津：天津人民出版社，2008，第79页。

67 1900年11月22日第72次会议第5项，载刘海岩等编《八国联军占领实录——天津临时政府会议纪要》，天津：天津社会科学院出版社，2004，第92页。

68 1901年7月1日第165次会议第20项，载刘海岩等编《八国联军占领实录——天津临时政府会议纪要》，天津：天津社会科学院出版社，2004，第336页。

69 萧祝文：《天津比商电车电灯公司》，载天津市政协文史资料研究委员会编《天津的洋行与买办》，天津：天津人民出版社，1987，第344—345页。

70 萧祝文：《天津比商电车电灯公司》，载天津市政协文史资料研究委员会编《天津的洋行与买办》，天津：天津人民出版社，1987，第345页。

71 Johan Mattelaer en Mathieu Torck (eds.). *A Belgian Passage to China (1870-1930)*. Published by Sterck & De Vreese, 2020, p.152.

72 《中国时报》（*China Times*）1906年2月28日。

73 京汉铁路总工程师让·沙多之胞弟。

74 Johan Mattelaer en Mathieu Torck (eds.). *A Belgian Passage to China (1870-1930)*. Published by Sterck & De Vreese, 2020, pp.152-153.

75 杨长河：《天津有轨电车开通的前前后后》，载中国人民政治协商会议天津市委员会、南开区委员会《天津老城忆旧》（天津文史资料选辑第76辑），天津：天津人民出版社，1997，第190—193页。

76 〔日〕中国驻屯军司令部：《二十世纪初的天津概括》，侯振彤译，内部发行，1986，第25—26页。

77 萧祝文：《天津比商电车电灯公司》，载天津市政协文史资料研究委员会编《天津的洋行与买办》，天津：天津人民出版社，1987，第345—346页。

78 Johan Mattelaer en Mathieu Torck (eds.). *A Belgian Passage to China (1870-1930)*. Published by Sterck & De Vreese, 2020, p.155.

79 Johan Mattelaer en Mathieu Torck (eds.). *A Belgian Passage to China (1870-1930)*. Published by Sterck & De Vreese, 2020, p.159.

80 萧祝文：《天津比商电车电灯公司》，载天津市政协文史资料研究委员会编《天津的洋行与买办》，天津：天津人民出版社，1987，第347页。

81 杨长河：《天津有轨电车开通的前前后后》，载中国人民政治协商会议天津市委员会、南开区委员会《天津老城忆旧》（天津文史资料选辑第76辑），天津：天津人民出版社，1997，第193页。

82 《天津比商电车电灯公司情况调查》（1949年4月16日），载天津市档案馆编《近代以来天津城市化进程实录》，天津：天津人民出版社，2005，第191—192页。

83 崇德堂是天主教耶稣会直隶东南代牧区在天津设立的办事处，位于今天津市和平区营口道22号。1873年开始，崇德堂开始经营房地产，房租与股票收入用于教区八个总本堂区的传教经费。

84 首善堂为天主教遣使会在天津的办事处，位于今天津市和平区承德道21号，其房地产收入为北京、天津、保定、正定教区以及北京文声修道院提供经费。

85 Historical Notes, 1921-1957: Brussels (Belgium), National Archives of Belgium, Crédit Foncier d'Extrême-Orient (cfeo), 8. See: René Brion and Jean-Louis Moreau, Inventaire des archives du Crédit Foncier d'Extrême-Orient et de sa filiale, la Société Hypothécaire de Tanger, op. cit. (note 2), pp. IX-XVI,

转引自 China Papers: The Architecture Archives of the Building Company Crédit Foncier d'Extrême-Orient (1907-1959), https://journals.openedition.org/abe/742；钱仲玫：《比商天津义品放款公司》，载天津市政协文史资料研究委员会编《天津的洋行与买办》，天津：天津人民出版社，1987，第328—338 页。

86 中国银行经济研究室编《全国银行年鉴·中华民国二十六年》，出版者不详，1937，转引自李天、周晶《比商义品公司对天津法租界城市建设影响研究》，《建筑学报》2012 年第 S2 期，第109 页。

87 Historical Notes, 1921-1957: Brussels (Belgium), National Archives of Belgium, Crédit Foncier d'Extrême-Orient (CFEO), 8. 转引自 China Papers: The Architecture Archives of the Building Company Crédit Foncier d'Extrême-Orient (1907-1959), https://journals.openedition.org/abe/742。

88 Notably: Chris Elder, *China's Treaty Ports: Half Love and Half Hate*, an anthology (Hong Kong; New York, NY: Oxford University Press, 1999) (*Literary anthologies of Asia*), 转引自 China Papers: The Architecture Archives of the Building Company Crédit Foncier d'Extrême-Orient (1907-1959), https://journals.openedition.org/abe/742。

89 CFEO was a founding partner of Credit Estates Company Ltd in 1937: Brussels (Belgium), National Archives of Belgium, Crédit Foncier d'Extrême-Orient (CFEO), pp. 463-472, 转引自 China Papers: The Architecture Archives of the Building Company Crédit Foncier d'Extrême-Orient (1907-1959), https://journals.openedition.org/abe/742。

90 Brussels (Belgium), National Archives of Belgium, Crédit foncier d'Extrême-Orient (cfeo), 1210-1325, 转 引 自 China Papers: The Architecture Archives of the Building Company Crédit Foncier d'Extrême-Orient (1907-1959), https://journals.openedition.org/abe/742。

91 Ren Brion, Jen-Louis Moreau. Inventaire Des Archives Du Credit Foncier D'Extreme-Orient Et De Sa Filiale, La Societe Hypothecaire De Tanger 1907-1991, 转引自李天、周晶《比商义品公司对天津法租界城市建设影响研究》，《建筑学报》2012 年第 S2 期，第109 页。

92 钱仲玫：《比商天津义品放款公司》，载天津市政协文史资料研究委员会编《天津的洋行与买办》，天津：天津人民出版社，1987，第330—335 页。

93 钱仲玫：《比商天津义品放款公司》，载天津市政协文史资料研究委员会编《天津的洋行与买办》，天津：天津人民出版社，1987，第335—338 页。

94 根据比利时布鲁塞尔皇家档案馆所藏地图计算，转引自李

天、周晶《比商义品公司对天津法租界城市建设影响研究》，《建筑学报》2012 年第 S2 期，第111—112 页。

95 李天、周晶：《比商义品公司对天津法租界城市建设影响研究》，《建筑学报》2012 年第 S2 期，第111 页。

96 杜小辉：《天津义品公司研究》，硕士学位论文，天津大学，第45 页。

97 Gabriel Van Wylick. L'architecture Contemporaine En Chine, op. cit., p. 102. Brussels (Belgium), National Archives of Belgium, Crédit Foncier d'Extrême-Orient (cfeo), 446. https://journals.openedition.org/abe/742.

98 Montreux (Switzerland), private archives Jean Volckaert. With all my gratitude to family Volckaert. On Gustave Volckaert (Ghent 1888-Uccle 1978): Thomas Coomans and Leung-kwok Prudence Lau, "Les Tribulations d'un Architecte Belge En Chine: Gustave Volckaert, Au Service du Crédit Foncier d'Extrême-Orient (1914-1954)" op. cit. (note 3), pp. 129-153. https://journals.openedition.org/abe/742.

99 Montreux (Switzerland), private archives Jean Volckaert. With all my gratitude to family Volckaert. On Gustave Volckaert (Ghent 1888-Uccle 1978): Thomas Coomans and Leung-kwok Prudence Lau, "Les Tribulations d'un Architecte Belge En Chine: Gustave Volckaert, Au Service du Crédit Foncier d'Extrême-Orient (1914-1954)" op. cit. (note 3), pp. 129-153. https://journals.openedition.org/abe/742.

100 Thomas Coomans. Les Tribulations d'un Architecte Belge En Chine: Gustave Volckaert, Au Service du Crédit Foncier d'Extrême-Orient (1914-1954). https://journals.openedition.org/abe/742.

101 Montreux (Switzerland), private archives Jean Volckaert. With all my gratitude to family Volckaert. On Gustave Volckaert (Ghent 1888-Uccle 1978): Thomas Coomans and Leung-kwok Prudence Lau, "Les Tribulations d'un Architecte Belge En Chine: Gustave Volckaert, Au Service du Crédit Foncier d'Extrême-Orient (1914-1954)" op. cit. (note 3), pp. 129-153. https://journals.openedition.org/abe/742.

102 赵雅博：《雷鸣远神父传》，台中：天主教耀汉小兄弟会，1990，第1 页。

103《致胞弟洛伯》，耀汉小兄弟会编译《雷鸣远神父书信集》，台中：天主教耀汉小兄弟会，1990，第26—27 页。

104 赵雅博：《雷鸣远神父传》，台中：天主教耀汉小兄弟会，1990，第60—61 页。

105 赵雅博：《雷鸣远神父传》，台中：天主教耀汉小兄弟会，1990，第94—97 页。

106《致赵主教（Msgr. Keynaud）》，耀汉小兄弟会编译《雷鸣远神父书信集》，台中：天主教耀汉小兄弟会，1990，第198 页。

107 赵雅博：《雷鸣远神父传》，台中：天主教耀汉小兄弟会，1990，第64 页。

108 来新夏主编《天津近代史》，天津：南开大学出版社，1987，第250—259 页。

109 赵雅博：《雷鸣远神父传》，台中：天主教耀汉小兄弟会，1990，第210—229 页。

110《致杜主教（Dumond）先生》，耀汉小兄弟会编译《雷鸣远神父书信集》，台中：天主教耀汉小兄弟会，1990，第135—138 页。

111《致法国驻北京公使（Conty）先生》，耀汉小兄弟会编译：《雷鸣远神父书信集》，台中：天主教耀汉小兄弟会，1990，第132—135 页。

112 赵雅博：《雷鸣远神父传》，台中：天主教耀汉小兄弟会，1990，第262—267 页。

113 赵雅博：《雷鸣远神父传》，台中：天主教耀汉小兄弟会，1990，第378—387 页。

114 赵雅博：《雷鸣远神父传》，台中：天主教耀汉小兄弟会，1990，第467 页。

115 赵雅博：《雷鸣远神父传》，台中：天主教耀汉小兄弟会，1990，第468 页。

116 赵雅博：《雷鸣远神父传》，台中：天主教耀汉小兄弟会，1990，第509—511 页。

117 Anne Splingaerd Megowan. *The Belgian Mandarin: Paul Splingaerd: The Life of Paul Splingaerd*. Philadelphia (PA): Xlibris Corporation, 2008.

118 Anne Splingaerd Megowan. *The Belgian Mandarin: Paul Splingaerd: The Life of Paul Splingaerd*. Philadelphia (PA): Xlibris Corporation, 2008 及 家 族 网 页 https://www.geni.com/people/Paul-Splingaerd-Lin-Fuchen/383089235820012375。

参考文献

中文文献

[1] 赵雅博. 雷鸣远神父传 [M]. 台中：天主教耀汉小兄弟会，1990.

[2] 费成康. 中国租界史 [M]. 上海：上海社会科学院出版社，1991.

[3] 来新夏主编. 天津近代史 [M]. 天津：南开大学出版社，1987.

[4] 李育民. 中国废约史 [M]. 北京：中华书局，2005.

[5] 刘海岩等编. 八国联军占领实录——天津临时政府会议纪要 [M]. 天津：天津社会科学院出版社，2004.

[6] 寿充一等编. 外商银行在中国 [M]. 北京：中国文史出版社，1996.

[7] 天津市档案馆. 近代以来天津城市化进程实录 [M]. 天津：天津人民出版社，2002.

[8] 天津市档案馆、南开大学分校档案系编. 天津租界档案选编 [M]. 天津：天津人民出版社，1992.

[9] 天津市地方志编修委员会编著. 天津通志·附志·租界 [M]. 天津：天津社会科学院出版社，1996.

[10] 天津市历史风貌建筑保护委员会、天津市国土资源和房屋管理局编. 天津历史风貌建筑（四卷）[M]. 天津：天津大学出版社，2010.

[11] 天津市政协文史资料研究委员会编. 天津的洋行与买办 [M]. 天津：天津人民出版社，1987.

[12] 熊性美、阎光华编. 开滦煤矿矿权史料 [M]. 天津：南开大学出版社，2004.

[13] 杨公素. 晚清外交史 [M]. 北京：北京大学出版社，1991.

[14] 赵尔巽等撰. 清史稿 [M]. 北京：中华书局，1977.

[15] 中国银行经济研究室编. 全国银行年鉴·中华民国二十六年 [M]. 出版者不详，1937.

[16] 中国人民政治协商会议天津市委员会、南开区委员会编. 天津老城忆旧（天津文史资料选辑第76辑）[M]. 天津：天津人民出版社，1997.

[17] 中国社会科学院近代史研究所翻译室. 近代来华外国人名辞典 [M]. 北京：中国社会科学出版社，1981.

[18]〔日〕中国驻屯军司令部. 二十世纪初的天津概括 [M]. 侯振彤译. 内部发行，1986.

[19]〔英〕雷穆森. 天津租界史（插图本）[M]. 许逸凡、赵地译. 天津：天津人民出版社，2008.

[20] 杜小辉. 天津义品公司研究 [D]. 硕士学位论文，天津大学，2014.

[21] 李天，周晶. 比商义品公司对天津法租界城市建设影响研究 [J]. 世界建筑，2012（s2）.

[22] 李晓春. 近代中国外商银行买办群体分析 [D]. 硕士学位论文，安徽师范大学，2006.

[23] 王苗、曹磊. 天津近代建筑师事务所发展研究 [J]. 天津大学学报，2013（4）.

[24] 汪敬虞. 十九世纪外国在华金融活动中的银行与洋行 [J]. 历史研究，1994（1）.

[25] 汪敬虞. 外国在华金融活动中的银行与银行团（1895—1927）[J]. 历史研究，1995（3）.

[26] 吴筹中、吴中英. 华比银行及其发行的钞票 [J]. 中国钱币，1993（4）.

[27] 吴景平. 关于近代中国外债史研究对象的若干思考 [J]. 历史研究，1997（4）.

外文文献

[1] Anne Splingaerd Megowan. *The Belgian Mandarin: Paul Splingaerd* [M]. 2008.

[2] Barbara Emerson. *Leopold II of the Belgium, King of Colonialism* [M]. Printed in Great Britain by Bulterand Tanner, 1979.

[3] Johan Mattelaer en Mathieu Torck (eds.). *A Belgian Passage to China (1870-1930)* [M]. Published by Sterck & De Vreese, 2020.

[4] Koen De Ridder. *The First Diplomatic Contacts between Belgium and China, Its Background and Consequences for Politics, Trade and Mission Activity* [M]. Leuven Chinese Studies IX. Belgium: Leuven University Press, 2001.

[5] Thomas Coomans. *China Papers: The Architecture Archives of the Building Company Crédit Foncier d'Extrême-Orient (1907-59)* [M]. ABE Journal [En ligne], 5|2014, mis en ligne le 01 décembre 2014, consulté le 19 décembre 2017.

[6] Thomas Coomans & Leung-kwok Prudence Lau. Les Tribulations d'un Architecte Belge En Chine: Gustave Volckaert, *Au Service du Crédit Foncier d'Extrême-Orient (1914-1954)* [J]. 期刊不详，2012.

电子文献

[1] http://blog.sina.com.cn/s/blog_4609f84b0102vg12.html.

[2] https://www.avae-vvba.be/5-banque-belge-pour-letranger.

[3] https://www.bnpparibasfortis.com/fr/votre-banque/patrimoine-historique-artistique/Article/consulter-les-archives-historiques-de-bnp-paribas-fortis.

[4] https://www.geni.com/people/Paul-Splingaerd-Lin-Fuchen/383089235820012375.

[5] http://www.thecurrencycollector.com/pdfs/Foreign_Banks_in_China_Part-II.pdf.

[6] www.weihsien-paintings.org.

第三部分 今日比利时与中国

Part III: Belgium and China Today

天津夜景（张建勇 摄）
Night view of Tianjin（photo by Zhang Jianyong）

第五章　新时代的交往

Chapter 5: Interactions in a New Era

1978 年谷牧访问比利时

1949 年中华人民共和国成立后，比利时继续承认于台湾之所谓"中华民国政府"为中国之合法政权。1971 年 10 月 25 日，比利时承认中华人民共和国为中国唯一合法政府。同日，时任驻法大使黄镇与比利时驻法大使罗贝尔·罗特希尔德签订《中华人民共和国和比利时王国建立外交关系的联合公报》，两国正式建立大使级邦交。

"文化大革命"结束后，中国重启经济建设进程。1978 年 5 月 2 日至 6 月 6 日，时任国务院副总理的谷牧率领中国经济代表团赴西欧访问包括比利时在内的五个国家，了解发达国家的经济发展水平，这是新中国成立后我国向西方国家派出的第一个政府经济代表团。这次访问之后的报告，推动了对外开放战略决策的制定，奠定了改革开放初期政策思路的雏形。"它和 1978 年 11 月的中共中央工作会议以及同年 12 月的三中全会一起，

Vice Premier Gu Mu's Visit to Belgium in 1978

After the establishment of the People's Republic of China in 1949, Belgium continued to recognize the so called "Government of the Republic of China" on Taiwan as the legitimate government of China. Until October 25, 1971, Belgium recognized the People's Republic of China as the sole legitimate government of China. On the same day, then Ambassador to France, Huang Zhen, and Belgian Ambassador to France, Robert Rothschild, signed the "Joint Communiqué on the Establishment of Diplomatic Relations between the People's Republic of China and the Kingdom of Belgium," and the two countries formally established diplomatic relations at the ambassadorial level.

After the end of the "Cultural Revolution", China restarted the process of economic development. From May 2 to June 6, 1978, Gu Mu, then Vice Premier of the State Council, led a Chinese economic delegation to Western Europe to visit five countries, including Belgium, to understand the level of economic development in developed countries. That was the first government economic delegation sent to Western countries

成为中国改革开放的三个转折点。"[1]

谷牧在回忆录中写道：

（中国）潜力巨大的市场对他们很有吸引力。我本来以为，按照国际交往对等原则，我遇到的会谈对象可能是副总理一级的人物。可是所到国家，同我会谈的都是总统或总理级的人物。法国总统德斯坦、联邦德国总统谢尔、瑞士联邦主席里恰德，都会见我们，比利时国王、丹麦女王也见了。这不是我谷某人如何，而是他们重视与中华人民共和国发展关系。[2]

谷牧副总理一行于 1978 年 5 月 18 日乘专机抵达布鲁塞尔，对比利时进行友好访问，在机场受到了比利时首相莱奥·廷德曼斯（Leo Tindemans）的热烈欢迎。在欢迎晚宴上，廷德曼斯首相说，"中华人民共和国已经多次表明了打算加速经济现代化的愿望"，"比利时方面完全准备采取合作的态度，这一合作符合我们两国的根本利益"。谷牧副总理指出："我们在社会主义建设中的方针是自力更生，同时我们也愿意同你们和其他国家发展科学技术交流和经济贸易往来，也要向外国一切先进的东西学习。"[3]

19 日，谷牧副总理一行在安特卫普港参观了码头、仓库。这时，一艘中国船正停泊在港口内。据港口负责人说，安特卫普港平均每星期接待一艘中国船。同一天，谷牧副总理还访问了贝尔电话公司一个生产由电子计算机控制的电话交换机工厂和安特卫普附近的一座核电站。随团的中国水利电力部长钱正英还参观了一个热电站。当天，谷牧副总理在布鲁塞尔访问了欧洲经济共同体总部，并会见了欧洲共同体委员会主席罗伊·詹金斯。[4]

20 日，谷牧副总理一行参观了一个蔬菜种植中心，

after the founding of the New China. The report that followed this visit drove the subsequent strategic decision to open up to the outside world and laid the foundation for the initial policy thinking of "reform and opening up." "Together with the Chinese Communist Party Central Committee Work Conference in November 1978 and the 3rd Plenary Session of the 11th Central Committee in December of the same year, Gu Mu's visit became the three turning points of China's reform and opening up."[1]

In Memoirs of Gu Mu, Gu Mu wrote:

The market (of China) with its huge potential was attractive to them. I had thought that, in accordance with the principle of reciprocity in international relations, the people I met with might be at the level of vice premier. But in all the countries I visited, the people I met with were all at the level of president or prime minister. President of France Valery Giscard d'Estaing, President of the Federal Republic of Germany Walter Scheel, President of the Swiss Confederation Willi Ritschard, all met with us, as well as the King of Belgium and the Queen of Denmark. It is not that I am somebody, but they value the development of relations with the People's Republic of China.[2]

Vice Premier Gu Mu and his party arrived in Brussels by special plane on May 18, 1978 for a friendly visit to Belgium, and received a warm welcome from Belgian Prime Minister Leo Tindemans at the airport. At the welcome dinner, Prime Minister Tindemans said, "The People's Republic of China has repeatedly expressed its desire to accelerate economic modernization", "Belgium is entirely ready to adopt a cooperative attitude, which is in the fundamental interests of our two countries." Vice Premier Gu Mu pointed out, "Our policy in socialist construction is self-reliance. At the same time, we are also willing to promote scientific and technological exchanges and economic and trade contacts with you and other countries, and we will learn all advanced things from foreign countries as well."[3]

一个农场和一个养猪场。下午，他在比利时农业大臣安托万·安布莱的陪同下，参观了设在比利时中部让布卢的国立农艺科学院，了解了这所科学院的种子改良、肥料、灌溉和植物保护等研究科目。

21日，谷牧副总理一行参观了布鲁塞尔以东一百公里林堡省的露天博物馆，那里展出了弗朗兹·马塞雷尔的木刻。中国人民在20世纪30年代就熟悉马塞雷尔，鲁迅先生曾把马塞雷尔的木刻介绍到中国来。1958年，马塞雷尔曾访问中国。[5]

22日，谷牧副总理前往布鲁塞尔以南60公里的沙勒罗瓦，参观了阿瑟克工厂生产大功率发电机和变压器的车间。随团的国家建委副主任彭敏则参观了普拉伊翁冶金公司的炼锌厂。中午，比利时国王博杜安在拉肯宫接见了谷牧副总理，并设午宴款待。晚上，谷牧副总理在布鲁塞尔举行告别宴会，答谢比利时政府的热情款待。比利时首相莱奥·廷德曼斯出席了宴会。在宴会上，谷牧副总理致辞说，在比访问期间，他和陪同人员，看到了比利时人民在工农业方面取得的重大成就和比利时先进的科学技术水平。谷牧副总理说，在许多方面，中国需要向比利时学习。廷德曼斯首相在致答词时说，中华人民共和国全面的和均衡的现代化的目标，是"令人鼓舞的"。他说："我相信，正如我经常说的那样，有才干和有能力的中国人民，是能够达到他们的宏大目标的。"[6]

回国后，考察团立即形成1.5万字的《关于访问欧洲五国的情况报告》呈报给中央领导同志。谷牧在报告中说："我们应当把欧洲当作争取第二世界的一个重点地区，进一步加强工作。"谷牧还提出：为了更大规模

On the 19th, Vice Premier Gu Mu and his party visited the docks and warehouses in the port of Antwerp. At that time, a Chinese ship was mooring in the port. According to the director of this port, the port of Antwerp received an average of one Chinese ship per week. On the same day, Vice Premier Gu Mu also visited a Bell Telephone Company factory producing computer-controlled telephone exchanges and a nuclear power plant near Antwerp. Chinese Minister of Water Resources and Electricity Qian Zhengying, a member of the delegation, also visited a thermal power plant. On the same day, Vice Premier Gu Mu visited the headquarters of the European Economic Community in Brussels and met with Roy Jenkins, President of the Commission of the European Communities.[4]

On the 20th, Vice Premier Gu Mu and his delegation visited a vegetable growing center, a farm and a pig farm. In the afternoon, accompanied by Belgian Minister of Agriculture Antoine Humblet, he visited the National Academy of Agronomic Sciences in Gembloux in central Belgium, to learn about research projects on seed improvement, fertilization, irrigation and plant protection at the academy.

On the 21st, Vice Premier Gu Mu and his delegation visited the open-air museum in Limburg province, one hundred kilometers east of Brussels, where the woodcuts of Frans Masereel were on exhibit. The Chinese people were familiar with Masereel in the 1930s when Mr. Lu Xun had introduced Masereel's woodcuts to China. Masereel visited China in 1958.[5]

On the 22nd, Vice Premier Gu Mu went to Charleroi, sixty kilometers south of Brussels, to visit the workshop of the Atelier de Constructions Electriques de Charleroi (ACEC) factory producing high-power generators and transformers. Peng Min, deputy director of the State Construction Commission, a member of the delegation, instead visited the zinc smelting Prayon Group. At noon, King Baudouin of Belgium received Vice Premier Gu Mu at Royal Castle of Laeken and hosted a luncheon. In the evening, Vice Premier Gu Mu held a farewell banquet in Brussels to thank the Belgian government for its warm

地引进国外技术设备，要有灵活的支付方式；在外贸体制上，应给地方、各部以一定的权力；必须进行以科技为主导的工业革命；加强技术交流，尽可能多派留学生到国外学习。

在后来的回忆录里，谷牧仅用"紧迫感"这个词简单地表达了当时的心情，事实上考察团已经被中西间真实的落差所震动。"已不是我们从苏联列昂节夫《政治经济学》上获得的那些老概念了"，他说道。考察团的紧迫心理和对中西差距的描述，也触动了当时中国的最高决策者们。在报告汇报会上，老帅叶剑英说："资本主义国家的现代化是一面镜子"，"出国考察，就是照镜子，解决我们自己的问题"。聂荣臻会前把报告看了五六遍，他说："引进什么，从哪个国家进，应该拍板了！"李先念也说："要利用西欧这个力量。"邓小平对谷牧说："引进这件事反正要做，重要的是争取时间。"之后，对利用西方国家的贷款和吸收外商投资，党中央基本上达成了共识，为日后被浓墨重彩书写的十一届三中全会夯实了基础。这次高规格的出访，也向国际社会传递了一个重要信号，即中国将走对外开放之路，有力推动国内改革。[7]随后，谷牧出任国家进出口管理委员会主任，着手制定《中华人民共和国中外合资经营企业法》。这是中国第一部利用外资的法律，吸收外商资金从此有了法律保障。

在中国的改革开放进程中，比利时创造了数个第一：比利时是最早向中国提供政府贷款的西方国家之一，也是最早向中国输出先进技术，同中国建立产业投资基金的西方国家之一。1979年比利时与中国签订了框架协议，两国的经济合作关系由此掀开了全新的篇章。比利时向

hospitality. Belgian Prime Minister Léo Tindemans attended the banquet. In his speech, Vice Premier Gu Mu said that during his visit to Belgium, he and his delegation had seen the significant achievements of the Belgian people in industry and agriculture and the advanced level of science and technology. Gu Mu said that in many aspects, China needed to learn from Belgium. In his reply, Prime Minister Tindemans said that the goal of a comprehensive and balanced modernization of the People's Republic of China was "encouraging." "I believe, as I have often said, that the talented and capable Chinese people are capable of reaching their ambitious goals," said Tindemans.[6]

After returning to China, the delegation immediately wrote a 15,000-word Report on the Visit to Five European Countries and presented it to the leading comrades of the Central Committee. In the report, Gu Mu said, "We should treat Europe as a key region in the Second World and further strengthen our work there." Gu Mu also proposed that, in order to bring in foreign technology and equipment on a larger scale, flexible payment methods should be available. In the foreign trade system, localities and ministries should be given certain powers. A technology-led industrial revolution must be carried out; technological exchanges should be strengthened and as many students as possible should be sent to study abroad.

In his memoirs, Gu Mu simply expressed the feeling of the time with "a sense of urgency," when in fact the delegation had been shocked by the real disparity between China and the West. "It is not the old concepts we have gotten from the Soviet Union Lev Leontyev's work - Political Economy," he said. The description of the gap between China and the West also shocked the top Chinese decision-makers of the time. At the report briefing, veteran marshal Ye Jianying said, "The modernization of capitalist countries is a mirror," and that "to go abroad on an expedition is to look in the mirror and solve our own problems." Nie Rongzhen read the report five or six times before the meeting, he said, "What to import and from which country? It's time to make the call!" Li Xiannian also noted,

中国无息贷款支持水净化、电视转播、电气化等建设。1981年3月29日谷牧再次到访比利时，随后比利时投入资金，参与建设上海贝尔电话设备有限公司。2003年中比在华设立直接股权投资基金，以前比利时投资上海贝尔公司所得利润也转入股权基金，用以支持中国创新型中小企业的发展。截至2018年，该基金的投资项目超过60个，金额超过30亿元人民币。2012年双方在比设立"镜子基金"，为比利时境内高科技成长型企业提供融资服务。两国金融合作进入新的发展阶段，为双边经贸关系发展提供了强大的资金支持和保障。[8]迄今，中国已成为比利时在亚洲投资最多的国家。[9]中比关系成为中欧关系的一个典范。

"We need to take advantage of what Western Europe has to offer." Deng Xiaoping told Gu Mu, "We need to bring in things from outside no matter what. The important thing is to buy time." After that, a consensus was formed on using loans from Western countries and attracting foreign investment, which laid a solid foundation for the Third Plenary Session of the 11th Central Committee. This high-profile trip also sent an important signal to the international community that China would take the path of opening up and strongly promote domestic reforms.[7] Subsequently, Gu Mu became the director of the State Import and Export Administration Commission and started to draft the Law of the People's Republic of China on Chinese-Foreign Equity Joint Ventures, which was the first law on the utilization of foreign capital in China.

Belgium has created several firsts among Western countries in the process of reform and opening-up. It was one of the first Western country to provide government loans to China; one of the first Western countries to export advanced technology to China and establish industrial investment funds with China. In 1979 Belgium signed a framework agreement with China, thus opening a whole new chapter in the economic cooperation between the two countries. On March 29, 1981, Gu Mu visited Belgium again and later Belgium invested in the construction of Shanghai Bell Telephone Equipment Co. In 2003 Sino-Belgian direct equity fund was established in China - the fund's purpose was to support the development of innovative small and medium-sized enterprises in China. By 2018, the fund has invested in over 60 projects with a value of over 3 billion RMB. In 2012, the two sides established the "Mirror Fund" in Belgium to provide financing services for high-tech growth companies in Belgium. The financial cooperation between the two countries has entered a new stage of development, providing strong financial support and guarantee for the development of bilateral economic and trade relations.[8] So far, China has become the country with the largest Belgian investment in Asia.[9] China-Belgium relations have become a model of China-Europe relations.

从"欧亚大陆桥"到"一带一路"

比利时地理位置重要，这使比利时成为全球贸易的中心。它是所有欧洲主要通道的交会处，位于英国利物浦港与意大利热那亚港之间的中心地带，该地带集中了欧洲60%的购买力和30%的欧盟消费者。[10]因此，可口可乐、卡特彼勒（工程机械）、UPS（国际快递）、丰田（汽车）、葛兰素史克（制药）、辉瑞制药、爱立信（通讯）、埃克森美孚（石油化工）和环球同业银行金融电讯协会等众多大型跨国公司，均将其欧洲总部设在比利时。[11]

随着全球化的迅速发展，物流成为世界各地企业的战略中心问题。而比利时由于地处欧洲中心，公路、铁路网络四通八达，并辅以港口、机场，以及大量价格低廉的仓储空间，早已形成高效快捷的"欧洲物流中心"。比利时境内的所有工厂与集装箱码头或货运空港的距离都不超过90公里。因此，出口货物在发货当天或48小时内均能抵达任何欧盟国家。另外，从中心仓库提取货物的货车能在24小时内将货物运抵国内的任何目的地并返回仓库。[12]

自2001年正式加入世界贸易组织（WTO）以来，中国逐渐成为"世界工厂"，中比两国之间的双边贸易额逐年递增，从建交之初的2000多万美元上升至2011年的291亿美元。[13]2011年5月9日，重庆至比利时安特卫普的"渝新欧"铁路货运正式开通，欧亚大陆桥开启了新的一页。这条陆上铁路货运线需要20天左右，比中国东部港口连接西欧港口的36天海运节省了约16天时间，大大缩短了运输周期，对开发中国西部和改变中国物流格局具有重要意义，同时也将刺激欧洲经济的

From "Eurasian Continental Bridge" to "Belt and Road Initiative"

Belgium's geographical importance makes it the center of global trade. It is at the crossroads of all major European corridors and located at the central area between the ports of Liverpool (UK) and Genoa (Italy), which concentrates 60% of Europe's purchasing power and 30% of EU consumers.[10] As a result, many large multinational companies, such as Coca-Cola, Caterpillar (construction machinery), UPS (international express delivery), Toyota (automobiles), Glaxo Smith Kline (pharmaceuticals), Pfizer, Ericsson (telecommunications), Exxon Mobil (petrochemicals) and the Society for Worldwide Interbank Financial Telecommunication (SWIFT), all have their European headquarters in Belgium.[11]

With the rapid development of globalization, logistics has become a central strategic issue for companies around the world. Belgium is located in the center of Europe with well-connected road and rail networks, supplemented by ports, airports, and a large number of inexpensive storage spaces. It has long become an efficient and fast-paced "European logistics center." All factories in Belgium are less than 90 km away from container terminals or cargo airports - export goods can arrive in any EU country on the same day of shipment or within 48 hours. In addition, trucks picking up goods from the central warehouse can deliver them to any destination in the country and back to the warehouse within 24 hours.[12]

Since its official accession to the World Trade Organization (WTO) in 2001, China has gradually become the "factory of the world", and the bilateral trade volume between China and Belgium has been increasing year by year, from more than 20 million U.S. dollars at the beginning of diplomatic relations to 29.1 billion U.S. dollars in 2011.[13] On May 9, 2011, the "Chongqing-Xinjiang-

现代丝绸之路——"中欧班列"
Modern Silk Road - "China Railway (CR) Express"

发展，促进中欧贸易的发展。[14]

2013 年中国提出建设"新丝绸之路经济带"和"21 世纪海上丝绸之路"的合作倡议，旨在借用古代丝绸之路的历史符号，积极发展与沿线国家的经济合作伙伴关系。为推动"一带一路"建设，2014 年国家主席习近平对比利时进行了国事访问，受到刚刚登基的菲利普国王热情接待，并访问了位于布鲁塞尔的欧盟总部。中欧班列也已成为丝绸之路经济带发展战略的重要组成部分，上升到国家战略的高度。

此后，中比之间又陆续开通多条中欧班列，包括以比利时为目的地的西宁至安特卫普（2016 年 9 月 8 日开行）[15]、唐山至安特卫普（2018 年 4 月 26 日开行）[16]、郑州至列日（2018 年 10 月 24 日开行）[17]、义乌至列日（2019 年 10 月 9 日开行）[18]四条线路，以及途经比利时的长春至汉堡（2017 年 10 月 13 日开行）[19]中欧班列。运输货物除了一些农业土特产产品之外，主要是汽车零部件、电子机械设备、阀门和服装等货物，以及近年来

Europe" railroad freight transportation was officially opened, opening a new page of the Eurasian Continental Bridge. Transporting goods on the railroad freight line between the eastern ports of China and the ports of Western Europe takes 20 days, which saves about 16 days compared with the 36 days of sea transport. It has greatly shortened the transport cycle, which is of great significance to the development of western China and the changing of logistics pattern of China. It will also stimulate the development of the European economy and promote the development of trade between China and Europe.[14]

In 2013, China proposed the construction of the "New Silk Road Economic Belt" and the "21st Century Maritime Silk Road," with the aim of actively developing economic partnerships with countries along the route, drawing from the historical symbols of the ancient Silk Road. To promote the construction of the Belt and Road Initiative (BRI), President Xi Jinping paid a state visit to Belgium in 2014, where he was warmly received by the newly crowned King Philippe. Xi also visited the EU headquarters in Brussels. The China Railway (CR) Express has also become an

2018 年比利时货物贸易进口 TOP15 国家和地区

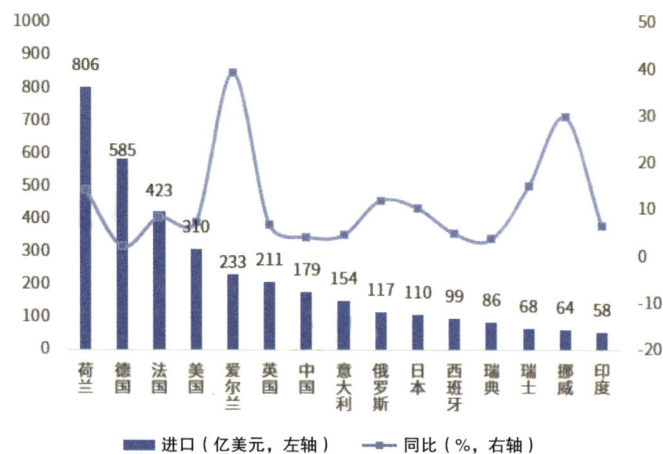

进口（亿美元，左轴） ■ 同比（%，右轴）

柱状数据（进口，亿美元）：荷兰 806、德国 585、法国 423、美国 310、爱尔兰 233、英国 211、中国 179、意大利 154、俄罗斯 117、日本 110、西班牙 99、瑞典 86、瑞士 68、挪威 64、印度 58

2018 年比利时货物贸易出口 TOP15 国家和地区

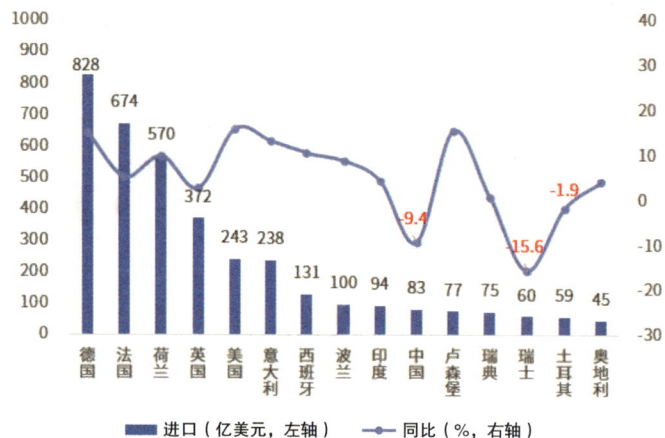

进口（亿美元，左轴） —— 同比（%，右轴）

柱状数据（出口，亿美元）：德国 828、法国 674、荷兰 570、英国 372、美国 243、意大利 238、西班牙 131、波兰 100、印度 94、中国 83、卢森堡 77、瑞典 75、瑞士 60、土耳其 59、奥地利 45

同比标注：-9.4、-15.6、-1.9

2018 年比利时货物贸易进出口 TOP15 国家和地区

注：比利时为进口原产国（地）、出口最终目的国（地），不包括经比利时转口的贸易。数据来源于欧盟统计局，前瞻产业研究院整理。

Top 15 countries and regions for Belgium's import and export of goods trade in 2018.

Note: Belgium is the country of origin for imports and the country of final destination for exports, excluding trade via Belgium for re-exports. Data from Eurostat, compiled by Qianzhan Industrial Research Institute.

跨境电子商务（世界电子贸易平台 eWTP）的货物。随着中国制造业的蓬勃发展，2017 年 6 月 30 日首批沃尔沃在中国大庆工厂生产的 200 余辆 S90 豪华轿车，通过中欧班列专列运抵大西洋沿岸的泽布鲁日港。此后，每年将有近 300 列"中欧班车"将中国制造沃尔沃轿车运送到比利时，然后转发到欧洲其他国家。时任中国驻比大使曲星表示，中比在"一带一路"框架下开展的务实合作取得了丰硕成果，必将推动中比贸易继续高位运行。[20]

当前，中比双边贸易额发展较为平稳，中国是比利时进口来源第七大国，是比利时第十大出口市场。据统计，2013—2018 年基本保持在 250 亿美元上下波动。2018 年比利时与中国双边货物进出口额为 261.2 亿美元。[21] 2019 年 1—7 月中国从比利时进出口商品总值为

important part of the development strategy of the Silk Road Economic Belt, rising to the level of national strategy.

Since then, several CR Express lines have been opened between China and Belgium, including four routes from Xining to Antwerp (started on September 8, 2016)[15], Tangshan to Antwerp (started on April 26, 2018)[16], Zhengzhou to Liège (started on October 24, 2018)[17], Yiwu to Liège (started on October 9, 2019)[18], and Changchun to Hamburg via Belgium (started on October 13, 2017)[19]. The goods transported are mainly car parts, electronic machinery and equipment, valves and garments, in addition to some agricultural products, as well as goods of cross-border e-commerce (World Electronic Trade Platform eWTP) in recent years. With the booming of China's automobile manufacturing, the first batch of more than 200 S90 luxury cars produced by Volvo at its Daqing plant in China arrived at the port of Zeebrugge on the Atlantic coast on June 30, 2017,

2012-2019年7月中国自比利时进、出口商品总值

中国对比利时出口商品总值（万美元）
中国从比利时进口商品总值（万美元）

2012-2019年7月中国从比利时进出口商品总值

中国从比利时进出口商品总值（万美元，左轴） 同比增长（%，右轴）

143.6 亿美元；2019 年 1—7 月中国对比利时出口商品总值为 105.3 亿美元；2019 年 1—7 月中国从比利时进口商品总值为 38.3 亿美元。[22] 两国经贸合作从传统的农业、化工、轻工业、原材料等行业逐步拓展到航空航天、高科技、生命科学和现代服务业等领域，成为中国与欧洲国家开展务实、互利合作的典范之一。

2018 年 10 月 17 日，中国与比利时签署《中华人

via a special CR Express train. Since then, there will be nearly 300 CR Express trains shuttling each year to deliver Chinese-made Volvo cars first to Belgium, and then to other European countries. Qu Xing, then Chinese Ambassador to Belgium, said that the practical cooperation between China and Belgium under the framework of "Belt and Road Initiative" has achieved fruitful results and would certainly continue to promote the high-level trade between China and Belgium.[20]

Currently, the bilateral trade volume between China and Belgium is developing relatively steadily. China is the seventh largest source of Belgium's imports and the tenth largest export market of Belgium. According to statistics, bilateral trade volume had been fluctuating above and below 25 billion U.S. dollars from 2013 to 2018. The value of bilateral import and export of goods in 2018 was 26.12 billion U.S. dollars.[21] The total value of China's export to Belgium from January to July 2019 was 10.53 billion U.S. dollars; the total value of China's imports from Belgium in the same period was $3.83 billion U.S. dollars.[22] The economic and trade cooperation between the two countries has gradually expanded from the traditional agriculture, chemical industry, light industry and raw materials to the fields of aerospace, high-tech, life science and modern service industry. It has become one of the models of practical and mutually beneficial cooperation between China and European countries.

On October 17, 2018 China and Belgium signed the Memorandum of Understanding between the Ministry of Commerce of the People's Republic of China and the Federal Ministry of Foreign Affairs, Foreign Trade and Development Cooperation of the Kingdom of Belgium on the Development of Partnership and Cooperation in the Third-party Market. Through the signing of the cooperation agreement and the establishment of a working group under the framework of the Economic and Trade Commission, the

民共和国商务部与比利时王国联邦外交、外贸与发展合作部关于在第三方市场发展伙伴关系与合作的谅解备忘录》。通过签署合作协议并在经贸混委会框架下成立工作组，中比第三方市场合作将逐步实现机制化、规范化。这项合作有利于发挥中国与比利时各自优势，将比利时企业在技术、服务、项目设计与管理经验等方面优势，与中国企业在基础设施建设、产能装备和制造、资金等领域优势相结合，共同开发第三方市场，共享市场合作机会和商业信息，拓展双边经贸合作新领域。这说明在一带一路的契机下，中比双方的经贸合作有了更深层次的发展。[23]

cooperation between China and Belgium in the third-party market will gradually be institutionalized and standardized. This cooperation is conducive to bringing into play the respective advantages of China and Belgium: combining the advantages of Belgian enterprises in technology, services, project design and management experience with the advantages of Chinese enterprises in infrastructure construction, capacity equipment and manufacturing, and capital, to jointly develop third-party markets, share market cooperation opportunities and business information, and expand new areas of bilateral economic and trade cooperation. This shows that under the opportunity of the Belt and Road Initiative, the economic and trade cooperation between China and Belgium has developed in a deeper level.[23]

九次访华的菲利普国王

现代欧洲王室是一个国家团结的象征。尤其是对比利时这样一个国土面积虽小、人口不多但内部有不同语言、关系复杂的国家来说，国王更是国家统一的黏合剂。比利时现任国王菲利普（Philippe Leopold Louis Marie，王号腓力一世）于1960年4月15日出生，是前任国王阿尔贝二世的儿子。他毕业于皇家军事学院，会开飞机和跳伞，曾先后就读于英国牛津大学和美国斯坦福大学，获得政治学硕士学位。2013年7月21日，53岁的菲利普宣誓继承王位。仪式上他用三种官方语言（荷兰语、法语和德语）宣誓。这被认为意义深刻，显示了他维护国家团结的信心，令比利时民众对他颇有好感。

比利时国王不仅是国家统一的象征，和平时期他们的最主要工作则是促进经济发展。为此，一般从作王储开始，他们即开始游历各国，了解世界。成为国王后，他们更是作为国家象征，积极进行外交活动，为本国企业寻找商机，铺平道路。例如，博杜安一世（Baudouin I，1951—1993在位）曾在1978年破格接见谷牧副总理率领的中国政府代表团一行；阿尔贝二世（Albert II，1993—2013在位）自1962年至即位前，任比利时外贸局名誉主席，率经贸代表团出访世界各国上百次，并于1975年和1993年两度以亲王身份访华，继位后也曾对中国进行国事访问。而现任国王菲利普则是目前为止访华次数最多的国王，曾经九次访问中国。

菲利普第一次来华是在1986年，行事低调、热爱旅行的年轻王储菲利普，像许多背包客一样，来到中国。在一个月的时间里，他不仅饱览了中国的壮美山河，还体验了淳朴热情的民俗风情，留下了美好的初印象。至

King Philippe Who Has Visited China Nine Times

The modern European royal family is a symbol of national unity. Especially for a country like Belgium, which is small in size and population but has different languages and complex relationships within, the king is the glue that holds the country together. Belgium's current King Philippe (Philippe Leopold Louis Marie, King Philip I) was born on April 15, 1960, the son of the previous King Albert II. Graduated from the Royal Military Academy, he can fly an airplane and parachute. He studied at Oxford University in the United Kingdom and Stanford University in the United States, and earned master's degree in political science. The 53-year-old Philippe took the oath of succession to the throne on July 21, 2013 in Belgium's three official languages (Dutch, French and German). This was considered highly significant and showed his confidence in maintaining national unity, which endeared him to the Belgian public.

Belgian kings are not only a symbol of national unity, but their main task in peacetime is to promote economic development. For this reason, starting from the time of being the crown prince, they began to travel around the world. When they became kings, they actively engaged in diplomatic activities as a national symbol. They also explored business opportunities for Belgian companies. For example, Baudouin I (1951-1993) received a delegation from the Chinese government led by Vice Premier Gu Mu in 1978, and Albert II (1993-2013) was the honorary chairman of the Belgian Foreign Trade Bureau from 1962 to his accession. Albert II visited China twice, in 1975 and 1993, as Prince, paid state visits to China after his succession. Having visited China nine times, the current King Philippe has made the most visits to China so far.

King Philippe first came to China in 1986. The young Crown Prince Philippe, a low-key, travel-loving man,

今，比利时王宫里还挂着他当年在中国农民家里吃饭的照片。[24] 成为国王后，菲利普将中国作为登基后进行首次国事访问的国家。2015年6月，国王夫妇率领了一个300多人的庞大代表团，其中包括比利时各大区的首脑和3位首相，其阵容之豪华在比利时外交史上罕见。

2015年6月23日，菲利普夫妇登上长城。

这次菲利普国王一行访华的首站是武汉，这一选择具有特殊意义。100多年以前，中比两国技术人员合作修建了著名的京汉铁路，汉阳铁厂的大部分资金和设备也同样来自比利时。这是两国成功合作的良好开端。他还发表演讲说："中国与比利时在地理、人口、历史、语言、文化等方面有着很大的差异。不过这些差异并非障碍，而是优势，通过交流，两国可以更为多彩。希望两国一直合作，分享知识，创造美好未来。"[25] 其后，菲利普国王一行又访问了北京、上海、深圳、苏州等地。在国家主席习近平的招待晚宴上，他说，此次访华印象深刻，收获良多，"我看到了中国的巨大变化"[26]。

came to China like many backpackers. In a month's time, he not only enjoyed the magnificent mountains and rivers of China, but also experienced the simple and warm folk customs, all of which left him a wonderful first impression. To this day, a picture of him dining in a peasant's house still hangs in the Belgian royal palace.[24] After becoming king, Philippe made China his first state visit. In June 2015, the King and his wife led a large delegation of more than 300 people, including the Belgium regional leaders and three prime ministers, an impressive lineup that is rare in Belgian diplomacy.

King Philippe and his wife visited the Great Wall on June 23, 2015.

The choice of Wuhan as the first stop of King Philippe and his delegation's visit to China is of special significance. More than a hundred years ago, Chinese and Belgian technicians cooperated in the construction of the famous Beijing-Hankou railroad, and most of the capital and equipment for the Hanyang Ironworks also came from Belgium. This was a good start to a successful cooperation between the two countries. He also gave a speech stating, "China and Belgium have great differences in geography, population, history, language and culture. But these differences are not obstacles, but advantages, and through exchanges the two countries can be more splendid. I hope the two countries will always cooperate and share knowledge to create a better future."[25] Later, King Philippe and his delegation visited Beijing, Shanghai, Shenzhen and Suzhou. At President Xi Jinping's reception dinner, King Philippe said his visit to China was impressive and rewarding, "I have seen the great changes in China."[26]

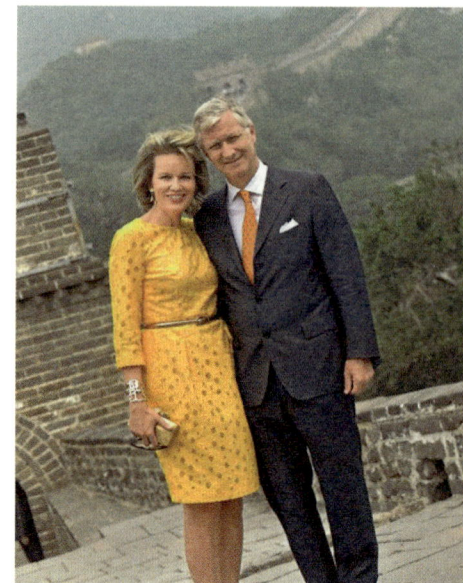

2015年6月23日，菲利普夫妇登上长城
King Philippe and his wife at the Great Wall on June 23, 2015

布鲁塞尔街头漫画。照片出自《欧洲心脏——比利时》（宋明江）

Street cartoon in Brussels. Photo from *Heart of Europe - Belgium* written by Song Mingjiang

丁丁与他的小狗白雪

Tintin and his dog Snowy

比利时的文化名人与文化符号

改革开放之后，中国的国门再次向西方打开，中国人对来自欧美的一切充满了好奇。自 1978 年国务院副总理谷牧访问包括比利时在内的西欧五国后，欧美的先进科技和文学艺术作品，被引进到中国。中国人开始重新认识比利时这个地处西欧的国家和那里的人民。

比利时被称作"漫画王国"，驰名世界的漫画家层出不穷，据说世界上每三个漫画家就有一个是比利时人。在布鲁塞尔，以漫画人物作为装饰的建筑物、地铁站、书店成了城市的一道亮丽风景。市中心 "新艺术"风格的漫画博物馆收藏了许多珍贵的原版画幅，是漫画艺术的百科全书。在这些闻名世界的漫画人物中，中国人最为熟悉的是丁丁和蓝精灵。

丁丁

丁丁在中国几乎是一个家喻户晓的漫画人物，是 20 世纪最受欢迎的欧洲漫画《丁丁历险记》（法语: *Les Aventures de Tintin et Milou*）中的主人公。这部漫画作品由比利时漫画家乔治·勒米以埃尔热（Hergé）为笔名创作，自 1929 年 1 月 10 日起在比利时报纸上开始双周连载，一共有 24 部作品。在中国改革开放之初的 20 世纪 80 年代，有两家出版社以连环画方式出版了除少数几种作品以外的全套丁丁历险记。截至 2007 年，即乔治·勒米出生后的 100 年，《丁丁历险记》被翻译成 70 余种语言出版，销售量突破 2 亿册。

"丁丁"的漫画故事以冒险为主，辅以科学幻想的内容，内容幽默，同时倡导反战、和平和人道主义思想，

Belgium's Cultural Figures and Cultural Symbols

After the reform and opening up, China's doors were once again opened to the West, and Chinese were curious about everything from Europe and America. Since 1978, when Vice Premier Gu Mu visited five countries in Western Europe, including Belgium, advanced technology, literature and artworks from Europe and America were introduced to China. Chinese began to reacquaint themselves with Belgium, a Western European country, and its people.

Belgium is known as the "Kingdom of Cartoons" and is home to many world-famous cartoonists, with one out of every three cartoonists in the world said to be Belgian. In Brussels, buildings, subway stations and bookstores decorated with comic book characters have become a beautiful scenery of the city. The "Art Nouveau" style Comics Art Museum in the center of the city houses a collection of rare original drawings and is an encyclopedia of cartoon art. Among these world-famous characters, Tintin and the Smurfs are the most known to Chinese people.

Tintin

Tintin is an almost household name in China and is the main character in *The Adventures of Tintin* (French: Les Aventures de Tintin et Milou), the most popular European comics of the 20th century. Created by Belgian cartoonist Georges Remi under the pseudonym Hergé, the comic strip was serialized biweekly in Belgian newspapers from January 10, 1929 and was published in a total of 24 volumes. In the 1980s, at the beginning of China's reform and opening up, two publishers published a complete set of Tintin's adventures in comic strip format, except a few other works. By 2007, 100 years after the birth of Georges Remi, *The Adventures of Tintin* had been published in over 70

张充仁与埃尔热
Zhang Chongren and Hergé

在西方国家非常著名。值得一提的是，二战爆发前，作者埃尔热在绘画《蓝莲花》时为搜集中国材料而结识了中国留学生张充仁，由此了解到神秘的远东世界，并在作品中揭露了日本在远东的野心，成为当时较早为欧洲介绍日本侵华情形的西方人之一。埃尔热与张充仁从此结下了深厚的友谊。战后两人彼此失去联系。埃尔热非常思念他的中国朋友，他把这种感情寄托到漫画中，在20世纪70年代成了《丁丁在西藏》，描述了丁丁寻找张氏的故事。两国于1971年建交后，埃尔热重新联系上张充仁。1981年张充仁受到埃尔热邀请访欧（当时埃尔热已经重病在身）。张氏访欧3个月，寓居埃尔热家，两年后埃尔热去世。这一段往事成为中比两国的友情佳话。[27]

蓝精灵

"蓝精灵"系列漫画是广泛流传了半个多世纪的世界经典童书，出自比利时漫画家贝约（Peyo）之手。小

languages and had sold over 200 million copies.

The comic story of "Tintin" is famous in the West for its adventure-based content, supplemented by science fiction, humor, while advocating anti-war, peace and humanitarian ideas. It is worth mentioning that before the outbreak of World War II, the author Hergé met Zhang Chongren, a Chinese student, when he was drawing *Blue Lotus* to collect Chinese materials from which he learned about the mysterious world of the Far East. In his work, Hergé revealed Japan's ambitions in the Far East and thus became one of the first Westerners to introduce Europe to the Japanese invasion of China. Hergé and Zhang Chongren formed a deep friendship from then on. After the war, they lost contact with each other. Hergé missed his Chinese friend so much that he put this feelings into his cartoons. In the 1970s, he completed *Tintin in Tibet*, depicting Tintin's search for Zhang. After the two countries established diplomatic relations in 1971, Hergé reconnected with Zhang Chongren, who was invited by Hergé to visit Europe in 1981 (when Hergé was already seriously ill). Zhang stayed at Hergé's house for three months during his visit to Europe. Hergé died two years later. This episode became a moving story of friendship between China and Belgium.[27]

Smurfs

The "Smurfs" comic book series, created by Belgian cartoonist Peyo, is a world classic children's book that has been widely circulated for more than half a century. The name Smurf originally came from three words: small, mushroom, and elf, because the Smurfs look like mushrooms and they are elves. When the animated films were introduced to China, the translators translated it into *Blue Wizards* in Chinese based on their dark blue skin color.

101 blue, three apples tall Smurfs live happily in the big forest and fight with the wizard Gargamel in a variety of catch and escape struggles. Although there are many Smurfs,

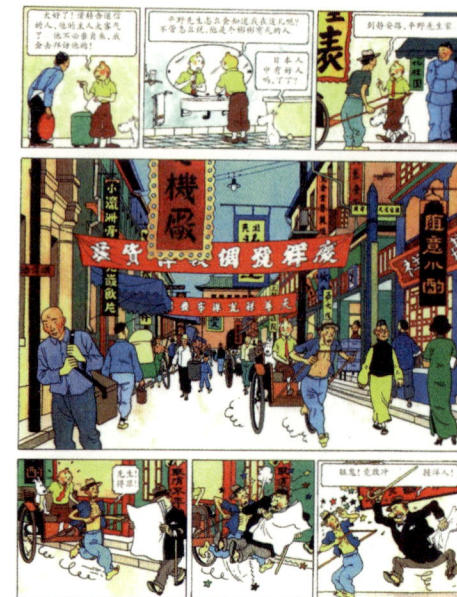

《蓝莲花》中，丁丁来到中国
In *Blue Lotus*, Tintin visits China

家伙们原名Smurf，这个词来源于3个单词：small（小），mushroom（蘑菇），elf（精灵），因为蓝精灵的外形很像蘑菇，他们又是精灵（elf），所以把3个词加在一起。而这部动画片引入中国时，译制人员依据它们的深蓝肤色，译成了《蓝精灵》。

101个蓝色的、3个苹果高的蓝精灵在大森林里快乐地生活，并与巫师格格巫展开各种各样你抓我逃的斗争。蓝精灵们数量虽多，个性却各有千秋，绝无雷同。作者通晓儿童心理，因此作品能启发儿童心智，传达爱和友谊，体现真、善、美，同时又幽默诙谐，是具有大智慧、大幽默的经典之作。"蓝精灵"自1958年面世后，风靡全球，被译成25种文字，销售2500多万册，改编的动画片曾在60多个国家播放。《蓝精灵》系列动画片最早由广东电视台引进到中国，1986年在央视播出，引起极大反响，是许多70后、80后童年记忆中美好的一部分。因此，2010年上海世博会"比利时·欧盟馆"的吉祥物选择了蓝精灵。[28]

"在那山的那边海的那边有一群蓝精灵，他们活泼又聪明，他们调皮又灵敏，他们自由自在生活在那绿色的大森林，他们善良勇敢相互都关心……"时隔多年，也许当初的小朋友们早把蓝精灵的故事忘得差不多了，

they all have different personalities and are never the same. The author understands children's psychology, so his works can inspire children's minds, convey love and friendship, reflect truth, goodness and beauty, while at the same time be humorous and witty. Since its release in 1958, "the Smurfs" has been popular all over the world and has been translated into 25 languages and sold more than 25 million copies. *The Smurfs* cartoon series had been played in over 60 countries was first introduced to China by Guangdong TV and broadcasted on CCTV in 1986, receiving great reception and becoming a part of the childhood memories of many post-70ers and post-80ers. Therefore, the Smurfs was chosen as the mascot for the "Belgium/EU Pavilion" at the 2010 Shanghai World Expo.[28]

"There is a group of Smurfs on the other side of the mountain and the other side of the sea. They are lively and smart; they are naughty and sensitive; they live freely in the big green forest; they are kind and brave and care about each other ... " After many years, perhaps those who were children at that time have forgotten almost all the stories of the Smurfs, but as long as they hear this familiar song, many childhood memories will come to their mind. However, it was not until many years later that people realized that this popular song was not an import, but an authentic Chinese original, with lyrics by lyricist Qu Cong and music by composer Zheng Qiufeng. The *Smurfs* animation series and the *Song of Smurfs* can be considered a classic example of

爵士乐、现代流行轻音乐中大量使用
Saxophone is heavily used in jazz
and modern pop music

但只要听到这首熟悉的歌曲,多少童年往事就会涌上心头。然而,直到很多年后,人们才知道这首脍炙人口的歌并非舶来品,而是地地道道的中国原创,由词作家瞿琮作词,作曲家郑秋枫谱曲。《蓝精灵》系列动画与《蓝精灵之歌》可视为当代中比合作的一个经典范例了! 29

阿道夫·萨克斯

当然,除了漫画人物,比利时还有一些真正的世界名人。比如乐器萨克斯管(Saxphone)的发明者阿道夫·萨克斯(Adolphe Sax,1814—1894)。

1814 年 11 月 6 日阿道夫·萨克斯出生在比利时瓦隆(Wallonie)大区的迪南。1840 年锐意进取的乐器制造师阿道夫·萨克斯根据波姆式长笛的原理发明了萨克斯管,并以自己的姓来命名这种新乐器。萨克斯管由金属制作,强弱幅度大,在声音的力度上可与其他铜管乐器媲美,也是其他木管乐器所不可及的,在音质上又有木管乐器的特点,并带有金属的明亮度。萨克斯管问世后,受到了当时很多音乐家的认可。1842 年阿道夫的好友、在巴黎音乐家圈中颇有影响力的柏辽兹(Hector Louis

contemporary Sino-Belgian cooperation![29]

Adolphe Sax

Of course, in addition to comic characters, Belgium has some real-world celebrities. Among them is Adolphe Sax (1814-1894), the inventor of the saxophone, the musical instrument.

Adolphe Sax was born in Dinant, Wallonie, Belgium, on November 6, 1814. In 1840 he invented the saxophone based on the principle of the Boehm flute, naming the new instrument after himself. Made of metal, the saxophone has a wide range of sounds, comparable in sound intensity to other brass instruments and unmatched by other woodwind instruments. In 1842, Hector Berlioz, a close friend of Adolphe and an influential musician in Paris, was so impressed with the saxophone that he introduced it to the public as a "modified open-hole tuba" and wrote an article about it in a journal, making it known to the world. Berlioz wrote: "The main characteristic of the saxophone is its wonderfully varied tone, deep and calm, emotional, soft and melancholy, like an echo within an echo, a marvelous sound that no other instrument can produce."[30]

The saxophone was first introduced to the military bands in 1845 when the French Military Ministry wanted to improve the obsolete military bands. This was followed by

阿道夫·萨克斯
Adolphe Sax

Berlioz）对萨克斯风非常赞赏，向公众介绍了这种"改造过的开孔大号"，并在刊物上撰文大力推介，使萨克斯为世人所知。他写道："萨克斯的主要特点是音色美妙变化，深沉而平静，富有感情，轻柔而忧伤，好像回声中的回声，在寂静无声的时刻，没有任何别的乐器能发出这种奇妙的声响。"[30]

1845年法国军事部打算改良陈旧的军乐队，于是萨克斯最先在军乐中崭露头角。随后欧洲的很多国家军队也逐渐引入了萨克斯，这使萨克斯很快以军乐乐器的形式享誉整个欧洲乃至全世界。法国作曲家比才（Georges Bizet）、圣桑（Charles Camille Saint-Saëns）等都在自己的作品中使用了萨克斯管。1910年以后，爵士乐在美国兴起，萨克斯管在爵士乐队、小号乐队中都扮演了不可或缺的角色，广受欢迎。

维克多·霍塔

维克多·霍塔（Victor Horta，1861—1947）是比利时乃至于世界"新艺术"（Art Nouveau）运动中最杰出的建筑设计师。历史学家倾向认为，他的作品代表了建筑的现代转型。他是最早将19世纪末20世纪初兴起的"新艺术"风格融入建筑的先锋之一，反对19世纪的"学院派艺术"（Academic Art），倡导艺术应体现在日常生活的各个方面，无论是建筑还是室内设计。[31]

霍塔于1861年出生于根特，从小喜爱建筑和音乐。他先学音乐，后习建筑。1878年在他17岁时，来到巴黎，同建筑师德布森（Jules Debuyson）一起工作。在那里，他受到正在崛起的印象主义和点彩画派艺术家的影响。1880年，他回到布鲁塞尔进入皇家美术学院学习。

霍塔
Horta

the gradual introduction of the saxophone into the armies of many European countries, which soon made the saxophone famous throughout Europe and the world as the military music instrument. French composers such as Bizet and Saint-Saëns used the saxophone in their own works. After 1910, with the popularization of jazz music in the United States, the saxophone played an indispensable role in the jazz and trumpet band.

Victor Horta

Victor Horta (1861-1947) was the most prominent architect of the Art Nouveau movement in Belgium and the world. Historians tend to believe that his work represents a modern transformation of architecture. He was one of the first to incorporate the "Art Nouveau" style that emerged in the late 19th and early 20th centuries into architecture, rejecting the 19th century "Academic Art" and advocating that art should be reflected in all aspects of everyday life, whether in architecture or interior design.[31]

Born in Ghent in 1861, Horta grew up loving architecture and music. In 1878, at the age of 17, he moved to Paris to work with the architect Jules Debuyson, where he was influenced by the rising Impressionist and Pointillist artists. In 1880 he returned to Brussels to study at the Royal Academy of Fine Arts. Because of his excellence in studies, he was appreciated by his mentor, Alphonse Balat, the architect to Leopold II. Horta became Balat's assistant and they co-designed the royal greenhouse of the Laeken Palace. In 1885 he started his independent practice and in that year he completed the design and construction of three residences, after which he built four public buildings in Brussels: Hotel Tassel, Hotel Solvay, Hotel Van Eetvelde and his own residence in Brussels, Maison & Atelier Horta. In the design and construction process, he developed his unique style by using steel as a supporting structure in the building and naturalistic style of decoration, blending the

因学业优秀，受到他的导师、利奥波德二世御用建筑师巴拉特（Alphonse Balat）的赏识，成为其助手，共同设计了拉肯宫（Laeken）的皇家温室。在这一工程中，首次使用了钢和玻璃这样的现代建材。1885年开始独立执业，这一年他完成了三幢住宅的设计和建造。此后他建造了布鲁塞尔四幢公共建筑，包括：塔索公馆（Hotel Tassel）、苏威公馆（Hotel Solvay）、伊特威尔德公馆（Hotel Van Eetvelde）和他自己在布鲁塞尔的住宅（即霍塔博物馆，Maison & Atelier Horta）。在设计和建造过程中，他在建筑结构上使用钢铁作为支撑结构，并采用自然风格的装饰手段，融合了艺术家的品位和工程师的技能，从而形成了他独特的风格。布鲁塞尔也因此成为新艺术运动最初的中心。[32]

啤酒

啤酒之于比利时，如同葡萄酒之于法国。啤酒起源于中世纪欧洲的修道院，是修道士们发明了啤酒。它的酿造有数之不尽的方法，使用的调料也不尽相同，可以说每家修道院都有自己特殊的秘方。在众多的啤酒中，其他国家的啤酒都无法与比利时啤酒的多样性、个性和成色相媲美。比利时啤酒有一千余种不同的品牌，每种场合都能找到相匹配的啤酒，清爽或浓烈、金色或褐色、果味儿或苦味儿、生啤或二次发酵……[33]除了标准的原料，包括水、大麦芽、啤酒花和酵母之外，不同的厂家还会添加不同的香草香料，所以风味各异。

直到今天，比利时的修道院依然保留着酿造啤酒的传统。独具特色的特拉普派（Trappist）修道士啤酒，其整个生产过程都是在修道院中完成，并由修道院中的

苏威公馆，1894年建成。照片出自《欧洲心脏——比利时》（宋明江）

Hotel Solvay, built in 1894. Photo from *Heart of Europe - Belgium* written by Song Mingjiang

塔索公馆
Hotel Tassel

资料来源（Source）：http://www.hortamuseum.be/Welcome.htm。

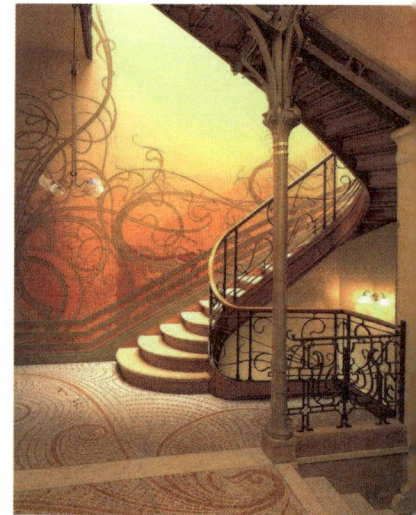

布鲁塞尔霍塔博物馆的室内设计。设计建造于1897—1900年。细节上出现了曲线为核心的"新艺术"运动特征，金属铸造的曲线形式栏杆和曲线图案的地板镶嵌、墙纸、灯具组成一体，风格典雅和谐，是"新艺术"运动设计的最杰出代表作品之一——

Interior design of the Horta Museum in Brussels. The museum was designed and built between 1897 and 1900. Details of the design featured the curves of the Art Nouveau movement. The curved form of metal casting railing and curved pattern of flooring inlay, wallpaper, and lamps are integrated in an elegant and harmonious style, truly one of the most outstanding representatives of the Art Nouveau movement

资料来源（Source）：http://www.hortamuseum.be/Welcome.htm.

taste of an artist with the skills of an engineer. Brussels thus became the original center of the Art Nouveau movement.[32]

Beer

Beer is to Belgium what wine is to France. It originated in the monasteries of medieval Europe, and it was the monks who invented beer. It is brewed in countless ways, using different spices, and it can be said that each monastery has its own special recipe. Among the many beers available, no other country can match the diversity, individuality and quality of Belgian beer. With over a thousand different brands of Belgian beer, there is a beer to match every occasion: refreshing or strong, golden or brown, fruity or bitter, draft or second fermentation ...[33] In addition to the standard ingredients, including water, barley malt, hops and

修道士酿造或在其监督下完成，且其销售利润必须直接用于支持修道院各项事务。特拉普派这个称号，相当于法国的"香槟"（Champagne），是由国际规范掌控，不允许随意命名。世界上只有7个修道院生产的啤酒有资格被称为"Trappist"，而其中6个位于比利时境内。[34]

而修道院的啤酒酿造方法和配方早已传到民间，并不断发扬光大。如今，在比利时，啤酒的生产厂家有400多家，其生产、调配和品尝的艺术已经到了一个相当高的水平，甚至高等学府里几乎都开设了啤酒酿造专业，如根特大学的啤酒酿造科学专业[35]、鲁汶大学的啤酒研究院开设了硕士学位课程。[36]

比利时人嗜好啤酒如同中国人嗜好饮茶。在啤酒馆点上一杯啤酒，边饮边聊，是比利时人休闲社交的一种方式，乃至形成一种社会文化。随着中国经济社会的发展，比利时啤酒酿造集团也开始在中国积极开拓市场。

yeast, different manufacturers add different herbal spices, resulting in a variety of flavors.

To this day, the tradition of brewing beer remains in the monasteries of Belgium. The distinctive Trappist monastic beer is produced in the monastery, brewed by or under the supervision of the monks of the monastery, and the profits from its sale must go directly to support the monastery's operation. The designation Trappist, the French equivalent of Champagne, is controlled by international standards and is not to be used arbitrarily. Only seven monasteries in the world can produce beer that qualifies as "Trappist," among them six are located in Belgium.[34]

The beer brewing methods and recipes of the monasteries have long been passed on to the public and have continued to flourish. Today, there are more than 400 beer producers in Belgium, and the art of production,

巧克力

比利时人认为巧克力是比利时的真正象征，是甜食中的极品。比利时以其口味广泛、种类繁多的"果仁巧克力"驰名于世。比利时人对巧克力的热情使得其制作成为一门艺术。制造者因力求推陈出新创造出种类更多的果仁巧克力，而被视作艺术家。为了保护比利时巧克力的形象，比利时政府甚至创建了"Ambao"标志，以保证使用100%可可原料生产的巧克力的品质。如今，比利时年产巧克力17.2万吨，全国有2000多家巧克力专卖店，比利时消费者年均食用巧克力10公斤。[37]

比利时巧克力中的招牌产品"果仁巧克力"，在雕刻精美的巧克力外层中包裹着不同口味的内馅儿，含在口中可以体味到缠绵悱恻的细腻感和香醇柔滑的味道，令人回味无穷。现在许多巧克力生产厂家仍然使用手工操作，坚持传统工艺，因此使比利时巧克力的质量得到保证。

1999年在中国开设了第一家比利时列奥尼达斯巧克力店。自从2001年比利时"凡情－蒂诺巧克力"（Valentino）来到中国，在上海、北京、沈阳、大连、苏州等城市发售以来，受到极大欢迎。[38]

blending and tasting has reached such a high level that beer brewing is offered at a major of study at almost all higher education institutions, such as Ghent University's Brewing Science program[35] and Leuven University's Beer Research Institute's master's degree program.[36]

Belgians are as fond of beer as the Chinese are of tea. Ordering a beer in a beer hall, drinking and chatting is a way for Belgians to relax and socialize, forming a unique cultural phenomenon. With the development of economy and society in China, Belgian beer brewing groups have also begun to actively explore the Chinese market.

Chocolate

Belgians believe that chocolate is the true symbol of Belgium. Belgium is famous for its wide range of flavors and varieties of "pralines." Belgian passion for chocolate has made the production of chocolate an art. The makers are considered artists for their efforts to create a wider variety of pralines. To protect the image of Belgian chocolate, the Belgian government even created the "Ambao" certification mark to guarantee the quality of chocolate made from 100% cocoa. Today, Belgium produces 172,000 tons of chocolate per year, there are more than 2,000 chocolate shops in the country and the average Belgian consumer consumes 10 kg of chocolate per year.[37]

"Praline", the signature product of Belgian chocolate, has a beautifully sculpted outer layer of chocolate wrapped in different flavors of filling. Many chocolate manufacturers are still working by hand, adhering to traditional techniques, thus guaranteeing the quality of Belgian chocolate.

The first Belgian Leonidas chocolate store was opened in China in 1999. Since the arrival of Belgian "Valentino" chocolates in China in 2001, they have been extremely popular in cities such as Shanghai, Beijing, Shenyang, Dalian and Suzhou.[38]

钻石

　　钻石玲珑剔透、耀眼夺目，在一些人眼中意味着财富和权力，在另一些人眼中则象征着爱情和美丽。全球开采出来的钻石有 80% 被送往比利时最大港口安特卫普，在那里被抛光、评估和交易，这使它成为世界钻石加工和贸易中心，被誉为"世界钻石之都"。最初的钻石加工业是 16 世纪由来自葡萄牙的几个犹太家庭开始经营，后逐渐发展起来。第二次世界大战期间，大部分钻石商携带存货设法逃亡伦敦，战后又返回安特卫普，使那里的钻石业再度蓬勃发展起来。[39]

　　钻石业在比利时是一项重要工业产品，占比利时出口总额的 7% 左右，约有从业人员 3 万名，有 1500 家公司经营钻石的加工和交易。世界上共有 21 家钻石交易所，其中 4 家在安特卫普。它的年营业额在 1996 年即达到 230 亿美元。自 1993 年以来，安特卫普每四年举办一次"精品珍宝"展（From The Treasury），集中展示历史上和当代独一无二的宝石和皇家宝石收藏，琳琅满目，美不胜收。[40]

Diamond

　　Diamonds are shining and dazzling, symbolizing wealth and power to some and love and beauty to others. Eighty percent of the world's mined diamonds are sent to Antwerp, Belgium's largest port, where they are polished, appraised and traded, making it the world's diamond processing and trading center and hence named the "Diamond Capital of the World." The diamond industry first started in the 16th century by a few Jewish families from Portugal, and has since developed. During the Second World War, most of the diamond dealers fled to London with their stocks, and returned to Antwerp after the war, where the diamond industry flourished again.[39]

　　The diamond industry is an important sector in Belgium's economy, accounting for about 7 percent the country's total exports, with about 30,000 employees and 1,500 companies engaged in the processing and trading of diamonds. There are 21 diamond exchanges in the world, four of which are in Antwerp. Its annual turnover reached $23 billion in 1996 alone. Since 1993, Antwerp has hosted the "From the Treasury" exhibition every four years, focusing on a unique collection of historical and contemporary gems and royal stones.[40]

安特卫普的钻石加工
Diamond-processing in Antwerp

驻比利时王国历任大使

李连璧（1973 年 12 月—1976 年 1 月）

李连璧（1917—2000），陕西华阴人。曾任西安学生救国会联合会主席、中华民族解放先锋队西北队部队长、中共中央西北局研究员、华县县长。新中国成立后，历任青年团陕西省委书记、西北工委副书记、中共陕西省委统战部副部长、陕西省人民委员会秘书长、外交部第二亚洲司副司长、驻波兰大使馆政务参赞、驻比利时大使兼驻卢森堡大使、驻欧洲经济共同体代表团团长、驻刚果大使，后任陕西省副省长、省第六届人大常委会副主任。

宦乡（1976 年 9 月—1978 年 3 月）

宦乡（1910—1989），贵州遵义人。1945 年冬至1949 年初，参加中国共产党地下活动，曾任上海《文汇报》副总编、天津《进步日报》（原《大公报》）党组副书记总主笔、中国人民政协会议筹备处副秘书长兼新闻处长。新中国成立后，进入外交部工作，历任欧洲司司长、驻英国代办处常任代办、外交部部长助理兼研究室主任。1976 年 1 月至 1978 年 9 月，任驻比利时、卢森堡、欧洲经济共同体大使。回国后曾任中国社会科学院党委书记、副院长。1982 年 7 月起兼任中国法学会副会长及国务院国际问题研究中心总干事党组书记、中国太平洋经济合作全国委员会会长、台湾研究会会长以及《世界经济报》名誉社长等职。

List of Chinese Ambassadors to the Kingdom of Belgium

Li Lianbi (December 1973 - January 1976)

Li Lianbi (1917-2000) was a native of Huayin, Shaanxi Province. He was the chairman of Xi'an Students' Salvation Association, captain of northwest branch of The Chinese National Liberation Vanguard, a researcher of the Northwest Bureau of the Central Committee of the Communist Party of China, and the Administrator of Hua County. After the founding of the People's Republic of China, he served as Secretary of the Shaanxi Provincial Committee of the Youth League, Deputy Secretary of the Northwest Labor Committee, Deputy Minister of the United Front Work Department of the Shaanxi Provincial Committee of the CPC, Secretary-General of the Shaanxi Provincial People's Committee, Deputy Director of the Second Asian Department of the Ministry of Foreign Affairs, political Counsellor of the Embassy in Poland, Ambassador to Belgium and Ambassador to Luxembourg, Head of the Delegation to the European Community, Ambassador to Congo, Vice Governor of Shaanxi Province and Deputy Director of the Sixth Standing Committee of the Shaanxi Provincial People's Congress.

Huan Xiang (September 1976 - March 1978)

Huan Xiang (November 1910 - February 1989), a native of Zunyi, Guizhou Province, joined the underground activities of the Communist Party from the winter of 1945 to the beginning of 1949, and served as deputy editor-in-chief of Shanghai *Wen Hui Newspaper*, deputy secretary of the party group and chief writer of Tianjin *Progressive Daily* (formerly *Da Gong Newspaper*), Deputy Secretary-General of the preparatory office of the Chinese People's Political Consultative Conference. After the founding of the People's Republic of China, he joined the Ministry of Foreign Affairs, where he served as Director General of the European Department, Permanent Chargé d'Affaires in the United Kingdom, Assistant to the Minister of Foreign Affairs and Director of the Research Office, and Ambassador to Belgium, Luxembourg and the European Community from January 1976 to September 1978. After returning to China, he served as Secretary of the Party Committee and Vice President of the Chinese Academy of Social Sciences, Vice President of the Chinese Law Society, Director General and Party Secretary of the International Studies Center of the State Council, President of the National Committee for China Pacific Economic Cooperation, President of the Taiwan Studies Association, and Honorary President of the *World Economic News*, etc. since July 1982.

康矛召（1978 年 5 月—1981 年 2 月）

　　康矛召（1919—1994），湖北武昌人。武汉大学肄业。1938 年赴延安参加革命，1943 年参与创办《山东画报》，兼任社长主编。解放战争时期任新华社华东野战军前线分社社长，1948 年任华东炮兵第三团政委，1949 年任华东野战军第八兵团政治部宣传部副部长。新中国成立后，作外交工作，历任驻印度大使馆、阿富汗大使馆参赞、外交部新闻司副司长、驻南斯拉夫临时代办、驻柬埔寨、毛里塔尼亚大使，驻比利时大使兼驻欧洲经济共同体使团团长和驻卢森堡大使。他热爱摄影艺术，对中国解放区和新中国的摄影事业做出了巨大贡献。

郑为之（1981 年 3 月—1983 年 2 月）

　　郑为之（1914—1993），广东遂溪人。1931 年加入中国共产党。1937 年毕业于暨南大学物理系。曾在上海从事党的秘密工作。1938 年后任中国人民抗日军事政治大学（简称"抗大"）一分校政治科员、山东国民抗敌自卫军政治副主任、东北抗日联军旅政治副主任、东北民主联军师政治部主任、第四野战军师副政委。新中国成立后，历任驻巴基斯坦大使馆参赞、驻丹麦大使、外交部美澳司司长、驻阿根廷、委内瑞拉大使、驻比利时大使兼驻卢森堡大使和驻欧洲经济共同体使团团长。后任国际问题研究所所长，曾为第六届全国人大外事委员会顾问。

Kang Maozhao (May 1978 - February 1981)

Kang Maozhao (1919-1994) was from Wuchang, Hubei Province. In 1938, he went to Yan'an to join the revolution, and in 1943, he participated in the founding of *Shandong Pictorial*, serving as director and editor-in-chief. During the War of Liberation, he served as the head of the Frontline Branch of the Eastern China Field Army of Xinhua News Agency. In 1948, he was appointed as the Political Commissar of the Eastern China Third Artillery Regiment. In 1949, he was appointed as the Deputy Director of the Publicity department of the Political Section of the Eighth Regiment of the Eastern China Field Army. After the founding of the People's Republic of China, he worked as a diplomat, serving as Counsellor of the Embassies in India and Afghanistan, Deputy Director of the Information Department of the Ministry of Foreign Affairs, Chargé d'Affaires in Yugoslavia, Ambassador to Cambodia and Mauritania, Ambassador to Belgium and Head of the Mission to the European Economic Community, and Ambassador to Luxembourg. He loved the art of photography and made great contributions to the field photographic art in China.

Zheng Weizhi (March 1981 - February 1983)

Zheng Weizhi (1914-1993), a native of Suixi, Guangdong Province, joined the Communist Party of China in 1931 and graduated from the Physics Department of Jinan University in 1937. After 1938, he served as a political officer at the First Branch of the Chinese People's Anti-Japanese Military and Political College (referred to as "Anti-Japanese College"), the Deputy Political Director of the Shandong National Resistance Self-Defense Force, the Deputy Political Director of the Northeast United Resistance Army, the Director of the Political Section of the Northeast Democratic United Division, and the Deputy Commissar of the Political Section of the Fourth Field Division. After the founding of the People's Republic of China, he served as Counselor of the Embassy in Pakistan, Ambassador to Denmark, Director of the U.S.-Australia Department of the Ministry of Foreign Affairs, Ambassador to Argentina and Venezuela, Ambassador to Belgium and Luxembourg and Head of the Mission to the European Economic Community, Director of the Institute of International Studies, and Advisor to the Foreign Affairs Committee of the Sixth National People's Congress.

章曙（1983 年 8 月—1985 年 8 月）

　　章曙（1925—1998），1925 年 5 月生于北京。1944 年，章曙进入武汉大学外文系学习，曾任武汉大学学生自治会宣传部长。1948 年 8 月来到晋察冀解放区参加革命。一年后，调至中共中央外事组，是最早一批新中国外交官之一。历任驻伊拉克使馆二等秘书一等秘书，驻联合国代表团政务参赞，联合国安全理事会事务司副司长，外交部西亚北非司副司长、司长，驻比利时大使兼驻卢森堡大使兼常驻欧洲经济共同体使团团长，后任驻日本特命全权大使。回国后任外交学院院长、党委书记。

刘山（1985 年 8 月—1988 年 3 月）

　　刘山（1927—2005），湖北沔阳（今仙桃）人。1948 年毕业于北京大学哲学系，同年加入民主青年联盟，1956 年加入中国共产党。历任外交部秘书处签证处科长、领事司处长、长沙铁道学院英语教研室主任、中国对外翻译出版公司编译室主任、副经理、外交部政策研究室副主任、驻比利时大使兼驻卢森堡大使和欧洲经济共同体使团团长。回国后曾任国务院外办副主任、外交学院院长兼任外交学院党委书记。

Zhang Shu (August 1983 - August 1985)

　　Zhang Shu (1925-1998), born in May 1925 in Beijing, studied at the Foreign Languages Department of Wuhan University in 1944 and served as the propaganda director of the Wuhan University Students' Self-Government Association. In August 1948, he joined the revolution in the liberated areas of Shanxi-Chahaer-Hebei, and one year later, he was transferred to the Foreign Affairs Group of the Central Committee of the Communist Party of China, becoming one of the earliest diplomat in the New China. He served as Second Secretary and First Secretary of the Embassy in Iraq, Political Counsellor at the United Nations Mission, Deputy Director of the United Nations Security Council Affairs Division, Deputy Director and Director of the West Asia and North Africa Department of the Ministry of Foreign Affairs, Ambassador to Belgium, Ambassador to Luxembourg and Head of the Permanent Mission to the European Community, and Ambassador Extraordinary and Plenipotentiary to Japan. After returning to China, he served as the President and Secretary of the Party Committee of Foreign Affairs College.

Liu Shan (August 1985 - March 1988)

　　Liu Shan (1927-2005), from Xiantao, Hubei Province, graduated from the Philosophy Department of Peking University in 1948 when he joined the Democratic Youth League. In 1956, Liu joined the Communist Party of China. He served as the Head of the Visa Division of the Secretariat of the Ministry of Foreign Affairs, Deputy Director of the Policy Research Office of the Ministry of Foreign Affairs, Ambassador to Belgium, Ambassador to Luxembourg and the Head of the European Economic Community Mission. After returning to China, he served as Deputy Director of the Foreign Affairs Office of the State Council, President and Secretary of the Party Committee of Foreign Affairs College.

夏道生（1990 年 2 月—1992 年 5 月）

　　夏道生（1932—），湖北武汉人。1951 年进入外交部工作，任驻匈牙利大使馆随员，曾在苏联东欧区和中国国际问题研究所工作。后历任驻加拿大使馆参赞、公使衔参赞、外交部政策研究室主任、驻比利时大使兼驻欧洲经济共同体使团团长。回国后历任国务院外事办副主任、中国人民外交学会副会长、外交部特别调研小组组长。

Xia Daosheng (February 1990 - May 1992)

　　Xia Daosheng (1932-), a native of Wuhan, Hubei Province, joined the Ministry of Foreign Affairs in 1951 and worked as an Attaché in the Chinese Embassy in Hungary. He served as Counsellor and ministerial Counsellor of the Chinese Embassy in Canada, Director of the Policy Research Office of the Ministry of Foreign Affairs, Ambassador to Belgium and Head of the Mission to the European Community. After returning to China, he served as Deputy Director of the Foreign Affairs Office of the State Council, Vice President of the Chinese People's Institute of Foreign Affairs.

丁原洪（1992 年 7 月—1997 年 2 月）

　　丁原洪（1931—），山东日照人。1949 年考入燕京大学西方语言文学系。1952 年年底提前毕业，入外交部工作。20 世纪 50 年代在罗马尼亚工作。其后在外交部苏联东欧司主管罗马尼亚事务。60 年代，作为中国政府代表团顾问、团员，参加中苏边界谈判。70 年代，作为外交部美国处处长，参与从打开中美关系大门到中美两国正式建交的全过程。80 年代，先后任外交部政策研究室副主任、主任。后历任驻联合国、瑞士、比利时大使兼任驻欧盟使团团长。回国后任外交部大使，负责亚欧会议。

Ding Yuanhong (July 1992 - February 1997)

　　Ding Yuanhong (1931-), a native of Rizhao, Shandong Province, studied at the Department of Western Languages and Literature at Yanjing University in 1949. Graduating early at the end of 1952, he was transferred to the Ministry of Foreign Affairs, where he worked in Romania in the 1950s. In the 1960s, he served as advisor and member of the Chinese government delegation to the Sino-Soviet border negotiations. In the 1970s, as the Director of the U.S. Department of the Ministry of Foreign Affairs, he participated in the process from the initial contact to the formal establishment of diplomatic relations between China and the U.S. In the 1980s, he served as Deputy Director and Director of the Policy Research Office of the Ministry of Foreign Affairs. Later, he served as Ambassador to the United Nations, Switzerland, and Belgium, and was also Head of the Mission to the European Union. After returning to China, he served as the Ambassador of the Ministry of Foreign Affairs and was responsible for the Asia-Europe Meeting.

宋明江（1997 年 2 月—2001 年 10 月）

　　宋明江（1939—），天津市人。1961 年毕业于北京师范大学中文系，后于北京外国语学院英语系深造，是新中国定向培养出国教授汉语的第一批代训生。尼克松访华后，调任美国驻华联络处首任中文秘书。后历任世界知识出版社编辑、《世界知识》杂志主编。1985 年调任驻英使馆参赞，后任外交部西欧司副司长、司长。1997 被任命为中国驻比利时特命全权大使兼驻欧盟使团团长。回国后任中国国际问题研究所所长兼党委书记，全国友协理事、外交学会理事等。

关呈远（2001 年 11 月—2005 年 1 月）

　　关呈远（1945—），黑龙江人。1964 年进入北京外国语学院学习。1972 年进入外交部工作，后赴法留学。回国后先后在外交部翻译室、驻瑞士使馆、外交部西欧司、驻法国使馆工作。后任外交部西欧司副司长、司长。2001—2004 年任中国驻比利时大使兼驻欧盟使团团长。2004—2007 年任中国驻欧盟使团团长。回国后任外交部外交政策咨询委员会委员、外交学会理事。

Song Mingjiang (February 1997 - October 2001)

Song Mingjiang (1939-), a native of Tianjin, graduated from the Chinese Department of Beijing Normal University in 1961 and later studied in the English Department of the Beijing Foreign Studies University, where he was one of the first students trained to teach Chinese abroad. After Nixon's visit to China, he was transferred to the U.S. Liaison Office in China as the Chinese Secretary. Later, he served as the editor of World Affairs Publishing House and the chief editor of *World Affairs*. In 1985, he was transferred to the Chinese Embassy in UK as Counsellor, and later became Deputy Director-General and Director-General of the Western Europe Department of the Ministry of Foreign Affairs. In 1997 he was appointed Ambassador Extraordinary and Plenipotentiary of China to Belgium and Head of Mission to the European Union. After returning to China, he served as Director and Secretary of the Party Committee of the China Institute of International Studies.

Guan Chengyuan (November 2001 - January 2005)

Guan Chengyuan (1945-), a native of Heilongjiang Province, studied at the Beijing Foreign Studies University in 1964. He joined the Ministry of Foreign Affairs in 1972, and then studied in France. After returning to China, he worked in the translation office of the Ministry of Foreign Affairs, the Embassy in Switzerland, the Western Europe Department of the Ministry of Foreign Affairs, and the Embassy in France. From 2001 to 2004, he served as Chinese Ambassador to Belgium and Head of Mission to the European Union, and from 2004 to 2007, he served as Chinese Head of Mission to the European Union. After returning to China, he was a member of the Foreign Policy Advisory Committee of the Ministry of Foreign Affairs and a member of the Board of Directors of Foreign Affairs College.

章启月（2005 年 2 月—2008 年 7 月）

　　章启月（1959—），出生于北京，北京外国语大学毕业。父亲是前驻比利时、日本大使章曙先生。1982年进入外交部工作，曾任职于纽约联合国总部秘书处和中国常驻联合国代表团，是独当一面的女参赞。1998—2004 年担任中国外交部发言人、新闻司副司长，后任驻比利时大使和驻印度尼西亚大使，2012—2014 年 6月担任外交部国外工作局局长，2014—2018 年任驻纽约总领事。2018—2021 年任驻希腊大使。

张援远（2008 年 8 月—2011 年 5 月）

　　张援远（1950—），生于黑龙江哈尔滨。1976 年毕业于加拿大多伦多大学。后进入外交部工作，任驻温哥华总领馆职员，曾在常驻联合国代表团任职，后任外交部翻译室参赞、主任，驻新西兰大使，驻比利时大使。

Zhang Qiyue (February 2005 - July 2008)

　　Zhang Qiyue (1959-), born in Beijing, is a graduate of Beijing Foreign Studies University. She is the daughter of Zhang Shu, former Ambassador to Belgium and Japan. She joined the Ministry of Foreign Affairs in 1982 and served in the Secretariat of the United Nations Headquarters in New York and the Permanent Mission of China to the United Nations, where she was the sole female counsellor. From 1998 to 2004, she served as spokesperson for the Chinese Ministry of Foreign Affairs, Deputy Director General of the Information Department, and later as Ambassador to Belgium and Ambassador to Indonesia. She served as the Director of Department for Diplomatic Missions Abroad of the Ministry of Foreign Affairs from 2012 to June 2014. She was Consul General in New York from 2014 to 2018. She serves as Ambassador to Greece from 2018 to 2021.

Zhang Yuanyuan (August 2008 - May 2011)

　　Born in Harbin, Heilongjiang Province, Zhang Yuanyuan (1950-) graduated from the University of Toronto, Canada in 1976. He later joined the Ministry of Foreign Affairs as a staff member of the Consulate General in Vancouver. He served in the Permanent Mission to the United Nations, and later as Counsellor and Director of the Translation Office of the Ministry of Foreign Affairs, Ambassador to New Zealand and Ambassador to Belgium.

廖力强（2011 年 5 月—2014 年 11 月）

　　廖力强（1964—），湖南醴陵人。1986 年进入外交部工作，历任驻塞内加尔使馆随员、外交部西欧司随员、外交部办公厅二秘、中央外事工作领导小组办公室参赞、外交部新闻司参赞、外交部办公厅参赞、驻比利时大使，2011—2014 年任外交部外事管理司司长，现任驻埃及大使兼驻阿拉伯国家联盟全权代表。

Liao Liqiang (May 2011 - November 2014)

　　Liao Liqiang (1964-), a native of Liling, Hunan Province, joined the Ministry of Foreign Affairs in 1986 and served as Attaché of the Embassy in Senegal, Attaché of the Western Europe Department of the Ministry of Foreign Affairs, Second Secretary of the General Office of the Ministry of Foreign Affairs, Counsellor of the Office of the Central Leading Group for Foreign Affairs, Counsellor of the Information Department of the Ministry of Foreign Affairs, and Counsellor of the General Office of the Ministry of Foreign Affairs. Later, he served as Ambassador to the Kingdom of Belgium from 2011 to 2014, Director General of the Foreign Affairs Management Department of the Ministry of Foreign Affairs, and currently Ambassador to Egypt and Plenipotentiary to the League of Arab States.

曲星（2014 年 12 月—2018 年 5 月）

　　曲星（1956—），山东莱州人。毕业于北京外国语学院和外交学院。1992 年毕业于法国巴黎政治学院，获政治学博士学位。1985 年起在外交学院执教，任教授兼博士生导师。后任中国驻法国大使馆公使、中国国际问题研究所所长。2014—2018 年任驻比利时大使。后任全国政协第十三届外事委员会委员、联合国教科文组织副总干事。代表作有《中国外交 50 年》、《中国外交新论》、《中国当代外交史》（副主编）、《中国外交史 1979—1994》、《邓小平的外交艺术》等。

Qu Xing (December 2014 - May 2018)

　　Qu Xing (1956-) is a native of Laizhou, Shandong Province. He graduated from the Beijing Foreign Studies University and Foreign Affairs College and received his PhD in political science from the Institut d'Etudes Politiques de Paris in 1992. Since 1985, he started teaching at Foreign Affairs College as the professor and doctoral supervisor. From 2014 to 2018, he was Ambassador to Belgium. He is currently a member of the Foreign Affairs Committee of the 13th National Committee of the Chinese People's Political Consultative Conference and Deputy Director-General of the United Nations Educational, Scientific and Cultural Organization (UNESCO). He is the author of *50 Years of Chinese Diplomacy*, *A New Theory of Chinese Diplomacy*, *History of Contemporary Chinese Diplomacy* (associate editor), *History of Chinese Diplomacy 1979-1994*, and *Deng Xiaoping's Art of Diplomacy*.

曹忠明（2018年9月）

曹忠明（1965—），浙江宁波人。1989年毕业于北京大学，后进入外交部非洲司工作，历任驻乍得大使馆随员、三秘，非洲司副处长、处长，驻法国大使馆参赞，非洲司副司长，驻马里大使，外交部干部司副司长、司长，2018年9月起任驻比利时大使。

Cao Zhongming (September 2018 - present)

Cao Zhongming (1965-), a native of Ningbo, Zhejiang Province, graduated from Peking University in 1989 and later joined the Africa Department of the Ministry of Foreign Affairs. He then served as Attaché and Third Secretary of the Embassy in Chad, Deputy Director and Director of the Africa Department, Counsellor of the Embassy in France, Deputy Director of the Africa Department, Ambassador to Mali, Deputy Director and Director of the Cadre Department of the Ministry of Foreign Affairs. He has served as Ambassador to Belgium since September 2018.

注释

1〔美〕傅高义：《邓小平时代》，冯克利译，北京：生活·读书·新知三联书店，2013，第222页。

2《谷牧回忆录》，北京：中央文献出版社，2014，第316—317页。

3《谷牧副总理离瑞士抵比利时进行友好访问 廷德曼斯首相设宴欢迎谷牧副总理》，《人民日报》1978年5月20日，第5版。

4《谷牧副总理访问欧洲经济共同体总部 詹金斯主席说发展中国与共同体的合作有重要政治意义 谷牧副总理说中国支持西欧联合，希望欧洲强大起来》，《人民日报》1978年5月22日，第5版。

5《谷牧副总理在布鲁塞尔举行告别宴会 比利时国王博杜安接见谷牧副总理》，《人民日报》1978年5月24日，第5版。

6《谷牧副总理在布鲁塞尔举行告别宴会 比利时国王博杜安接见谷牧副总理》，《人民日报》1978年5月24日，第5版。

7谷牧：《我国对外开放国策的酝酿和起步》，《党的文献》2009年第1期，第21—27页；袁晓江：《1978年谷牧率团考察欧洲五国》，《百年潮》2017年10月，第13—22页。

8朱琳慧：《2018年中国与比利时双边贸易全景图（附中国与比利时主要进出口产业数据）》，前瞻产业研究院，2019年8月30日，https://www.qianzhan.com/analyst/detail/220/190828-796c2e0c.html。

9比利时驻华大使馆：《走进比利时——比利时王国与中华人民共和国建交40周年特刊》，北京：世界在线外交传媒集团，2011，第54页。

10尽管英国宣布于2021年1月1日脱欧，但其新的到欧盟以外其他国家的通道短时间内尚难以全部调整完毕。

11比利时驻华大使馆：《走进比利时——比利时王国与中华人民共和国建交40周年特刊》，北京：世界在线外交传媒集团，2011，第57页。

12比利时驻华大使馆：《走进比利时——比利时王国与中华人民共和国建交40周年特刊》，北京：世界在线外交传媒集团，2011，第58页。

13《中国和比利时两国各领域交流合作不断加深》，中国政府门户网站，2012年9月18日，http://www.gov.cn/jrzg/2012-09/18/content_2227281.htm。

14《比利时安特卫普港至中国重庆的铁路货运正式开通》，中国政府门户网站，2011年5月10日，http://www.gov.cn/jrzg/2011-05/10/content_1860646.htm。

15《综述：中比合作亮点闪耀》，中国政府网，2017年5月30日，http://www.gov.cn/xinwen/2017-05/30/content_5198167.htm。

16《唐山港开通中欧班列》，人民网，2018年4月27日，http://pic.people.com.cn/n1/2018/0427/c1016-29954445.html。

17《中欧班列（郑州）比利时线路开通》，中国政府网，2018年10月25日，http://www.gov.cn/xinwen/2018-10/25/content_5334362.htm。

18《首列义乌—列日中欧班列抵达比利时》，新华网，2019年10月26日，http://www.xinhuanet.com/2019-10/26/c_1125155787.htm。

19《长春至汉堡中欧班列首发》，新华社，2017年10月13日，http://world.people.com.cn/n1/2017/1013/c1002-29586532.html。

20《首列"中欧班列"沃尔沃专列抵达比利时》，《光明日报》2017年07月03日，第10版。

21朱琳慧：《2018年中国与比利时双边贸易全景图（附中国与比利时主要进出口产业数据）》，前瞻产业研究院，2019年8月30日，https://www.qianzhan.com/analyst/detail/220/190828-796c2e0c.html。

22《2019年1—7月中国从比利时进出口商品总值统计》，华经情报网，2019年9月16日，https://www.huaon.com/story/466667。

23朱琳慧：《2018年中国与比利时双边贸易全景图（附中国与比利时主要进出口产业数据）》，前瞻产业研究院，2019年8月30日，https://www.qianzhan.com/analyst/detail/220/190828-796c2e0c.html。

24刘美林：《九访中国的比利时国王》，《环球人物》2015年第18期，第47—49页。

25《特写：比利时国王菲利普访问湖北》，新华网，2015年6月23日，http://www.xinhuanet.com//politics/2015-06/23/c_127938346.htm。

26刘美林：《九访中国的比利时国王》，《环球人物》2015年第18期，第47—49页。

27王炳东：《比利时漫画、埃尔热和丁丁》，载北京外国语大学编《比利时研究文集》，内部出版，2001，第94—100页。

28宋明江：《欧洲心脏——比利时》，上海：上海锦绣文章出版社，2013，第33—34页。

29《〈蓝精灵之歌〉遭误会20年 百分百国产获鲁迅奖》，四川新闻网－成都日报，2011年08月10日，http://ent.sina.com.cn/m/f/2011-08-10/03103382286.shtml。

30李强：《萨克斯全科教程》，北京：中国青年出版社，2002，第2—3页。

31王受之：《世界现代建筑史》，北京：中国建筑工业出版社，1999，第75—76页。

32宋明江：《欧洲心脏——比利时》，上海：上海锦绣文章出版社，2013，第29—30页。

33比利时驻华大使馆：《走进比利时——比利时王国与中华人民共和国建交40周年特刊》，北京：世界在线外交传媒集团，2011，第24页。

34宋明江：《欧洲心脏——比利时》，上海：上海锦绣文章出版社，2013，第29—30页。

35 https://www.ugent.be/bw/biotechnology/en/research-units/schoonmeersen/research/brewing-sci-tech.

36 https://onderwijsaanbod.kuleuven.be//opleidingen/e/CQ_55500634.htm#activetab=diploma_omschrijving.

37比利时驻华大使馆：《走进比利时——比利时王国与中华人民共和国建交40周年特刊》，北京：世界在线外交传媒集团，2011，第31页。

38比利时驻华大使馆：《走进比利时——比利时王国与中华人民共和国建交40周年特刊》，北京：世界在线外交传媒集团，2011，第31页。

39比利时驻华大使馆：《走进比利时——比利时王国与中华人民共和国建交40周年特刊》，北京：世界在线外交传媒集团，2011，第36页。

40宋明江：《欧洲心脏——比利时》，上海：上海锦绣文章出版社，2013，第82—83页。

参考文献

中文文献

[1] 北京外国语大学编.比利时研究文集 [M].北京,北京外国语大学,2001.

[2] 比利时驻华大使馆.走进比利时——比利时王国与中华人民共和国建交40周年特刊[M].北京:世界在线外交传媒集团,2011.

[3] 谷牧.谷牧回忆录 [M].北京:中央文献出版社,2014.

[4] 李强.萨克斯全科教程[M].北京:中国青年出版社,2002.

[5] 宋明江.欧洲心脏——比利时 [M].上海:上海锦绣文章出版社,2013.

[6] 王受之.世界现代建筑史[M].北京:中国建筑工业出版社,1999.

[7] 〔美〕傅高义.邓小平时代 [M].冯克利译.北京:生活·读书·新知三联书店,2013.

[8] 谷牧.我国对外开放国策的酝酿和起步 [J].党的文献,2009（1）.

[9] 刘美林.九访中国的比利时国王 [J].环球人物,2015（18）.

[10] 袁晓江.1978年谷牧率团考察欧洲五国 [J].百年潮,2017.10.

[11]《人民日报》.

电子文献

[1] 中国驻比利时大使馆网站，http://be.china-embassy.org.

[2] 外交政策咨询委员会网站，http://fpag.fmprc.gov.cn.

[3] 新华网，http://www.xinhuanet.com.

[4] 人民网，http://pic.people.com.cn.

[5] 中国网，http://www.china.com.cn.

[6] 鲁汶大学网站，https://www.kuleuven.be.

[7] 根特大学网站，https://www.ugent.be.

[8] 前瞻产业研究院，https://www.qianzhan.com.

[9] 华经情报网，https://www.huaon.com.

后记

Afterword

在本书编译出版过程中，天津社会科学发展研究中心诸位同事做了大量的工作：安红女士负责本书的排版、美术设计以及美术编辑工作；唐倩女士负责本书中鲜见影像史料的搜集整理工作，补缺还原了诸多史实；姜雨晨女士负责本书的全书校对工作，提出许多宝贵意见；牌梦迪女士负责全书的中英文审校工作，在此一并致以谢意。

In the process of this book's publication and translation, colleagues from the Tianjin Development Research Center of Social Sciences have provided tremendous assistance: Ms. An Hong was responsible for the layout, art design and art editing of the book; Ms. Tang Qian was responsible for the collection and arrangement of the rarely seen visual historical materials in the book, filling in the gaps and restoring many historical record; Ms. Jiang Yuchen was responsible for the proofreading of the entire manuscript and made many valuable comments; Ms. Pai Mengdi was responsible for proofreading and improving the Chinese to English translation. We would like to express our gratitude to them.

图书在版编目（CIP）数据

比利时在天津的历史遗迹 / 张畅，刘悦，（美）杨溢
(Yi Edward Yang) 著 . -- 北京：社会科学文献出版社，
2023.5
　ISBN 978-7-5228-1544-2

　Ⅰ.①比⋯ Ⅱ.①张⋯ ②刘⋯ ③杨⋯ Ⅲ.①中外
关系－国际关系史－史料－比利时－近代 Ⅳ.
① D829.564

中国国家版本馆 CIP 数据核字 (2023) 第 045980 号

比利时在天津的历史遗迹

著　　者 / 张　畅　刘　悦　　〔美〕杨　溢（Yi Edward Yang）

出 版 人 / 王利民
责任编辑 / 王玉敏
文稿编辑 / 王亚楠
特约编辑 / 姜雨晨
责任印制 / 王京美

出　　版 / 社会科学文献出版社 · 联合出版中心（010）59367153
　　　　　　地址：北京市北三环中路甲 29 号院华龙大厦　邮编：100029
　　　　　　网址：www.ssap.com.cn
发　　行 / 社会科学文献出版社（010）59367028
印　　装 / 北京盛通印刷股份有限公司

规　　格 / 开　本：880mm×1230mm　1/12
　　　　　　印　张：26　字　数：290 千字
版　　次 / 2023 年 5 月第 1 版　2023 年 5 月第 1 次印刷
书　　号 / ISBN 978-7-5228-1544-2
定　　价 / 298.00 元

读者服务电话：4008918866